PENGUIN BOOKS

THE FALL OF PARIS

Sir Alistair Horne was born in London in 1925, and has spent much of his life abroad, including periods at schools in the United States and Switzerland. He served with the R.A.F. in Canada in 1943 and ended his war service with the rank of Captain in the Coldstream Guards attached to MI5 in the Middle East. He then went up to Jesus College, Cambridge, where he read English Literature and played international ice-hockey. After leaving Cambridge, Sir Alistair concentrated on writing: he spent three years in Germany as correspondent for the *Daily Telegraph* and speaks fluent French and German. His books include *Back into Power* (1955); *The Price of Glory: Verdun 1916* (Hawthornden Prize, 1963); *The Fall of Paris: The Siege and the Commune 1870–71* (1965); *To Lose A Battle: France 1940* (1969); *Small Earthquake in Chile* (1972, paperback reissued 1999); *A Savage War of Peace: Algeria 1954–62* won both the *Yorkshire Post* Book of the Year Prize and the Wolfson History Award in 1978 (revised paperback edition 2006). His other publications include *The French Army and Politics 1870–1970* (1984), which was awarded the Enid Macleod Prize in 1985, *Harold Macmillan, Volumes I and II* (1988–91), *A Bundle from Britain* (1993), a memoir about the USA and World War II; *The Lonely Leader: Monty 1944–1945* (1996); *Seven Ages of Paris: Portrait of a City* (2003); *Friend or Foe: A History of France* (2004) and *The Age of Napoleon* (2004). In 1969 he founded a Research Fellowship for young historians at St Antony's College, Oxford. In 1992 he was awarded the CBE; in 1993 he received the French Légion d'Honneur for his work on French history and his Litt.D. from Cambridge University. He was knighted in 2003. He is currently working on an authorised biography of Henry Kissinger, as well as a second volume of his own memoirs.

ALISTAIR HORNE

THE FALL OF PARIS

THE SIEGE AND THE COMMUNE 1870–71

PENGUIN BOOKS

PENGUIN BOOKS

UK | USA | Canada | Ireland | Australia
India | New Zealand | South Africa

Penguin Books is part of the Penguin Random House group of companies
whose addresses can be found at global.penguinrandomhouse.com.

First published by Macmillan 1965
Revised edition first published by Papermac 1990
Published in Penguin Books 2007

019

Printed and bound in Great Britain by Clays Ltd, Elcograf S.p.A.

ISBN: 978-0-141-03063-0

www.greenpenguin.co.uk

Penguin Random House is committed to a
sustainable future for our business, our readers
and our planet. This book is made from Forest
Stewardship Council® certified paper.

For CAMILLA

'. . . Paris goes her own way. France, irritated, is forced to follow; later she calms down and applauds; it is one of the forms of our national life. A coach passes flying a flag; it comes from Paris. The flag is no longer a flag, it is a flame, and the whole trail of human gunpowder catches fire behind it.

To will always, this is the fact about Paris. You think she sleeps, no, she wills. The permanent will of Paris—it is of this that transitory governments are not enough aware. Paris is always in a state of premeditation. . . . The clouds pass across her gaze. One fine day, there it is. Paris decrees an event. France, abruptly summoned, obeys. . . .

This smouldering between Paris the centre and France the orbit, this struggle which resembles a swaying of the forces of gravity, this alternating between resistance and adherence, these bursts of temper of the nation against the city followed by acquiescence, all indicate clearly that Paris, this head, is more than the head of a people. The movement is French, the impulsion is Parisian. . . .'

From the Introduction by Victor Hugo to the *Paris Guide*, 1867.

Contents

PART ONE
THE SIEGE

PART TWO
THE COMMUNE

List of Illustrations

List of Maps

Foreword

DURING the crisis of June 1940, the French Government led by Paul Reynaud, having abandoned Paris and making its uneasy way towards Tours and Bordeaux, left strict instructions with the Prefect of Police in Paris, Roger Langeron: he was to stay in the city, along with his whole force of *agents de ville*, in order to forestall the possibility of a Communist *coup* in the absence of the Government. They were to await the arrival of the German military command so as to ensure that no barricades went up in Clichy, Belleville, and the eastern and south-eastern suburbs. Of course there was no hint of a *coup*, and, at the time, the French Communist Party was largely leaderless and in full disarray. Monsieur Langeron contacted the German authorities as soon as they arrived, assuring them that the Paris police force of 15,000 was at their disposal. Order was preserved.

Of course M. Langeron and his superiors had learnt from past experience and were well aware of the terrible weight of history, the compelling pull of historical memory and precedent in the apparently endless conflict of Paris versus France, in that order. May 1795, the collapse of the Prairial Days and the occupation of the Fauborg Saint-Antoine by the Army had looked after Paris for a time: thirty-five years, something of a record, as it would turn out. The switch-overs of 1814 and 1815 had been effected painlessly, thanks to the good sense of the Provisional Government in insisting on the rapid deployment within the city of the Allied troops. Paris had remained quiet. Louis XVIII had even set up his Court within a city in which his brother had been murdered: both a measure of his own confidence, reinforced, it should be added, by the presence of a substantial Royal Guard, and a striking example of his desire to reign as *le Roi de la Concorde* and the King of Forgiveness. He had been remarkably successful in both objectives. But he had been old and ill, and his foolish successor had not appeared to have forgotten or forgiven anything.

And so, after a blessed pause of thirty-five years, the whole obscene business had started up again in the murderous July Days of 1830, with some hundreds of victims later commemorated by name on the July Column. In order to avoid further bloodshed, Charles X had left Saint-Cloud for Rambouillet and had made his leisurely way to the coast, embarking for England. At the same time, the incurably silly, posturing Lafayette had made a second appearance, indeed a Second Coming, on the balcony of the old Hôtel-de-Ville, where he was able to persuade the usurper, Louis-Philippe, to drape himself in the tricolor flag, a gesture that did the trick, at least for the time being.

But, so it was said, the July Monarchy had turned out, almost from the start, to be unglamorous and therefore *boring*, the greatest crime that any modern French regime could commit. The King of the French himself, it was alleged, was a crashing bore, who talked too much, especially to gathered firemen, and who carried a green umbrella. Guizot, too, his sensible minister, had gone on too long (only eight years in fact), so he too had had to go, along with *Le Roi Bourgeois*. Of Lamartine it had been said at the time: '*M. de Lamartine était de ceux qui étaient devenus révolution-naires pour se désennuyer.*' And there had been many more like him at the time (as, indeed, there still are). This had brought a new round of killing in February 1848. Louis-Philippe, like his predecessor Charles X, had had the decency to go off quietly, landing at Newhaven, and heading first of all for Eastbourne, before settling in Surrey.

The elections of that year had given an enormous majority to moderate provincial royalists; they had also been seen, as they were meant to have been seen, as a massive vote against Paris. The June Days had followed, accompanied by much of the usual silliness: *Marchons sur Varsovie* (a very long march indeed) and exploding in a new topography of barricades in the east central districts of the city. The fighting between the insurgents on the one side, and the Army and the National Guards, who had been brought in from the western districts or from the provinces, had been savage; there had been atrocities on both sides, hostages had been summarily despatched, including the Archbishop of Paris. The repression that had followed had been ferocious; many insurgents had been shot, many others had been deported to Algeria; and there had thus been created a new generation of Parisian avengers, especially among the widows or the female companions of the victims.

Haussmanisation had, if anything, made matters rather worse, by accentuating the class contrasts between one quarter and another, and by thus creating artisan ghettoes in the east and the north-east of Paris. The Butte des Moulins had been levelled, displacing an unruly population eastwards and rendering the Palais-Royal harmless from then on. But it had also made the wealthy western districts wealthier, the exclusive domain of middle-class families and their numerous servants, and the area had been further extended westwards by the taking in within the city's boundaries of Neuilly, Chaillot, Passy and Boulogne.

So the principal theme of Alistair Horne's remarkable book, and one eloquently proclaimed by its title, *The Fall of Paris*, is the decisive crushing of the place, as it would be, once and for all. So it might be seen as a hopeful theme, albeit one realised at extraordinary bitter human cost:

many, many more victims than those of the Terror of 1793–4. Adolphe Thiers, the man who, more than any other, had decided to settle accounts with the violent and dangerous city, with its strident claims to revolutionary universalism, has suffered much at the hands of historians, at least until the recent reassessment by Patrick Bury and Robert Tombs in their well-documented biography. It is clear from the present book that in suddenly removing his Government to Versailles, and in thus handing over the city to the bewildered, directionless Commune, he not only acted with decision, but that there could not have been an alternative line of action open to him. He (and his ministers) had got out, had succeeded where the unfortunate Louis XVI had failed. At different times, by a variety of advisers, none of whom had taken the trouble to study the ground or to take a look at maps, Louis had been counselled to head for Rouen or for Bourges. Thiers had at least managed to get his hastily packed Government, as well as a clutter of Generals, to the relative safety of Versailles. The surprised leaders of the Commune had done the rest, by failing to pursue him there at a time when they still had the advantage of numbers. So it could be said, in view of what finally happened, at the cost of an appalling bloodbath on a scale unequalled in the nineteenth century, that the little man had saved France from its capital. And for this he deserves considerable credit. Of course, the conflict was not just one between the Provisional Government on the one side, and the quarrelsome leaders of the Commune, supported by the inhabitants of the eastern and north-eastern districts on the other. There were the Prussians to be considered as well. The author is rightly concerned at all times to keep them in the picture throughout. As it turned out, their presence somewhat facilitated the task of the Thiers Government by sealing off most of the northern exits from the Capital.

As in any chronicle of events, dramatic or banal (in this case the former), there is the usual assortment of villains, sillies, the sensible, the victims and the pathetic, and the uncommitted, mere witnesses, in this case most of them American and English. The villains are readily identifiable: the apostles of hate: Rochefort, Pyat, Rigault, Ferré. There is a whole army of sillies, led, from behind, by France's National Bore, her *Pompier National*, Victor Hugo, in full trumpeting bombast and Parisian Universalism, the City of Light. Here he is, as quoted by Mr Horne, calling the peaceable cities of France to rise up in defence of their cordially (and rightly) hated capital: 'Lyons,' he enjoins it, familiarly, 'take thy gun; Bordeaux, take thy carbine; Rouen, draw thy sword' (this addressed to the most pacific and prudent of French cities), 'and thou, Marseilles, sing thy song, and become terrible.' One is glad to note that none responded to such declamatory appeals. There is more Hugolian bombast later on: 'Paris', he announces, 'is resolved to let itself be buried under its own ruins rather than surrender,' (he got the ruins). Later the old fool berates us, the English, for standing aside while the Capital of Civilisation is under siege. So it is with satisfaction that we hear of an English chronicler describing one of Hugo's speeches as 'of unexampled silliness'. He survives the Commune, of course, goes into exile, makes himself a nuisance in Brussels, so that the Belgian authorities sensibly move him on, and he ends up for a bit in Luxembourg. There are plenty of other sillies, though none on the Hugolian scale: they include the posturing Gambetta, the intolerable Louise Michel, the trying Elizabeth Dimitrieff, and the exhibitionist Bergeret.

Of the sensible, one would give first place to the patient Jules Favre. But Gladstone and his Foreign Minister, Granville, deserve more than a mention. They both expressed sympathy at the plight of France, and resolutely refused to get involved. Some might accuse them of smugness, I think they were just showing remarkable good sense.

The victims of these terrible events are innumerable, 22,000 or more, many of them are nameless, though many could be identified through the courts-martial documents in Vincennes. Two notable victims at once come to mind: the obstinate, honourable Louis Rossel, a regular Army officer, the son of a French Protestant and of a Scotswoman, who eventually joined the Commune out of patriotism and who attempted to bring a minimum of discipline into *fédéré* ranks. The other is the Archbishop of France, Mgr Darboy.

What adds to the horror of this chronicle of war and violence is a topography that one associates with the early pictures of Sisley: the valleys of the Seine, the Marne, the rivers often in flood, the riverside villages under snow, a reassuring list of place names, many within walking distance of Paris; and which is evocative of week-ends and happy leisure: Villiers, Champigny, Joinville, Epinay-sur-Orge, Bougival, Rueil, Gennevilliers, Issy, Le Point-du-Jour. Comfortable houses in ochre-coloured stone, with green shutters, are revealed unroofed and with gaping holes in their walls, there are uneven lines of broken poplars, and war has come to a peaceful, previously banal, rather pretty countryside.

There is little place for humour in this account of war and revolution, revolt and repression. But I would single out the 'lamb offered to one British correspondent [that] ironically turned out to be a wolf.' And here is *La Semaine Sanglante*, with Paris burning, as seen from the fashionable *Pavillon Henri IV*, on the Terrasse de Saint-Germain, high up above the great bend of the Seine: a number of buildings appear to be alight, one of them seems to be the Louvre, 'a large lady exclaimed: "Let's hope he doesn't mean the department store!"' She seems to have got her priorities right.

*   *   *   *   *

In this new edition of *The Fall of Paris*, the author has incorporated much
of the work published since the book first came out in 1965, including the
large number of books that were published in 1971 for the Centenary of
the Commune. His book offers much the most comprehensive account of
the War itself, the long Siege, the near-famine, the almost accidental
proclamation of the Commune, in an atmosphere of holiday rejoicings
and light-heartedness, and the terrible course of events that ensued. It is a
brilliant account of one of the most sombre periods of modern French
history. At the time of the present *Bicentenaire* of another Revolution, it is
as well to be reminded that revolutions are not just about dancing in the
streets, *la fête populaire* and similar light-hearted occasions for collective
joy, but that they are also about lynchings and corpses in the streets.

Richard Cobb
Wolvercote, May, 1989

Preface

TODAY the thought of a European war between Germans and Frenchmen seems to belong to a remote era years away. This past half century of peace—already longer than the interval between the Franco-Prussian war and 1914—remains *the* outstanding historical achievement of the much criticized and little-loved European Common Market. But the conception of this book dates back to the 1950s, when—as a young foreign correspondent in Germany—I lived among the visible legacy of that last bout of Franco-German hostility, which was then still all too tangible and too close for comfort. Yet relations between France and Germany, the root of evil in the world I grew up in, had already taken a sudden miraculous turn; and, in contemplation of this happy fact, I began thinking of a book which might trace the lethal course of these relations over the preceding century. War has a curious way of crystallizing the more peaceful trends of history, and of pointing up the developments of the intervening years; as I later found Theodore Zeldin observing in his impressive *France 1848—1945,** the French Army in particular also 'acts as a magnifying lens revealing aspects of national problems, and of personal tensions, more clearly than they can be seen in civil society.'

Thus my projected book was to be woven around three great battles, decisive in their own war, and in wider historical contexts as well. They were to be Sedan 1870, Verdun 1916, and Sedan 1940. There were many links—tactical, strategic, historical, and psychological—connecting the battles in this blood-sodden corner of France which made the project seem a fascinating one. Then a first visit to the sinister battlefields of Verdun engendered emotions that were never to leave me alone. As I read deeper and deeper, Verdun assumed predominance in my mind; subjectively, it almost seemed *the* central event in the war which, though ended seven years before I was born, overshadowed my childhood. And, more than any other battle I had ever read of, it seemed not only to symbolize the whole war, but to have affected the destinies of nations far beyond the actual conflict. Gradually it overlaid the rest of the trilogy, and out of it came a book called *The Price of Glory: Verdun 1916*. This in turn was followed, as the third leg of the trilogy, by *To Lose a Battle: France 1940*.

*Zeldin, T, p. 105, Oxford 1973–7.

But while writing *The Price of Glory* I found myself constantly having to refer back to 1870, and I knew that when I had finished the current project I would return there. Then once again the ground began to shift beneath my feet. Historical research is like a moving staircase; one thing is certain, that when you come to the end you will have journeyed far from your starting-point. As I set forth on the Franco-Prussian War, the brief encounter at Sedan—which sealed the fate of the Second Empire—began to be eclipsed by the long-protracted Siege of Paris as the supreme drama of the war. At Sedan the French never had a chance, the issue having already been decided, militarily, elsewhere; at Paris there was a chance, if not of actually winning the war, at least perhaps of gaining less humiliating terms in the peace that followed. And what was lost at Paris, by France, was much more than just a battle.

The greatest difficulty in writing about the Siege of Paris was to separate it from the infinitely grimmer civil war that followed on the heels of the departing Germans. In the event, the two episodes proved inseparable; once again the escalator jolted forward, and I found myself confronted by the Commune as historically the more portentous of the two.

In purely military terms, Paris fell twice in the space of six months; first to Bismarck, secondly to the French Government forces under Thiers. But she also fell in more than one sense; pride, as well as her traditional role of being the prime centre of European power, were involved (the latter never to be restored), and finally there was the grim fall of morality that accompanied the repression of the Commune.

Some of the episodes related in this book will hardly be palatable to Frenchmen born now, and in recording them the author exposes himself to certain obvious charges. The Battle of Verdun, hideous tragedy though it was for both sides, has justly come to be regarded as France's 'finest hour', but both the Siege and the Commune lie somewhere at the other end of the scale. Edmond Goncourt, a Parisian himself, advised in the middle of the Siege that 'posterity should not presume to relate to future generations of the heroism of the Parisians of 1870'. As the Commune crumbled in May 1871, some twenty thousand Parisians were slaughtered by their fellow-countrymen; and, for all our recent conditioning, the modern mind boggles at setting such occurrences inside what passed for the world's most civilized city.

It is not always easy to place an episode in its right historical context. Yet it was, in fact, all not so long ago; the daughter of a young Englishman Edwin Child, who witnessed many of the events recounted in this book was still alive when I wrote *The Fall of Paris*; Pétain, whose long, sad life ended in 1951, was a schoolboy outside Paris during the

Siege and lived to play a vital part in two World Wars; Joffre, who manned the Paris ramparts as a volunteer gunner, was to lead the French Army from 1914 until Verdun ruined him; Mayor Clemenceau of Montmartre, who by a slight twist of fate might have been shot by either the Communards or the Government forces, survived to impose the Versailles Treaty on the defeated Germans of 1918. Winston Churchill was born four and a half years after the Commune was suppressed; Lenin, a few months before the Franco-Prussian War broke out; while Karl Marx was then fifty-two. There were also links with the past; among the many who defended Paris with their oratory was Victor Hugo, old enough to remember the Grand Army of the first Napoleon in which his father had been a general; and among the spectators on the Prussian side were Generals Burnside and Sheridan, veterans of the more recent American Civil War.

Karl Marx's paper on the Commune, 'The Civil War in France', which he wrote while 'Bloody Week' was still raging in Paris (although he himself got no closer to the seat of war than the British Museum), must be rated one of the all-time classics of journalism. His facts were astonishingly accurate; but he then proceeded to distort them for his own dialectic ends. One of the other principal difficulties in writing the present book was that it was virtually impossible to find any published sources on the Commune that are not violently *parti pris*: either Marxist or bourgeois in sympathy. Similarly, French accounts of the Siege, strongly subject to contemporary emotions, have to be treated with caution. Fortunately, there exists a wealth of 'neutral' rapportage, not to be found in two subsequent 'World' Wars. Britain—as well as the U.S.A.— was a non-belligerent, and the correspondents of the leading British papers ranged far and wide with the forces of both sides during the Siege, and subsequently under the Commune. Journalism was still an honoured trade, and their accounts—reinforced by others such as the official reports of a shrewd and level-headed American Minister, Elihu Washburne— were as literate, often superbly so, as they were objective. With the advent of the telegraph (and later the balloon from Paris), and in the absence of all forms of censorship, the Franco-Prussian War received a quicker and more accurate coverage than any war before, or since.[1]

In the further pursuit of objectivity, I advertised in various American and British journals, inquiring after unpublished sources on the Siege and the Commune, and expecting to get perhaps three or four responses. Instead, to my astonishment, I received well over a hundred, many containing balloon letters actually flown out of besieged Paris. Much of the original material in this book was thanks to

[1] One instance of this was the grand manoeuvre of MacMahon's Army in August 1870, bringing him eventually to Sedan, which was lost to the sight of the Prussians—until they read about it in *The Times*.

the kindness, and trust, of these correspondents, to whom I am more indebted than I can say. Space does not, unfortunately, permit me to express my appreciation to all of them individually, but I feel I must single out those few to whom I owe particular gratitude: Miss E. Child, for placing at my disposal the letters, journals, and mementoes of her father, Edwin Child—a rich source of unpublished material subsequently bequested to King's College, London; Major-General Sir E. L. Spears, Bt., for letters written to his grandfather, Edward Louis Hack;[1] the Hon. Mrs. Mervyn Herbert, for access to the papers of Dr. Alan Herbert; Mrs. Stewart-Mackenzie of Seaforth, for the loan of the letters of her grandfather, Colonel the Hon. John Stanley; the Hon. Nancy Mitford and the Hon. Lady Mosley, for putting me on to both the Stanley papers and the writings of their grandfather, Thomas Gibson Bowles; Miss Clare Blount, for the loan of the letters of Sir Edward Blount; Mrs. C. H. Cole, for the papers of her great-uncle, Benjamin Wilson; Mr. Keith Brown, for the letters of his grandfather, William Brown; and, among my French correspondents, particularly to M. G. Antoine Girot, for providing access to the papers of his great-granduncle, Louis Péguret.

In addition, I must express my thanks individually to the following, here and in the United States, for various documents kindly loaned, or assistance given: Mr. R. C. Buss, Mr. E. G. Pierce, Miss Helene B. Lawrance, Miss Rosemary Meynell, Mr. H. T. Glover, Miss Patience Harbord, Mrs. Laura Strang, Mrs. M. F. Carter, Mr. Frederick J. Burnley, Mrs. W. M. Denham, Mr. Stephen Z. Starr, Mr. C. H. Gibbs Smith, Mr. Maurice Lyon, Mrs. V. Young, Mr. Francis C. Blount, the Royal Naval College, Dartmouth, the Société Jersiaise, and the Wallace Collection.

I am especially grateful to Professor Michael Howard (whose excellent book, *The Franco-Prussian War*, in itself requires a separate note of indebtedness), Sir Isaiah Berlin, and Dr. A. L. Rowse for advice and suggestions made at different stages of the book. Much painstaking research and sifting of the unpublished material was carried out for me in the earlier phases by Mr. Michael Wheeler-Booth, whose help was invaluable to me. I am also profoundly indebted to Mr. Robert K. Windbiel and Mr. Robert Yeatman, for reading the manuscript with critical eyes, and particularly to Mrs. Venetia Pollock, who also performed the same service for my earlier

[1] In view of General Spears's own role as a key eyewitness of events in France during both World Wars, his connection—through his grandfather and the Rafinesque family—with the Siege of Paris and the Commune imparts perhaps an additional interest.

book, *The Price of Glory*; and lastly to Mrs. Renira Horne, both for her valuable criticisms, and support. Needless to say, any errors that remain in the text are mine alone.

Finally, I must record my thanks to Mrs. C. M. James and Mrs. A. R. Bruce for the arduous labour of transcribing my notes and typing the manuscript, and to Mrs. James additionally for preparing the bibliography as well as assisting on various points of research.

*   *   *   *   *

Over the ensuing years, I have been indebted to numerous correspondents and other authors who have provided helpful comments and new material; out of the many, I would like to mention, in particular, Mr. Frank Jellinek, Mr. W. M. McElwee MC of Sandhurst, and Mr. Michael Rosen of San Francisco. Though limited by space, in this new edition I have tried wherever possible to incorporate corrections, amendments and new material. Over the intervening years, events have taken place that modify, perhaps, previous perceptions, particularly of the Commune; Vietnam, Afghanistan, civil strife in the Lebanon and the *événements* of 1968 in Paris itself, at once spring to mind. But, for all these revised perceptions, I have personally come across few new sources that cause one radically to amend the historical record of 1870–1. Among the recent works to be found listed in the revised bibliography at the end of this book, in addition to the monumental two-volume *oeuvre* by my colleague of St. Antony's College, Oxford, Theodore Zeldin, *France 1848–1945*, and Eugene Weber's provocative *Peasants into Frenchmen*, I would however like to draw special attention to *The War Against Paris, 1871* by Robert Tombs, for its thoughtful new perception of the role of Thiers' 'Versailles Army' in the reconquest of Paris from the Communards.

Alistair Horne
Turville, March 1989

PART ONE

THE SIEGE

The Great Exhibition of Paris, 1867

1. The Greatest Show on Earth

THE winter preceding the year of 1867 had been one of those, rare
enough in Paris, that just never seemed to end. Spring itself was so
far no more than a prolongation of the season of sleet and snow, whose
gloom had served to intensify the shadows pressing in upon Louis-
Napoleon's Second Empire. Pessimists and the ubiquitous critics of
the regime were hastening to predict that the Great Exhibition,
intended as a brilliant cameo of the reign which would distract uneasy
minds, would never get off the ground. Indeed, a bare ten days
before the official opening on April 1st, a sea of mud had prevented the
Emperor from travelling by coach from the Tuileries to inspect
progress at the Champ-de-Mars. The next day five hundred workmen
were set to work clearing the roads, while an even larger task force
rushed preparations on the exhibition grounds.

To the astonishment of most of Paris, the Cassandras were con-
founded. Unlike its predecessor in 1855, which Queen Victoria had
visited and which had opened a fortnight late while exhibits were still
uncrated (reminding cynical Parisians of a theatre where the curtain
went up with the actors *en déshabillé*), the Great Exhibition began with
faultless punctuality. True, with the signs of winter and haste not yet

erased, it gave some the heart-rending presentiment of attending 'the baptism of a puny child that seemed born only to die'. Then as April passed, the sun suddenly came out, all at once the shadows cleared, and even Haussmann's pampered, opulent Paris had to admit that she had given birth to the spectacle of the epoch.

The focus of the Exhibition, a few yards from where the Eiffel Tower stands today, was a vast elliptical building of glass 482 metres long, set in a filigree of ironwork, not unlike London's own Crystal Palace. So high was the dome, marvelled Théophile Gautier, 'that one had to use a machine to reach it, and the roof with its red arcades breached by the blue of the sky gave you a sensation of the immensity of the Coliseum'. Inside this huge pavilion all the leading countries of this new industrial era had ranged exhibits depicting the peak attained by human civilization. 'There art elbowed industry,' added Gautier, 'white statues stood next to black machines, paintings hung side by side with rich fabrics from the Orient.' The pavilion was divided into seven regions, each representing a branch of human endeavour, where the various nations of the world exhibited their most recent achievements. It was the year that Lister introduced antisepsis, and Nobel invented dynamite; in other spheres of activity, Russia annexed Turkestan, and the U.S.A. bought Alaska from Russia. Among her exhibits, America, just recovering from the Civil War, had sent a complete field service or 'ambulance', as it was then called, representing the peak of military medicine of the day. But the crowds passed it by, bestowing more attention upon a patent new piece of American furniture, described as a 'rocking chair'. Britain had sent locomotives and imposing bits of heavy machinery, as well as a mass of Victoriana that attempted (with limited success, Paris thought) to combine comfort with elegance. There were displays of a new featherweight 'wonder' metal, 'aluminium'—so precious in its rarity that the Emperor himself had ordered a special dinner service made of it. In the science section which, with machinery, comprised the nucleus of the Exhibition, there were also some marvellous products of a substance known as 'petroleum'; a name which no one thought would cause a particular shudder in Paris in a few years' time.

From Prussia had been sent, among other things, an equestrian statue of the venerable King Wilhelm I. Parisians found it slightly ridiculous, but were too polite to say so. Rather more eye-catching was an immense 50-ton gun exhibited by a Herr Krupp of Essen, who had started life as a manufacturer of railway wheels. Firing a 1,000-lb. shell which weighed as much as two small cannon, it was the biggest thing the world had ever seen, and for this it won a prize. At the Crystal Palace in 1851 Herr Krupp had also shown some of his new steel cannon (the rest of the world was still casting them in bronze), but though women had found them 'enchanting', he had gained practically no orders. So this time he took the bold step of presenting the monster to his king; an extravagant but awkward gift. French military men eyed Herr Krupp's exhibit with perhaps more attention than they would have done had that nation of comic professors and beer-swilling bombasts not astonished Europe by trouncing Austria in a staggeringly short campaign the previous year. But for the moment the world was all peace, and the menacing black gun seemed to belong as much to the past as the droll collection of cannibal arms exhibited by missionaries at a near-by stand. Paris as a whole was not unduly impressed; any more than she was by the grave Prussian officers with their mutton-chop whiskers who showed such flattering interest in the relief plans of all the great French fortresses which their hosts had obligingly placed on show. Besides, thought Paris, the Krupp gun—like its progenitors—was gross and ugly, and therefore to be regarded as of no serious account.

More appropriate to the mood of the moment than the grim products displayed by Krupp, so it seemed, was Louis-Napoleon's own contribution of a statue of a robust nude reclining upon a lion— entitled 'Peace'. As might perhaps be expected, the beautiful and the frivolous formed an important part of France's exhibits, which occupied nearly half of the total ground space of the Great Pavilion. Edwin Child, a twenty-year-old Briton serving as a jeweller's apprentice in Paris, was quite overcome by the 'fabulousness' of the jewellery. In the diary that he was to keep so meticulously in the midst of the dramatic events of the next four years, he wrote goggle-eyed of 'rich peacocks, birds of species as yet unknown, tiaras of diamonds, rubies, emeralds, etc., but in such profusion as even to rival the palace of Aladdin . . . one might go on for ever in describing it'. Less frivolous, however, was one of the main keynotes struck by the Exhibition as a whole, in which the Emperor himself had shown a special interest, and this was the life of the worker in the new industrial age. There was a special section devoted to 'bon marché' goods (though someone remarked superciliously that it slightly gave the impression of a shabby bazaar). Scattered around outside in the park lay complete 'model' workers' dwellings, among which Louis-Napoleon in person was an exhibitor (tactfully he was given a prize). Denizens of Belleville and the other less salubrious working-class slums of Paris came and gazed at these in silence, wondering from what bourgeois dream of Utopia they could have emanated. At the very heart of the Exhibition the social achievements of the Second Empire (and they were by no means trivial) were to be found summed up in an imposing gallery, entitled 'The History of Labour'. But there were one or two events, perhaps too recent, perhaps too apparently insignificant, that went unrecorded. In this same year of 1867, a German-Jewish professor exiled in London published a weighty book called *Das Kapital*. While, in Paris, the Great Exhibition was reaching its glittering climax, in Lausanne the 'International' held its second Congress; and seldom had France known a year with more industrial stoppages.

Beside the 'History of Labour' gallery stood that of the *Beaux-Arts*. Imposing as were its contents, however, the dead hand of the Academicians had deliberately excluded all the rising talent that was in any way controversial. Works by Ingres, Corot, and Théodore Rousseau crowded the walls, but Pissarro, Cézanne, Monet were all rejected, as were Courbet and Manet; though the last two had managed to obtain permission to erect, at considerable personal cost, private pavilions outside, where for 50 centimes you could go to jeer at the *Déjeuner sur l'herbe*. Indeed, it was really in the outer space surrounding the immense dome that the chief magic of the Exhibition lay; a magic that tended to distract the visitor from the more solid displays within. Walking through it reminded one of a voyage round the world, and visitors of the epoch were suddenly astonished to discover for the first time how shrunken the telegraph, the steamship, and the soon-to-be-opened Suez Canal were making the world seem. French was a language hardly heard. Each nation had erected stalls and kiosks where pretty girls or ferocious tribesmen served their customers in bizarre national costumes. Russians wandered about with their little steppe ponies among Yakut and Kirghiz *yurts*; while Mexicans in gay ponchos ogled a reconstruction of the Roman catacombs, pigtailed Chinese wandered serenely round a replica of the Green Mosque of Bursa. Bosomy maidens from Bavaria dispensed beer to morose Andalusians, who in turn were wooed by Arab coffee-vendors, with their raucously insistent calls and magnificent robes. Via the port of Antwerp, one reached an Inca palace; an avenue of sphinxes guarding the Egyptian Temple led to the Swedish house of Gustavus Vasa. Inside the temple, the blackened flesh of a mummy, dead two thousand years, was unbandaged before the shocked eyes of the Goncourt brothers.

Above this extraordinary panoramic babel, as an unread augury of a less distant future, bobbed and hovered a double-decker captive balloon in which Nadar, the famous photographer, took visitors—a dozen at a time—for flights over the exhibition grounds; while up and down the Seine new excursion boats capable of carrying a hundred and fifty passengers made their first appearance. They were called *bateaux-mouches*.

Whether you regarded it from aloft in the *Géant* or the *Céleste*, from the river, or merely on foot, the Champ-de-Mars presented an unbelievable ensemble of brilliance, mediocrity, and simply execrable taste, but above all of dazzling colour beyond the palettes of even that garish new school not yet named 'Impressionist'. In this era of the Suez Canal and Indian nabobs, of the Japanese print and the first of the European interventions in China, the influence of the Orient predominated. It was especially so as dusk came on. Then, the Goncourts remarked, 'the kiosks, the minarets, the domes, the beacons made the darkness retreat into the transparency and indolence of nights of Asia.... And the banners, the flames, the unfurled flags of the nations gave us an impression of walking on a street of the Middle Empire.' With nightfall, too, life on the Champ-de-Mars assumed a new allure. Cheap food, wine, and entertainment attracted all Paris; you could dine excellently for 80 centimes, and Edwin Child recorded that even on his apprentice's pittance he could afford 'a jolly good oyster supper and white wine'. At the same time in one of the casinos he also noted (though far from prudish) being 'nearly disgusted with the masks ... bordering on the obscene'. There was indeed something for everybody's taste. Simple provincials came to gaze and gape at the city women wearing the new, svelte, seductively reduced line, with which the English couturier, Worth, had finally—that same year— dethroned crinoline with all its protective billows. From all over Paris the *demi-monde* in its various ranks converged; the *cocodés* and *cocodettes, lorettes, grandes horizontales,* and *petits crevés* jostled disapproving men in black selling Bibles. Pimps and pickpockets mingled with the swarm of street performers and the charlatan salesmen of patent hair-restorers and arsenic-based rejuvenators that were said to have killed off the Duc de Morny. All night, and week after week, the Capuan revels continued amid the *kiosques* with their provocative girls in national dress, offering an infinite variety capable of satisfying all but the most jaded appetite. Even the Goncourts, profoundly knowledgeable about Second Empire life, were evidently stirred by what they saw:

At the English buffets in the Exhibition, there is a fantastic quality in the lustre of the women, in their crude pallor and their flaming hair; they are like the whores of the Apocalypse, something terrifying, frightening, inhuman.

As the weeks went by, illustrious guests and visitors poured into Paris from every corner of the globe. The city resembled one enormous inn, bearing a sign of '*Complet*' at the entrance. Prices soared, and in protest at being driven from their garrets by the sudden increase in rents, students in the Quartier Latin threatened to 'go and camp in the Jardin du Luxembourg'. They were spurred on by an angry young man with a bushy beard called Raoul Rigault, who was later to achieve some notoriety during the days of the Commune, but now no one paid much attention to their plight. There were too many other things to occupy the mind, and what more than the resplendent arrival of the various monarchs and their retinues ? There was the Prince of Wales, smiling appreciatively on the frivolous city he adored, and the Princess Royal, shocking it by her dowdy gowns; the Pasha of Egypt, the Sultan of Turkey, Kings of Greece, Sweden, and Denmark, Kings and Queens of Belgium and Spain; the brother of the Mikado of Japan, the King of Prussia and the Tsar and Tsarina of All the Russias. Only Franz-Josef of Austria, and his brother, unhappy Maximilian of Mexico, were conspicuously absent. Seldom had there been such a concourse. It comprised, as Prosper Mérimée remarked cynically, 'a *table d'hôte* quite as amusing as that which Candide encountered in Venice'. No less than the cantonment on the Champ-de-Mars, Haussmann's bright new Paris seemed to have been built specifically for these arrivals to the Exhibition. The straight wide boulevards imparted a pomp to the coach processions, flanked by the Imperial *Cent Gardes*, who with their blazing breastplates were themselves refulgent like gods of mythology; for all of which Edwin Child could only find the French word *féerique*. Almost daily there was a procession, with the Emperor seeming to be constantly in attendance at a station to meet a royal train.

Great was the excitement in Paris when it was announced that the King of Prussia and the Tsar would arrive in close succession at the beginning of June. Although the latter was the real guest of honour (high politics decreed it so), it was King Wilhelm of Prussia and his massive Chancellor, Count von Bismarck, who attracted all eyes. On the train they passed positions the old king had occupied in 1814, when he had contributed to the downfall of his present host's uncle. Though some Parisians detected a note of typical Teutonic tactlessness as the King complimented them, ecstatically, on 'what marvellous things you have done since I was last here!', on the whole they thought his behaviour quite unexceptionable. In fact he stole many hearts by always doing the right thing; for instance, by his kindly display of affection for the fragile Prince Impérial, then recovering from an illness. A comfortable figure projecting an image of some benevolent country squire, he set the nervous French at ease, and indeed seemed utterly at ease himself; as someone remarked uncharitably after the event, he explored Paris as if intending to come back there one day. Even the terrible Bismarck, whose great stature made Wickham Hoffman of the U.S. Legation think of Agamemnon, positively glowed with goodwill. Beauties of Paris society surrounded him, admired his dazzling White Cuirassier uniform and the enormous spread eagle upon his shining helmet, and attempted to provoke him; but in vain. In conversation with Louis-Napoleon, he dismissed last year's Austro-Prussian war as belonging to another epoch, and added amiably 'Thanks to you no permanent cause of rivalry exists between us and the Court at Vienna'. The festive atmosphere temporarily obscured the full menace of this remark.

On April 12th, the Emperor attended the première of one of the great entertainments to be produced in honour of his Royal guests: Offenbach's *La Grande Duchesse de Gérolstein*, with the immortal Hortense Schneider (persuaded not without difficulty) playing the lead role. *La Grande Duchesse* was an event of international importance. Of all its galaxy of talent, no one represented the spirit of the Second Empire in all its irony and gay hedonism more than this migrant from a Cologne synagogue choir, Jacques Offenbach. For years the orchestras in the Bois had had their repertoires full of the lilting tunes from *Orphée aux Enfers* and *La Belle Hélène*, the regimental bands marched to Offenbach, and only last year Paris had been driven to a frenzy by the *cancan* from *La Vie Parisienne*. Now here was this new triumph about the amorous Grand Duchess of a joke German principality, embarking on a pointless war because its Chancellor, Baron Puck, needed a diversion. Its forces were led by a joke German general called Boum, as incapable as he was fearless, who invigorated himself with the smell of gunpowder by periodically firing off his pistol into the air. The farce, tallying so closely with Europe's private view of the ridiculous Teutons, was too obvious to be missed. When the Tsar came to see it, his box was said to have rung with unroyal laughter. Between gusts of mirth, members of the French court peeped over at Bismarck's expression, half in malice, half in apprehension, wondering if perhaps King Wilhelm's lack of tact about his previous visit to Paris had not been revenged to excess. But nobody appeared to be showing more obvious and unrestrained pleasure than the Iron Chancellor himself; one might almost have suspected that the pleasure was enhanced by the enjoyment of some very secret joke of his own. In the interval, crowned heads jostled each other to enter Hortense's dressing-room, and the more fortunate were honoured at her home, gaining her the unkind nickname of *le Passage des Princes*. Overnight *La Grande Duchesse* became the jewel of the Exhibition.

Day after day the sparkling entertainments continued. On April 29th it was the first night of Gounod's new opera, *Roméo et Juliette*; his greatest, Paris thought. On June 21st, as a demonstration of just how liberal the Empire was becoming, and could afford to become, Louis-Napoleon permitted a revival of *Hernani*, proscribed since 1852, the work of that incorrigible old revel in exile, Victor Hugo. It nearly backfired; the occasion was marked by a noisy anti-Bonapartist manifestation, amid a clamour to bring back Hugo. (Fortunately by this time most of the visiting dignitaries had already returned to their homes.) And all the time the giggles and laughter echoed from behind the *cabinets particuliers* in the restaurants and from the private establishments. Never had prostitution in all its various degrees found Paris such a paradise. On the Champs-Élysées one of the Goncourts overheard a *cocotte* boasting to her friend: 'I'll tell you frankly; one's making eight hundred francs; one lives on three, and puts five hundred in a Savings Bank.' Writing to his friend, Panizzi, about the *opéra bouffe* arrival of the Sultan, Prosper Mérimée expressed the thought that 'all these great personages come to see Mademoiselle Thérésa[1] and Mademoiselle Menken. These ladies are doing brilliant business and have raised their prices, like the butchers; like them they too are selling fresh meat, or what passes for it.' The more prudish critics of the regime were heard to remark: 'If I were the Emperor I wouldn't be flattered that people came to visit me in order to carry out public orgies.'

Few nights passed without one of the magnificent balls in which the Second Empire so excelled. At the great embassies they waltzed till dawn to the latest Strauss number, 'The Blue Danube'. At the Tuileries, where the Empress gave a ball in honour of her Russian guests, and the great Strauss himself led the orchestra, the gardens had been rendered even more enchanting by cordons of that new invention, electric light, which made the extravagant uniforms and jewels so glitter and flash that once again *féerique* was the only word that sprang to mind. As red and green Bengal lights were reflected in it, water cascading over stucco rocks from specially constructed fountains 'looked like a torrent of fiery lava *en miniature*', wrote one guest. 'No one thought of dancing. Everyone wanted to listen to the waltz. And how Strauss played it!' Then the Emperor took to the floor with the Queen of Belgium, the Crown Prince of Prussia with the Empress.

When could this dream of a Thousand and One Nights ever end, what would replace it ? But the climax of it all was to come with the great review at Longchamp. Again it was organized principally for the delight of the Tsar, yet Louis-Napoleon also had in mind how nothing impressed the King of Prussia more than a good parade, and

---

[1] The renowned vaudeville star of the 'Alcazar'.

he was a man whom it was desperately important to impress. Sixty thousand troops were to have taken part—though, in the event, somehow only thirty-one thousand could be mustered. But in the vibrant sunshine, their sheer panache quite obscured such a numerical deficiency. From the great fortress of Mont-Valérien perched high above the racecourse, a cannon thundered out. The Emperor was arriving, escorted by Spahis on magnificent black chargers, and with the Tsar on his right and King Wilhelm of Prussia on his left. Led by the veteran Marshal Canrobert, the French troops marched and rode past their Emperor: grenadiers in high shakos, light infantry in yellow-striped tunics, chasseurs with green plumes, cavalry with their long lances and awe-inspiring helmets, fierce, turbaned zouaves in red and blue, accompanied by the little *vivandières* who skipped saucily along with small kegs of brandy slung, St. Bernard-like, round their necks. Then came the artillery, caparisoned as for a royal tournament, with superbly polished weapons that had seen service in the Crimea and at Solferino. To anyone who had inspected the Krupp monster on the Champ-de-Mars, the little brass cannon did seem somewhat antique; an observation not escaping the hard eyes of Bismarck, and which no doubt added savour to the private joke he had so enjoyed at *La Grande Duchesse*. But on this intoxicating June day these were ungrateful thoughts, drowned by the great roars of '*Vive l'Empereur !*' as each detachment swept past the Imperial stand. The review terminated with a massed cavalry charge of ten thousand cuirassiers, carabiniers, scouts, lancers, and hussars. Within five yards of the royal guests they halted, in perfect unison, saluting with drawn sabres. Amidst the wild applause of the spectators, the Tsar and the King of Prussia solemnly saluted their host, bowed to the Empress Eugénie, and then warmly congratulated Marshal Canrobert. It was, even the anti-Bonapartists had to admit, possibly the most memorable day of the reign. Nothing like it had ever been seen before —nor ever would again.

The Tsar, certainly, was impressed, and was almost effusive in the compliments he paid his host. Louis-Napoleon was delighted. The unattended new danger of Prussia in European affairs had dictated that his most important task during the Exhibition should be, in the unfortunate absence of Austria, to woo Tsar Alexander II, and the visit had not started off too auspiciously. There had been serious thought as to whether he should have come to Paris in the first place; it was after all the uncle of this new Emperor of the French who had caused the burning of his uncle's Moscow, and memories of the Crimea were recent enough still to hurt. On his arrival a wide detour of the procession had been carefully planned by Louis-Napoleon, so as to avoid the Boulevard Sébastopol; yet despite these precautions there had been shouts from the crowd of 'Long live Poland!', and the Tsar had reached the Tuileries in ill humour. But the seductive soft charms of Paris in early summer, the brilliant spectacles lavished upon him as well as the attentive courtesy of his host, had begun to thaw the Russian ice, and as they drove together from Longchamp, he had never seemed in better humour. Then suddenly something terrible happened. A twenty-two-year-old Polish patriot called Berezowski leaped out of the crowd and fired a pistol at the Tsar. He missed, but the white gloves of the Tsarevich were spotted with blood from a wounded horse. Louis-Napoleon was distraught; 'Sir', he said gallantly, 'we have been under fire together; now we are brothers-in-arms.' The Tsar, shaken by this all-too-nearly successful preview of the dreadful death fate was storing for him, was icy. In one second all Louis-Napoleon's dreams for an accord with Russia seemed farther off than they had ever been.

There was talk of calling off the great ball to be held in the Tuileries that night. Somehow the shot fired at the Tsar had extinguished a portion of the blaze of light generated by the Exhibition. The police state once again revealed itself beneath the benign, almost liberal, countenance of the Empire. A heavy hand descended on 'subversive elements' in the Paris population, and even the 'rebel' artists were told that their private exhibitions outside the Champ-de-Mars would no longer be permitted. On June 11th a still outraged Tsar left Paris. Three days later the Prussian entourage followed, and the *Chefs de Protocole* stood at the station wondering if all the banalities of goodwill that had been uttered did not now ring a little hollow. As the lights dimmed, so people once more became aware of things standing in the dark shadows. Before long there was more bad news. On June 19th the Emperor Maximilian I of Mexico, Franz-Josef's brother and Louis-Napoleon's puppet, abandoned by his French protectors to the mercy of the Mexican nationalists, was shot at Querétaro. Ten days later the news was brought to Louis-Napoleon just as he was distributing prizes at the side of the Sultan of Turkey. This time all celebrations were at once cancelled, for with the death of the unhappy Maximilian died the hopes of the Bonapartes' last foreign adventure. At top speed Manet produced a huge painting of the tragedy, but was forbidden to hang it in his gallery, on the grounds that it might be construed as reflecting upon imperial policy. Next there came reports that that old trouble-maker, Garibaldi, was on the move again in Italy, while in the Assembly the Orleanist, Thiers, was up to mischief. There were predictions of a bad harvest in France, portending a rise in food prices, and news from Algeria of cholera and famine.

Despite all this, the Exhibition with all its accompanying revelry carried on insouciantly throughout the summer and into the autumn. Towards the end, Emperor Franz-Josef of Austria paid a belated visit, though grieving a dead brother and with a sister-in-law driven insane by the tragedy, and too injured by France ever to offer either the friendship or alliance that Louis-Napoleon so badly needed. At the beginning of September Baudelaire, paralysed by syphilis, died aged forty-six in a madhouse; two months later workers began the dreary task of dismantling the Great Exhibition and a long line of Seine barges queued to remove the debris, the unrecognizable papier-mâché fragments of the gaudy pavilions and ephemeral kiosks. Soon the Champ-de-Mars was once again an empty field. With the departure of his last guests, Louis-Napoleon, as the shadows mounted round him once again, began to suffer pain from the stone for which the past excitement had acted as a distracting opiate. An atmosphere of after-the-ball-is-over descended on the city at large. Some sensed that the Exhibition had been the last rocket of the imperial fête, and that all there was left now was the smell of powder. Sober heads began to tot up the accounts. On the surface, there was no gainsaying the spectacular triumph of the Exhibition; even the Assistant Secretary at the American Legation, Wickham Hoffman, had to admit grudgingly that it was 'the most successful ever held except our own at Philadelphia'. A staggering total of fifteen million people had visited it, three times as many as its predecessor in 1855. But had it done as much for the unemployed as it had for industrial progress ? Would it bring France new prosperity at home, and above all had it brought her any new friends ? Or had the foreigners who came simply departed more aware of France's weaknesses and resentful at her triumphs ? Certainly no one would challenge Comte Fleury's famous remark, 'In any case, we had a devilish good time', which seemed to apply to the Exhibition as much as to the Second Empire as a whole. But there was also something in a nostalgic reflection made by Gautier as he mused on the Champ-de-Mars in sadder days three years later, when it seemed to him as if whole centuries had passed since 1867.

'C'était trop beau !'

The Tuileries Ball, 1867

2. Empire in Decline

C'était trop beau!

THE words may have been spoken in partial hindsight, but who during those *féerique* months of 1867, when the Empire seemed to have reached a peak of splendour, could have foreseen then what tragic reversal of fortune lay ahead for France, and particularly for Paris herself, within a passage of less than four years time? Who could have imagined that the scene of that glittering triumph, the Tuileries Ball, would be reduced to ashes, together with so much of central Paris; the Emperor disgraced and in exile; the Empire already little more than a dim memory? History knows of perhaps no more startling instance of what the Greek tragedians called *peripeteia*, the terrible fall from hubristic, prideful heights. Certainly no nation in modern times, so replete with apparent grandeur and opulent in material achievement, has ever been subjected to a worse humiliation in so short a time. Within just three years of the closing-down of the Great Exhibition, badly beaten French soldiers would be encamped upon the Champ-de-Mars; *la ville lumière* besieged by that amiable, courteous King of Prussia, her lights extinguished through lack of fuel, her epicurean populace reduced to a diet of rats. A few months

14

more, and that same king would be crowned emperor over the prostrate body of his former host's fallen Empire; his coronation followed by one of the harshest peace settlements ever imposed by one European state upon another.

Who, in 1867, could have predicted all this? Yet there was still worse to come. Less than two months after the war against the Prussian invader had ended, and the first Siege of Paris had been lifted, there would occur in March 1871 the savage civil war for ever to be associated with the name of the *Commune de Paris*. Before this new conflict was over, during the last desperate days of May 1871 some twenty thousand men, women, and children would be massacred in the streets of Paris by their own countrymen; a blood-bath which made the Terror of 1793–4 with its twenty-five hundred executions protracted over fifteen months seem restrained by comparison, and which exceeded by far in numbers those killed by enemy action during the four months of Prussian siege. Out of the Commune's brief revolutionary reign in Paris, and above all out of its brutal repression, would grow a deep-rooted bitterness that still gnaws at the heart of French politics today.

The Commune poses a set of problems rather different from those of the Siege. In order of importance, essentially military issues become replaced by social and ideological themes. Without the lessons and legends derived from the Commune, there would probably have been no successful Bolshevik Revolution in 1917, and its influence behind another French military disaster—that of 1940—cannot be obscured. In the light of all that has transpired since, the Commune appears as the more historically significant of the two events; certainly it is still regarded as such in the Communist world today. Even though the Siege and the Commune seemingly constitute two quite separate subjects, about each of which a flood of literature has been written, they should not in fact be treated in isolation. The Commune emerged directly from the Siege; without the Siege, the Commune of 1871 could never have happened; without an account of the Commune, the story of the Siege is incomplete. Many of the *dramatis personæ* are the same in both events, and, above all, Paris herself remains the grandly tragic heroine, common to each act.

And yet, however clearly the sparks which ignited the Commune may be traced to the Siege, there exist factors in the background, unconnected with the Siege, which contributed fundamentally to the explosive content of proletarian Paris. For an understanding of this, one has to turn back to examine the diseases concealed by the alluring façade of the Second Empire; as indeed one also must in order to find an explanation of why Louis-Napoleon's Army which had presented so brave and glittering a spectacle at the Great Exhibition should perform so dismally only three years later.

*   *   *

As memories of the Great Exhibition faded away and the Empire rushed on towards its extinction, in the three years of life remaining to it the sounds of revelry still lingered on, the masked balls continued. Just as in England the Victorian code became inseparable from the name of the sovereign, so from its very origins Second Empire society had never shown itself more loyal than in its eagerness to follow the paths indicated by its pleasure-loving Emperor. During the early days of the reign, the *haut monde* escaping from the bourgeois virtuousness of Louis-Philippe's regime had sought consciously to recapture the paradise of Louis XV. In the Forest of Fontainebleau courtesans went hunting with their lovers, attired in the plumed hats and lace of that period. In Paris nothing set the tone of the epoch nor typified it more than those masked balls which so impassioned Louis-Napoleon, and at which he loved to appear as a Venetian noble of the seventeenth century. While the masks permitted their wearers to escape into a Walter Mitty world of fantasy, so the peacock extravagance of the occasions themselves bedazzled and distracted the eye from the more unpleasant realities that lay just beneath the surface. Each ball was more luxurious than the last, and throughout the reign those at the Tuileries occurred with such regularity as almost to resemble a non-stop carnival.

Few were more memorable than the one held at the Ministère de la Marine in 1866 where the guests were required to form *tableaux vivants* of the four continents. A procession of four crocodiles and ten ravishing Oriental handmaidens covered in jewels preceded a chariot 'in which was seated Princess Korsakow *en sauvage*', noted an English guest. 'The fair diplomate gratified us by the sight of one of the best-shaped legs it has been my good fortune to see for many a day; we could judge of its proportions above the knee, as the flesh-tinted maillot which covered while it did not conceal the limb, was of the most zephyr-like texture.' Next came Africa, Mademoiselle de Sèvres, mounted on a camel fresh from the deserts of the Jardin des Plantes, and accompanied by attendants in enormous black woolly wigs; finally America, 'a lovely blonde, reclined in a hammock swung between banana trees, each carried by negroes and escorted by Red Indians and their squaws'. Three thousand guests came, and the cost of this one ball alone was put at four million francs.[1]

---

[1] £160,000 or $800,000.

As the prevailing styles decreed, the women at these balls emphasized their bosoms to the limits of decency (sometimes beyond): they were magnificent, outrageous, and predatory animals. There was the Marquise de Gallifet (whose husband was to play so sinister a role in Paris during the last days of the Commune), sometimes clad as a great white swan, at others as Archangel Michael, her breast sheathed in golden armour. And there was the nineteen-year-old Comtesse de Castiglione, Louis-Napoleon's most ravishing and dangerous mistress, who once appeared at the Tuileries as a provocative Queen of Hearts; which drew from the Empress the deadly shaft that 'her heart is a little low'. What went on in the antechambers to these entertainments the rest of Paris suspected, without needing to hear about Madame X, who had once returned to the ballroom with the Duke de Morny's Légion d'Honneur imprinted upon her cheek.[1] To the prudish or the uninvited, these balls seemed thinly veiled orgies, and indeed the scene more often resembled Rubens than Watteau.

A Victorian visitor to Paris in 1870, Lady Amberley,[2] wrote to her mother: 'We have been each night to the play and are much disgusted with the badness of the morals they exhibit. I hope real life is not as bad.' A curious film of hypocrisy slicked over the surface of the Second Empire; Flaubert was prosecuted in 1857 for offending public morals by *Madame Bovary*, Manet was subjected to most virulent Press attacks for the 'immorality' of his *Olympia* and the *Déjeuner sur l'herbe;* and women smoking in the Tuileries Gardens were as liable to arrest as were young men bathing without a top at Trouville. But underneath, in fact, the morals of the Second Empire were every bit as bad as Lady Amberley feared, and probably worse. *Nana* was its ikon, and its motto the rhetorical question from Offenbach's *La Belle Hélène* that required no answer:

> *Dis-moi, Vénus, quel plaisir trouves-tu*
> *À faire ainsi cascader ma vertu?*[3]

From top to bottom Paris was obsessed with love in all its forms as perhaps never before. In 1858 the Goncourts confided to their journal, almost with a note of surprised discovery: 'Everybody talks about it all the time. It is something which seems to be extremely important

---

[1] It was also said of the Duc de Morny, the Emperor's natural half-brother and ablest counsellor, that he kept a casket containing portraits of his conquests in all strata of society, photographed naked and usually with flowers adorning their private parts.

[2] The mother of Bertrand Russell.

[3] 'Tell me, Venus, what pleasure you find
In robbing me thus of my virtue'?

and extremely absorbing.' Even in their own circle, where some of the greatest intellects of the times gathered, few evenings went by without Sainte-Beuve or another holding forth on sex on an almost schoolboy plane. According to Paris police records, during one month in 1866, 2,344 wives left their husbands, and 4,427 husbands left their wives; there were some five thousand prostitutes registered at the Prefecture, and another thirty thousand 'free lances'.

The greatest of the *grandes horizontales*, 'La Païva', once asked Ponsard the playwright to compose some verses in honour of her sumptuous new staircase (in what is now the Travellers' Club on the Champs Elysées), and he replied with a single line adapted from *Phèdre*: '*Ainsi que la vertu, le vice a ses degrés*.'[1] Certainly this was true of the Second Empire, where all was meticulously, one might almost say decorously, organized. There was a place, a step on the staircase, for everyone. A married woman, driven from her home on account of some revealed indiscretion, could establish herself at one of several levels within the *demi-monde* before the barrier of actual prostitution was crossed. At the top of the social staircase, immense fortunes passed through their hands. Even Egyptian beys could be ruined in a matter of weeks. Louis-Napoleon supposedly gave the Comtesse de Castiglione a pearl necklace costing 422,000 francs, plus 50,000 a month pin-money; while Lord Hertford, by reputation the meanest man in Paris, gave her a million for the pleasures of one night in which she promised to abandon herself to every known *volupté* (afterwards, it was said, she was confined to bed for three days). La Païva, who adopted the splendidly suitable motto of *qui paye y va*, herself spent half a million francs a year on her table. Among the other *grandes horizontales* were Cora Pearl, an English *demi-mondaine*, born Emma Crouch and seduced at fourteen, and Giulia Barucci, a favourite of the Prince of Wales. Typical of her profession, she was described as having the manner of a patrician, 'but of education, of pudicity, of any concern for convention, not a shadow'. Her whole talent lay in the art of the courtesan.

For clients the *grandes horizontales* drew from the idle rich dandies like Feuillet's '*Monsieur de Camors*', who described his day as follows: 'I generally rise in the morning. . . . I go to the Bois, then to the club, and then to the Bois, and afterwards I return to the club. . . . In the evening if there's a first night anywhere I fly to it.' Everything in the Second Empire seemed designed for their greater convenience; there was even a newspaper, the *Naïade*, made of rubber—so that it could be read while wallowing in the bath. Later, as the fortunes of the rich

---

[1] 'Vice, like virtue, has its steps up and down'.

dandies poured away into the same bottomless chasms, they became known as *petits crevés*, to whom, in their debauched tastes, there was no more diverting spectacle than watching a turkey dance on a white-hot metal plate. For their delectation, as well as for those lower down the social scale, there were the semi-amateurs: the *comédiennes* (whom it was said the Bois de Boulogne 'devoured in quantity'), the *lorettes* with their apprentices called *biches*, the *grisettes*, and the *cocodettes*. All could be picked up by the bushel at 'Mabille's', or at the circus which on opening night reminded the Goncourts of 'a stock exchange dealing in women's nights'. For the Bohemians there were the *grenouillères*; unattached, easy-going young women who hopped from garret to garret, like the English art student who declared she was for 'free love and Courbet!' Still lower down the scale, there were the pathetic children such as the little girl recorded by the Goncourts who had offered her fourteen-year-old-sister, while 'her job was to breathe on the windows of the carriage so that the police could not see inside'. Finally, below the stairs, for the working men of Paris there were innumerable cabarets where his pitifully few sous could find him a low woman, or—more usually—make him obliviously drunk on raw spirit.

To this picture of unrestrained libertinism under the Second Empire, there was a grim reverse side. The brilliant masked balls would soon be no more than a memory as ephemeral as that of an Offenbach first night, the beauties would vanish across the stage with only a vaguely seductive scent to mark their passage. But something infinitely more sinister lingered on. Syphilis was rampant, and still virtually incurable. Many of the great men of the age were to die of it; among them de Maupassant, Jules Goncourt, Dumas *fils*, Baudelaire, and Manet. Renoir once remarked, almost regretfully, that he could not be a true genius because he alone had not caught syphilis. This terrible disease was symptomatic of the whole Second Empire; on the surface, all gaiety and light; below, sombre purulence, decay, and ultimately death.

With that peculiar ease the French have for unloading upon an individual the shortcomings of the nation at large, blame for all that was wrong with the Second Empire, all that was corrupt in it, was sooner or later to be heaped upon the man at the top. As far as its morals were concerned, the Second Empire was perhaps justified in pointing an accusing finger. 'The example', as the Goncourts heard someone complain at Princesse Mathilde's, 'comes from high up.' One of the few traits Louis-Napoleon shared with his illustrious uncle was the remarkable sexual potency of the Bonapartes. The incessant string of mistresses and paramours, which so shocked the virtuous Eugénie, lasted as long as his health. Even his marriage has been

c

attributed to the fact that, in an endeavour to seize the impregnable fortress by guile, Louis-Napoleon entered Eugénie's bedroom one night by a secret door, unannounced, but was so frustrated in his desires as to be left no alternative but the marital bed. The power of the Emperor's gallantry was indeed attested by no less a person than Queen Victoria. 'With such a man,' she wrote in 1852, 'one can never for a moment feel safe', but when, three years later, during a drive through the Bois, her host appears to have flirted with the thirty-five-year-old queen as no one ever had before, her views were quite changed: 'I felt—I do not know how to express it—safe with him.'

It was not in matters of morality alone that the Emperor could be held responsible for setting the tone of the epoch. For only in kind was Louis XIV's 'L'État, c'est moi !' less true of Louis-Napoleon. Upon his shoulders rested the whole weighty fabric of the Empire that he had re-established. As the years passed it became more and more evident that, should this main pillar ever be removed, the structure it supported would instantaneously collapse. And the pillar was crumbling.

As long as historical speculation proves profitable, the character of Louis-Napoleon will engage biographers. Seldom has so controversial a character held the sceptre of such power in Europe. It would be hard to name an opposite not contained in him: outrageous audacity and great personal courage wrestled with timidity; astuteness with almost incredible fallibility; seductive charm with its antonym; downright reaction with progressiveness and humanity ahead of their age. Machiavelli jousted with Don Quixote, and the arbiter was Hamlet. All these conflicting components tended to lead to the same cul-de-sac; whatever Louis-Napoleon intended for his people, the final result was usually the opposite. Above all, he pledged them 'the Empire means Peace', but gave France her most disastrous war; Canute-like, during the terrible floods of 1855 he had declared, 'I give my honour that under my reign rivers, like revolutions, will return to their beds and not be able to break forth'; yet in his wake France was plunged into the bloodiest revolt in her history. 'If surnames were still given to Princes', said de Girardin, the journalist, 'he would be called the Well-Meaning.' It was fair comment.

To look at, he had none of the presence of his great uncle, the first Napoleon. As a young man, Chateaubriand noted him as being 'studious, well informed, full of honour and naturally serious'. Later, to a guest who met him while in exile in England at Lady Blessington's, he was 'a short, thickish, vulgar looking man without the slightest resemblance to his imperial uncle or any intelligence in his counte-nance.' Those who saw him in his full glory enthroned at the Tuileries were disappointed to find a man with dull eyes and a large moustache. In the cruelly unflattering circumstances of Sedan, Bismarck's biographer, Dr. Moritz Busch, remarked that the defeated Emperor seemed a little unsoldierlike. 'The man looked too soft, I might say too shabby. . . .' In many ways, Louis-Napoleon was an extraordinarily talented man. His reading during the long years in prison had made him much better educated than the average ruler of the day. Taking up chemistry, he had written a treatise on beet sugar competent enough to be accepted seriously by the industry, and a pamphlet on unemployment gained him considerable (though ephemeral) popularity with the workers. In 1860 he began work on a major life of Julius Caesar, for which Roman *ballistæ* were re-created to hurl missiles about in the grounds of St.-Cloud. First and foremost his inventiveness took a military bent. An excellent horseman, as early as 1835 his *Manuel d'Artillerie* impressed the professionals, and a few years later he was busy improving the current French Army musket. By 1843 he was recommending something ironically similar to the Prussian system of conscription that would eventually be his ruin, and even as Bismarck's captive at Wilhelmshöhe he soon busied himself collecting material on Prussian military organization.

The real tragedy of Louis-Napoleon was that for him the time was out of joint. Under other, simpler circumstances he might—who knows?—have proved one of the great beneficial rulers of Europe. At his back was the constant warning of the insecurity of his, and his dynasty's, position. He knew that he had ridden into power through a technical split between the royalist parties, that many considered him a usurper (which indeed he was); and he knew that it was *l'ennui*—that deadliest of all French diseases—with the bourgeois dullness of poor King Louis-Philippe which had paved the way for him, Louis-Napoleon, and how easily this fickle jade could turn against him too. Therefore for all these reasons France had to be distracted, and like other French leaders before and after him, he was forced into the pursuit of that equally fickle mistress, *la gloire*. At home he would implant the glorious and indelible stamp of his reign on a brilliantly rebuilt Paris. Abroad, grandiose foreign adventures would leave their mark on the world; and, finally, when all else failed, he would distract by gigantic Exhibitions. Unfortunately, most of his schemes were destined to end in dangerous failure because of his erratic character. '*Il ne faut rien brusquer*' was one of his favourite maxims, but it was something which in fact he never stopped doing. De Morny, the most valuable of his advisers, remarked in despair that 'the greatest difficulty . . . is to remove obsessions from his mind and to give him a steadfast will'. George Sand regarded him as 'a sleepwalker', a view that was later upheld by his conqueror, Bismarck, who saw him as 'really a kindly man of feeling, even sentimental; but neither his intelligence nor his information is much to speak of . . . and he lives in a world of all sorts of fantastic ideas'. But still the abysmal tragedy of Louis-Napoleon's reign might have been averted had he not found himself confronted with the two most adroit and dangerous statesmen of the nineteenth century: Cavour, and Bismarck.

Having deemed it necessary to sustain his seizure of power in 1851 by instituting an authoritarian regime, Louis-Napoleon had then set to work to create internal prosperity as one way of diverting French minds from the loss of their essential liberties. In the early years of the Second Empire (admittedly cashing in on the groundwork laid by his predecessor) he had been strikingly successful, and prosperity had become an acceptable substitute for the majority of Frenchmen. In their hedonistic materialism, more than one resemblance might be found between Louis-Napoleon's Second Empire and the 'You've-never-had-it-so-good' England of the 1950's but the big difference was that under the Second Empire economic expansion was real. In its short duration, industrial production doubled and within only ten years foreign trade did the same. Gold poured in from new mines in California and South Africa. Mighty banking concerns like the Crédit Lyonnais and the Crédit Foncier were established, the latter especially designed to stimulate the vast new building programme. In the cities there sprang up huge stores like the Bon Marché and the Louvre. The railway network increased from 3,685 kilometres to 17,924, so that all of a sudden the Riviera—formerly the haunt of only a few eccentric English at Cannes—became a Parisian resort. Telegraph lines radiated out all over the country, and shipbuilding expanded as never before. Guizot's exhortation of 'enrichissez-vous' applied with even more force to the Second Empire. Men like Monsieur Potin the grocer became millionaires overnight; and, as Daubet's unhappy *Nabab* discovered, scandals and vicious intrigues could reduce them to nothing again just as quickly. Speculation raged:

> C'est une frénésie, une contagion,
> Nul n'en est à l'abri, dans nulle région . . .[1]

The contagion spread to the summit of the Establishment, with even the Duc de Morny tainted; while he was Ambassador to St. Petersburg Bismarck recalled that de Morny had used the diplomatic bag to send

---

[1] 'It's a frenzy, a contagion,
No one is sheltered from it, in any region.'

trainloads of valuables back to France duty-free, which were later auctioned and reputedly brought him a profit of some 800,000 roubles. Yet out of this cauldron a new wealthy bourgeoisie had arisen, installing itself solidly and comfortably in the châteaux from which its forebears had driven the aristocrats. As ostentatious as any European aristocracy and determined not to be driven out in its turn, the bourgeoisie was the chief political mainstay of the regime that was responsible for its good fortune; though it had little favourable to say of its benefactor. Never before had France as a whole been more prosperous, and in a remarkably short time she had established herself as one of the world's leading industrial powers. Her population at the census of 1866 had grown to 37½ million, but the most remarkable feature was the immense growth of the big cities, especially Paris, as a result of this industrialization.

The Second Empire's greatest surface achievement (in fact its one truly ineffaceable landmark) was Baron Haussmann's rebuilding of Paris. In 1859 the old 'Farmers-General' wall around the city had been demolished, and seven new *arrondissements* incorporated. At one leap Paris, now with a population of two million, spread out as far as the circle of protective forts that had been constructed by Louis-Philippe. In the centre of the city 20,000 houses were demolished and 40,000 new ones were built at an enormous cost (inflated by the arts of profiteers). Great boulevards cut through the evil-smelling higgledy-piggledy alleys of old Paris, and the city essentially as it stands today was born. Haussmann was more a financier and an engineer than a man of high artistic sense, and his new Paris provoked violent controversy. The conservative Goncourts said it made them think of 'some American Babylon of the future', but George Sand thought it a blessing to be able to walk without 'being forced every moment to consult the policeman on the street corner or the affable grocer'. To an innocent from abroad, like Edwin Child, Haussmann's Paris seemed 'about the most magnificent town, I should think, in the world; all houses being six, seven and eight storeys high and everything so different and so far superior in elegance, utility, sociability, etc., to London . . .'. But away from the centre there were still rural scenes beyond the Arc de Triomphe; there were fields where the Trocadero now stands, and windmills at Montmartre; Passy had the air of an isolated village, and Auteuil was regarded as 'just about the end of the world'. In his beloved Bois de Boulogne, the Emperor himself had done much landscaping, cutting new drives and creating artificial cascades.

But for Haussmann aesthetics had been only one of several considerations. Health and crime were two others. In the course of demolition, many of the festering abscesses of the old city had been lanced; the traditional plague-breeding spots as well as the lairs of assassins and rogues, such as the Buttes-Chaumont. In this city where riot and revolution had become almost a regular feature of life, there was one further aim all-important to the mind of the precariously installed Louis-Napoleon. The acute eye of Queen Victoria had spotted, during her visit of 1855, that he had had the streets of Paris covered with macadam, 'to prevent the people from taking up the pavement as hitherto'. Later on, it would have been apparent to any military observer what excellent fields of fire Haussmann's long, straight streets afforded, what opportunities to turn the flank of a barricade there were for troops debouching from their oblique intersections, and how easy the wide boulevards made it to transport riot-breakers from one end of Paris to another. They had, thought Haussmann, at last succeeded 'in cutting through the habitual storm-centres'. But in fact, with what force will be seen later, he had to a large extent achieved the defeat of his own purpose.

In no way did Louis-Napoleon earn the title of 'the Well-Meaning' more than in his endeavours to improve the miserable lot of the French working man, and herein lay the source of perhaps the saddest paradox of his reign. It was the section of France for which he strove hardest, yet when the crunch came, the working class provided his most violent enemies. Louis-Napoleon's far-reaching social reforms included the setting-up of institutions of maternal welfare, societies of mutual assistance, the establishment of workers' cities, homes for injured workers; also projected were shorter working hours and health legislation; the loathsome prison hulks were abolished and the right to strike granted. The Emperor's own personal contribution to charitable works was considerable, and in his efforts to ingratiate himself with the workers he even decreed that, instead of being named after his mother, Reine Hortense, a new boulevard over the covered-in St.-Martin canal should be given the name of a worker, Richard Lenoir. But many of Louis-Napoleon's more progressive ideas were frustrated by the greed of the new bourgeoisie and the conservatism of the provinces, facts which did not escape the notice of the workers of Paris.

As much as anyone else he was aware of the problems and the dangers; ominously, he told Cobden 'It is very difficult in France to make reforms; we make revolutions in France, not reforms.'

Under the surface life in fact had altered little, with both economic and political problems sharpening the French workers' discontent. They alone it seemed had been left out of the general wave of 'enrichissez-vous', as was typified by the fact that between 1852 and 1870 the wages of a miner in the Anzin collieries increased by a mere 30 per cent, while the company's dividends had tripled. Though workers' wages had increased, almost nowhere had they kept up with the rise in the cost of living. In Paris, for example, the average daily wage rose only 30 per cent over the duration of the Second Empire, while the cost of living rose a minimum of 45 per cent. Conditions were particularly harsh for the workers of Paris, where, as one unfortunate by-product of Haussmann, their rents roughly doubled during the period, so that by 1870 they ate up one-third of their wage packet. Meanwhile food could take another 60 per cent, which left very little over for the other good things of life. Bourgeois chroniclers of the period claimed that the workers of Paris had little taste for meat; the truth was that they simply could not afford it, and it was no coincidence that in 1866 butchers first sold cheap horsemeat (thereby introducing a taste which in four short years would be forced upon a much wider Parisian clientele). Indebtedness was general, and Parisian workers seemed to spend half their lives at the pawnbrokers of the *mont-de-piété*, where the family mattress was the standard pledge. According to Prefect Haussmann himself, in 1862 over half the population of Paris lived 'in poverty bordering on destitution', and of these the lot of the 17,000 women earning only between 50 centimes and 1·25 francs a day was particularly atrocious. For the 3·81 francs which (in 1863) was the average wage, the Parisian worker was required to labour eleven long hours a day. Bad as the conditions of Victorian England were, even apprentice Edwin Child noted how much harder life was in Paris, with his own day beginning at 5 a.m.

The high rents of Haussmann's new city gradually forced the workers out into insalubrious slums on the fringes that were every bit as evil as those demolished in the centre. By comparison, their places of work were often 'palaces'. The *cabarets*, which increased in number immeasurably during the Second Empire, offered slightly less sordid refuges where for a few sous the worker could obtain temporary Lethe. Drunkenness became worse than it had ever been. With it all went a heavy increase in child mortality, a desire for idleness, and a taste for white-hot political discussion within the safety of the *cabaret*.

What life below the glittering façade of the Second Empire was actually like for a great many Parisians has never been more vividly described than by the Goncourts. Jules's former mistress, a midwife called Maria, had gone to deliver a child at the upper end of the Boulevard Magenta, and there she found

a room where the planks that form the walls are coming apart and the floor is full of holes, through which rats are constantly appearing, rats which also come in whenever the door is opened, impudent poor men's rats which climb on to the table, carrying away whole hunks of bread, and worry the feet of the sleeping occupants. In this room, six children; the four biggest in a bed; and at their feet, which they are unable to stretch out, the two smallest in a crate. The man, a costermonger, who has known better days, dead-drunk during his wife's labour. The woman, as drunk as her husband, lying on a straw mattress and being plied with drink by a friend of hers, an old army canteen attendant who developed a thirst in twenty-five years' campaigning and spends all her pension on liquor. And during the delivery in this shanty, the wretched shanty of civilization, an organ-grinder's monkey, imitating and parodying the cries and angry oaths of the shrew in the throes of childbirth, piddling through a crack in the roof on to the snoring husband's back!

Hogarth could hardly have done better.

'Above, wealth increases; below, comfort disappears' was a reasonable enough summing-up of the period. Throughout Louis-Napoleon's reign, for all his good intentions, the gulf between the workers and the rest of the population grew wider and wider, and in Paris it was particularly exacerbated by the works of Haussmann. Whereas in the old days different streets had coexisted side by side, often with the intimacy of village life, now the spiralled rents of the rebuilt *arrondissements* had resulted in a kind of resentful apartheid. Far from 'piercing' the traditional trouble-centres of Paris, Haussmann had in fact merely created new and infinitely more dangerous ones, solidly proletarian and 'Red' *arrondissements* like Belleville and Ménilmontant, where in the latter days of the Empire no police agent would dare appear alone and where—as the Commune was to show—concentration had made the work of organizing a revolt easier than it had ever been.

It was not merely the physical plight of the workers that made relations between the classes increasingly bitter; after all, in the industrial nineteenth century the majority of workers still regarded poverty and misery as part of their ineluctable lot. There were other factors for discontent under the Second Empire, philosophical and political, that at the moment were less easily classified. Workers who had the time and strength to think began to be gnawed by the fear that, as the gulf between *patron* and employee widened, not only was the latter's relative prosperity diminishing, but also any say he might have in the actual development of the new industrial system, which was turning out increasingly to his disadvantage. It was a fear that was by no means confined to the French worker, as 1848 had shown, but there lay a particular, dangerous legacy behind French frustrations. After each of the three major uprisings within the past century, the Great Revolution of 1789, the July Days of 1830, and the February and June uprisings of 1848, the French workers felt in retrospect that they had been swindled. It was mostly their blood that had flowed at the barricades, but on each occasion the bourgeoisie had somehow slyly reaped the benefits. The resentment was particularly keen among Paris workers, who with some justification regarded themselves as initiators of all three revolutions; and above all their memories smouldered from the most recent one. During the June insurrection of 1848 a higher proportion than ever before of the several thousands killed in Paris were workers. In the resistance to the *coup d'état* of December 1851, which Louis-Napoleon himself quelled with unmitigated brutality, some 160 were killed in Paris, most of them workers, and in the regime of terror that followed 26,000 were arrested and transported in hulks. Henceforth the Parisian proletariat, more politically conscious than any other, would never forgive Louis-Napoleon for destroying the Republic *they* had created; nor would they forget the way the *petit bourgeois* had betrayed them when they were so brutally mown down on these last occasions. Only three ingredients were required to spark off a new and even more menacing explosion: a diminution of the vigilant police state, weapons, and organization.

The last of these three requirements, organization—something virtually unknown to workers in the past—was growing apace, feeding upon at the same time as it nourished their resentments. Louis-Napoleon's attitude towards it was disastrously ambiguous and contradictory. At first he granted the workers the right to strike (which they used to the full), but forbade them the right to affiliate. Gradually, half-heartedly—partly as a manœuvre to play the workers off against the growing power of the Orleanist bourgeoisie—he permitted the workers to form unions under close police supervision. But below the surface things were already seething. In 1863 French representatives attended the first meeting of the International Working Men's Association, organized by Karl Marx whose new and more violent teachings were beginning to replace, in France, those of the venerated Socialist, Proudhon. In 1867, the year of the Great Exhibition, the International held its second Congress; *Das Kapital* was published, and Marx's supporters staged their first successful demonstrations in Paris. Though still in its infancy, with its receipts for 1867 totalling only £67 and Marx himself regarding most of its 70,000 members as 'ragamuffins', by 1870 the French branch of the International was capable of organizing a big strike at Creusot; more important, it had established itself as a centre for revolutionary propaganda and conspiracy.

The opponents of Louis-Napoleon were, however, by no means confined to those who wore blue smocks. Undoubtedly the façade of

the Second Empire owed much of its frivolous brilliance to the fact
that the mass of the bourgeoisie turned to the pursuit of pleasure as
an outlet for energies that would otherwise have been channelled into
political activities, were these not so heavily restricted under the
Empire. At the same time this façade successfully, but treacherously,
concealed the mounting resentments below, which are normally to
be found when the lid is placed on French liberty. In the early days
of the regime, the Corps Législatif had been so shorn of its powers
that it could do little more than place a parliamentary stamp upon
projects already packaged by the Imperial Cabinet. Political meetings
were virtually banned, and censorship of the Press was complete.
There was only one organ of the 'official Opposition', *Le Siècle*, and this
was by no means unfettered. Heavy-footed police inspectors also
breathed down the necks of writers and artists. As Gautier grumbled
to the Goncourts (who, together with Baudelaire and Flaubert, had
all suffered petty persecutions): 'What can you do when they won't
have any sex in a novel? ... Now I'm reduced to writing a con-
scientious description of a wall; and even so, I'm not allowed to
describe what may be drawn on it, a phallus for instance.' Once even
a famous actor was nearly arrested when seen blowing his nose upon
a handkerchief which bore an effigy of Napoleon I.

Following Orsini's assassination attempt of 1858, there had been a
further tightening-up of the dictatorship with the passage of a law
providing summary powers of expulsion without trial. On Louis-
Napoleon's coming to power a large number of Socialist deputies had
been proscribed and expelled from France. With them went Victor
Hugo and many extreme Republicans, such as Louis Blanc, Ledru-
Rollin, Félix Pyat, and Charles Delescluze, who would later come
back into the public eye with some force. From their place of exile
they kept up a barrage of violently hostile propaganda upon the
regime. Among the poorer classes the absent Victor Hugo became a
legendary figure, and his worshippers included the young illegitimate
daughter of a *châtelain* and his chambermaid, who was later to make
her mark in the Commune: Louise Michel, the 'Red Virgin'. Inside
France a steady clientele of journalists filled the Sainte-Pélagie gaol,
which—by no means disagreeable as nineteenth century prisons went
—they turned into a veritable club for sedition.

At the more 'respectable' end of the Opposition spectrum stood the
Legitimists, who favoured a return of the Bourbon claimant, the
exiled Comte de Chambord, and at their side the Orleanists who
regretted the departure of the good old Louis-Philippe. Even the
Emperor's own cousin, Princesse Mathilde, whose influential salon
the Goncourts frequently attended, made little secret of her Orleanist

sympathies. Then came varying shades of Republicans, ranging from the 'moderates' to the downright revolutionaries. The salon of the talented Madame Juliette Adam was a rendezvous where such 'moderates' as the veteran Adolphe Thiers and Jules Favre, the lawyer, could often be found; as well as another younger and more flamboyant advocate, Léon Gambetta, who, regarded as an 'intransigent' or 'radical', stood a shade further towards the more violent-hued end of the spectrum. Still further down came extreme Republicans like Henri de Rochefort, a rebel against an aristocratic lineage, who with his angular figure, quixotic quiff of hair, and the most vitriolic pen of the age was to become a deadly landmark in the last days of the Empire. Finally, tinted with the most burning shades of red came a hotchpotch of revolutionaries: Jacobins, Blanquists, Proudhonists, Anarchists, and later Internationalists. They included old hands like Blanqui, who had first taken up arms against the government of France at the age of twenty-two, in 1827, and who flitted mysterious and ghost-like about Paris usually only one leap ahead of the police; and irreconcilables reminiscent of Robespierre, such as Delescluze. Both men in their early sixties, by the end of the Empire they had spent forty-seven years of their combined lives in various prisons and penal colonies.

Scattered through the spectrum and confined to no particular layer of it were most intellectuals, some Academicians, and especially the writers, who hated the regime passionately for its interference in their work. The artists in opposition were also activated by motives of varying altruism and self-interest; they included the veteran and unquenchable crusader Daumier as well as young painters like Manet and Pissarro and Renoir, for whom the Establishment principally represented the philistine *nouveaux riches* of the bourgeoisie who refused to buy, or take seriously, their 'new' art; above all, there was Courbet, who with some ostentation flung back the Légion d'Honneur offered him in 1870. Much less easy to define in their resentment towards the Second Empire were the various malcontents, the inevitable angry young men and the elder *déclassés* of whom Taine said: 'In the attics of students, in the garrets of Bohemia, and the deserted offices of doctors without patients and of lawyers without clients there are Brissots, Dantons, Marats, Robespierres and Saint-Justs in bud.' Out of the typical background of Left Bank studentry came a young man called Raoul Rigault, who spent most of his spare time in the Bibliothèque Nationale inflaming his thoughts through perusal of Hébert's scurrilous *Père Duchesne* of 1790. Sentenced to prison three times before the age of twenty-four, during one of his flights from justice, starving and desperate, he ran into Renoir in the middle of the

Forest of Fontainebleau. Renoir equipped him with a painter's smock and palette, and concealed him for some weeks. It was a chance encounter that was later to save Renoir from becoming known to posterity merely as a talented young painter whose promise had been cut short by Communard bullets.

Superimposed upon all these diverse groups there was the inescapable perversity that traditionally makes government in France a hazardous occupation; 'France', explained Prévost-Paradol, 'is republican when she is under the Monarchy, and she becomes royalist again when her Constitution is republican'.

All things considered, it was perhaps hardly surprising that Louis-Napoleon was forced to distract France by recourse to 'la gloire', that hardy panacea for Gallic ailments. 'The Empire is Peace', he promised as he came to power, but within two years Frenchmen were dying on the Alma. Though it makes even less sense than it did then, the Crimean War was possibly the only one of his foreign adventures to bring Louis-Napoleon benefits, ephemeral as these might prove to be. At last the wounds in Anglo-French amity that were left over from the era of the first Bonaparte seemed to be healed; Louis-Napoleon danced with Queen Victoria in the Waterloo Room of Windsor Castle, and on her return visit she stood before the tomb of wicked 'Boney' as the organ at the Invalides played 'God Save the Queen'. From then on things became progressively worse for Louis-Napoleon abroad. Much of the trouble stemmed from the blind pursuit of his belief in the sovereignty of peoples; like many of his ideals that were noble in theory, this 'Principle of Nationalities' was well in advance of his era and still more in excess of his powers. The wily Cavour soon spotted how this, plus the urge for la gloire, would make Louis-Napoleon an admirable champion of Italian nationalism, and so—with the aid of Castiglione's irresistible person—seduced him for his own ends. Embroilment in Italy at first brought France glorious—but costly—victories at Magenta and Solferino against the never very martial Austrians in 1859. It also, of course, lost her Austria's friendship, and by grabbing Nice and Savoy from Piedmont as part of his 'fee', Louis-Napoleon greatly impaired Italian affections. Later, through the logic of his Principle of Nationalities, Louis-Napoleon found himself pledged to protect the Pope to the extent of mowing down the popular Garibaldians at Mentana, thereby sacrificing most of the remaining goodwill he had accrued among Italians. At the same time the 'Principle' led him to show sympathy for Polish aspirations of independence—which cost him mighty Russia's friendship, while not benefiting the unhappy Poles; most dangerous of all, the example that he had set in the unification of Italy morally forced him not to interfere with Bismarck's scheme to unite the German principalities under Prussia, which eventually was to cause his downfall.

Had Louis-Napoleon succeeded in his pursuit of '*la gloire*', the dynasty might have been assured a much longer life in France, whatever the forces arrayed against him at home, and the Commune would never have happened. As things turned out, it constantly eluded his grasp, and his awareness of this forced him out on to still more dangerous quicksands in its quest. In 1866 Prussia flattened Austria, after a lightning campaign of unsurpassed brilliance which ended at Sadowa. The largest obstacle to German unification was eliminated and overnight Prussia appeared as a new and deadly challenge to France's traditional status in Europe. Moreover, to Louis-Napoleon who had placed his money on Austria, Bismarck's triumph came as a personal slight. To repair his ruffled pride he ill-advisedly demanded 'compensations', as a reward for his neutrality. These would principally have been at the expense of little Luxembourg, but they also included claims to German territory on the left bank of the Rhine. The over-all result was that Britain now took fright that France had dishonest intentions towards her protégé, Belgium; Germans of both North and South were united in their resentment of French demands; and Bismarck squared up to the fact that sooner or later France would have to be fought before German ambitions could be realized. Louis-Napoleon received no 'tip' (this was how Bismarck contemptuously termed his policy of 'compensations') for his services, and once again '*la gloire*' proved elusive. Next, Louis-Napoleon's craziest adventure of all—the creation of a Latin-Catholic Empire in Mexico into which he had been pushed by his Spanish Empress—collapsed in ruins. The French forces, commanded by an ill-starred general called Bazaine, were forced to evacuate, leaving Louis-Napoleon's puppet 'Emperor', Maximilian, to be shot by Mexican nationalists; and here the only net gain was American hostility.

The year of the Great Exhibition and the calamity in Mexico, 1867, marked the turning-point of the reign. As the fateful year of 1870 approached and all Louis-Napoleon's foreign designs were seen to have ended in disaster, his subjects grew more and more restless. As the Government relinquished its electoral manipulations of the early days, at each successive election the Republicans showed themselves to be increasingly powerful, until in 1869 they had captured Paris and most of the big cities. All else having failed, Louis-Napoleon turned in despair to reform at home. He would convert the regime into a 'Liberal Empire', himself into a constitutional monarch. But it was too late. When the new Law on the Press was passed, repealing the tough laws of 1852 and lifting censorship, it was like the genie released from the bottle. The 'yellow' Republican Press began to insult the ruling family in a way that had never before been seen outside a time of revolution. The attack was spearheaded by Rochefort's *La Lanterne* with its brick-red cover; a kind of *Private Eye* of the times, but an infinitely more deadly scourge. For three months it provided Paris with its greatest amusement since *La Grande Duchesse*.[1] Then Rochefort was sentenced to a year's imprisonment. He chose instead to flee to Brussels (later he was amnestied and returned in triumph to Paris). But the damage was done; a mortal blow had been struck at the respect of the Empire, and the irreverence was contagious. With the Law on Assemblies relaxed, the 'Red' Clubs of the extreme Republicans once again began to meet, now in an atmosphere of impassioned hatred against the regime far exceeding anything known in the revolutionary year of 1848. 'Moderation is Death' became the slogan, and worship of the ancestors of 1793 one of the most popular themes. Meanwhile the Government stood aside, quoting to itself as comfort the parable of the cats of Kilkenny, and hoping that the Clubs too would eventually wipe each other out.

Typical of the new, inflammatory atmosphere was the 'Baudin Trial'. Baudin was an obscure revolutionary who had found a fleeting moment of glory in the uprising against Louis-Napoleon in 1851, when he had leaped on top of a barricade crying 'I'll show you how one dies for 25 sous a day', and was promptly shot. On All Soul's Day, 1868, his name was 'rediscovered' on a neglected tombstone. There were demonstrations and cries of '*Vive la République !*', and Delescluze opened in his paper *Le Réveil* a fund to provide the martyr with a more suitable memorial. The Government foolishly rose to the fly, and brought Delescluze to court. Delescluze was defended by young Gambetta, who astutely turned the trial into a devastating indictment of the Empire. The Government was made to look ridiculous (something inexcusable in France), and Gambetta and Delescluze became idols in their respective spheres.

By 1870 it could with justice be said that France had become one of the most truly democratic parliamentary monarchies among the major powers; there was more liberty than under Louis-Philippe, the Press and political life were as unrestrained as during the Second

[1] The first issue of *La Lanterne* opened with the oft-quoted words: 'France contains, according to the *Almanach Impérial*, thirty-six million subjects, not counting the subjects of discontent.' Instead of an estimated circulation of four thousand, it promptly sold one hundred thousand copies.

Republic. Yet the extreme Republicans continued to preach revolution and even assassination against the Emperor, regarding every fresh relaxation—the amnesty of the Republican exiles, the appointment of a former anti-Bonapartist, Ollivier, to take charge of the new 'Liberal Empire'—as a sign of weakness. In a way they were right. Louis-Napoleon had been greatly debilitated by the deaths, in 1865, first of his shrewdest lieutenant, the Duc de Morny,[1] and later of Walewski and Troplong. There was little new blood available, and old tired faces seemed to surround him. Worst of all, about 1867 the Emperor himself began to show himself tired, worn out with the cares of governing, and foreign ambassadors noted how his conduct of affairs was becoming increasingly dilatory and infirm. At one point, von der Goltz reported to Bismarck that 'the Emperor seemed to have lost his compass'. When Ollivier summoned up courage to tell him that people thought his faculties were declining, Louis-Napoleon (according to the Goncourts) replied impassively, and no doubt thinking of his private life, 'That is consistent with all the reports I have received'. The truth was that the unhappy man was also beginning to suffer the tortures of the damned from an enormous stone on the bladder. Unable to sleep, he was forced to leave his retreat at St.-Cloud because of the noise of the clowns at a nearby fête, and the only sympathy he received from his subjects was: 'What ingratitude on the part of the clowns, whom he had so protected throughout his reign!'

To an English observer who watched the young Prince Impérial drilling his troop of fellow boy cadets, Louis-Napoleon now 'huddled in his seat, was a very minor show', whereas the Empress struck 'a splendid figure, straight as a dart, and to my young eyes the most beautiful thing I had ever seen . . .', who 'dominated the whole group'. As the powers of the Emperor declined, so those of his consort rose. In the eyes of her faithful admirer, Mérimée, 'there is no longer an Eugénie, there is only an Empress. I complain and I admire . . .'. Others were less admiring. To them Eugénie—cold but capricious and unpredictable, adventurous and aggressive—was the single most disastrous influence upon the Emperor in his later years.

In 1869 the last of the great Tuileries masked balls was held; the Empress Eugénie appeared magnificently attired as Marie-Antoinette. As the menace from across the Rhine grew simultaneously with the Republican clamour at home, it seemed a remarkably ominous choice

[1] De Morny was also Louis-Napoleon's half brother; he once said of himself 'I am a very complicated person. I am the son of a Queen, the brother of an Emperor, and the son-in-law of an Emperor, and all of us are illegitimate.'

September 4th, 1870. Rochefort at the Hôtel de Ville

3. The Disastrous Six Weeks

NOT unlike that other year of catastrophe forty-four years later, 1870 arose wreathed in a warm smile of hope. In France, the 'Liberal Empire' which Louis-Napoleon had introduced under the ministry of Émile Ollivier at the end of the previous year seemed so full of promise that there was even a momentary upswing in the popularity of the Emperor. In a plebiscite held to approve the new Constitution (even though its terms, like those of most such referenda, were something of a swindle), the Government won an apparently striking success with a majority of nearly six million out of a total poll of nine million. Over Europe as a whole such a spring of content had not been seen for many years, so that by June the new British Foreign Secretary, Lord Granville, could justly claim not to discern 'a cloud in the sky'. Peace was everywhere. But as summer developed it was a particularly trying one; in fact one of the hottest in memory. There were reports of drought from several parts of France, with the peasants praying for rain and the Army selling horses because of the shortage of fodder. It was just the kind of summer when tempers fray.

Then, at the beginning of July, a small cloud had passed across the sun. To fill the vacant throne of Spain, Bismarck suddenly advanced a Hohenzollern candidate, Prince Leopold of Sigmaringen. So violent, however, was the alarm expressed in France at this threatened act of 'encirclement' that the candidate was promptly withdrawn. Relieved, Lord Granville chided the French Government for resorting to such strong language, and the *Illustrated London News* devoted its July 16th frontispiece to Queen Victoria dispensing prizes amid the peaceful surroundings of Windsor Park. Manet began to make plans for his holidays at Boulogne, and the clouds seemed to have evaporated. But the truth was that France, like a mass of plutonium, had reached the 'critical' stage. Ever since Sadowa she had not forgotten the apparent Prussian affront to her grandeur, and in 1868 one of her most intelligent men, Prévost-Paradol, had predicted that no French Government, however patient, could stand idly by while Prussia proceeded to unite Germany under her, without eventually 'drawing her sword'. When dashing General Bourbaki of the Guard heard that the Prussians had climbed down over Spain, he hurled his sword down to the ground in disappointed rage. The country's mood, that of a great power which sees its position of eminence being speedily eroded, was dangerous, and the Press, led by *Le Figaro*, now set to whipping up flames of bellicosity by inflammatory articles. After all the failures of Louis-Napoleon's foreign policy in previous years, mounting pressure was applied upon the Government to seize this opportunity of pulling off, at any cost, a brilliant coup. Neither the Emperor (who still heard his cousin Prince Napoleon's whispered warning that an unsuccessful war would mean the end of the dynasty) nor Ollivier actually wanted war. But the ailing ruler was being pushed hard, on one side by his heavy-handed Foreign Secretary, the Duc de Gramont, who has never forgiven Bismarck for calling him 'the stupidest man in Europe', and on the other side by his own Eugénie who, pointing to the Prince Impérial, declared, 'this child will never reign unless we repair the misfortunes of Sadowa'.

Gramont now began to adopt towards Prussia a plaintive, hectoring tone. It was not enough that Prussia had retracted; she must be humbled for her presumption, and accordingly Gramont cabled his Ambassador in Prussia, Bénédetti, to keep the crisis hot. The King, who was taking the waters at Bad Ems, received Bénédetti on July 13th with the greatest courtesy. No one wanted war less than he; the unification of Germany he regarded as 'the task of my grandson', not his. But behind him was Bismarck, determined not to wait two generations, who had long since calculated that a war with France would provide the mortar he needed to cement together the present rather loose structure of the German federation. The pretext, however, had to be most carefully selected; one that would cast France in the least favourable light, from the point of view of the other nations of Europe as well as that of Prussia's own German allies. As he once remarked, 'A statesman has not to make history, but if ever in the events around him he hears the sweep of the mantle of God, then he must jump up and catch at its hem'. With France showing herself determined to press for further diplomatic victories, to twist the knife in the wound, Bismarck thought he heard the sweep of the mantle. At Bad Ems, King Wilhelm had become irritated by the importuning of Bénédetti for a guarantee that the Hohenzollern candidature would never arise again. He declined to give such a guarantee, also refusing a request by the French Ambassador for a further audience. A telegram giving an account of his interview with Bénédetti was then despatched to Bismarck in Berlin; without actually fudging it, as he has frequently been accused of doing, Bismarck sharpened the tone of the dispatch before handing it to the Berlin Press and expediting it to every capital in Europe.[1]

In fact, even with Bismarck's editing, the famous Ems Telegram hardly seemed to contain a *casus belli* (certainly not according to the usage of modern diplomatic language, where the tone in which de Gaulle rejected Britain's application to join the European Common Market in 1963 might be construed as only a shade less uncivil). But, although in the eyes of even French historians 'never had an international cataclysm been unleashed over such a futile pretext', the telegram was enough to entice Louis-Napoleon's head into the noose. Throwing to the winds his favourite maxim of *Il ne faut rien brusquer*, he plunged France into perhaps the most *brusqué* action of her whole existence.

On July 15th France declared war. At once she found herself branded as a frivolous aggressor with neither friend nor ally. 'The Liberal Empire goes to war on a mere point of etiquette', declared the *Illustrated London News*. Austria had made it clear she would only join France in the event of a successful invasion of southern Germany. Italy would do nothing so long as there were French troops in Rome. Russia, where Tsar Alexander II was still annoyed at Louis-Napoleon's encouragement of the Poles and further piqued by the apparently insultingly light sentence passed on Berezowski, his would-be assassin at the Great Exhibition, was coldly neutral. The United States had not forgotten the Mexican adventure, and all hopes of British support were torpedoed on July 25th when Bismarck cunningly arranged for *The Times* to print the damning text of French proposals for a Franco-

---

[1] Bismarck's version of the Ems Telegram stated that the King had 'refused to receive the Ambassador again, and had the latter informed by the adjutant-of-the-day that His Majesty had no further communication to make to the Ambassador.'

Prussian partition of Belgium. Only the Irish, who had regarded
Louis-Napoleon's 'Principle of Nationalities' as being in their own
interest, were on France's side. Gladstone's Britain, having declared
herself neutral in 1866, had virtually relinquished any influence in
European affairs; in any case she was preoccupied with domestic
thoughts, so she too would remain, once again, strictly neutral; although
sentiment was generally behind Carlyle when he contrasted 'noble,
patient, deep, pious and solid Germany' with 'vapouring, vainglorious,
gesticulating, quarrelsome, restless and oversensitive France'. But
few thought the 'noble' Prussians had much of a chance. On July 17th,
Lady Amberley wrote to her mother indignantly, 'It makes one
miserable to think of that lovely Rhine a seat of war', while Delane
of *The Times* declared: 'I would lay my last shilling on Casquette
against Pumpernickel.' Fortunately for Delane nobody accepted his
wager, but it was not the last occasion when an editor of *The Times*
would be wrong about Germany.

A young American woman, Lillie Moulton, who dined at the
Palace of St.-Cloud on the eve of the declaration of war, noted:
'The Emperor never uttered a word, the Empress sat with her eyes
fixed on the Emperor and did not speak to a single person. No one
spoke.' But outside, in both nations, scenes of unparalleled exultation
greeted the advent of war.

In Germany, where memories were invoked of the fourteen French
invasions that had taken place between 1785 and 1813, the whole of
Bonn University, a thousand students, joined the colours. In London,
British bystanders gave a cheer to the trainloads of young Germans
as they left Charing Cross on their way to join up, chanting '*Nach
Paris !*' In Paris something like hysteria reigned; mobs in the street
sang the banned Marseillaise and shouted '*Vive la guerre !*' endlessly,
while the more erudite recited de Musset's

> *Votre Rhin, Allemand . . .*
> *Où le Père a passé,*
> *Passera bien l'enfant.*[1]

The Zouaves paraded a parrot that had been taught to screech '*À
Berlin !*' *Le Figaro* opened a subscription fund to present every soldier
in the Army with a glass of brandy and a cigar; and an enterprising
publisher advertised a *French-German Dictionary for the Use of the
French in Berlin.* On every hand, alleged Prussian 'spies' were
seized and roughed up. For a very small minority in Paris, life con-

---

[1] Your Rhine, German . . ./Where the father has passed/The child can certainly pass
too.

tinued virtually unmarked by the outbreak of war; young Edwin Child was too preoccupied by the pursuit of an attractive compatriot called 'Carry', and Edmond Goncourt too distracted by grief at the recent death of his inseparable brother, for either even to note the event in their respective diaries. There were also a few dissentient voices. Flaubert wrote to his 'dear master', George Sand, 'I am mortified with disgust at the stupidity of my countrymen. . . . Their wild enthusiasm prompted by no intelligent motive, makes me long to die, that I may be spared the sight of it. . . . Oh, why cannot I live among the Bedouin?' From the very first, the war was markedly less popular in the provinces than in Paris, and Eugene Weber[1] tells us how the knocking out of front teeth was a regular self-mutilation resorted to, so as to avoid conscription (without them, it was impossible to tear open a musket cartridge), especially in the South West provinces farthest from Paris. From her country retreat in July 1870, George Sand also recorded the contrast between Paris 'braying with enthusiasm' and the provinces where the overwhelming feelings were 'consternation and fear'. The contrast remained throughout the war in some rural areas; Weber tells how, in one village, 'a French patrol saw the people running to greet it with food and gifts, only to turn away when they realised the men were not Prussians.'

Exultation could hardly have been so widespread were it not for supreme confidence. Even Gambetta considered it safe to go off on holiday in Switzerland. Frenchmen still regarded Bismarck's Germany with the kind of amused contempt that Prussians reserved for Austrians. 'Gérolstein' was the model, and who could be frightened by an army under command of a 'General Boum'? Also, it was encouraging to think that German society was perhaps just as decadent as the Second Empire, if one could judge from accounts (which had delighted Paris) of the German princelings at Baden-Baden who had tripped round the famous Cora Pearl and her girls, chanting

> We will give anything, even Germany,
> To go and drink champagne tonight
> With Madame Cora, tra la la.

Of course, there were those who were less sanguine. Mérimée, writing to his friend Panizzi about the enthusiasm for the war and the high morale of the soldiers, added, however, 'I am afraid the generals are not geniuses', and a few days later 'I am dying of fear'. From Washington, Prévost-Paradol, newly appointed French Ambassador,

---

[1] Eugene Weber, pp. 102–4, 519, *Peasants into Frenchmen, the Modernization of Rural France 1870–1914*, 1977.

warned his countrymen, 'You will not go to Germany, you will be crushed in France. Believe me, I know the Prussians'. Then he committed suicide. But, just like the warnings Baron Stoffel, the French Military Attaché in Berlin, had been sending the army, Prévost-Paradol's forebodings also went unheeded. It was more comfortable to place one's faith in the smug pronouncement of the Military Almanac, which rated the Prussian Army as 'a magnificent organization, on paper, but a doubtful instrument for the defensive, and which would be highly imperfect during the first phase of an offensive war'.

In fact, whether on paper or in practice, the Prussian Army of 1870 was a magnificent instrument by any standard. At the top, the King was the first professional soldier to rule Prussia since Frederick the Great; it was a matter of pride to him that he could inspect eighty-seven battalions in twenty-two days, and under his mantle nothing had been too good for the army. Although the combined population of Prussia and the Northern Confederation, at thirty million, was less than that of France, a system of universal service and of reserves organized on a regional basis that was far in advance of the era enabled the German states to produce an army of 1,183,000 men within eighteen days of mobilization. Nothing on this scale had ever been seen before. Moltke, possibly a greater organizer than a strategist, had devoted his entire genius to the creation of the General Staff, recruited from the élite of Potsdam. For this great body of troops it provided a brain and nerves such as no other nation possessed. No single item was left to chance. Railways built in Germany in recent years had been planned with a particular eye to military needs, especially the requirements of mobilization, and a highly trained corps of telegraphists ensured excellent communications. All aimed at a maximum speed of concentration, for an offensive campaign that would hit the enemy hard before he was ready; the technique would be employed again by the Germans in two later European wars. The Army was issued with maps of France showing roads not yet marked on maps of the French Ministry of War, and when later the Prussians constructed a 'turning' railway around Metz, it was reported that a survey had been carried out secretly three years previously. With the invading army came a regular system of military government (virtually unheard of before the twentieth century), including such refinements as a Post Office functionary dispatched to check that the accounts of the enemy's postmasters corresponded to book entries. The Teutonic 'organization man' had arrived.

The gay uniforms of the French Army, the joyous fanfares and the dashing officers with their fierce, emulative 'imperials' and expansive confidence made a striking contrast to the Prussians' sober disdain for any kind of superfluity. In weapons, the French had a distinct advantage in their cartridge-firing *chassepot* rifle with nearly twice the range of the Dreyse 'needle-gun'. But they had nothing to compare with the steel breech-loading cannon which Herr Krupp had given Prussia, and which the French military leaders had refused to take seriously. The Prussian guns were superior in range, accuracy, and rapidity of fire, and while the French shells tended to burst noisily but harmlessly in the air, the Prussian percussion-fused shells exploded with demoralizing effect at the foot of their targets. Apart from the renowned *chassepot*, the French Army placed its faith in a secret weapon called the *mitrailleuse*. A development of the six-barrelled American Gatling gun, and a primitive precursor of the machine-gun, it consisted of a bundle of twenty-five barrels, which, by turning a handle, could be fired all together or in very rapid succession. In the early days of battle, French newspapers published sketches showing a soldier at his *mitrailleuse* looking in vain, after a few minutes' cranking, for one remaining target. But the much-vaunted weapon had two grave defects; it was as large, unwieldy, and vulnerable as a cannon, but without the latter's range; and it had been such a secret weapon that it was not issued to the Army until a matter of days before mobilization.

In leaders, the imposing triumvirate of Bismarck, Moltke, and Roon would have required an opponent closer to the stature of the first Napoleon than of his nephew. The Prussians had the edge on the French both in that elusive quality, the will to conquer, as well as in actual battle experience; for them, Sadowa had been what Spain and Poland were to be for the Third Reich. France's generals were second-raters by almost any criterion, and all particularly short on initiative. Bazaine, MacMahon, Canrobert, Bourbaki had been skilful at chasing Algerians in Algeria, Mexicans in Mexico; there had of course been wars against European powers in the Crimea and Italy, but they had been long ago, and the victories at Magenta and Solferino had lulled the Army into that complacency so fatal to victorious nations. Poor Bazaine, who was later to find himself locked up in Metz with 200,000 men, had previously never commanded more than 25,000, and that only in manœuvres. And at the very summit of the Empire the divine spark of leadership was lacking, with Louis-Napoleon now desperately stricken by the stone in his bladder 'as big as a pigeon's egg'.

Although in some respects Louis-Napoleon possessed greater military ability than most of his advisers, on matters of life and death he had been tragically impotent to assert his will. Against strong opposition from the Artillery Committee he had succeeded in pushing through the *chassepot*, but he had been forced to finance the *mitrailleuse* out of his own pocket, and completely defeated in his efforts to modernize the artillery. Thus, despite Marshal Lebœuf's famous boast about the Army being ready down to the last gaiter-button (which wits claimed was largely true, as there was not a gaiter in store anyway), it went to war with muzzle-loading brass cannon that were, compared with the products of Herr Krupp, about as obsolete as the Emperor's Roman *ballistæ*. Worst of all, however, parsimonious and complacent politicians had repeatedly frustrated his attempts at reforming Army organization so as to introduce something resembling Prussia's compulsory service. The feudal system of 'substitution'— or 'blood tax'—whereby a rich man could 'buy' a less affluent citizen to take his place with the colours still prevailed, and it was as demoralizing as it was inefficient. The Left had vigorously attacked any expansion of arms spending, with Jules Favre questioning what possible interest there could be for Prussia to war with France; although later no faction would be quicker to chastise the regime for its incompetence in prosecuting the war. For the *Garde Mobile*, the territorials that were to provide the answer to the Prussian reservists, Marshal Niel, the Minister of War, had asked for 14 million francs and got 5. Then, typical of Louis-Napoleon's bad luck, Niel—perhaps the one man who might have reformed the Army—died in 1869. Extremely unpopular in the provinces the *Garde Mobile* was still little more than an idea as France entered the war.[1]

[1] Following Louis-Napoleon's 1851 *coup d'etat*, the French Army had come to be recognized as the defender of the hierarchy; a situation which suited the bourgeoisie, but alienated the Republican foes of the Second Empire, who saw it now as an instrument of authoritarian repression. Indeed, under Louis-Napoleon the Army was widely used—instead of the police—to break strikes as well as to head off revolution. Conversely, the Army saw its own role as being one of upholding the existing regime, rather than attempting to alter or influence the political scene in any way; this despite the fact that some 30 per cent of the officer corps came from the nobility (or at least claimed to) and might therefore have been expected to support a restoration of the monarchy, while—as seen by the way they voted *Non* in Louis-Napoleon's various plebiscites—many others were at best lukewarm Bonapartists.

So, throughout the Second Empire, the Army cadres—worrying less about its legitimacy than they perhaps might have done—remained 'loyal' and 'reliable'. On the other hand, the divisive effect that the Army's role in the coup of 1851, and subsequently, had on the political scene bore the most baneful consequences for the state of France's military preparedness by 1870. Especially was this so when it had come to opposing Louis-Napoleon's military laws crucial to modernizing universal service, and providing the reserves, such as Moltke was churning out on the other side of the Rhine. Universal service in France was a farce anyway, with a system of substitution whereby the moderately affluent bourgeois could, for a modest sum (of perhaps 1500 francs), purchase a substitute. The results were not all that dissimilar to those of college deferrals to the draft permitted in the US during the Vietnam War; the Army got the rag-tag-and-bobtail, the élite stayed out.

During those first days, France's highly centralized mobilization machinery produced scenes of indescribable chaos. Soldiers from the Pas de Calais had to rejoin their depots in the south, or in the west, finally to be sent to fight in the east. The whole nation surged with men travelling frenetically to and fro. A retired major watching the commotion at the Gare de l'Est said 'It was like that during our embarkments for the Crimea and Italy; the memory reassures me'. But the commanders found less cause for comfort. On the third day of mobilization, General Micheler telegraphed in despair: 'Have arrived at Belfort. Can't find my brigade. Can't find the divisional commander. What shall I do ? Don't know where my regiments are'. When travel-weary troops finally reached their destination, there was often nowhere to sleep because the tents could not be found. Magazines were discovered to be empty. Gunners became separated from their guns. In Metz, France's chief war depot, there were no stores of sugar, coffee, brandy, or rice—and worst of all no salt. At Douai, a gunner general reported 'finding a fine stock of horse-collars, but one-third of them were too narrow to fit any animal's neck'. From Brest, the Admiral Commanding complained that he was putting to sea without charts of the Baltic or the North Sea; and in a final display of combined arrogance and incompetence, the only maps issued to the Army were of Germany, not France. They were never to be used. Summing up the horrible improvidence with which France went so gaily to war against the finest army since the *Grande Armée*, Émile Zola wrote of a 'Germany ready, better commanded, better armed, sublimated by a great charge of patriotism; France frightened, delivered into disorder . . . having neither the leaders nor the men. nor the necessary arms'.

On July 28th, Louis-Napoleon rode forth in command of his armies with the Empress's last words—'Louis, do your duty well'—still

While in the Provinces conscription had continued to be bitterly resisted, in Paris the Right mistrusted a conscript army that smacked of the *levée en masse* for obvious political reasons, and clamoured for a strong professional *armée de métier*, not just as a bastion against the menace abroad, but at home too. The Left saw this, saw the muskets pointing at them, and reacted accordingly. Thiers, the historian who described himself as a 'monarchist who practises republicanism', had studied the lessons of the First Empire and always believed in the superiority of professional armies. But most Republicans agreed with their colleague, Jules Simon, who declared during the debate on the Draft Law of 1867, just three years before war began, 'We want an army of citizens which would be invincible on its home soil, but incapable of carrying a war abroad.' Battling the creation of a *Garde Mobile*, the territorials that might have provided the answer to the Prussian reservists, Simon accused the Government's intent of being 'the organization of war; ours, exceptionally defensive, is the organization of peace'. In vain did Prévost Paradol criticize the left-wing opponents of 'the strong army', on the grounds that 'defensive' war demands as skilful soldiers as 'offensive' war.

ringing in his ears, but with not a single Army corps at full strength. As he passed through Metz, suffering constant pain, to an eighteen-year-old called Ferdinand Foch he gave the impression 'of a man utterly worn out'. Moltke had over 400,000 men in supreme fighting trim and 1,440 guns concentrated on the far side of the Rhine, against the less than 250,000 partially organized men that Louis-Napoleon had been able to muster. Nevertheless, goaded on by the bellicose Paris mob and his own beloved Eugénie, once again breaking his principle of 'ne rien brusquer' he decided on an 'attaque brusquée', without waiting for his own mobilization to be completed. His strategic plan, in so far as he had one, was to advance rapidly eastwards into Germany, in the hopes of swinging the South German states, and eventually the reluctant Austrians, into the war against Prussia. It was about as realistic as most of his ideas on foreign policy. Capturing Saarbrücken from weak German advance forces on August 2nd, he gained for France her one victory of the campaign (one of those to take part in it was the perplexed General Micheler, who had at last caught up with his troops and his Divisional Commander). All Paris revelled in the triumph, and at the news that the fourteen-year-old Prince Impérial had had his baptism of fire, picking up as a souvenir a Prussian bullet that fell nearby; a telegram was read out on the Bourse, reporting the capture of the Prussian Crown Prince by Marshal MacMahon; and enraptured Parisians made a famous tenor sing the Marseillaise from the top of a horse-drawn bus.

But the rejoicing was short-lived. Rapidly appreciating that the French Army was divided by the line of the Vosges mountains, Moltke deployed his forces so that they could concentrate with overwhelming superiority against either half. The first blow fell at daybreak on the 4th when men of General Abel Douay's division in MacMahon's Army were caught breakfasting at Wissembourg in Alsace by troops of the Crown Prince, proving that the latter was still very much at large. The French fought heroically but were overrun by sheer weight of numbers, and became demoralized when their general was killed by a shell. But this was still only a skirmish. The main blow fell two days later at Wœrth when MacMahon, deceived as to the numbers the Prussians could bring against them, allowed himself to be brought to battle by the Crown Prince, with more than twice as many infantry as himself. The Prussians suffered so heavily that they could not pursue, but the result was a resounding French defeat. On the same day, the other half of the French forces, optimistically entitled 'The Army of the Rhine' and commanded by the Emperor himself, suffered an equally crushing defeat at Spicheren to the left of the Vosges and close to the scene of the earlier French success at Saarbrucken. In fact, this battle was not part of Moltke's itinerary. At that moment he was actually holding back his First and Second Armies, awaiting the success of the Third on his left. But the impetuous General von Steinmetz, drawn by the sound of shooting, precipitated his First Army into the battle.

At Spicheren, if the French had been worth their salt (Bazaine and three divisions were doing nothing nine miles from the battle), the day should have been turned into a Prussian disaster. As it was, Prussian casualties outnumbered the French by 5,000 to 4,000, and at Wœrth both sides lost about 11,000 men. The two French defeats were far from decisive, but the troops' morale (already upset by the disorder of mobilization, and the undisciplined, drunken scenes accompanying it) had been seriously shaken; chiefly by the Prussian artillery which had torn great holes in the ranks of the infantrymen long before the Prussians came within range of the deadly *chassepot* or the *mitrailleuse*; and by the ineptitude their leaders had displayed.

After Spicheren and Wœrth, the French never again left the defensive. So brilliant and often irresistible in the attack when that spirit of *furia francese* is uppermost, they have never been good at the kind of fighting withdrawal at which the British soldier so excels. After Wœrth and Spicheren the long, disheartening retreat began. On August 12th, the Emperor handed over the supreme command to Marshal Bazaine. Disastrously, order and counter-order from panic-stricken Paris caused the forces under the two marshals to divide, with MacMahon falling back on Châlons-sur-Marne, the Aldershot of France, and Bazaine on Metz. There was a brief pause while the outside world formed a reappraisal of the Prussians; discovering the Royal Guard, the *Illustrated London News* wrote glowingly that 'a finer or more martial looking set of fellows can be found in no European Army'. Also in England, the Amberleys who had been so shocked by Second Empire morals typified Liberal reactions when they wrote 'we are in great delight at their two defeats and hope the Prussians may push on now to Paris and so end the war soon'.

Bazaine, upset by another extemporized attack on his rear, decided to pass through Metz and fall back on the ancient fortress of Verdun, eventually to join up with MacMahon's forces. But after all the French vacillations and changes of plan, time was running out. On August 15th, the vanguard of Bazaine's retreating column found the only road to Verdun cut by Uhlans of Moltke's fast-moving Second Army, between the villages of Rezonville and Mars-la-Tour in the middle of the Woëvre Plain. The following day a desperate encounter took place, degenerating rapidly into a 'soldier's battle', with the Germans distinctly outnumbered and, for once, their staff-work falling down. By 2 p.m. every foot soldier and every gun had been thrown into the battle, but the Germans were saved by cautious Bazaine's fear of his left flank being turned. Losses were heavy, 17,000 for the French and 16,000 for the Germans, with a son of Bismarck shot in the thigh. That night the battle was broken off, each side claiming a victory. But it was Moltke's men who held the field, astride Bazaine's escape route.

Meanwhile, Moltke was bringing up the whole strength of his First and Second Armies, and Bazaine had withdrawn to a position of what he considered to be 'exceptional strength', at Gravelotte, a few miles back on the road to Metz, where just twenty years earlier a small triumphal arch had been built to celebrate Louis-Napoleon's visit to Alsace-Lorraine. Behind the enemy guns, the tired French could see from their positions the blue outline of the Meuse hills surrounding Verdun in the distance; to them, as much as to the Germans of forty-six years later, it represented the never-to-be-attained Promised Land. On August 18th, 188,332 Germans supported by 732 guns moved in to attack 112,800 Frenchmen with only 520 guns. For the first time the bulk of both Armies were involved, and among the spectators General Sheridan, late of the American Civil War, had arrived to watch (from the German side) what would be perhaps the most decisive day of the war.

Wounded during the retreat through Metz, Bazaine, a promoted ranker, galloped from one threatened battalion to another, comporting himself all that day like a valiant brigadier, but never once like an Army commander. His attention was distracted by the costly efforts of the uncontrollable Steinmetz against his left flank; though, in fact, resting on a ravine, it was the strongest part of his line. But his right hung in the air at St.-Privat in the open Woëvre, which Canrobert had done little to fortify because—typically—the Army's entrenching tools had been left behind in Châlons. As dusk was gathering, the Prussians (for whom the day so far had gone far from brilliantly) swung round to attack at St.-Privat, led by the Guards. It was the end. Through the night Bazaine's Army flooded back in disorder into the sanctuary of Metz. The 20,000 casualties they had inflicted (the highest of the war) to their own 13,000 attested, nevertheless, to the heroism with which the French—though disillusioned and exhausted, outnumbered, out-generalled, and out-gunned—had fought that day. The Prussians, who had committed a number of almost catastrophic errors, had been severely shaken, with the Guards losing nearly all their officers, but, once again, the balance had been tipped largely by sheer offensive spirit.

In Paris the optimism engendered by the first fleeting triumphs had been replaced by a much darker mood. On August 7th, Edwin Child wrote in his diary (it was his first mention of the war): 'In con-

sequence of disastrous news from the seat of war Paris was in a state
bordering upon madness. I myself saw 3 or 4 Germans nearly
punched to death, but for the interference of the police they would
have been, in the evening. Excited mobs *partout parlant la politique*,
in many cases even destructive. Several of the largest cafés being
forced to close'. The next day he started packing up his employer's
jewellery for dispatch to London or Geneva, which he thought 'a most
ridiculous precaution as business happened to be rather brisk'. But
everywhere people seemed to be expecting the arrival of the Prussians
before the gates of Paris at any minute. On the 14th, four days even
before Gravelotte, Child discovered that the entrance to the Bois de
Boulogne had already been blocked by fortifications. Edmond de
Goncourt, who managed to enter the Bois, experienced great emotion
at the sight of the beautiful trees being felled. These days, he commented, had given the population of Paris 'the look of an invalid;
one sees on these faces, yellow, strained and drawn, all the heights
and depths of hope through which the nerves of Paris have passed
since August 6th'.

Meanwhile, news of the first defeats had caused the fall of Ollivier
in favour of General de Montauban, Comte de Palikao (he had
acquired his title after a triumph over Chinese peasants in 1860),
who was to be both President of the Council and Minister of War.
The Left, now abandoning all vestiges of pacifism, relentlessly assailed the Government for its martial shortcomings, with Jules
Favre demanding that the faubourgs of Paris be armed, preparatory to
a *levée en masse*. Although at the time few shared Prosper Mérimée's
pessimism that this measure would only provide 'a new Prussian
Army around our necks', no one would later regret Favre's proposal
more than Favre himself. On August 16th there was a brief glimpse of
what might be expected. Mounting disorder, provoked by the extreme
Republicans, culminated in a serious insurrection in the working-
class quarter of La Villette. A fire station was attacked in an attempt
to acquire arms, and several wretched firemen were killed. One of the
instigators, a man called Eudes, was sentenced to death but saved by
subsequent events to play an important role during the Commune.
On the day of the La Villette affair, Mérimée prophesied to Panizzi
'We are heading inevitably towards a Republic, and what a Republic!'

It was also on August 16th that the Emperor arrived at Châlons,
in a third-class railway carriage. There he found all the signs of a
beaten army. Exhausted soldiers lay about, 'vegetating rather than
living' as one staff officer described them, 'scarcely moving even if
you kicked them, grumbling at being disturbed in their weary sleep'.
Generals crept through the camp in dirty uniforms, afraid to show
themselves to their men. Drunks reeled everywhere, and discipline

hardly existed any more. Among the worst were the eighteen battalions of *Gardes Mobiles* from Paris, whose officers proved quite impotent to prevent them shouting, in response to the exhortation of *'Vive l'Empereur!'*, *'Un–deux–trois! Merde!'* Eventually they had to be dug out of the brothels and drinking-dens of Châlons and sent back to the capital. Out of the remaining debris MacMahon was feverishly trying to constitute a new army.

On the day after his arrival, Louis-Napoleon called a momentous conference at which the fate of the Empire was to be decided. It was attended by his cousin, the unattractive but astute Prince Napoleon (known as 'Plon-Plon'), MacMahon, and a new personality, General Louis Jules Trochu, commanding the recently formed XII Corps. Aged fifty-five, Trochu had behind him (certainly by Second Empire standards) so distinguished a military career that one might well wonder why he was still a mere corps commander, and a freshly promoted one at that. As a young captain under Louis-Philippe he had been specially selected by the great Marshal Bugeaud to be his aide in Algeria, and he had remained with him until his death. In the Crimea, Trochu had commanded a brigade with great flair, and had been badly wounded during the storming of Malakoff. At Magenta and Solferino he had been unique among the French divisional commanders in manœuvring his units with an almost peacetime precision, and his coolness under fire was quite outstanding. Then for the next ten years his career seemed to languish. As the Franco-Prussian War opened, he was to be found humbly offering to take a division to the front, but instead had been sent to command an inactive corps in the Pyrenees. The reason why Trochu's promotion had lagged was partly that he was politically distrusted, regarded as an Orleanist—or worse—and both hated and feared by the Empress. In 1867 he had increased his disfavour in imperial eyes by publishing a tract called *L'Armée Française* in which he had placed his finger all too accurately on most of the things that were wrong with the French Army, not sparing the Government.

But this was not the only reason for the blighting of Trochu's career. He was, so it seemed, something remarkably rare in a French general—unambitious. His dislike of the regime could not entirely explain, first, his desire, on the death of his patron, Bugeaud, 'to re-enter into the most complete obscurity'; nor, subsequently, a series of refusals of important jobs. These had included the command of the Chinese expedition (Palikao got it instead) which would probably have carried with it a marshal's baton, and which Trochu had declined on the grounds of his father's illness. Was there something lacking in the man? Nevertheless the correctness of his warnings about the state of the French Army had now made him a Cassandra. This—coupled to his known political orientations—had acquired him so sudden and great a popularity in Paris that on August 7th a hundred deputies of both Right and Centre had put his name forward as a successor to Ollivier. But Trochu had once again lost himself the job; this time by demanding as a condition that he be allowed to mount the tribune to reveal all the errors of the Government since 1866. Clearly this was not the time for such an inquest, and instead—to get him out of Paris—Palikao gave him the job of forming the XII Corps in Châlons.

On August 10th, Trochu had addressed an important letter to the Emperor's War Council. In it he spoke already of a 'Siege of Paris', adding:

... the essential conditions for all sieges, imperatively necessary for this one, is that the struggle should be supported by a relieving army ... to act by repeated attacks against the Prussian Army, which would as a consequence be incapable of a complete investment, and to protect the railways and major roads from the south by which the city would be provisioned ....

The force to provide this 'relieving army' he thought could only be Bazaine's, then assembled before Metz, which should at once retreat on Paris. Accurately he predicted that

at the present time you still have three routes with which to effect this retreat. In four days you will have only two. Within eight days you will have only one; that of Verdun. That day the Army will be lost.

As it turned out, August 17th, the day the Châlons conference opened, was in fact the day of Gravelotte, but news neither of this battle nor of Rezonville was yet known, so it was still assumed that Bazaine was retreating towards Châlons. At the conference, Prince Napoleon at once vigorously supported Trochu's proposal. The Emperor was listless and silent, and seemed to have no will-power left; at their first encounter he had shocked Trochu by asking him hopelessly 'Where is the King of Prussia?', and throughout the conference it was clear to Trochu that the Prince was now 'the only Napoleon who counted'. Feebly the Emperor suggested he should consult Eugénie, but he was brushed aside, and eventually Trochu's proposals were agreed to. Trochu himself was to return as Governor of Paris, charged with its defence. Thus the strategy was laid for something not unlike that which was executed by Joffre and Galliéni on the Marne in 1914, though the relative strength of the forces available for it were more closely those of Weygand in June 1940. Still, there might have been a chance ....

But on the afternoon of the 17th the dread news arrived that

Bazaine's retreat had been cut off at Rezonville. Once again Louis-Napoleon wavered, and telegrams from Palikao and Eugénie began to arrive from Paris. On no account must he return to Paris with his forces, bearing the stigma of defeat. If he did, the dynasty would surely topple. A strong diversion against the Prussians was called for. '*Louis, fais bien ton devoir*', the words could not be forgotten. Then came fragmentary news that Bazaine had lost at Gravelotte and was now penned in at Metz. MacMahon was ordered to set forth with his 'Army of Châlons' to Reims, instead of Paris, and meanwhile in Paris Palikao was devising a staggering flanking operation that would simultaneously cut in two Moltke's armies, and save Bazaine. After more disastrous vacillation, MacMahon received orders to march towards Montmédy on the Belgian frontier. With him went the Emperor, no longer in military command and a political ruler in name only, carried along like an unwanted parcel in the baggage train of his army, a phantom racked with pain, forbidden to return to his capital, and with no other option but to chase after his Nemesis. The march to the culminating tragedy at Sedan is vividly described by Émile Zola in *La Débâcle*. Old crones on the route jeered at the dispirited, bedraggled soldiery: 'Cowards, cowards!' The hundreds of stragglers brought the Army into further disrepute with the locals; French farmers barred their doors and threatened to fire on the starving troops begging for food. The Army disappeared into the forest wilderness of the Argonne, out of sight of the world. For several days Prussian Intelligence puzzled as to what MacMahon's intentions could be. Then, on August 23rd, *The Times* reported ' . . . the imminence of some great movement . . . Marshal MacMahon is executing strategical movements, which Marshal Bazaine will support at the proper moment'. These revelations reached Moltke on the night of the 24th, but still Moltke pondered; could anyone commit such a folly as to leave Paris uncovered and move across the front of superior enemy forces? But by the following night the pattern was clear. At once the ever-vigilant Uhlans were on the track; now like a pack of wolves, waiting for the stragglers; now like beaters, driving the frightened coveys towards where the guns lie in wait. On those torrid last days of August MacMahon's men, harried incessantly by the Prussian cavalry, must have shared the emotions of their great-grandsons under the torrent of the Stukas, wondering where their own Air Force was.

Meanwhile, Trochu, the new Governor, had reached Paris. On the journey, which had taken nearly twelve hours, his train had been held up by an immense train filled with equipment, labelled—the horrible irony of it—'For the Siege of Mainz'. On the 18th, he had at once issued a lengthy and orotund first proclamation—precursor of many to come—calling for 'not only calm in the street, but calm in your homes, calm in your hearts . . . in sum, the grave and restrained serenity of a good nation'. Finally, he added (for those who cared) the promise that when he had completed his task 'I shall return to the obscurity from which I came'. But at once his plans were upset by the news that what had been agreed at the Châlons conference was abandoned and that not even MacMahon now stood between the Prussians and Paris. Worse still, he found himself thwarted in his every effort to prepare Paris for the now inevitable siege. When he had been received at the Tuileries the Empress was as cold as ice, and accused him of scheming a return of the Orleanists, to which he had replied acidly that he could not see how even their presence 'could simplify a situation that had become so perilously complicated'. There had been a stormy session with Palikao, who had told him that his powers as Governor were 'purely nominal' and from then on assiduously boycotted his office. On August 25th, Trochu wrote a letter to Palikao, complaining that ' . . . the city and its defenders could be surprised by the arrival of enemy columns' and that since taking over his post

I have received from the Government neither verbally nor in writing, neither directly nor indirectly, neither in confidence nor otherwise, any communication whatsoever relative to the movement of the Prussian Army. The defence of Paris is reduced . . . to the rumours of the newspapers. . . .

This having been said, he seems to have lapsed into a characteristic lethargy and, once more, to have withdrawn from responsibility.

As the French leaders, preoccupied by their internecine squabbles, fiddled in Paris, on August 30th the Prussian Third Army, which had executed a grand right wheel, caught up with MacMahon at Beaumont-sur-Meuse, some fifteen miles south-east of Sedan. It was the hundredth anniversary of that prophet of German destiny, Hegel. There was a battle, and that evening French cavalry blades gave a ball at Douzy (did they recall Brussels on the eve of Waterloo ?), attended by hopeful ladies come from Sedan to watch a triumphant battle the following day. But MacMahon, realizing that he no longer had any prospect of breaking through to Metz still sixty miles away, retired into the small citadel town of Sedan, the birthplace of the great Turenne, one of France's more successful generals in past wars with Germany. It was also destined to be the scene of a second dreadful French disaster, in 1940.

The second of France's Armies was now trapped, with its back against the Belgian frontier seven miles away and two powerful Prussian Armies moving in rapidly on the other three sides. In the

E

forthright words of one of the French corps commanders, General Ducrot, '*Nous sommes dans un pot de chambre et nous y serons emmerdés !*' There were rations in Sedan sufficient only for a few days. The situation was hopeless. Nevertheless, right up to the last minute, the French cavalry attacked out from Sedan in a series of desperately gallant charges, worthy of the First Empire. They were commanded by General the Marquis de Gallifet, whose wife had been so renowned for her dazzling costumes at the imperial masked balls, and who was himself to play a rather less admirable role in the last days of the Commune. Would the cavalry try yet again, asked Ducrot? 'As often as you like, *mon général*,' Gallifet is reported to have replied, 'so long as there's one of us left.' Once again they charged, to be shattered by the German guns, this time drawing forth praise from the watching King of Prussia himself: 'Ah! The brave fellows!', words that are still carved on the memorial above Floing. Soon after dawn on September 1st, MacMahon himself was severely wounded at Bazeilles on the outskirts of Sedan. He was replaced by a General de Wimpffen, recently arrived from Algiers, a man of (even by Second Empire standards) unbounded confidence in his own ability. By mid-morning he was still talking of 'pitching the Bavarians into the Meuse'. But chaos inside Sedan had now reached catastrophic proportions; cannons were jammed wheel to wheel with refugee waggons and the wretched Emperor's baggage train, with shells from four hundred Prussian guns bursting in their midst; soldiers were trampled to death trying to get through the gates about to close on the approaching enemy. During the last hours, Louis-Napoleon rode among his wavering troops outside the walls, his face rouged in order to hide just how ill he was, hoping a Prussian cannon would grant him an honourable release, but twice forced by pain to dismount. Finally, he ordered a white flag to be hoisted over the citadel. Though de Wimpffen promptly had it taken down again, crying 'I will have no capitulation', eventually even he had to bow to the inevitable.

On a hill outside Sedan, General Sheridan put down his telescope and remarked to Bismarck 'the battle is won'. Bismarck replied, calmly, he should be glad to think so but saw no signs of it yet. Like a Mongol empire ruled from the saddle, the whole power of Prussia seemed to be present; the King, Moltke, Roon the Minister of War, Bismarck gigantic in his *Pickelhaube* and spurs. There was also a host of German princelings, and reporting the deeds of the day was Mr. Russell of *The Times*. America's General Sheridan was present too. At 6.30 that evening, a French general rode slowly under a flag of truce through the Prussian lines that were reduced to silence by a sense of the moment. To the King he handed a brief note from the French Emperor:

N'ayant pas pu mourir au milieu de mes troupes, il ne me reste qu'à remettre mon épée entre les mains de Votre Majesté. Je suis de Votre Majesté le bon frère.[1]

Bismarck dictated a reply. The terms were hard. Later de Wimpffen arrived to plead for something better, on the grounds—with a touch of prophecy—that

a peace based on conditions which would flatter the *amour propre* of the Army and diminish the bitterness of defeat would be durable, whereas rigorous measures would awaken bad passions and perhaps bring on endless war between France and Prussia.

Bismarck replied harshly, describing France as 'a nation full of envy and jealousy', and adding 'We must have territory, fortresses and frontiers which will shelter us from an attack on her part'. The next day, at the humble house of a weaver in Donchéry, the Emperor met Bismarck to capitulate with 104,000 troops. With their men, Ducrot and Gallifet moved into the degrading misery of a temporary prisoner-of-war compound. There was a ragged last cheer of '*Vive l'Empereur !*' from the Zouaves, and Louis-Napoleon passed on his way to imprisonment in Germany; to Schloss Wilhemshöhe that had once been the seat of his uncle Jérôme, King of prostrate Westphalia. On the capitulation the whole Prussian Army encamped at Sedan sang forth Luther's 'Old Hundred' in thanksgiving, then began to pack their equipment with shouts of '*Nach Paris !*'

It was indeed beginning to look as if, from the German point of view, victory was now only a matter of marching. Of the two Armies with which Louis-Napoleon had intended to cross the Rhine, one—MacMahon's—had surrendered; the other—Bazaine's—was immured, with little hope now of relief, at Metz. What other forces, what weapons, remained to France ? A few fortresses, such as Strasbourg, Belfort, Toul and Verdun in the east, Péronne, Lille and La Fère in the north, were intact. There were plenty of arms still in provincial depots, which the incompetent commissariat had so far proved incapable of distributing; just as there were strewn about France various scattered regular units which, in the chaos of mobilization or of subsequent manœuvres, had not yet arrived on any battlefield. There were also numbers of territorial *Mobiles* units, formed or forming. But there was no third army ready and on a war basis, to replace the other two, and the mood in the provinces, never as keen on the war in the first place as Paris, was hardly one of red-hot enthusiasm. Thus, between Sedan and the capital, Moltke's victorious

---

[1] Since I could not die in the midst of my troops, I can only put my sword in Your Majesty's hands. I am Your Majesty's good brother.'

forces could expect to meet with little more than a few ill-organized groups of *franc-tireurs*. Many, like the observing General Sheridan, felt that in the immediate future 'the taking of Paris was but a sentiment'.

For two days contradictory rumours flitted across Paris. One minute there would be universal rejoicing at news of some miraculous success, or that the King of Prussia had gone mad, and a rush to the windows to hang out flags and light lamps. Half an hour later another dispatch would arrive; away went the flags, and out went the lamps. It was not until the afternoon of the 3rd that definite news of the capitulation reached the Government. The Empress flew into a terrible, Spanish rage, then retired to her room to weep. Palikao was stunned. On recovering his senses, he at once warned the commander of the 1st Division to stand by for trouble—thereby deliberately short-circuiting Trochu, the Governor. But what was to come happened with barely a scuffle.

That night there was a midnight session in the Corps Législatif at which Palikao confirmed the worst rumours. Jules Favre promptly tabled a motion calling for the abdication of the Emperor, but supporters of the Empire still held a majority and managed to stall off a decision with constitutional arguments. But outside in the Paris streets—that parliament of its own—pressure was mounting. Of the first reactions to the news of Sedan, Edmond Goncourt jotted in his journal:

Who can describe the consternation written on every face, the sound of aimless steps pacing the streets at random, the anxious conversations of shopkeepers and concierges on their doorsteps, the crowds collecting at street-corners and outside town halls, the siege of the newspaper kiosks, the triple line of readers gathering around every gas-lamp? . . . Then there is the menacing roar of the crowd, in which stupefaction has begun to give place to anger. Next there are great crowds moving along the boulevards and shouting: 'Down with the Empire! Long live Trochu!' And finally there is the wild, tumultuous spectacle of a nation determined to perish or to save itself by an enormous effort, by one of those impossible feats of revolutionary times.

The next day, September 4th, was a beautiful sunny Sunday; it was, as someone remarked afterwards, the century's only day of revolution when there were neither barricades nor rain. Early that morning the crowds began to assemble again, now chanting in unison:

'*Déchéance ! Dé-ché-ance ! Dé-ché-ance !*'[1]

---

[1] Meaning, in this context, 'abdication'.

Gradually the women and children disappeared and the crowds assumed the look of a manifestation, though not yet of an uprising; a manifestation that was slowly converging upon the Corps Législatif. There the futile debates of the previous night had been resumed in an atmosphere of hubbub, rendered more chaotic by the intervention of outsiders who had infiltrated into the Chamber. Its Imperial Police guardians, as apprehensive as anyone about their immediate future, had suddenly become unaccustomedly polite, explaining amiably 'There's a session going on to overthrow the Government', and allowing individuals to enter on the flimsiest of pretexts. Outside, the Palais Bourbon was still protected from the mob by a cordon of regular troops, but at midday the situation became thoroughly confused with the arrival of the National Guards. Edwin Child had met them on the Place de la Concorde as he was returning from church, 'in steady silent march with drums beating, the silence almost choking in its expressiveness was broken here and there by the cries of *À bas l'Empire, Vive la République!*'.

The Paris National Guard was a kind of militia which, under the Second Empire, had originally been formed chiefly from the 'reliable' bourgeoisie, but in the emergency of August the Government had been pressed to expand it on more democratic lines, and it was already thoroughly permeated with Republican sympathizers. Its arrival at the Palais Bourbon threw the regular troops there, commanded by an elderly and infirm general (who died of apoplexy a few weeks later), into complete bewilderment. Thus about a hundred National Guardsmen were permitted to enter the building as 'reliefs' for the overburdened police. With them agitators and leaders of the extreme Left made their way inside, reappearing at the windows to exhort their followers still outside to emulate their example. In a matter of minutes, the mob had invaded the Chamber itself, where they found the Deputies presciently packing up their belongings. Republican spokesmen like Picard and Crémieux tried to orate to the crowd, the latter forced to stand up on a step-ladder because of his small stature. Repeatedly the President, M. Schneider, called for order and then in despair left his seat; whereupon it was occupied by two young men who diverted themselves by ringing the presidential bell. At this moment of pandemonium, Jules Favre judiciously appeared and drew off the mob by telling it that 'it is not here but at the Hôtel de Ville that we must proclaim the Republic'. There were good precedents for this piece of inspiration. It was on the Place de Grève[1]

---

[1] In the Middle Ages the Place de Grève (now Place de l'Hôtel de Ville) had become a traditional gathering-place for dissatisfied or unemployed workers; hence the expression *en grève*, on strike.

outside the Hôtel de Ville that the revolutionary Municipal Government of Paris had been created in 1789, and it was from this building
that the Provisional Government had ruled France after the proclamation of the Second Republic in 1848. Thus a cavalcade now set
forth from the Palais Bourbon for the great Gothic pile of the Hôtel de
Ville, flanked by the National Guard, whose muskets had in the
meantime sprouted unmartial garlands of flowers. Favre and Crémieux
went on foot, carried along by the mob, Picard in a coach.

At the Hôtel de Ville they found a scene of even greater chaos than
the one they had just left. Their opponents to the Left of them, the
darlings of the extremist clubs—Delescluze, Pyat, Millière—had
beaten them to it and were already in the process of forming a rival
Government. There now ensued a scene in which the machinery of
democracy can seldom have been seen to function in a more curious
manner. Inside the Hôtel de Ville, politicians, demagogues, and men
of the people who had been fortunate enough to gain entry scribbled
down 'lists' of a new Government on scraps of paper; usually, and
naturally enough, heading each list with their own name. They then
ran to the windows and threw out their list to the waiting mob below;
whoever caught it read out the names, and according to the mob's
response so a candidate was elected or not. The potentially explosive
situation between the two groups of Republicans, the 'moderates'
and the 'ultras'—or 'Reds'—was averted by Jules Favre who—with a
lawyer's ingenuity—proposed that the Government of the new
Republic of France should be composed of the Deputies from Paris.
The Parisian mob, as might have been expected, gave its approval and
on this basis the Government was formed. But the air once again
became charged by the unattended arrival of that arch rabble-rouser,
Henri de Rochefort. Released from prison[1] by the mob with Eudes
and others, pale and emaciated from his sojourn there, but entwined
like a maypole with coloured ribbons and flowers, he now appeared
borne upon the shoulders of the crowd. On all sides delirious voices
acclaimed him the saviour of France ('Poor France!' muttered Goncourt), and carried in triumph into the Hôtel de Ville. To pacify the
mob, the new Government (wisely enough) offered Rochefort a sinecure job. Standing on a window-sill of the Hôtel de Ville, Gambetta
with dramatic flourishes now proclaimed the Republic.

All the new Republic needed was a leader. The thoughts of Favre
and of his fellows immediately turned towards the man whose name
had been called out by the mob nearly as often as Rochefort's:
General Trochu. Over the past few days, Trochu, his bad relations

---

[1] He had been imprisoned the previous year for writings offensive to the
regime.

with the Empress and Palikao hidden from no one, isolated and aloof from it all, the one general whose reputation was still untarnished, had rapidly assumed the stature of a god in Parisian eyes. Far from making any gesture to save the regime (though he had only recently assured the Empress of his fidelity), he had remained locked in his headquarters at the Louvre while the Palais Bourbon was being stormed and had not left it until all was over; later, in his memoirs, blaming Palikao for having kept him completely in the dark. As the mob passed the Louvre on its way to the Hôtel de Ville, Trochu rode out on horseback and soon spotted Favre's tall figure with its great head of hair. Favre had told him of the invasion of the Corps Législatif, and called upon Trochu to join in the march upon the Hôtel de Ville. Offered the post of President, Trochu accepted it with no great enthusiasm; having first been assured by his future colleagues that they would 'resolutely defend religion, property and the family'. At a time when the country was involved in a life-or-death struggle, it was perhaps a strange primary consideration.

The remainder of the Government posts were filled amid an almost indecent scramble for spoils on the part of some of the new leaders. Crémieux was observed advancing on the Ministry of Justice in the Place Vendôme as fast as his small legs would carry him, accompanied by a horde of ragamuffins, while Gambetta and Picard—both after the same office—arrived at the Ministry of the Interior simultaneously. Gambetta triumphed, however, through the cunning *de facto* ploy of instantly dispatching telegrams signed 'The Minister of the Interior, Léon Gambetta'. Favre was appointed Vice-President and Minister of Foreign Affairs, and Picard had to content himself with Finance. Étienne Arago became Mayor of Paris. Thiers declined office, and of the extreme Left only Rochefort was brought into the Government. Louise Michel recalled Favre genially greeting Ferré and young Raoul Rigault on the threshold of the Hôtel de Ville as '*mes chers enfants*', but already there were those who wondered how long the peace between the two sets of Republicans would last. Edmond Goncourt for one, though certainly no supporter of Louis-Napoleon, had misgivings about the new regime:

I cannot explain why, but I have no confidence; it does not seem possible to rediscover in this boastful *plebs* those first soldiers of *la Marseillaise*. They seem to me simply cynical cads, full of fun and frolic, playing politics; lads who have no feeling under the left breast for the vast sacrifices of the nation. *Oui, la République.* . . .

One thing was certain; as in the case of past revolutions, France was now ruled by a Government formed by Parisians, of Parisians, and for Parisians. The views of the rest of the country had never been considered for one moment.

Among his first duties Trochu took it upon himself to notify Palikao of what had transpired. Trochu found a broken man who had just received word that his son had been mortally wounded at Sedan. His head resting between his hands, Palikao hardly seemed to take anything in, and then announced that he was leaving for Belgium. Meanwhile the Empress had already fled. Courageously she had stayed on at the Tuileries that afternoon long after the invasion of the Palais Bourbon, until two old friends, Nigra and Metternich, the Italian and Austrian Ambassadors, had come and urged her to flee. At first she refused. She remembered the humiliation in which Louis XVIII had left, forgetting even his slippers, and how poor old Louis-Philippe and Amélie had scuttled out of these same Tuileries in an open coach, taking only fifteen francs with them, and leaving their dinner to be finished by the revolutionaries. She had long sworn that none of this would happen to her. But it was already late. The servants were beginning to desert their imperial mistress, flinging off their livery and pilfering as they went. The mob gathering outside could be clearly heard within; then a clatter of muskets in the courtyard and rough voices on the main staircase. Fortunately something still held the mob back, perhaps the memory of Louis-Napoleon's ruthlessness during the *coup d'état* of 1851. The Empress at last consented to leave. It was too late to use the gate on the Place du Carrousel, which was filled with people, so the Empress, accompanied by the two ambassadors and her lady-in-waiting, Madame Lebreton, left by a side door and scurried through the galleries of the Louvre. At the Rue de Rivoli exit the diplomats a little ungallantly placed the two heavily veiled women in a carriage and left them to their fate. At first they went to the house of a State Councillor in the Boulevard Haussmann, but he had already gone. It was the same story at the house of the Empress's Chamberlain in the Avenue de Wagram. Eventually, in despair, she thought of her American dentist, Dr. Evans, the man who had bought up the Civil War ambulance after it had been shown at the Great Exhibition.

The handsome and popular dentist was at home, entertaining two ladies. At once he offered his services. The next day at dawn he smuggled the Empress out of Paris in his own coach, telling the sentries on the barricades that he had with him 'a poor woman on her way to a lunatic asylum'. Two days later the party safely reached Deauville, where Dr. Evans persuaded an Englishman, Sir John Burgoyne, to take the Empress over to England. It was an extremely rough passage, and the Empress landed feeling so unwell that she had to be taken to see a doctor; by a strange coincidence it was the same that had attended the seventy-five-year-old Louis-Philippe after his flight in 1848.

So the Second Empire ended. The faithful Mérimée wrote to Panizzi that day: 'Everything is collapsing at once'; and six weeks later he died broken-hearted in Cannes. The rest of imperial society made its way, with Palikao, to Brussels; passing *en route* that most famous of returning exiles, Victor Hugo, and his ménage. As they encountered the beaten remnants of the Sedan army, Hugo wept and remarked to his companions: 'I should have preferred never to return rather than see France so humiliated, to see France reduced to what she was under Louis XVIII!'

In Paris the mob had now occupied the Tuileries, finding all the sad signs of an unintended departure; a toy sword half-drawn on a bed, empty jewel cases strewn on the floor, and on a table some bits of bread and a half-eaten egg. In the time-honoured sequence of French revolutions, the mob quickly set about effacing the traces of the fallen regime. Just as at the onset of the 'Hundred Days' the fleurs-de-lis had been unpicked from the Tuileries carpets and replaced with Napoleonic bees, so now all the N's and imperial eagles were chiselled and ripped off the public buildings, and busts of the deposed Emperor joyfully hurled into the Seine. At the main entrance of the Tuileries, later in the afternoon of September 4th, Goncourt saw scribbled in chalk the words 'Property of the People'. A young soldier was holding out his shako to the crowd and crying 'For the Army's wounded', while others in white shirts had climbed up the pedestals of the peristyle columns and were shouting out 'Free entry into the bazaar!'

Throughout the city an atmosphere of unrestrained carnival reigned, and evidently no-one had time to share Goncourt's sober thoughts about the new regime. It was a sparklingly sunny day, no blood had been shed, and all Paris now turned out in its Sunday best to celebrate the most joyous revolution it had ever had. George Sand, aged sixty-six, rejoiced: 'This is the third awakening; and it is beautiful beyond fancy. . . . Hail to thee, Republic! Thou art in worthy hands, and a great people will march under thy banner after a bloody expiation. . . .' On the afternoon of September 4th, Edwin Child noted how 'the army fraternized with the citizens, carrying the butt end of their muskets in the air, and the town presented more the appearance of a grand national *fête*, than that of the capital of a country that has just received the shock of the greatest capitulation and defeat known in history'. There were some incredible scenes. Juliette Adam, long an enthusiastic Republican, thought that the Concorde presented 'a marvellous spectacle':

From the chestnut trees of the Tuileries just as far as the horizon of

Mont-Valérien and the hills bathed by the Seine, the scene is on so grand a scale, the crowd feels such a real communion of ideals and desires, that poetry and enthusiasm invade even the coldest and most insensitive hearts. Everything provokes admiration, everything fascinates the vision of these deeply moved Parisians! Around the lamp posts, red crêpe flutters in the breeze ... water gushes and sings in the fountains; the dome of the Invalides glitters in the sun ....

On the Pont de la Concorde she noticed a young worker in a red fez who had been singing the Marseillaise non-stop for the past three hours, clinging to one of the candelabra. Amid all the celebration, there was a universal intangible feeling that everything was somehow going to be all right now. All had been the fault of the Emperor and his extraordinary mediocrity—no one else's, certainly not France's—and now that had been purged. The new sixteen-year-old wife of Paul Verlaine (whose marriage conscription had postponed) voiced the mystique of *La République* that was so widely shared when she asked, longing for assurance: 'Now that we have her, all is saved—that's so, isn't it? It will be like in ....' 'Like in '92, she wanted to say', explained Verlaine. '*They* won't dare to come now that we have *her*', a workman said, echoing Madame Verlaine. After all, what quarrel could the Prussians have with poor France, now that she had rid herself of the wicked Bonaparte? What the Parisians could not see in this hour of extraordinary rejoicing was the solid German phalanxes, advancing ever closer, nor hear the German Press at home shrieking for the destruction of 'the modern Babylon'.

After Sedan: Troops encamped on the Champs-Élysees

4. Paris Prepares

WHILE Paris continued to exist in a jubilee atmosphere, effacing the last relics of the Second Empire and, in that time-honoured continental manner, changing street names so that the Rue du 10 Décembre reappeared as Rue du 4 Septembre, the new Government settled down to surveying its assets. With a quarter of a million men captive, one way or another, at Sedan and Metz, little enough remained of the Army Louis-Napoleon had taken to the wars six weeks previously. General Vinoy's newly formed XIII Corps which, fortunately, had moved too slowly to reach Sedan in time, was now in fact the last major unit left to France. Bedraggled, jaded, and dispirited, its return to Paris had reminded an American observer of the 'floating in of a wreck upon the beach'. In a letter to their daughter, an English couple wrote 'There seems nobody here to direct anything—soldiers arriving, worn out with fatigue, and no better rooms to be found for them than a bed on the damp earth in the Avenue de la Grande Armée—not even straw, on which to lay their weary limbs. . . .' Part of General Vinoy's corps was also sprawled out in an encampment where that far-away memory, the Great Exhibition of 1867, had once stood. It contained virtually only two good regular regiments, the 35th and 42nd, which had been recalled from Rome where they had constituted the pontifical guard.

A bric-à-brac of other troops escaped from Sedan and elsewhere, numbering perhaps 10,000, made up the total to somewhere over 60,000. There were also 13,000 well-trained naval veterans, including marines and gunners with their weapons, which someone had far-sightedly ordered to Paris; as well as a sprinkling of well-disciplined units formed of gendarmes, customs officers, firemen, and even foresters. Then there were a force of over a hundred thousand *Mobiles*, or '*Moblots*', young Territorials from the provinces who had been organized too belatedly to have received more than the sketchiest training. These included twenty-eight battalions of Bretons, many of whom spoke no French and were regarded with contempt by the proletarians of the Paris National Guard (the feeling was mutual), although they were to prove themselves to be among the most reliable of Paris's defenders. Thus with this concentration of forces upon the capital, Trochu had virtually denuded the rest of France.

Finally, there was the Paris National Guard. At the outbreak of hostilities this had numbered only 24,000 volunteers. Then it was expanded to some 90,000, and the Government of National Defence now vastly augmented it by introducing compulsory registration. Its members were paid 1·50 francs a day and—as a Republican sop to the extreme left-wingers of Belleville—were allowed to elect their own officers. To everyone's astonishment the enrolment of the National Guard produced some 350,000 able-bodied males; a fact which in itself revealed the inefficiency of France's war mobilization. What was to be done with this great untrained mass of men? Only a small percentage of them would be required to fill the role for which they were originally intended, that of relieving the regulars and *Mobiles* on the fortifications. And who was to control the unruly elements of the city, now that they had rifles placed in their hands? From the first Trochu and the regular Army generals had doubts about the National Guard's military value; 'We have', said Trochu, 'many men but few soldiers'. But nobody could then foresee what a terrifying crop would spring from this sprinkling of dragon's teeth.

The force, actual and potential, of over half a million men was supported by more than 3,000 cannon of varying sizes. Some of these guns were mobile field artillery, some were mounted in floating batteries and *chaloupes*[1] of the Seine flotilla (they had originally been

[1] The *chaloupes* were mostly converted *bateaux-mouches* that had made their debut at the Great Exhibition of 1867.

designated for service on the Rhine), but about half of the ·heavy pieces were stationed in the city's external fortifications. And herein lay Paris's principal hope of surviving a siege. The whole city was surrounded by an *enceinte* wall, 30 feet high and divided into ninety-three bastions linked with masonry 'curtains'. In front of the wall was a moat 10 feet wide, and behind ran a circular railway supplying troops to the ramparts. Beyond the moat, at distances varying between one and three miles, lay a chain of powerful forts. There were sixteen in all, each mounting between fifty and seventy heavy guns and each within artillery range of its immediate neighbours. From Vauban's day until the Maginot Line, the French have been unrivalled in the building of fortifications, and every one of the Paris forts was placed in a superbly commanding position. The most powerful of all was Mont-Valérien, perched on its great hill in the loop of the Seine to the north of St.-Cloud. Today, though the wall has gone and Paris has long since enveloped the line of forts, they still offer fascinating and unexpected panoramas out over the city.[1] Unfortunately, however, the forts which had been built on M. Thiers's instance in 1840 were already to some extent out of date by 1870. Nothing had been done to incorporate the lessons about plunging fire learned from the Crimea, and worst of all the range of heavy cannon had roughly doubled during the past thirty years. As a result, several of the forts could be commanded by artillery fire from neighbouring heights (notably those of Châtillon at the south), from which parts of the city itself could actually be bombarded. And then, as Viollet-le-Duc, that great restorer of medieval fortresses who was then serving as a colonel of the Engineers pointed out, there was something marvellously anachronistic about a modern city like Paris, in a country as centralized as France, withdrawing into its keep, while abandoning the country at large to the marauders.

Yet, however grave its deficiencies, the line of forts filled out a circumference of nearly forty miles; which meant that any investing army would be required to occupy a front of approximately fifty miles for a siege to be watertight, and this might require every spare soldier of even Moltke's vast army. Meanwhile, to make up for the valuable time lost in August when his every endeavour as Governor had been thwarted by Palikao, Trochu set to work energetically to supplement the defences. Twelve thousand labourers were employed digging improvised earthworks in the weak places and laying electrically-fired landmines; the catacombs were sealed, and elaborate barrages

[1] Many of the Paris forts are still in use as barracks for the Army or security forces; one of them, more recently, was the scene of execution of condemned O.A.S. officers.

placed across the Seine; the beautiful trees in the Bois were felled to
make barricades and provide fuel; and Bessy Lowndes, an Englishwoman living out at St.-Cloud, watched while a huge gun was installed in the former Emperor's park there. There were inevitable
delays owing to legal wrangles over land appropriation, and personal
tragedies as houses on the outskirts of Paris were demolished to improve fields of fire. There was the sad story of M. Flan, a famous
vaudeville artist of the Second Empire, who had retired with his
magnificent library to Neuilly. Now the engineers came to tell him
that his house was to be demolished that same evening; 'But it will
take at least a week to shift my library'—'So much the worse for your
bibliothèque!' That night the poor man took a room in a neighbouring hotel and was found dead of a broken heart in the morning.
As work progressed, Goncourt paid a visit to the interior circular road
running behind the ramparts and noted 'the lively animation and
grandiose movement of the National Defence':

Throughout the length of the road, the manufacture of fascines, gabions,
sand-bags, and in the trenches the digging of powder magazines and
petroleum stores. On the paving of the former customs barracks, the
dully echoing thud of cannon-balls tumbling off waggons. Above, on the
ramparts, gunnery practice by civilians; below, musketry by the National
Guard. The passage of silent groups of workers; the passage of the blue,
black and white blouses of the *Mobiles*; and in a kind of grassy canal
where the railway runs, the flashing-past of trains with only their super-
structures visible, red with military trousers, stripes, epaulets and caps
of this completely martial population, improvised in the midst of the
bourgeois population. And amid all this, everywhere the uncontrolled
scurrying-about of little open carriages, displaying slightly infatuated
feminine curiosity.

For a visit to the fortifications was rapidly replacing a drive in the Bois
as the smart Parisian's favourite Sunday-afternoon entertainment.

In the centre of Paris, the Tuileries stables and gardens had been
turned into a vast artillery park, and with grim foresight common
graves were dug in the wasteland at Montmartre to prevent the
possible spread of disease. As it was discovered that there were only
two hundred rounds per heavy gun, Dorian, the vigorous new Minister
of Works, ordered the rapid transformation of Paris factories into
munitions plants and cannon foundries. Trainloads of treasures from
the Louvre were shipped off to Brest (Goncourt had watched while a
weeping functionary crated up *La Belle Jardinière*, 'as if in front of a
dead sweetheart when she is being nailed into her coffin'), and the
empty galleries became another arsenal. The *cocottes* and other
members of the profession that had grown so inflated under the

Second Empire were chased off the boulevards and into workshops making uniforms. The partially completed new opera-house was turned into a military depot, the Gare du Nord became host to a flour-mill, and most of the theatres (closed in national mourning after Sedan) became hospitals, as did other such large buildings as the Luxembourg, the Palais Royal, the Palais de l'Industrie, and the Grand Hôtel. At the Bourse were billeted staff officers of the National Guard. On the top of the highest buildings, including the Arc de Triomphe, were installed semaphore stations; many of these were later taken over by the Jesuits, doubtless because of the legendary excellence of their grapevine communications.

Of all the factors confronting a city about to stand siege none is obviously more fundamental than the state of its provisions. How long would Paris be able to feed its vast population ? It was a question the new Government asked itself daily. Fortunately the most efficient of Palikao's late Government, Clément Duvernois, had as Minister of Commerce shown great initiative in amassing foodstuffs inside the city. The Bois de Boulogne had been transformed into an incongruously bucolic scene; 'As far as ever the eye can reach,' wrote the *Manchester Guardian*'s Paris correspondent, 'over every open space, down the long, long avenue all the way to Longchamp itself, nothing but sheep, sheep, sheep! The South Downs themselves could not exhibit such a sea of wool.' In the Bois alone, there totalled some 250,000 sheep, as well as 40,000 oxen, and there were even animals grazing in the smaller city squares. But by one grave oversight, Duvernois had overlooked the need for milch cows, which was later to cause terrible suffering among the children. On the outskirts of Paris Goncourt watched a cavalcade of market-gardeners, bringing into Paris all that 'must not be left for the enemy, carts of cabbages, carts of pumpkins, carts of leeks . . . .' In the forest around Paris murderous public hunts were carried out to prevent any game falling into Prussian hands. Unfortunately the sight of all the beasts in the squares and groaning granaries encouraged Parisians in the belief that the city was more than well provided for, and therefore few thought of accumulating more than modest private stocks of food. The poor, in any case, could not afford to.

The Government itself had little idea just how much food it had in stock, or indeed how many mouths there were to feed. Vaguely it calculated there was enough flour and grain to last for eighty days and fuel for about the same time; and this in itself was assumed to be comfortably in excess of what might be required, on the Micawberish reckoning that before little more than a month was up Paris would be rescued by the provinces she had abandoned, or by some more or less divine form of intervention. Certainly no one imagined that there would be a siege lasting well over four months. Thus, although a rudimentary system of price controls was established, there was no idea of rationing. The actual control of supplies lay in the hands of the mayors of the twenty different *arrondissements*, which resulted in some grave inequalities. Eventually, and inevitably, high prices and interminable queues became the only effective method of rationing. From the very first this danger had been loudly predicted by Blanqui and the Socialist factions, and as early as September 14th the Central Committee of Workers had urged the Government to have all food expropriated and equitably distributed. Later that month, Labouchere, writing as the 'Besieged Resident' of the *Daily News*, wrote gaily to his paper 'I presume if the siege lasts long enough, dogs, rats and cats will be terrified'; little did he know that he would soon be eating more than just his words.[1]

It was here that the Government of National Defence made one of of its worst miscalculations. No effort was made to get useless mouths out of the city; and indeed it was hardly reckoned that any effort would be needed. The herdsmen driving their beasts into the city were confronted daily with a solid mass of impatient coaches leaving it; and there were fearful scenes of chaos at all the railway stations, which—as departing Britons discovered to their sorrow—already refused to accept any luggage. Many foreigners and most of the *corps diplomatique* had pulled out; including Lord Lyons, the British Ambassador (which was to be a source of great bitterness to the remaining British community), but with the important exception of the American Minister, Mr. E. B. Washburne. Edwin Child's employer, M. Louppe, hastened off to Geneva with most of his jewels, but Child himself, although he had got his passport ready, finally decided to stay and see the fun. There were many Frenchmen who with their passion for excitement shared his feelings, and ' *Il faut être là*' became an impulsive slogan.

The trains seemed to bring people in as fast as they took them out. 'One might have thought Paris was the only safe place upon earth', an English commercial traveller called Brown wrote to his wife in England; 'thousands were crowding in all directions towards the barriers. . . . Men, women and children of all classes were carrying, wheeling or dragging some kind of vehicle, and the richer ones

[1] In passing, it is perhaps worth comparing the measures taken by the Russians prior to the Siege of Leningrad, at nine hundred days the longest and most terrible in history. Already by mid-July 1941, more than two months before the actual investment of Leningrad, stringent rationing had been introduced and by August 24th more than one-fifth of the total population had been evacuated.

employed carts of every description from the costermonger to the brougham.' There was an additional factor which was not without its impact upon the thrifty Parisians; the Government ordained a 'fine' on any resident leaving the city, proportional to their rents.

As Lord Lyons left, so young Tommy Bowles, who had been sailing on a private yacht in the Solent when the revolution took place, arrived to constitute himself *de facto* Special Correspondent of the *Morning Post*. Among his journalist colleagues hastening to Paris, Bowles was preceded by Henry Labouchere, who was to gain fame as the 'Besieged Resident' of the *Daily News*. An Englishman with Huguenot ancestry, 'Labby' was something of a character. Aged thirty-nine at the time of the siege, in his youth he had once joined a Mexican circus in pursuit of a lady acrobat. Lover, wit, cynic, stage manager, and diplomat; he had filled all these roles, and had then been elected to Parliament in 1865, where—as a radical and a republican—he was to be apostrophized by Queen Victoria as 'that viper Labouchere!' Inheriting £250,000 at approximately the same time as he lost his seat, Labouchere bought a quarter share in the *Daily News* and promptly appointed himself to Paris; an appointment which was to treble the paper's circulation. During the September 4th 'Revolution' he had terrified his companion and fellow-radical, Sir Charles Dilke, by 'making speeches to the crowd in various characters . . .', causing Dilke to fear they would both be seized as Prussian spies. Thick and fast flowed other curious British and Americans into the city, so that enterprising estate agents were soon circulating advertisements that read; 'Notice for the benefit of English gentlemen wishing to attend the Siege of Paris. Comfortable apartments, completely shell-proof; rooms in the basement for impressionable persons.' Thus, with the influx of foreigners, refugees, outsiders, and—above all—the armed forces, instead of having 1,500,000 inhabitants to feed as the Government estimated, there were in fact considerably over 2,000,000.

By mid-September a truly remarkable transformation had occurred in Paris. As a Frenchman, Louis Péguret, wrote to his mother in the provinces, 'If you saw Paris today, you would be astonished. It's no longer a city, it's a fortress, and its squares are nothing more than parade-grounds. Everything is cluttered up with soldiers and *Mobiles* carrying out manœuvres in rivalry against each other.' The Champ-de-Mars was a seething mass of troops, among whom Edmond Goncourt ironically spotted pedlars selling paper and pencils for them to write out their wills. Observing the workers out at St.-Denis, the ubiquitous Goncourt noted that 'everybody who eats or drinks outside the *cabarets* holds a rifle between his knees', and grocers had taken to

F

selling sugar clad in National Guard képis. There was indeed 'a smell of saltpetre in the air'.

This new-found martial enthusiasm had its unpleasant side: a mounting obsession for uncovering Prussian 'spies'. A M. Patte wrote to a friend in England; 'We are surrounded by spies. The other day ... we arrested two German spies, disguised one in Garde Mobile and the other in woman [sic]; under the dress he had a loaded pistol and a German letter.' Nobody—least of all anyone with a foreign accent or any eccentricity of dress—was safe. Among the first foreigners to be arrested was young Tommy Bowles of the *Morning Post*, as a suspected 'Uhlan', and soon after his release he watched a 'very handsome and elegantly dressed lady' picked up wearing mens' clothes, and claiming that she had 'been in the artillery'. She too was released when her case was discovered to have a simple, romantic explanation to it. Another Englishman saw a woman dragged off triumphantly by the National Guard, amid exclamations of 'It is Madame de Bismarck!', and from this episode he concluded that 'it was positively dangerous for any flat-breasted female of more than the ordinary height, and with the suspicion of down on her upper lip, to venture on the streets.' A Philadelphian and his daughter were seized while sketching in the Bois, and the Anglo-American school attended by one of Minister Washburne's sons was ransacked by troops after an innocent pigeon was reported to have flown out of its garden and over the ramparts. After the Germans had arrived at the gates, a spinster's garret was broken into because people in the street mistook the flapping of her scarlet and green macaw for some kind of semaphore signalling to the Germans, and as the Siege wore on such episodes became commonplace.

Often the 'spy-mania' led to situations that were far from comic. On September 16th, eighty-year-old Marshal Vaillant, the head of the fortifications committee, was manhandled by a mob which claimed he had been spying out the defences, and came within an inch of being shot out of hand. According to Bowles, one wretched drain-worker was actually 'stalked by three hundred National Guards and ... blown to pieces the next time he put his head out of his sewer'. Suspicions were whipped up further by the Paris Press, with even *Le Figaro* alleging that a consignment of French uniforms had been intercepted on its way to the King of Prussia's headquarters; the most rational of men became susceptible, and Goncourt himself admitted that one day as he passed the shuttered mansion of La Païva he wondered 'if this has not been a great bureau of Prussian espionage in Paris'. For the foreign community in particular things became so dangerous that one Englishman at least was to be found advertising in the press, 'Mr. Crummles is not a Prussian, having been born at Chelsea'. Eventually, special passports were issued; nevertheless, by the end of the Siege one English doctor could claim he had been arrested no less than forty-two times.

There was no mistaking the miraculous extent to which Trochu seemed to have repaired the morale of the shattered Army, and by September 13th he felt he was able to risk a mass military parade of the troops in hand. Stretching all the way from the Bastille to the Étoile, it struck one of Trochu's staff officers, Captain d'Hérisson, as 'the finest review I have ever seen'. In the background there were distant rumbles as the last Seine bridges were blown up, but there was comic relief when an elderly admiral with long white whiskers was carried out of sight by a bolting horse. Trochu took the salute astride a magnificent steed, which did not bolt; the drums beat and the bugles sounded, and there were rousing and reassuring shouts of 'Long live Trochu!' that were heartily echoed by the civil population. Certainly there had been nothing quite like it since that famous Longchamp parade held by Louis-Napoleon for the Tsar and the King of Prussia in 1867. The following day Trochu exhorted the Paris National Guard to 'be completely confident in the knowledge that the *enceinte* of Paris, defended by the resolute effort of public spirit, and by three hundred thousand rifles, is unapproachable'. An eminent British banker in Paris who watched the review, Edward Blount, felt so reassured by what he had seen that he wrote to a friend in London expressing the conviction that the French 'will not accept dishonourable conditions—I mean by this territory or ships. They will rather fight to the end, and, when Paris is lost, retreat to the last fortress left in France'. Tommy Bowles was already full of praise for Trochu, thought that Paris 'will fight and fight well', and sharply criticized the English armchair critics who didn't agree. An Englishwoman on her last trip to Paris came away feeling more respect for the Parisians than hitherto, and thinking that they would not easily give in; while Mr. Brown wrote his wife on the day of the review 'If it ever comes to fighting (*which I do not think it will*), I do not think Paris will fall.' Of the British community in Paris, one of its most distinguished members, Dr. Alan Herbert, was in something of a minority when he wrote to his brother, the Earl of Carnarvon, 'I believe the Parisians will not allow a regular siege. The general impression is that it is not possible to support one. . . .' and again the following day 'I do not believe that there will be any serious defence of Paris. . . .', predicting (on more certain ground) that after the war 'we shall very likely have a revolution more or less bloody'. In England, *The Times*, which had had its nose badly put out of joint by

the unexpected performance of 'Pumpernickel', had now switched
to supercilious forecasts of how long the 'city of luxury and pleasure'
could take it.

As the Prussians drew closer, one thing was fairly apparent; there
had seldom been a more powerfully armed fortress than Paris, or
one apparently so strongly defended. The big question, and one which
nobody seemed to bother to ask at the moment, was just how, and
with what long-term strategy, the new leaders were going to use these
considerable assets. The commissars of Leningrad in 1941 had had a
generation of absolute power and a ready-formed ruthless apparatus
upon which to base their conduct of affairs, but the Government of
National Defence could claim no such advantage. Its men had spent
a lifetime in hopeless and helpless opposition; they had been swept
into power before being able to formulate any united policy, or
forward strategy; and by conviction they were kindly-minded
liberals, not revolutionary Dantons. Fundamentally theirs was a
weak position in that they had no other title to be in power than the
acclaim of the Paris mob. The Government's enemies to the Left
were to taunt it constantly that it regarded its chief function as being
to maintain order, and thus the 'bourgeois' *status quo*, as much as to
make war on the Prussians; and there was more than a grain of truth
in it. There was certainly truth in Rochefort's complaint that there
were too many lawyers in the Government. Jules Favre, who with his
high hat and badly-made legal frock-coat might have been a Daumier
model, seemed to set the tone. Ollivier once remarked unkindly that
Favre 'considered a political discourse was just one more counsel's
speech', and it was perhaps typical of his eloquent oratory that,
having assured the immortality of his client, Orsini the bomb-thrower,
he had then abandoned him to the death sentence. Simon, Ferry,
Picard, and Crémieux were all lawyers; old Garnier-Pagès, whose
long white hair, neatly parted over his forehead, flowed at the back
past an enormous collar and down on to his shoulders, spoke as
windily as any advocate; Gambetta was also a lawyer, but he was a
different proposition altogether, as will be seen later. But it was
Trochu, the man of September 4th, whose personality predestined
what the Government of National Defence was to become, and
in whose mind the strategy (such as it was) for the whole siege
was determined.

In his portraits, one sees a short man with a round and bony head;
bald, but with a waxed moustache and the inevitable little 'imperial'
of the epoch. He had a lively voice and there was a look of intelligence
in his eye. He enjoyed iron health, a phlegmatic, even temper, and
was capable of working eighteen hours a day. He was a pipe-smoker.

As he had told his colleagues on his appointment as President, '*Je suis Breton, catholique et soldat*' (to which the cynical Rochefort remarked that all this was 'a matter of perfect indifference'). His father had striven, against great hardship, to make a living as a farmer on wind-swept Belle-Île off the Brittany coast. In 1866 Trochu's elder brother had died, leaving eleven destitute children. Trochu, whose wife was barren, adopted the seven younger children and brought them up as his own. His long, rather sermonizing letters to them, constantly referring to '*la philosophie de la vie*', are in the true tradition of the provincial bourgeois of the age, as well as being revealing of Trochu's character. In his distinguished work *L'Armée française* of 1867 he had also harped on the urgency of finding a 'moral philosophy' to replace that of material self-seeking in the Army. Profoundly religious, he would have been extremely contented in the contemplative and sanctified atmosphere of a monastery. Jules Favre wrote 'With Trochu, the Christian philosopher dominates the soldier'. It was true; though he was an extremely able soldier, it was as a military thinker rather than a man of action. Washburne, the American Minister, who was once received by the new President in slippers and dressing-gown, thought that 'he did not look much like a soldier', and General Burnside was equally surprised during a visit he paid him. On that occasion Trochu had spoken for half an hour on how wicked France had been, how she had fallen away from the Catholic faith and how the sins of her people were now being visited upon her, and then he burst into tears. Even among a Government of lawyers, he could outdo any of them when it came to longwinded, tedious speechifying. As Maxime du Camp remarked unkindly, 'When he spoke, he believed himself; and as he spoke without cease, he always believed himself'. His lack of worldly ambition, commented on earlier, made him a kind of Ferdinand the Bull among generals, but at the same time he was a man of great personal honour. As the Siege progressed, he would steadfastly refuse any privileges and insisted on drawing the same rations as the troops; to the astonished annoyance of their colleagues, he and Rochefort alone declined the 20,000 francs salary the new Government had voted itself. After the war, he would accept neither the Légion d'Honneur nor the marshal's baton that were offered him.

Trochu was by nature a Cassandra, and from the moment of his taking office he was frankly pessimistic about the prospects for Paris. As early as August 18th he had told the Empress's Council on his return from Châlons that '*tout etait perdu*', and he admitted later in his memoirs that the rejection of his plan to have Bazaine and MacMahon fall back on Paris 'had extinguished in my eyes the last

gleam of salvation ... Paris besieged could no longer expect help
from outside and must inevitably fall after a defence of long or short
duration. ...' By prolonging the defence of Paris as long as possible,
Trochu as a regular Army officer felt that at least the honour of the
Army could be salved; and that was the most that could be expected.
Throughout the Siege, in contrast to the fiery and optimistic Gambetta,
this question of 'honour' was to occupy his thoughts quite as much
as success, in which he never really believed. Part of his pessimism
lay in the misgivings he felt right from the start about the forces at
his behest; if the best of the regular Army had been so mauled by the
Prussians, how could this armed rabble in Paris do any better? Although he had drawn the last of France's Army into Paris, he feared
that its quality would render any adventurous strategy immensely
hazardous. 'I had neither any strategic, nor tactical idea', he later
admitted in a passage of his memoirs that was to be ferociously
attacked by his enemies. And it was roughly true; such little strategy
as he devised was strictly opportunist and entirely dependent upon
Moltke's intentions. 'In our Government deliberations', wrote
Rochefort *ex post facto*, 'we were just like a gardener who, instead
of watering his plants, waits for rain, certain that it will come sooner
or later.' Obsessed by the experience of his old chief, Marshal
Bugeaud, at the Siege of Saragossa in 1808 (which lasted eight
months), Trochu was convinced that Paris's only hope was to sit
tightly on the defensive and wait for the Prussians to pound themselves
to death against the forts and bastions of the city. But what if they
never attacked. ...?

In mid-September this was a thought that did not greatly exercise
the Government, and still less the populace in whose hearts confidence had grown by leaps and bounds since the grand review of the
13th. The mood reflected by Goncourt and his circle on September
6th, when they had parted at Brébant's with the words 'perhaps in a
fortnight the Prussians will be dining at this table', had completely
evaporated. Indeed, once more there was possibly more confidence
than was healthy. The continuing superlative weather certainly
helped to allay anxieties; though it was a little marred by the dust and
the occasional unpleasant smell, since the street-cleaners and water-
carts seemed to have gone out with the Empire, and most of the
sewage-disposal men had apparently been Germans. An atmosphere
of benevolent unity—something not seen in Paris for many a year—
was now displayed by all segments of the population. The Place de la
Concorde had become a kind of open-air patriotic theatre, and
Britons in Paris began to weary of the never-ending strains of the
Marseillaise. America—the first nation to do so—had recognized the

new Republic, and Washburne conveyed her 'congratulations'. The Bourse fluttered optimistically upwards as Italy, Spain, and Switzerland followed suit, and beliefs were revived that the rest of the world could not possibly leave Paris in the lurch for long. Mr. Brown passed on to his wife the rumour that 'we hear America has put in a word to say she cannot look upon France being further humiliated ...', and Paris buzzed with other *canards*—that Britain and Russia would soon intervene, that the Prussians would give up the war as they had declared that only Louis-Napoleon was their enemy. Above all, there was growing incredulity that Paris, *la ville lumière*, the marvel of the world, should really be compelled to submit to the fate of any ordinary provincial fortress. If there was to be a siege, it was society that would be shut out from Paris, not vice versa, and this was clearly a situation that the world would not long tolerate.

All this was typified by that vigorous septuagenarian, Victor Hugo, who—with a military képi perched permanently on his head—had hardly drawn breath since his return from exile. On September 9th he had issued an eloquent appeal to the Prussians:

It is in Paris that the beating of Europe's heart is felt. Paris is the city of cities. Paris is the city of men. There has been an Athens, there has been a Rome, and there is a Paris.... Is the nineteenth century to witness this frightful phenomenon? A nation fallen from polity to barbarism, abolishing the city of nations; German extinguishing Paris.... Can you give this spectacle to the world? Can you, Germans, become Vandals again; personify barbarism decapitating civilization?... Paris, pushed to extremities; Paris supported by all France aroused, can conquer and will conquer; and you will have tried in vain this course of action which already revolts the world.

A Briton in Paris commented scathingly, 'He writes as if he were King of France, or President, at least', but the Prussians appeared to be unimpressed, so Hugo now turned all his rhetorical passion to whipping his countrymen into a state of frenzy:

Let the streets of the town devour the enemy, let windows burst open with fury... let the tombs cry out... despotism has attacked Liberty. Germany is assailing France.... As for Europe, what do we care about Europe?... She can come to us if she likes. We do not ask for help. If Europe is afraid, let her remain so. We shall do a service to Europe, that is, to all.....

and elsewhere:

Lyons, take thy gun; Bordeaux, take thy carbine; Rouen, draw thy sword; and thou, Marseilles, sing thy song, and become terrible!

Deserters from the Battle of Châtillon

5. The Investment

WITH inexorable speed Moltke's forces were now closing in on the capital. There would be many ways in which the Franco-Prussian War represented a turning-point between classical forms of warfare and those of the twentieth century. But the continuous post-1914 front, formed by mass armies standing shoulder to shoulder, had not yet arrived. As at Waterloo, armies still wheeled and manœuvred in relatively compact formations with the aim of seeking out and bringing to battle the enemy's principal forces, rather than of invading and occupying his territory. It was in Paris that what was left of the French Army now lay, and additionally Paris was capital of one of the world's most highly centralized countries. Thus, upon the Prussian General Staff, Paris now exerted a doubly irresistible magnetism; for once Paris and the forces there could be made to surrender, would not France herself inevitably have to sue for terms? For the time being, the rest of France could be left virtually in a vacuum. With the exception of Prince Frederick-Charles's force, comprised of elements of the First and Second Army, encamped about Metz, and lesser units detailed off to invest Strasbourg and the other fortresses, as well as guarding lines of communication, the bulk of the German Army moved towards Paris.

Down the three principal convergent roads they poured, two

Armies strong, sustained by a consumption of looted wine so enormous that the accompanying General Sheridan reported 'two almost continuous lines of broken bottles along the roadsides all the way down from Sedan'. Hardly had Louis-Napoleon offered up his sword than Moltke turned about his great masses amid cries of '*Nach Paris!*' so that already by September 4th King Wilhelm had reached Rethel and the following day he was at Reims. There columns of curious German troops filed past the altar where Joan of Arc had unfurled her standard and where the Kings of France had been consecrated. The following week the Prussians were marching down the beautiful Marne where forty-four years later, almost to the day, another Moltke's dreams of reaching Paris would fall to pieces. On September 15th a train that had set forth from the Gare du Nord was seized by Prussian outriders at Senlis, twenty-seven miles north of Paris, and that same day Moltke held a council-of-war at Château-Thierry at which, with his usual methodical detail, he allotted his commanders the positions they were to assume around Paris. Like the claws of a crab, the Army of the Meuse under the Crown Prince of Saxony (the impetuous General Steinmetz having been relegated to a governorship in Poland) was to envelop the north of Paris, while the Prussian Crown Prince's Third Army swung round the southern side. On September 17th the encircling movement began. To their surprise, the Saxons found themselves permitted to move in close under the northern forts of Paris without opposition, and by the 18th Crown Prince Frederick had already crossed the Seine south of Paris, cutting the railway to Orléans. The following day Lord Lyons and the last of the *corps diplomatique* to leave Paris made a hasty exit, with the Papal Nuncio, Monseigneur Chigi, formally bestowing his blessing upon both the opposing camps as he passed through the lines.

Back in Germany the surrender at Sedan had been greeted with wild scenes of jubilation. Berliners had garlanded with laurels the statues of national heroes on Unter den Linden, and on all sides a new note of aggressive belligerence had begun to be heard. General von Blumenthal wrote down in his journal, 'We ought to crush them so that they will not be able to breathe for a hundred years', and Lutheran pastors preached fire-eating sermons about the men of Israel pursuing the Philistines. In their appreciations, however, the leaders were rather less sanguine. After the September 4th revolution, King Wilhelm himself had been heard to remark gloomily, 'The war is only just beginning now. They will now bring about the *levée en masse*.' Bismarck, claimed General Sheridan, 'dreaded' the establishment of a Republic, and did not approve of the movement of the German armies on Paris so soon after Sedan. From a purely tactical point of view, the 122,000 infantry and 24,000 cavalry with which the investment had been carried out seemed dangerously inadequate for laying siege to a city with half a million armed men in it, along a fifty-mile perimeter, which would allow an estimated density of only one infantryman per yard. Moltke prayed that the stunned French would not discover the numerical weakness of the besieging force until it was properly dug in, or until Frederick-Charles' army was released from the siege of Metz; on the other hand, Prussian Intelligence reckoned that supplies in Paris could only suffice for a siege lasting, at the very most, ten weeks. Added to this, a letter had been received from a Prussophile Englishman (admittedly he sounded like something of a crank) warning of terrible pits and traps laid in the woods around Paris. All in all, as the Prussian forces moved into their siege positions, with the precision of the tumblers of a well-designed lock, everything dictated the utmost prudence. There was certainly no idea in the mind of that thin-lipped, cautious gambler, Moltke, of a sudden brutal thrust that might break the line of the Paris forts before the defenders had a chance to weigh up their opponents.

From the French point of view, as the Prussian Crown Prince's army moved westwards past the southern line of forts towards Versailles, its exposed and extended flank offered something as temptingly vulnerable as that which the famous Governor of Paris, Galliéni, spotted in 1914, precipitating the Battle of the Marne. Alas, though, this apparently golden first opportunity was to reveal that Trochu was no Galliéni (nor, it must be admitted, were his troops those of France in 1914). In their movement around both sides of Paris, the Prussian reconnaissance units had been agreeably surprised to meet with hardly any resistance and to discover that no major French force had been installed outside the ring of forts. But on September 19th an action took place, developing into the first real battle of the siege, which was to have a doubly pernicious influence on all of Trochu's subsequent operations.

Just to the south of Paris rises a feature called the Châtillon Plateau. Today it is intersected by route N20 to Orléans, and on it stands a nuclear research centre. From the city its eminence is not obvious, but it affords even today—although the city suburbs have grown up around it—one of the most remarkable panoramic views of Paris. Standing there you feel you can almost reach out and touch the domes of the Panthéon and the Invalides. Three of the principal forts guarding that side of Paris were dangerously vulnerable to enemy heavy batteries placed on the Châtillon Plateau; worse still, as Paris was to discover later on, from it monster guns such as Herr Krupp had exhibited in 1867 could actually strike at the heart of Paris itself. On the plateau were a number of small French outposts held by XIV Corps, now commanded (together with XIII Corps) by General Ducrot. Captured in the *pot de chambre* of Sedan, the general had managed to escape (Bismarck claimed he had broken his parole and would, if caught, be shot) and was now Trochu's right-hand man, as fiery and vigorous as ever. His outposts at Châtillon could see the Crown Prince's army moving steadily along the main road to Versailles across his front with its flank turned almost insolently towards him. The sight was too much for this peppery veteran, who had been present at so many of the summer battles where French forces had been repeatedly crushed by resting too much on the defensive. He urged Trochu to allow him to throw in an attack on the Versailles road which, if successful, would assure French tenancy of the Châtillon heights at the same time as it severed a line of communication essential to a close investment of Paris.

With words that were to seem increasingly typical as the Siege proceeded, Trochu instructed Ducrot '... you could probe his [the Crown Prince's] flank, but with the greatest circumspection'. To Ducrot, fuming, this was far from adequate; either he must strike with full force before the enemy could establish himself at Châtillon, or do nothing at all. Trochu, defending himself *ex post facto*, accused Ducrot of wanting to implement 'an act of high military imprudence', adding (not without reason) that if he had permitted Ducrot to throw in his XIII Corps as well, 'the Siege of Paris would have ended there'. Thus a compromise operation was agreed on, the purpose of which, said Trochu (again *ex post facto*), was merely to make the Germans think they could not take Paris without a hard fight.

Shortly after dawn on the 19th Ducrot's men issued forth on France's first major action since the disaster at Sedan. Ducrot's operational plan was simple, for 'one could not expect more from such raw troops. Alas! They were unfortunately even rawer than the Commander-in-Chief thought ....' On the right, attacking through what are now charming woods and pleasure parks at Meudon, were a regiment of Zouaves which, far from being the legendary tough veterans of North African *razzias* ('the friends of my dear Guards' as Queen Victoria had once called them), was composed largely of young recruits. Although for most of them this was their first battle they had absorbed all the tales of terror their elders had to tell about the Prussians. There had been the usual muddle of the *Intendance* with ammunition not arriving on time, but now it had reached the Zouaves and they were huddled together distributing it. Suddenly shells from a well-trained Prussian field-gun battery descended among them. Some of the young Zouaves panicked and a chain-reaction set in. Nearby a battalion of unblooded *Mobiles*, alarmed by the desperate cries of the Zouaves, began firing at each other in the early-morning mist. In the midst of this incipient chaos, the gallant Ducrot himself arrived 'at the gallop'. Exhorting, cajoling, threatening, he was able to bolster up the courage of the faltering *Mobiles*, but the Zouaves were beyond repair. With those baneful exculpatory cries of '*Nous sommes trahis*'—'we are betrayed'—all too frequently heard on battlefields where fortune has deserted French arms, they decamped in groups towards Paris, and the sight of the renowned red pantaloons fleeing provoked less chic infantrymen to follow suit.

The streets of Montparnasse were soon full of deserters. There Goncourt met a small platoon of returning Zouaves. 'They said that they were all that remained of a body of two thousand men of which they had been part. Farther away, a terrified *Mobile* was relating that the Prussians numbered a hundred thousand in the Bois de Meudon, that Vinoy's Corps had been dispersed like shot out of a gun. . . . One sensed in all these accounts the madness of fear, the hallucinations of panic.' Later, this time near the Madeleine, he met more Zouaves, whom he studied with the analytical interest of the diarist: 'the expression of the deserter is empty, dull, glaucously diffuse; he can concentrate on nothing, can resolve on nothing.' Other Parisians were less detached; to troops who claimed that their officers had abandoned them, an American overheard a 'red hag' retort 'Perhaps *you* left them at the front'. Louis Péguret, who had just reported for service with the 115th Battalion of the National Guard, found himself besieged by the fugitives: 'They said it was intended they should be massacred, because they had been sent into battle without cartridges. They lied, for we inspected their pouches, and, not only did they have ammunition, but not a single packet of cartridges had been undone, not a single shot had been fired by these cowards.'

At the front, Ducrot was attempting to consolidate, urging that the Châtillon redoubt, a last toe-hold on the vital plateau, should be held at all costs. But for all the work Trochu had ordered done on the lines of forts, virtually nothing had been carried out so far beyond the permanent fortifications. Thus the redoubt by itself was clearly indefensible, and the final decision was imposed upon Ducrot when he discovered that some inspired official had, the previous evening, ordered the destruction of the waterworks at Choisy-le-Roi which alone supplied water to the Châtillon Plateau. Reluctantly the order to retreat within the line of forts was given, and—although various unsuccessful attempts were made during the remainder of the month to dispute the issue—this vital position was abandoned to the enemy. The Prussian Crown Prince could barely believe his good fortune, but because of prevailing fears of the precariousness of the investing forces, no attempt at a follow-up was made. As the French later admitted, the southern forts were still by no means ready to repel a full-scale attack, and a rapid pursuit on the heels of the demoralized Châtillon fugitives might well have ended the war then and there. But this was no more Moltke's way of waging war than it was Montgomery of Alamein's.

On September 20th Uhlans from the two Prussian armies joined hands near Versailles, which surrendered without a shot. The Siege was set. Paris was now severed from the rest of France; unlike Leningrad, where the besieging Nazis suffered the disadvantage of never being able completely to close the iron ring around the city. That same day the Crown Prince of Prussia stood on a height overlooking the city and gazed down at the glistening gilt dome of the Invalides that seemed so incredibly close. W. H. Russell of *The Times* who was with him thought it 'as fair a sight as eye could see', and then lay down to have a good look at the fortifications with his telescope. 'Men were working in the trenches with a will. As I swept the line of Vanves I caught sight of an officer in an embrasure looking earnestly up in the direction of the plateau through his glass, and evidently directing the gunners at the piece by his side. I could look straight down into its muzzle'. This magical view of the invested city immediately evoked in the Crown Prince's mind memories of 'the fine warm Sunday in the year 1867 on which the fountains played here in honour of my father and the Tsar Alexander . . . .' At his former host's abandoned palace of St.-Cloud, where the staircase was dominated by a huge oil-painting of his mother-in-law, Queen Victoria, arriving there in state only fifteen years previously, the Crown Prince now found upon a desk a stack of invitation cards headed '*Impératrice Régente*'. How swiftly and ruthlessly the wheel of Fortune had swung about! Here was what had long been Europe's greatest military power abjectly humbled, and the enemy capital—that Babylon of modern times—stretched out before Prussia's grasp.

In Paris the mood (as described by Goncourt) in the days immediately preceding the Battle of Châtillon had been one of 'Let them come, let the cannon thunder! It's been too long!' When in fact the first cannon began to be heard in the distance, the streets filled with people anxious for news. Initially there were the usual *canards* of a 'great victory'. Then the appearance of the abject flotsam from Châtillon brought with it the truth. Retribution for this first setback was promptly exacted on the wretched deserters. Angry crowds seized them on the roads into Paris, spitting in their faces and threatening to lynch them, until the *Garde Nationale* escorted them—with many prods of rifle butts—into the centre of the city. Even the liberal-minded Madame Lambert wrote in her journal, 'I could have watched, without flinching, while they shot the deserters'. (A week later Tommy Bowles in fact watched twenty-one of them 'marched round the ramparts with their hands tied behind their backs, their coats turned inside out, and then led forth from the Porte de Maillot to be shot . . . .' But he added, 'There are those, however, who maintain that they were not shot at all, but brought back by another gate with their coats turned the right side out', and indeed there is no record that any were actually shot). Trochu's official communiqué, couched in the age-old military formula for minimizing a catastrophe, said baldly: 'Some of our soldiers withdrew with a regrettable precipitation. . . .' But there was no disguising the seriousness of Châtillon. With its loss vanished French hopes of maintaining any positions in advance of the ring of forts, which now automatically became the line of investment. Worse still, the performance of the Zouaves confirmed in Trochu's mind all his pessimism about the troops under his command, so that henceforth he would view any major offensive out of Paris with the greatest reserve.

Some small consolation was found by the Parisians the day after Châtillon when they were told that a large mine had been exploded under a number of German spectators who had assembled to gloat over Paris from their newly-won position, and throughout the rest of September various small-scale engagements were fought nearby in attempts to retrieve something from the disaster. At Villejuif on September 23rd, the French troops already showed themselves in a much better light, but strategically the situation remained unchanged.[1] Of these French attacks General von Blumenthal, Chief-of-Staff to the Prussian Crown Prince, wrote in his journal: 'Our lines are so weakly held that, if the enemy should attack at one point with the whole of his force concentrated, we must be beaten back and have our line cut through. Fortunately, he does not understand his business, and wastes his strength striking out blindly in all directions'.

*   *   *

[1] After Villejuif a prematurely optimistic little jingle went the rounds:
'Bismarck, if you go on,
Of all your Prussians there will be left barely one,
Bismarck, if you go on,
Of all your Prussians, there will be left not a one.'

On the same day that Ducrot's men were doing battle on the Châtillon Plateau, Jules Favre was discussing peace with Bismarck at Ferrières fifteen miles to the east of Paris. Ever since the deposition of Louis-Napoleon the new Republican Government had cherished illusions that peace on honourable terms had only to be asked for, provided of course the right way of asking could be found. A flurry of diplomatic activity had ensued. On September 6th Favre and Thiers told Lord Lyons that they wished the neutral powers to mediate on the basis of reparations, but no cession of territory. To this latter point Favre committed himself irrevocably, and rashly, in a circular letter to the chancelleries of Europe in which he declared that France would never surrender 'an inch of her soil nor a stone of her fortresses'. In their interview with Lord Lyons, Thiers had tried to impress the British of the urgency of a solution by emphasizing the 'Red menace' in Paris, and indeed the following week Lyons was reporting back to Lord Granville, the Foreign Secretary, his own belief that 'the Reds within are more likely to give permanent trouble than the Prussians without'. On September 7th, Favre was begging Washburne to 'intervene to make peace', and two days later he despatched Thiers to London on a similar mission. There Thiers found sympathetic courtesy, but was offered nothing more substantial by the Gladstone Government which, not uncharacteristically, was too preoccupied with domestic reforms. From London he travelled to Vienna, from Vienna to St. Petersburg, from St. Petersburg to Florence, even at one point withdrawing the Comtesse de Castiglione temporarily from oblivion in order to try those well-proven charms upon Bismarck, on France's behalf. But nowhere did he gain more than evasive half-promises. Europe was by now thoroughly in awe of Prussia.

After Thiers had left London, Favre decided to communicate directly with Bismarck and ask for an audience. Bismarck agreed, and —still full of optimism—Favre set out for Meaux where King Wilhelm had last been reported to have his headquarters. In fact, the two parties passed each other on the road and, fatigued, Favre had to retrace his footsteps to Ferrières where Bismarck was sleeping. Rapidly his illusions were dispersed as he discovered Bismarck disposed to negotiate no less harshly with him, the plenipotentiary of the Republic, than he had with de Wimpffen, Louis-Napoleon's man, at Sedan. Deep into the night he pleaded with Bismarck in the great Rothschild palace at Ferrières, which Crown Prince Frederick amiably described as 'a chest-of-drawers standing with its legs in the air'. But on every point the agile lawyer was out-manœuvred. Bismarck, who had often expounded the advantages of smoking during negotiations, studied his adversary with cool detachment, puffing

smoke at him, while Favre, a non-smoker, fidgeted nervously. The
new, extortive temper of the triumphant Prussians was reflected in all
Bismarck said. At last, with unmodified brutality, he posed Prussia's
demands: Alsace and part of Lorraine. 'I am certain', he added with a
touch of prophecy, 'that at a future time we shall have a fresh war
with you, and we wish to undertake it under every advantage'. Favre
pointed out that no French Government could survive yielding to
such a demand. 'You want to destroy France!' he exclaimed, and then
burst into tears.[1] Bismarck went on to make it clear that the Prussians
would not even consider a temporary armistice without the prior
surrender of the fortresses of Toul and Strasbourg, which were still
holding out.

The interview was at an end. To one of Bismarck's entourage,
Favre as he left the Château de Ferrières looked 'crushed and depressed, almost despairing'. Apart from humiliation, only one thing
had been achieved for France; the beginnings in a shift of British
public opinion. Queen Victoria had herself telegraphed King Wilhelm
to beg him 'to display magnanimity' at Ferrières, and she had been
manifestly snubbed. Moreover, as the harshness of Bismarck's terms
were revealed, the feeling spread in Britain that Prussia was no longer
the injured party and had now put herself in the wrong by her determination to continue the war. But what immediate value could
France derive from this incipient British sympathy?

Back in Paris the Provisional Government was shocked and outraged by what Favre had to tell. Gambetta at once telegraphed the
Prefects of Paris: 'Post up in all Communes the summary of Favre's
interview with Bismarck. . . . Paris, incensed, swears to resist to the
end. Let the provinces rise up!' For France, with her back pinned to
the wall by the rapacity of the Prussian General Staff, it now seemed
there was no option but to fight tooth and nail. A decisive watershed,
not only in the course of the Franco-Prussian War, but in the whole
history of European relations, was about to be traversed. Henceforth
warfare would no longer be a polite contest between professional
armies on the eighteenth-century model, but a jungle-law 'survival of
the fittest' struggle between peoples—of a kind of which the French
levée en masse of the 1790's had provided a foretaste. An indelible
mark would be carried by Europe into the twentieth century.

Gambetta's telegram immediately posed the question: how in

---

[1] The cynical Bismarck gave this version of Favre's tears: 'He seemed to be
crying and I endeavoured in a fashion to console him; but when I looked a little
closer, I positively believe that he had not shed a tear. He intended, probably, to
work upon my feelings with a little theatrical performance, as the Parisian
advocates work upon their public'.

fact were the unoccupied provinces to be marshalled for total war; in particular, so that they could march to the aid of Paris ? Since Trochu had virtually stripped the country of its last organized forces (now incarcerated in Paris), new armies would also have to be raised. After the revolution of September 4th, opinion in the provinces where Bonapartism was strongest had been frankly apathetic, and many local commanders were paralysed by a lethargy of despair. But, as the actual approach of the Prussians provoked new fears, the last news reaching Paris from outside before the investment was more encouraging; Gustave Flaubert, now a lieutenant in the local *Garde Nationale*, was writing (perhaps rather optimistically) to his niece from Rouen about 'armies being forced; in a fortnight there will be perhaps a million men about Paris,' and to Maxime du Camp (on September 29th) 'I guarantee that within a fortnight all France will rise. Near Mantes a peasant has strangled a Prussian and torn him apart with his teeth. In short there is now a genuine will to fight. . . .' But who was to exploit and canalize this will; in fact, to lead the provinces ? As soon as the Government of National Defence had come into power, there had been discussions as to whether it should stay in Paris, or retire into the provinces. Few of its members then seriously believed that any army was capable of totally blockading Paris from the rest of France; but what really decided the issue was the instinctive belief that 'Paris *was* France'. After a great deal of discussion, by September 11th the Government had decided to stay put and instead send Crémieux as a one-man delegation to Tours. Crémieux was seventy-four, inexperienced and (like so many of his colleagues) a talkative lawyer rather than a man of action. Almost at once the confusion and chaos at Tours proved too much for him, and—just two days before the investment—Glais-Bizoin and Admiral Fourichon were sent as reinforcements. It was a remarkably inept selection, for they too were old and doddery and were at once equally overwhelmed by events. What was needed was a Churchill. But was there such a man among France's new leaders, and even if there was how could he be got out of besieged Paris ?

On September 23rd a possible answer to the second question was sent, literally, from above. A number of balloons had been located in Paris; though most of them were in various states of disrepair, including the famous *Céleste*, which had dazzled visitors by its captive flights over the Great Exhibition of 1867, now described as being like a 'sieve'. One of them, the *Neptune*, had been sufficiently patched up, however, to be wafted out of Paris on the 23rd, over the heads of the astonished Prussians. Its intrepid pilot, Duruof, had landed safely at Evreux beyond the enemy's reach with 125 kilograms of dispatches, after a three-hour flight. Four other balloons took off in quick succession, with (astonishingly enough) none of their crews being shot down, captured, or otherwise coming to grief. The blockade seemed to have been broken, and a means of communicating with the provinces created reliable enough for the Minister of Posts, M. Rampont, to decree the establishment of a regular 'Balloon Post'.

As soon as the idea was mooted of ballooning a new plenipotentiary to Tours, the fearless Ducrot volunteered. As France's most vigorous military leader, with an untarnished reputation, he would have been a good choice; but, as Bismarck had placed a price on his head, the risks of his balloon descending in the Prussian camp were considered too grave to undertake; besides, Trochu considered him indispensable in Paris. Few other voices in the Government had quite matched Ducrot's enthusiasm. Rochefort had become unusually silent, and Favre—declaring (according to Trochu) that 'the post of peril was in Paris'—turned positively green at the thought of the hazardous voyage. As Trochu admitted afterwards with commendable honesty, 'Monsieur Gambetta was the only one of us who could regard without apprehension the prospects of a voyage in a balloon', and as Minister of the Interior Gambetta did seem to be a logical choice when it came to organizing a *levée en masse* in the provinces. Gambetta's more remarkable attributes were not then apparent. He was only thirty-two and of an extremely unpromising physical appearance. The son of an Italian grocer living in Cahors, he was described by Rochefort as 'inclined to thinness, with long black hair, a Jewish nose, and an eye which protruded so terribly from its socket as to lead one to fear lest it should escape altogether . . .' (an operation later cured this defect). His morals were deplorable, some of his personal habits worse, and a careless Bohemian life had prematurely aged him so that his beard and his mass of unkempt black hair were already streaked with grey. But before the age of thirty he had established himself as one of the great orators of France, and above all his meridional blood endowed him with something notably lacking in the other men of September 4th—passion. One of his staunchest admirers, Minister Washburne (who had also been among the first to recognize his qualities), recalled how at the famous Baudin Trial where he had first made his name, Gambetta 'poured forth a torrent of eloquence, denunciation and argument which seemed to completely stun the court . . . Mirabeau, in his palmiest days in the National Convention, was never his superior'. In the judgment of another contemporary, 'There was authority even in his laugh . . . and it seemed natural for others to obey as for him to command.' All that he seemed to lack was military experience.

The decision to entrust Gambetta to a balloon was reached on October 3rd, but it was not until four days later that a favourable wind allowed him to start. By 11 a.m. on the 7th, a huge crowd had assembled round the launching-pad that had been set up in the Place St.-Pierre, Montmartre, the highest point of Paris and close to where the Sacré-Cœur now stands. There had been a big disappointment the previous day when the count-down ceased after two small trial balloons had disappeared into thick fog at an altitude of a few hundred feet. But now all augured well. There were loud cheers as Gambetta arrived, wrapped up in a great furred cloak prepared by some kind feminine hand. A farewell embrace from the veteran Socialist, Louis Blanc, a command of *'Messieurs les voyageurs, en ballon !'*, and Gambetta climbed into the open wicker basket. The crowd commented on Gambetta's apparent nervousness, on the paleness of his normally florid face, on how he clutched at the rigging and how an additional rope had to be thrown round the shrouds to prevent his falling out. His apprehension was more than understandable. From a man embarking on this kind of balloon journey in 1870 probably at least as much real courage was demanded as from an early American or Soviet astronaut in the 1960's; and for the balloonists there were no helping hands or batteries of computers on earth, ready to guide them down, no flotillas standing by to pick them out of the sea, and only in the matter of 're-entry' did they have more control over their flight than the astronauts. Over their head billowed a great bag of highly inflammable coal-gas that needed just one stray enemy bullet to turn it into a ball of flame. Needless to say, no other Minister of any nation had yet entrusted himself to such a vehicle, even for the briefest flight. As the anchor ropes were cast off, Gambetta managed to recover his nerve sufficiently to unfurl a tricolour, displaying a characteristic sense of theatre. Teams of men guided the unpredictably bobbing, flimsy elephant into the air so as not to foul nearby roofs. At last the *Armand Barbès* began to rise freely, spinning and jigging with a sickening motion, accompanied by great cries of *'Vive la France ! Vive la République !'* from below, until it slowly disappeared out of sight to the west. If this was not actually France's 'finest hour' of the war, it was certainly the beginning of it.

The National Guard at Rifle Practice

6. Trouble on the Left

JUST after the Battle of Châtillon, Henry Labouchère made 'a few calls' around Paris. Everyone 'seemed to be engaged in measuring the distance from the Prussian batteries to his particular house. One friend I found seated in a cellar with a quantity of mattresses over it, to make it bomb-proof. He emerged from his subterraneous Patmos to talk to me, ordered his servant to pile on a few more mattresses, and then retreated.' But once a momentary panic at the imminence of an all-out Prussian assault had passed, a more sober and resolved mood began to reveal itself among the populace at large. The Châtillon reverse seemed to have administered a sharp (and in many ways salutary) corrective to that feverish optimism which had dominated Paris since September 4th. In a balloon letter home, Edwin Child described '... the streets and people very quiet. All that enthusiasm has cooled down. Were it not for the enormous consumption of newspapers the difference of Paris ordinary and in a state of siege would be almost imperceptible'. Strolling along the banks of the Seine on the

Sunday after Châtillon, Goncourt noticed that 'the placid fishermen' were now all wearing a képi of the *Garde Nationale*, while a friend of O'Shea of *The Standard* was rebuked for playing billiards. Even Rochefort, the new Director of Barricades, was to be found administering a mild sedative with an order that citizens should curb their patriotic zeal and not 'spontaneously' erect barricades without reference to his commission; since some had been built so close behind the ramparts as to hinder seriously their defence!

The passing of the gaudiness of the early days left a vacuum which was beginning to be occupied by something dangerously like boredom; dangerous, because Paris knows no more promising incubator of revolt and kindred diseases than that most dreadful of states, *l'ennui*. The theatres and the opera had closed their doors, a ten o'clock curfew had descended on the cafés following Châtillon, and the streets at night had become so dark and deserted that they reminded Tommy Bowles of London. As early as September 25th, Edward Blount, the banker, was writing '. . . the evenings are awfully dreary . . .', which Labouchere endorsed with a characteristic Fleet Street complaint that by 11 o'clock at night 'one would have supposed oneself in some dull provincial town at three in the morning'. By October 21st, more than a month since the investment in which no major action had been initiated by either side, Bowles seemed to be regretting his yachting-holiday decision to throw up the gay life and come to Paris, grumbling 'it is a melancholy fact that life is getting dull here'.

What the Siege was beginning to mean to a sensitive and intelligent Parisian was (as so often) admirably summarized by Goncourt, who on October 15th wrote in his journal:

To live within oneself, to have no other exchange of ideas than something as undiverse and limited as one's own thought, rotating around one obsession; to read nothing but thoroughly predictable news about a miserable war; . . . to enjoy modern life no longer in this early-to-bed city; to be able to read nothing; . . . to be deprived of all that provided recreation for the mind of educated Paris; to miss all that was new and all that renewed [literally, *à manquer du nouveau et du renouveau*]; finally to vegetate in this brutal and monotonous state of affairs, war, thus is the Parisian imprisoned in Paris by a boredom comparable to that of a provincial city.

The lack of news from outside was without doubt the chief contributory cause of this incipient boredom. Many who underwent the Siege considered in retrospect that this was a worse privation even than the subsequent food shortage, and it soon revealed itself as a most pernicious psychological factor, operating on a multiplicity of levels. After only a week of isolation, Minister Washburne confided to his diary: 'I wish there could be a balloon to come in, for this absence of all intelligence from the outside world is becoming unbearable.' But it was a vain wish, as it became quickly apparent that although balloons could leave Paris with impunity, a return flight was quite another matter. When in October a copy of the *Journal de Rouen* was somehow smuggled into the city, and reprinted *in extenso*, Child remarked that 'whoever had said 3 months ago that a Provincial paper a fortnight old arriving in Paris would cause a sensation would have been laughed at; however such was the case'.

One immediate result of the news blockade was a plethora of incredible rumours, which, since no one could refute them, the Paris Press printed with avidity. On September 29th it was reported that the Prussians were in retreat towards the coast, an anonymous American being quoted as having 'heard them pack up last night'. The following week the Duc d'Aumale was advancing from Le Havre at the head of an army; a magical tunnel had been dug to connect Paris with the provinces, through which sheep and cattle were now pouring into the city; and among a mass of 'secret weapons' invented was a deadly new *mitrailleuse* that could slaughter the enemy three thousand at a time. Moltke was dead and the Crown Prince of Prussia dying; the Prussians outside Metz had been so reduced that any resident wanting to leave the city was chloroformed, in order that he might not notice their weakness as he passed through the lines; Prussia had been so drained of regular troops that the *Landsturm* were about to launch a revolution in Berlin; and there were even rumours of revolution in England. On October 24th when an *aurora borealis* turned the sky blood-red, it was said that the Prussians were firing the woods round Paris in the hopes of 'smoking out' the Parisians.

Hand in hand with these spurious reports went column after column of the kind of nonsensical bombast that particularly infuriated the British correspondents in Paris. 'In order that Paris, whose genius has given her the empire of the world, should fall into the hands of the barbarians', declared *Le Figaro*, 'there must cease to be a God in heaven. As God she exists, and as God she is immortal. . . .' Another paper complained of the world looking on impassively 'at the ruin of a nation which possesses the most exquisite gifts of sociability, the principal jewel of Europe and the eternal ornament of civilization'. There was, snorted Labouchere, 'nothing like having a good opinion of oneself'. When later, after a new series of disasters, an American read in a morning paper the comment 'Thank Heaven, we can subsist for a while on our antecedents; they are sufficiently illustrious', he was reminded of the boy on Bunker Hill, who, asked by a stranger what people there lived on, replied 'Pumpkin Pies and Past Recollections'.

The example for this bombast was set from the top, by Trochu with his passion for long-winded grandiloquence and Spartan aphorisms; and certainly as long as Victor Hugo breathed there would be no shortage of material. On September 21st he had marked the anniversary of the First Republic with yet another of his florid orations, proclaiming that 'Paris, which has been accustomed to amuse mankind, will now terrify it. The world will be amazed. . . .' These mock heroics may have reduced sympathy for Paris's plight among the foreign community, but they were lapped up with the greatest zeal by the Parisians. Despite the lack of real news (or perhaps because of it), there had never been a greater demand for newspapers in Paris. Some forty-nine new ones were actually started during the Siege, and to Labouchere it was a constant mystery where they obtained their newsprint. What was even less easy to understand, in the light of subsequent developments, was the fact that throughout the Siege the Government made no effort to control by censorship the steady outpouring of harmful rumours, of bombast, and later of violently seditious attacks on itself. (By comparison, it is worth noting that one of the very first steps taken during the Siege of Leningrad was the confiscation of all radio sets and the disconnection of telephones.)

Every hue and shade of French politics was represented by this mass of Parisian journals. On the extreme Left were three notable organs which, not satisfied by a simple effusion of bombast like most of their competitors, had already started baring their teeth at the new Government. There was *La Patrie en Danger* and *Le Réveil*, edited respectively by Blanqui and Delescluze, those two professional revolutionaries who between them had spent so much time in various imperial gaols; but the most scurrilous of all was Félix Pyat's *Le Combat*. Pyat was sixty years old, and in common with Blanqui and Delescluze had passed twenty-nine of these in prison, and much of the remainder in exile. His experience had given him a remarkable sixth sense which somehow enabled him to turn up invariably at the critical moment of a revolution or a conspiracy; more remarkable still was his facility for disappearing when things went wrong. His companion in exile, Louis Blanc, once remarked of him to Juliette Lambert: 'His mistrust is extraordinary; in London we never knew his address. His best friends were kept in ignorance of it. Félix Pyat never even told it to Félix Pyat for fear that Félix Pyat would betray it'. Having helped precipitate the June uprising of 1848, when others came to pay the bill Pyat had vanished, and in May 1871 this slippery figure would be one of the few leading Communards to wriggle out of the net. His appearance belied his outstanding lack of physical courage; slightly resembling Louis-Philippe, he has been described by one writer as 'superbly tall, with a romantic mane and beard, proud leonine gaze and a voice that could carry incredible distances . . . the purest romantic terrorist that ever flung a paper bomb . . . ' Pyat was a kind of backroom Rochefort, devoid of the latter's appeal for the masses, but almost as brilliant a journalist and even more capable of being seduced into folly by the power of one of his own metaphors. It was Louis Blanc again who described him as 'a distinguished man of subtle ideas and sensible speech. But as soon as he writes he becomes a madma:., incapable of controlling himself. . . ' To Rochefort he was simply 'a misanthrope embittered by twenty years of exile, grumbling at not filling the position in the Republic that was his due'. A renegade bourgeois, no one was more effective at enraging the class he had deserted; at the same time, among the extreme Republicans there was no one whose political ideas were more ineffectual and inchoate than Pyat's.

Returning from exile in London when the Empire fell, Pyat had launched *Le Combat* on September 16th. His first stunt had been to set up a subscription fund for a 'rifle of honour' to be bestowed upon any Parisian sniping the King of Prussia, and it was only a matter of time before *Le Combat* was making it plain that it would equally welcome the dispatch of General Trochu. The uneasy truce between the 'Reds' (as they had become known in more moderate circles) and the Government which had followed September 4th had not survived the initial disaster at Châtillon. In their assaults on the Government, *Le Combat* and its allies were now thoroughly representative of proletarian opinion in Paris, while at the same time they fanned the embers. Behind this rapidly growing opposition to the Government were a number of complex causes, not altogether explicable in terms of pure reason. The extreme belligerence of proletarian France towards the Prussians has already been noted, but is worth commenting on again; especially since it is a phenomenon that contrasts strangely with the tendency in intervening years for left-wing and 'popular' movements all over the world to become indentified with anti-militarism. At the beginning of the Siege, elements from Belleville held daily patriotic manifestations outside the American Legation, on which Hoffman, the Assistant Secretary, commented acidly, 'Day after day Washburne was called out to thank them for this *démonstration patriotique*; I got very heartily sick of it.' However odd its flavour from time to time, this left-wing patriotism was nevertheless ardent and sincere, but there was also a strongly particularist element to it. For it was Paris, sacred Paris, that was now more directly in danger than the rest of France, and Paris had to be defended *à outrance*. To its working classes especially Paris was France, while the rest of the country consisted principally of feudal landowners, reactionary peasants, and clerics. Paris was the sacred city of revolution, and as Dantonesque memories were revived of how the foreign invaders were repelled in 1792, so for the first time there began to be heard clamours for the rebirth of a *Commune de Paris* which, like its famous predecessor, would in some mystical way repeat the miracle.

As far back as the year of the Great Exhibition, Prosper Mérimée had remarked that 'the bourgeois regard war with horror; but the people . . . are longing to eat Prussians', and since September 4th the divergence between the two classes in Paris had become if anything wider. As the Siege progressed it seemed likely to grow wider still; for one thing, though the harshness of Bismarck's terms at Ferrières had temporarily united all France in favour of continuing the war, the supreme binding element of terror with which the Nazis (in their folly) confronted Leningrad by stating their intention of destroying the city and its whole population, regardless of surrender, was absent. To the property-owning and commercial classes, the war as it dragged on was bound to equal a waste of material assets; assets which the Paris proletariat had never possessed. Meanwhile, in the latter's minds, the war since September 4th had taken a vital ideological turn. Before that date, there had been a somewhat equivocal situation where the Prussians were also enemies of *the* enemy, Louis-Napoleon. But now they were threatening the Republic, the glorious new revolution, which had to be defended at all cost. And not only against the Prussians.

Old hands like Blanqui, Delescluze, and Pyat could recall all too vividly how in those previous revolutions the bourgeois had usurped the workers' birthright, and they had fears that it was going to happen all over again. Every utterance from the moderate camp claiming that the 'Reds' constituted as grave a menace as the Prussians was seized upon as a warning of what to expect. Sooner or later the treacherous bourgeois would do a deal with the reactionary Prussians, and conjointly they would then set about stamping once more on the *true* Republicans of Paris. Favre's interview with Bismarck was itself regarded with gravest mistrust, as revealed by Blanqui writing in *La Patrie en Danger* of September 22nd: 'Since the Fourth of September the Government of the so-called National Defence has had only one thought: peace. Not a victorious peace, not even an honourable peace, but peace at any price . . . it does not believe in resistance. . . .' Every fresh military setback, every sign of flaccidity (of which there was to be no shortage) on the part of Trochu and his colleagues, henceforth came to be interpreted as evidence of ill faith, of collusion; worse, of treachery.

From all sides they bombarded the Government with suggestions on how to conduct the war more vigorously, while at the same time

seizing the opportunity of pushing through whatever municipal reforms they could in areas of Paris under their control. As early as
September 15th a body describing itself as the 'Central Committee of
the Twenty *Arrondissements*' published a manifesto demanding
'Municipal elections, the control of the police and the election and re-
sponsibilities of all magistrates to be placed in the hands of these
municipalities, absolute rights of the Press, the right to hold meetings
and to form affiliations, the expropriation of all essential foodstuffs. . . .'
A week later the Central Committee issued another manifesto, declaring 'Point One: The Republic may not negotiate with an enemy
occupying its territory. Point Two: Paris is resolved to let itself be
buried under its own ruins rather than surrender. . . .' This then went
on to demand the suppression of the Prefecture of Police and the
election of an all-powerful *Commune* of Paris. At Belleville a meeting
of 3,000 'citizens' unanimously 'deposed' the mayor of the 19th
arrondissement, ordaining his 'immediate arrest by the citizens'. The
innate anticlericalism of the extreme Republicans was not long in
bursting to the surface; on October 9th, a letter published by a
Citizen Berthydre outraged bourgeois opinion by suggesting that
churches should be used to house the 'brave National Guard' as well
as cattle and sheep, and not long afterwards *La Patrie en Danger* was
dictating that 'all the hospitals must be purged of priests who are to
be arrested, armed and placed before the patriots in the most dangerous
places'. Meanwhile, fresh grist was added to the 'Red' mill when, at
the end of September, the Government feebly adjourned the holding
of municipal elections from one day to another, finally announcing on
October 8th that they would postpone them altogether until the
Siege was raised.

And now a source of power potential such as the Paris extremists
had never known before was there to lend immense amplification to
their voices. The *Garde Nationale* had rapidly established itself as *the*
storm-centre of the Left. From the Government's point of view it
was turning out, in more ways than just one, worse even than the most
sceptical regular soldiers, like Trochu, had predicted. Originally, in
the minds of such rosy-spectacled liberals as Ernest Picard (and,
indeed, Gambetta too), the creation of the *Garde* would fulfil three
functions: it would quickly produce a mass of trained soldiers; it
would provide relief for the poor of Paris, now confronted with widespread unemployment; and it would keep the 'Reds' quiet by giving
them an outlet for their bellicosity. But in only the second respect had
the Government hopes shown any likelihood of vindication. For their
services, National Guardsmen received the handsome emolument of
1·50 francs a day, and their wives half-pay (Pyat had promptly

demanded that 'unmarried wives' should be accorded the same benefits).[1]
Undoubtedly it was to save a great many of the poorer Parisians from
starvation during the Siege, but even these benefits had their built-in
dangers, as the shrewd eye of young Tommy Bowles quickly noted:
'These thirty sous will constitute a formidable difficulty when the war is
over, for the recipients have already come to consider they have a right to
State pay, and will strongly resist its withdrawal. . . .'

Whether through the allure of the thirty sous, or genuine patriotism,
in sheer numbers the recruitment of the National Guard had been an
unexpected success, and the initial enthusiasm in its ranks quite
enormous. Between September 5th and 13th alone, 78 new battalions
(each of roughly 1,500 men) had been formed, and by the end of the
month the National Guard numbered 360,000 men; twice as many as
had been anticipated by the Government. Everybody seemed to be
in it; Cresson, later Prefect of Police, alleged that no less than 25,000
fugitives from justice had enrolled, while an Englishman calling at
Rothschilds in the city met Monsieur le Baron himself in uniform,
waiting to go on duty on the fortifications. Each battalion was composed on a regional basis, and the proletarian units from Belleville
and Ménilmontant presented a marked contrast to those from the
richer *arrondissements*, who sometimes provided themselves with
seductive young *vivandières*, got up like the regimental daughters of
comic opera. Uniforms presented an extraordinary motley: some
battalions were clad in chocolate brown, some in brilliant green, while
others (presaging 1914–18) wore a romantic *bleu horizon*, and in the
earliest days the *Garde* mounted watch on the ramparts in anything
from tartan to sheepskins. But the force quickly divided itself into
two components, proletarian and bourgeois, and equally quickly there
sprang up grievances at the size and composition of each others'
forces. In the opinion of at least one critical British observer, Labouchere, there was absolutely no doubt in the early days as to which of
the two rival sets gave the better impression (though this was an
opinion he later changed): 'I have been struck with the difference
between one of these poor fellows who is prepared to die for the
honour of his country . . . and the absurd airs, and noisy brawls, and
the dapper uniforms of the young fellows one meets with in the
fashionable quarters. It is the difference between reality and sham. . . .'

To command the National Guard, Trochu had appointed General
Tamisier, a regular officer of bourgeois origins who completely shared

---

[1] The total of 2·25 francs was rather more than half the average pre-war Parisian
worker's wage, but of course made no allowance for the rapid rise in food prices during
the Siege.

his superior's misgivings about 'irregular' forces, and whose only recommendation in the eyes of the 'Red' battalions was that he had spent seventeen days in prison for having helped try to suppress Louis-Napoleon's *putsch* in 1851. Jules Favre later remarked of him: 'Authority floated in his hands and his courage, which would have done wonders before the enemy, was impotent to vanquish the timidity of his character.' And, more scornfully, the leader of one of the Belleville battalions, the flamboyant Flourens, regarded him as 'a fine old man, of the stamp of a retired grocer, who must twenty years ago have had some energy'. But in the 'Red' battalions the real power lay in the hands of the demagogues, for they had insisted on the right to elect their own officers—to which the Government had weakly consented. The elections proceeded, regardless of any military qualifications, and it was usually the notorious soap-box orators and the red-hot revolutionaries who grabbed the top ranks. Quoting a 'dandy' he met one day at his club, Bowles recounts a typical situation: ' "What bores me is that my sergeant is my *concierge*. He drinks a good deal at the wine-shop of our quarter, and so he was known, and so, *ma foi*, they elected him. Fancy, I was obliged to ask his permission to come and dine!" ' It was hardly surprising that discipline in the *Garde* as a whole was all but non-existent. In one of its very first engagements, troops from one of its battalions had broken into a nunnery and dressed themselves up in nuns' clothing'. Later, a 'curious-looking' colonel arriving to inspect a unit of the *Garde* was exposed as a woman; the mistress, in fact, of the real colonel, who had not wished to break up his game of cards. Such episodes—added to the contrast between the noisy braggadocio of some of the battalions and their actual performance when confronted with the enemy—established the *Garde* as an object of ribaldry in Paris; which, if nothing else, at least helped maintain Parisian spirits as the Siege wore on.

Too many Parisians agreed with Labouchere's cockney coachman— 'Why, sir, giving them fellows *chassepots* is much like giving watches to naked savages'; or with Prosper Mérimée, who had predicted gloomily to his friend, Panizzi, as early as August: 'Paris is quiet, but, if one distributes arms to the *faubourgs* as Jules Favre demands, here is a new Prussian Army that we shall have upon our necks'. Nothing would convince the military that the *Garde* could be turned into proper soldiers, and nothing could dispel from bourgeois minds Machiavelli's warning that 'he who commands the defence of a town will shun arming the citizens tumultously as he would shun a reef'. And indeed, if they could have read what Karl Marx would be writing to his old friend, Dr. Kugelmann, from London in a few weeks time, the Paris bourgeoisie would have felt even more cause for fear:

'. . . however the war may end, it has given the French proletariat practice in arms, and that is the best guarantee of the future.'

So no function more active than that of standing watch on the ramparts well behind the actual front, and of helping keep order in the city (although in the long run they created graver disturbances than they quelled) was entrusted to the *Garde Nationale*. Tommy Bowles watched them at work: 'They make holes and fill them with spikes; sow their ramparts with nails, points upwards, and propose even to cover these with broken glass, as if the Prussians were so many cats.' Edwin Child, who in October joined a kindred body, the *Garde Civique*, found himself delegated to supervising the distribution of meat at his local butcher, and in despair transferred to the *Garde Nationale* the following month. But, as will be seen later, he was to find service there even more disillusioning. Louis Péguret, a young Frenchman with left-wing sympathies who joined the 115th Battalion on September 16th, found his duties confined to drilling twice a day, and a week later his first 'operation' seems to have been to square the eternal triangle: '. . . arresting and conducting to the *Commissaire* a man, his wife and another woman. You can see it's not very perilous. . . .', but at least he felt that out of the uniform issued him he would eventually be able to cut 'a magnificent pair of trousers and fine waistcoat'.

To the *Gardes* the sense of their uselessness was understandably demoralizing; as they whiled away the time smoking, drinking, playing cards, and gossiping, the boredom became chronic and led to graver maladies. Paul Verlaine the poet, newly married to a sixteen-year-old bride, had joined the 160th Battalion, standing duty near Issy at the south of Paris: 'At first, it was veritably charming, veritably, and I am in no way exaggerating. To begin with, it was that delicious month of September with its sharp, pale mornings. . . .' Then he describes the infiltration of 'bad habits'—of heavy drinking, culminating in 'the first quarrel of our youthful household . . . it happened after I had returned home excessively vinous (to be more precise, it was absinthe) from the ramparts. My wife burst into sobs. . . .' It marked the beginning of the breakdown of their marriage, and the formation of a vice that eventually ruined Verlaine and drove him into the arms of Rimbaud.

Drunkenness, the opium of the masses under Louis-Napoleon and now an inevitable by-product of the National Guard's enforced indolence, was to become one of the worst scourges of the Siege. Even when Paris was approaching her last rat, the alcohol never ran out; you could buy a lot of cheap wine on 1·50 francs a day, and besides it kept you warm. 'Even the *cochers de fiacre* are drunk upon their boxes, to an extent that is really astonishing', Tommy Bowles was remarking in November. 'It is the thirty sous pay that does it all.' A few years previously, General Grant had banned all alcohol in his army, but this was a measure that was beyond the courage of Trochu. So the *Garde* spent its days in the *bistros*, and it was by no means unusual to see them marching to their posts in crooked, erratics lines. Disaffection spread, and the consumption of so much fiery liquor seemed only to add further heat to the anti-Government passions of the 'Red' *Gardes*.

Next to drink, the greatest distraction for the proletarian battalions was to spend their evenings listening to the inspired orators at one or other of the 'Red' Clubs. Closed during the last days of the Empire, the first of the Clubs to reopen its doors was the Folies-Bergère (not to be confused, in the *spectacles* it offered, with its modern successor), but 'reactionary pressure' forced it to emigrate eastwards, where it became, more suitably, the Club des Montagnards. In the dense and smoky atmosphere, the audience came to seek warmth and shelter (until the gas was extinguished at 10 p.m.) amid this mass of sulphurous humanity, as well as reassurance against the perils of the outer world; but the Clubs also acted as substitutes for 'the theatres and *salons* of the people'. Even when the theatres slowly reopened in October, the Clubs with their wild, often nonsensical, stars combined with the brilliant interpellations of Parisian wit from the hall still presented a steady, very cheap, and extremely amusing source of entertainment. Typical of what the Clubs offered at this level was the blasphemous orator who exclaimed that he would like 'to scale heaven, and collar the Deity . . .' to which a wag in the audience rejoined: 'Why don't you go there in a balloon?' The output of sheer nonsense from the Clubs was quite remarkable, and was undoubtedly what in part prompted U.S. General Burnside's famous remark after visiting Paris under truce in October: 'It's a madhouse inhabited by monkeys'. At one of the Clubs, Tommy Bowles could recall 'the original flag of Joan of Arc' being gravely produced. There was always a strong element of anti-religious obsession, and frequent declarations in favour of free love. Above all, the Clubs pullulated with suggestions to the Government on how to win the war, and even more brilliant inventions; including *escargots sympathiques* which were to carry messages in their shells through the Prussian lines. There was remarkably little time for any serious discussion of such unmilitary topics as Socialism.

The credulity of the audiences, as Goncourt noted (a shade superciliously) after the opening of the Club de Montmartre, was astonishing:

It is touching to see how these flocks of men are duped by the printed and spoken word, how marvellously deficient is their critical faculty.

The sacrosanct word 'democracy' is able to fabricate a catechism even richer in miraculous fairy stories than the old one, and these people are quite ready to gulp it down devoutly.

For all the sheer amusement value of the Clubs, the violence of their unchecked attacks on the Government soon began to take root insidiously. Any orator could be certain of frenzied applause whenever he compared the timidity and indecision of the men in the Hôtel de Ville with the ruthlessness of '93; or whenever he mentioned the Terror or the mystical Commune. Still intoxicated by the memory of how the Government had itself been brought to power by the popular voice of the mob, the Clubs developed an ever-expanding view of their own importance, to the extent that Pyat, typically, was soon offering Trochu the advice that before undertaking any new operation he should 'consult the Clubs'. But perhaps the most ominous feature of the Clubs was that it was here that the darlings of the mob really electioneered for, and were appointed to, senior military posts in the National Guard.

The kind of officers elected by the proletarian battalions included a dull-witted worker called Mégy, who—on the strength of his once having shot an Imperial policeman come to arrest him—was made an ensign. There was Johannard, a flower-vendor and East End Casanova, who applied to command the 109th Battalion but was given a lieu-tenancy in consolation: 'Citizens,' he had declared in his own support, 'there is no need to have ever touched a rifle to be a major or a general; men of war reveal themselves on the field of battle; you shall see my deeds.' (Actually he caught smallpox and never went near the front.) And there was Sapia, commanding a battalion at Montrouge, a 'Red' who wrote on paper embossed with a coronet to which he apparently had no claim, who had spent time in a lunatic asylum and had once had himself photographed in the pose of blowing out his brains. Above all, there was Gustave Flourens, who now thrusts himself forcefully upon the Paris scene.

About the same age as Gambetta, Flourens was the son of a re-spectable, indeed illustrious, physician who had been a member of the Collège de France. His brother was a *Conseiller d'État* under Louis-Napoleon and later became (despite the notoriety Gustave attained) a Minister of Foreign Affairs under the Third Republic. With a brilliant academic brain himself, Flourens had inherited his father's chair at the Collège de France for a brief time until dismissed for publishing a revolutionary pamphlet. A Byronic knight-errant in the service of Liberty, whatever its name and however Utopian, Flourens had gone to Crete to offer his services against the Turks. But the Greeks evidently found him too troublesome, and he narrowly escaped being deported back to France. Eventually he drifted home, where involvement in an inept Socialist conspiracy against Louis-Napoleon landed him in gaol. Hardly had he been released than he challenged to a duel one of the most renowned swordsmen of the time, Paul de Cassagnac, and was promptly run through the chest. He recovered, and when Rochefort was arrested in turn, it was Flourens who led the erection of barricades in the last year of the Empire. Subsequently he had fled to England (which he thought 'could be great, if only she had no Lords and no Bible'). In August 1870, estimating that the Empire was finished, Flourens made his way to Switzerland, and thence into France; where he was immediately arrested as a Prussian spy. After the September 4th revolution, he was released by personal intervention of Rochefort and finally reached Paris, where the left wing greeted him with only less acclaim than it had greeted the great Rochefort himself.

Flourens' flamboyant allure, his biting eloquence, and sheer panache promptly gained him leadership of the five Belleville battalions of the *Garde*; but there was absolutely nothing proletarian about him. He paraded in a magnificently embroidered uniform of his own design that had a strong Grecian flavour, with five rings on the sleeves (though, as a *commandant*, he was in fact only entitled to four), and was usually mounted on one of the two finest horses once belonging to the Imperial Stables, 'Capitan' or 'Passiflor', which he had requisitioned for himself. Fair-haired (though prematurely balding), with a beard and flowing red mustachios, an aristocratic nose and commanding blue eyes, he was so tall and slender as to look almost effeminate. Some of the roughnecks under his command nicknamed him 'Florence', but appearances deceived. His consumption of women was notable ('Where is your mistress, Flourens?' he had once been assailed, to which he retorted acidly, 'Humanity is my mistress!'). And, while he shared Rochefort's mob appeal, Flourens was a man of action—which Rochefort was not.[1]

'The blood was boiling in our veins, the earth burning under our feet', admitted Flourens, and certainly *his* blood was beginning to boil over at the inaction of Trochu's Government. For its members, he had nothing but contempt; Favre was 'this Judas who helped the Empire last for eighteen years . . .', Ferry 'an eighteenth-grade lawyer', and even Gambetta was dismissed as *'un révolutionnaire*

---

[1] Even though, at times, braggadocio tended to exaggerate his deeds: after the battle of Châtillon Tommy Bowles claimed to have seen Flourens, talking 'as if he had directed all the movements, and had been the sole hero of the day; the fact being that he only arrived on the ground when everything was over, and that he had no business to be there at all'.

manqué'. At Trochu's obsession with minor irrelevancies of civic administration during the siege, he mocked scathingly:

Imagine the Greeks of the Eastern Empire getting in a frenzy to find out whether the light that emerged from the navel of Jesus Christ was organic or inorganic, while the Turks were in the act of putting their ladders up against the wall of Byzantium!

(The comment might have applied with equal force too to the 'Opposition', the Red Clubs.) Why, asked Flourens, had Trochu not been harassing the enemy every night since the day the Siege began? Why was there no plan? Why had a *levée en masse* throughout France not yet been proclaimed? Above all, why was the vast military potential of the *Garde* being so outrageously wasted? The whole defence of Paris, Flourens was beginning to conclude, was 'nothing but a lie and a farce'.

The patience of Flourens was reaching breaking-point, and by October 5th the 'Red' leaders had talked themselves into taking action. That day the Belleville and Ménilmontant battalions of the National Guard, some 10,000 men, headed by a resplendent Flourens and accompanied by their bands, marched to the Hôtel de Ville. While the bandsmen thundered out the Marseillaise on the Place outside, Flourens presented his demands to Trochu in person, in the name of the whole *Garde*. They were: an immediate sortie by the *Garde*; modern *chassepots* instead of the old *tabatière* muskets; new uniforms; immediate municipal elections; and a vague request that Garibaldi be called to aid the Republic. Trochu explained that 'purposeless sorties by large masses of undisciplined men ... were hazardous', while Dorian, the Minister of Works and the one man in the Government universally respected, told Flourens 'I could more easily give you cannons then *chassepots*'. Trochu, who throughout the interview had deferentially addressed Flourens as '*Monsieur le major*', ended by sermonizing him in a parental fashion: 'I could be your father. Your place is at the ramparts, and not at the Hôtel de Ville.' Captain d'Hérisson, one of the aides present, was astonished by the mildness with which Trochu treated the demonstration. 'I was simple enough to believe that violent hands would be laid upon the Major of the Ramparts and that he would be cast into the deepest of dungeons until the end of siege'. But not at all. The *Garde* was allowed to march off unmolested, booing as they went both Trochu and their own general commanding, Tamisier, and loudly cheering Flourens. 'Then', added d'Hérisson, 'everybody went to dine.'

Thus the first demonstration against the Government ended, with Flourens evidently realizing that he had not yet the support to force

H

the issue further. But three days later a second, noisier, and far less disciplined march was made on the Hôtel de Ville. This time Flourens prudently played no part; instead the leader was the semi-demented Sapia. There also marched with him a far saner and eventually more significant figure, Eugène Varlin, commander of the 139th Battalion and one of the French leaders of the International, who had returned from exile in Brussels. Cartridges had been issued, and the mob which accompanied the Belleville *Garde* that day had a menacing air absent during the previous manifestation. One of its members attempted to pull Captain d'Hérisson off his horse, and spat in his face. Apoplectically, General Tamisier shouted 'Do you hear the cannon? Pretty moment you choose to sow discord!', which hardly helped matters. For the first time there were cries in unison of '*Vive la Commune !*', and the atmosphere in the Place de l'Hôtel de Ville resembled one of revolt rather than of demonstration. But on this occasion, forewarned by what had occurred three days earlier, Trochu had taken the precaution of having some 'loyal' battalions of the *Garde* from the bourgeois *arrondissements* standing by. Now, for the first time, the two factions faced each other stolidly, armed and glaring. It was an ominous preface to what was to come. Yet, confronted with the rival *Gardes*, even the fieriest Bellevillite sensed that Sapia had overstepped the mark, and a strange thing happened. Suddenly, in the midst of a rabble-rousing diatribe, Sapia was seized by some of his own men, bound, bundled into a waggon, and handed over to Trochu outside his office at the Louvre. All that was now needed to disperse the 'Reds' was a short speech from Jules Favre and a violent shower of rain.

The following day Blanqui in his *La Patrie en Danger* was predicting, not without accuracy, that henceforth '. . . the good Germans will await phlegmatically the end of our cattle and our flour. After which, the Government of National Defence will declare in unison that Paris has defended herself heroically, and that it is now time to think of the *pot-au-feu*. . . . October 8th will mark in history the day that the first article of the Capitulation of Paris was written by bourgeois bayonets; the others will follow of their own accord. . . .' Flourens wrote to Rochefort urging that he should 'not remain any longer with the traitors'. But Rochefort, who, like many a rebel placed in a position of authority, was enjoying it, declined, although asseverating that he had 'descended to all but the most impenetrable cellars of my conscience . . .' At the same time, the Government let it be broadcast that, as a result of Flourens's demands of the 5th, it had speeded Gambetta on his way to organize the provinces; it temporized on the holding of municipal elections, but otherwise did little else. Little, that is, except to fling the unfortunate Sapia (who had been delivered so opportunely into the Government's hands) into the Mazas Prison. An example should be made of him, Trochu was determined. He would be court-martialled. (He was, but, to Trochu's fury, acquitted.) Kératry, the Chief of Police, wanted to follow up by arresting Flourens and Blanqui, but found that none of his men would risk such a duty when the victims were safely in their stronghold at Belleville. His further suggestion, that Flourens be deviously lured to General Tamisier's H.Q. and then seized, was rejected indignantly by Trochu; whereupon Kératry resigned and took the next balloon out of Paris.

After these two discouraging events, Labouchere summed up gloomily: 'What will be the upshot of this radical divergence of opinion between the two principal classes which are cooped up together within the walls of Paris it is impossible to say. . . .'

October 31st, the Government besieged at the Hôtel de Ville

7. The Triple Disaster

On October 7th, Juliette Lambert (alias Madame Edmond Adam) visited Fort Montrouge to sample life at the front line. Standing at her side the fort commandant suddenly spotted through his telescope 'a Prussian officer, seated in an armchair on a balcony of one of the prettiest houses of L'Hay. This officer, armed with a spy-glass, was insolently observing the fort. "Clear the balcony", ordered the commandant.... Bang! The cannon-ball hit the house; balcony, armchair, Prussian officer, all disappeared.... I let out a cry of victory ... it was a beautiful day....'

It would be hard to judge which was more remarkable, the magnification of the commandant's telescope or the accuracy of his cannoneer, as the village of L'Hay stood at least two miles away. Even allowing, however, for an element of exaggeration, the incident recorded by the ardent Madame Lambert was typical of the operations to which the battle for Paris had now settled down: sniping, outpost skirmishes, artillery duels, minor pinpricks here and there. At the time of Châtillon, Paris had reminded Minister Washburne of

Washington after the Battle of Bull Run: 'nothing was completed and the confusion everywhere was immense. Had the Prussians known the weakness of Paris, they could have come right in. . . .' But since then the city fortifications had become so well established that to Washburne they seemed just about impregnable; and in any case it was now quite clear that the Prussians had no intention of trying to take the city by storm. By their unobliging attitude, one of the main pillars of Trochu's strategy had been swept away (if it had ever existed), and a 'phoney war' had set in, wherein neither side seemed prepared to undertake any major initiative. But time, however, was clearly not on the side of the besieged. As October drew to a close, chilly damp weather replaced September's superb Indian summer, and the lengthening nights brought a gloomy warning of the winter to come. O'Shea of the *Standard* reported that a National Guardsman had dropped dead one cold night in the Rue de Clichy, and depression was penetrating into the austere and draughty encampments of even the regular Army and the *Mobiles*. Officers were beginning to feel the nervous strain of gross and continued inaction, and impatience was no longer by any means the sole prerogative of Flourens and Belleville. A young Englishman, Charlie Carter, acting as tutor to General Ducrot's nephews, grumbled in a letter to his sister Fanny:

. . . The Prussians have been here a month and more and *nothing* has been done. Nothing but false reports are constantly going about to excite or soothe the popular feeling, as the case may require. Every day it is the same, '*La Province* is rising up with the utmost energy, etc.', why it's been doing so the last 2 months and if it does nothing more, it isn't much use.

Given the French temperament, something seemed bound to crack.

On October 27th, it did. To the north-east of Paris, just under four miles outside the city walls, lay the isolated hamlet of Le Bourget. Beyond it disappeared the endless plain of northern France. (Today the village is contiguous with urban Paris, while out of the plain has been carved the modern airport). With little apparent strategic value to either side, it was one of those featureless positions in featureless country that in the First World War would have been destined to become a name in no-man's-land, changing hands untold times to satisfy the whims of local commanders. On the investment of Paris, Le Bourget had become an uneasy outpost in Prussian hands. Uneasy, because to some extent it was dominated by the two most powerful forts north of the *enceinte*, the Fort de l'Est and Aubervilliers, and it was flanked by St.-Denis, the ancient village in whose cathedral repose the bones of the French kings, which was itself a powerfully fortified and strongly garrisoned fortress. At the same time, Le

Bourget was also extremely vulnerable to artillery placed on the gently rising heights to the north, all of which lay in Prussian hands. Despite this consideration, to the French commander at St.-Denis, an ambitious brigadier called Carey de Bellemare, Le Bourget presented an irresistibly enticing morsel. All at once he could bear the temptation no longer, and—acting entirely on his own initiative—on the night of October 27th he sent some 250 *francs-tireurs* to attack it. A company of the Prussian Guard was caught by surprise, and the following morning the French found themselves in occupation of Le Bourget. Having sent in a further two battalions of reinforcements, and feeling that tenancy was now assured, on the 29th de Bellemare set off for Paris to convey the good news personally to Trochu. So delighted was he with his success, that, according to Trochu, he promptly requested to be promoted *général de division*. His delight was certainly not shared by Trochu, whose immediate reaction was that Le Bourget was both inessential and indefensible, and that de Bellemare's initiative was only 'increasing the death roll for nothing at all'. Trochu was, he professed, even more surprised by the General's departure from the line at such a time, and on such a mission. Then, while de Bellemare was still in the room, a telegram was handed to Trochu, reporting that the Prussians were counter-attacking at Le Bourget. 'That is where *you* should be!' exclaimed Trochu. But, to his further astonishment de Bellemare was back again that same afternoon, claiming that the attack was nothing but a 'false alarm', and once again pressing his suit for promotion.

The Paris Press, however, thirsty for a triumph at any cost, had refused to associate itself with Trochu's dubiety and at once proclaimed the first great victory of the Siege. Even the sceptical Labouchere had been induced to enter in his diary for the 30th: 'We really have had a success.' Alas, a few hours later he was angrily correcting himself: 'So we have been kicked neck and crop out of Bourget.' The Prussian counter-attack of the afternoon of the 29th had in fact, as de Bellemare told Trochu, been successfully warded off. But it was no more than a reconnaissance in force which revealed to the Germans that they would have to bring up a much greater force to regain the village. In the meantime, with their customary speed the German guns had been rushed up and began to pound the village relentlessly, throwing in some two thousand shells. At 8 o'clock the next morning, 6,000 bayonets of the Prussian Guards division swept into the attack in loosely deployed formations: a new technique which, together with the preliminary 'softening-up' barrage, provided a remarkable preview of a First World War action. Hurriedly the French ordered up reinforcements. General Hanrion, bringing up a column of men, sent his own son back to speed it up; the young *sous-lieutenant*, having accomplished his mission, returned only to be shot down close to the spot where he had left his father. On the other side, Prussian tempers were raised by the shooting of a colonel who had ridden up to a French unit waving white handkerchiefs, and still more by finding scrawled on a wall close to Le Bourget's *'Pensionnat de Demoiselles'* the provoking words 'Prussian devils—you won't see your wives again'. As the Prussians fought their way into the village, the action degenerated into house-fighting, becoming one of the most bitter of the whole war. The French reinforcements were too little and too late, but the defenders had to be winkled out house by house. Major Ernest Barcuche, son of one of Louis-Napoleon's Ministers and commanding a battalion of *Mobiles*, shot himself rather than surrender. Gradually the fight narrowed down to the little Church of St.-Nicholas, where from behind the overturned pulpit another major, Brasseur, put up a gallant last-ditch resistance against huge odds. By midday on the 30th Le Bourget was once again in Prussian hands. Visiting the battered and bloodstained church shortly afterwards, Archibald Forbes, the *Daily News* correspondent attached to the Saxon Armies, noted that 'the Virgin had a bullet-hole through her heart'.[1]

Le Bourget cost the French nearly 1,200 men, most of whom were captured, and the Germans 477. The battle had annoyed the Prussian General Staff almost as much as it had Trochu. Blumenthal considered it 'a perfectly unnecessary fight', while the humanitarian Crown Prince Frederick thought that 'possession of that village was not of such great importance that it had to be retaken with such relatively heavy losses'. In Paris, for once even the eager Ducrot had been in agreement with Trochu over the uselessness of de Bellemare's action. So a communiqué was issued explaining the unimportance of Le Bourget, duly written off as 'not forming part of our general system of defence'. This was of course true; its sole importance to the French was in so far as any extension of the siege lines was an advantage, and provided that such extension was tenable. Compared with vital Châtillon, Le Bourget was both less easy to hold and strategically far less valuable. But the real significance of the episode lay in morale, not strategy. Here was what the Paris newspapers had led the populace to believe was the first big victory of the Siege apparently frittered away and turned into defeat through what looked like yet another display of ineptitude and lethargy by the Government. The build-up made the ensuing disappointment all the sharper. Yet before its full impact could be felt, another sledge-hammer blow of still worse news came down on top of it.

[1] Today the gloomy little church still stands on the way to the airport, with traces of Prussian bullets and its walls hung with primitive murals commemorating the battle.

On September 27th, Strasbourg had surrendered after a gallant defence culminated by a bombardment which, destroying the magnificent old library and killing many civilians, had provided a savage foretaste of the twentieth century. Towards the end food had begun to run out, and the inhabitants literally forced to live on the famous but indigestible *pâté de foie gras*. Meanwhile, Metz, better provisioned, had continued to hold out, pinning down an entire Prussian Army. But as October advanced, the population, swollen by Bazaine's enormous force inside the walls, was also beginning to suffer from hunger. On October 14th bread rationing had been introduced; most of Bazaine's transport mules and many of his cavalry horses had already been eaten. The most decisive shortage, however, was of salt. It may sound trivial, but without it none of those brilliant French sauces could be prepared that made palatable otherwise unpleasant dishes such as the rats that would soon become a stable diet of Paris, and because of this deficiency the children of Metz, covered in scorbutic sores, were beginning to die in depressing numbers. All the time the stolid Bazaine, according to Robinson of the *Manchester Guardian* who was in Metz, 'smoked by day and played billiards by night', having made no attempt to break out during the seventy days the siege had lasted. His friends insisted: 'The Marshal is a deep one; he has some hidden movement to make which will cover his name with glory. . . .' But Bazaine had nothing up his sleeve, and on October 29th he was forced to surrender a starving city to Prince Frederick-Charles's forces. The last of Louis-Napoleon's armies, 6,000 officers and 173,000 men, marched out; ragged, sick, demoralized, and many wretchedly and sullenly drunk. As Bazaine himself rode forth into captivity, women spat at him, and immediately the news reached Tours Gambetta had Bazaine proclaimed a traitor.

History's verdict on Bazaine is that he was an indifferent general and an unenthusiastic Republican, and probably nothing worse.[1] But as even one of France's own historians has remarked of one of her least endearing national characteristics: 'In France we have to have traitors. It is impossible to admit that we should be beaten without someone's treachery.' Thus it was as a traitor that Bazaine was hauled before the courts after the war, sentenced to death and then—after a reprieve—to life imprisonment; a fate remarkably similar to that which overtook another *Maréchal de France* seventy years later, the

[1] Bazaine's dilemma was one of legitimacy, happily unknown to members of a British or American officer corps, but which was to dog French history right through the Second World War to the Algerian War of the 1950's. Maintaining a perhaps misplaced loyalty towards the deposed Emperor, Bazaine was articulate in detesting the new Republican Government and he rejected its authority. 'I had no government,' he declared as his trial. 'I was, so to speak, my own government.'

aged Pétain. Whether Bazaine was guilty or innocent, or whether he had any alternative to surrender, the fall of Metz was a grave blow to French fortunes. It meant that the whole of Frederick-Charles's Second Army was now free either to join in the Siege of Paris, or to carry the war against the new armies Gambetta was levying at Tours.

In England a judgement that typified changing British emotions towards the war was expressed by the *Illustrated London News*: 'Germany is thought to have had enough of triumph, France enough of punishment.' But the Supreme Arbiter evidently did not agree.

Reports that Bazaine was negotiating for the surrender of Metz had begun to reach the Government in Paris on about the 26th. Trochu told Rochefort, who told Flourens (with a caution to keep it quiet), who promptly told Pyat, who headlined *Le Combat* on the 27th 'FALL OF METZ'. The Government immediately, and clumsily, denied the story, stigmatizing the paper a 'Prussian organ', and *Le Combat* was burnt on the streets by outraged citizens. On the 29th Rochefort wrote a letter of resignation from Victor Hugo's house. The next day the evacuation of Le Bourget was announced; on hearing the news Juliette Lambert declared: 'I cannot express the chagrin, the discouragement, the rage and the despair which invaded me, I slumped into a chair without knowing where I was'. On Monday the 31st, after a weekend of rising excitement, rumour and counter-rumour, the Government was forced to admit the truth of *Le Combat*'s story.

Then, as a final blow to the *guerre à outrance* faction, it was revealed that Thiers had just returned from his travels with a four-power armistice proposal. He was in fact urging the Government to accept the latest Prussian terms—which included the cession of Alsace and an indemnity of two milliard francs—and the word had quickly got around the left-wing strongholds that a 'peace-at-any-price' sell-out was being prepared by that old enemy of the working class. The Mayor of Montmartre, a fiery young radical called Georges Clemenceau, that morning posted up an *affiche* declaring: 'The municipality of the 18th *arrondissement* protests with indignation against an armistice which the Government could not accept without committing treason.' Coming in such swift succession, the combined force of the three blows shocked bourgeois Paris and was altogether too much for the Paris 'Reds'. On the afternoon of 'Black Monday'—which happened to be Hallowe'en—the storm broke.

All through the previous day, Tommy Bowles had noted 'ominous threats uttered by the crowds on the boulevards'. It was, he predicted, 'not unlikely that we may have troubles', and others of the British Press corps shared his fears. So did Edmond Adam, Juliette Lambert's husband, who had replaced Kératry as Prefect of Police.

Through Picard, the Minister of Finance, he warned the Government that an insurrection might well be in the offing and recommended that precautionary measures be taken. But Trochu, expressing utter confidence in his own popularity, had merely replied, 'I shall be responsible for order'. At 8.30 on Monday morning Adam had gone to Trochu in person and repeated his warnings, only to be brushed away again with the remark 'we are a Government born of public opinion . . . consequently, *mon cher préfet*, we only employ moral forces'. Unconvinced, Adam at once went to the Place Vendôme and ordered ten reliable battalions of the National Guard to stand by to cover the approaches to the Hôtel de Ville. Later he followed this up with an order for a further ten battalions to be held ready. From the earliest hours of Monday morning everything indicated that Adam's fears were by no means groundless. Felix Whitehurst, one of the British community in Paris, was writing up his diary when

a rather stronger storm of drums and trumpets set in than even we have been accustomed to during the last six weeks, and, as we have drums and trumpets on the brain, of course we took glass and went to the balcony to inspect. Thousands of National Guards were marching in every direction, and as they were not, as a rule, in heavy marching order, were too clean to be coming from, and too late to be going to, the forts or fortifications, it struck us that something was in the air . . . . I marched off at once to the Hôtel de Ville. As I passed along the Rue de Rivoli, I saw on every side the signs of a brewing storm. All the concierges were outside their gates, and their wives, who should have been 'doing the first floor' were talking to other conciergeresses, who should have been 'doing' the 'entresol' and the 'second'. Men in trousers with red stripes were carefully putting up their shutters. . . .

Several of the British correspondents had already reached the Hôtel de Ville. There the first sight that struck O'Shea of the *Standard* was 'a forest of umbrellas'. 'Most of the men were in uniform, or had some prompting of uniform, if only a cap with a red band; and all were excited. . . .' There was angry talk about Le Bourget, and O'Shea heard a Belleville Mrs. Malaprop lashing the Thiers peace mission with repeated shouts of '*Pas d'amnistie!*' Elsewhere Bowles innocently asked an angry demonstrator why he was yelling *À bas Trochu!*' to be told, 'Well . . . because he's come unstuck'. The din was growing tremendous and individual slogans were constantly drowned by raucous blasts of bugles and drums, and chants of '*Vive la Commune!*' Occasionally from the first-floor windows of the Hôtel de Ville, some gesticulating authority would appear to make a speech that no one could catch. Meanwhile, O'Shea noticed that the pavement outside the building itself was only held by 'a scant line of Breton *Mobiles*' and was being 'gradually encroached upon'. At about midday,

Labouchere reckoned there were some 15,000 people outside the Hôtel de Ville, most of them National Guards. Nearly all were either unarmed or else carrying their muskets butt uppermost; a traditional sign that the soldiery was on the side of the Parisian mob.

Conspicuous by their absence were the 'Red' leaders. So far the demonstrations in front of the Hôtel de Ville bore all the signs of being spontaneous and unplanned, and indeed it seems that Flourens and his associates were almost as taken by surprise as Trochu. That very morning they were holding a council in Belleville to discuss the situation, when news of the gathering demonstrations reached them. Quickly it was proposed that the Belleville battalions of the National Guard should march on the Hôtel de Ville, overthrow the Government, and replace it with one headed by Blanqui, Delescluze, Pyat, Flourens, and Victor Hugo. Some heated discussion followed, and it was clear that not all the Belleville officers of the *Garde* shared Flourens' enthusiasm for the project. After October 5th Flourens had been deprived of his command of the five battalions (to which he was in any case not entitled), and now he led only a small élite which he had majestically christened the *Tirailleurs de Flourens*. Both Flourens and the dissenting Belleville *Gardes* were equally mindful of the unfortunate fate of Sapia, and thus it was with only his '*Tirailleurs*', some 400 strong, that Flourens and the other members of the 'new' Government set forth for the centre of Paris.

At the Hôtel de Ville the situation was rapidly deteriorating. For a while Arago, the Mayor of Paris and a herculean figure, had held the fort by bellowing back at the mob like an angry bull through the closed grille that protected the entrance. Suddenly a shot was fired; it was never discovered by whom or by which side. Several others followed. No one was hit, but the mob scattered backwards in haste, revealing in the empty space *Mobiles* with bayonets at the ready. There was a momentary panic and word ran round that Trochu had given orders for his Bretons to massacre the 'sovereign people of Paris'. Meanwhile Arago, realizing that matters were getting beyond him, decided to summon by telegraph all the absent members of the Government. Trochu at once buckled on his sword, put on his epaulets and his cross of *Grand Officier de la Légion d'Honneur*, and with two aides courageously rode out from the Louvre through booing crowds. Before leaving his office, he issued strict instructions to his Chief of Staff, General Schmitz, not to 'move either a man or a gun without my personal order in writing'. Favre had been discussing armistice terms with Thiers over lunch when the telegram arrived, but he too promptly left, picking up Picard on the way who (not without cause) grumbled all the way 'We are sticking our heads into a mouse-trap'. Not one of the various members of Trochu's Cabinet converging on the Hôtel de Ville seems to have thought of bringing with him any forces.

Soon after the arrival of the Ministers, the mob recovered its nerve, and—no doubt goaded on by the actual sight of the objects of their wrath—surged forward again. This time their impetus carried several hundred into the building before the *Mobiles* could close the gates again. The major in command of the three companies of *Mobiles* within the vast building, threatened with being overwhelmed by the invaders, drew his sword. His men rushed to his assistance, striking right and left with their rifle-butts. At this point, Trochu, who had been discussing in the first-floor conference room whether the mob could be drawn off with a promise of immediate municipal elections, appeared on the stairs and ordered the *Mobiles* to offer no resistance, but to withdraw to their barracks. He then returned to his discussions, locking himself and the Cabinet in, and leaving Arago and others to harangue the invaders on the staircase. Twice Rochefort (whose resignation Trochu had refused) was sent out as an appeaser, but even this former darling of the mob had evidently lost his old touch. After angry hands had tried to pull him down and voices actually cried '*À bas Rochefort!*' he simply walked out in disgust; disappearing for ever from the Hôtel de Ville and the Government which he had forsaken.[1] At least once Trochu himself left the conference in an attempt to pacify the mob by what he described as '*objurgations patriotiques*' in one of his famous, verbose orations. Inside the '*Salon Jaune*' situated on the western corner of the Hôtel de Ville with two windows facing the Seine and two overlooking the mob seething in the Place outside, the Government was stolidly continuing its debate, with Picard urging that a date be fixed immediately for the long-promised elections. Some time after 3 p.m., an abatement of the occasionally deafening tumult from the corridor seemed to indicate that enthusiasm among the insurgents was beginning to wane, and that some were actually departing. Then all of a sudden there was a flurry of trumpets, the doors of the '*Salon Jaune*' burst open, and in strode Flourens, magnificently booted and spurred and carrying a great Turkish scimitar.

Behind Flourens came Blanqui, Delescluze, Pyat, Millière, and most of the 'Government' proposed that morning in Belleville. One notable absentee was Hugo, whose invective had done so much to raise the temperature of the 'Reds' to its present level, but who was now prompt to dissociate himself from the results. To make himself heard and his will felt above the hubbub, Flourens leaped up on to the

---

[1] Rochefort in his memoirs gives a different, and not wholly plausible account of his departure; one of the invaders, he claimed, told him 'they're fighting at Belleville. You alone can prevent a disaster', and then dragged him off by force.

conference table. Up and down it he strode, issuing orders right and left, kicking over inkwells and scuffing up the green baize with his spurs, his boots on a level with Trochu's nose. Labouchere, who had infiltrated in Flourens' wake, heard him (before being hustled out again by the mob) call upon both Trochu and the Trochu Government to resign, an invitation which Favre politely declined. Millière then passed up to Flourens a draft order decreeing the arrest of Favre, but Flourens refused to sign it on the grounds that the insurgents had insufficient force with which to effect an arrest. Despite the Government's refusal to be deposed (which manifestly discountenanced the 'Reds'), the process of replacing it now ensued regardless. Once again the spectacle of September 4th was repeated, with a snow-flurry of paper slips descending on the expectant mob in the Place below. Many of the lists of the 'Committee of Public Safety' (as the traditionalist-minded 'Reds' intended to call themselves) began with the name of Flourens, especially those that the brash major had scribbled out himself. But it was Dorian whom the mob most persistently called for, just as less than two months ago it had in its fickleness howled for Trochu: Dorian, former industrialist and now Minister of Works, the most universally respected man in the 'old' Government.

A reluctant candidate, who sped from one group to another displaying a truly remarkable diplomatic flair, Dorian affably told the 'Reds' that he could not, under the circumstances, accept their offer. Confusion and indecision set in, revealing the 'Reds'' lack of planning behind the coup of that day, as well as their inherent disorganization that was to feature so largely in bringing them to disaster the following spring. Swiftly the insurgents broke up into groups and caucuses to discuss a substitute for Dorian. As Lissagaray, the 'official' historian of the Commune, later wrote, 'Each room had its own government, its orators, its *tarentules*.... Thus that day which could have revitalized the defence vanished in a puff of smoke. The incoherence of the *avant-garde* restored to the Government its virginity of September.' Tempers rose. The insurgent leaders began to quarrel among themselves; Blanqui declined to have Flourens on his 'list', and Delescluze did not want Pyat. Meanwhile more and more of the mob were pressing into the Hôtel de Ville, the real *canaille* of Paris, many of them drunk. With no particular political aims, some invaded and looted the kitchens; furniture was smashed and a superb plan of Paris drawn up by Haussmann himself was cut to pieces. As they surged up the great staircase, even the heavy iron banisters were seen to give menacingly. Reaching the rooms where Flourens and the 'Red' leaders were wrangling, these agents of the 'dark people' added to the chaos by themselves standing on tables and demanding a hearing.

As he opened his mouth, one was neatly felled by a heavy inkstand hurled from out of the mob; another incessantly blew a trumpet, while a third beat a drum. Blanqui became submerged, was kicked, had his venerable white beard pulled by toughs who did not recognize the frail old man, and was buffeted hither and thither, until he collapsed in a corner half-senseless. The air inside the Hôtel de Ville had become almost unbreathable. Of it, the fastidious Captain d'Hérisson remarked:

The mob brought with it its particular odour. The smell of its pipes and cigars alone contended with a stink as of wet dogs . . . and of dried sweat which exhales from a mass of troops, especially when those troops are dirty and have only been partially washed by the rain.

Throughout this spectacle of mounting bedlam Trochu had maintained an almost superhuman sang-froid. While Flourens and his fellows paced up and down the conference table above him, he had calmly puffed away at a cigar, observing their antics. One of the British correspondents claimed that 'a sardonic smile played round the soldier's mouth', and in some curious way he seems almost to have enjoyed the humour of the situation. Then, as the 'Red' leaders began to row among themselves and the mob grew more unruly, Trochu quietly removed his epaulets and decorations and handed them to one of his aides. His conduct, thought O'Shea, was thoroughly 'noble', and it set an example that was followed by the rest of the Government—with the possible exception of Garnier-Pagès. The old man with his comic high collar and flocks of white hair divided neatly down the centre had collapsed completely when, in the midst of expatiating to the mob 'I have witnessed three glorious revolutions', he was rudely told to 'shut up'. Sobbing and laughing at the same time he mumbled to Flourens, 'I am going home, to my family; and tomorrow I shall no longer take any part in politics'. Otherwise the calm inspired by Trochu, while it averted any incident that might easily have led to bloodshed, also had a subversive effect on the insurgents, torn as they were by indecision and fraternal wrangles. The sergeant of the *Garde* detailed off to keep Trochu under surveillance appears to have been particularly impressed by the general's bearing. Proudly explaining that he had served a long time in the Zouaves, he treated Trochu with marked deference, and while the bickering was at its height remarked to him, '*Voyez-vous, mon général,* these are the sods who have made us take arms at the double, and led us here without knowing what to do'; and then yelled to Flourens at the top of his voice:

Florence, ma vieille, tu faiblis ![1]

[1] Florence, old girl, you're weakening!'

It was now beginning to get dark. The Trochu Government had been held captive for several hours, and so far no serious attempt had been made to liberate it from the outside. To the exterior world it looked as if the 'Reds' had pulled off a *fait accompli*. The ever-vigilant Goncourt, having read on people's faces signs 'of the great and terrible things that are in the air', had made his way through the rainy darkness and sodden crowds to the Hôtel de Ville. There the sight of 'the workers who had led the movement of September 4th sitting on the sills with their legs dangling outside' told him the worst. 'The Government had been overthrown and the Commune established. . . . It was all over. Today one could write: *Finis Franciae.* . . .' At this moment, with superb irrelevance, he was asked by an old lady if 'the price of Government stock was quoted in my paper'. As he walked home, he saw a young National Guardsman 'running along the middle of the Boulevard, shouting at the top of his voice 'To arms, damn you!' Gloomily he speculated: 'Civil war, with starvation and bombardment, is that what tomorrow holds in store for us?' His pessimism was shared by Minister Washburne, who had come away from a visit to the Hôtel de Ville at six o'clock with the conviction that 'the revolution had been practically accomplished, and that we should have a genuine Red Republic'.

Though Flourens and his '*Tirailleurs*' had achieved what looked effectively like a siege within a siege, the blockade of the Hôtel de Ville was in fact as far from perfect as a 'Red Republic' was from establishment. Jules Claretie, who had tried to enter the building, had been told by a 'Red' sentinel, 'You cannot pass without a *laissez-passer*. . . . Signed by whom, I don't know, but it has to have a blue stamp'. But despite this requirement, he had got in and out again without much difficulty. As the hours wore on numbers of the *Tirailleurs* had wandered off to find food and drink—or just to get out of the pouring rain—and the blockade became even laxer. Somewhere about this time, Picard, who had been so unhappy about going to the Hôtel de Ville in the first place, managed to slip out undetected through a small side door and safely reached the Ministry of Finance in the Place Vendôme. From his office there, the only member of the Government at large, he set about organizing the liberation of his colleagues.

Well might it be asked why, with the enormous forces at the Government's disposal in Paris, this liberation had not already been effected. The answer was simply that there was no one to give the orders. General Tamisier, the commander of the National Guard, was a prisoner in the Hôtel de Ville, and so was Edmond Adam, the Prefect of Police; General Schmitz, like a good soldier, was still

awaiting written orders from Trochu. Ducrot, commanding the most
powerful and dependable units in Paris, was isolated in his H.Q. out
at Porte-Maillot, and heard no rumour of the uprising until about
5 p.m., roughly the time when Picard was making his escape. The
fire-eating general, who had long wanted to settle the 'Reds' once
and for all with a 'whiff of grapeshot', promptly and on his own
initiative ordered a whole infantry division to arms, plus one battery
of 12-pounders and one of *mitrailleuses*, and stood by to march on the
Hôtel de Ville.

As officers sent out on reconnaissance returned with progressively
worse news and still no orders arrived from Schmitz, Ducrot became
almost overwhelmed with impatience. Finally, at 6.30 p.m. a telegram arrived from Picard, calling on Ducrot to report to him at the
Ministry of Finance. Preferring to remain at the head of his 'ex-
peditionary force', instead he dispatched a major from his staff to tell
Picard that he was only waiting for the word 'go' to enter the city
and 'chase out the insurgents'. Ducrot's emissary found Picard in
his office, surrounded by people, in an atmosphere dense with hubbub
and movement.

All over Paris drummers had beaten out the *rappel* (a sound that
struck a chill in the hearts of people in whom it was associated with
the 'Terror' of the Great Revolution), calling all the National Guard
to arms, and already the Place Vendôme was crammed with loyal
battalions. Picard told the major what he had done, and at once gave
the authorization for Ducrot to march. On his way back to the Porte
Maillot, the idea occurred to Ducrot's emissary to call in on General
Schmitz at the Louvre. There he was confronted with even greater
confusion than *chez* Picard, with order heaping upon counter-order.
Schmitz, though completely distracted, agreed to transmit Picard's
authorization to Ducrot by telegraph. At about 8.30 p.m. the major
was in the act of mounting his horse to return to Ducrot, when who
should appear on the threshold of the Louvre, surrounded by an
immense crowd and wearing the *képi* of a simple National Guardsman,
but Trochu himself?

One of the 'loyal' battalions of the National Guard to obey
Picard's summons, the 106th commanded by Major Ibos, had marched
to the Hôtel de Ville, where the heavy rain had already thinned out the
mob outside, and had managed to penetrate the building. There had
been some buffeting with the proletarian Guards there, but no shooting.
Indeed, the 106th seems to have been greeted with a certain amount
of *bonhomie* by the rival elements, who no doubt expected to convert it
to their cause. Reaching the '*Salon Jaune*', Ibos found Flourens still
pacing the conference table, and immediately leaped up beside him.

Something resembling a brawl ensued, during which a section of the maltreated table collapsed. In the uproar that followed (perhaps aided by the turning of a blind eye by Trochu's disgruntled guard, the ancient Zouave), a posse of Ibos's men surrounded the Head of State, hustled him down the stairs and thence out of the Hôtel de Ville, with Jules Ferry clinging to his wake. More than one account describes Trochu as being literally carried off in the arms of a gargantuan National Guardsman; a version he strenuously denied, though admitting that someone did thoughtfully remove his general's *képi* with its tell-tale gold braid and replace it by his own.

On regaining his headquarters, Trochu, apparently greatly shocked to learn of the orders that had just been transmitted to Ducrot, at once countermanded them. His motives seem to have been governed less by fear that the Prussians might choose this moment, when Ducrot's forces were deployed elsewhere, to launch an all-out assault on the city, than by fear of the carnage his subordinate would wreak upon the mob. Post-haste Ducrot's major rode forth with his new orders, but was astonished to learn at Porte-Maillot that the general, finally overcome by impatience as he had been once before, at Châtillon, had already left for Paris at the head of an immense column at 7.30 p.m. Meanwhile, Ducrot had sent on ahead another orderly, Captain Neverlée of the Dragoons, to inform Schmitz at the Louvre of his impending arrival. Neverlée too was turned about by Trochu with orders for Ducrot to halt immediately and report in person to the Louvre. By the time Neverlée returned, Ducrot had reached the Étoile. Although fuming with rage, he did what he was told. On his arrival at the Louvre, Ducrot forcefully represented that the Government 'had to act immediately with energy, crush the insurgents and liberate their prisoners by force'. He begged Trochu to let him fire into the mob; he could disperse it in five minutes, and his *Mobiles* were eager to sink their teeth into the *Garde*. Trochu refused. The prevailing view was that extreme methods should be shunned, that the remaining members of the Government held by the insurgents— Favre, Simon, Arago, Dorian, Le Flô and others—should be liberated by negotiation, and that repressive measures should be postponed till the morrow.

After several voices had raised themselves in support of Ducrot, however, Trochu produced one of his typical compromises. The 'loyal' National Guard that had congregated in the Place Vendôme would alone march to surround the Hôtel de Ville; while at the same time two battalions of *Mobiles*, notably Bretons, that were housed in the nearby Napoléon Barracks would carry out an ingenious Trojan-horse tactic. There was, as one of Trochu's staff pointed out, a subterranean tunnel some one hundred yards long linking the barracks with the Hôtel de Ville, built by Napoleon I so that the Hôtel de Ville could be garrisoned against an uprising within five minutes. In all probability its existence was unknown to the insurgents, who could be taken by surprise by armed *Mobiles* emerging in their midst. At about 10 p.m., with drums beating and trumpets sounding, the 'loyal', bourgeois *Garde* marched out of the Place Vendôme, headed by Jules Ferry.

The scene now switches to the Prefecture of Police where Juliette Lambert had spent an afternoon of 'mortal anguish'. That morning her husband, Edmond Adam, the Prefect of Police, had gone to the Hôtel de Ville in response to Arago's call. To distract herself from worrying about Adam, Juliette paid a vist to Fort Romainville at the east of Paris. On her way back she had passed through Belleville, which she found 'in full mutiny'. The 'menacing' faces everywhere filled her with alarm. Reaching the Hôtel de Ville she interrogated the huge crowd in the Place as to what was going on within: 'They answered quite gaily "*tout est fini*". I continued my questions and understood nothing from the replies'. The worst seemed to be confirmed by the appearance of Flourens, riding in triumph among the mob on one of his splendid mounts, to the acclaim of his supporters, whom 'he thanked with a look, with a gesture, or with words'. Returning to the Prefecture at about 4.30 p.m., she learned to her great concern that Adam had still not returned from the Hôtel de Ville and that nothing further had been heard of him. For two nerve-racking hours she waited. Then news of Adam arrived, via an extraordinary figure: Frontin, a retired police superintendent now serving with the National Guard. According to Frontin, Adam had been taken with the Government, but it was some hours before his identity had been revealed. There were then angry howls of 'Arrest him' and, as chief of the mob's traditionally greatest enemy, the police, prospects looked extremely unpleasant for Adam. At this moment, however, Frontin appeared, 'arrested' him, briskly marched him down the corridors of the Hôtel de Ville, and 'escorted' him to freedom, whence Adam had immediately reported to Schmitz at the Louvre.

Juliette stayed on at the Prefecture, awaiting her husband's return; then suddenly three to four hundred insurgents appeared on the Quai outside. At their head was a young man who, until that morning, had been a simple clerk at the Prefecture and who had only come to notice through the unusual interest he had shown in the police dossiers. His name was Raoul Rigault, the fugitive that Renoir had helped in the Forest of Fontainebleau a few years earlier. Rigault now stalked into the Prefecture, producing a paper signed by Flourens stating that he, Rigault, was to replace Adam as Prefect. Pouchet, Adam's deputy, coolly and deferentially informed Rigault that only an hour previously he had received a similar order appointing someone else, and politely suggested that Rigault return to sort matters out with Flourens. Rigault flew into a tantrum, called Flourens *'idiot, bruyant,*[1] *imbécile !'* and stamped out again. A short while later another note arrived from Flourens, this time begging the Police to look for his horse, which had strayed in the mêlée outside the Hôtel de Ville, and ending with the P.S. 'Please remit the horse to the bearer'. Next, the 'Scarlet Pimpernel' figure of ex-Superintendent Frontin reappeared, this time very smartly dressed and carrying a rifle, with fresh news about Adam. The Prefect, it appeared, had gone on to the Place Vendôme, in quest of the National Guard battalions he had ordered to stand by that morning, only to be told that twenty-five had been despatched to the Hôtel de Ville, but that most of them had strayed on the way. It was disheartening news. Then Trochu had been released and the plan to reoccupy the Hôtel de Ville drawn up; whereupon Adam had promptly volunteered to lead the detachment which was to 'Trojan horse' the insurgents.

Midnight passed anxiously at the Prefecture. Once again, the good Frontin materialized, mysteriously, 'as if through a wall'; now disguised as one of Flourens' *'Tirailleurs'*, and bearing a vivid account of the successful recapture of the Hôtel de Ville. Down the subterranean passage Adam and his men had crept, lighting the way with resin torches, and up through a trap-door in the cellars of the Hôtel de Ville, where they gave a terrible fright to a group of insurgents brewing up peacefully around a fire. The alarm was sounded, but too late; Adam and the Breton *Mobiles* swiftly reached the main staircase. Adam, continued Frontin's bulletin.

wishes that the Hôtel de Ville be evacuated and that there should be no killing. It's not as easy as that. There are some bright lads who refuse to come down. The *Mobiles* are at the bottom of the great staircase, ready to fire; the Belleville *'Tirailleurs'* are at the top, ready to reply. The Prefect is in the middle of the staircase, alone, backed by one side to pacify the others so that they can then be pushed outside. If there's a shot, the first one will be for him! The insurgents threaten to kill M. Jules Favre, if the *Mobiles* advance. The Prefect replies that if they touch M. Jules Favre, M. Jules Simon, or any of the other prisoners, not one of *them* would get out alive. 'We are the stronger', says he, 'Look out of the windows. . . .'

'I am going to see if *M. le préfet* is still on his staircase', ended Frontin, and once again slid out into the night.

[1] 'Loud-mouth'.

Out of the countless, and often conflicting, accounts of that extra-ordinary day, little can be certain, but Frontin's story of the re-entry into the Hôtel de Ville seems to have been reasonably accurate. There now ensued lengthy parleys aimed at effecting a bloodless evacuation of the building by the insurgents, in which Dorian and Delescluze (who, in the course of this evening of wrangling, had now emerged as the 'Red' with the greatest qualities of leadership) played the principal roles. On and on the negotiations dragged, until Ferry with his force of loyal National Guards surrounding the exterior of the building could hardly desist from intervening. At last an agreement was reached; the Government would hold immediate elections and there would be no reprisals against any of the insurgents; in return, the Government captives would be released and the Hôtel de Ville peacefully evacuated. Dorian's promises were endorsed by Adam and Ferry, and hands were shaken all round. At 3 a.m., the march-out began. Heading the procession, farcically reminiscent of guests going in to a banquet, came General Tamisier arm-in-arm with Blanqui; then came Dorian with Delescluze, and the rest of the Government amicably paired off each with an insurgent leader. The latent comedy of the situation seemed an appropriate epilogue to all that had gone before that day. Conspicuously absent alone was the slippery Pyat who, true to form, had 'disappeared' the moment the tide seemed to be turning. At the rear of the notables was Adam, keeping a wary eye on his *Mobiles* and exhorting the 'Red' Guards-men to shoulder their muskets, instead of carrying them dejectedly butt downwards: 'You have not been conquered.' Until 5 a.m. the defile continued. There had been, Adam estimated, between seven and eight thousand men inside the building. Then Adam returned to bed, 'broken with fatigue, but contented', according to his wife. The ever-attentive Minister Washburne, before turning in that morning, noted 'all the streets deserted and the stillness of death everywhere. What a city! One moment revolution, and the next the most profound calm!' The astonishing uprising had ended as suddenly as it had begun, and without a single casualty; it was indeed, as Flourens remarked cynically, 'Trochu's only successful military operation during the whole siege'.

Alas for France, what ended in the small hours of November 1st was in one sense only a beginning. Later that morning, the weary Adam was woken by Picard in person, his habitual gaiety completely restored. 'Well, Adam', he cried, 'have you given orders for the arrest of Messieurs Pyat, Blanqui, Delescluze, Flourens, and Millière, and the other leaders of last night's invasion? It has been done, hasn't it?' Adam was shattered. The Government, he told Picard, had solemnly promised that there would be no reprisals. No, replied Picard, the honour of the Government was not committed; he for one had not been consulted. All that day there were bitter arguments in the Government Council, with Adam taking part. From the earliest Ducrot had been applying pressure on Trochu to carry out swift justice, including the summary execution of some of the leaders as an example, and the Ministers themselves were still seething with outrage at the indignities they had suffered. Finally it was decided that Ferry and Adam's promises to the insurgents constituted only 'an armistice'. There was a heated row between Adam and Ferry when Adam declared that this was simply casuistry, and that he would refuse to break his word.

The next day the Government insisted and Adam resigned. More than any other figure on the Government side, he had been the real hero of October 31st, and his departure represented a serious loss. Dorian, whose honour was also involved, suffered the pangs of being pulled in two directions; with full justification he explained, 'I make cannon. . . . If I stopped, soon neither a bullet nor a cannon would be made', and so, tearfully, he decided against resigning. A new Prefect of Police, Cresson, was appointed, who wasted no time in rounding up the principal insurgents. Twenty-two were arrested and flung into the Mazas. They included Blanqui, Millière, Vermorel, Vallès and Eudes (for the second time since the war began). The net brought in even the elusive Pyat, and Flourens was arrested while actually at the front line with his battalion—though not until a month later. In addition, sixteen battalion commanders of the National Guard were cashiered; all of whom, including Karl Marx's future son-in-law, Longuet, subsequently became Communards.

Even a right-winger like Jules Clarétie, the journalist, considered the arrests to be 'pitiful, useless, dangerous'. A sour sense of betrayal now permeated the whole of left-wing Paris, and what little prestige still remained to the Government vanished with the realization that the double-dealers among it included even the once-revered Dorian. To the existing list of grievances was added a new bitterness that would have incalculable results when the Siege was ended. Optimistically Tommy Bowles wrote: 'The day will have taught the Parisians one thing, that the dreaded *spectre rouge* is a very harmless turnip-headed ghost after all.' Events were to prove him horribly wrong. Nor were the arrests the only respect in which the Left felt it had been double-crossed. After the *entente* with Dorian, Deescluze claimed—probably in good faith—that the insurgents had been promised elections to replace the Provisional Government. What actually took place, on November 3rd, was nothing more than a plebiscite requesting an answer of 'yes' or 'no' to a vote of confidence in the Government. The result was 560,000 to 53,000; which was regarded by the Government as a notable victory, and by the 'Reds' as a manifest swindle—which indeed it was. Worthy of note, however, was the fact that three of Paris's twenty mayors had declared themselves in sympathy with the uprising of October 31st, including Clemenceau of Montmartre.

Among the other immediate consequences, Victor Hugo protested against the abuse of his name on the 'Red' Government 'lists' without his consent; Rochefort resigned once and for all and joined the artillery of the National Guard; and General Tamisier was replaced as commander of the Guard by General Clément Thomas, an even more unfortunate choice than his predecessor in that he was detested by the Left for his brutal repression of the uprisings of 1848. From now on the Government never again risked meeting in the Hôtel de Ville, and among its members mistrust of the military value of the National Guard reached a new zenith. Finally, to Thiers who returned on the night of November 2nd to the Prussian camp with the aim of pursuing the armistice talks, Bismarck—having been well informed of what had transpired and realizing how much the French hand had been weakened—regretted that he could not continue the talks, on the pretext that the Government by whom Thiers had been sent probably 'no longer existed'.

Balloon Factory at the Gare d'Orléans

8. A Touch of Verne

WHEN, at the beginning of October, a Frenchwoman in Prussian-occupied Versailles first saw a balloon rising out of Paris, she exclaimed in the hearing of Russell of *The Times*: 'Paris reduced to that! Oh good God! Have pity on us!' Yet the balloons of Paris were to constitute probably the most illustrious single episode of the Siege. To the average person today, the Siege of Paris evokes principally two images: rat-eating and balloons. The first represents the depths to which a modern civilization can be reduced; the second, the zenith of its resourcefulness in adversity.

The development of the balloon had always been a preserve of the inventor nation. De Montgolfier's first 'hot-air' balloon of 1783 was a perilous device in which the passengers had to stoke a fire with straw and wood immediately beneath the highly inflammable paper envelope; so perilous, indeed, that Louis XVI had proposed that the first manned flight be made by two criminals under sentence of death. In fact, it was carried out by Pilâtre de Rozier and the Marquis d'Arlandes, who flew for twenty-five minutes across Paris, at a height of three hundred feet. Almost simultaneously, a French physicist, Professor Charles, was experimenting with a hydrogen-filled balloon, which made its first ascent from the Tuileries in December 1783. When someone cast doubts on the usefulness of Charles's invention,

121

one of the spectators, Benjamin Franklin, was provoked to make a famous retort: 'Of what use is the new-born baby?' Two years later, Blanchard managed to cross the Channel in a *charlière* (throwing out even his own trousers in an endeavour to maintain altitude), for which feat he earned £50 and a life pension from Louis XVI. But the unfortunate de Rozier was killed while emulating Blanchard that same year, and in 1819 Madame Blanchard, the wife of the Channel-crosser, died in a balloon crash over Paris.

As early as 1793, the French were using balloons for military purposes—to carry dispatches over the heads of the enemy—and the following year Robespierre established an '*École Aérostatique*' at Meudon. This was closed down by Napoleon I; perhaps one of the few instances where he showed less prescience than his tragic nephew. For Napoleon III at least appreciated the military potentialities of balloons, and had employed a man called Nadar to spy out Austrian positions at Solferino. At the Siege of Venice, the Austrians themselves had tried to set fire to the city with numerous small unmanned paper balloons, each carrying an incendiary bomb; but fortunately (and true to form), all had landed within their own lines. During the American Civil War, the North used captive balloons to photograph Confederate lines at the battles before Richmond, and McClellan is said to have derived considerable advantage from their intelligence. Later the balloons were even linked by telegraph to the ground. But when the South brought into service a fairly effective rifled anti-aircraft gun, and after a balloon bearing a Yankee general had broken loose, nearly delivering him to the Confederates, the North apparently began to lose interest.

The next recorded military employment of balloons, and the first time that they were used to carry mail on a big scale, was at besieged Metz (appropriately enough the pioneer de Rozier had been a native of Metz). The service was initiated by an enterprising Englishman, G. T. Robinson, of the *Manchester Guardian*, the only British staff correspondent there, as a means of getting his reports out after runners had refused bribes of up to 1,000 francs. Because of the shortage of raw materials (all the sulphuric acid required to manufacture hydrogen had been used up in making soda water), it was impossible to send up manned balloons from Metz, so that many were to fall into enemy hands. Robinson's first balloon had a ladder driven through it by a clumsy French worker, but despite all handicaps one successfully took off on September 15th, carrying 8,000 letters, and thereafter they were launched at a rate of nearly one a day. The service continued until October 3rd, by which time it had transported over 150,000 letters and dispatches.

Louis-Napoleon, on his return from
Germany, 1871

General Trochu

General Ducrot

Léon Gambetta

Cattle and the sheep in the Bois de Boulogne just before the Siege

The Crown Prince of Prussia views Paris from the
heights of Châtillon

'How one could have used the balloons to surprise the enemy.'—From a drawing by Cham

'My passport? Here it is!'—From *Souvenirs du Siège de Paris*

Felix Pyat

Victor Hugo

Gustave Flourens

Henri de Rochefort

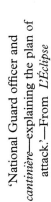

'Garde nationale sédentaire—Partisan of peace to the bitter end.' —From *L'Éclipse*

'National Guard officer and *cantinière*—explaining the plan of attack.'—From *L'Éclipse*

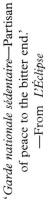

'No news!'—From a drawing flown out with Fonvielle on the *L'Égalité*, Nov. 24th

'The queue for rat meat.'
—From a drawing by Cham

Alan Herbert's hen, 'Una', who
survived the Siege

Edwin Child in National Guard
uniform

Child's 'identity card' issued by
the Commune

Below: Child's bread ration card
issued during the last days of
the Siege

The lynching of Vincenzoni, February 1871

The revictualling of Paris: distribution of the English food

When the Siege of Paris began, there were only seven existing balloons in the city, most of them in disrepair. Symbolically, the *Impérial*, which had arrived just too late to observe the dynasty triumph at Solferino, was in shreds; the *Céleste*, which by giving captive flights had dazzled visitors to the Great Exhibition of 1867 with French prowess, was described as being as gas-tight as a 'sieve'. But undismayed the intrepid French aeronauts at once went to work; literally, with paste-pot and paper. Within two days of the closing of the ring, the first balloon was prepared for flight, but burst while being inflated. That same day, however, Nadar carried out a successful reconnaissance of the Prussian lines. The corpulent Nadar was a man of many talents—photographer, caricaturist, journalist, and a friend of the Impressionists (it was in his house that Renoir held one of his first exhibitions). In Jules Verne's *De la Terre à la Lune* he appeared under the anagram of 'Ardan', and seven years before the war he had flown in the double-decker *Géant* all the way to Hanover. He also appears to have been an astute businessman; Nadar's enemies later accused him of dropping advertisements for his own company over the Prussian outposts, instead of propaganda leaflets!

On September 23rd, Durouf made his successful solo flight to Evreux, and three days later the Minister of Posts, M. Rampont, decreed the establishment of a 'Balloon Post'. Among the first to be invited to send a letter by it was the eighty-six-year-old daughter of the inventor, Mlle de Montgolfier. Two kinds of epistle were permitted, '*monté*' and '*non-monté*', according to whether the balloons were manned or not; the former limited to small sheets resembling today's air letters, not exceeding four grammes in weight, and costing the standard 20 centimes; the latter to be simply postcards bordered, for the benefit of the enemy should they fall into his hands, with such slogans (in stilted German) as 'Crazy people, shall we always throttle each other for the pleasure and pride of kings ?' and 'Paris defies her enemy! All France is rising; death to the invaders!' As it was, only one '*non-monté*' balloon (the fifth) left Paris, to be shot down by the Prussians after a flight of only a mile, so that this service was subsequently abandoned.

After Durouf, balloons took off at a rate of about two or three a week, usually from an empty space at the foot of the Solférino Tower on top of Montmartre, or from outside the Gare du Nord and the Gare d'Orléans. Godard, one of a family of veteran aeronauts, got away successfully suspended from two small balloons lashed together and appropriately named *Les États-Unis*. Tissandier, flying in the patched-up *Céleste*, which in peacetime had never been capable of staying in the air for more than thirty-five minutes, managed to reach

Dreux (fifty miles from Paris) after passing so low over Versailles that he could see Prussian soldiers sunbathing on the lawns. Lutz, travelling aboard the *Ville de Florence*, found himself descending rapidly into the Seine, and was forced to jettison a sack full of top-secret Government dispatches. Remarkably enough, it was returned to him on landing by some peasants, and he managed to escape with them through the Prussian lines to Tours, disguised as a cowherd. Another unfortunate, faced with a similar crisis, threw his lunch pack overboard in mistake for ballast; yet a third threw himself out, but fortunately landed in a soft beet-field. The crew of the seventh (unnamed) balloon fell into a swamp just outside Paris, and for hours lay in icy water with Prussian bullets skimming over their heads, but they too escaped. It was not only as postmen that the balloons acted; later, one perilously carried a consignment of dynamite destined for Bourbaki's Army; and another took up a scientist who merely wanted to study an eclipse of the sun—an event that provoked amusement among the British correspondents, coming as it did at the height of the fiercest battle of the Siege.

Writing home on September 30th, Edwin Child remarked sceptically: 'This letter the glorious French Republic has promised to forward by means of a balloon but the writer has about as much confidence in the punctuality of a balloon, as a Parisian lady has in the '*parole*' of a 'man of honour''. The letter did in fact arrive, but looking back from this age of science, it does seem little less than miraculous that so many of the French balloonists succeeded in getting through. It was not until the eighteenth flight on October 25th that a manned balloon (curiously enough named the *Montgolfier*) fell into Prussian hands. Equipment was incredibly primitive. The balloons themselves were constructed simply of varnished cotton, because silk was unobtainable, and filled with highly explosive coal-gas; thus they were exceptionally vulnerable to Prussian sharp-shooters. Capable of unpredictable motion in all three dimensions, none of which was controllable, in inexperienced hands they had an unpleasant habit of shooting suddenly up to six thousand feet, then falling back again almost to ground-level. Huddled in their baskets (which Bowles noted to his horror were only 'the height of a man's waist, with just enough room for two people to sit or rather squat'), devoid of any protection from the elements, the balloonists suffered agonizingly from cold as the winter grew more bitter. The most useful items of equipment carried on board were a six-hooked anchor and a 150-metre 'trail' rope. The latter was invaluable as a form of automatic ballast, depending upon how much of its weight was deposited on the ground, as well as for slowing down a descending balloon. Often the aeronauts carried no compass, and after a few minutes of twisting, giddy progress they had in any case lost all sense of direction.

To every corner of France – and beyond – the winds blew them, and they seldom had the remotest idea where they were on landing. Added to this, since a frustrated Bismarck had proclaimed that he would submit any apprehended balloonists to the fate of common line-crossers, there was always the prospect of a Prussian bullet at the end of each flight (although, on hearing the Prussian threat, another 172 aeronauts had promptly volunteered). It was perhaps hardly surprising that Bowles and his fellow correspondents should at times find balloonists demanding a £100 'bonus' before accepting their dispatches.

> *Audace humaine! effort du captif! sainte rage!*
> *Effraction enfin, plus forte que la cage!*
> *Que fault-il à cet être, atome au large front,*
> *Pour vaincre ce qui n'a ni fin, ni bord, ni fond,*
> *Pour dompter le vent, trombe, et l'écume, avalanche?*
> *Dans le ciel une toile et sur mer une planche.*[1]

Thus wrote Hugo of these early cosmonauts, and indeed, faced with the unknown and the uncertainty of their conveyance, their 'audacity' cannot be exaggerated. But in the exhilaration of the moment – the sense of escape from the imprisonment of Paris, the champagne effect of altitude, the silence, and the beauty – fear seems to have been relegated to a minor role. After his flight, Gambetta described himself as 'stupefied at the total obliteration of the picturesque in the boundless expanse beneath'; Durouf claims to have been preoccupied by the spectacle of the Prussian cannon-balls rising and falling back below him; Buffet, flying at night, by the lights of the ramparts that seemed to 'surround the city with a girdle of fire'; and another balloonist by hearing a cock crow at two thousand metres in the extraordinary silence of the sky. Cheerfully and defiantly, crews uncorked wine in their precarious baskets to toast 'Death to the invaders! *Vive la France!*' as they sailed over the Prussian lines.

In the deserted halls of the Gare d'Orléans, Eugène Godard, veteran of some eight hundred flights, had set up an assembly line for fabricating balloons, and scattered across Paris were small ancillary workshops. Conducted by Nadar to a former dance-hall at Montmartre,

[1]'Human audacity! the struggle of the prisoner! blessed rage!
At last, eruption stronger than the cage!
What does that creature, atom with generous brow, require
To conquer that which has no end, nor edge, nor base,
To tame the wind, tornado, sea-foam, avalanche?
In the sky a canvas, and over the sea a shelf!'

Théophile Gautier found some sixty young women sewing away with furious industry, reminding him of the 'humming of old-fashioned spinning-wheels'. At the Gare du Nord, where rails already rusted over with grass beginning to grow between them made Bowles think of the Sleeping Beauty, the completed balloons were varnished; stretched out, partially inflated, like rows of massive whales. In the waiting-rooms here and at the Gare du Nord, sailors were busy braiding ropes and halliards. The specifications were rigid; each balloon had to have a capacity of two thousand cubic metres at least, and be capable of lifting four people, plus an additional five hundred kilogrammes in weight.[1] For each satisfactory product, the factory received 4,000 francs (of which 300 were earmarked for the pilot), but there was a 'penalty clause' imposing a 50-franc fine for every day delivery fell behind schedule. (In fact, the economics of the operation proved highly favourable to the Government, since each balloon could carry 100,000 letters, bringing in a revenue of 20,000 francs.)

Where could sufficient numbers of trained aeronauts be found to man the balloons ? Soon the 'professionals' would all have flown out of Paris. Godard solved this by setting up a training-school within the factory. Baskets were suspended from the station girders, containing all the essential controls to simulate flight—valves, ballast, guide-ropes, etc. Godard's sailors in particular (possibly because they were less prone to sea-sickness) proved themselves markedly proficient in a short time; of the 65 balloons that left Paris during the Siege, only 18 were piloted by professionals, 17 by volunteers, and the remaining 30 by sailors.

A more intractable problem was that the balloons afforded only a one-sided means of communication. 'With the aeronaut', sighed Gautier, 'flew our thoughts too, our messages for our absent loved ones, the very beating of our hearts, all that is good, tender, and delicate in the human soul. On this fragile paper even those who affect a stoical smile have shed a tear.' But how could the 'absent loved ones' acknowledge this outpouring of affection and anxiety ? The balloons were, of course, unsteerable. 'People dreamed only of balloons', remarked Gautier. 'They interrogate the wind and sound the depths of the sky. Chemists and scientists share but one idea, to control the direction of the balloons'. A Government grant of 40,000 francs was made to a well-known naval engineer, Dupuy de Lôme, to construct a steerable balloon, and he produced a drawing of a cigar-shaped vehicle with a propeller rotated by a man and a supplementary sail. Even before the war, Tissandier (who later piloted the *Céleste* out of Paris) had contemplated the possibility of building a

[1] This meant that one balloon alone consumed the equivalent of seven tons of coal, out of Paris's total stocks of some 73,000 tons.

huge 'dirigible' propelled by a 400 h.p. steam engine, and now cranks besieged him with futuristic ideas; even Victor Hugo contributed his. They ranged from sails, oars, and rockets to the harnessing of ten thousand pigeons. *La Petite Presse* of November 7th reported that, in an experiment at the Jardin des Plantes, it had been proved that four eagles could shift a five-ton waggon; a story that was taken up in all credulity by the *Pall Mall Gazette*, which insisted that 'four or six powerful birds were harnessed to the balloon, and were guided by an aeronaut by means of a piece of raw flesh fastened to the end of a long stick, which was held in front of their beaks'. There was a proposal by an Englishman to run an aerial telegraph wire to Paris, borne high over the lines between two balloons a hundred kilometres apart, and someone even proposed that Paris could be victualled by a thousand Montgolfier balloons, each bearing a single cow.

One balloon, the *Duquesne*, actually left. Paris equipped with a propeller hand-driven by three beefy sailors; but it still flew in the opposite direction to that intended. The most serious, and persistent, attempts to balloon back into Paris were made by Tissandier. By October 19th, he was at Chartres, waiting for a favourable wind that would waft him towards Paris. The whole city was plunged into darkness as the greedy balloon consumed its last gas, and was still only partly expanded. Then an excited officer rushed up to warn Tissandier to take off at once, as the Prussians were close at hand. But a strong gust of wind blew the under-inflated balloon into a tree, where it exploded. At the beginning of November, Tissandier was trying again, this time from Rouen. For a week he waited. At last the wind seemed right, and he leaped into the basket of the *Jean Bart*. As the balloonist took off, someone thrust a piece of paper into his hand, which he took to be an important dispatch, only to discover to his disgust that it was a brochure from a local tailor. The *Jean Bart* disappeared for three hours into thick clouds and fog. When it emerged, Tissandier saw that he had hardly moved and that the wind was beginning to turn against him. On a third attempt he narrowly escaped being blown out to sea. Right up to the capitulation of Paris, the balloonists were still trying. But none ever succeeded in making the return journey.

Other methods devised for communicating with Paris included a submarine, and glass globules that were to be floated down the Seine (but unfortunately it froze); and one balloon even carried with it divers' suits with a similar project in mind (but unfortunately it landed in Bavaria). Five messenger dogs were used (unsuccessfully) and several brave foot-couriers tried to run the blockade. With great ingenuity, they secreted minuscule messages in hollow buttons, in the soles of their shoes, and even in slits under their skins; but most of them were caught and several were shot. Only one, a postman called Létoile Simon, succeeded in making the trip both ways, and he was awarded the *Médaille Militaire*.

The humble carrier-pigeon was to prove the only means of breaking the blockade in reverse. In Paris there was an expert in microphotography called Dagron, who before the war had invented a ring called a 'Stanhope' containing a tiny photograph magnified by a gem-like lens, a novelty that had sold in vast quantities at the Great Exhibition of 1867. Early on November 12th, Dagron and his equipment had set out from Paris in two balloons. the *Niepce* and the *Daguerre*. Both were blown towards the east; before the horrified eyes of Dagron in the *Niepce*, the *Daguerre* came down and was promptly seized by Prussians. When the crew of the *Niepce* desperately tried to gain altitude by heaping out ballast, the sacks of sand proved to be rotten and burst in the gondola. All fell to bailing out the sand with Dagron's photographic beakers; some of the precious equipment had to be jettisoned too, but the *Niepce* escaped. Eventually Dagron reached Tours, where, although badly handicapped and delayed by the loss of equipment, he set up the first microphotography unit ever to be employed in war. Government dispatches in Tours were reduced to a minute size, printed on feathery collodion membranes, then rolled into a pellicle; so that one pigeon could carry up to 40,000 dispatches, equivalent to the contents of a complete book. On reaching Paris, the dispatches were projected by magic lantern and transcribed by a battery of clerks. Sometimes one pigeon-load alone would require a whole week to decipher and distribute. As well as carrying official messages, the pigeons were entrusted with a vast amount of precious personal correspondence. In England in late November, the G.P.O. announced facilities for sending letters, via the French Post Office, into Paris; they were to consist of no more than twenty words, the charge for which was fivepence per word; the announcement ending with the caution that the French Post Office 'cannot guarantee the safe delivery of this correspondence, and will not in any way be responsible for it'. The front page of *The Times* was also frequently filled with advertisements from relatives of the besieged, microfilmed in entirety to the size of a small snapshot, and relayed by pigeon.[1] Another device were the '*oui ou non*' letters sent by '*ballon-monté*' containing four questions, each with a number. The replies

[1] One of the cherished myths of *The Times* history was that, during the Siege, microphotographed copies of its front page were also flown *into* Paris by pigeon. This particular *belle légende* was finally shot down by *The Times* itself, following some learned research, a hundred years later. An analysis carried out by a Mr. John Hayhurst, of the British Ministry of Technology, of all micro films received in Paris revealed that none had a front page of *The Times* on it, thereby effectively destroying claims made by the paper shortly after the siege ended. [*The Times*, 4/2/70.]

pigeoned back into Paris were published in Government bulletins.

In the course of the Siege, 302 birds were sent off, of which 59 actually reached Paris. The remainder were taken by birds of prey, died of cold and hunger, or ended in Prussian pies.[1] Some of those captured on board the *Daguerre* were released by the Prussians, carrying demoralizing 'deception' messages. But they were betrayed by their suspiciously Germanic wording, as well as by being signed by an 'André Lavertujon', who had in fact never left Paris. The great drawback to the pigeon post was its unreliability and, as the days grew shorter, the arrival of the pigeons—unable to fly by night—became increasingly erratic. One, released at Orléans on November 18th, did not in fact reach Paris until February 6th, a week after the Siege ended. But although, for reasons that will emerge later (which were far from being entirely the fault of the balloonists or the pigeons), the strategic role of the aerial posts was limited, their effect on civilian morale in Paris was incalculably great. A *Daily News* correspondent in the provinces noted 'one of the most plaintive of the laments sent from Paris was "we have had no pigeon for eight days".' During such a hiatus spirits slumped. When the war ended, there was serious talk of rewarding the noble birds, which some compared to the geese of Rome, by the incorporation of a pigeon in the city coat of arms.

As more and more balloons safely reached unoccupied France, the Prussians were not allowing this threat to their blockade to go un-contested. In the occupied areas stern orders were issued for all scattered dispatches to be handed over to the Prussian authorities, and after his warnings of draconian reprisals had gone unheeded, Bismarck himself ordered Alfred Krupp to design a special anti-balloon cannon. When at last it arrived, it was an ingenious fore-runner of modern weapons, described by the Crown Prince of Prussia as 'resembling a rocket battery', and by others as 'a long mobile barrel mounted on an axis, more resembling a telescope than a cannon'. It could allegedly fire a 3-lb. grenade to a height of 2,000 feet, yet seems to have been strangely ineffective. An American adventurer called Wells who offered the Prussians to take to the skies as a 'balloon-interceptor' ended in a crash, and Wells transferred his services to the French at Bordeaux. Other attempts to install sharp-shooters in balloons apparently ended in equal disaster. The most effective challenge to the French balloonists was provided by the Prussian observation-posts set up all round Paris, which reported the course of the balloons leaving the city along Moltke's incomparable telegraph network. This resulted in their being shadowed during much

[1] As a counter-measure, the Prussians imported falcons; to which one of the many Paris 'inventors' suggested that pigeons be equipped with whistles, to frighten off the predators!

of their flight over occupied territory by detachments of vigilant Uhlans, waiting to pounce upon any descending balloon. The new technique began to have its successes. First, the *Montgolfier* was seized on landing in Alsace after a three-hundred-mile flight. Two days later the *Vauban* carrying Reitlinger, a special emissary of Jules Favre, descended in a forest near Verdun, and Reitlinger only reached the Belgian frontier after the narrowest of escapes from Uhlan patrols. That same day the *Normandie*, bearing among others the young nephew of Worth, the English *couturier*, also came down near Verdun. Worth, Cuzon the pilot, and another passenger all jumped out prematurely, leaving the wretched remaining passenger, Manceau, soaring aloft like an arrow in the lightened balloon. Manceau managed to release the gas valve, redescended, but panicked when still some thirty feet from the ground. He likewise jumped out, breaking his leg. All four were seized by Prussian patrols, badly treated, and threatened with a firing-squad. This probably would have been their fate, had not Worth been a British subject on whose behalf repeated representations were made in London.

Next, on November 4th, the *Galilée* was captured near Chartres with 420 kilograms of mail, followed on November 12th by the *Daguerre*. The prospects began to look so grave that the French now decided to send up their balloons only by night, in order to baffle the German observers. This change of schedule resulted, as winter drew in, in some of the grimmest and most dramatic flights of the Siege. After taking off at 1 a.m. on November 25th, the *Archimède* came down at dawn in Holland and would undoubtedly have been blown out to sea had its flight lasted a few minutes longer. In December the *Ville de Paris* landed at Wetzlar in Germany, believing it to be Belgium, and five days later the *Chanzy* ended up in Bavaria after an eight-hour flight. But no flight was more perilous or more remarkable than that of the sister balloon of the *Archimède*, the *Ville d'Orléans*, about which more will be heard later.

By a real miracle, until November 28th and the thirty-fourth balloon, there had not been one single fatality. That day a young sailor called Prince climbed aboard the *Jacquard*, announcing (so it was said): '*Je veux faire un immense voyage—on parlera de mon ascension !*' The next day Prince and the *Jacquard* were spotted from the Lizard lighthouse, disappearing out into the Atlantic. His dispatches were picked up from the sea, but not Prince, and his death is today marked by a small commemorative plaque in the Gare d'Orléans. Altogether some 65 manned balloons left Paris during the Siege. They carried 164 passengers, 381 pigeons, 5 dogs, and nearly 11 tons of official dispatches, including approximately two and a half million letters. Six landed in Belgium, four in Holland, two in Germany, one in Norway, two were lost at sea, but only five fell into enemy hands. The news they exported of Paris's continued resistance did much to stimulate sympathy abroad for the French cause, as well as kindling hope in the provinces. But above all, the knowledge that the city was not entirely cut off from the outside world, the ability to communicate, however haphazardly, with relatives there, and to learn that other French forces were still resisting the enemy somewhere in the provinces, went far towards countering that deadly ailment, l'ennui, and towards restoring Parisian morale.

Although it was by far the most practical, the balloon was by no means the only scientific development to occupy fertile Parisian minds during the Siege. Inventions and ideas of all kinds poured into the Government by the hundred, so that even before the investment it was forced to set up a Comité Scientifique to deal with this flood of ingenuity. One of the first serious propositions placed before it had been the mining of Versailles and St.-Cloud; the mines to be fired electrically from Paris so as to prevent the Prussians setting up gun batteries there. Fortunately—although some forbears of 'Dr. Strangelove' on the Committee seem to have regretted it—this proposal was turned down.[1] But most of the ideas reaching the Committee formed a fascinating catalogue of science fiction and sheer fantasy. One suggested the poisoning of the river Seine where it left Paris; another the 'decomposition' of the air surrounding the Prussians; and a third the loosing of all the more ferocious beasts from the zoo—so that the enemy would be poisoned, asphyxiated, or devoured. There was a considerable vogue for adaptations of 'Greek fire' that would consume him by fire in various ways, and someone proposed a 'musical mitrailleuse' that Siren-like would lure the Kultur-lovers by playing Wagner and Schubert, and then scythe them down. Another ambitious soul suggested hitching a sledge-hammer worthy of Vulcan, weighing ten million tons and encompassing fifteen miles, to a series of balloons and cutting the ropes over Moltke's H.Q. One less murderous, but equally disagreeable, idea came from a doctor who suggested replenishing Parisian fuel supplies with gas distilled from human corpses.

Some of the 'inventions', though almost nonsensically futuristic in 1870, are not unfamiliar now. There was the 'mobile rampart', a precursor of the tank;[2] there were shells that would emit 'suffocating

---

[1] St.-Cloud was in fact gutted early in the Siege by a shell from French guns at Mont-Valérien.

[2] A visionary, heavily armoured 'land monitor', dating back to 1854 and invented by an Italian engineer called Balbi, which was to be propelled by steam, was actually offered to Mayor Clemenceau of Montmartre; so it was alleged when Clemenceau was Premier of France in World War I. Clemenceau had opened up public subscriptions to build one large and two small 'monitors', with a view to breaking the Prussian stranglehold; but before any model could be developed the war had been lost. [From Mid-Week Pictorial: an Illustrated Weekly, Vol. VII, No. 13, 30 May 1918, p. 23; Letter from M. Rosen, 30/4/72.]

like fire[1]. One diabolical scientist proposed bombarding the Prussian lines with bottles containing smallpox germs, and a suggestion to use balloons filled with explosive as 'flying bombs' was prudently dropped on the grounds that Prussian reprisals against Paris would be infinitely more lethal. Parisian scientists were constantly preoccupied by the quest for a 'super-explosive' with which to erase the besiegers, and one employed on this project was the inventor of the Orsini bombs, which had come so close to extinguishing Louis-Napoleon. Labouchere, who met him, expressed fears of his being 'hoist with his own petard' and indeed experiments resulted in several fearful accidents. Among them was one involving the inventor of the best hand-grenade produced during the Siege, who inconveniently blew himself to pieces in his laboratory.

In advocating their wares, the inventors could be most persuasive; even so sceptical an observer as Tommy Bowles appears to have been impressed by the 'frock-coated, keen-eyed little chemist, who has within his knowledge more effectual and terrible methods of warfare than all the cocked-hats in Europe ever covered'. He assured Bowles that he had invented a devastating explosive which he claimed could 'blow the Prussian Army off the face of the earth', as well as a 'means of decomposing water itself, and turning it into consuming flames'. (The encounter prompted Bowles to prophesy, a little optimistically, that 'when war becomes a mere duel of skill between chemists its glory is gone, and, when the risk of it is so enormously increased, its attractions will disappear as well'). The Paris Press was particularly susceptible to the most Laputan projects, and a great clamour was aroused in the papers when the Scientific Committee declined the 'invention' that would have decomposed the air around the stricken Prussians.

As noted in another chapter, many of these—such as the 'sympathetic snails', a design for a 'hot-water rifle', and the unleashing of the lions from the zoo—originated from the fetid atmosphere of the Red Clubs, and as often as not received the ardent support of Pyat's *Le Combat*. But none was more exotic than Jules Allix's '*doigts prussiques*': pins dipped (appropriately) in prussic acid, with which the women of Paris could defend their virtue. These were to be ancillary to a remarkable corps created by Félix Belly, called the 'Amazons of the Seine'.[2] In October, the British correspondents had all been intrigued

[1] In *Le Combat*, Pyat went wild about this weapon, 'which, adhering to and corroding the flesh, forces men under the impact of violent pain to relinquish their position and take flight'.

[2] The 'Amazons' seem to have had a precedent in the '*Vésuviennes*' of the 1848 Revolution who, equipped with 'Greek fire', were to strike some fearful fiery blows for feminist rights.

by recruiting placards that had sprung up on walls throughout Paris. The redoubtable ladies were to be dressed in black pantaloons with orange stripes, a black hooded blouse, a black képi with an orange band, and a cartridge pouch slung across the shoulder. Armed with a rifle, their intended role was 'to defend the ramparts and the barricades, and to afford to the troops in the ranks of which they will be distributed all the domestic and fraternal services compatible with moral order and military discipline'. Ten battalions were to be raised, and their expenses were to be met by a 'sacrifice' on the part of the 'Amazons'' richer sisters of bracelets and jewellery. Enrolments would be accepted at 36 Rue Turbigo, said the proclamations, which were signed '*Le Chef Provisoire du premier bataillon,* FÉLIX BELLY.' The Amazons were quickly wedded by Allix to his '*doigt prussique*', which he reasoned was a more feminine weapon than a rifle, describing its usage as follows: 'The Prussian advances towards you—you put forth your hand, you prick him—he is dead, and you are pure and tranquil'. Alas, although Belly claimed 15,000 applications, this fearful secret weapon never materialized. The Government, less concerned by the implications of the 'fraternal services' which the Amazons were to perform at the front than by the fact that Belly was apparently collecting enrolment 'fees', intervened. For a while, however, Paris at least had something to laugh about; Belly disappeared from sight; Allix later represented the 8th *arrondissement* in the Commune and ended up in a lunatic asylum.

Belly, if the allegations were true, was not alone in utilizing the inventive craze as a means of personal aggrandisement. One resourceful Parisian made handsome profits through a factory manufacturing false 'trophies' of war, where he produced Prussian *Pickelhauben* and sabres by the score, as well as forging 'next-of-kin' letters that were certified to have been removed from a Prussian corpse; and O'Shea remembered an 'ingenious rascal with a bandaged head who paraded a pair of human ears in a jar of spirits of wine on the boulevards, and brought down a flush of coppers by making believe that they were his own, sliced off by the Barbarous Prussians'.

As the orators of the Clubs produced one fantastical invention after another, so the great intellects of France in the various Academies occupied their time with equal irrelevancies. Carrying on its usual curriculum of discussions on medieval grammar and Coptic characters, the nearest the Academy of Inscriptions and Letters came to contemporary affairs was a lecture in November on 'The Provisioning of Besieged Towns in Antiquity'; while the Academy of Science busied itself with such topics as differential equations and the eclipse of the sun.

By and large, apart from the balloon and pigeon post, the inventors
of Paris gave birth to little that was of practical use during the Siege.
There were perhaps no more than three such developments: a primitive armoured train, powerful electrical searchlights which were
employed to protect the Paris forts against surprise attack by night,
and an unpalatable synthetic foodstuff called *osseine* derived from bone
and gelatine. In fact, the greatest achievements lay in the production
of more conventional weapons, such as cannon, *mitrailleuses*, and
rifles, during the Siege, and for this the credit belongs to one man:
Dorian, the Minister of Works. In more ways than one, Dorian—a
peacetime industrialist—proved himself to be *the* outstanding member
of the Trochu Government, and as an organizer he was unexcelled.
Under him, every available workshop and factory in Paris was set to
producing munitions; the *Conservatoire des Arts et Métiers* became a
vast cannon plant; and even along the smart Rue de Rivoli the sound
of hammering came from basement windows where weapons were
being forged. Great ingenuity was used to circumvent grave shortages
in raw materials; steel was replaced by alloys of bronze and tin, there
was even talk of using that new rare metal, aluminium, and somehow
saltpetre for gunpowder was recovered from old plaster. Even the
bells of St.-Denis Cathedral were melted down. By the end of
September, Dorian's workshops were already turning out 300,000
cartridges a day, and when the Siege ended no less than 400 cannon
and a large number of *mitrailleuses* had been manufactured in Paris.
Haste and carelessness led to a series of disastrous accidents in
powder-mills (one apparently caused by a plumber soldering on the
roof), and it was later claimed that many of the breech-loading guns
were unsafe; but—since most of the arms plants had been shifted to
the provinces before September, and equipment had to be improvised—it is perhaps remarkable that anything was produced at all.
No less remarkable was the means of financing the cannon, some
two hundred of which were subsidized through popular subscription,
launched by Victor Hugo. The inhabitants of the poorer, 'Red',
arrondissements considered that many of these had actually been
'bought' by them, and their pride in the results of their sacrifices
was justifiably immense. In mid-December a National Guardsman
wrote to his sister in the provinces that these cannon were now being
delivered at a rate of twenty-one a day: 'you know that's really something, every five days, a hundred guns. . . .' It was also to become one
of the immediate causes of the outbreak of Civil War when the Siege
ended.

Wounded in the Théâtre-français

9. 'Le Plan'

WITH the 'Red' leaders in gaol, awaiting a possible death sentence, the greatest danger confronting Trochu's conduct of the war—that of a revolution inside Paris—seemed to have been averted. Belleville was sullenly in check; but for how long? Yet, as November arrived and the Siege approached the end of its second month, neutrals inside Paris sensed a distinct plunge in morale. On November 6th, Labouchere reported: 'I never remember to have witnessed a day of such general gloom since the commencement of the Siege. The feeling of despair is, I hear, still stronger in the army.' Gloom had thoroughly infected Labouchere himself; should a peace be signed on the latest Prussian terms, wrenching Alsace-Lorraine away from France, he predicted: 'within ten years we shall infallibly be dragged into a Continental war'. Only in the date did he err. On November 12th, Washburne wrote despondently: 'I might as well stop my diary, for there is absolutely nothing to put down. There are now no military, nor even political movements, the streets are becoming more and more vacant and the people more and more sober....' To maintain morale, the Paris Press had to fall back as a surrogate for more striking events on the doings of one Sergeant Ignatius Hoff of the 107th of the Line. Hoff was a shadowy figure who, employing Mohican tactics, specialized—like a latter-day commando—in the nocturnal throat-slitting of German sentries. Each night he returned with a collection of *Pickelhauben*, and by November his alleged tally had reached twenty-seven. He was swiftly built up into an almost legendary hero; much as air aces like the great Guynemer were singled out for beatification from the amorphous carnage of the First World War.

But even the exploits of Sergeant Hoff could not suffice to distract Parisians from the uglier facts of life that were now becoming apparent for the first time. In his entry for November 12th, Washburne added: 'During the last few days the suffering has greatly increased.' It was true; about the same time Tommy Bowles recorded an ominously symptomatic observation. He had been watching fishermen haul in a seine net from a lake at the Bois de Boulogne. Not a fish was in it. The following day he was reporting that milk had run out, and on the 16th Washburne wrote: 'Fresh meat is getting almost out of the question.... They have begun on dogs, cats, and rats.... The gas is also giving out.' One of the first to try the new fare was Labouchere, who rated his introductory *salmi de rat* as 'excellent—something between frog and rabbit'. But it was still a novelty. Yet another grim aspect of siege life—the threat of epidemics —began to intrude itself upon the scene; already during one week of November smallpox had claimed five hundred victims.[1]

All this, coming so soon after October 31st's revelation of public discontent, made even Trochu realize that something had to be done swiftly and dramatically. The time had come for a major military effort. But where, and how?

For some time the wags of Paris had been talking about '*le plan Trochu*'. It was a word he was extremely fond of; even when he sat down to a game of piquet (according to Labouchere) he would warn his opponents, '*J'ai mon plan*', and if he lost he would leave the table grumbling, 'nevertheless, my plan was a good one'. A little ditty was beginning to make the rounds:

---

* One of the first victims, much mourned, was little Giuseppina Bozzacchi the ballerina. The previous May, Bozzacchi as Swanilda had delighted Paris in the Second Empire's last glittering première, Delibes's *Coppélia*. She was only seventeen.

Je sais le plan de Trochu,
Plan, plan, plan, plan, plan !
Mon Dieu ! Quel beau plan !
Je sais le plan de Trochu :
Grâce à lui rien n'est perdu.[1]

Later, a story was also put around by Trochu's enemies that he had
confided his mysterious 'plan' into the hands of his lawyer, but in
fact the documents when examined proved to be a blank! Trochu in
his memoirs hotly denies this slander; admitting, with perfect truth,
that he had never had any plan at all.

Indeed, in so far as there was any military plan, it was Ducrot's.
There was no one in 1870 more representative of the best tradition of
French generals than Ducrot; ardent, courageous to a fault, enterprising, but seldom rewarded by success. In 1914 he would have been
and out-and-out supporter of Foch; in Algeria of the 1950's, of General
Massu and perhaps even of the O.A.S. He was a true disciple of
l'attaque à outrance. Before the war Ducrot had warned Louis-
Napoleon that the Army was not ready to fight Prussia, but that if
war were inevitable the only way to win would be with a *Blitzkrieg*
through the southern states of Germany. Captured with the Emperor
at Sedan, the humiliation had driven him to escape, in circumstances
which Bismarck claimed constituted a breach of parole. He was, in
Trochu's words, *'un véritable homme de guerre'*, and ever since the
setback at Châtillon he had been champing at the bit to lead a major
action. In the earliest days of the Siege, Trochu and Ducrot had both
agreed (erroneously) that the forces in the provinces would never
amount to much, and that, therefore, if the Prussian ring round Paris
were to be burst, this would have to be done from the inside. There
were three points which seemed to offer the best prospects of a breakthrough: between the Marne and the Seine to the south-east of Paris;
on the Plain of St.-Denis to the north; and across the peninsula
formed by the meanderings of the Seine at Gennevilliers to the north-
west, one of the favourite painting grounds of the Impressionists. Of
these, Ducrot considered the last alone combined both tactical and
strategical advantages. The investing enemy forces in the Gennevilliers peninsula were less securely organized, and once their lines
there had been pierced Ducrot's men would find themselves in unoccupied, friendly territory, which would not be the case in other

[1] 'I know Trochu's plan,
    Plan, plan, plan, plan, plan!
    My God! What a fine plan!
    I know Trochu's plan,
    Thanks to him, nothing is lost.'

directions. Moving north-westwards along the Basse-Seine via Rouen, Ducrot would then reach out for Le Havre, gaining a port through which Paris could be revictualled, linked with the French Armies of the provinces, and perhaps even supplied with fresh arms from overseas.

Such was Ducrot's 'plan'. He had, he says, just completed his studies of it when he heard, on October 7th, of Gambetta's flight out of Paris. Immediately he presented the plan to Trochu. The pessimistic Trochu was by now thoroughly convinced that no attempt at breakthrough would succeed, but for want of any better suggestion both he and his Chief of Staff, General Schmitz, accepted Ducrot's plan in principle, which henceforth became '*le plan Trochu*'. Ducrot was allowed to go ahead with preparations, to the extent of carrying out a limited operation at Malmaison on October 21st that aimed at securing the left flank of the breakthrough. It was tentatively planned that the attempt should be made between November 15th and 20th, by which time Ducrot (whose chief concern still lay in the quality of his troops) hoped to have a corps of fifty to sixty thousand well-trained men available. Meanwhile Trochu—until October 31st—remained sceptical towards the plan's probability of success and phlegmatic in his efforts to push it, even hesitating to comply with Ducrot's requests that Gambetta be kept fully informed about the operation. The 'Red' uprising, however, was enough to alarm Trochu into backing *Le Plan* with new zest.

But before *Le Plan* could go any further, all was upturned with a sudden, miraculous piece of news from Tours.

*   *   *

After his departure from Paris on October 7th, Gambetta had had an eventful flight. The balloon sailed over the Prussian lines at less than 2,000 feet, its occupants watching nervously while enemy riflemen below took pot shots at them. Hastily throwing out ballast, the pilot rose to safer altitudes before any harm could be done. After a few hours, he opened the gas valve and attempted to land on an empty space, but peasants came running up to warn the balloonists that they were in Prussian-occupied territory. They took off and later, spotting a group of men who looked like *franc-tireurs*, tried to land again. These were in fact Prussians. Fortunately their arms were stacked, and by the time they could grab them the balloon was rising rapidly once more; however, a bullet actually grazed Gambetta's hand. After this hair-raising escape, the pilot allowed some time to elapse before trying a third landing. Eventually they came

down near Montdidier, at 3.30 p.m., and just a quarter of an hour
ahead of the Uhlans. Despite his unnerving experiences, that same
evening Gambetta issued a rousing proclamation, announcing his
arrival, and calling the provinces to arms. Within forty-eight hours
of his arrival at Tours, far exceeding the powers accorded him by
Trochu, he had taken over the Ministry of War from old Crémieux
while remaining Minister of the Interior, thus establishing himself as
a virtual dictator. As his right-hand man he appointed Charles de
Freycinet, only a little older than himself and almost equal to him
in boldness and will-power. A civil engineer, Freycinet shared Gambetta's civilian contempt for the orthodox military who had hereto-
fore proved themselves so singularly unsuccessful in their own profession. He was a brilliant organizer, though neither this talent nor
his and Gambetta's combined spirit and drive could quite compensate
for their lack of military know-how.

The situation which Gambetta and Freycinet inherited in October
was hardly an encouraging one. The peasantry in unoccupied France
was largely indifferent to the struggle; since the fall of the Empire,
political wounds had reopened everywhere, with Orleanists, Bonapartists, and Republicans all clawing at each other. Many of the local
authorities were still run by ardent, conservative supporters of
Louis-Napoleon, who showed a reluctance to heed instructions
emanating from the Republican Delegation at Tours. In the big cities,
such as Lyons and Marseilles, there had been serious 'Red' disorders
similar to that of October 31st in Paris. And there were also the same
heated conflicts between the regular Army and those who urged the
creation of Republican National Guard Forces. Gambetta, in one
of his earliest reports back to Paris, wrote disgustedly: 'The country
districts are inert, the bourgeoisie in the small towns are cowardly,
and the military administration either passive, or desperately slow.'
Inside the occupied areas, harsh and Teutonically thorough repres-
sions of *franc-tireurs* and telegraph line-cutters, coupled with heavy
fines levied upon the communities where they were active, had
terrorized the inhabitants. Yet, in fact, this occupied territory still
only amounted to a small fraction of the vast surface of France.
Beyond the German lines of investment around Paris, all of the
country to the south, south-west, and west remained free; as did most
of the north, too, as far as Amiens and even further. It contained a
reservoir of anything up to a million men of military age, which
could be tapped. Moreover, the pinning-down of Moltke's forces
around Paris and Metz provided valuable time for the provinces to
regain their breath, and their morale—and for Gambetta to reorganize.

Despite the failure of his predecessors, the 'Old Men of Tours', to cope with the Augean problems confronting them, Gambetta's impact was immediate. He drove his senior generals to daily despair, but between them he and Freycinet miraculously raised armies with a speed which the generals could never have achieved; certainly far beyond anything that Trochu or Ducrot had anticipated.[1] Volunteers from all over France flowed into Tours, 'their chests bristling with enormous daggers', and arms began to arrive from depots all over the country—as well as from Britain and America. Above all, Gambetta, with his meridional passion, his Churchillian invective, managed to instil into his forces something that had been long lacking in France—the will to win. After General de la Motte Rouge on October 11th had lost Orléans to the Bavarian General von der Tann with only 28,000 men, Gambetta immediately sacked him, threatened him with court martial, and replaced him with General d'Aurelle de Paladines. A divisional commander in the Crimea, Aurelle had a magical touch with his troops that made him appear to be the perfect complement to Gambetta. By the beginning of November he had transformed a beaten, demoralized rabble into something resembling an Army; meanwhile, the Germans, their lines precariously extended in pursuit of what must have seemed to them little more than a colonial punitive expedition, were committing mistake after mistake unworthy of the great Moltke.

Pushed hard by Freycinet and Gambetta, Aurelle moved in with 100,000 men to strike the Bavarians in France's first major offensive since the fall of Louis-Napoleon. On November 9th, a battle was fought at Coulmiers some ten miles west of Orléans. Von der Tann was outnumbered by more than three to one; for once the French artillery, now supplied with percussion fuses, was as effective as the enemy's; and by nightfall von der Tann was forced to retreat, beaten, and with his personal baggage abandoned to the French. Had the French cavalry shown more persistence, defeat would probably have been turned into annihilation; but as it was Gambetta's forces had won for France her first clear victory of the war. The next morning Orléans was reentered, and for several days the scenes of jubilation there astonished by their fervour members of the Anglo–American ambulance left behind with the German wounded.

Valid as the reasons for rejoicing were, the victory at Coulmiers was, alas, but part of a strategical error which was to pave the way to France's final catastrophe. In his first apprecaitions, Gambetta,

---

[1] Well might one speculate upon what would have happened had Gambetta held Trochu's command in Paris, while the vigorous Ducrot had ballooned to Tours in his place; certainly, under Gambetta, the 'torrential sortie' out of Paris would have been attempted—and before it was too late.

vésted with absolute authority and complete freedom to communicate with the remainder of unoccupied France, saw himself now as the sole arbiter of the nation's strategy; clearly, the supreme planning could no longer reside with Trochu and Ducrot locked up in Paris. To Gambetta, the amateur strategist, the objective was equally clear; Paris must be relieved from the outside, and by the most direct route. This meant via Orléans, a distance of less than seventy miles as the crow flies. But Gambetta committed a cardinal error in overlooking the tenuousness of his communications with Trochu. For whereas the balloon service had already provided a tested and reliable means of Paris informing and instructing the provinces, signals in the reverse direction had to depend solely upon the spasmodic, insecure, and quite unreliable pigeon post; for this reason it would obviously be a great deal easier for Tours to co-ordinate with Paris's plans than *vice versa*.

Thus, while throughout October Paris had been pursuing Ducrot's plan, aimed at linking up with the provinces along a north-westerly axis, Gambetta was planning to join hands with the Paris garrison from almost the opposite angle. At least part of the fault for this divergency of strategy seems to lie in Trochu's procrastination in informing Gambetta. On his own admission, he first told his deputy, Favre, of Ducrot's Basse-Seine project during the first fortnight of October. 'Have you briefed Gambetta?' asked Favre. 'No', replied Trochu, advancing by way of explanation his doubts about Gambetta's ability to make a serious effort in the provinces. Favre and other members of the Government insisted that Gambetta be informed at once, but it was not until the 14th that this was actually undertaken, by means of a friend of Gambetta's called Ranc who was intending to balloon out of Paris. In case Ranc should fall into enemy hands it was decided to give him no written orders; instead, he was summoned to the Louvre and there personally briefed by Trochu. After the war, to Trochu's indignation, Ranc denied having received any instructions at all for Gambetta. It does seem likely that, bearing in mind Trochu's habitual long-windedness and his early pusill-animity towards Ducrot's plan, nothing so precise as a clear-cut order was issued for Ranc to convey. Certainly Gambetta claimed he took Ranc's dispatch as no more than a suggestion, and one that did not happen to attract him. As follow-ups to Ranc's mission, more definite orders to Gambetta were, however, sent on the 19th, 23rd, and 25th of October. But by this time Gambetta was thoroughly committed to his Orléans strategy. Like Nelson, he turned a blind eye to Trochu's signals, later insisting, disingenuously, that they had never been seriously discussed at Tours as constituting anything so definite as a plan, and at the same time failing to inform Trochu of his own project. By November 10th, Trochu—thoroughly frustrated —had still heard no word from Gambetta and now sent yet another dispatch, this time specifying that Bourbaki be sent to establish himself on the Basse-Seine. But it was too late; Aurelle's troops were at that moment reoccupying Orléans, and Gambetta was already considering his next move.

On November 14th the news of Coulmiers was brought to Paris by a line-crosser, Ernest Moll, a farmer whom the Prussians had used as a guide. The city exploded in a delirium of joy. 'We have passed from the lowest depths of despair to the wildest confidence', exclaimed Labouchere. 'I am so happy', declared Juliette Lambert, 'that I would willingly give myself up to arrogance. Yes, we have a success. . . .' Strangers kissed each other on the boulevard; *Le Figaro* saw the hand of God at work, and acclaimed Aurelle a modern Maid of Orléans. In the excitement, the revolt of October 31st and the growing food shortage were forgotten. At long last the spell of defeats had been broken!

At the Louvre, however, once the initial excitement had subsided, the Government was far from sharing the exultation of the boulevards. Gambetta's success struck at the heart of *le plan*, which had now gone far towards fruition. The whole weight of the Paris Army had already been shifted towards the north-west; immense preparations had been made, including the construction of pontoon bridges; and the sortie was scheduled to begin within the next week. To the non-military members of the Government with their simple civilian understanding of logistical problems, the solution was straightforward; 'Cheer up, *mon cher général*', was the cautious Picard's immediate reaction, 'here's a stroke of good fortune which will perhaps save us from proceeding with our heroic folly'. If nothing else, public opinion, of which, since October 31st, the Government was increasingly mindful, and which was already ejaculating slogans of '*Ils viennent à nous*; *allons à eux !*'[1] was forcing the Government's hand. But Trochu, aware of the ponderous technical difficulties involved, hesitated. Then, on November 18th, a second message arrived from Gambetta, urging him to co-operate by striking southwards towards Orléans. This decided the Government. The next day Trochu told a shocked Ducrot that his offensive would now have to be transported lock, stock, and barrel to the other side of Paris. For the third time in two months, Ducrot fumed with rage and frustration; as he put it his disappointment was 'not less than his embarrassment'.

---

[1] 'They are coming to us; let's go to them!'

It was hardly an exaggeration to say, as Trochu did, that what Ducrot was now being asked to perform was 'the most extraordinary *tour de force* of the Siege of Paris'. Through the Paris streets had to be shifted 400 guns, 54 pontoons, and 80,000 men with all their supplies and equipment.

Worst of all, whereas Ducrot had selected the Gennevilliers peninsula in the first place because the enemy was relatively weak there, the route connecting with Gambetta's advance from Orléans now lay across the famous Châtillon Plateau, wrested from Ducrot at the end of September, which had since become perhaps the strongest sector of the whole Prussian line. Quickly discarding this approach, Ducrot decided instead to mount his attack south-eastwards across the Marne, before its confluence with the Seine. Once he had broken through the ring, his intention was to swing westwards to meet up with Gambetta's forces somewhere in the area of Fontainebleau. In contrast to the Basse-Seine project, however, his new line of advance lay through territory controlled by German Armies, and an attack across the Marne necessitated complicated bridging operations in the face of the enemy. With five weeks in which to prepare the previous offensive, there was, he claimed, only five days for the planning of this one; therefore certain omissions were inevitable.

With all the activity involved in transposing Ducrot's Army, it was impossible that the enemy should not have learnt something of what was afoot. In any case, as has been demonstrated on other occasions in France's military history, good security is not where her most formidable talents lie. Despite Trochu's assertion that only five officers were in on the original plan, most of the British correspondents seem to have gleaned details of it, and by the beginning of November it was being freely discussed among Goncourt's circle at their favourite dining place, Brébant's, where derisive laughter met the suggestion that Trochu was planning to 'lift the blockade of Paris within a fortnight'. As early as October 21st, when Ducrot was carrying out his preliminaries at Malmaison, the Crown Prince of Prussia noted in his diary admissions by French prisoners that 'a sortie on the largest scale is being planned against Versailles and Saint-Denis, with the object of bringing into Paris a convoy of provisions from Rouen'; and as soon as Gambetta had begun to march on Orléans, even before the Battle of Coulmiers, the Crown Prince was predicting a major sortie out of Paris in that direction. On November 16th, while Trochu was still making up his mind, Moltke ordered the Third Army, as 'a temporary measure', to concentrate its forces on the left bank of the Seine south of Paris, showing that he was fully aware of the potential threat. By November 27th,

Bowles was reporting, 'I have had confided to me nothing less than General Trochu's famous plan, and have witnessed the preparations for its execution'; officers had even boasted to him 'that in eight days we shall be in communication with the outside'. Also on this same day Jules Claretie noted the demolition of the barricades at Nogent-sur-Marne so that the artillery could pass; while, after dinner that evening, General von Blumenthal received a telegram warning that the French had thrown a bridge across the Marne near Joinville, opposite the Württemberg division. The next day orders were sent out to reinforce the division. Finally, on November 30th, Labouchere wrote that Ducrot's new plan had been 'confided to me by half a dozen persons, and, therefore, I very much question whether it is a secret to the enemy'.

Still dubious about Gambetta's prospects, and perhaps (belatedly) also influenced by security considerations, Trochu had once again procrastinated before notifying Tours of the change in plan, and the date of the new sortie: November 29th. Not until the 24th, only five days before the attack, did he finally dispatch a message; and then it was prevented from reaching Gambetta in time by probably the most extraordinary mishap of the entire war. The balloon to which Trochu entrusted the crucial intelligence was called, appropriately enough, the *Ville d'Orléans*. The thirty-third to leave Paris, it carried a crew of two: Rolier, the pilot, and Béziers. Since Prussian anti-balloon measures had made daylight flights increasingly risky, the *Ville d'Orléans* took off from the Gare du Nord under cover of darkness, shortly before midnight. As dawn came up, the two men saw that a heavy fog obscured the earth. Lacking anything but the most primitive navigational instruments, they had not the faintest idea of their position, but—as they had set off in a propitiously moderate south-south-east breeze—comfortably assumed that they were heading towards unoccupied north-western France. In the utter stillness of the ether, Béziers thought he heard beneath them something like the sound of continuous railway trains. Then the fog rolled away, and to their horror the aeronauts realized that the noise was in fact waves. As Béziers noted down in his log: 'The sea for us, that's death!' By mid-morning the *Ville d'Orléans* was still flying out over the sea. At last they sighted a number of ships; Rolier came down as low as he dared, and let out the 120-yard guide-rope in the hopes that a ship might be able to grab it. But, as the ships seemed quite oblivious to their cries and signals for help, they decided to seek the safety of greater heights by jettisoning ballast. Among the objects sacrificed to the waves was a 60-kilogramme bag of dispatches containing the vital message on which hung the fate of Paris.

The balloon rose into dense cloud, and once again the earth vanished out of sight. It became bitterly cold, and the two men's moustaches turned to icicles. In noble devotion, Béziers took off his mantle to protect the carrier pigeons; though at this point it must have seemed that the prospects of survival for both birds and men were extremely low. On and on the balloon sailed. Then, just before 2.30 p.m., it began to descend rapidly. Out of the clouds the top of a pine tree suddenly emerged; a sight no less welcome than the coastline of Greenland must have been to the Vikings. It was too much for the half-frozen men who had begun to abandon hope. Without hesitation they leaped out, falling (according to Béziers) twenty metres into deep, soft snow. The unweighted balloon promptly soared and disappeared, carrying with it their food and clothing, as well as the unfortunate pigeons. The aeronauts climbed down a precipitous mountain, and walked and stumbled for hours without finding any signs of civilization; least of all any clue, as to what part of the world they had landed in. Was there any terrain like this to the west of Paris? Where were they? In the Vosges mountains? The Black Forest? But what about the sea they had traversed? Exhaustion was setting in, and several times Rolier collapsed in the snow. Then, as night was falling and it seemed only a matter of time before Rolier succumbed to a lethal urge to sleep, they came across a ruined cabin, where they spent the night. The next day they resumed their march and eventually reached a poor hovel, tenanted but empty. They ate what they could find, and a few hours later two peasants clad in furs appeared, speaking a strange language. The French tried to explain their presence by drawing sketches of their balloon; but without success.

It was not until one of the peasants lit a fire with a box of matches marked 'Christiania' that Rolier and Béziers realized that they had landed in the centre of Norway! In fifteen hours they had travelled nearly nine hundred miles from Paris; it was a voyage worthy of the imagination of Jules Verne. The aeronauts were taken to Oslo (then called Christiania), fêted by blonde young women draped in *tricolores* and banqueted for several days like visiting gods, then returned home.[1] Astonishingly enough, both their balloon with its pigeons as well as the sacks of dispatches jettisoned into the sea eventually turned up, safe and sound. The latter were brought in by a fishing boat, and at once expedited to France by the French Consul. But they

---

[1] Béziers, a born adventurer, tried a month later to run the blockade on foot into Paris, carrying dispatches. He was captured, imprisoned in a cellar, and told that he would be shot, but somehow managed to escape.

were to reach Tours too late for Gambetta to do anything about co ordinating with Trochu's break-out.

Inside Paris, Trochu was just as much in the dark about Gambetta's advance towards him—so essential to the success of the 'Great Sortie' on which the city's defenders were staking their all—as Gambetta was about Trochu's plans. In actual fact, after the recapture of Orléans, Aurelle seems to have been stricken with mental paralysis, or alarmed by his own success. For the best part of a fortnight he had sat still, vigorously disputing the next move with Freycinet. During this lost fortnight (a fatal one for France), when Aurelle had bogged down at Orléans and Ducrot was switching fronts in Paris, Prince Frederick-Charles was marching the Prussian Second Army rapidly westwards from Metz, whose surrender had released it. By the end of November it was firmly in position between Orléans and Paris, able to intervene in either direction.

The Great Sortie—Ducrot crosses the Marne

10. The Great Sortie

ABOUT the time that the Government was pinning its hopes on the break-out across the Marne, the voice of Victor Hugo was heard once more. This time he wrote, more soberly, in a new poem entitled '*Paroles dans l'Épreuve*';

> *Nous arrivons au bord du passage terrible;*
> *Le précipice est là, sourd, obscur, morne, horrible;*
> *L'épreuve à l'autre bord nous attend; nous allons,*
> *Nous ne regardons pas derrière nos talons;*
> *Pâles, nous atteignons l'escarpement sublime,*
> *Et nous poussons du pied la planche dans l'abime.*[1]

[1] Words during the Time of Trial
We arrive at the edge of the terrible crossing;
The precipice is there, veiled, dark, gloomy, horrible;
On the other side awaits the ordeal; we go,
We do not look behind us,
Pale, we reach the sublime escarpment,
And we kick the plank into the void.

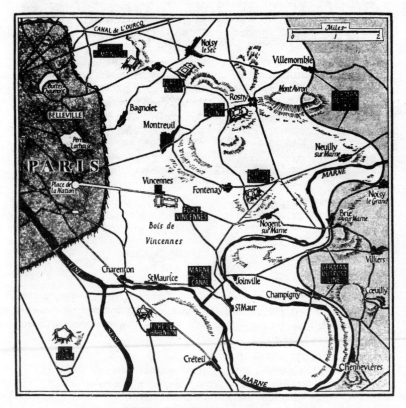

MAP 1.   The Great Sortie

The feeling that Paris, and behind her France, had reached the brink of an abyss—or at least a Rubicon—was one shared by all Parisians as the hour of the 'Great Sortie' drew closer, but they were perhaps less pallid in their apprehension than the poet. Despite the last distribution of fresh meat to civilians having been made on November 21st, spirits had never been higher. That day Mr. Brown wrote to his wife in Kentish Town: 'The most perfect order reigns and the resignation of the people to support the privations is admirable beyond all praise, they are as gay as ever and determined to support the Government they have chosen to the last extremity. . . .' The next day, Edwin Child, now a proud member of the National Guard, was writing enthusiastically to his mother: 'A tremendous battle is expected day after day. There will be more than 200,000 men engaged upon the French side. What has been done in Paris since the Siege is nothing less than marvellous. This modern Babylon celebrated for its dolls and bonbons now makes cannons, mitrailleuses, converts ancient guns into modern ones, makes shots, shells and gunpowder by ton. . . . 100,000 men have been selected from out of the National Guard, armed and fully equipped for war, and a finer set of men it would be difficult to find. . . . The flower of the nation. . . .' He ended by declaring he would 'like to see every Prussian exterminated', adding a derogatory note for the neutralist Mr. Gladstone. On the 27th, the seventieth day of the Siege, Washburne remarked that 'Paris has never before been so tranquil, and never before has there been so little crime. You do not hear of a murder, robbery, theft, or even a row, anywhere.'

Everywhere in these last few days there was a sense of urgent preparation, and nowhere more so than among the National Guard. Under the pressure of the repeated demands that the Guard participate in actual fighting, culminating in the outbreak of October 31st, the Government had yielded to the extent of forming special *Compagnies de Guerre* of the youngest and fittest which would march with the regulars in the 'Great Sortie'. 'If our brave brothers succumb', their new commander, General Thomas, told them, 'on us be the duty to avenge them!' Endlessly they drilled themselves in the empty spaces around Paris, and a new vigour and sense of purpose seemed to have entered their movements. O'Shea of the *Standard* watched some Guard battalions, in a weird multiplicity of uniforms, march off to the front after a review outside the Opéra. He thought the accompanying *vivandières*, with their gaudy 'Bloomer costumes', plumed hats, *tricolore*-painted brandy-kegs slung from the hips, and Roman daggers or even little ivory-handled pistols tucked into their belts, a little too theatrical; but he admired the regimental bands composed of pensioners who made brave attempts to wheeze out the *Chant du Départ*; and, above all, thought he detected for the first time 'the groundwork of discipline'. The Belleville battalions, despite orders not to take their colours to the outposts, nevertheless marched with pennants on which had been embroidered Phrygian caps to distinguish them from the bourgeois units.

On November 26th, all the gates to the city were closed (giving the Prussians final confirmation of what was about to happen), and in the stampede to get in Goncourt saw a poor old man knocked over on a drawbridge, his spine broken. On the 28th, Washburne recorded that all the American ambulance waggons had been ordered to stand by to move at 6 a.m. the next morning; 'there is something in the atmosphere and the general appearance of the city that betokens unusual events. The day is damp, chilly, gloomy and cloudy, but the streets are filled.' That night, awoken by an immense cannonade which even out at Versailles had deprived an anxious King of Prussia of his sleep, Goncourt climbed up to the roof of his building. There, 'in a night without stars', he saw

from Fort Bicêtre as far as Fort Issy, over the whole stretch of this great semicircular line, a succession of small dots of fire that flicker up like gas-jets, followed by sonorous echoes. These great voices of death in the midst of the silence of the night stir one. After some time the howling of dogs joins in with the thunder of the cannon; frightened voices of awoken humans begin whispering; cockerels, men and women, everything lapses back into silence and my ear, straining out of the window, could hear nothing more than the cannonade in the distance, far in the distance, resembling the dull noise that an oar makes when it strikes the side of a boat.

On rising the next morning, Parisians found their walls plastered with proclamations heralding the Great Sortie. One, emanating from Trochu, was his shortest yet; the other, addressed by Ducrot to the Second Army (of which he was now the commander), ended on a note of immortal magnificence, evocative of all the military *grandeur de la France*. 'As for myself,' he declared, 'I have made up my mind, and I swear before you and the entire nation; I shall only re-enter Paris dead or victorious. You may see me fall, but you will not see me yield ground. So do not halt, but avenge me. *En avant donc ! en avant, que Dieu nous protège !*' Parisian hearts beat loudly; how could the day not be won when the commander himself could make such a vow ? 'Here is a *real* soldier!' cried Juliette Lambert.

Behind the scenes all was far from well. Bowles, who had passed the whole of the previous day at outposts near Issy, had picked up sinister 'whisperings of "pontoons" and bridges having become a difficulty at the last moment'. At dawn on the 29th Trochu, was at his battle H.Q. in Fort Rosny 'when General Ducrot, in a state of indescribable agitation, came to report to me that a sudden rise in the level of the Marne had temporarily rendered our operation impossible'. In the first stage of the breakthrough, Ducrot's primary objective was the heights around Villiers on the left bank of the Marne. All the Marne bridges having been blown at the time of the investment, everything depended on the provision of sufficient pontoons so that bridgeheads could be established at Bry and Champigny on either side of the Villiers loop. The pontoons had been successfully towed across Paris from the original site of the sortie, and by the night of the 28th were in readiness at Charenton. At 11 p.m., Ducrot's chief engineer, Krantz, had given the order to advance the pontoon-train from the Seine into the Marne, through the St.-Maurice canal which lay just in French hands. Headed by the tug *Persévérance*, the canal was safely negotiated, but at Joinville it was brought to a halt. Here the Marne is perhaps a little wider than the Thames at Maidenhead, but even under normal conditions the current is much swifter. Now the debris of the destroyed Joinville bridge had formed a kind of barrage across the river; two out of three arches were blocked, though the third was navigable, provided there was no substantial rise in the water. This was a danger foreseen by Krantz, and ideally—as Ducrot admitted— the river under the other arches should have been cleared to avert it. But there had been no time; it was one of the 'omissions' which had had to be risked. And heavy rains had in fact swollen the Marne, so that torrents of angry water were surging through the one clear arch. The puffing *Persévérance* was brought to a standstill. It retired, fired its boilers almost to bursting-point, and then tried to charge the bridge again. This time it gained ground, and there seemed hope of its getting through, when three pontoons foundered, with their crews; causing a lengthy delay before another attempt could be made. At its third effort the *Persévérance* succeeded, but by now it was clearly too late to hope of getting the pontoons in position before daybreak.

Once again Ducrot saw all his plans collapsing about him, and it was in a state bordering on despair that he came to see Trochu. What was to be done? Call off the whole operation? Immediately both generals agreed that of this there could be no question; apart from anything else, the threat of revolt in Paris by a disappointed mob was still too grave to be risked. Not for the first or last time this factor, more than any military consideration, was the deciding one. So the main offensive would be postponed twenty-four hours, until the Marne subsided; meanwhile the subsidiary actions planned to be thrown in on the wings would still proceed that day, unsupported. It was a decision that hardly pleased Vinoy, who was to execute the principal of these diversions, and the lost twenty-four hours were just long enough for Moltke, now precisely aware of Ducrot's intentions, to push a division of Saxons in behind the weak Württemberger force covering the focal point of the line.

Paris, remained happily unaware of the latest hitch in '*Le Plan*'. In transports of delight, Juliette Lambert exclaimed (prematurely) in her journal: '*Enfin! Enfin!* Yesterday, while we were at the opera, the Great Sortie began! This great action, which Paris has been awaiting for two months, has been launched. What emotions are ours...!' All through the 29th, Goncourt observed a general mood, quite alien to the city, of 'concentrated meditation. In the public vehicles no one speaks; everybody has retired within himself, and women of the street regard what goes on round them with a blind man's stare.... Any man who speaks, who suggests knowledge, is besieged.' Little knots of anxious citizens hovered outside Government buildings and on the main thoroughfares leading to the battlefield, hoping for fragments of news. The strain of the suspense was intolerable. By the evening Goncourt found himself unusually irritable with his circle at Brébant's.

On the other side of the ramparts, Bismarck's secretary, Dr. Moritz Busch, who happened to be visiting an officer's mess, found the lieutenants in confident high spirits: 'having all sorts of fun... singing the song of the Eleven Thousand Virgins of Cologne'.

The first news to be posted up outside the Hôtel de Ville was encouraging to the Parisians. 'All General Ducrot's divisions have crossed the Marne!' As usual, Paris fastened on this early glimmer of hope, building out of it a resounding victory. Bourse prices ran up their biggest gains since September, and Louis Péguret, writing to his sister in the provinces, related how, at the ramparts that morning 'some artillerymen told us that the battle was receding farther and farther from Paris towards the South; a little more and the Armies of the Loire and Paris will join hands.' O'Shea overheard an old man say that 'he did not think they should go to Berlin! Mainz would be far enough.' Then, at 9 p.m. that night, out came an official communiqué stating baldly, 'The object the Governor had in view has been attained'. To anyone acquainted with the Government's delicate fibbery and still capable, after ten weeks of siege, of reading between its lines, it was only too plain that Ducrot had not broken through.

At the front the initial, and seemingly most delicate, stage of the operation had in fact gone off smoothly. By dawn on the 29th Ducrot had assembled enough pontoons to throw across bridgeheads at both

Champigny and Bry. Under cover of a tremendous barrage from Fort Nogent and from guns massed in the St.-Maur peninsula, the French succeeded in capturing and holding these two towns, without too much difficulty, during the morning. It was when they surmounted the steep escarpments leading up on to the Villiers plateau that they first ran into serious trouble. The Württembergers had established their centres of resistance in the parks of two châteaux, one at Cœuilly and the other at Villiers, and from positions carefully prepared behind stone walls in these parks their invisible riflemen directed a murderous fire on the attackers. The owner of the Château de Cœuilly, who had fled into Paris on the approach of the Germans, was with Ducrot, patriotically laying the French guns on to his own property (the *châtelaine* of Villiers, with perhaps equal courage, stayed in her home throughout the battle), and his shells exacted a heavy toll among the defenders. Three times the French attacked with a heroism which showed that, despite the long saga of defeats, the legendary *furia francese* was not totally dead. But each attempt collapsed, leaving heaps of blue-and-scarlet figures to enliven the seared winter grass, none closer than 150 yards to the park of Cœuilly. Casualties reached almost 1914 proportions; one regiment, the 42nd, lost its colonel and four hundred men. At Villiers the story was the same. Here it was the Zouaves, determined to erase the shame of their performance at Châtillon; but driven to despair at being decimated by a well-entrenched enemy (once again, a foretaste of the First World War) who never revealed himself.

The start of the Great Sortie had thrown the journalists of Paris into a frenzy of activity, and, accompanied by Gustave Doré and other war artists, they rushed about in little groups, trying to get first hand accounts from the returning wounded. But, not unlike the eminent war correspondents derided in Evelyn Waugh's *Scoop*, most of them were satisfied with composing lurid descriptions of the fighting from a judicious distance. Of the Anglo-American contingency, hardly any troubled to get a *laissez-passer* to visit the front during the whole Siege. The outstanding exception was the least experienced, Tommy Bowles, and it is his eyewitness report of November 30th that seems the most trustworthy, as well as the most vivid. Bowles had established himself on a hill at Créteil, just west of the St.-Maur loop of the Marne and only five hundred yards from the Prussian lines, and from here he had a spectacular view of Ducrot's men attacking southwards towards the Mesly heights in support of the main Champigny–Bry thrust. Shot and shell from the St.-Maur batteries whistled over the heads of the troops waiting in reserve behind Bowles. These included, he noted, the 170th (Belleville) Battalion of the

National Guard, at the front for the first time, and he was curious to see how it would behave. From a battery of field guns

... I saw the French skirmishers dotted thickly along the flank of the hill at a distance of 300 yards, and, a short distance beyond, the Prussians firing on them from the wood. In a minute or two the fusillade began in earnest—a rolling, rattling, crackling fire, which now and then swelled into a continuous roar. The road on the right was partially hidden by trees, but I could see the Prussian barricade indicated by an incessant curtain of white smoke, which distinguished it from the rest of the line, where the action was yet indicated only by little detached puffs. Suddenly the smoke of the barricade cleared off and was not renewed, and the instant after I saw a swarm of men running rapidly at and disappearing behind the barricade, which was thus taken at the point of the bayonet. The skirmishers on the left nevertheless continued in their position, running only to and fro along their line, while the Prussians kept up a vigorous fusillade, as we knew in the battery, for the balls occasionally fell around us, we being on higher ground and in the line of fire. Over the Marne I could see the red trousers swarming up the hills beyond Champigny, and the artillery alternately galloping up and firing, while the Prussian line had already—this was eleven o'clock—disappeared over the crest.

The prospects looked favourable, but, half an hour later Bowles was reporting that the action to his immediate front

... seemed to warm, and some of the French skirmishers began to fall back—in very good order, however—firing and turning slowly. Wounded men, pale and bloody, now began to arrive, some borne on *brancards*.
For half an hour I followed the action from my post; but then impatience got the better of me, and I took horse and rode along towards the front. . . .

Reaching a captured Prussian barricade, Bowles was met

... by a crowd of breathless men swarming around and through it, and running to the shelter of a wall on the right of the road. Beyond I could see others running up, and as I foresaw confusion I thought it best to return, which I did under a considerably increased accompaniment of balls. As I re-entered the village and came upon the supports, I was eagerly questioned by officers and men. '*Nous battons en retraite, n'est-ce-pas?*' said they, feverishly; and I was forced to reply that I thought so. The Belleville Battalion was there, and their remarks were not calculated to inspire confidence in their courage. '*Nous sommes battus*', they said, looking with pale faces at one another, while some of them silently left the ranks, and walked with a careless air towards the rear.
Advancing again, I found that the skirmishers were huddled up rather than rallied behind their wall, while the road, which before had been perfectly deserted, was covered with stragglers making for the village in

a weary, downcast way. To them from the front came a gendarme, who rode about furiously, asking them, 'Are you wounded?' and on the negative reply, bidding them with oaths to return to the front. I saw that the fortune of battle had, indeed, distinctly turned. The French were now running fast back over the crest of the hill, and the supports had retired with the artillery into the valley in a line with the village on the right. As I was looking I saw the Prussian artillery appear on the hill, make a half turn, and send a shell instantaneously into the village, where it blew a house behind me into shatters. . . .

It was now half past twelve. I returned to the Place in the centre of the village opposite to the church. Such a scene as there grew up before me in a moment or two I hope I shall never behold again. The pavement was covered with wounded men, generally half-undressed, and lying there helplessly, while one surgeon was doing his best to attend to them. In the middle of the Place a seething mob of soldiers of all arms struggled and wrestled to get through the village, without order, without leaders, without any idea what to do or whither to go, unless it were to avoid the Prussians. Every moment the mob increased, with every moment the panic became greater and the struggle to get through fiercer. They fought with each other, they swayed to and fro, a moving mass of men and gleaming arms, they pressed out on either side till they filled the little Place, and trampled even on their wounded comrades, whom the first comers had avoided. It was not an army that was retreating, it was not even a respectable mob. But this attack was but a diversion, and the main result of the engagement was entirely successful. . . .

Here Bowles was deceived. What he had witnessed was all too faithful a miniature of that which was to follow in the afternoon on the Villiers plateau. Riding about the front with utter fearlessness on a magnificent white charger, pushing defaulters back into the line at the point of his sabre, Ducrot watched the frontal assaults on Villiers and Cœuilly bog down. He had expected the Villiers plateau, key to the whole operation, to be a tough nut to crack frontally and therefore had detailed off the whole of III Corps, led by General d'Exea, to carry out a powerful flanking operation. D'Exea was to cross the Marne further upstream at Neuilly, capture Noisy-le-Grand, and then move on Villiers from the north-east. He was the Blücher of that day, but a Blücher who did not arrive in time. His crossing of the Marne was badly slowed up by the shortage of pontoons, so that not until midday had the bulk of III Corps got across. Furiously Ducrot kept training his glasses on his left flank, but still no sign of d'Exea. Then at last he saw a dense mass of men approaching him from the direction of Noisy. His heart leaped, and he sent off a cavalry detachment to hasten the tardy d'Exea towards his objective. But the scouts were met with a volley of rifle shots; the force spotted by Ducrot was in fact the first body of Saxons ordered up by Moltke to reinforce the Württembergers. Coolly Ducrot commanded the men around him to lie down, take aim, but hold their fire. Not until the enemy were at point-blank range did Ducrot give the order to fire; he himself 'broke his sword in the body of a German soldier', and the Saxons fell back in disarray.

At last one of d'Exea's divisions, commanded by the de Bellemare of Le Bourget fame who had at last received the promotion he coveted, was seen advancing slowly from its bridgehead. But to Ducrot's intense rage it was advancing in the wrong direction; not on Noisy-le-Grand, but obliquely towards Bry which had been in French hands since early morning, where it only further encumbered an already saturated area, getting hopelessly mixed up with troops of other divisions. It was now 3 p.m., and it was clear that there could be no flank attack on Villiers that day. Still the costly frontal attempts continued, but in vain. In another hour the short winter day began to fade, leaving the French spearhead precariously perched on the Villiers plateau to face the dreaded Prussian counter-attacks that could be expected the next day. By that evening Ducrot knew the Great Sortie had failed. The sensible thing he knew, too, would have been to withdraw back across the Marne; but once again fear of the Paris mob overruled good sense. Besides, after his flamboyant proclamation, how could he return—alive, but unvictorious?

The various diversionary efforts on other parts of the front had also ended in costly failures. At Choisy-le-Roi and L'Hay alone Vinoy had lost a thousand in dead and wounded, and 300 prisoners. Only at the north of Paris had the Marines, operating from St.-Denis under Admiral de la Roncière le Noury, scored a minor success in taking a village called Épinay-sur-Seine; but this was itself to have unattended repercussions as disastrous as the failure at Villiers. In Paris, the Government rivalled the street in its eagerness to read unqualified success into the random bulletins reaching it from the front. On the late afternoon of the 30th, Jules Favre, its acting head, drafted a hasty dispatch for Gambetta reporting a successful crossing of the Marne, as well—*en passant*—as the capture of Épinay. Two balloons, one propitiously called the *Bataille de Paris*, the other *Jules Favre No. 2*, were standing by to carry this vital message, so that for once there would be no delay in informing Tours. Strong and favourable winds wafted both balloons swiftly to the west, but disaster nearly overtook the *Jules Favre No. 2* when it was blown out over the Brittany coast. With great luck the pilot managed to make a crash landing in Belle-Île, ripping off in his descent the roof of a house which, by the wildest of coincidences, belonged to no other than the brother of

Trochu himself. According to Henry Vizetelly of the *Illustrated London News*, his mother, aged eighty-four had been 'praying during the night for some sign from heaven that her son would yet save France, and she had interpreted the noise of the crashing rafters in a favourable sense.' The crew of the balloon were badly injured, but by the evening following its dispatch the news from Paris was in Gambetta's hands. His hopes were raised no less high than Mme Trochu's had been, and with as little justification. Of Épinay Gambetta had never heard, but on glancing at the map his eye at once lit upon an Épinay-sur-Orge, a few kilometres south of Orly. Joy of joys! This must mean not only that Ducrot had broken out across the Marne but that he was now well on his way to the rendezvous at Fontainebleau. Issuing a dramatic order of the day, he instructed his generals, Aurelle and Chanzy, to march on Fontainebleau post-haste, without pausing to concentrate. Thus it came about that the amateur strategist allowed himself to commit one of the deadliest sins known to the professional—the division of his forces. And meanwhile the most professional of Moltke's army commanders, Prince Frederick-Charles, had arrived from Metz and was all set to strike his first blow against the Army of the Loire.

The casualties for that one day, though smaller than during the great battles of the summer, had been painfully heavy. The French had lost, by Ducrot's reckoning, 5,236 men, 4,000 of these around Villiers and Cœuilly alone, and the Germans 2,091. That night smart clubs on the Champs-Élysées and humble *bistros* alike mourned many a friend who had dined there only a few nights earlier. The commander of II Corps, old General Renault, who had seen half a century's service, received his forty-fifth wound; his leg was amputated and after four days of delirium in which he raved constantly against Trochu, he died. One of the brigade commanders on Bowles's front, La Charrière, had also been hit three times, and the third proved mortal. Colonel Franchetti, Ducrot's most spirited cavalry leader, had been wounded by a stray shell, and died shouting deliriously, 'Follow me, my friends! It's hard, but we'll get there. *Vive la France!*' Captain de Neverlée, Ducrot's emissary on October 31st, who had informed his friends on the eve of battle that he would not survive the morrow, fell gallantly before Villiers; and somewhere on the battlefield the mysterious, heroic commando Sergeant Hoff was missing. Ducrot, seen constantly galloping in front of the Prussians with a mad frenzy as if, knowing he could not return 'victorious', he were seeking a stray bullet, had had at least one horse killed under him. Trochu too experienced several miraculous escapes.

All day the wounded had streamed back before the eyes of the shocked Parisians, with faces bearing (said Goncourt) 'the horrible anxiety of their wounds, the uncertainty of amputation, the uncertainty of life or death'. They came in files of blood-bedaubed horse-drawn buses and in *bateaux-mouches* that deposited them on the *quais* of the Seine. Owing to the primitiveness of surgery in those days, exacerbated by the traditional ineptitude and squalor of French military hospitals, the badly-wounded knew they could rarely look forward to a happy outcome of their suffering. The plight of the wounded at the front was particularly appalling. Chaos among the ambulances had not helped. Felix Whitehurst, a British voluntary worker, noted that many had been sent out so full of attendants that there was room for only one casualty in each, and that at Champigny there had been such a jam as to prevent them deploying on to the field. Then there had been a disgraceful muddle over linen urgently required for 1,500 wounded at Nogent; Whitehurst had gone into Paris and, after a three-hour wrestle with French bureaucracy, got it—only to find on his return that the wounded had been moved on else-where. A French staff officer admitted to him that it 'beats the worst mess of the worst days of the Crimea'. The *Daily Telegraph* corrrespondent recorded handing his cherished reserve of chocolate to a wretched casualty who had lain all night without receiving food, soup, or medical care, and many of the wounded whom it had been impossible to collect had been left out on the battlefield overnight, their wounds freezing in the sudden bitter cold. Prussian outposts were astonished to see French soldiers apparently more concerned to strip the horse carcasses of their last ounce of flesh, and root up a forgotten cabbage here and there, than to carry in their fallen comrades.

Among the numerous ambulances (including those staffed by Americans and Britons, about which more will be said shortly) involved in this work of mercy, a colourful figure was to be found on the battlefield: Monseigneur Bauer, Archbishop of Syracuse and Chaplain-General to the Army. His had been an unusual career; born a Hungarian Jew, involved as a young man in the 1848 uprising in Vienna, he had then taken orders. In 1868, by now a naturalized Frenchman, he became Empress Eugénie's personal confessor, and it was he who had blessed the Suez Canal. Renowned even during the Second Empire for gallantry of a distinctly un-ecumenical flavour, Mgr. Bauer ended up some thirty years later once again a layman, defrocked, and married to a beautiful young Jewish artist. Despite his links with the deposed regime, he enjoyed great popularity with the troops; possibly on account of his Rabelaisian qualities, as well as his considerable courage. On the Marne battlefield the prelate presented an admirable, but incongruous, figure; prancing about on horseback in long purple boots and breeches, with a broad-brimmed ecclesiastical hat on his head, a large gold crucifix and a diamond-studded order around his neck, and a huge episcopal ring on his finger. At his side rode a mounted 'bodyguard' of four ecclesiasts equally bizarre in their trappings, a standard-bearer holding aloft a banner with a large Red Cross, and under his command were several hundred lay *Frères Chrétiens* acting as stretcher-bearers. Tirelessly, and quite contemptuous of the Prussian bullets that came his way, he rode about the field directing the succour of the wounded. 'He is', said Labouchere (though it must have been second-hand, as that distinguished correspondent had not stirred far from his quarters in the Grand Hôtel during the battle) 'as steady under fire as if he were in a pulpit'.

But all the efforts of Mgr. Bauer and the various ambulances could not suffice to bring in more than a tithe of the agonizing wounded. The army was low on ammunition and it was clear to Ducrot that it was in no condition to renew the offensive, so on December 1st a twenty-four hour truce to remove the wounded was requested, and granted. Meanwhile the Prussians were preparing a massive counter-attack. They unleashed it the following morning, even before it was fully light. Ducrot was at his battle H.Q. giving orders to the chief of the *Ambulances de la Presse*, Ferdinand de Lesseps of Suez fame, when the cannonade broke out. Quickly he mounted his horse and rode off towards it. On the road to Champigny he met 'an avalanche of vehicles, infantrymen, cavalry, all descending at full speed towards the Marne'. Somehow he managed to stop their flight, but the spectacle he found at Champigny itself was even more depressing; '. . . the Grande Rue is full of *Mobiles*, and soldiers of all arms, running in every direction; a ration convoy trying to advance adds still further to the disorder, the confusion; . . . words, exhortations, threats have no effect at all on this torrent of fugitives forever increasing. . . .' With awful regularity shells from Prussian big guns fell amid this tangle, exploding on the granite *pavee* with terrible effect. Bowles, who was once again on the spot, could find no other word for it than 'a perfect rout'. Later, other French units managed to stage a rally and all day desperate fighting continued. But the next morning, under cover of a fog and the cannons of St.-Maur, Ducrot's army evacuated its bridgeheads to recross the Marne.

At 3.15 that afternoon, so the Prussian Crown Prince's Chief of Staff, General von Blumenthal, noted in his journal, he received a telegram which 'informed me that the enemy appears to be in retreat on Joinville. . . .' After dinner I played whist for the first time, and during the game had the unspeakable joy of receiving a message from

Viebahn, telling of a brilliant victory won by the Grand Duke of Mecklenburg.'

But in Paris the populace for a day or two still lived in the illusion that the break-out might yet take place, as the official communiqués were less than enlightening. On the disastrous day of December 3rd, a M. Patte was writing happily to a lady friend in London that 'just now the guns make the most dreadful noise, but we hear it, I can say with pleasure, as it is the cannon which announces to us the deliverance . . .'. Not until the 5th was Ducrot's admission of defeat manifest. It was a bright, cold, bracing morning. Not a drum was to be heard anywhere. Goncourt spoke for all Parisians when miserably he entered in his journal: 'the heights and depths of hope; this is what kills you. One believes oneself saved. Then one realizes one is lost. . . . Today the recrossing of the Marne by Ducrot has thrown us back into the darkness of failure and despair.'

The ebullient Ducrot himself was no further from despair. By the night of November 30th, he had already concluded that Paris herself was lost. After the battle there had been some bitter recriminations in the high command; General Blanchard, one of his corps commanders, had actually tried to provoke Ducrot to a duel by declaring (it was an allusion to the famous 'dead or victorious' proclamation) 'I wish to know if your sword is as long as your tongue'. Ducrot had replied by offering his resignation, and requesting to revert to the ranks. The request was refused. Then, in the midst of all this misery and acrimony, on December 5th yet another deadly blow descended. It was a letter from Moltke, addressed to Trochu, studiously polite, but informing him of the crushing defeat that Frederick-Charles and the Grand Duke of Mecklenburg had between them inflicted upon Gambetta's divided forces, resulting in the recapture of Orléans.

In three days the Great Sortie had cost 12,000 officers and men; it had failed, and at the same time the relieving army from Tours had been stopped in its tracks. The plight of Paris now seemed hopeless. But still the fear of Red revolution, combined with the revealed harshness of Prussian peace terms, purged any idea of capitulation from the minds of the Government. The Siege would go on, though since the supreme military effort had failed it would henceforth be merely a matter of survival and attrition.

If the Government of National Defence could derive any consolation at all from the results of the Great Sortie, it was that it had at last managed to lay hands on the illusive firebrand, Flourens. In hiding since October 31st, he had heard that his *Tirailleurs* had been in action and had lost three men killed (presumably in the rout that Tommy Bowles had witnessed); impatiently he went off to join them at Maisons-Alfort, and was promptly arrested on his return to Paris by order of General Thomas. But the seizure of Flourens was of itself a petty enough success.

Could *Le Plan* ever have succeeded? Could anything have lifted the Siege by November? Military history frowns upon 'ifs', but it does seem that *if* Tours and Paris could have co-operated in Ducrot's original plan, and it had taken place, as projected, within the first fortnight of November (i.e. before the arrival of Frederick-Charles), the break through to Le Havre might well have succeeded. Even once the plan had been switched Gambetta's forces might, if properly handled, also have reached Fontainebleau in time to help Ducrot; but whether Ducrot could ever have got that far remains open to doubt. The strategy of the second plan was fundamentally at fault; breaking out across the Marne, Ducrot would have had his flanks open to German attacks on both sides all the way to Fontainebleau, and would probably have been destroyed between the Marne and Seine. Bismarck, who had seen this, remarked calmly on hearing of the sortie on November 30th 'Where could they go? . . . . They would put their heads in a sack. Such an attempt would be the best thing that could happen for us.'

Despite Bismarck's confidence, however, the French attempt had succeeded in throwing the Prussian military leaders into considerable alarm for a short time, aware as they were of the tenuousness of their siege ring about Paris. At Versailles, there had been serious talk of crisis measures to be taken in the contingency of a break-out, and, though light in comparison to French casualty figures, the fresh losses suffered so long after the war had seemed over at Sedan made an unpleasant mark in German minds. For weariness over the prolongation of the war had set in both at home and at the front, and perhaps for this reason alone there existed some purpose in the Paris forces keeping up an aggressive attitude for as long as they were able.

The American Ambulance at Work on the Battlefield

11. The Outsiders Within

As the war dragged on, and Prussia showed herself apparently incapable of bringing it to a speedy conclusion, there was an additional fear never very far from Bismarck's mind. Might others among the great powers be tempted to intervene, and thus rob the Germans of the completeness of victory?

The Austro-Hungarians, still mindful of their chastisement at Sadowa, had made it clear they would only enter the war on the condition (unfulfilled) of early French victories; thus it was the ever-unpredictable British on whom Bismarck kept an eye, with the other squinting over his shoulder at the Russians behind him. At the beginning of the war, there had been widespread sympathy in Britain for the Germans—from the top down. Queen Victoria acclaimed her son-in-law Fritz's first victory over MacMahon at Frœschviller as 'wonderful news', while Lady Russell in a letter to Kate Amberley[1] commenting on Sedan exclaimed, 'Thank God that punishment has

[1] Her daughter-in-law, and mother of Bertrand Russell.

162

fallen on the right hand!' But since Sedan there had been a distressing reversal of British public opinion, perhaps summarized in a letter Lady Amberley received from an English radical towards the end of the Siege: 'Abt the war I think the Prussians were right at 1st but in its present phase my sympathies are intensely & most painfully French.' Sir Charles Dilke, M.P., who had visited the August battle-fields under Prussian auspices, declared, 'I began to wish to desert when we saw how overbearing success had made the Prussians and how determined they were to push their successes to a point at which France would have been made impotent in Europe. . . .' By November both the prolonged resistance of suffering Paris and Gambetta's courageous efforts in the provinces had begun to play strongly upon traditional British compassion for the underdog. In London there were manifestations in favour of British assistance to France, and the iconoclastic Bradlaugh had found several excuses to hit out at the Queen's Germanic ties. Even *The Times* had been provoked into protesting against German brutality, and such ardent francophobes as Thomas Carlyle were finding themselves increasingly isolated.

More and more the thoughtful in Britain suffered from concern at the true scope of Prussian ambitions, as revealed by the bombastic utterances of her leaders, and at the kind of Europe that would emerge from the war. In December the *Illustrated London News* wrote:

·The war may or not be over when Paris shall have capitulated. . . . But it will not have ended in another sense, when the peace shall have been signed . . . . It may be neither next year nor the year after that the lessons of the last two months will bear fruit, but that they will bear it we have no doubt at all. . . .

In an even more remarkable prophecy, Karl Marx predicted from Highgate as early as September that any German victory which led to the dismemberment of France would inevitably end 'by forcing France into the arms of Russia', followed by a new war of revenge; 'and', he added in a letter of the same month, 'a war No. 2 of this kind will act as the midwife to the inevitable social revolution in Russia'.

Dilke, a radical supporter of the Gladstone Liberal Government, held that 'if Gladstone had been a great man' and had threatened to intervene with the Royal Navy against whichever side attacked the other, the Franco-Prussian War would never have broken out. (One might well speculate as to whether, had Dilke's advice been taken, 1914 too would not then have been averted—or at least postponed.) But in July Gladstone had determined upon neutrality, and as the war progressed—whatever the pressures of public opinion at home—nothing would deflect him from his steadfast course. To one of Jules

M

Favre's emissaries, Frédéric Reitlinger, who reached England at the time of the Great Sortie, the Grand Old Man had sermonized (according to Reitlinger): 'War is a terrible disaster for humanity. Are there any circumstances which may justify a Government throwing a country into war?...' His Foreign Secretary, Lord Granville, had added: 'we have neither the right nor the power to interfere in an affair which does not concern us'; and 'France has given an exhibition of military courage which has aroused the admiration of the world, but there is also a *civil courage* which a great people must not neglect, and which is even greater and more admirable than military courage.' Such was the tenor of British policy in those days, and even the subsequent sinking by *German* action of five British colliers in the lower Seine, which aroused widespread anger in Britain, was not sufficient to alter it.[1]

From Bismarck's point of view the gravest risk of outside intervention (and, for Britain, the most serious threat to her standard of neutrality in Europe) came at the end of October from the other end of Europe. Russia, admittedly to some extent provoked by Bismarck himself, decided to seize the opportunity of denouncing the clauses in the 1856 Treaty of Paris which neutralized the Black Sea. The two powers responsible for enforcing this legacy of the Crimean War were Britain and France; Britain's naval position in the Eastern Mediterranean seemed threatened, and she was faced with the prospect of once more fighting Russia, but this time—with France otherwise occupied—alone. To Bismarck, anxious to keep the war—and the peace—a strictly bilateral affair, any spread of hostilities would have been most undesirable. Instead he proposed a conference, which was accepted by the powers concerned. But such a conference would also, he realized, have proved injurious to Prussian interests in so far as it must almost certainly have led to a general attempt by the European powers to settle the Franco-German dispute; which in turn might well mean a 'soft' peace for France, with no annexations. Bismarck wanted to deal with France by himself. Thus, with his usual diplomatic cunning, he temporized; chiefly through placing a multiplicity of obstacles in the way of any French delegate attending the London Conference until victory was in the bag.

Gladstone's efforts to remain on good terms with both combatants resulted, as such endeavours so often do, in pleasing neither side. On the German side, there was constant annoyance at Britain's Olympian offers of mediation; coupled, as the true strength of Bis-

[1] Some of the collier crews marched in protest through London, holding a Union Jack covered with muddy marks and inscribed 'trampled on by the feet of Germans'.

marck's hand became increasingly apparent, with a certain '*übermensch*' contempt for Britain's ineffectuality on the European scene. Before the war was over, Archibald Forbes, the *Daily News* correspondent attached to the German Army of the Meuse, would record a conversation with a young officer who 'benignantly announced that the Queen Elizabeth Regiment would, before two years were over, be besieging Windsor Castle. . . .' Queen Victoria's exhortatory, but unspecific, telegrams urging 'magnanimity' upon King Wilhelm, as well as the steady flow of advice to her daughter, the Crown Princess, provoked mounting resentment in the Berlin Press—ably fanned by Bismarck. Already at the end of October Crown Prince Frederick was noting in his journal 'I regret to observe that the German Press, but in especial the 'inspired' papers in Berlin, continues its spiteful attacks on England. . . ,' and by mid-December he was deprecating that 'In Berlin it is now the order of the day to vilify my wife as being mainly responsible for the postponement of the bombardment of Paris and to accuse her of acting under the direction of the Queen of England. . . .' German public opinion was also highly sensitive to the unfavourable trend in British sympathies; but, as Gambetta's levies proved to be more and more troublesome, its most tangible source of resentment was the flow of British arms being sold to the French armies in the provinces.

In the earliest days of the war, French opinion too had been scandalized by the unfriendly attitude then prevailing in the British Press, but once Paris herself was threatened it was widely assumed, not only that sympathies would switch, but that Britain herself would actively enter the lists to rescue the Fount of Civilization. Leaders of all sides (with Hugo well to the fore) applied themselves to this theme; early in October, Louis Blanc, the veteran Socialist, addressed a pamphlet 'To the English People', among whom he had spent so many years in exile. 'Civilization', he declared, 'is, for the moment, a prisoner in Paris'. After trying to bring home to Londoners just what to be besieged might mean to them, he ended with the admonition: 'A nation which by its indifference sanctions the saturnalia of force risks, and deserves, to submit to them.' The words summed up the feeling of most Parisians, and, when the British knight-errant showed himself totally unmoved by all appeals, great was the sense of bitterness, almost of betrayal. During the Great Sortie, M. Patte wrote caustically to his friend in London, Mrs. Macpherson, 'The influence of Britain in Europe is down; England is now a merchant's country as America is . . .', and—later—Gulielma Rafinesque to her brother, Louis Hack; 'I am really ashamed of England for her indifference. I suppose she is afraid of the Prussians, they seem to be very strong—

enfin!' It was a sentiment that grew to be echoed by many of the
Britons sharing the Parisian lot; in his letters home, Edwin Child
frequently deplored the pusillanimity of Gladstone in the strongest
terms, while William Brown wrote his wife, 'I cannot understand
England's neutrality, it is void of all self-respect or respect of Englishmen abroad. . . .' He longed 'for a Pitt or a Palmerston in the place
of a Gladstone and Granville . . .'.

There were indeed times when it was positively unwise to fly a
Union Jack in Paris. When, following the fall of the Empire, Parisian
street names were changed, the Press demanded (according to
Labouchere) 'that the Rue de Londres should be rebaptized on the
ground that the name of Londres is detested even more than Berlin';
and when the British colliers were sunk, Felix Whitehurst noted down
in his diary, 'We are so hated that this news was as good as that of a
victory'. In an article of September, entitled 'English Spies', *Les
Nouvelles* had proposed that all the British should be shot at once.
But, for the most part, the odium was directed specifically against
the British correspondents in Paris. In December one of the Red
Clubs passed a vote calling for the arrest of all of them, and at least
once Labouchere himself was denounced (by *Le Gaulois*) as a German
spy.

Apart from the acrid reports they sent home on the French conduct
of the war (which were picked up from time to time by the Parisian
Press), the British Press corps did tend towards eccentricities capable
of generating the worst suspicions among a neurotic population. Here
Labouchere, liable with the least encouragement to impersonate a
demagogue of 1792 and harangue the crowd, occupied an eminent
position; there was also the nameless representative of *The Times* who
provoked an amused admission of envy from his colleague, Tommy
Bowles: 'He rides about—insecurely on a horse, or securely in a
brougham—covered with Geneva Crosses, and in a gorgeous uniform,
with a violet velvet collar, and a képi covered with gold lace and
embroidery.' (The Germans too appear to have had their share of
eccentrics among the British correspondents; of one, described as
'Dr. S—', Russell of *The Times* wrote unforgettably:

His long grey hair falls in tangled masses on his shoulders . . . his tall,
lank figure is draped in an old Arab Burnous, which he requisitioned in
his march through France; and his loose baggy breeches are thrust into
a pair of dilapidated Wellingtons. He is a man of science; well read; a
scholar in many things; and yet in his old age he has come trooping here
from home as the correspondent of more than one paper. . . . He attached
himself to the 2nd Company of the 5th Jægers, and his medical knowledge—or rather his readiness to lend a hand to a wounded or sick man—

his pluck and cheerfulness, recommended him to the officers and men, who laughed at him and liked him.

Apart from his headgear, in the course of the campaign, 'Dr. S—' had managed to collect some 'not valueless spoils of war—vases and China from St.-Cloud, pieces of Sèvres, etc.', picked up 'as trophies of his pen and tourniquet.').

Of all the British resident in Paris, by far the most personally popular was a tall figure with a grizzled moustache, who, 'accompanied by a black and tan retriever dog, made his way from one Mayoral centre to another, leaving at each place a large packet of bank-notes for the relief of the poor of the district'.[1] His name was Richard Wallace and he was the natural son of the unmarried Marquis of Hertford—who in turn was the son of the depraved 3rd Marquis upon whom Thackeray had modelled the wicked Lord Steyne in *Vanity Fair*. The 4th Marquis supplemented several of the vices of his father by becoming, in addition, renowned as one of the meanest men of his age. During the potato famine he never gave a penny to help his starving Irish tenants, and when Louis-Napoleon and the Empress called on Hertford at Bagatelle, his sumptuous villa in the Bois, they usually came—with supreme tact—at teatime, so as not to put their host to any undue expense. As the Marquis was dying of cancer in 1869, Goncourt recalled how he had once boasted 'When I die I shall at least have the consolation of knowing that I have never rendered anyone a service'. But he was also a multi-millionaire and had amassed one of the finest private art collections in Europe (which, indirectly as a result of the Siege, was to end up as a gift to the British nation). To all this Richard Wallace, who had lived all his life in France, had been appointed heir, and he swiftly made up for the iniquity of his forebears by displaying an almost boundless generosity. At his own expense, Wallace organized two full-scale ambulances[2] to operate during the siege; one to serve the French wounded, and the second for the benefit of sick and destitute Britons. Repeatedly there appear in contemporary diaries such entries as 'December 5th. Mr. Wallace has given eight thousand pounds for coals for the poor.' 'December 26th. Mr. Wallace has again distinguished himself by his munificence. He has given about twenty thousand pounds in charity.' By the end of the siege, Wallace's private contributions are estimated to have totalled 2,500,000 francs,[3] an enormous sum in those days.

[1] The description is from Bernard Falk.

[2] An 'ambulance' in 1870 parlance denoted rather more than today; it was usually a field hospital plus its means of collecting the wounded. One of Wallace's ambulances possessed at least fifty beds.

[3] Roughly £100,000, or 500,000 dollars.

In return for his generosity to the Parisians, Wallace was to receive an assortment of honours; when the conservatory at the Jardin des Plantes was shattered by Prussian shells, two prize camellias that survived were presented to Wallace; the last balloon to leave Paris, and later a boulevard, were named after him; he was awarded the Légion d'Honneur, and even the Jockey Club opened its doors to him. Yet it was the British community in Paris which probably owed most to Wallace. As the Siege progressed, many of the foreigners in Paris fell into as great a state of need as the most indigent Parisian; their sources of employment had often withered away, and, cut off from their homes, they found themselves left with limited sums of capital which the spiralling costs of food soon eroded away. Obviously the worst off were the German nationals unable to escape from Paris before the Siege, and who now found themselves stranded in a hostile city which grudged them their every mouthful of food. But at least they had Minister Washburne, who had been requested to act on behalf of the North German Federation, looking after their interests; in addition to those of the American community in Paris. A whole floor of the U.S. Legation was fitted up to house impoverished Germans, and although he had to turn many hundreds away, by the end of the Siege Washburne was actually supporting some 2,400 'enemy aliens'.

The British, however, far more numerous than either the Germans or the Americans,[1] had no representative of the flag to whom they could turn. On September 18th, as has been noted previously, Lord Lyons, the British Ambassador, and most of his staff had left Paris for Tours. The representatives of only six nations remained in Paris: Switzerland, Denmark, Sweden, Belgium, and Holland—and of course Washburne of the U.S.A. In December Washburne was granted discretion by Washington as to whether he too should leave Paris, but he chose to remain. With Lord Lyons had also departed the British Consul, and at the beginning of November he was joined by Wodehouse, the secretary who had assumed seniority at the Embassy; finally, in December, Colonel Claremont of the Horse Guards, the Military Attaché, departed. There was now no official left in the British Embassy, save a concierge whose duty, according to one disgruntled Englishman, was 'to shrug his shoulders to all enquiries and reply in the most amiable manner possible "I cannot give you any information!"'

Before Claremont departed, he placed Edward Blount, the banker, in charge of the Embassy. But Blount found himself in a highly

---

[1] There were approximately 4,000 in Paris during the Siege, compared to only 250 Americans.

invidious position; he had neither funds nor authority, and was not in fact officially appointed Consul until January 24th, a few days before the capitulation. One of Blount's few official actions was to marry Wallace to the former *parfumerie* assistant with whom he had been living for the past thirty years,[1] though doubts about the legality of the ceremony induced Wallace to repeat it at a mayoral office after the Siege. The 'bolting' of the British diplomats provoked considerable anger, both among the British in Paris and at home. Tommy Bowles regarded it as 'the most extraordinary and monstrous thing', and recommended that on his return—the Ambassador's expense account should be overhauled. In the House of Commons, Sir Robert Peel denounced Lord Lyon's departure as an 'ungenerous and unmanly flight;' though, as Gladstone pointed out in defence of Lyons, it was not really his fault, in that he had acted 'on the direct injunctions of the Government at home', and the British Ambassador's 'primary duty is to take care of the interests of his country. . .'. Gladstone added, rather unconvincingly to those whose sole livelihood lay in Paris, that 'there was no occasion for any to reside in Paris who could get out of it'.

Over nine hundred British subjects had indeed been persuaded to leave before the completion of the Prussian investment, but some four thousand still remained in the city. Although at various times efforts were made to evacuate more of these, only small driblets succeeded in obtaining a *laissez-passer* through both the opposing lines. On September 22nd Labouchere had watched sceptically while four Britons clambered gaily into a carriage loaded 'with hampers of provisions, luggage, and an English flag flying'. They got as far as the Pont de Neuilly, where they were seized and taken before General Ducrot who told them unkindly 'I cannot understand you English; if you want to get shot we will shoot you ourselves to save you trouble.' The threat evidently did not deter the insouciant Britons from trying afresh the next day; after which Labouchere claimed 'nothing has been heard of them since'. At the end of October, forty-eight Americans and a few British presented themselves at the outposts with official permits; the Americans were let through, but—to their chagrin—the British were turned back on the grounds that their

---

[1] This seems to have been one family failing from which Hertford's descendants could not escape. Some years after the Siege, when Wallace had acquired a baronetcy and total respectability, his son—himself also born out of wedlock—announced his wish to marry a woman by whom he had already had a number of children. The shock was too much for Wallace, who is said to have exclaimed 'Is there to be no end to bastardy in this family ?', thereby creating an irreparable breach with his heir.

permits had not yet received clearance from Prussian Headquarters at Versailles. On November 8th, however, Wodehouse of the Embassy succeeded in getting through with seventy-five of his compatriots, of whom twenty-six travelled at Wallace's expense, having been given 100 francs each by him as well as a packet of provisions for the journey. And this was about the sum of those who left Paris. As explained by Trochu, the Government of National Defence was reluctant to allow large batches of foreigners to leave the city, because 'the effect is so demoralizing to the army and the citizens'. It was a policy which puzzled many Britons when at every turn they were accused of being so many 'useless mouths', or worse.

Following the departure of the Ambassador and his staff, Wallace took it upon himself to look after the interests of the abandoned Britons in Paris, through an organization called the British Charitable Fund (B.C.F.). Dr. John Rose Cormack (later knighted for his work), the head of one of Wallace's ambulances, was Chairman of the B.C.F., and another doctor, Alan Herbert—the younger brother of the Earl of Carnarvon, who had been practising medicine in Paris since 1859— was its hard-working secretary. In London Herbert's brother Carnarvon, as Patron of the B.C.F., did much to raise funds for the besieged Britons; but in effect it was from the pockets of wealthy Britons in Paris, such as Wallace and Blount, that most of the charity flowed.

As hardships in Paris became increasingly oppressive, this charity was often desperately needed. To Carnarvon, Alan Herbert wrote that one of his team, the Reverend Dr. J. W. Smyth, who made regular rounds of the British community, 'told me he never had seen so great distress'. Speaking to Labouchere in mid-October, Herbert admitted that the Paris Britons were more numerous than he imagined; 'he estimates their number at about 4,000, about 800 of whom are destitute.' The B.C.F. was then 'helping to keep alive 502 people'; two months later Herbert confided to Labouchere, in some despair, that the Fund already had a thousand names on its list, while 'unknown and mysterious English emerge from holes and corners every day'. Labouchere added the comment that 'If the siege goes on longer it is difficult to know how all these poor people will live', and by January those drawing relief from the B.C.F. were to number 1,200. To control the doling-out of relief, Herbert instigated 'a system of tickets', or ration cards, which appear to have worked more fairly than that sponsored by the Parisian authorities—as will be seen in the following chapter. In exchange for Herbert's tickets, each Briton on the B.C.F.'s list received a weekly ration of two ounces of Liebig's meat extract, one pound of rice, between eight to twelve pounds of bread, and a small sum of money: one franc per individual, three francs for a family of four to five members. To check up on possible frauds, Dr. Smyth and two sharp-eyed spinsters, Miss Ellen (who later married the Reverend Doctor) and Miss Annette Sparks, kept up a round of visits to those Britons claiming 'extreme poverty'. The relief these received was not much, but to many it was to mean the difference between probable starvation and survival.

If Parisian animosity towards the British had Gladstonian neutrality as its focal point, the principal and recurrent bone of contention against the United States was that the American Minister was withholding news from the city. Before food became seriously scarce, news from outside was by far the most eagerly sought-after commodity in Paris. And in this respect Elihu Washburne was uniquely privileged. After the Siege was over, an admiring American lady, Lillie Moulton, remarked to him 'What would those shut up in Paris have done without you ?', to which Washburne replied with becoming modesty 'Oh I was only a post-office'. In fact, because of his appointment to represent North German interests in Paris, Washburne had been granted by Bismarck the unique privilege of being the only diplomat allowed to send sealed dispatches out of Paris; he was also permitted—and this was of far greater value—to receive one copy of *The Times* per week, sent by the U.S. Legation in London. The proviso attached, however, was that he should keep the contents of his weekly newspaper strictly to himself. Throughout the Siege he was under constant pressure to divulge his knowledge. One Parisian journal pleaded eloquently 'We gave you Lafayette and Rochambeau, in return for which we only ask for one copy of an English paper', and on one occasion old Père, the doorman at the Legation, was offered a bribe of 1,000 francs for the latest *Times*. Washburne appears to have used his discretion in handling this much-coveted privilege; certain selected British correspondents were evidently allowed occasional access to the closely guarded copies of *The Times*, and from time to time Washburne disseminated carefully edited fragments of news to the city at large. But it was a thankless task. 'If we gave the Parisians news', commented his assistant Wickham Hoffman, 'they said that we gave them only bad news. If we withheld it, they said that we were withholding the news of French victories. . . .' Then Labouchere thoughtlessly wrote in the *Daily News* 'Go to the Legation of the United States on any day, and there you find the latest London journals lying on the table'.

The fat was in the fire. At the end of December, Bismarck, having read Labouchere's comment, wrote to Washburne complaining that he had abused the American mail privileges. Washburne replied with cold dignity that the U.S. Legation 'had endeavoured honorably to discharge our duties as neutrals; that we had acted according to the best of our judgments under this sense of duty; that we proposed to continue to act as we had done; and that if the German authorities could not trust us, they had better stop the bag altogether. . . .' He concluded with a pointed reminder of what he had done to look after Bismarck's precariously placed compatriots in Paris. In due course Bismarck apologized; but Washburne had meanwhile instructed his opposite number in London to cease sending *The Times*, so as to avoid any further such accusations from the besieging camp. Labouchere now grumbled (with little enough reason) that, since his ticking-off by Bismarck, Washburne mounted a 'grim guard' over his reading matter, and Washburne himself noted being 'daily violently assailed' by a portion of the Paris Press as a "Prussian representative" and a "Prussian sympathizer" because of his secretiveness. In fact, thus deprived of his English newspapers, he was to end the Siege little better informed on external events than the average Parisian.

*   *   *

Apart from this one source of friction, in Parisian eyes the American image remained indisputably more popular than that of the British; for which there were several contributory reasons. First the distant and introversive United States of 1870 were never *expected* to take a position on European affairs; so there was no sense of disappointment here. Secondly, with the American residents in Paris so outnumbered by the British, they were less likely to aggravate sensibilities with their presence, or expose themselves to the charges of 'useless mouths'. Thirdly, there was the very solid and impressive presence of Washburne himself. But perhaps above all the popularity of the Americans stemmed from the demonstrative usefulness of the American Ambulance during the Siege.

When it was all over, even Ducrot himself was forced to admit the grave shortcomings of the French medical organization. After Sedan, there had been only 6,000 hospital beds available in Paris, which was 'far from being sufficient'. By the beginning of the Siege this had been raised to 13,000, and eventually to 37,000. The various religious bodies had formed 'ambulances' on their premises, as had the railway companies on the sites of their disused stations. Inside the Théâtre français, a nostalgic Gautier found 'wounded lying about in the foyer, where once the critics used to pace about'. Schools and courtrooms had also been turned into hospitals, and the biggest occupied the floors beneath Labouchere in the Grand Hôtel; while the *Société de la Presse* itself operated a highly active ambulance.

On the surface the results seemed imposing; but only on the surface. In September the Government had ordained two kinds of 'ambulance'; the first category comprised of properly constituted hospitals capable of receiving the most severely wounded; and the second, *'ambulances privées'* which could only partially fulfil requirements and were allowed to take in the lightly wounded. The latter formed a particular source of abuse. The authorities had little or no control over them; Ducrot claimed that when his soldiers got into them they could no longer be located—'their stay prolonged itself indefinitely, and they never reappeared in their units'. The 'private ambulances' provided an attractive source of occupation for the *grandes dames* of Paris; 'The wounded soldier has become an object of fashion', recorded Goncourt. They also offered refuges for ablebodied men dodging active service; until the police were ordered to arrest anyone wearing a Red Cross who was unable to produce his certificate as an *infirmier*. With some relish Labouchere watched a *petit crevé*[1] 'arrayed in a suit of velvet knickerbockers, with a red cross on his arm borne off to prison, notwithstanding his whining protests'.

Rivalry for patients among the 'private ambulances' was acute; Goncourt relates of one rich man who had converted his house into a hospital, then, distressed to find he had no inmates, paid a local hospital 3,000 francs for a casualty! At the beginning of the siege, Louis Péguret of the National Guard wrote his mother that 'Madame Massieux [a liquor-vendor] has urged me to have myself brought to her if I am wounded; she has transformed her *boutique* into an ambulance, and she has assured me that I shall lack nothing. I accepted her offer with great pleasure, hoping that Providence will do me the favour of giving my place to some other unfortunate.' Everywhere Red Cross flags were to be seen flying from private domiciles; from his window in the Grand Hôtel alone, Labouchere could count fifteen. There were, criticized O'Shea, 'too many toy ambulances in Paris, and too few serious ones'.

The proliferation of ambulances of various kinds led to bitter internecine squabbles ('There never existed in this world such unhappy families as these humane societies are now in Paris', claimed Tommy Bowles at the beginning of January); which in turn led, on the battlefield, to appalling chaos. According to Ducrot, their arrival on the scene frequently 'paralyzed' the work of the divisional and corps ambulances. Among several similar blunders, a British voluntary ambulance worker, Felix Whitehurst, records how on one occasion

---

[1] Labouchere defined *petits crevés* as 'those youths who are best described by the English expression "nice young men for a small tea-party" '.

the *Ambulance de la Presse* received orders to send two hundred waggons to collect wounded at St.-Denis:

Rather astonished, they got together as many conveyances as they could,
and went off to the last resting-place of French kings. When they got
there they found that wrong directions had been given; the wounded had
been carried into Paris by the *Intendance Militaire*, and instead of two
hundred carriages being required, it was intended to say there were
about two hundred wounded.

But worst of all was the picture in the base hospitals in Paris. There
were insufficient doctors, nurses were untrained,[1] methods primitive
and conditions appallingly unhygienic. Juliette Lambert noted being
deeply disturbed by the terrible cries of the wounded having limbs
amputated in the Palais de l'Industrie, and later in the Siege she was
shocked to see 'one of our great surgeons weep in telling me that, in
his hospital, he had not saved a single amputation case'. The deadly
killer was septicaemia, often complicated by gangrene, for which—
in their practical application—Lister's principles of antisepsis had
not yet produced a remedy. Most hospitals had a 'death shed' into
which any man that contracted septicaemia was immediately
removed; 'The simple reason', explained an American surgeon, 'was
that their presence under the same roof with their comrades would
mean certain death for all.' The situation in the Grand Hôtel, the
biggest 'ambulance' in Paris, which housed five hundred wounded
moved there from the Palais de l'Industrie, was particularly atrocious;
even though, according to Labouchere, the size of its staff outnumbered the patients. It was reputed that a man could not cut his finger
in the germ-ridden atmosphere of the Grand Hôtel and reach the
door alive. When Bowles visited it, he found the wounded

packed three, four, and five in each of the little rooms which the company
was wont to let to single travellers at high prices. Ventilation cannot be
said to be imperfect, for there is none; and the dead, as many as fifty
at a time, are placed, 'packed like biscuits', in the centre of a gallery into
which the rooms open. The stench is something terrible, and only last
night a French gentleman said to me, 'To be taken there is death'.

All in all, the state of the Parisian 'ambulances' showed little
advance over what Lord Raglan's men had suffered in the Crimea.
And the nearest resemblance to any Florence Nightingale upon the
scene lay in the presence of the American Ambulance, which owed

---

[1] Goncourt, perhaps harshly, describes some of them as 'old whores, fat,
superannuated *lorettes*, delightedly preparing themselves to mess about with
the wounded with sensual hands, to find erotic pleasure in the amputations'.

its existence to Dr. Thomas Evans, the handsome and enterprising dentist who had assisted the Empress Eugénie to flee from Paris. After the Great Exhibition of 1867, Evans had (for no very clear reason) bought up the whole collection of up-to-date medical equipment of the American Civil War exhibited in Paris, and when war broke out he had organized an ambulance and presented all this equipment to it, plus 10,000 francs. In charge of the American Ambulance was Dr. Swinburne, as Chief Surgeon, who based his work on Civil War experiences. There it had been proved that the most effective way of combating septicaemia was by ensuring perfect ventilation. To the astonishment of the French with their native horror of *courants d'air*, the American Ambulance housed its two hundred wounded in draughty tents, kept warm only by a stove placed in a hole in the ground which dried and heated the earth beneath the tent. The results were miraculous: whereas four out of every five died in the purulent confines of the Grand Hôtel, four out of five of Swinburne's amputation cases survived.

The British correspondents were constantly singing Swinburne's praises, and even Dr. Alan Herbert, working in Wallace's British Ambulance, had to admit that its American counterpart was 'one of the shows of today'. On any battlefield the American Ambulance was always (according to Tommy Bowles) the first to arrive; at the Great Sortie it brought in eighty wounded men, one of them dying in the arms of Washburne's son; and at a later engagement its field clearing-station was actually hit by Prussian shells. Its fame spread fast; Labouchere said, 'It is the dream of every French soldier, if he is wounded, to be taken to this ambulance.[1] They appear to be under the impression that, even if their legs are shot off, the skill of the Aesculapii of the United States will make them grow again'. It may have been a mild exaggeration, but certainly there was no mistaking the efficacy of Evans's and Swinburne's team; nor the Parisian gratitude which their work of mercy gained for the United States.

[1] Some French officers evidently carried cards with requests to this effect printed on them.

Death of Castor and Pollux

12. Hunger

ONCE the bitter disappointment at Ducrot's failure in the Great Sortie had passed, purely military considerations no longer predominated in Parisian minds. There was now a topic that had become far more grimly immediate. On December 8th, Goncourt noted in his journal: 'People are talking only of what they eat, what they can eat, and what there is to eat. Conversation consists of this, and nothing more.... Hunger begins and famine is on the horizon.' Among his circle, Goncourt found Théophile Gautier lamenting 'that he has to wear braces for the first time, his abdomen no longer supporting his trousers'. Goncourt himself was finding the salted meat distributed by the Government 'inedible', and described how he had to kill one of his own chickens. The execution had been carried out ineptly, 'with a Japanese sabre. It was terrible, the bird escaped from me and fluttered about the garden, without a head'. Minister Washburne, better off than many a Parisian, confided 'I sigh for the doughnuts and hot rolls at Proctors', and another American recalled with apparent envy how, at a concert in November, a young lady 'received, instead of a bouquet, a—piece of cheese'.

Cheese, along with butter and milk, was now little more than a memory of the past, and the vast herds of cattle and sheep that in September had filled the Bois, as well as every vacant plot in Paris, had vanished. Fresh vegetables had run out; for one franc a day and at considerable risk to themselves, 'marauders' were sent out under the protection of *Mobiles* to grub about in 'no-man's-land'. Augustus O'Shea recalled recognizing one of them, a coloured Martiniquais, who only two months earlier had sold him a pair of gloves in a smart shop of the Rue de la Paix, and whom he now encountered seedily dressed and 'staggering under a bag-net of cauliflowers'. Before the Siege began, Bismarck had predicted in his cynical fashion that 'eight days without *café au lait*' would suffice to break the Parisian bourgeoisie, and even the Government of National Defence had not seriously reckoned on a blockade lasting more than two months, at most. Now, with Christmas, the hundredth day was already approaching.

Early in October Paris had begun to eat horsemeat, first introduced by Parisian butchers four years previously as a cheap provender for the poor. *Pour encourager les autres*, to create a wider fashion for hippophagy, the *Commission Centrale d'Hygiène et de Salubrité*, had treated itself to a sumptuous and well-advertised banquet, the menu of which read:

> *Consommé de cheval*
>
> *Cheval bouilli aux choux*
>
> *Culotte de cheval à la mode*
>
> *Côte de cheval braisée*
>
> *Filet de cheval rôti*
>
> *Bœuf et cheval salés froids*

From that moment, horse became very much *à la mode*, establishing a taste which still provides the principal source of revenue of many a Parisian butcher. To a '*belle*' who (exceptionally) had refused to dine with him, a frustrated Victor Hugo wrote:

> *Je vous aurais offert un repas sans rival:*
> *J'aurais tué Pégase et je l'aurais fait cuire*
> *Afin de vous servir une aile de cheval.*[1]

[1] I would have offered you a meal beyond compare:
I would have killed Pegasus and had him cooked,
So as to serve you with a horse's wing.

As belts were tightened, many a superb champion of the turf ended its days in the casserole; among them were the two trotting horses presented by the Tsar to Louis-Napoleon at the time of the Great Exhibition, originally valued at 56,000 francs, now bought by a butcher for 800. But it was from mid-November when Paris first realized the supplies of fresh meat were exhausted (though the shock was largely absorbed by the excitement at Gambetta's triumph at Coulmiers), whence originated the exotic menus with which the Siege is immortally coupled. It was then that the signs 'Feline and Canine Butchers' made their debut. Although it was known that carnivores at the zoo were being nurtured on stray dogs, at first the idea of slaughtering domestic pets for human consumption provoked great indignation; a member of the Rafinesque family recorded how 'the cart of a dog-and-cat butcher from which emanated lamentable barks and miaows was assailed by a crowd which was moved and perhaps disgusted. In the scuffle that followed five dogs escaped at the gallop whilst the crowd cheered.' But soon necessity bred familiarity, and by mid-December Labouchere was reporting in a matter-of-fact way, 'I had a slice of spaniel the other day' (though it made him 'feel like a cannibal'), and recounting without comment a week later how a man he had met was fattening up a huge cat which he meant to serve up on Christmas Day, 'surrounded with mice, like sausages'. As more and more of the two traditional domestic enemies became reconciled in the cooking-pot, Gautier claimed that they seemed to grow instinctively aware of their peril:

Soon the animals observed that man was regarding them in a strange manner and that, under the pretext of caressing them, his hand was feeling them like the fingers of a butcher, to ascertain the state of their *embonpoint*. More intellectual and more suspicious than dogs, the cats were the first to understand, and adopted the greatest prudence in their relations.

Next it was the turn of the rats. Although, together with the carrier-pigeon, the rat was to become the most fabled animal of the Siege of Paris, and from December on a good rat-hunt was one of the favourite pastimes of the National Guard, the number actually consumed was relatively few.[1] Apart from the (probably exaggerated) fear of the diseases they carried, on account of the lavish preparation of sauces required to make them palatable rats were essentially a rich man's dish; hence the famous menus of the Jockey Club, featuring

[1] According to one contemporary American calculation (although on what it was based is not revealed), only 300 rats were eaten during the whole Siege, compared with 65,000 horses, 5,000 cats, and 1,200 dogs.

such delicacies as *salmi de rats* and 'rat pie'. With the passage of time menus grew even more exotic as the zoos were forced to surrender their most precious inmates. Hugo was sent some joints of bear, deer, and antelope by the curator of the Jardin des Plantes; kangaroo was consumed at Goncourt's favourite haunt, Chez Brébant; and at a butcher's on the fashionable Faubourg St. Honoré O'Shea found the carcases of wolves on display. Because of the danger involved in killing them, the lions and tigers survived; as did the monkeys, protected apparently by the exaggerated Darwinian instincts of the Parisians, and the hippopotamus from the Jardin des Plantes, for whose vast live-weight no butcher could afford the reserve price of 80,000 francs. Otherwise no animal was exempt. By the end of December, even the pride of the Jardin d'Acclimatation, two young elephants called Castor and Pollux, were dispatched after several disgracefully inept attempts with explosive bullets. Like most of the bigger animals the poor creatures were bought by Roos, the opulent proprietor of the Boucherie Anglaise. Visiting his premises on New Year's Eve, Goncourt describes how 'in the midst of nameless meats and unusual horns, a boy was offering some camel kidneys for sale'; while on the wall 'hung in a place of honour, was the skinned trunk of young Pollux' which the butcher was pressing upon a group of women for 40 francs a pound. "You think that's dear ? But I assure you I don't know how I'm going to make anything out of it. I was counting on three thousand pounds of meat and he has only yielded two thousand three hundred!"' Obviously shocked at the price, Goncourt concluded, 'I fell back on a couple of larks'.

Opinions varied sharply on the merits of these unaccustomed dishes. One Englishman wrote his wife that 'horseflesh is excellent and the French cooks make the best of it; the flesh of the Mule and Ass is equal to veal. . . .' On first eating horse in November, Tommy Bowles exclaimed in rapture: 'How people continue to eat pigs I can't imagine', but a few weeks later he had changed his tune: 'In spite of all attempts, I cannot eat horse', adding almost enviously that 'A *franc-tireur* tells me that he made an excellent dinner off crow and dahlia root'. By the first days of January he was recording: 'I have now dined off camel, antelope, dog, donkey, mule and elephant, which I approve in the order in which I have written . . . horse is really too disgusting, and it has a peculiar taste never to be forgotten.' Goncourt declared that horsemeat gave him nightmares, while Verlaine recalled how a dinner of burnt horse provoked the second scene of his marriage, 'and—the first blow'. Juliette Lambert also appeared to agree with Bowles, writing to her daughter at the end of December about the hump of camel she had bought: 'It was divine! What a dinner!' As

N

time went on, people's palates became more discriminating; there
was a noticeable price differential between 'brewery' and sewer rats,
and Wickham Hoffman of the American Legation declared that
among horses light greys were greatly preferable to blacks. Of the
zoo animals, he thought elephant was 'tolerably good', but reindeer
was the best. One French 'expert' described dog as being 'fine, fresh,
rosy, covered with very white fat; stimulating to the appetite when well
prepared'. Professor Sheppard, another American, made the agreeable discovery that 'rats, to my surprise, taste somewhat like birds',
while cat 'tastes something like the American grey squirrel, but is
even tenderer and sweeter'. And on the whole most people, ranging
from the fastidious Labouchere to the Earl of Carnarvon's brother,
Dr. Alan Herbert, seemed to agree with Sheppard about the superiority of cat; while the robust Edwin Child betrayed little concern
about the taste of what he was eating—so long as it was food.

Before the food shortage had reached its full gravity, and to those
that could afford them, these bizarre victuals also provided a rich
source of humour. Le Figaro related how a man was pursued through
Paris by a pack of dogs, barking loudly at his heels; he could not
understand their interest until he remembered that he had eaten a
rat for breakfast. A similar cartoon in one of the illustrated journals
depicted, sticking out of a man's mouth, the tail of a cat which had
dived down his throat in pursuit of its natural prey. After a dog
dinner at Brébant's, Hébrard was heard to comment, 'At our next
dinner they'll be serving us the shepherd'; but in fact the Parisians
were never quite reduced to cannibalism.

Some of France's best scientific brains had been employed to
devise additional ways of supplementing the dwindling food supplies.
In the latter days of the Siege a bread, named 'pain Ferry' after the
responsible Minister and composed of wheat, rice and straw, made its
appearance. One Frenchman said, 'It seemed to have been made from
old Panama hats picked out of the gutters', while to Professor Sheppard it tasted of 'sawdust, mud and potato skins'. As a kind of synthetic milk, the Comité Scientifique recommended a nauseous-
sounding brew of glucose, albumen (or gelatine), and olive oil;
unfortunately there was no olive oil in Paris. One of its more successful developments was the 'osseine' mentioned earlier, made out of
bones and gelatine, which was sold widely in the last days of the
Siege for making bouillon, at one franc a kilogram. Unfortunately,
in Paris's anguish speculators were also swift to glimpse opportunity.
Appalling concoctions of bogus foodstuffs—above all of milk for
desperate mothers—appeared on the market; doctored pumpkins
were sold as apricot marmalade, and jams fabricated from horse

gelatine and molasses were sold at 1·40 francs a pound; cooking-grease was adulterated with candles, and Goncourt overheard arsenic being recommended as a good antidote to hunger. Few butchers were above taking advantage of their sudden emergence as the most powerful (and most detested) section of the community; cat, said Professor Sheppard, was frequently sold as 'an otter, or a rare species of hare, or an extraordinary small and odd kind of sheep', and a lamb offered to one British correspondent ironically turned out to be a wolf. There were also ingenious rackets whereby valuable racehorses, bought at knackers' prices, were switched for old hacks of equivalent weight and were somehow kept alive until they made a handsome profit for their new 'owner' when the Siege ended.

Despite the quite sensible entreaties of Blanqui and the left wing, no effort was made by the Government to establish proper control of food distribution until too late, and then the measures were ineffectual and unfair. In the earliest days the Government had set up price controls on a number of staple foods, but these were feebly enforced and soon short-circuited by a rampant black market. Meat rationing was introduced in mid-October; it started at 100 grammes per person per day, was reduced in November to 50 grammes, and later to 30—or roughly one ounce—but it encompassed none of the 'exotic' meats mentioned above. Restaurants were also instructed in October to serve but one plate of meat to each client; notices were posted up, but little attention paid to them in any place where money could speak. Labouchere noted that 'in the expensive cafés of the Boulevards, feasts worthy of Lucullus are still served', and the situation altered little as the months passed. Bread was not rationed until the last days of the Siege, though false rumours of it provoked panic and riots in mid-December. No measures were ever taken to counter hoarding. The prudent well-to-do lived off their own private stocks purchased before the Siege began, but far more reprehensible were the speculators who sat on foodstuffs until prices seemed sufficiently attractive. Some made a killing from beetroots bought in October at 2 centimes a piece, and later sold for 1·75 francs. Panicked by the rumours of premature peace that followed Thiers' armistice talks, others released some of their butter hoards so that prices dropped by two-thirds with revealing abruptness.

Because it was more profitable to sell 'under the counter', but also because the disgracefully inefficient system of distribution meant that often their shops were genuinely bare, traders took to putting up their shutters for long periods. This resulted in endless, heartbreaking food queues; a word that one British correspondent (who would not live long enough to see mid-twentieth-century Britain)

found hard to translate—'There is no equivalent in English—happily!'
Such a queue; he discovered, was often 'more than a couple of hundred strong. Its outer edge towards the street was kept by armed
Gardes Nationaux, who, patrolling like sheepdogs here and there,
suppressed with difficulty the almost continual disputes'. Hour after
hour the wretched housewives waited ('to have any certainty of a
basketful one had to be on the spot by three in the morning' claimed
O'Shea), often leaving empty-handed, with hatred in their hearts
equally for the *petit bourgeois* as represented by the heartless butcher
and for the rich bourgeois who could afford to buy without queuing.

Virtually the only effective rationing was achieved by that most
unfair of all criteria—by price. Regardless of the Government's
attempts at price controls, the cost of most foodstuffs soared as the
weeks went by, as its shown by the following table:[1]

	First two weeks of the Siege	*December 10th to 24th*
	francs	francs
Butter	4·00 per lb.	35·00 per lb.
Eggs	1·80 a dozen	24·00 a dozen
Fowl	6·00	26·00
Rabbit	8·00	40·00
Cheese	2·00 per lb.	30·00 per lb.
Fresh pork	1·10 per lb.	— (non-existent)
Cat	—	6·00 per lb.
Rat	—	0·50
Potatoes	2·75 per bushel	15·00 per bushel[2]
Carrots	1·20 per box	2·80 per lb.
Cabbage	0·75 each	4·00 each[3]

Even this table barely reflects the full extent of price rises, as
these had already been substantial by the time the investment of
Paris was complete; compared with pre-war days, for instance, the
prices of butter had risen by over one-third, and potatoes and rabbits
had more than doubled. The price that some people were prepared to

[1] Extracted principally from detailed weekly accounts of prices kept by
Professor Sheppard.

[2] By the following week potatoes had risen to 28·00 francs per bushel.

[3] The official rate of exchange in 1870 was approximately 25 francs = £1,
or 5 francs = 1 dollar. What this means in terms of today's money is hard to
assess accurately, though it may be taken—as a very rough guide—that the £
sterling of 1870 had something like four times the purchasing-power of the £
of 1965; perhaps a more useful guide is the fact that, in 1870, the average wage
of the Parisian worker was less than 5 francs a day.

pay for uncontrolled foods seemed limitless. O'Shea recalled that a friend of his had been offered a fat poodle for 100 francs; on December 19th Washburne recorded eating mule meat at '2 dollars per pound in gold'; on Christmas Day he saw a goose in a shop being sold for 25 dollars, while Sheppard noted that a turkey which could still have been bought for 100 francs the previous week had had its price pushed up to 180 francs for Christmas (before the war it would have fetched 10 francs). Towards the end of the year, Francisque Sarcey studied a 'crowd of loiterers huddled around a turkey, just as in other times one used to see them in front of the great jewellers on the Rue de la Paix'. The comparison was hardly exaggerated, and indeed at least one jeweller had found it more profitable to transform his premises into a provision shop, displaying elegantly in the window (according to O'Shea) 'a dead rabbit . . . flanked by a plate of minnows and three tiny sparrows; while higher up half-a-dozen hen-eggs were arranged in a circle, like a necklet of pearls'.

Even by this time there was, claimed Sarcey, still 'an enormous quantity of rabbits and poultry', so that for the affluent the Siege offered inconvenience but never real hunger. Before the investment began all those who could afford it, and had foresight, had laid in substantial reserves. At the beginning of December, Labouchere noted that there were still three sheep hoarded in the cellar of the British Embassy ('Never did the rich man lust more after the poor man's ewe lamb that I lust after these sheep'). Bowles had a friend 'who possesses two sheep and a pig, and I am happy to say that I am on the best of terms with him, as well as with another who has got a cow and produces fresh butter', while another Englishman, Henry Markheim, recalled eating roast beef in a restaurant on December 20th, and being assured by the proprietor that there was a further week's supply in his cellar. Edward Blount kept two live cows as well as two horses throughout most of the Siege. On November 17th he wrote in a letter 'Paris can stand out for two months more. . . . I have still fresh meat of the cow I killed, for breakfast, and milk and butter from the one still living . . . we dine well at the Jockey Club. In fine we get enough, and people do not complain . . .', though four days later he noted 'dreadful misery in the poor quarters of the town'. Throughout November and December he managed to live on his salted cow; his horses were requisitioned, but spared after a personal appeal to Jules Favre, and not until January 1st was he forced to kill his remaining cow, which kept him in meat for the remainder of the Siege, so that as far as he was concerned he was able to say comfortably 'I think a little starvation does no harm'. The experiences of Dr. Alan Herbert were not dissimilar. At the end of November, he was writing to his brother, the Earl of Carnarvon: 'Good stock of provisions; enough, if necessary, to last till end of January .... If there should be an amnesty, beg Fortnum and Mason to send immediately hams, tongues, potted meats and *cheese* ...'. He too had a reserve of livestock, including a hen called 'Una', to whom he became so attached that he would not permit her to be sacrificed;[1] a fact which suggests that, as well as being tender-hearted, the doctor can never have been quite reduced to the extremities shared by some of the more hard-up Britons in Paris, whom he did so much to help.

The American Legation had also laid in a large stock of food for its dependents, including canned hominy and grits. Some thirty of its members dined off traditional turkey ('at twelve dollars a piece') on Thanksgiving Day; on December 13th, Wickham Hoffman wrote to a colleague 'We ate (four days ago) a sucking pig, a roast duck, truffles and fresh butter. This is not famine—and all washed down with Château Margaux 1850.... I was a guest'; and on Christmas Day his Minister, Washburne, sat down unashamedly to an eight-course menu beginning with oyster soup. Some senior French officers seem to have looked after themselves just as well as the diplomats; Wickham Hoffman recalled in astonishment one three-hour 'breakfast' with a general commanding a forward position, at which 'we had beef, eggs, ham, etc., and from what I heard I should say that he and his staff breakfasted as well every day'. One Parisian also describes a fabulous dinner in the Rue de Ponthieu, given by a French naval captain just two weeks before the capitulation to celebrate the installation of a new mistress: 'Domestics in breeches and silk hose served us *foies gras truffés*, filets of steak of real beef—no Jardin des Plantes hippopotamus—enormous Argenteuil asparagus, grapes from Thomery that had escaped Prussian surveillance, and bucketfuls of the finest champagne'. The author concluded that really the only hungry ones in Paris were those who 'suffered from voracious appetites'. Restaurants seemed remarkably unaffected, and inversely so in proportion to their expensiveness; after the Siege was over, Goncourt and his friends presented to *Chez Brébant* a medallion bearing the inscription:

'DURING THE SIEGE OF PARIS A FEW PEOPLE ACCUSTOMED TO FOREGATHERING AT MONSIEUR BRÉBANT'S ONCE A FORTNIGHT NEVER ON ONE SINGLE OCCASION PERCEIVED THAT THEY WERE DINING IN A CITY OF TWO MILLION BESIEGED SOULS'.

It was a remarkable and revealing testimony.

[1] 'Una' survived the Siege and followed her master back to England as a household pet. When she died she was stuffed and mounted in a glass case and remains to this day in Tetton House, Alan Herbert's old home (see illustration, between pages 130 and 131).

For those with even a little money, the situation was rarely worse than it was for the average Briton during the direst moments of the U-Boat blockade in the First World War. Edwin Child on his apprentice's pay (though no doubt aided by a youthful and insouciant digestion) describes dining, at the end of the year, off 'two plates of meat (couldn't say of what) with sauces and preserved green peas. Found it remarkably good anyhow and relished it as such.' But in a letter home a short time later he admits: 'the *Garde Nationale* helps me a great deal as outside Paris we are fed and inside are paid 1½ francs a day, but when it costs 2 francs each meal this does not go far'. Many of the British correspondents wrote of eating a slice of Pollux's trunk (though the genuine article must have been almost as rare as bits of the True Cross), but even a young elephant will not go far among two million people; especially at 40 francs a pound. Apart from the plight of the indigent foreigners in Paris, which has been noted earlier, for the hundreds of thousands of the really poor in Paris, who had found it a struggle to keep their heads above water under the high cost of living of the Second Empire, and who could not now afford rats because of the cost of the essential sauces, jokes about strange foods were hardly funny. Starvation was never very far away. In the third week of December, Labouchere was shocked to find in slums off the Boulevard de Clichy women and children sitting, 'half-starved', on their doorsteps. 'They said that, as they had neither firewood nor coke, they were warmer out-of-doors than in-doors. . . .' Prostitution spread as women, like one young girl who accosted Goncourt, sold themselves for a crust of bread; the restaurants benefited, for the poor sold them their ration cards when they were unable to pay for the food. In December the sight of convoys of small coffins carried by weeping parents up to Père Lachaise cemetery became a daily occurrence as the lack of milk made infant mortality soar. Apart from the children, it was the women of the poor who suffered most. At least the men had, most of them, their 1·50 francs a day from the National Guard, little enough of which reached their wives. The habit of the *bistro* formed under Louis-Napoleon had assumed a still stronger hold, as representing the only barrier against boredom and cold, and even—corroborating an axiom of Hippocrates—as the surest way to appease hunger. And there was never any shortage of wine or alcohol. In the poorer districts, drunkenness was never more widespread, nor more wretched. So while the women and children of proletarian Paris queued and died, the men got drunk; all the while fuming against the Government.

For all the suffering, with the exception of the children, very few Parisians actually died of starvation during the Siege. Once again, by way of comparison, it is perhaps worth returning to the Siege of Leningrad. Within the first month of war starting in June 1941, rationing was introduced, and by November this had already been reduced to below subsistence-level. That month the first cases of death by starvation were recorded: 11,085. There was no question of such exotic meat substitutes as rat or elephant; during the first winter of the Siege the population of Leningrad was reduced to eating 'pancakes made of sawdust, jelly made from carpenter's glue ... raw bran pancakes made from powdered wall-paper glue and containing an insect repellent'. People died at their work and in the streets; and by January 1942 the death rate had risen to as high as an estimated 9,000 a *day*.

* * *

Apart from her apparently bottomless cellars, Paris—accustomed as she was to both demanding and supplying more diversions than most other cities—had few enough resources with which to distract her mind from the reality of hunger. Promenades around the fortifications, enlivened with an occasional peep through telescopes at the Prussian lines, continued to provide the principal Sunday occupation; the philosophical, motionless gudgeon fishermen still found diversion on the banks of the Seine, and, although their efforts became less and less frequently rewarded with success, the curious crowds they drew never diminished.[1] But, as the weather grew more bitterly cold, these pastimes began to pall. Instead, rat-hunting became the vogue, with the *Paris Journal* offering helpful hints on how to 'fish for sewer rats with a hook and line bated with tallow'. Spy-chasing, rumour-mongering, and scurrility continued to keep minds busy, ably abetted by the wilder elements of the Press; although Blanqui's *La Patrie en Danger* folded up on December 8th for want of funds. There were still plenty of lengthy parades and patriotic demonstrations to keep both body and emotions warm; many of them in the Concorde before the statue of Strasbourg, which had become a kind of shrine.

Meanwhile, a new and enduring source of entertainment had been provided by the publication of the Tuileries papers, replete with the most salacious revelations of corruption and vice under the Second Empire. Labouchere recalled seeing the copy of a receipt from Miss Howard, showing how as the Emperor's mistress she had received five million francs, and even he admitted to being shocked at the

---

[1] According to George Orwell, in *Down and Out in Paris and London*, no dace have been caught in the Seine since the Siege of Paris.

discovery of what an 'El Dorado of pimps and parasites, panders and wantons' the Imperial court had been. Meretricious booksellers made a heyday out of the disclosures, shouting to passers-by *'Demandez la femme Bonaparte ! Ses amants, ses orgies !'* The virtuous and frigid Eugénie was usually the butt of the obscene caricatures resulting from the release of the Tuileries papers; one showed her in the nude, being sketched by the Prince de Joinville, and another dancing a *cancan*, her petticoats flung up over her head, for the delectation of the King of Prussia, who was drinking champagne on a sofa, while Louis-Napoleon hung, encaged, from the wall. All this, encouraged and even sponsored by the Trochu Government, appalled Goncourt as many other Parisians by its 'lack of gravity, of restraint, of what is proper'; and indeed there was something shamefully frivolous in the way Paris could continue to blame the *ancien régime* for its present terrible dilemma. Against the protests of the austere Blanqui, the theatres which had closed in September reopened at the end of October. Their comeback was led by the Théâtre français with excerpts from *Le Misanthrope* and a lecture on 'Moral Nourishment During the Siege', and on November 5th the Opéra had also reopened, but with a dismally depleted cast as most of the singers had made haste to leave Paris before the investment. The bill of fare offered by the theatres was equally impoverished, and a performance seldom ended without some patriotic polemic. Labouchere recorded a typical evening at the Comédie française, consisting of 'a speech, a play of Molière's without costumes, and an ode to Liberty'. Young Sarah Bernhardt was among the actresses to take part in the many fund-raising productions, devoted to hospital charities and the purchase of cannon; it was a role that she was to repeat, though aged and minus a leg, in another war, nearly half a century later. At these performances nothing was more popular than a fiery reading of of Victor Hugo's *Les Châtiments*, the embittered attack on Louis-Napoleon that he had written when in exile, and of which 22,000 copies had been sold by mid-December.

In fact, outside the Red Clubs, Hugo himself remained one of the most fertile sources of entertainment in the besieged city—at the same time as he entertained himself. Visiting him one night in December, Goncourt found 'the God' dressed in a red pea-jacket with a white scarf round his neck, surrounded by actresses and conversing about the moon. Later, Goncourt recounted with obvious envy and admiration how the septuagenarian had somehow maintained his noteworthy libidinous energy during the Siege, unimpaired by malnutrition or the lack of heat:

Every evening towards ten o'clock, leaving the Hotel Rohan, where under the pretext of keeping his grandchildren, he had housed Juliette,[1] he returned to the *Maison Meurice*, where one—two—even three women awaited him . . . and through the window of the ground floor, where Hugo had selected his room, Madame Maurice's maid while strolling in the garden, used to see—morning and evening—naked portions of strange priapics.

'This', commented Goncourt, 'seems to have been Hugo's main occupation during the Siege'. Such demands on his time did not, however, hinder the vigorous old man from proclaiming, in December, as a gesture of contempt at the Government's inertia, that he intended to go out single and unarmed against the enemy; an intention which drew a large crowd outside his house, attempting to dissuade him—which it succeeded in doing.

All the time the flow of bombastic proclamations and heroic couplets continued, though the tone had become more sober.

> *Les cercles de l'enfer sont là, mornes spirales;*
> *Haine, hiver, guerre, deuil, peste, famine, ennui.*
> *Paris a les sept nœuds des ténèbres sur lui.*[2]

wrote Hugo; as December progressed, all seven spheres of hell were well established in the city, and there was no distraction sufficient to dispel their effect. Goncourt compared the lethal boredom provoked by the Siege to that of 'a tragedy which reaches no climax'. Occasionally the tragedy was relieved for a moment by the advent of falsely optimistic news, as on December 8th when it was widely rumoured that Bourbaki had reached Chantilly. 'Nothing is more painful', wrote Goncourt, 'than this situation where one does not know whether the armies of the provinces are at Corbeil or Bordeaux, or even whether they exist or not. Nothing crueller than to live in obscurity, in the night, in complete ignorance of the tragedy that threatens you. . . .' By December 15th, Labouchere sensed that 'a dead, apathetic torpor has settled over the town'. It was having its effect on the Army. Slackness was on the increase, particularly in the forts where boredom was most acute. At Fort Issy an officer reported that roll-calls, normally taken by an officer, had been passed on to a sergeant-major, then to a sergeant, and finally on to a mere corporal. Absenteeism rose. Clearly, with the mounting lack of food and fuel, the onset of hard winter and the failure of the Great Sortie, morale was slipping.

---

[1] His mistress Juliette Drouet.
[2] 'The regions of hell are all there, sombre spirals,
    Hate, winter, war, mourning, disease, famine, boredom,
    Paris has the seven nodes of the underworld upon her.'

But it was perhaps extraordinary that it had not already slipped further. In a letter dated December 12th to Fish, the American Secretary of State, Washburne noted with surprise that the recapture of Orléans 'seems to have made but very little impression on the people of Paris', and there were even going the rounds such jokes as 'The Army of the Loire is cut in two . . . so much the better! that now gives us two armies!' Among the pious Catholics of Paris, there was still a belief that the patron saint, Ste. Geneviève, would somehow intervene with a miracle before it was too late. There were people too who found encouragement in the increasing flow of cannon from Dorian's factories; one National Guardsman, Louis Péguret, wrote to his sister in the provinces on December 17th '. . . now everything is functioning very well, and every day we feel stronger, for every day our armament becomes more considerable, our young troops more hardened to war.'

That there had been no recurrence of the October 31st demonstrations after the bitter disappointment of the Great Sortie was doubtless in part due to the narcotic effects of hunger and cold, and to proletarian Paris's preoccupation with the mere struggle to survive. But there were two other factors. In a curious way, the city had grown acclimatized to the routine of Siege life—it was almost hard to remember any other form of existence. And at the same time, a new element of pride, a more sober kind of pride, was growing among the population; having come so far, Paris could not now give in. M. Patte, writing to an Englishwoman, spoke for the defiant mood of many Parisians:

Pascal has said thinking of the Christian Church: '*Il y a plaisir d'être dans un vaisseau battu par l'orage, lorsqu'on est assuré qu'il ne périra pas.* . . .'[1] Well, I say that of Paris, of France: '*Elle ne périra pas!*' They said, she was daid [*sic*]; but she moves and they say now; she is not daid.

* * *

Following the failure of the Great Sortie, there had been the inevitable post-mortems and soul-searchings in the Government, protracted over several days. Ducrot, better placed than anyone to know by what margin the attempt was defeated, was now convinced that, militarily, Paris had expended her last hope. Moltke's letter informing Trochu of the recapture of Orléans he regarded as a sign

· [1] 'There is pleasure in being in a boat whipped by the storm, when one is sure that it will not perish. . . .'

of war-weariness on the part of the enemy, and urged the Government to utilize it as an excuse for reopening the stalemated armistice negotiations. This was, he argued, France's last chance of obtaining reasonable terms from the Prussians; if the war were allowed to drag on further, they would only be more prone to making France pay for the extra cost to themselves; and meanwhile the French bargaining-power could only diminish. Favre and Picard agreed with Ducrot, but almost more than any other member of the Government, Trochu was in favour not only of continuing the fight, but of making another major attempt at a sortie. It seemed a curious reversal of form; in the days when there had been any hope at all of a Parisian initiative suc-ceeding, Trochu had played the role of Cunctator; now, when prospects were, to say the least, poor, Ducrot appears as the pessimist, attempting to lay a restraining hand upon his chief.

One of the factors encouraging Trochu was the report of successes being registered by Gambetta's recently constituted Army of the North, commanded by General Faidherbe. Following the eclipse of d'Aurelle and the defeat of Chanzy at Orléans, Faidherbe, a colonial soldier and former Governor of Senegal, had emerged as the ace in Gambetta's hand. A strict disciplinarian, he had managed to impose upon his force some of the military virtues, such as obedience, which were notably lacking among many of Gambetta's other levies. Within a week of the failure of the Great Sortie, Gambetta ordered Faidherbe to move towards Paris with a view to assisting a break-out through St.-Denis, towards the north-east. On December 9th, though racked with fever, Faidherbe seized Ham on the river Somme, thereby severing the rail link between Reims and Amiens. The local enemy commander, General von der Groeben, panicked and ordered the evacuation of Amiens. Although Faidherbe's action was little short of brilliant, it was of necessity a limited and ephemeral one, for he had fewer than 50,000 men, of whom probably only about half could be considered as effectives. And Ham was at least sixty-five miles away from Paris. Yet the news of its capture was sufficient for Trochu; and Ducrot, acting for all his new pessimism like a good military subordi-nate, at once threw himself into the plan for a new sortie to link up with Faidherbe somewhere north of Paris. The sector chosen was Le Bourget, the scene of the disaster precipitated by de Bellemare in October. On this flat plain, Trochu reckoned that his infantry would be able 'to form proper battle lines', under heavy covering fire from the fortresses of the north, and even Ducrot agreed that they would have the advantage of their batteries not being constantly dominated from superior heights as they had been on the Marne.

The operation began on December 21st. On the previous day,

Goncourt, paying a visit to his brother's grave, had encountered the
National Guard preparing to move at Place Clichy:

They are in grey cloaks with, on their backs, large packs surmounted
with tent pickets. Women and children surround them, keeping them
company until the last minute. A little girl carrying a tiny pack on her
back, with a ship's biscuit as make-believe army rations, is clutched
between the legs of her father. Young women, at the same time embarrassed and a little frightened, hold the rifle of a brother or a lover
who has made his way into a wineshop. . . .

Juliette Lambert, woken at dawn in another part of Paris by the same
spectacle, found that the sound of the drums and the singing of the
Marseillaise aroused in her 'an extraordinary emotion': 'A sortie
was going to be made, and the National Guard was going to be used!
It will win, I feel it, I am sure, because we are at the apogee of patriotic
exhortation and of courage.' Her optimism echoed the surprising
resurgence of morale after the failure of the Great Sortie, but it was
shared by few of the war correspondents in Paris; Bowles wrote on
December 19th 'I greatly fear a great disaster', and his views were
largely shared by a totally unconcerned Bismarck, engulfing great
portions of wild boar sent from his Varzin estates and complaining, as
news of the new sortie came in, 'there is always a dish too much'. The
strategy of the Paris leaders, he remarked between mouthfuls, reminded him of 'a French dancing-master, who is leading a quadrille,
and shouting to his pupils, now Right! now Left! . . . *Il va de ci, il
va de là. Comme là queue de notre chat.*'

For, once again, the Prussian High Command had got to know
about the impending sortie at least as early as the population of Paris.
It had been the old story of poor security; on the 18th Trochu had
issued one of his lengthy proclamations; the next day the city gates
had been closed. All of this reached German ears by means of the
Paris Press, and urgent activity at the forts adjacent to Le Bourget
had revealed to them the exact locality of the sortie. Since (and
doubtless as a result of) de Bellemare's action in October, the Prussians had already greatly strengthened their positions around Le
Bourget, and now the whole of the Second Guard Division was
alerted. With all advantage of surprise forfeited, the thermometer next
threw in its lot against the attackers. On the 15th, Blumenthal had
been noting in his journal 'very warm and unhealthy weather', but on
the eve of the sortie the mercury plunged. From the moment the
French assault troops began to advance across the flat, coverless plain
in the searing cold of the 21st, the operation resembled with tragic
fidelity what their grandsons were to experience in the First World

War. According to Archibald Forbes[1] of the *Daily News* who was in
the Saxon camp, 'the French fire was quite furious, half a dozen guns
flashing out at once; but it seemed wild. The Germans' was regular
as the beats of a pendulum of a clock.' Shells from well-established
Prussian cannon tore into the massed formations, and men fell cursing
an enemy they never saw. In many ways it was worse than Villiers;
certainly the attackers saw even less of the enemy infantry. An armoured train of *mitrailleuses* scuttled back and forth, but the invisible
enemy infantry seemed impervious to its bullets. Some of the French
troops, notably the Marines, fought with great gallantry, sustaining
heavy losses; by the evening of the 21st the Prussians could count
some 250 dead on the southern approaches of Le Bourget alone.
Once again, there were serious lapses in the higher command; for no
very clear reason, a whole Army Corps holding St.-Denis stood idly
by throughout the day without giving Ducrot's men any support.
And, once again, there were reports of *défaillances* among the National
Guard; according to Labouchere, 'One battalion did not stop until it
had found shelter within the walls of the town.'

Near Drancy Labouchere ran into Ducrot: 'The General had his
hood drawn over his head, and both he and his aide-de-camp looked
so glum, that I thought it just as well not to congratulate him upon
the operations of the day.' From the other side of the lines, Forbes
spotted a man galloping about on a white horse, whom he thought
'might have been Ducrot himself', trying to rally the forward troops;
'but all was of no use. He could not get his fellows' steam up . . . the
battalions went about, the white horse bringing up the rear at a slow
walk, as if marching to the funeral of his honour. . . .' When it was
clear that the frontal attack on Le Bourget had failed, Trochu (who
had assumed over-all command of the battle from Fort Aubervilliers)
ordered that saps and parallels be dug, as if laying siege to a town.
The order was utterly unrealistic; the frozen ground far too hard to
dig. That day it had already been so cold as to prompt O'Shea to
remark of the attackers: 'How they could have fingered a trigger is
more than I can make out. It was as much as one can do to hold the
telescope for a minute', but by nightfall the temperature had fallen
to −14°C. (about 7°F.) It was difficult even to erect tents on the
exposed and concrete-hard ground; there was no fuel for fires, and
through the usual sloppy muddle of the *Intendance*, some French
troops were left out on the battlefield for thirty-six hours without
food or wine. Bowles found them miserably attempting to huddle

---

[1] Forbes was to become of the most renowned war correspondents of his day,
and the author of biographies on both Louis-Napoleon and the Emperor
Wilhelm I of Germany.

together in shallow holes; to Ducrot the plight of his troops 'made one pity to see them ... heads wound about with scarves, their blankets folded and re-folded round their bodies, legs enveloped in rags. . . .' They no longer resembled soldiers; it was indeed, as Ducrot described, 'Moscow at the gates of Paris'. The next day Felix Whitehurst with the British Ambulance, spotting a white flag waving in no-man's-land, found a slightly wounded man who had tied a handkerchief to his tent-pole to attract attention; but he had frozen to death in the night, unfound. Another party came across a poor peasant, shot while trying to dig up vegetables, his knife still frozen to his hand. Sentries froze to death at their posts, and a total of over 900 frostbite cases were reported.

'The cold', said O'Shea, 'literally froze the martial ardour out of the French.' Back into Paris the Army shambled; never had suffering been greater, never in the war had French troops looked quite so wretched. Juliette Lambert who saw them on the 22nd felt all her previous hopes disintegrate; 'there was the desolation of desolations among the officers, revolt among the troops'. Apart from the frostbite victims, the French had suffered over 2,000 casualties (including a general whom some said had been shot by his own troops); compared with 14 officers and less than 500 men lost by the Prussian Guard. Meanwhile, unbeknown to Paris, Faidherbe had been beaten back by the grim-faced Manteuffel, and with him Paris's last chance of relief from the outside. The Government's reputation fell to a new low, with red placards springing up all over Paris demanding the resignation of Trochu. After the second battle of Le Bourget Ducrot declared, 'Hope of forcing the lines of investment abandoned even the most intrepid hearts', and finally, on the 22nd, the Government felt itself forced to send to Tours a balloon message warning that Paris would have no rations left after January 20th.

The prospects for Christmas could hardly have been gloomier.

Gambetta's Army of the Loire in Retreat

13. Over the Hill

ALTHOUGH the Prussians constantly seemed all too well informed about conditions in Paris, the defenders knew little of what life was like for the besieging forces. Perhaps it was just as well, for on the few occasions when Trochu's men captured an enemy redoubt it depressed them to discover just how solidly and how comfortably the invader had installed himself. W. H. Russell, *The Times* correspondent attached to the Prussian Crown Prince's army, remarked: 'I could not but compare the extraordinary energy or gusto with which the German Line regiments worked with the lassitude and dislike for siege works exemplified by our soldiery in the Crimea'. On his expeditions, Russell noted how each village around Paris had been transformed. He marvelled how, out of many a pleasant villa, 'the Prussians had made the most of them and thrown up beams inside for their men, and pierced them with loopholes, strengthening the line with stockades and wooden block-houses. Thus every village around Paris is a little fortress. Each is connected with the other by

trenches, and the approaches are covered with abattis, with emplace-
ments for field-guns'. Viollet-le-Duc, the expert on medieval fortresses then serving under Trochu as a Lieutenant-Colonel in the
engineers, was also vastly impressed by what he saw of the Prussian
positions once the Siege was over: ' . . . there is not one metre of
earth shifted without purpose. The least fold in the ground is utilized'
In open country between the fortified villages, the Prussians had dug
deep shelters in the shape of a cone. At the centre of the cone was a
large fire, around which, in cold weather, the troops slept, their
heads pointing outwards. One such cone was taken during the Great
Sortie and the contrast it offered with the miserable, wet, cold and
exposed positions of the French was more than distressing. It was a
contrast that would be repeated with dismal regularity as the German
entrenched themselves upon French soil forty-four years later.

In these fortifications, life was reasonably agreeable and secure.
Occasionally nightfall brought an unpleasant shock when someone
infringed the strict blackout precautions; but otherwise French shellfire did little to upset the leisurely routine of life. Out of the line,
the besiegers spent their time pleasantly enough, rowing on the lake
at Enghien or skating when the winter set in, or just goggling at the
wonders of Versailles. At first, as the Parisians by driving in all herds
and collecting all food within range of the metropolis had created a
kind of 'scorched earth', provisions had been scarce and extremely
expensive. But the admirable quartermasters of the Prussian Army
soon had an efficient system of supplies flowing direct from the
Fatherland. Army rations were supplemented with regular parcels
of *Wurst*, smoked cheese, and tobacco from sweethearts and well-
wishers at home. Archibald Forbes, the correspondent of the *Daily
News* with the Saxon forces to the north of Paris, recorded eating as
guest of the 103rd Regiment in the front line a sumptuous Christmas
dinner comprising sardines, caviare, various kinds of *Wurst*, boiled
beef and macaroni, roast mutton, and ending with luxuries long unheard of inside Paris—cheese, fresh butter, and fruit. By comparison
with the well-being of the Saxons, he was deeply moved by the suffering of French prisoners taken at Le Bourget, 'so ravenous with hunger
that the men grubbed in the gutter after turnip-tops and bones, and
turned over dirt-heaps in search of stray crusts of bread.'

For the Germans, excellent wine 'liberated' from French cellars was
also plentiful. But, despite this looting of cellars—the prerogative of
the conqueror everywhere—gratuitous vandalism was not excessive.
When the Siberian cold of December struck, doors, furniture,
panelling, and sometimes even grand pianos were smashed up for
firewood. This was, however, a common necessity of war in which—

o

as many an absentee French household discovered to his sorrow after the Siege—his own side was by no means retrograde; Edwin Child himself records in his diary for December how, during the freeze-up he and others of his company of the National Guard demolished an entire railway station to provide fuel. On the whole, the besiegers were well behaved and relations with the inhabitants could have been much worse. At Versailles, even a Frenchwoman confided to Russell that 'much as she detested the Prussians, she must admit that a woman could walk with greater immunity from affront along the Boulevards after dark than she could have done when the French troops were in garrison'. But, as many Prussians discovered, molestation was superfluous; in a time of hunger blandishments of chocolate and sugar have a remarkable way of purchasing smiles—if not more. So morale was excellent—and so was the troops' health, at least until the end of December.

Bismarck had made his first Siege headquarters in the Rothschilds' Château de Ferrières, where he received Jules Favre at the end of September. In the grounds there was a statue to Austria beneath which some ardent pan-Germanist had inscribed *'Heil dir Germania! Thy children are all one!'* and in a washerwoman's cottage Bismarck's entourage had been amused to find a copy of *Les Liaisons Dangereuses*. Bismarck himself had been less amused when the Rothschild steward insisted there was no wine in the house, for he claimed that to his certain knowledge 'there were more than 17,000 bottles'. However, the fabulous game-birds in the park at Ferrières offered compensation, and soon the steward proved more compliant. Bismarck's secretary, Dr. Moritz Busch, who kept a detailed account of the great man's tabletalk, reveals that when he was not throwing out brutally cynical observations on how to deal with France, or complaining at his treatment by Moltke and the King, or discoursing on the joys of hunting in his native Pomerania, conversation tended to revolve round the theme of food. At length the Iron Chancellor would propound to his court his special recipes for roast oysters; grumble that once upon a time he could devour eleven hard-boiled eggs for breakfast, but now he could only manage three; boast how in his diplomatic training he and his fellows practised drinking three-quarters of a bottle of champagne while negotiating. 'They drank the weak-headed ones below the table, then they asked them all sorts of things ... and forced them to make all sorts of concessions ... then they made them sign their names. ...' It was a revealing insight into the art of 'blood and iron' diplomacy.

Early in October, somewhat reluctantly, Bismarck moved his headquarters to Versailles, where the King had already set up court.

There the gluttonous obsession with the pleasures of his vast stomach continued, spiced by a liberal flow of offerings from adulators at home that prompted the faithful Busch to make entries like the following: 'Today's dinner was graced by a great trout pasty, the love-gift of a Berlin restaurant-keeper, who sent the Chancellor of the Confederation a cask of Vienna March beer along with it, and—his own photograph!' Even within Paris, few can have been so concerned with what they were eating: 'December 8th ... we had omelettes with mushrooms, and, as several times previously, pheasant and sauerkraut boiled in champagne....' 'December 13th ... we had turtle soup, and among other delicacies, a wild boar's head and a compote of raspberry jelly and mustard, which was excellent'. By comparison with some of these bizarre collations, a simple *salmi de rat* might almost have seemed more digestible, and at times even Bismarck rebelled. On December 21st he interrupted a mealtime discussion on the French sortie of the previous day to exclaim: 'There is always a dish too much. I had already decided to ruin my stomach with goose and olives, and here is Reinfeld ham, of which I cannot help taking too much, merely because I want to get my own share.... And here is Varzin wild boar, too!' At times the table talk ran to speculation on the bill of fare of the besieged, with one learned Herr Doktor dictating that elephant's trunk must be 'something like the tongue, and must taste like tongue'. Lightly the talk would stray to thoughts of cannibalism, to which Bismarck contributed: 'I believe I have read that they prefer women, who are, at least, not of their own sex....'

Such was the way in which, while Parisians drew in their belts ever tighter, life went on in the arch-enemy's household.

For all his gluttony, however, there was a certain Puritan simplicity about Bismarck's existence. Edward Blount who dined with him after the Siege noted that 'wax candles for instance, were stuck into black wine bottles; in one corner was a hard-looking campbed....' It was a simplicity shared by the Prussian royal court which had installed itself at Versailles, amid all the relics of extravaganza of the *Roi Soleil*. Of this kingdom in a saddle which had followed the victorious armies from the Rhine, all the principal components were present. There was the old King himself, august, courteous, usually to be seen dressed in Wellington boots, regimental overalls and a double-breasted uniform frock-coat, buttoned up to the throat; austerity in his early life had left with him a curiously unroyal habit of marking the level of wine left in the bottle at the end of each meal, and until quite late in life he had made do without a bathroom in his palace in Berlin. There was the Crown Prince of Prussia, a noble, bearded figure, smoking a short pipe that bore a royal eagle on its porcelain bowl. He was, for a Teutonic knight, strangely haunted by humanitarian anxieties[1] that set him apart from his fellows, and so restless that members of his staff complained they never had a chance to sit down in the evening. There was the stern-faced, moustachioed Minister of War, General von Roon, and of course there was the brooding genius who had brought them all to Versailles: Moltke, upon whose smooth, monastic features Russell of *The Times* could never look without being reminded of a 'calculating machine'. And everywhere—'as plenty as blackberries', wrote one Englishwoman—were the kings and princes, grand dukes and dukes, landgraves and margraves of the lesser states and principalities of Germany, each determined that their share in the greater glory of Prussia should not be neglected. A young Yorkshireman, Charlie Carter, thought 'all the swells . . . as healthy and stunning as possible', but what impressed Charles Ryan, an American surgeon, was their essential homeliness; how they 'walked about the streets munching alternately a piece of raw ham or sausage from one hand'. The businesslike, rather sombre display of the Prussian leaders had also struck Russell the moment he had arrived at Versailles; in contrast with the glittering French troops he had seen, there was 'little lace of gold or silver; but little glitter, save of button, spur, or scabbard . . .'.

Versailles was thoroughly, incongruously pervaded by the Lutheran spirit. The Crown Prince recalled how, when he had first arrived in September, his army had held an open field service of thanksgiving at the foot of the great terrace: 'I think Louis XIV would have turned in his grave. . . . We sang the same hymn, '*In Allen Meinen Taten*', that was chanted before marching off for the front on July 31st at Spires'. In the private chapel of Louis XIV, the royal entourage regularly attended sermons imbued with a great deal of the Sword of Gideon. All the ground-floor galleries of the great palace had been turned into a hospital and were filled with wounded Germans. The air was filled with the terrible odour of gangrene, and Bismarck raged at the poor medical conditions that prevailed; '. . . the rooms were cold, because they were not allowed to be heated for fear of spoiling the pictures on the walls. As if the life of a single soldier were not worth more than all the lumber of pictures in the château . . . .' Burials were frequent, and the French populace grew accustomed to the military bands playing the solemn strains of '*Wie Wohl ist Mir, O Freund der Seelen*'. On the sacred lawns outside the palace, where hitherto it had been almost a crime to set foot, the King and his staff

---

[1] During the war, he once shocked a German writer by declaring 'I hate this slaughter. I never desired the honours of war, and would gladly have left such glory to others . . .'.

unconcernedly exercised their horses. There were decoration ceremonies at the nearby Château Beauregard, once the home of Louis-
Napoleon's mistress, Miss Howard. Every day there was a steady
stream of visitors: American and British generals, frock-coated
politicians from Germany, and portraitists come to paint the leaders
against suitable backdrops of the city of Paris at their feet.

To a casual visitor, life at Versailles as the Siege dragged on gave
the appearance of calm monotony. But beneath the surface, all was
far from calm. First of all there was the overriding political problem
of German unity, closer to Bismarck's heart than any of the more
immediate issues raised by the war. Assiduously he had been working
behind the scenes to get the German states to agree to cap the triumph
over France by promoting the King of Prussia to be Emperor of all
Germans, thereby achieving the ultimate goal in his work of unification. Worry over the recalcitrance of Southern Germany had begun
to affect Bismarck physically; his varicose veins, which had troubled
him during the Austro-German war, were once again giving him
pain. Negotiations with the Bavarians, he complained to the faithful
Busch, had nearly collapsed on the most trivial of points; 'You
would never guess; it was the question of collars or epaulets.' Then,
on November 23rd, an excited Chancellor visited Busch:

'We have got our German unity, and our Emperor!' There was silence
for a moment. Then I begged to be allowed to take the pen, with which
he had signed the document.... Two empty champagne bottles stood
on the table. 'Bring us another', said the Chief to a servant, 'it is a great
occasion.'

But it was still far from plain sailing. When the old King first heard
of the suggestion, according to his heir, it 'put His Majesty quite
beside himself with displeasure . . . [he] held that the matter came
just as the most inopportune time possible'. . . . Bismarck grumbled
that he would remain in office not one hour after the war ended, and
there was repeated speculation as to whether the Iron Chancellor
might be about to retire. However, on New Year's Day, Archibald
Forbes heard the chaplain of a Saxon division preach words that in
contexts of a later epoch would have a peculiarly sinister ring: 'Already one race, one people, we are now one nation. . . .' Bismarck
had got his Empire.

Then came the question of German peace aims. What should
France be made to pay for Louis-Napoleon's war? Moltke and the
victorious General Staff, supported by public opinion at home,
wanted the whole of Alsace-Lorraine, the fair cities of Metz and
Strasbourg. Bismarck, with those far-sighted pale-blue eyes fixed
on the distant future, saw the dangers to Germany of having a

revanchiste France on her frontier, spoiling for an opportunity to grab back the lost territories. But the generals countered that the farther this frontier could be pushed back, the safer Germany would be. On this issue, Bismarck—and, later, a whole generation of European youth—were to be the losers.

Bitter divisions had also arisen over the actual conduct of the war, as it had dragged on and on beyond the capitulation at Sedan. Somehow at Versailles the spirit of the court of Louis XV, its intrigues and jealousies, had infected those stolid Teutons. When his thrusting but successful cousin, Prince Frederick-Charles, was created a field-marshal, the Crown Prince questioned peevishly: 'For how long will the possesion of this rank he has laid claim to satisfy his boundless ambition and overweening vanity?' Moltke was at odds with Roon, because he could not keep pace with demands for men and material. All the soldiers were in conflict with Bismarck, and many of them viewed the Crown Prince with suspicion, considering him too tender-hearted, and circulating ugly whispers as to the English-Liberal influence of his wife, Queen Victoria's daughter. The High Command no longer presented a picture of a well-oiled machine with all its components running in smooth unison, presided over by an infallible 'calculating machine', and harnessed to a task the achievement of which was a foregone conclusion. Fears of grave military reverses were never far away. None of this could of course be seen by the hard-pressed French; had Trochu been granted the gift of omniscience he might well have been persuaded to follow more energetically (though he declared it was constantly in his thoughts) the maxim of Suffren: '*Allez jusqu'à votre dernier coup de canon, c'est peut-être celui-là qui sera le salut*'.[1]

To begin with, at Versailles, chosen more for reasons of prestige than of strategy, the Prussian High Command felt itself constantly menaced, with the least French activity to the west of Paris capable of causing panic. Then, as long as there were substantial French armies at large in the provinces and another army intact in Paris, Prussian minds would be nagged by the fear of being caught between two fires. In early November, when Aurelle was registering his initial successes round Orléans, there had been serious talk at Moltke's headquarters of raising the Siege of Paris. Complaining of 'the inexpressibly distressing manner in which the operations of our armies are being conducted', von Blumenthal wrote at the time that 'the King fancies our own position in front of Paris to be extremely hazardous and will not sanction any troops being sent away. I have not been so depressed

[1] 'Go on until you fire your last shell, that is perhaps the one which will win.'

for a long time.' The prospect of having to lift the blockade was again voiced, briefly, during Ducrot's attempt to break out at the end of November. On December 16th, when Faidherbe was active round Amiens, the Crown Prince, who shared to the full his father's gloom about the way the war was going, entered in his diary: 'It looks more and more as though our military situation is once more to become critical in the north, as it already is in the south. . . . His Majesty's outlook on the immediate future is of the blackest. . . .' The recuperative powers of the French, as exploited by Gambetta, repeatedly dismayed him: 'It is positively amazing how quickly, after an Army has been beaten and put to flight, ever fresh masses of men are again got together and armed, which in their turn fight well.' Perhaps the most realistic fear of the Crown Prince was of a French flying column slashing the besieging army's tenuous link with its rear. It was a fear by no means limited to him alone: 'What would happen', speculated Dr. Busch anxiously as late as mid-December, after Faidherbe had pointed the way by cutting (temporarily) the railway from Reims to Amiens, if the French with 300,000 men from the south-east were fall on the thin line of our communications with Germany ? We might then easily be compelled even to give up Paris.' To a military historian it does seem astonishing that Gambetta did not think of such an operation until so late in the war—far too late, as will be seen shortly.

It was not only the French defenders who suffered from the phenomenal cold that struck in December. Even from the comparative luxury of Bismarck's quarters, Dr. Busch wrote 'in spite of the big beech logs which were burning in my fireplace, I could not get reasonably warm in my room . . .' and a fortnight later Russell was complaining that he was 'shrivelled up with cold'. How much worse it was for the men in the line can be imagined. The funeral ceremonies at Versailles became increasingly frequent, noted Russell, as more and more of the German wounded succumbed. By January, the sick list had reached thirty to forty men per company, and sometimes higher. With the fall in health, morale showed an alarming decline too. General von Stosch had reflected the expectations of every German private when he wrote home on November 23rd: 'I think that we shall be home by Christmas.' But, like MacArthur in Korea, he was to be sadly disappointed. A bitter Christmas came and went, with the troops still entrenched round Paris and the end of the war no nearer in sight. Daily the official communiqués repeated a formula that would become extremely familiar to Germans in 1914–18: 'Nothing new before Paris.' Photographs of sweethearts and next of kin were getting grubby and well-thumbed. Among his Saxons, Forbes noticed drunkenness sharply increasing.

The protraction of the war was noticeably affecting the leaders too. By November, the King was tormented with recurrent nightmares provoked by anxieties lest the retreat from Orléans might turn into a rout; Blumenthal was suffering badly from some nervous malady, and Bismarck's health was not improving. As Russell explained in a letter to Lord Carnarvon on January 7th, Bismarck was 'laid up and had varicose veins united with indiscriminate appetite—beer and champagne—great eating—no exercise—and mental labour.' To Russell on New Year's Eve, the Crown Prince 'expressed the utmost weariness of the war, because it was a useless expenditure of blood and prolonging of misery and suffering to all. . . .' Even Bismarck was prone to depression. He confided to his wife: 'The men are freezing and falling sick; the war is dragging out; the neutrals are interfering in our affairs . . . and France is arming.' Time no longer seemed to be on the Prussian side. The Crown Prince predicted sombrely:

The longer this struggle lasts, the better for the enemy and the worse for us. The public opinion of Europe has not remained unaffected by the spectacle. We are no longer looked upon as the innocent sufferers of wrong, but rather as the arrogant victors, no longer content with the conquest of the foe, but fain to bring about his utter ruin. No more do the French appear in the eyes of neutrals as a mendacious, contemptible nation, but as the heroic-hearted people that against overwhelming odds is defending its dearest possessions in honourable fight. . . . Bismarck has made us great and powerful, but he has robbed us of our friends, the sympathies of the world, and—our conscience.

Clearly something had to be done to hasten the end of the war, and there now seemed only one way left to achieve this. Bombard Paris into submission! It was a measure which public opinion at home now demanded with mounting impatience. When the Siege began, three courses had presented themselves to the Prussians: to take the city by frontal assault; to starve it out, like Metz; or to pound it with the mighty cannons of Krupp until, like Strasbourg, the civilian population cried for an end. Because of the effectiveness of the permanent fortifications of Paris, and the enormous casualties they could wreak upon an attacking infantry, the first course had never been seriously considered. On October 8th, the Crown Prince had written 'I count definitely on starving out the city', and it was a view shared at that time by all factions of Prussian leadership. Two weeks later, after Paris had already given the Prussians their first surprise by their determination to resist, von Blumenthal delivered a detailed appreciation:

I do not think that we can hope for the bombardment of Forts Issy, Vanves, and Montrouge before the 10th of November. . . . The forts will then have to be bombarded for at least four or five days, sapping pushed on, and batteries established in the second position. The two forts, Issy and Vanves, can then be assaulted by storm on the 1st of December. The real difficulties of the situation will then only begin; namely the attack on the *enceinte*. If we do succeed in capturing the *enceinte* by storm, it could not be before the 1st of January—a result which the mere investment of the fortress should bring about of itself by that date. It is impossible that Paris can be provisioned for so long. I am of the opinion that we ought not to think of a bombardment, but trust entirely to starvation.

Von Blumenthal had submitted his appreciation to Moltke, who 'agreed with me entirely' Upon this optimistic and erroneous supposition, Moltke based his strategy, and no priority was attached to preparing a siege train of heavy guns round Paris. His artillery commander, General von Hindersin, had been left behind in Sedan to organize transportation back to Germany of the 'booty'.

When he did arrive, in the way that military men have of pressing their own wares, von Hindersin immediately began canvassing for an early bombardment of Paris. His case soon gained, for political reasons, the support of Bismarck, followed by that of the King. But no issue was to divide the Prussian leaders with greater acrimony. On the other side, the anti-bombarders comprised the Crown Prince —for humanitarian reasons—and Moltke and most of the generals, with the exception of von Roon whom Bismarck had won over. Moltke's attitude was purely based on military considerations. Bismarck, in whom a layman's light-hearted regard for the problems of the military combined with rooted cynicism about French character, gaily reckoned that 'two or three shells' would suffice to scare Paris into capitulation, but Moltke—observing the minimal effect that French cannonades obtained upon his own positions—opposed any bombardment until at least 250 heavy guns could be assembled with an initial supply of 500 rounds each. And this effort, declared Moltke, must represent 'a lead weight tied to the legs of the Army'. There were mountainous logistic difficulties. All four of Moltke's Armies in France were supplied from a primitive railway network which converged at one bottleneck, Frouard on the Moselle, before linking with a single line to Germany. Only one line fed the forces of investment; even this was unviable until the fortress of Toul fell on September 25th, and daily it was jammed with the immense everyday requirements of a besieging army. Moreover, until Strasbourg and Metz were reduced by the end of October, the 250 heavy guns required for Paris were simply not available.

As October passed and the French showed no signs of surrender, Moltke—as a prudent commander, although maintaining his reservation

—realized he would have to provide for an eventual bombardment. Valuable time had already been lost, and it was obvious that further long delays could not be avoided. Even when the railway had been cleared as far as Nanteuil-sur-Marne, von Blumenthal noted that the Crown Prince's Army (to whom the burden of the bombardment would principally fall) had fifty-six miles to haul its ammunition, while 'we have only 600 carts in the siege park, and require at least 1,700'. Roads were so bad that it took the heavily laden waggons as long as nine days to make the return trip between Nanteuil and the siege park set up at Villacoublay, and many collapsed under their loads. With the freeze-up, fresh tribulations arrived. There was also the problem of the range of Herr Krupp's super-heavy guns, which, with a maximum of 5,600 metres, would reach no farther than the suburbs of Paris, unless the forts to the south of Paris were first silenced and then the guns moved forward again.

On November 20th, Bismarck was relaying vexedly the latest discussion about the bombardment to the sympathetic ears of Dr. Busch; 'I said to the King once more, so late as yesterday, that it was now full time for it, and he had nothing to say against me. He told me that he had ordered it, but the generals said they were not ready.' Blumenthal's account of the same meeting describes him as going so far as to declare to Bismarck 'that I would rather retire than permit it'. Blumenthal's nervous twitch was getting markedly worse, and so was Bismarck's indisposition. On the 28th, the latter grumbled to Busch: 'If they would give me the command-in-chief for four-and-twenty hours . . . I should give just one order–"fire!"'. . . If we had only begun the bombardment four weeks ago, we should in all probability have been by this time in Paris. . . .' As it was, the eager artillerist, General von Hindersin, had himself been forced to tell Bismarck only a few days previously that the bombardment could, in any case, not begin on January 1st. But meanwhile pressure at home was beginning to make itself felt more and more at Versailles. 'Make haste and bombard Paris, and have done with it', O'Shea read in one letter found upon a dead German, and it typified the attitudes of countless German wives and sweethearts. The Press, undoubtedly pepped up by the conniving Bismarck, was now roaring for the final act, and a little jingle made the rounds:

> *Bester Moltke, sei nicht dumm,*
> *Mach doch endlich: Bumm! Bumm! Bumm!*

Then, by the second week in December, things had reached such a pitch that a cable arrived from the Governor of Berlin expressing fears of insurrections. With gleeful *Schadenfreude*, Bismarck from his sickbed had the message passed on to the King.

There was an important Council of War on December 17th. Although Bismarck was excluded from it, Moltke had been swung round. The Crown Prince, though now in the minority, still staunchly resisted Bismarck and the generals. His was the sole voice to be raised pleading on humanitarian grounds within the German camp at that time, and well may one speculate how much happier the fate of twentieth-century Europe might have been, had not an untimely death[1] wrenched this well-intentioned kindly figure from the German throne, leaving it instead to his son, young Wilhelm II. Even the policy of starving Paris into submission had disturbed him, and in his diaries he reveals himself to have been constantly worrying about the fate of the children in the city. As the threat of the bombardment drew closer, Russell wrote in a letter to Lord Carnarvon how the Crown Prince had confided to him: 'I pass sleepless hours when I think of the women and children'; and as the guns actually blazed out he was to be tortured by the recent discovery 'that at Strasbourg, as a result of the siege, a hospital for children who have lost limbs has had to be established'. But on December 17th the victory was once again Bismarck's. It was agreed that first of all there should be an experimental bombardment of Mont Avron, an isolated plateau beyond the line of forts to the east of Paris where the French had established themselves in support of the Great Sortie. If that succeeded, the southern forts would be subjected to an all-out pounding, following which the city itself would become the target. It would begin just as soon as the guns and their ammunition were ready.

*　　*　　*

Out beyond Prussian Versailles, in the country still in French hands, Gambetta was persisting in his endeavours to carry on the *guerre à outrance*; even though deprived of the comfort of knowing just what alarm his activities were still capable of provoking at enemy H.Q. But the month of December brought little comfort of any kind. The defeat at Orléans and the failure of the Great Sortie had marked the watershed in the affairs of Gamebtta's armies, and since then morale had slumped. In many areas, the war had become a broken-backed guerilla affair conducted by irregular *franc-tireurs*, in which atrocities led to savage counter-atrocities with the civilian population bearing the brunt of Prussian reprisals. There were more and more

---

[1] On his death, his brother-in-law, the future Edward VII, wrote to his son George: 'Try . . . never to forget Uncle Fritz. He was one of the finest and noblest characters ever known; if he had a fault, he was too good for this world.'

cases of Gambetta's soldiery being refused shelter and support as
weariness with the ruinous war grew among the civilians of the
provinces. Under the endless miles of dispiriting retreat, the papier-
mâché soles of hastily made boots disintegrated, leaving many
soldiers barefooted in glacial conditions. They cursed Gambetta
when they heard of such optimistic utterances as one telegram sent
from Bourges in December: 'Things are getting better here very fast
and a few days from now you will hear news of us. Fine cigars, keep
cheerful. . . .' Corruption was rife among the generals—one was
noted for setting up his headquarters in a local brothel—and discipline
in many units was non-existent. As the Crown Prince remarked, 'It
is typical of the French how, so long as the struggle lasts, even when
they are in the field against their will, they always fight bravely, but
directly it is all over they throw to the winds, so to speak, all that is
generally expected of soldiers.' Woes beset Gambetta on every side.
Bakunin the anarchist had made an appearance in Lyons, over which
for a brief time the Red Flag had flown and a Commune presided;
in Marseilles on October 31st, an adventurer called Cluseret who had
fought in the American Civil War had carried out a revolt rather
more successfully than Flourens in Paris; there were uprisings in
various parts of the south, all of which had to be quelled. Finally,
the Prussian advance had forced Gambetta to take the humiliating
step of evacuating his 'Government' from Tours to Bordeaux,
thereby creating a precedent to be followed in two successive wars.

One after another, he had fallen out with his generals after they
disappointed him. Aurelle had been sacked and submitted to vitu-
peration in which his conduct was approximated to Bazaine's, and
under such accusations of treachery more than one general preferred
to relinquish his command. There was no escaping the fact that by
January all Gambetta's armies in the field which might have relieved
Paris had failed. Chanzy, for all the remarkable spirit that he still
managed to instil into the Army of the Loire, had been pushed back
to Le Mans and largely neutralized. Faidherbe, though performing
wonders in the north in Flanders and Artois until he was brought
to bay at St.-Quentin, clearly had no hope now of breaking through
to join Trochu. It was little wonder that Gambetta was reported to
be looking old and depressed. But true to his character he still refused
to abandon hope, and there remained to him one trick comprising
two rather dog-eared cards.

While Louis-Napoleon was still on the throne, that great Italian
champion of liberal causes and the downtrodden, Giuseppe Garibaldi,
had actually contemplated launching his volunteers into an invasion
of France. But when the new Republic was proclaimed and France

became the underdog, his sympathies performed a rapid turnabout. On October 7th, accompanied by his sons, Ricciotti and Menotti, and collecting several thousand troops as he went, the leonine old warrior landed in Marseilles; his fingers bent with rheumatism, his legs so lame from past wounds that at times he had to be carried in a litter, but he was still indomitable. In Tours, Crémieux greeted the news with 'My God—we needed only *that!*' and the Garibaldians were assigned an unimportant role in the south-east of France, to keep them out of mischief. This Garibaldi quickly turned to good advantage. On November 19th, Ricciotti and 560 men (plus one of the ubiquitous *Daily News* correspondents) attacked the German garrison at Châtillon on the upper reaches of the Seine (not to be confused with the Châtillon on the southern fringe of Paris), some 120 miles south-east of Paris. The Germans there numbered nearly a thousand, but Ricciotti succeeded in capturing 167 of them as well as much booty, and in killing the colonel in command. Ricciotti then withdrew, with a loss of only three killed and twelve wounded. This brilliant *coup de main* threw the local German forces into great anxiety, the ripples of which reached Versailles; for Châtillon was but sixty crow's-flight miles away from the Prussians' single supply-line to Paris. As the Crown Prince gloomily predicted: 'Should the Gari-baldians succeed in falling on Vitry-le-François or any other point of our railway lines, they would be in a position to cut off for the moment all our communications with the frontier and home.' A week after Châtillon, less successfully, Garibaldi risked a pitched battle in attempting to retake Dijon, and narrowly escaped disaster at the hands of General von Werder. But Garibaldi's exploits had belatedly kindled a bright vision in the mind of that amateur strategist, Gambetta.

In mid-December, but not until mid-December, Gambetta decided to expedite Bourbaki, the last of his generals, with an army one hundred thousand strong, to join up with Garibaldi and raise the Siege of Paris by severing Prussian communications through a right hook aimed at Lorraine. The choice could hardly have been less fortunate; had it been Chanzy or Faidherbe the prospects might have been much better. But Bourbaki the dapper Guardsman, object of that merry jingle of Empire days,[1] was still Imperialist at heart, as unenthusiastic about Gambetta and the Republic as he was about continuing the war itself. In turn his civil superiors lacked confidence in him, and indeed he had little confidence left in himself; as he

---

[1] *Ce chic exquis*
Par les Turcos acquis,
Ils le doivent à qui?
A Bourbaki!'

grumbled to one of his young officers who had proposed a night operation, 'I'm twenty years too old. Generals should be your age.' Transporting Bourbaki's army to the south-east proved too great a strain for Freycinet's railways, and in the arctic weather the troops suffered appallingly. When they reached the Dijon area, ill fed and ill clad, their fighting value was sharply diminished. There was much confusion in liaising with Garibaldi, combined with inept staff-work and an uninspiring example set by Bourbaki; and climatic conditions were such that only a Russian army could have attacked with vigour. Yet, despite all this, under the new threat von Werder was forced temporarily to evacuate the important centre of Dijon, causing once again gravest alarums at Versailles. As late as January 14th, the Crown Prince was offering fervent prayers: 'We trust to heaven that, in his extraordinarily strong defensive position, he will succeed in holding back General Bourbaki'.

But it was altogether too late. Secretary Wickham Hoffman of the U.S. Legation in Paris who had served as a colonel under General Grant at the Siege of Vicksburg was one American Civil War veteran who was astounded that 'no serious effort was ever made to cut the German lines of communication'. He later recalled how General Sheridan, the Unionist Cavalry leader, had exclaimed to him—despite his pro-German sympathies, and using a word reminiscent of the *mot de Cambronne*—that if he 'had been outside with thirty thousand cavalry, he would have made the King * * * *'. Sheridan in fact had the lowest opinion of the employment of cavalry by both sides in the Franco-Prussian War, and had Gambetta possessed the services of a Jeb Stuart, or even of Sheridan himself—let alone of a Robert E. Lee—the outcome of the Siege and indeed the whole war might well have been different. Certainly, that a serious initiative against Moltke's communications was not contemplated much earlier must be rated one of the worst strategical errors of the Tours Government. The Prussian commander dispatched to repair the damage done by Bourbaki, General von Manteuffel, himself admitted that the Garibaldi–Bourbaki campaign might well have been, for the French, 'the most fortunate of the war of 1870–71'. As it was, it was to provide the final French catastrophe of that war.

Prussian shells fall in Montparnasse

14. Paris Bombarded

ON the cold morning of December 27th, a French colonel called Heintzler and his wife were giving a breakfast party for several friends at the recently acquired outpost of Avron. Suddenly the party was spoiled by a heavy Prussian shell which burst without warning in the room. Six of the breakfasters were killed outright, the host and hostess were gravely wounded, and only the regimental doctor and a servant emerged unscathed. Two days later Felix Whitehurst recorded seeing the remains of the six victims in his hospital: 'but it was such a human ruin that no individuality could be recognised'. Ceaselessly during those two days Prussian guns of a calibre hitherto unknown continued to plunge their huge shells down on Avron. A grim new phase of the Siege had opened.

The Avron plateau was a magnificent natural feature due east of Paris, with commanding views on all sides. But it lay beyond the line of French forts, like an island, isolated from Fort Rosny by a deep and wide ravine. It had been seized by the French to support Ducrot's Great Sortie, and should logically have been abandoned when the Sortie failed, but it was the kind of textbook position that military men are habitually reluctant to give up. Despite the fact that the artillery was commanded by Colonel Stoffel, the enlightened former Military Attaché in Berlin who had done his best to warn France what to expect of Moltke's army, little had been done during the four weeks of French tenancy to organize Avron's defences. Beyond the usual half-heartedness and procrastination, there was the sheer incapacity of undernourished men to dig in the frozen earth. Entrenchments had been prepared to withstand little more than field-artillery fire. As O'Shea remarked, *the earth had hardly been stirred*. Forbes, who on the other side of the lines was watching the Saxons vigorously felling trees as they brought up their huge guns, was amazed that the French should remain apparently deaf, and blind, to all the fracas of these preparations. To bombard this one small position, Moltke had brought up seventy-six of his heaviest guns: Krupp steel 24-pounders which in fact threw 56-lb. projectiles, and even bigger Krupp pieces that could fling a shell of 110 lb. Later, an observer told O'Shea in awe how he had seen one crater thrown up at Avron by the Krupp guns measuring four and a half feet across and a yard deep; not much by twentieth-century standards, but a record for those days. The shallow French entrenchments were swiftly shattered; young troops unnerved by this hideous new experience ran screaming to the rear; and one after another Colonel Stoffel's gun positions were silenced. All day the searing bombardment continued. The next day the German gunners re-sighted their pieces, and the shelling was resumed with even more lethal accuracy. Trochu came out to survey the scene, as did Tommy Bowles, and both displayed their customary courage under fire. But by the 29th the French were left with no alternative but to evacuate the whole plateau.

After the forty-eight-hour German bombardment, the Avron plateau presented a forlorn picture. Even the battle-hardened Forbes who visited it in the wake of the Saxons was appalled:

No man who long followed this war but must have become so familiar with the aspect of slain men, that the original thrill and turn of the blood at the sight had faded into a memory of the past, at which he all but smiled when it dimly recurred to him; but the terrible ghastliness of those dead transcended anything I had ever seen, or even dreamt of, in the shuddering nightmare after my first battle-field. Remember how they had been slain. Not with the nimble bullet of the needle-gun, that drills a minute hole through a man and leaves him undisfigured, unless it has chanced to strike his face; not with the sharp stab of the bayonet, but slaughtered with missiles of terrible weight, shattered into fragments by explosions of many pounds of powder, mangled and torn by massive fragments of iron.

It was a reaction more or less novel to war correspondents—until 1914, and before familiarity with mutilation bred insensibility.

On the other side, O'Shea was staggered how Avron had been 'literally shaven' by the huge projectiles; but at the same time he noted shrewdly that 'their very dimensions militated against their destructiveness in instances, as they penetrated to such a depth that their large splinters at bursting lodged in the ground, harmlessly displacing the clay'. And in fact the German shells, filled only with black powder (since T.N.T. was yet to be invented), caused less than a hundred casualties. It was their moral, rather than their physical effect, that drove the French off Avron. But the German success was sufficient to have a telling influence upon both sides. In Paris, morale suffered a serious setback at this first unequivocal sign that the enemy's offensive potential might be stronger than the Paris defences. The cannonade, heard all too plainly in the centre of the city, sounded a deadly harbinger in Parisian minds of what lay in store for themselves. Wrote Washburne: 'The Parisians are "low down" today, and I think Trochu is going down. But he is as hard to get rid of as some of the officers we had during the time of the Rebellion.' At Versailles Avron was regarded as a 'dummy run' that had exceeded all hopes. Even the Crown Prince was forced to admit 'we have enjoyed a fine success we never expected', and his principal supporter in the anti-bombardment camp, Blumenthal, declared that the 'brilliant' results at Avron had now persuaded him; 'it is quite possible that the time has come when a bombardment of the forts and a portion of the city may be successful'. For, he concluded, it was apparent 'the French are no longer making a serious stand'. On New Year's Eve, after a long session, the King of Prussia gave the order for the bombardment of Paris to begin as soon as possible. It was an act fertilizing the ovum of a new monster and a new myth that would long affront and appal world opinion, under the name of 'Teutonic frightfulness'. The Crown Prince wrote in his diary: 'May we not have to repent our folly. . . .!'

In order that the heavy guns could bombard the city unmolested from close-in positions, the southern forts had first of all to be silenced. From Fort Issy, a French corporal of the *Mobiles* wrote to his father on New Year's Day '. . . in short, life is tolerable; but alas I have an idea that I shall not long enjoy this relative well-being . . . there is bombardment in the air.' Vigorously the garrisons were set to work filling sandbags and carrying out other last-minute preparations on the defences. On January 5th, the same corporal was again writing to his father: 'At 8 o'clock he [a fellow soldier] had just opened one of our windows looking out on to Châtillon, to empty a

certain mess-tin *from which one does not eat*, when a shell, passing
over his head, traversed our barrack room to explode I don't know
where. . . . In a flash, everybody was at the bottom of his bed, leaping
into his boots.' Within a short time Prussian 220-mm. guns firing
from the dominating Châtillon heights (wrenched from Ducrot in
September) had smashed most of the gun embrasures, turned the interior court into a zone of death, and rendered uninhabitable the
barracks that faced outwards. Supplementing the heavy guns the
Prussians also employed a weapon the French gunners disliked even
more: low-trajectory 'rampart guns' firing a 20-mm. projectile that
could penetrate ramparts and kill at 1,300 yards, and thereby make
repair work on the defences extremely unpleasant. By 2 p.m. on the
same day, the guns of Issy had been silenced; as the French were to
discover again in 1914, their fortifications were simply not adequate to
face the latest products of Herr Krupp. The story was similar at Fort
Vanves, where nine guns had been swiftly knocked out and urgent
pleas for support addressed in vain to Forts Issy and Montrouge.
Only Montrouge still replied with any vigour, but as Moltke later
wrote, 'the forts never again got the best of it'. Yet even to his shrewd
gaze the long-term, material inefficacy of the huge shells of that day
remained unrevealed, as indeed it had been during the success at
Avron. Throughout the bombardment in which as many as 60,000
shells were rained down on it, Fort Vanves lost only 20 men killed
out of its garrison of 1,730. Likewise, only 18 were killed and 80
wounded out of 1,900 in Issy. Although three out of four of Issy's
barracks were destroyed, the ramparts remained intact and in none
of the forts was any breach made in the actual defences. These facts
were not, however, apparent to Moltke; the demonstrative results at
Issy and Vanves were that the Prussian siege batteries could now
move forward as much as 750 yards nearer to the heart of Paris.

Even as the forts were still being pounded into submission, on
January 5th the bombardment of Paris proper began; in the coldly
technical words of Moltke, 'an elevation of 30 degrees, by a peculiar
contrivance, sent the shot into the heart of the city'. What was
probably the first shell burst in the Rue Lalande on the Left Bank,
scattering its fragments over a baby asleep on its cradle. Other great
masses of iron furrowed up the Montparnasse Cemetery, whose
occupants were beyond harm, but one which fell near the Luxembourg
literally sliced in two a little girl on her way home from school.
Tragedy followed on tragedy; Henry Markheim, writing under the
sobriquet of the 'Oxford Graduate', recorded morbidly how he had
seen, that first day, 'an old woman's head blown off', and three days
later his own house near the Invalides was struck; one unhappy

mother, said Juliette Lambert, returned home to find her two children obliterated by a shell; among the foreign community, a young American—Charles Swager of Louisville, Kentucky—who had come to France 'for his health', had his foot carried away and died a month later from the injury; six women were killed in a food queue; in the Quartier Latin a *cantinière* of the National Guard was killed in her bed, and in a *bistro* several tipplers were killed by a shell bursting in a street that must have seemed, to the survivors, appropriately named—Rue de l'Enfer. Wrote Goncourt on the 6th: 'The shells have begun falling in the Rue Boileau. . . . Tomorrow, no doubt, they will be falling here; and even if they do not kill me, they will destroy everything I still love in life. . . . On every doorstep, women and children stand, half frightened, half inquisitive. . . .'

The shells fell at a rate of between three and four hundred a day: a small proportion of those devoted to the southern forts, yet they fell with a regularity that reminded Goncourt of 'the action of a steam-engine piston'. In general, the bombardment did not begin before 10 p.m. and went on for four or five hours at night, which Dr. Alan Herbert thought was 'very good-natured' of the Prussians. Sir Edward Blount disagreed, noting on January 17th: 'The noise is tremendous, and even in the Rue de la Paix I cannot sleep', although nothing had fallen closer than the Invalides. The range of the German cannon, using heavily increased charges and firing at maximum angles, surprised both sides. No shells actually fell on the Right Bank of the Seine, though one reached the Pont Notre-Dame, but hitherto unheard-of ranges of 7,500 yards were steadily registered. The domes of the Panthéon and the Invalides became favourite targets, and the areas around them suffered the most heavily. The Salpetrière Hospital, a prominent building with a large Red Cross on its roof and two thousand aged women and a thousand lunatics, was hit repeatedly, giving rise to the suspicion that the Prussians were deliberately firing on hospitals. The Odéon Theatre, also in use as a temporary hospital, was hit twice, and shells ruined the priceless collection of orchids under glass in the Jardin des Plantes. Other shells hit the beautiful church of St.-Sulpice off the Boulevard St.-Germain and destroyed a painting of the Last Judgement. More usefully, hits scored on the balloon workshops in the Gare d'Orléans forced this highly inflammable industry to seek refuge in the Gare de l'Est; at the same time they also hit the house of the daughter of the inventor of the balloon, Mlle de Montgolfier, killing two men.

Although the doughty eighty-six-year-old spinster was one who refused to budge, the unnerving and ever-present threat of death or mutilation without warning in the middle of the night—not unlike what Londoners experienced from the V.2 rockets in 1944–5—drove many inhabitants of the Left Bank from their homes. They numbered perhaps as many as 20,000. The refugees reminded Théophile Gautier of a 'migration of Indians carrying their ancestors rolled in bison skins; the women follow, pressing against their meagre breast a pale suckling which they try to envelope in a shred of shawl. . . . Other fugitives walk bent beneath the weight of some piece of furniture; nothing more picturesquely sinister than this cortege advancing in the shadows, lit up by the livid reflection of the snow and the red fire from the shells.'

Even Goncourt's circle was affected, with the Germanophile Renan being among the first to retire under the hail of Teutonic steel. The refugees added yet another strain to the already extenuated provisioning system, and many on leaving their *arrondissement* were threatened with total loss of their rations.

After the initial fear of the unknown had passed, indignation became the principal reaction to the bombardment; indignation that reached a climax on January 11th with the solemn funeral of six small children, killed by the same shell. It was the defilement of the *ville lumière*, the holy city, as much as the random disembowelling of innocent children or the shelling of hospitals that outraged most Parisians, while the affront to humanitarian principles earned France stronger support abroad than at any other time during the war. Edward Blount, then acting as Consul in the absence of any senior British representative, wrote: 'At first I did not believe that the Prussians picked out particular buildings, churches, hospitals, etc., but as they have thrown their missiles into the Salpetrière, it appears to me that they must have meant it. . . .' (The volcanic Rochefort, strangely enough, was one who did not believe 'the enemy laid their batteries intentionally on the hospitals', but when, in answer to a protest from Trochu, Moltke replied to the effect that he hoped soon to push his guns near enough to spot the Red Cross flags more clearly, the Prussian case was hardly assisted.) Most of the British correspondents felt particularly disgusted by the brutality of the indiscriminate bombardment. Bowles commented: 'It might perhaps have been expected that the God-fearing and laws-of-war-respecting Prussians would have followed the ordinary usages in such cases, and would have given notice before bombarding a city full of defenceless people . . .' and O'Shea even more outspokenly condemned the bombardment as 'a Massacre of Innocents, a Carnival of Blood'. 'Although I was a neutral', he wrote in his memoirs published sixteen years later, 'and individually suffered nothing from this bombardment, it kindled ire and resentment in my breast; and now, although I have erased many very bitter reflections in my diary, I look back upon it with loathing.' Even Russell at Versailles, who had been led to believe by the Prussian High Command that shells were not to be thrown into the city, was shocked to 'see their guns were fired at the very highest angles consistent with safety and I could watch the explosions far inside the enceinte . . .'. One of the few dissentient voices in Paris itself was that of Felix Whitehurst, who observed with dispassionate logic, and some justification: 'Like a door, a city must be *ouverte ou fermée*. If it is an open city, the law of nations says you must not fire on it, only summon it, and then take it by an attack. If it is a fortified city, behind forts, you may bombard it when and how you can.' Nevertheless, all the principal nations made diplomatic protests to the Prussians—with the exception of the unrepresented British, which, as Edward Blount remarked, 'produced a painful effect'.

But as relief grew at the relatively little damage and casualties caused, indignation was rapidly replaced by a remarkable indifference to the bombardment. In a manner somewhat reminiscent of the London blitz, this new common menace temporarily united the various strata of Paris society as it never had been at any other stage of the Siege. Already by January 8th, Washburne could write: 'The carelessness and nonchalance of the Parisians in all this business is wonderful. . . . Ladies and gentlemen now make excursions to the Point du Jour to see the shells fall.' The bombardment in fact became a valuable distraction from the drab grimness of Siege life. Wrote another American, Nathan Sheppard: 'Last night we were a thousand or two strong on the Place de la Concorde, looking at the bombs. Everybody enjoyed it hugely.' The normally unadventurous Labouchere left his hotel for the Point du Jour to 'see myself what truth there was in the announcement that we were being bombarded'. There he found that speculators 'with telescopes, were offering to show the Prussian artillerymen for one sou'. Later he overheard a mother threatening an undisciplined child, 'If you do not behave better I will not take you to see the bombardment'. In his favourite vein of cynicism,[1] Labouchere remarked how 'the number of persons who have been

---

[1] A certain degree of indifference to the suffering inflicted by the bombardment seems to have rubbed off on the British correspondents themselves. While walking with the representative of *The Times* one day, Labouchere came across a man 'with his legs shattered, his head in the lap of a girl who was crying bitterly'. They did their best for him, but the man was evidently beyond hope. Professional instincts then asserted themselves; 'Shall you give a description of what we have seen?' *The Times* enquired politely, 'It was on my side of the road.' Labouchere replied 'No, we both saw it, and it belongs to both of us'. Finally the two journalists tossed for sole rights, and *The Times* won.

all but hit by shells is enormous'. Everybody had his bombardment anecdote, and with the acute commercial sense of the true Parisian, small boys made a killing in the sale of shell-fragment souvenirs. Juliette Lambert overheard one street urchin saying to another 'I tell you that the shells are falling here! You can see the hole, it's a good place!', and towards the end of the Siege Goncourt suffered some anxiety on a bus through 'a man in a white overcoat, holding out a shell to the conductor of the omnibus: "Hold this for me while I get on, and be careful! For Gods sake, be careful!"' Familiarity bred a remarkable degree of contempt; a Professor of History lecturing at the Collège de France when a shell exploded said calmly 'If it does not incommode you, Messieurs, we shall continue!', and an absent-minded friend of Jean Renoir was heard to inquire in the middle of the bombardment 'Who's firing?'

Life went on remarkably as usual. Pails of water were ordered to be kept at the ready in every house, and doors left unlocked in case passers-by should seek refuge from the shells. Most of the prizes from the Louvre had already been evacuated to Brittany before the invest-ment began; the Venus de Milo had been crated up and stowed in a secret vault by the Prefect of Police; and now stacks of sandbags en-cased the Arc de Triomphe and such works of art as the *Chevaux de Marly*. Goncourt noticed on January 9th an absence of people in the streets of the Left Bank, and the local bus service was disrupted when a shell fell on the depot, killing eight horses; but otherwise 'there is no panic or alarm. Everybody seems to be leading his usual life, and the café proprietors, with admirable sang-froid, are replacing the mirrors shattered by the blast of exploding shells.' Indeed, in some hearts the beginning of the bombardment had awoken new optimism. Trochu for one reckoned that the all-out Prussian attack he had awaited so long was about to begin; while National Guardsman Edwin Child noted in his diary for January 5th: 'A most terrible cannonade going on all day, we were in hopes of being sent out.' Expectations, however, had soon been dashed and he added gloomily: 'but it seems as if we should make a campaign without a chance of fighting *tant pis ou peut-être tant mieux*'. Four days later, he was con-tenting himself with dodging shells at the Point du Jour: 'after a few minutes I could tell by the sound whether they would fall to the right or left and when I fancied one was likely to come unpleasantly close I ran behind a tree. Returned homeward without a scratch, and in Rue Rivoli met Maria and her mistress. Walked to Trocadero as-sisting them in turns to a slide.' The following day, after an extensive exploration of the Left Bank, he drew an important conclusion that other Parisians were also reaching: 'Became more and more convinced of the impossibility of effectually bombarding Paris, the houses being built of such solid blocks of stone that they could only be destroyed piecemeal. One bomb simply displaces one stone, in spite of their enormous weight. . . .'

The Prussian bombardment was proving a failure. Although Herr Krupp had personally offered Roon six of the 560-mm. giant mortars firing a 1,000-lb. shell that had been displayed at the Great Exhibition of 1867, none of these were actually delivered, and the other guns used—monsters as they were by nineteenth-century standards—were simply inadequate to the task. Added to this, the increased charges used had caused a large number to wear out, or blow up in the faces of their crews. Thus, when the final reckoning came to be made, it was found that in the three weeks the bombardment of Paris lasted only 97 people were actually killed and 278 wounded, and 1,400 buildings were damaged for an expenditure of approximately 12,000 shells; while the Prussians themselves lost several hundred gunners to French counter-battery fire.[1] Well might Washburne declare on January 16th that the bombardment 'had not so far had the effect of hastening a surrender. On the other hand, it apparently had made the people more firm and determined.'

Again, the inefficacy of the bombardment was concealed from the initiators. From Versailles on January 8th, Russell of *The Times* could see 'Paris burning in three distinct quarters. . . . It was a calm, frosty night—moon shining, stars bright—lights in the windows of Versailles—noise of laughter and tinkling of glasses.' At the other side of the city, Forbes observed a 'continuous white streak of smoke' above the southern *arrondissements*, and in a flight of fancy compared the 'death pall hanging over Paris to Dumfries in the midst of the cholera epidemic in 1832'. One of the first indications the Prussians received that their 'terror weapon' was not as terrible as they had hoped was when a ravishing French widow, Mme Cordier, the sister of none other than the gallant General de Galliffet of Sedan fame, requested permission to *enter* the city. Russell found her in deep mourning, leaning on the arm of a Prussian staff officer; 'the neatest small feet in the highest heeled of boots, a little dog trotting after her. Everything about her, face, figure, waist, was petite, except her eyes and her cavalier.' The obviously smitten Russell explained chivalrously that her request was motivated by a desire to reward 'the devotion of a M. de B.— who is inside the walls.' Blumenthal added in astonishment, 'She drove from Tours in a well-equipped carriage, in complete insouciance of the many shells flying over her head.' The day

[1] By comparison, the winter shelling of Leningrad in 1941–2 resulted in a total of 519 civilians killed, and 1,447 wounded.

Mme Cordier obtained her free pass to visit her lover, the Crown Prince was revealing himself once more prey to all the doubts and anguish he had hitherto harboured about the bombardment: 'Weeks ago Count Bismarck promised himself the most prodigious results, once three shells had exploded in the place, yet on this the fifth day of the bombardment these still remain unrealized.' Roon, he noticed, was now suffering from chronic asthma and Bismarck 'only just recovering from nervous rheumatic pains in the feet'. Three days later, on January 12th, the Crown Prince commented on hearing that Prussian shells had fallen among a Parisian church congregation: 'Such a piece of news wrings my heart.'

But at Versailles there was in the offing another event, one of the most momentous in modern European history, to distract Prussian minds from the shortcomings of the bombardment. In a solemn ceremony within that glittering hall where only so few years ago Queen Victoria had danced with Louis-Napoleon amid all the splendours of the Second Empire, King Wilhelm I of Prussia had himself proclaimed Kaiser of the Germans. At last Bismarck had had his way. W. H. Russell described the scene in the Hall of Mirrors:

It is 12 o'clock. The boom of a gun far away rolls above the voices in the Court hailing the Emperor King. Then there is a hush of expectation, and then rich and sonorous rise the massive strains of the chorale chanted by the men of regimental bands assembled in a choir, as the King, bearing his helmet in his hand, and dressed in full uniform as a German General stalked slowly up the long gallery, and bowing to the clergy in front of the temporary altar opposite him, halted and dressed himself right and front, and then twirling his heavy moustache with his disengaged hand, surveyed the scene at each side of him.

Russell's comment on this extraordinary event taking place beneath a painting of Frenchmen chastising Germans within the great palace which bears the inscription '*à toutes les Gloires de la France*' was— 'What a humorous jade Fortune is!' But the humour was barely apparent to a Frenchman like Goncourt who mourned prophetically: 'That really marks the end of the greatness of France'. Not only had something of the old order of Europe died; to the injury of the bombardment of Paris an appalling insult had been added, and the combination of the two would jointly inject a special bitterness into Franco-German relations for the next three-quarters of a century.

On the eleventh day of the Prussian shelling, Markheim, the 'Oxford Graduate' remarked, 'the prospect of possible starvation is fraught with such unknown terror that it renders us quite callous to the dangers of bombardment'. These 'unknown terrors' of starvation

were not very far distant for a great many Parisians, and now January
brought with it a new form of suffering, one that malnutrition greatly
exacerbated. The cold! Fuel was now running desperately short,
causing, as O'Shea noted, 'the greatest privation'. Already by November 20th coal-gas, urgently required for the balloon service, had been
stringently rationed and largely replaced by oil; five days later oil
was requisitioned, and the streets of the *ville lumière* plunged into
darkness. And it seemed as if even the elements had deserted the
Parisian cause; first there had been the abnormal autumn rainfalls,
producing the Marne floods that had helped wreck Ducrot's Great
Sortie; and now—since the onset of the savage freeze-up in mid-
December—Paris was gripped by the bitterest winter in living
memory. Wrote O'Shea, 'We might be able to rattle a four-in-hand
across the Seine . . . that is, if we had not eaten the team in advance';
and Wickham Hoffman of the American Legation, not normally given
to exaggeration, related how hungry rats had apparently broken into
the kitchen of a compatriot, eaten the grease off some unwashed
plates, then later died of cold in his bedroom. With coal gone, wood
was rapidly running out, and there were no horses to transport what
little remained. To keep warm in her house, Juliette Lambert noted
that she needed 100 kilogrames of wood per day, while in fact she was
entitled to only 75 kilograms *a week*; 'What is one to do?' As in every
privation, it was worse for the poor. Markheim, who visited Belleville
with his mother shortly after Christmas, was shocked to see that

scarcely a vestige remained of the young saplings that peopled this outer
line of boulevards, except here and there a stump with the bars of the iron
fence that protected the tree lying wrenched and twisted on the soil.
Further on, huge trunks lay prostrate, around which swarmed an eager
crowd of women and children, hacking with their puny hatchets at the
twigs and bark. . . . All Belleville had turned out into the streets, and
swarmed in ant-like procession, *divina vis populi*, each one bearing away
his portion of the spoil, branch, log, faggot, sweepings of small twigs
shovelled into aprons and pinafores—a desperate struggle for existence.
Hard by was the cemetery of Père la Chaise. . . .We paused awhile to
look into a long wide trench which the diggers were carrying through the
eastern slope of the hill. . . . Sorrowing relatives gazed tearfully at the
closely packed *fosse commune*, crushing its dead in such tight embrace.
'Never mind', quoth a grave-digger, who recked not of the agonies of the
tomb, 'there's room enough for all of 'em. . . .'

Soon, when their own neighbourhood had been denuded, the
frantic fuel-scavengers began to descend on the more fashionable
parts of Paris. 'I hear', wrote Washburne on December 27th, 'that
several yards were broken into last night. The high board fences

enclosing the vacant lots on the Rue de Chaillot, near the legation, were all torn down and carried off last night.' That same day, on the Avenue de l'Impératrice (today the Avenue Foch) Goncourt had run into

a menacing crowd, surrounded by terrible female faces, hooded by a Madras, and giving the impression of Furies, among the rabble. . . . The explanation is a depot of wood for making charcoal which they have begun to pillage. The cold, the freeze-up, the lack of fuel to heat their minute rations of meat, has thrown this female populace into a fury and they hurl themselves upon trellis-works, plank barricades, ripping up everything that comes to their enraged hands. In their work of destruction, these women are assisted by appalling urchins, who place step-ladders up against the trees in the Avenue de l'Impératrice, breaking off anything they can reach, each dragging behind him his small faggot, tied by a string, held by a hand plunged in pocket.

Three weeks later, it was the turn of the Champs-Élysées themselves. There Goncourt watched 'a cloud of children, armed with hatchets, knives, anything that would cut, slashing off pieces of bark with which they filled their hands, their pockets, their pinafores, while in the hole left by the felled tree, one could see the heads of old women, engaged in digging up with picks all that remained of the roots.' Meanwhile, in a contrast so typical of the Siege, at a nearby café there were 'seven or eight young Mobile officers, parading and coquetting around a *lorette*, deciding on a menu of fantasy and intellectual imagination for dinner'.

Protection against the cold was in no way assisted by the dilapidated state of clothing. The fuel shortage had closed down most of the laundries, and men took to wearing their shirts inside out: 'Imagine', Louis Péguret boasted to his sister, 'I have worn a shirt for 39 days!' Even women of the upper classes, recorded Tommy Bowles, 'are now dressed, without exception, in sombre and modest attire which makes them look like refined upper-housemaids', though Felix Whitehurst qualified this by declaring; 'It is not that there are no fine garments, but to go out decently dressed would now expose you to risk of arrest as a Prussian spy, or that which is worse, to be recognized as an Englishman.' Again, want was most acute among the poor, many of whom had been forced to pawn their meagre garments in order to buy food. At the end of December the Government had made allocations of flannel, and, in one of their many acts of charity during the Siege, the Rothschilds supplied the poor with clothes for some 48,000 children and a similar number of adults. But still none of this was sufficient, even though augmented by a new suggestion of the Laputan inventors of Paris: shirts made of newspaper (euphemistically

christened *flanelle de Santé*), which the newspapers themselves
boasted could 'be worn a consecutive month without ceasing to be
comfortable!'

Hand in hand with malnutrition and the cold came that inevitable
concomitant, disease. Smallpox cases mounted rapidly, as did typhoid,
now that the Siege forced Paris to draw most of her drinking water
unfiltered from the foul Seine. Outbreaks were worst among the
overcrowded and insanitary slums, but under the circumstances it
was perhaps little short of miraculous that no major epidemic occurred during the Siege. Still, January brought an alarming increase
in the number of deaths; Labouchere complained from his hotel
sanctuary, 'they nail up the coffins in the room just over mine every
night'. As may be deduced from the table below, it was pneumonia
caused by the cold that particularly helped to augment the mortality
figures:

Cause	DEATHS 1st week of Siege	10th week	18th week (January 14th—21st)
Smallpox	158	386	380
Typhoid	45	103	375
Respiratory ailments	123	170	1,084
All causes	1,266	1,927	4,444

What these statistics do not reveal is that the highest mortality rate
lay among infants, deprived of milk and warmth, then among the
women, followed by the old and unemployed. As the Russians themselves were to discover during the Siege of Leningrad, anyone who
was occupied—even the National Guardsman warming himself in the
bistro while his wife queued for food—had a better chance of survival.

By mid-January the Government felt forced to take a step which
stripped the last illusion about the state of Paris's food supplies.
Bread, the staff of life, was rationed to just over half a pound per adult
per day, and half this amount for children under five; though its
quality was bad enough to cause more infant deaths from enteritis.
'Black, heavy, miserable stuff, made of flour, oat-meal, peas, beans
and rice,' commented Washburne. 'The cook put a loaf of it in my
hands and I thought it was a pig of Galena lead. . . .' The ration of
meat (when there was any to be had) had now also been reduced to
roughly a quarter of a pound a week for adults. 'Personally I am pretty
well', Edward Blount could continue to write, 'I still have one horse

and some cow, biscuits and *confiture*, but the misery around me is frightful.' It was no exaggeration. Those foreigners who could yet afford to dine out were regularly shocked by the pinched and wan faces of children begging at the doors of the restaurants. Labouchere records visiting the house of an absent friend to find 'three families installed in it—one family, consisting of a father, a mother, and three children, were boiling a piece of horse meat about four inches square, in a bucket full of water. This exceedingly thin soup was to last them for three days. The day before they had each had a carrot.' On January 7th, Goncourt with his usual aptness summed up the outlook of a dying city; 'The sufferings of Paris during the siege? A joke for two months. In the third month the joke went sour. Now nobody finds it funny any more, and we are moving fast towards starvation....'

Strategically, the situation confronting Trochu at this time was aptly likened by one of the Britons in Paris to that of 'a king left alone on the board, with enough room for a certain number of moves until the final mate'. As in the chess parallel, only a miracle could now save Paris and the pious Trochu's first move after the Prussian bombardment began was to pray for one. Informed by a historically-minded chaplain that it was the anniversary of the repulse of the Huns from the gates of Paris, fourteen centuries earlier, by Ste. Geneviève, Trochu promptly framed another of those renownedly verbose proclamations announcing how he had invoked the intercession of the city's patron saint. When the Cabinet was informed, the effect upon its more anticlerical members—as Trochu himself admitted—was more explosive than any Prussian shell, with Jules Ferry leaping out of his chair as if one had just gone off underneath him. The proclamation was quashed, accompanied by the brutal advice from Victor Hugo to 'Throw your prayer-book to the dying, General, and let's have a breakthrough in a hurry'. Instead, Trochu was permitted to declare on January 6th, even more rashly, 'The Governor of Paris will not capitulate'. Thus, with miracles barred by the Republican *laïcs*, the Government was forced to consider a more pragmatic approach to the city's last moves. The leaders were now seriously divided. Ducrot had long since lost any hope of military success; all he could suggest was that the Paris forces be split into penny-packets and infiltrated through the Prussian lines to join up with Gambetta, and for himself he requested—typically—that, as there was nothing left for him to achieve in Paris, he be allowed to balloon out also to fight with Gambetta. Trochu and a majority felt that the city should hold out as long as the food lasted, and make one last major attempt at a sortie. In this desperate counsel they were swayed, as so often in the past, by yet another exaggerated dispatch from Gambetta, revealing Bourbaki's march, which in one grand sweep would sever the enemy's lines of communication. But not even the most hardened optimist on Trochu's staff now gave a sortie any prospect of success.

It was not, however, until a Government session on January 15th that the possibility of surrender was actually mentioned. Then, as on the eve of the Great Sortie at the end of November, not military considerations—nor even the problem of food—precipitated a fateful decision. As Ducrot was to remark on the Siege in retrospect, 'virtually the whole defence revolved around a single thing! *fear of a rebellion.* . . . One was constantly obliged to face two enemies: one which, night and day, tightened his ring of fire and steel, the other which at every instant was awaiting the moment to hurl itself upon the Hôtel de Ville. . . .' Upon the first suggestion that the city should now surrender, one doubt immediately presented itself to all minds: would the Reds permit a surrender ? Although Flourens and their other leaders gaoled after October 31st still languished in the Mazas, neither the Red newspapers nor the Clubs had in any way reduced the violence of their attacks upon the Government. It was a source of amazement to Washburne, as it was to most foreigners in Paris, that the Government had taken no further action. Now, with matters growing more desperate, the angry voices reached a new pitch. There were proposals from the Belleville Clubs that the Government should march out through the Prussian lines, preceded by choirs of virgins; there were outcries of 'you are 400,000 strong, and you let them shell us!'; but above all, and louder than ever before, came the demands for a *sortie torrentielle* of the citizenry of Paris, of the National Guard. These were backed up by red-dyed posters that surreptitiously appeared all over Paris on January 6th. Drafted by Delescluze and signed by 'The Delegates of the Twenty *Arrondissements*', these called for the Government to be instantly replaced by the mystical Commune, and—once again—for the immediate employment in battle of the National Guard. That the working population of Paris after all its suffering should still be so ardent for battle was astonishing, but it was also unmistakable. As Corporal Louis Péguret of the National Guard, who sympathized with the Reds, wrote at the beginning of January, 'The majority, the mass of inhabitants have redoubled their energy to resist, and desire whole-heartedly to march on the Prussians to crush them.' (On the other hand, among the bourgeoisie, the slogan 'Rather Bismarck than Blanqui' was beginning to be heard with increasing regularity.) Word of emotions prevailing in Paris had even reached Versailles; on January 16, Blumenthal recorded, 'It looks as though in Paris a catastrophe were about to happen to the present rulers there. According to the Parisian newspapers, red-hot speeches are being made in the working mens' clubs of the Belleville quarter, and they are calling for a Commune—i.e. a Reign of Terror.'

On that same day, after its usual procrastinations, the Government of National Defence made up its mind, one of its members having sown the seed of an idea with the remark: 'When there are 10,000 National Guards lying on the ground, opinion will calm down'. It was an idea that at this late hour was even popular with the generals, despite their past contempt for the military virtues of the National Guard; for the regular Army, and particularly the provincial *Mobiles*, were getting increasingly fed up that the Parisians had not taken their fair share in the fighting for their city. So it was decided. In three days time a last attempt at a sortie would be made—what Trochu described, *ex post facto*, as the 'Supreme Effort' (although it was patently a little late in the day for such an effort); this time throwing in the National Guard. It would be based on a plan by Trochu's deputy, General Schmitz, and would strike to the west of Paris, towards Buzenval in the sector nearest to Versailles. It was also, needless to say, the sector most strongly defended by the Prussians, and if it had any strategic justification at all it was the vague idea of linking up with Chanzy who was supposedly, once again, waiting in the wings.

The Liberation of Flourens

15. Breaking-Point

FOR all its considerable numbers, and the length of time these had now been under arms, the National Guard could still by no stretch of the imagination be termed a formidable force. There were good battalions, and good commanders—like Arthur de Fonvielle, the brother of Wilfred the balloonist, who had fought for Shamyl in the Caucasian wars against the Russians. But these were in the minority. What Parisians remembered was how the swaggering Belleville units had turned and fled at the first cannon-ball during the Great Sortie; how others had done the same at the second Le Bourget; and the ubiquitous indiscipline and drunkenness of the National Guard as a whole. One battalion had been sent out to Fort Issy as relief for the exhausted garrison, but was returned the following day by the fort commandant with the explanation that it had arrived drunk and fought among itself all night, and that he preferred to make do with his worn-out

225

men. Another, the 200th, reached Créteil during the Great Sortie in such a state of intoxication that it had to be dispatched to the rear by General Thomas himself. Following this episode, the peppery old general made a public example of the battalion, declaring that in such circumstances the National Guard constituted an additional danger; an action by which he, according to d'Hérisson, 'signed his own death warrant'. In the boredom of its idleness, the Guard had an excuse for their drunkenness; and all too little preventive discipline was ever enforced. One admiral did try to cure the drunks by placing them in a post of danger for several nights; but more typical was the case of the grocer who, according to Whitehurst, declined to go on guard 'because it is cold and wet'; or of the entire 147th Battalion which refused to march to the outposts because their wives had received no allowances during their last tour of duty. To the Bellevillites there was indeed something fundamentally undesirable about discipline. 'Of what use is discipline?' an orator at the Club Favier had asked, with an unusual display of (perhaps misdirected) logic, when Flourens's *Tirailleurs* were dissolved; 'How has it served us to the present time? It has resulted in our being beaten by the Prussians. It was the disciplined troops which lost at Reichshoffen, at Forbach, at Sedan; it was the disciplined troops which capitulated at Metz.'

With some justification he might also have asked what was the point of the National Guard at all? Month after month it had been given no other tasks than to stand guard passively on the walls or to quell disorders in Paris (admittedly, most of the latter it had caused itself). Something of the grinding boredom and sense of futility emerges from the diary entries of Guardsman Edwin Child; even though, in the enthusiasm and optimism of youth, he continued almost to the bitter end to hope for a more gallant and purposeful role. On December 1st, during the Great Sortie, he begins:

Up at 7. Reunion at 8 o'clock of our company at its usual place (Gare St. Lazare). We then marched to Champs Elysées, behind the Palais d'Industrie, and met the 3 other companies and went through the '*école de bataillon*' under our Commandant, about 2 hours of it. In afternoon retired several articles, trousers, etc., and had them changed for various reasons, too large, etc. ...

December 2nd. Up at 7. Reunion of the Company at 8, no drill but in place of it a few words of advice and warning from the Captain, order to fetch our '*capotes*', military overcoats, at 2 p.m. ... Upon fetching overcoat at 2, were ordered to be ready fully equipped by ½ past, rushed to *magasin*, put on coat and knapsack and managed to be on time, marched to the Madeleine and there remained under arms, in hourly expectation of being ordered outside, till 7 p.m., when we fetched our cartridges, being told to hold ourselves ready for ½ past 3 a.m. Not a very much admired order as all of us were almost frozen, after standing nearly 8 hours without any exercise.

December 3rd. Up at ¼ to 3. Dressed myself with all the appurtenances and proceeded to Madeleine but on arriving there met the Sergeant Major who told us the movement had been countermanded, none to my chagrin by any means, it having snowed best part of night, returned without grumbling to my bed and rose again at 8, dressed a second time but without *sac ou bidons* and proceeded to our *place de réunion*, where we received commands to rest at our homes and hold ourselves ready at any moment to start. . . .

December 4th. Up at 7. Had a jolly good breakfast and then walked to our *rendez-vous* and from there to the Madeleine where we remained about 1 hour, but at last about ½ past 10 we heard the long-wished for order *'Bataillon ! par ½ sections, en ligne ! marche !'* and then with drums beating and smiling faces we were fairly en route in search of glory, we traversed the Rue de Rivoli, Bastille and left Paris by the Porte de Charenton. . . .

Child's battalion arrived at Créteil near the Marne just as the defeated troops were returning from it, following the failure of the Great Sortie. The action was over. Child continues:

December 5th . . . Under arms at 1 p.m. for the inspection of our guns. Afterwards had a stroll along the Marne and watched the *artillerie* and the Mobiles crossing the river upon a bridge of boats, a very picturesque sight, the sky being of a spotless blue and it being a clear frosty day; after this I went marauding trying to find something to soften my bed. . . .

December 6th. . . . Amateur concert (one squad) in eve, obliged to do my share, gave them *Rule Britannia*. Were warned that an attack was hourly expected so could only sleep by fits and starts. . . .

On the 11th, after ten days in the line without seeing a shot fired, Child returned to Paris:

By the time we arrived at the Madeleine, we were smothered in mud from head to foot and myself I was almost dead with fatigue the distance being about 14 kilometres and not being yet *endurci* to the weight of the sack upon my shoulders. . . .

Once again, on December 18th, on the eve of the second Battle of Le Bourget, Child's battalion was ordered to stand by.

. . . Up at 4, at 5 under arms and en route for our *Grande Garde* (outpost) this time in the trenches and directly in front of the Fort of Montrouge; the bullets of which whistling over our heads and shaking our frail habitation composed of loose stones piled one upon the other almost to pieces and about our ears. . . . At 11 I was ordered on service at the guard house, guard every four hours, the post being almost a sinecure, remained there till Tuesday morning. . . .

December 23rd. Rose about ½ past 4, prepared coffee and at 6 started with full *accoutrements* to act as reserve and in case of need to support a party of sailors at work making a new trench more in advance; close to where we were hidden, behind a wall, was a pond that was speedily turned into a series of slides, and that kept the blood in circulation, it being fearfully cold. We were not wanted during the day so about 6 returned to our quarters, made up a good fire and tried to sleep but found it impossible the cold being too intense, in spite of our blankets and capotes, so smoked away the night. . . .

December 24th. Sliding, etc., anything to keep warm. . . .

December 25th (Christmas Day). . . . Card playing. 3 times on guard. 2 hours day & 2 separate hours at night. At 5 p.m. with 14 others volunteered, to make a short reconnaissance in the village of Bagneux, which lay right in front of us. Reached about 20 of the houses but without discovering the enemy. . . .

December 27th. At 10 a.m. with several others went to Fort Montrouge and fetched some targets that we afterwards fixed in a large field, where the rest of the company was each man firing 4 shots (put 2 in). Afterwards retired to our quarters and amused ourselves as best we could cleaning our guns, etc. . . .

December 28th. We were rather lucky. this time being in a shed hid by a wall with a stove in the middle red hot; to obtain wood, had to walk some distance and demolished a railway station (Cachan) entirely, roof, floor, doors and everything. Was nominated or rather proposed as Corporal a vacancy having occurred, but in consequence of a few remarks as to nationality, I retired from the 'contest' to prevent any disagreement, and at the request of the Captain. Fearfully cold, freezing hard.

Back in Paris on January 5th, Child then records how his battalion marched to Place de la Concorde;

. . . there being passed in review by the General Clément Thomas, commander-in-chief of the National Guards, who naturally much gratified with our martial appearance, etc., etc., all 'bunkum' as Americans would say. . . .

Disillusion had begun to set in; by January 12th, Edwin was ruminating gloomily:

. . . Wonder whether I shall see the end, or leave my carcase to rot in the field of battle, cannot say that I much care which way it is, but would like to stick a Prussian before the latter arrives. . . .

What kept the National Guard plunged in this heart-breaking futility was partly the whole bourgeois *Weltanschauung* of nineteenth-century France, its roots deeply implanted in the Terror of '93. Even so normally lucid an intellectual as Goncourt could hardly be rational when speaking of the proletariat, as witness when on December 29th he wrote 'I am above all astonished at the demoralization of the working class caused by the luxury of well-being which the Emperor provided. I see this class become completely flabby. From everything that was virile, martial, enterprising about it, it has become loquacious and extremely economic with its skin. . . . The National Defence has found nothing but cowards in the battalions from La Villette. The debauchery of the National Guard exceeds anything that the imagination of a well-brought-up man could invent. . . .' If anything, bourgeois views of the proletarian National Guards had—not surprisingly—hardened in the course of the Siege, as a result of fresh fears awakened by the various demonstrations—and particularly that of October 31st. Ducrot in his summarizing remarks on the National Guard referred to 'the conscienceless mob, what M. Thiers rightly called the "vile multitude", which we armed.' All the way through the Siege, just as the bourgeoisie never lost its fear, so the professional soldiers never abandoned their contempt of the National Guard, and Trochu readily seized upon such excuses as the poor showing of the Belleville units at the Great Sortie to disband whole battalions. No attempt was ever made to give the National Guard any proper training, and deaf ears were repeatedly turned to all appeals to equip it with *chassepot* rifles, in place of the obsolete *tabatière* muskets. It was a disastrous example of half measures; and no wonder that the *Garde* performed so poorly on the few occasions they had been under fire! In response to popular pressures, the Government had raised 400,000 National Guards; it had trained them and armed them insufficiently to be of any military value, but just enough to constitute the most potent revolutionary threat the nineteenth century had yet seen.

Just what use *could* have been made of the Paris National Guard is suggested by the heroic performance of its equivalent, the *Opolchenie*, at the beginning of the Siege of Leningrad. Although some of its units were thrown into battle after only one day of training, they fought with great courage and tenacity actually alongside the regular troops at the front, and, out of 300,000 volunteers (a number of whom were women), four divisions were all but wiped out while others suffered about 50 per cent casualties.

On January 18th the National Guard began its approach march to the west of Paris, ready to attack the world's most efficient professional army. Goncourt was there watching them:

It was a grandiose, soul-stirring sight, that army marching towards the guns booming in the distance, an army with, in its midst, grey-bearded civilians who were fathers, beardless youngsters who were sons, and in its open ranks women carrying their husband's or their lover's rifle slung across their backs. And it is impossible to convey the picturesque touch brought to the war by this citizen multitude escorted by cabs, unpainted omnibuses, and removal vans converted into army provision waggons.

There did indeed seem to be present a flicker of the spirit of the taxicabs speeding to the Marne in 1914, and Juliette Lambert also was struck how the National Guards marched 'behind the bands, eager to act, and resolved to dare all in this last effort to save our Paris'. (But, although half of the nearly 100,000 men earmarked for the sortie came from the National Guard, once again Edwin Child was disappointed. The 18th, the day after his 23rd birthday, found him at the other side of Paris, 'playing cards in the afternoon with an unusually fine music of cannons to while away the time'. The following day when the sortie was in full swing, after more card-playing, he was ordered back into the city: '*Sac au dos* at 4 p.m. for Paris, but from some mismanagement rested under arms till $\frac{1}{4}$ to 7 then moved forwards but felt fatigued before starting.')

Among the regulars waiting to go into the attack, Tommy Bowles, who as usual had pressed forward as close to the front as he could get, found a rather different mood: 'They showed little enthusiasm, I thought, their drums and trumpets were silent, and even the perpetual chatter and badinage which usually mark the progress of a French regiment were absent. . . .' Spirits were not improved by the inevitable chaos in the assembly areas, due to poor staff-work, such as in the past had preceded almost every initiative by the Paris garrison. Only two bridges across the Seine were available, and incredibly enough no orders had been given to remove the barricades on them, so that a hopeless tangle of men, guns, and ambulances piled up against these. There ensued, noted Bowles, 'endless confusion and delay'. To make matters worse, once again the weather played traitor to the French. A sudden thaw on the 17th had turned the frozen earth to slippery, treacherous mud, and an opaque mist[1] rendered

[1] On hearing Trochu had complained that, because of the mist, he could not see his troops, Rochefort was heard to remark savagely: 'Thank God; if he could see them he would recall them!'

even more difficult the process of disentanglement. The front of the attack lay immediately under the guns of Mont-Valérien, across the root of the same Gennevilliers peninsula where Ducrot had originally wanted to break out in October. Trochu's plan was to move simultaneously with three columns: Vinoy on the left against Montretout, Bellemare towards Buzenval in the centre and across what is now St.-Cloud racetrack, and Ducrot on the right marching over the scene of his earlier undertaking at Malmaison. This time it was Ducrot himself who was critically late; his delay, wrote O'Shea acidly, 'explained by the circumstance that he had some seven and a half miles English to traverse in the dark, on a railway hampered by obstructions, and a high-road occupied by a train of artillery which had lost its way. This occurred not in Cochin-China, but a short drive from Paris, on a bit of country every feature of which could have been mastered in half an hour by an intelligent huntsman, with the aid of the staff-maps and a reconnoitring glass.'

Scheduled to begin at 6 a.m., the attack was postponed for several hours, and finally went in without Ducrot. The delay, continued O'Shea, was not 'the only blunder which dislocated Trochu's conception. The men of the National Guard had been kept under arms, packs on their backs and four days' provisions, making in all a burden of four stone weight, from two in the morning. The Line, too, were haggard and worn with fatigue, and marched without elasticity of step when they got the word to go forward at ten o'clock.' Yet the French chalked up some surprisingly encouraging initial successes. On the left Vinoy's Zouaves, retrieving the name they had lost at Châtillon, took by surprise a Posen regiment at Montretout (an indication that even some of Moltke's forces were no longer fighting with their usual mettle), and advanced into the outskirts of St.-Cloud itself. In the centre, Bellemare actually secured a foothold on the Garches–La Bergerie plateau, from which the Prussian guns could dominate the attacking French and which was a vital defence to Versailles. There, the whirr and rattle of the French *mitrailleuses* little more than two miles away had drawn the German Emperor on the second day of his reign to the aqueduct of Marly, whence he and his court watched the battle with anxiety. On his way to join the Emperor, Bismarck met a musketeer who 'gives us to understand we are in a bad way, the enemy being already in the wood on the hills behind La Celle'. His secretary, Dr. Busch, noted down in his diary serious fears that the French 'might press on further and force us to evacuate Versailles', and the Crown Prince went so far as to reveal that on the following morning, when he 'arrived at the Prefecture for the usual report with His Majesty, the *fourgons* were standing there ready loaded, and all preparations had been made for a hasty departure!' Gone was the festive mood of yesterday's coronation; the Hall of Mirrors where the glittering kings and princes were now being replaced by rows of Prussian wounded had become, according to W. H. Russell, 'a valley of lamentation'.

But in fact Bellemare, unsupported by Ducrot on his right, was soon stuck. The adventurous Bowles, who was on the spot, considered that

the officers, if they had been worth their salt and capable of leading their men, might, I am convinced, have taken the whole of Garches, batteries and all; but they seemed to lose their heads, and not to know what to do or whither to go, though I am sorry to say a few of them solved the latter question by going 'back again' down the valley. Their defects were of course not without influence upon the men.

By the afternoon, the Prussian guns had checked the attack all along the line, the French had lost their initiative without taking any of the key points, and Bowles left the battlefield that evening gloomily predicting that 'the real struggle will begin tomorrow under anything but favourable conditions'.

Ducrot had arrived on the scene, and as usual was observed conspicuously mounted on his white charger, well ahead of his troops; once again, his incredible good luck preserved him unscathed, but his temerity did nothing to alter the course of the battle. With comparable courage, two women serving as *cantinières* seized the *chassepots* of fallen soldiers, and themselves fell in the front rank. There were grimmer scenes recorded that day. Trochu's aide, Captain d'Hérisson, was struggling with a mount unnerved by a near miss, when he saw his orderly gallop past him: 'He was still in the saddle. But one of the fragments of the shell had torn away the whole of the lower part of his stomach, and had carried away his intestines. The upper part of his body was only attached to the lower part by the spinal column, and there was an enormous red, gaping space from his sides to his thighs. He threw up his arms and fell, while his horse, hit in the withers, galloped off into space to the accompaniment of the clink of the empty stirrups. A cold shiver ran through me.' To Labouchere, 'The most painful scene during the battle was the sight[1] of a French soldier felled by French bullets. He was a private in the 119th Battalion, and refused to advance. His commander remonstrated. The private shot him. General Bellemare, who was near,

[1] Labouchere, however, appears to have got no closer to the actual battlefield than he had on past occasions, so the 'scene' was probably not observed at first hand, though it has been corroborated by other witnesses.

ordered the man to be killed at once. A file was drawn up and fired on him; he fell, and was supposed to be dead. Some *brancardiers* soon afterwards passing by, and thinking that he had been wounded in the battle, placed him on a stretcher. It was then discovered that he was still alive. A soldier went up to him to finish him off, but his gun missed fire. He was then handed another, when he blew out the wretched man's brains.'

On the whole, and particularly at Montretout, the National Guard had fought with unexpected distinction. But on Bellemare's crucial front, Bowles now witnessed an ominous occurrence;

... on the crest of the hill, the fighting·was going on heavily, and our first line, composed of Mobiles, was skirmishing in the woods some thirty yards in front. Just then a regiment of National Guards was brought up by an aide-de-camp to support them, and very pretty they looked, coming up the hill at a run, with fixed bayonets, the colonel puffing heavily in front, and the aide-de-camp brandishing his sabre and cheering them on. When they got a little below me, however, and began to hear the balls singing past their heads, they ducked to a man, with unanimity that was positively comic, slackened speed, stopped by common consent, and then falling flat on their stomachs, opened fire to the front on the Mobiles!'

It was not the only episode where the wretchedly trained National Guard lost its head. In one regiment observed by d'Hérisson, 'the drummer beat the charge; the colonel gave the word of command, '*En avant!*' the regiment shouted, '*Vive la République!*', and—nobody stirred. That went on for three hours—Ducrot appeared on the scene in person and shouted '*En avant!*' He was answered by shouts, but nobody moved.' A Colonel Rochebrune was killed by what was later asserted to be a bullet from one of the *tabatière* muskets issued to the National Guard; and as darkness fell, Trochu's own party was fired upon by some disorientated National Guards, who claimed to have mistaken them for Uhlans, and a young lieutenant, de Langle de Cary, received a bullet through the chest.

It was virtually the last salute that Trochu would receive from his army. That night he recognized the Buzenval sortie had failed, and the next morning orders to withdraw were issued. But it was more than the Army's tenuous threads of discipline could withstand. Wrote Ducrot:

Hardly was the word retreat pronounced than in the rear areas on the left the débâcle began... everything broke up, everything went.... On the roads the muddle was terrifying ... across the open country the National Guards were taking to their heels in every direction..... Soldiers, wandering, lost, searched for their company, their officers.

As the National Guard streamed through the streets of Paris there were once again those piteous cries of '*Nous sommes trahis*', and this time few Parisians doubted that they were nearly at the end of the line. The Buzenval battlefield presented a horrible spectacle; members of the American Ambulance told Washburne 'the whole country was literally covered with the dead and wounded, and five hundred ambulances were not half sufficient to bring them away'. Trochu called for an armistice of two or three days, but there were those who claimed that he did so as much to underline the facts of life to the Reds as to bury the dead. The facts were certainly shocking enough; for a total of only 700 Prussian casualties, the French had lost over 4,000 in dead and wounded, of which 1,500 were from the National Guard. After the war Trochu testified that in his estimate they had themselves been responsible for one-eighth of the French casualties, but there was no doubting that in its aim of the 'bleeding' of the National Guard the Government had been eminently successful. To O'Shea it was 'an indisputable crime' to throw in the National Guard at Buzenval, and few of his fellow correspondents disagreed with him.

Bowles accompanied the defeated, bedraggled army back inside the city walls: 'On my return to Paris I found the Avenue de la Grande Armée lined on each side by a dense crowd of people eager for news.... They listened sadly in little groups to the complaints of marching, counter-marching, hunger, want of rest, and bad leadership which constitute the staple of the National Guards' account of the affair.' Earlier another Englishman, William Brown, had remarked on a disturbing new phenomenon in Paris: 'Since last night a strange change has come over the city; an enormous number of troops have left last night and some cannonading took place late, but gradually died away towards morning. All the National Guard have left; a terrible silence reigns around; not a shot is heard and everybody demands what this means; can it be that we are at last victorious and have forced the enemy's positions and so are fighting beyond the lines, and in consequence out of hearing ? Or can it be a calamity too sad to think of ... ?' By the 21st, all Paris knew what the silence signified; it was, explained Goncourt, 'the silence of death, of the kind caused by a disaster in a great city. Today one no longer hears Paris live. All faces have the look of faces of the sick, of convalescents'. More simply, Juliette Lambert just wrote: '*Paris est perdu !*'

Trochu had returned on the afternoon of the 20th from his battle-post at Mont-Valérien where, as he said in a superlative piece of understatement, 'my presence was no longer useful'. Immediately a joint session of the Government and the Mayors of Paris was summoned, at which he was called upon 'to explain myself concerning the military situation and my personal intentions'. Trochu replied that militarily all was lost, and that he himself 'formally refused to assume the responsibility for any new operation which would be a slaughter without any goal that was strategically justifiable'. The meeting became stormier than any in the past, with coals of fire heaped from all sides upon the Governor's head for the failure of the Buzenval sortie. Particularly violent in their recriminations were the Mayors, led by one Georges Clemenceau of Montmartre, who still demanded a continuation of the war at all costs, saying much the same thing with the same degree of savagery as, when Premier of France forty-seven years later, he would growl, '*Moi, je fais la guerre*'. But the influential Favre, Trochu's deputy, now favoured capitulation; for, during Buzenval, he had received word that Chanzy had been utterly crushed at Le Mans, losing 10,000 men. The Army of the Loire no longer existed. Now a bitter and unseemly scene took place between the two leaders, with Favre reproaching Trochu for his promise that he would 'never surrender', and Trochu retaliating by blaming Favre for his insistence that he would 'cede neither an inch of territory nor a stone of our fortresses'. Dorian, who relayed the episode to Rochefort, admitted that, in spite of the pain it caused him, he felt an almost irresistible desire to laugh 'when he heard them throw their respective boastings in each other's face'.

But on one point all factions were agreed: Trochu must go. When it was put to him, the General declared that it would be inconsistent with military honour for him to resign. The Government must replace him. After lengthy discussions, the following compromise was arrived at: Trochu would be relieved of his military command, but retain the Presidency; on the other hand, the Governorship of Paris would be suppressed. This last represented a final resort to casuistry that was as typical of this Government of lawyers as it was remarkable. When Trochu had made his rash promise, he declared, 'The *Governor of Paris* will not capitulate'; therefore, it was argued with that insuperable logic of the French, if the Governor no longer existed, no promise would be broken. The way to capitulation was now open; although some of the British in Paris were reminded of Byron's immortally cynical line from *Don Juan*, 'And whispering "I will ne'er consent"—consented'. But who would replace Trochu? Finally it was decided that the tough old Commander, Vinoy, would take over the military reins and that to Favre would be entrusted the invidious task of negotiating an armistice.

As Trochu left his headquarters, his staff were shocked to hear him mutter with uncharacteristic profanity about his sacrifice, '*Je suis le*

Jésus-Christ de la situation!' On the 22nd, Edward Blount called to find him calm but abandoned, alone 'with Madame Trochu and one faithful member of his staff', but still exuding a curious kind of self-satisfaction; 'He asked me whether I would ever have thought it possible, with the kind of army left in Paris, demoralised, half starved, with nothing in abundance, except drink, to make an effectual stand against the splendid and highly disciplined troops of the invaders'. Few mourned the departure of this Hamlet among generals, who had led Paris, for better or for worse, from the first days of the Siege. Labouchere was among the kindest when he commented, 'So poor Jonah has gone over, and been swallowed up by the whale.' Victor Hugo, who had been responsible for many of the crueller puns on Trochu's name running round Paris—such as '*trop lu*', or 'the past participle of the verb *trop choir*'[1]—composed a mocking little epitaph:

> . . . *Soldat brave, honnête, pieux, nul,*
> *Bon canon, mais ayant un peu trop de recul . . .*[2]

Washburne wrote, 'Trochu is dethroned, having remained long enough to injure the cause', and later added that he had 'proved himself the weakest and most incompetent man ever entrusted with such great affairs . . . too weak for anything, weak as the Indian's dog which had to lean against a tree to bark'. But Trochu had never had any tree against which he could have leaned. Although he 'had much to answer for', as O'Shea noted rather more charitably, 'in the entire cabinet there was but one good Minister, Dorian—that because he was a practical man, a man of business. The rest were phrasers and praters.' Wickham Hoffman, who regarded Trochu as 'a strange compound of learning, ability, weakness, and fanaticism, and I have little doubt that he confidently anticipated the personal intervention of Ste.-Genevieve to save her beloved city', also reckoned that 'had Vinoy or Ducrot been in command from the beginning, the result might have been different'. But nobody was under any illusion that the advent of Vinoy could affect the issue now; it was, said Goncourt, simply 'the changing of doctors when the invalid was on the point of death'.

As Vinoy took over, Belleville, still overflowing with rage at the futile slaughter of its National Guards, and realization of the imminence of 'surrender, burst out in its last—and most violent—

---

[1] Meaning, literally, to have 'fallen excessively'.

[2] 'Soldier brave, honest, pious, null,
A good cannon, but with too much recoil'.

revolt of the Siege. Shortly before one o'clock on the morning of January 22nd, a band of armed men appeared at the gates of the Mazas prison and demanded the release of Flourens and the others imprisoned after October 31st. They induced the prison Governor to receive a deputation of three or four men; these promptly seized the gates and let in their comrades. The Governor (who seems to have acted with remarkable feebleness, and was indeed later arrested for complicity) handed over Flourens and the rest, merely requesting a 'receipt for their bodies'. With drums beating, the insurgents then marched to the *Mairie* of the 20th *arrondissement*, where they pillaged all the food and wine stored there and set up a headquarters. In the course of the night, Flourens prudently evaporated, but the following afternoon his liberators headed—once more—for the Hôtel de Ville. Delescluze, Arnould, and other Red leaders had been conferring at a nearby house on the Rue de Rivoli, while, as usual, Blanqui was detachedly watching developments from a nearby restaurant. As on past occasions, the demonstrations began peacefully enough; there was much angry invective hurled against the Government, intermingled with cries of '*Donnez-nous du pain!*' No member of the Government was in the Hôtel de Ville, so a deputy of Ferry, Gustave Chaudey, came out to meet the mob leaders, warning them that this time the building was well defended by armed Breton *Mobiles* behind every window. This time, the Government forces under Vinoy were ready and determined.

Despite Chaudey's intervention, at about three o'clock two to three hundred National Guards of the 101st Battalion arrived from the Bastille, armed to the teeth, and led by such extremists as Razoua, Malon, Louise Michel, wearing a képi and clad in a man's uniform, and the two semi-lunatics, Sapia who had led the October 8th disturbances, and Jules Allix of *doigt prussique* fame. They took up a menacing position in front of the Hôtel de Ville, and then a solitary shot was fired—probably, but not certainly, by the National Guard. Panic seized the crowd, and there were shouts of 'They're firing on us'. Sapia's men now got down on one knee and fired a carefully directed volley into the Hôtel de Ville. There, Adjutant Bertrand, a Warrant Officer of the Finistére *Mobiles* who was standing just outside the gate, was hit and badly wounded. Immediately a peremptory command was given, followed by a devastating fusillade crackling out of every window in the great building. For the first time during the Siege, Frenchmen were firing at, and killing, other Frenchmen. It was a terrible omen of what was to come, and Gustave Chaudey would later die for having, presumptively, given the *Mobiles* the order to fire. Meanwhile, a sharp-eyed Breton levelled his sights on the gesticulating Sapia and knocked him down, mortally wounded. Jules Clarétie, a Republican journalist who had just arrived on the Place, describes how 'the desperate crowd stampedes, tries to get away in all directions. The firing continues all the time. The windows of the Hôtel de Ville open and the *Mobiles* reply. People fall around me. On my left, I see a young man sink down in the yellow mud that has been diluted by a penetrating light rain; and on my right, a spectator in a top hat, killed outright.' Louise Michel, who was to win her nickname 'the Red Virgin' that day, was driven to a frenzy by the sight of the mob being shot down. Firing from the cover of an overturned omnibus, she admitted shooting to kill and flayed those of her fellows who merely peppered the walls of the Hôtel de Ville. For half an hour the exchange of fire went on, until the arrival of reinforcements sent by Vinoy. The National Guard dissipated, overturning more omnibuses to cover its retreat, and leaving five dead and eighteen wounded—women and children among them—in the empty Place.

On his way to the Hôtel de Ville that Sunday evening, to discover what was going on, Washburne met 'an acquaintance, a young surgeon in the French Navy, who was profoundly agitated and profoundly depressed'. Telling him about the shooting, the surgeon remarked 'that nobody knew what would come next, but that, at any rate, France was "finished".' Certainly it seemed that, as the Siege was running to its end, a dreadful new phase was bound to begin. In fact the January 22nd uprising had been no full-scale attempt at revolution; the numbers of the insurgents were far fewer than on October 31st; none of the principal Red leaders—Delescluze, Blanqui, Pyat, or even Flourens—was involved; and up to that day the great majority of the National Guard was still opposed to violence. But the shooting changed everything, and Paris hardened into two irreconcilable camps. Echoing the bourgeois attitude, which now saw Red revolution just round the corner, a *Mobile* corporal in Fort Issy (whence the 101st National Guard had once been returned because of its 'uselessness') wrote to his father: '...those miserable bastards...they are nothing but cowardly bandits far more dangerous for us than the Prussians; the Bretons fired on them— so long live the Bretons!...' But now Vinoy did what bourgeois Paris felt Trochu should have done months ago; he ordered the suspension of *Le Combat* and *Le Réveil*, the closing of all the Red Clubs, and the indictment of Delescluze and Pyat before a military tribunal. (But Pyat, as always, had vanished into thin air.)

After the January 22nd uprising, 'civil war was a few yards away', Jules Favre wrote in retrospect, 'famine, a few hours'. Though he may have exaggerated the proximity of starvation (subsequent estimates suggest that there was still enough food for another ten days), the fear of civil war had suddenly become very real. Rather than attempt to fight a war on two fronts, the Government considered it imperative to obtain an armistice with the least delay. There would not even be time to consult Gambetta and the Tours Government. On the 23rd, Jules Favre called for Captain d'Hérisson, Trochu's former staff officer, and entrusted him with a dispatch for Bismarck. He was enjoined to the utmost secrecy; 'God only knows', said Favre, 'what the Parisian populace will do to us when we are compelled to tell them the truth.' D'Hérisson sped to the parley-point on the Pont de Sèvres, where in October he had met the American generals Burnside and Forbes bound on another armistice mission to Paris. He arranged for a cease-fire at 6 o'clock that same evening, and immediately returned to collect Favre. Together they crossed the Seine in a row-boat, made dangerously leaky by bullet-holes: Favre— an incongruous figure in his top hat and badly made lawyer's frock-coat—and d'Hérisson, immaculate in his red-striped trousers, frantically bailing with an old saucepan. On landing, Favre was escorted at once to Bismarck's residence. 'You have grown whiter since Ferrières, M. le Ministre', he was greeted. Playing with the distraught old lawyer like a cat with a mouse, when Favre first mentioned with pride the resistance of Paris, Bismarck revealed the same brutality he had shown at Ferrières; 'Ah! you are proud of your resistance ? Well, sir, let me tell you that if M. Trochu were a German General I would have him shot tonight. . . . Do not talk to me of your resistance. It is criminal!' That night Favre dined with Bismarck, who reported gleefully to the Crown Prince that he had 'developed a perfectly wolfish hunger', eating even the second night 'a dinner intended for three'.

The armistice talks continued on the 24th, which, the Prussians noted auspiciously, happened to be the anniversary of the birth of Frederick the Great. Bismarck, secure in the knowledge of possessing all the cards, was hard and uncompromising, but Favre obtained terms sufficient for him to return to Paris for his Government's approval. The only outstanding point was whether or not the National Guard should be allowed to retain its arms. On the 25th, 26th, and 27th he was back again with Bismarck, this time accompanied by a General d'Hautpoul, as military representative, whose strange conduct the Prussian Crown Prince and Dr. Busch both ascribed to drink; though Favre, more charitably, insisted he was reeling from sheer emotion. Bismarck was clad in the uniform of a White Cuirassier; the same that had made Paris stare during the Great Exhibition, those brilliant days of only three and a half years ago which now seemed to belong to another century. 'He looked a giant', said d'Hérisson. 'In his tight uniform, with his broad chest and square shoulders, and bursting with health and strength, his proximity overwhelmed the stooping, thin, tall, miserable-looking lawyer, with his frock-coat wrinkled all over, and his white hair falling over his collar. A look, alas! at the pair was sufficient to distinguish between the conqueror and the conquered, the strong and the weak.' Such was the new balance of power in Europe. Immediately the conversation returned to the National Guard. Having heard Favre say that France needed to keep at least three regular divisions to maintain order, Moltke declared that he could accept only two and that the National Guard would have to be disarmed. With some passion, Favre cried out, 'I cannot at any price have the National Guard disarmed. That would mean civil war.' To this, Bismarck replied coldly, 'You are being foolish. Sooner or later you will have to bring reason to the National Guard, and you gain nothing by waiting', and he added cynically, 'Provoke an uprising then, while you still have an army to suppress it with.' According to Bismarck, Favre 'looked at me in horror, as much as to say, "What a bloodthirsty fellow you are!" '

Finally Favre was allowed to keep the National Guard under arms, but Moltke insisted, in exchange, that he be allowed to retain only one regular division. It was to prove a disastrous compromise for the French forces of order. For the rest of the terms, the Army was to surrender its arms and its colours, but the officers would be left their swords; an armistice would be granted to Paris immediately, and would extend to the rest of France in three days' time; Paris would pay a war indemnity of two hundred million francs, surrender the perimeter forts to the Prussians, and throw the rampart guns into the moats, but no Prussian troops would enter Paris for the duration of the armistice, which was to last until February 19th; during this time an Assembly would be freely elected, and would convene at Bordeaux to discuss whether or not to resume the war, or on what terms to conclude a definitive peace treaty; and meanwhile the Prussians would do all in their power to permit the revictualling of Paris. As a last favour, Favre begged for Paris to be allowed to fire the final shot of the Siege—which he was granted. It was January 27th, and noting that it was also the thirteenth birthday of his heir, Prince Wilhelm,[1] the Crown Prince of the new German Reich added in his diary a pious wish that history was to make sound somewhat ironic: 'May he grow up a good, upright, true and trusty man, one who

[1] The future Kaiser Wilhelm II.

delights in all that is good and beautiful, a thorough German who will one day to learn to advance further in the paths laid down by his grandfather. . . . It is truly a disquieting thought to realize how many hopes are even now set on this boy's head.'

That same night Favre and his entourage left Versailles, looking, thought one of the Germans, 'like poor culprits, who are tomorrow to go to the scaffold. They made me sorry for them.' Back in Paris, Favre begged his fifteen-year-old daughter to keep him company as the cannons ceased firing. At the stroke of midnight, standing on a balcony of the Quai d'Orsay, he heard the last distant rumble fade, and then collapsed sobbing into the child's arms.

*   *   *

News of the armistice was received in Paris with a mixture of rage and stupor. Thanks to the indiscretion of the Prussian officer who had first received the request for peace talks that Favre sent via d'Hérisson, the city had known what was afoot from the 24th. Leaving Chez Brébant that night, Goncourt found that 'on the Boulevard, the word capitulation, which it might have been dangerous to pronounce a few days ago, is in all mouths.' In low voices he and his circle had been discussing the dire news during which one of them, Du Mesnil, intoned gravely, 'There is a danger. And that is, one doesn't know whether, the capitulation having been signed, it will not be rejected by the virile portion of Paris.' The next day Edwin Child resigned from the National Guard. During the riots of January 22nd, his battalion had been called to arms, offering Child his last chance of the Siege to fire a shot in anger, but he, 'not having much desire to be killed in a street riot, was exempted as "*étranger*".' By the 25th he had had enough:

Gave my resignation to the Captain, feeling heartily disgusted with the whole affair. 400,000 men capitulating, granted half of them no use as soldiers, *soit* 200,000. I pity the people, but scorn the chiefs. After the entire confidence placed in them by the people something might have been done, had half the population been sacrificed to the enemy there would have been no recriminations . . . . The population seem as if paralysed and unable to comprehend their position, and the Government are afraid to say the word 'capitaulation' so call it 'armistice'. What an end of 20 years uninterrupted prosperity, and what a lesson to a nation fond of flattery and calling itself the vanguard of civilisation. 'Pride goeth before destruction', etc.

And the following day:

Went to *appel* at 11. For the last time there heard read before my company that '*le Garde Child, volontaire étranger, a été rayé de la compagnie, sur sa demande*,[1] henceforth having no longer the right to call myself a soldier, having endured a bloodless campaign of 40 days duration without hardly seeing the enemy or firing a shot. And for such services they talk about giving everyone a medal. Why I should be ashamed to wear it!

In its proclamation announcing the surrender, the Government however did its best to keep up the mystique of the city's heroism: 'The enemy is the first to render homage to the moral energy and to the courage of which the entire Parisian population has just given an example. . . .' Among the Press, *Le Siècle* echoed: 'Paris has compelled the respect of Europe', and *Le Soir*: 'France is dead! *Vive la France !*' Of the few to strike a more sober note, *Le Temps* pleaded, 'It is time to have an end of the charlatanism of rhetoric, which is one of our chief plagues', and the left-wing *Rappel* warned ominously, 'It is not an armistice, it is a capitulation. . . . Paris is trembling with anger.' To the private citizen, however, the capitulation evoked a symbol of death without hope. At the burial of Régnault, reckoned by some to be the most promising painter in France, who had been killed at Buzenval, Goncourt recorded 'an enormous crowd. Over this young body of dead talent, one wept for the interment of France'; and as the guns fell silent a tearful Juliette Lambert scribbled down, 'I should like to die at this hour'. Among even the moderate left wing, bitter hatred and resentment flared against Favre and his accomplices; Corporal Louis Péguret of the National Guard wrote to his sister, '*Enfin ca y est !* . . . . Paris has capitulated! The Government consoles us by saying "Armistice", but for people who are more honest and of greater faith this word is translated *capitulation*. What can we do ? We can only curse and execrate their name, and tell our children one day to condemn their memory. . . .'

At Fort Issy, as the garrison was about to march out, the Colonel addressed his men: 'Soldiers! You have had to lay down your arms. Officers! You may keep yours; but I want to say to all of you; you were all, all of you, worthy of carrying them'. Then with a brisk gesture he unbuckled his belt, handed his sword over to his orderly, took up his cane and headed the forlorn exodus from the fort, past a group of Prussian soldiers waiting to take it over. It was finished. After one hundred and thirty days, the Siege was over. On January 30th, Jules Clarétie the journalist wrote, 'The forts are occupied. Paris is enveloped by a dense fog which seems to carry the sorrow of its fall. . . . One sees disarmed *Mobiles* wandering about, dejected soldiers, and sailors; sandbags and equipment are being handed back,

[1] 'Guardsman Child, foreign volunteer, has had his name removed from the company at his own request.'

the bloodstained stretchers folded up. . . . *Mais quoi!*' he concluded in a note of that indestructible French buoyancy, 'Behind this fog hope has not left us.'

The war might have ended for Paris, but in the provinces it still continued. Rumours of Favre's armistice had only reached the unconsulted Gambetta at Bordeaux on the 27th, throwing him—not unreasonably—into a thoroughly meridional rage. At once he issued a denial, declaring, 'We cannot believe that negotiations of this kind could have been undertaken without the Delegation being previously notified.' On January 27th Favre had in fact dispatched a thirty-year-old volunteer called Lacaze aboard the *Richard Wallace*, the last but one balloon to leave Paris, with instructions to inform Gambetta of the armistice; but, in the final tragedy of the Siege, Lacaze never reached his destination. The *Richard Wallace*, named after Paris's great British benefactor, was last seen sailing out over the Bassin d'Arcachon near Bordeaux. Why Lacaze never opened the gas-valve as he crossed the coast has never been explained; perhaps he had a heart attack; possibly he passed out from prolonged malnutrition; or perhaps, quite simply, he could not bear to return to the soil of a conquered and humiliated France. Whatever the cause, a small plaque in the Gare du Nord still commemorates the second, and last, fatality of the brave balloonists of Paris.

Thus it was only on the morning of the 29th that Gambetta was awakened by a curt telegram from Favre, informing him of the capitulation. Outraged, his first instinct was to refuse to comply, and he issued a decree urging that the armistice be utilized 'as a school for instruction for our young troops'. But even he now began to realize that the fight was hopeless, and when Favre's emissaries reached Bordeaux on February 6th the Churchillian dictator of the provinces greeted them with his resignation.

There was, however, still one disaster of the war, emanating from the exiguity of Favre's instructions to Bordeaux, which had yet to be played out. Down in the south-east corner of France, Bourbaki had received no word of the surrender. After the brief success in forcing a temporary evacuation of Dijon, his campaign had gone progressively awry. Two Prussian armies under Werder and Manteuffel were now pressing his ragged, starving, and beaten forces back into the icy slopes of the Jura by the Swiss frontier. Their plight was desperate: 'As there were no leaves on the trees for the men to eat.' wrote Rochefort, 'they tore the bark from the trunks and ate it, while the horses gnawed the wood of the gun-carriages before falling dead on the road.' Bourbaki himself tried unsuccessfully to commit suicide, and finally the remnants of his army straggled over into Switzerland

R

to beg refuge there. It was, to quote Michael Howard's classic study, *The Franco-Prussian War*, 'one of the greatest disasters that has overtaken a European army'.

And so ended the most disastrous war in the long course of French history.

By comparison with what defeat cost the nation, and with the lives that would be forfeited to redeem this defeat half a century later, the total French losses were not excessive; some 150,000 killed and died of wounds, and a similar number of wounded (the German totals were only 28,208 and 88,488 respectively). During the Siege of Paris itself, French military casualties (including the National Guard) totalled only 28,450, of which less than 4,000 were killed. According to Professor Sheppard's figures, deaths from all causes during the Siege amounted to 6,251; of these, only six persons are listed as having died 'apparently from want of food', though there were a further 4,800 infants, infirm, and aged 'whose death may be said to have been hastened by want of food or by bad food'.[1]

But, in Paris, the real killing had yet to begin.

[1] One final comparison to the Siege of Leningrad may here be relevant; according to Léon Goure, 'at least 1,000,000 to 1,250,000 persons, or about one-third of Leningrad's war-time population, are unaccounted for and may be presumed to have died from the effects of starvation, cold, and illness, most of them during the winter and early spring of 1941–42'. And even during Henri IV's three months' siege of a far smaller Paris in 1590, 12,000 are said to have died from hunger and disease.

PART TWO

THE COMMUNE

'Purification' after German troops leave Paris

16. The Uneasy Interlude

As the guns fell silent, the divergent emotions of shame at the capitulation and of satisfaction that it was all over were immediately overshadowed by one thought common to all Parisians. Food! In his first letter home after the cease-fire, ex-Guardsman Child wrote to his parents on January 30th: 'Once more a free and enlightened citizen, capable of judging of my own actions and for the moment without being humbugged by Colonel, Commandant, Captain or any other species of the coward race whatever, the moment I can leave this gay(?) city I shall pay a visit to the native hearth and trust to your parental feelings to prepare me a good substantial welcome, in the shape of roast beef or a leg of mutton, fresh eggs (etc.). . . .' With relief in sight, the longing became almost more agonizing than during the last days of the Siege. To his brother-in-law Louis Hack in London, Jules Rafinesque wrote: 'I do not think that we will die of hunger since the revictualling approaches—oh, Loulou, provided the first leg of lamb that is given to us to eat is tender and well done! ! enough jam, more nectar, more nectar!'

Matters soon proved to be worse than even the Government had suspected. In its last display of incompetence, it had gravely overestimated the food stocks remaining in the city: earlier, Jules Ferry had appointed two officials to keep account of the dwindling stocks as a check on each other, but—incredibly enough—it appears that instead of being compared, their two estimates had been added together. Thus on the actual day of capitulation there was probably no more than a week's food left at the present subsistence-level. Archibald Forbes, the *Daily News* correspondent attached to Moltke's Army of the Meuse, managed to ride into Paris on the 31st, and was much shocked by the emptiness of the foodshops.[1] The whole city, he noted, 'was haunted by the peculiar half-sweetish, half-fetid odour which horse flesh gives out in cooking . . .', and he was constantly alarmed lest his own well-fed steed be seized and devoured. What few wares the shops had to offer now commanded astronomical prices: 2 francs for a small, shrivelled cabbage; 1 franc for a leek; 45 francs a fowl; 45 francs a rabbit (generally cat); 25 francs a pigeon; and 22 francs for a 2-lb. chub. A few days later, Forbes's colleague with the Crown Prince was still more appalled by the sight of the hungry Parisians begging for bread on the bridge at Neuilly; it was, he declared, something 'not soon to be forgotten'. Nor could the well-fed Prussian soldiery, engaged in oiling their rifles and mending worn equipment, look on unmoved at 'delicate ladies, with jewels on their fingers, grubbing in the fields of frosted vegetables'. Clearly, the revictualling of Paris had become a matter of the utmost urgency. But although each day more and more herds of cattle were to be seen being driven by French peasants towards the hungry city, France herself—the countryside devastated and communications disrupted —could do little. Even the former enemy showed his anxiety; the Kaiser himself instructed that six million army rations be sent into Paris; while fortunately, with remarkable prescience, the Prussians had begun repairing bridges and railway tunnels well before the armistice.

It was to Britain and America that Paris chiefly turned in her hour of need. The response was immediate. Mr. Gladstone's Government requisitioned Navy ships loaded with Army stores; at Deptford, twenty-four great ovens were set to work night and day baking bread and hard-tack; the Lord Mayor's Relief Fund was inundated with donations. According to Edward Blount, who was responsible for distributing the food in Paris, in the early days of February alone the London Relief Committee sent 'nearly 10,000 tons of flour, 450 tons of rice, 900 tons of biscuits, 360 tons of fish, and nearly 4,000 tons of fuel, with about 7,000 head of livestock'. Some $2,000,000-worth of food was sent from the United States, but much of it was held up at

[1] Forbes also found himself besieged by news-starved Britons, bombarding him with such questions as 'Is Ireland quiet?'

Le Havre because no one could be found to unload the ships. The British experienced similar difficulties. On January 31st Blount, writing to his wife that 'the misery is appalling', added, 'We hope for provisions at the end of the week, but the railways are in an awful state. There is no way of getting to Boulogne or Calais. I am overloaded with work. . . . I bought horse flesh, which I distributed among my own clerks and others to save them from starvation.' There were also hitches, such as when the French authorities insisted on sending back pheasants included by thoughtful British donors, on the grounds that 'these things are for the aristocracy and not for the people—it would be more prudent not to distribute them'.

But gradually the food supplies began to reach Paris. On the morning of February 4th a British correspondent recorded being awakened by drums heralding the arrival of the first convoy; on the 7th, delegates from the Lord Mayor's Relief Fund arrived and the trickle of food became a torrent. Two brothers called Lyon, coming to collect notes for lectures they intended to give in England in aid of the hungry, passed on the outskirts of the city 'a long train of provisions; each waggon labelled in large letters "The Gift of the British Government". We felt proud of our country and went into Paris a couple of inches taller on that account.' For a nation not over given to such demonstrativeness, there were immediate responses of gratitude; Jules Ferry telegraphed the Lord Mayor, declaring that 'In the extremity of its misfortunes, the voice of the English people has been the first that has been heard by it from outside with an expression of sympathy. The citizens of Paris will never forget. . . .' Much of the resentment felt towards Britain because of her 'splendid isolation' during the war vanished. The food had come only just in time; the unloading of the first of the British food waggons at Les Halles provoked an uncontrollable riot, accompanied with pillage and leading to a deplorable wastage of the precious victuals. Eggs, vegetables, butter, and chickens were trampled underfoot, while for seven hours the police seemed powerless to intervene.

The plight of the foreign communities in Paris, many of whom now had no resources left with which to buy the relief foodstuffs, was every bit as bad as that of the Parisians, and once again the generous Richard Wallace came to the aid of his indignant British, adding to the many thousands of pounds he had already given away during the Siege. Blount also dug deep into his own pocket, and as acting Chargé d'Affaires was inundated with pleas; while his first communication from the still absent British Ambassador, Lord Lyons, included a request for him to 'look after' the Ambassador's niece at the Carmelite Convent, adding—with a touch of pomposity—'I am sure you will not begrudge the labour which you will add to your many good works.' Many of the British also had their own private sources of relief; a kind friend of O'Shea's rode in from Versailles with a leg of mutton concealed in his saddle-bag, while William Brown, the commercial traveller who had written his wife on January 18th explicitly requesting her to order from Crosse and Blackwell 'the day communication is open . . . 2 good-sized hams, 1 dozen concentrated milk, 1 dozen two-pound tins of boiled beef, 1 dozen kippered herring, 1 dozen assorted jams, 1 dozen half-pound packets of Apps's cocoa', did not receive the parcel until February 23rd. Dr. Alan Herbert's family seem to have been particularly solicitous for his welfare. In the last days of the Siege his brother, the Earl of Carnarvon, had received from Versailles a touching letter from a former servant, one Martin Harper, now courier to Russell of *The Times*, saying that he had 'bespoken two legs of mutton, four chickens, one goose', etc., to take in to Alan Herbert, and that 'My Lord need not feel yourself at all under my obligation, for I always did like Mr. Herbert'. The Earl meanwhile had dispatched his own ration-bearing emissary, Louis Gleissner, from London; but both were beaten to it by another brother, Auberon Herbert, M.P., who, carrying a piece of beef in his satchel, mysteriously infiltrated into Paris immediately after the cease-fire and seems to have been one of the first foreigners to enter. Others hastened at the first opportunity to Versailles, to find—like Tommy Bowles—a square meal of 'omelette, *sole au vin blanc*, and a *Chateaubriand*'; while on February 5th Edwin Child records how he and his friend Albert 'couldn't resist' buying a fowl and some fresh butter that had just arrived from Versailles. They 'had it cooked by our concierge and ate it with the family of the latter. It seemed as if happy times were again in store, may it prove so. Lovely day.'

By the second week in February, revictualling had had its effect. With it a remarkable change could be detected in the physiognomy of Paris. One of the *Daily News* correspondents commenting on the 'incredulity' of visitors to Paris remarked 'these visitors go into the restaurants and see plenty of food there, which they can eat with pleasure, and they conclude that there has been no great suffering . . . .' But once again, as during the Siege, there had been grave inequalities in the distribution of food; so the poor often remained acutely, and resentfully, hungry. On January 31st Auberon Herbert had written to Odo Russell of the Foreign Office: 'There does not seem in Paris real distress except among the poorer classes; there it exists, and is likely to increase.' His prediction was correct, and three weeks later Dr. Alan Herbert wrote his brother, Carnarvon: 'though fresh meat is to be had, the price is out of the means of the poor, and work is but slowly beginning. . . . I have seen more scurvy since the capitulation than I did during the siege.'

Sooner or later the foodstuffs pouring into Paris would restore the bodies of the besieged, but it could do little to repair the insidious damage wreaked upon the minds and souls of Parisians. Psychologically, they were in anything but a fit state to face the humiliation of an unprecedented defeat, or of the crushing peace terms that lay ahead. The sheer drabness of the city which, with most of the fine trees on its boulevards felled and many houses gaping from shell damage, bore little enough resemblance to the sparkling Paris of 1867, was in itself hardly a tonic to morale. It was true that the sense of humiliation was something shared by all Frenchmen, but only Paris was afflicted with the additional burden of a neurosis loosely diagnosed as 'obsidional fever'. Like the workings of an invisible parasite, the neurosis had gnawed away progressively during the Siege and only now was the full extent of the canker's inroads revealed. Boredom, malnutrition, the anxiety and uncertainty of what tomorrow would bring, the unbalancing effects upon a habitually highly-strung population of cycles of excessive optimism followed by blackest disappointment, these were among the causes that had produced the canker. But above all others there had been the soul-destroying sense of isolation from the rest of humanity. Many Parisians agreed with Saint-Edmé, the secretary of the Scientific Committee, that by far the worst privation of the Siege—even worse than the lack of food—had been the lack of news from outside. Even Washburne, better off than almost anyone else in this respect, recorded in the last fortnight of the Siege: 'It seems to me as if I had been buried alive.'

In a pathological study of the Siege, one French doctor analysed the symptoms of 'obsidional fever' as including such phenomena as spy-mania, mistrust and defiance of authority, the resplendent but hollow verbosity stemming from a need for self-assurance, and fear-created persecution complexes that pointed accusing fingers at the usual variety of 'enemies'—Freemasons, Jews, and Jesuits. With unprecedented fickleness even for France, the neurosis transformed heroes of one day into traitors of the next. Nowhere was this more graphically displayed than in the abrupt reversal of attitudes towards the legendary Sergeant Hoff. In the early days Hoff with his daring nocturnal forays had been the darling of Paris. Then he had disappeared on the field of battle at Champigny and the whole city had mourned. But by the beginning of January rumours were circulating that he was in fact a Prussian spy; which, of course, explained why he had been able to obtain helmets and other enemy trophies with such facility. There was, declared one paper, 'a woman in the affair . . . she had received 7,000 francs from Sergeant Hoff over a matter of weeks. Seven thousand francs from a simple sergeant, that sounds fishy. . . .!' But no more solid evidence was ever produced to substantiate this calumny against poor Hoff.

The effect that obsidional fever had upon people's minds was far from being illusory. Early in January Julliette Lambert recorded a series of terrible nightmares she had suffered; 'For six days it seems as if all the centipedes in the world having traversed my brain attached themselves to it, and had to be torn off one by one, each time opening the seams of my mind.' Nerves badly scarred by the Siege now had to cope with the deadly vacuum created by the capitulation. At one point in November, Goncourt had noticed that there was one aspect of Siege life that 'almost made you love it'. It was the excitement of living in the 'continual flutter of a war that surrounds you, that almost touches you, of being brushed by danger, of one's heart always beating a little fast; this has a certain sweetness'. Now all that was over, and as Goncourt had presciently foreseen, 'this feverish pleasure will be succeeded by boredom that is very empty, very empty, very empty'. Boredom, *l'ennui*, once more that deadliest of Gallic ailments. Now Paris was a city of men shuffling aimlessly about, staring without purpose into shop windows; regular troops and *Mobiles* waiting to be sent back to their homes, National Guards with no employment, *petits bourgeois* with no trade. To the innocent bystander, after all these months of war and privation, the scene might seem peaceful enough. But not very far beneath the suface, in the vacuum left by the capitulation, a dangerous ferment was bubbling up. Apart from anything else, for the past four months the civil population had been educated to kill Prussians; and the vast majority had been given no opportunity of an outlet for these deliberately fostered, violent urges. They remained unquenched; and in the debasement of such a defeat many Parisians, like frustrated children, were ready to kick any object at hand.

To cope with the maladies of Paris would have required leaders profoundly versed in the art of psychology; but, alas, the new Government of France was to prove itself as deficient in this respect as its predecessor had been in the conduct of war.

Most of those who could now hastened to escape from what had been their prison over the past four months, and from the fetid atmosphere prevailing in Paris. At first, it was not easy, as permits had to be obtained from both the French and Prussian authorities; but Labouchere, who was himself shortly to seek re-election to Parliament, was amused to note that some 23,000 Parisians applied to leave the city on the pretext that they were standing as provincial candidates·

for the new Assembly. Then as controls were relaxed, they began to leave in such numbers that one Parisian believed many Frenchmen were intending to emigrate from the country for good. Degas departed for Château Ménil-Hubert, and Manet went to recuperate at Arcachon, both having served in the Paris National Guard; Berthe Morisot was taken by her parents to stay with Puvis de Chavannes; Monet and Pissarro remained in England where they had fled during the war; while Renoir was among the few who returned to Paris. At least 100,000 people are estimated to have left Paris during the armistice weeks alone; and most of these came from the middle-class bourgeoisie who could afford to leave, or who had somewhere to go. On the road they passed the poorer denizens of the suburbs, returning from evacuation in the provinces to what the war had left of their homes, accompanied by truck-loads of furniture and provisions. There were also the richer, more prosperous Parisians, who, having left the city before the investment, were now coming back to check on their property or to collect their rents. But many of them too would leave Paris again as soon as their objectives were achieved. These were regarded by the proletarian segments of Paris, bound ineluctably to the capital by the economic facts of life, with even less favour than the members of the bourgeoisie who were now leaving. There was also another aspect of the exodus which did not escape the attention of the disgruntled Red leaders, still seething with rage at the killings of January 22nd; it meant the substantial reduction in the number of bourgeois battalions of the National Guard on which the Government had relied to keep order in Paris in the past. Here was an ominous factor in what was to come.

With the armistice, many of the principal personalities of the Siege also left Paris and thus disappear from this story. Most of the British correspondents like Bowles, O'Shea, and Labouchere (now covered in fame as the 'Besieged Resident' that would help him gain popular support for re-election to the House of Commons) hastened home, emaciated and not a little disgusted by all they had seen; of the other British and Americans who had seen the Siege through, Richard Wallace, Dr. Alan Herbert, Minister Washburne, and his assistant, Wickham Hoffman, all remained in Paris after brief sorties outside. In a state of ecstasy, Edwin Child reached home by mid-February, but a few days later he found himself falling asleep in the middle of a Covent Garden pantomine, and by March 3rd he was on his way back to Paris. General Ducrot faded into a disgruntled semi-retirement, while Trochu withdrew to the oblivion that he had always promised would be his destination once he had completed his wartime role. Into his place now steps a toughly resilient little figure, who for over a generation had already played a variety of roles both on and off the political stage of France: Adolphe Thiers.

On February 8th, France went to the polls to elect a new Government, which, as stipulated by the armistice conventions, would assume the responsibility of accepting or rejecting the permanent peace terms offered by Germany. The auspices for holding elections could hardly have been less promising. For an acceptable basis, the sponsors had to reach back beyond the Second Empire, as far as the Electoral Law established by the Second Republic in 1849. This decreed universal suffrage, with the voters of each *département* selecting their deputy from a long list, rather than voting for two or three candidates put up by the individual parties. The name on each list receiving the highest number of votes was elected; candidates were allowed to have their name placed on a plurality of lists, and could thus in fact be elected for more than one *département*.[1] When this duplication occurred, by-elections had to be held subsequently. There were only eight days for electioneering, and in the forty-three *départements* occupied by the Germans it was actually forbidden. By comparison, in neurotic Paris the brief campaign was accompanied with great heat and confusion. There an impressive multiplicity of platforms was to be found—Labouchere heard one candidate open his address with '*Citoyens, je suis le représentant du* go-ahead *!*'—but in the country at large the contenders fell into two principal groups, the 'list for peace' and the list for continuation of the war. If the latter comprised principally the left-wing firebrands of Paris, those standing on the 'list for peace' were essentially conservatives from rural France. Most of the old familiar names—Favre, Simon, Garnier-Pagès, Glais-Bizoin—appeared on the lists; to the disgust of many like Goncourt, who was outraged that they should 'have the presumption, these men, to present themselves for election!' On polling day, there also arrived a feeble reminder from an almost forgotten voice; Louis-Napoleon, still a captive in Germany. In a proclamation beginning with a curiously familiar ring, the late Emperor declared that he had been 'betrayed by fortune', and reminded France that he was still its 'real representative', while any other Government was 'illegitimate'.

But Louis-Napoleon's intervention—a rather pathetic echo of his uncle's bold sortie from Elba—hardly assisted Bonapartist prospects. When the votes were counted, they revealed that only a score of his supporters had been returned, and most of these by faithful Corsicans. The elections resulted in an astonishing and overwhelming victory

[1] As it turned out, Thiers was elected by twenty-six different constituencies, Gambetta by ten.

for the 'list of peace'. Out of 768 seats (though because of duplication and other causes in fact only 675 could be filled immediatly), the vast majority had been won by deputies with conservative, Catholic, and rural sympathies. Over 400 of them were monarchists, though they were divided in their loyalties between the Legitimists who backed the exiled Comte de Chambord, and the Orleanists (the larger faction) who rallied behind Louis-Philippe's son, the Duc d'Aumale. No more than 150 genuine Republicans had been returned, and these too were divided between the 'respectable' moderates of the ilk of Jules Favre and the extremists to the left of Rochefort; of whom there were approximately 20, mostly Deputies of Paris. Within a space of less than six months, the Government of France had veered from Bonapartist imperialism to a liberal Republic, and now back again to an ultra-conservative majority with royalist leanings. The swing was bound to be unsettling, on top of everything else, but was not perhaps as startlingly illogical as it seemed. The Empire was blamed for having started the war, the Republic with having prolonged it and lost it. Both factions were discredited, so now the provinces turned back with nostalgic hope to what at the moment seemed like the Golden Age of the last monarchy, of Louis-Philippe. There was also no doubt that the provincial conservatives were further urged along their path by what they had heard about the Reds' behaviour in Paris during the Siege, and how feebly the Republican Government had dealt with them, and they deeply feared the pranks which these Reds—if given another chance—might play with property, religion, and all else that was dear to them. That the 'brutal rurals' (as the Parisian proletariat stigmatized them) should have won so complete a victory over Paris was in itself not altogether surprising or unfair, for in 1871 more than 80 per cent of the country was still employed on the land.

Yet even allowing for this fact, neither the Electoral Law, which allocated Paris[1] only 43 seats out of 768, nor the results took into account the real or imagined pre-eminence of Paris in France. It was her tradition to look upon the provinces with superior contempt. Under the Bourbons, for a noble to be exiled from Paris to his country estates was a fate worse than death. Before the war, France had reminded the historian, Taine—as he remarked to the Goncourts—'of Alexandria in its heyday. Below Alexandria there dangled the valley of the Nile, but it was a dead valley.' Now, more than ever before, the four months of isolation had given Paris a sense of apartness from the rest of the country; more than ever it seemed to lend force to Danton's famous piece of arrogance, '*Paris, c'est la France*'. With the deeds and sufferings of Gambetta's levies concealed from

[1] The *département* of the Seine.

their view, Parisians naturally concluded that they themselves had borne the principal weight of the war. Their attitude was typified by Corporal Pégeurt of the National Guard writing to his sister on December 19th; 'we realize that France is coming to the aid of France, that is to say the provinces knowing very well that at this moment their destiny is being played out within the walls of Paris'. Not for the first time, Paris by the end of the Siege had inflated herself into that dangerous state of blind pride which the Greeks called *hubris* and which almost invariably preceded a calamitous fall. 'O city, you will make History kneel down before you', Victor Hugo had declaimed. But would the rest of France now also genuflect? In assuming that she should, Paris in her neurotic state was building herself up for a bitter disillusion.

News of the elections hit Republican Paris like a thunderbolt, The extremists had suffered particularly, for her 43 seats had been allocated to the city as a whole, and not by *arrondissements*, so that only a handful of their leaders—including Delescluze, Pyat, and Millière, with such assorted allies as Gambetta, Garibaldi,[1] Rochefort, Clemenceau, and Victor Hugo—had been elected. To the left wing, therefore, the elections represented a defeat only less terrible in kind than the capitulation, and henceforth the peace-seeking, conservative country squires would become paired with the Prussian conquerors. For during the Siege the Parisian proletariat and its ideologues had felt that, as well as fighting the enemy outside, they were also fighting for the ideal Republic; above all for their birthrights, promised by the Great Revolution, of which they had been successively defrauded by the bourgeoisie and the provincials. After those few glittering moments of September the Republican dream had never seemed closer to fulfilment, but now it looked as if the fraud was going to be repeated all over again. A chasm had been opened between the provinces and aggrieved Paris which every fresh act of the new Assembly was to widen.

First, there was the election of a man to be head executive of the new Government. The choice fell naturally enough upon Thiers, who, as head of the 'list for peace', had been elected by no less than twenty-six different constituencies; compared to Gambetta (whom Thiers derided as a *fou furieux*) with only ten. A powerful majority of the new Assembly now appointed Thiers to the post of supreme power in France, and he promptly set about forming a Government composed

[1] Although Italian, Garibaldi qualified for election in that he had been born in the former Savoyard territory of Nice; similarly, Richard Wallace, as another French-born foreigner, had also wished to stand for the Assembly, and resented the implied slur when—after all his charitable work during the Siege—he could not gain nomination.

of like-minded men. A small, white-haired, gnome-like figure, with a bespectacled and owlish face of sallow tint, Thiers was already seventy-three but had lost none of his ruthless vigour. He was a consummate politician with almost half a century of experience in the tortuousness of French government, and his knowledge of French history was equally profound. From the very first he gripped the reins with a firmness that neither Trochu nor Favre could have achieved, dominating both the Assembly and the Government. In Thiers's long career, his first mentor had been Talleyrand; he had helped Louis-Philippe to the throne, under whom he had three times been *Président du Conseil* and there was no reason to suspect that he had relinquished his Orleanist leanings. He had steadily opposed Louis-Napoleon during the Second Empire, and had refused to take office under the Republic proclaimed on September 4th, although he was willing to play along with it. Thiers once claimed: 'By birth I belong to the people; my family were humble merchants in Marseilles; they had a small trade in the Levant in cloth, which was ruined by the Revolution. By education I am a Bonapartist; I was born when Napoleon was at the summit of his glory. By tastes and habits and associations I am an aristocrat. I have no sympathy with the bourgeoisie or with any system under which they are to rule.' On the other hand, by instinct he was considerably less sympathetic towards poverty, or any of its manifestations. In 1834, when a serious revolt had broken out in Lyons and threatened to spread to Paris, Thiers—then Minister of the Interior—cunningly put the word about that the Lyons revolutionaries were winning the day, thus drawing the dissident Parisian leaders into the open and provoking a revolt which was harshly crushed. For the ensuing 'massacre in the Rue Transnonain', immortalized by Daumier, the left wing would always hold Thiers responsible, and it knew that it could now expect little but hostility from the new Assembly.[1] Thiers, a supreme realist, was also dedicated to concluding 'peace at almost any price' with Germany, and the choice of words was perhaps ominous when one of the *Daily News* correspondents, referring to the peace terms, remarked that 'If France is ruined, she is at least sure to get from M. Thiers *un enterrement de première classe*'.[2] In the course of Thiers's latest mandate, thousands of Parisians would require interment, but it would be far from 'first-class'.

[1] What the proletariat thought of Thiers was depicted by a woman who shouted at him (according to Maxime du Camp), 'with a terrible Bordeaux accent: "Monsieur Thiers, you are a man of talent, you have written books, you have a brilliant wit; but you are a scoundrel [*canaille*] because you are a bourgeois and you have no love for the people..."'.

[2] 'A first-class funeral'.

Because Gambetta and his Delegation had evacuated themselves there on December 10th, after being driven out of Tours, it was at Bordeaux that the new Assembly first met. By its second meeting in Bordeaux's eighteenth-century Grand Théâtre, on February 13th, the Assembly witnessed a scene which graphically revealed its mood. Garibaldi, attempting painfully to rise to speak, was booed and finally silenced by shouts of 'No Garibaldi!', 'No Italian!', and 'Let him hold his tongue!' A spectator with a long black beard was heard to shout from a box, 'You rural majority, listen to the voice of the towns', and then the President cleared the galleries. Garibaldi also left and was loudly applauded outside; he declared that he had come to France to fight for the Republic and that he felt his mission was now over. That night, clad in his familiar red shirt and broad-brimmed hat, he departed for Caprera, never again to return to an ungrateful France. He was, as Hugo truthfully remarked, 'the only French general never to be defeated in the war'; but, more than this, in the eyes of the left wing he was *the* hero of the Republican cause and the insult cut deep.

Thiers's most immediate task on his accession to power was to con-clude a peace treaty with the conquerors. Time was running out. The armistice was due to expire on the 19th, but he managed to gain an extension; first to the 24th, and then again to the 26th. On February 21st he arrived at Versailles, and for six days the talks dragged on. Thiers at once proved a tougher negotiator than Favre. On the 26th, Bismarck, still unwell, testily refused any further extension of the armistice and declared that if a treaty were still not concluded, the German forces would resume hostilities against 'whatever they could find to fight'; to which Thiers replied, by warning the Iron Chancellor that such an action would incur the odium of all Europe. Finally, that night, the treaty was signed. On his way back to Paris, Thiers broke down and wept in his coach. France was to lose all Alsace, and most of Lorraine, two of her fairest and most valuable provinces, in-cluding the bastion cities of Metz and Strasbourg. By hard negotiating and appealing to the greed for glory of the Prussian military, Thiers had managed to save the city of Belfort (which, despite a long siege, had never capitulated) in return for subjecting Paris to the shame of a triumphal march by the conqueror. The Germans had demanded the payment of an unprecedented war indemnity of six milliard francs, or £240 million; but they acceded to strong British representations that France could never pay this amount, and it had accordingly been reduced to five milliards—still an astronomical sum.[1] Until it was paid off, France was to submit to partial occupation. 'The peace

---

[1] £200 million, or $1,000 million.

terms seem to me so ponderous, so crushing, so mortal for France', groaned Goncourt when he heard of them, 'that I am terrified the war will only break out again, before we are ready for it'. Even beyond the frontiers of France, there were many Europeans who agreed with him.

On February 28th Thiers presented the Treaty to an appalled Assembly for ratification. Edgar Quinet declared prophetically that 'the ceding of Alsace-Lorraine is nothing but war to perpetuity under the mask of peace', which was approximately what Thiers had warned Bismarck. Victor Hugo made a speech (as a contemporary British chronicler described it) of 'unexampled silliness', but predicted that 'the hour will sound—I can feel already the coming of that immense revenge'. The France of 1792 would 'stand upright again! Oh! then she will be a power to reckon with. We shall see her, at a single stroke, resume possession of Alsace, resume possession of Lorraine! Is that all? No, we shall see her, at a single stroke, resume possession—mark well my words—of Trèves, Mayence, Cologne, Coblence . . . of all the left bank of the Rhine as well.' Having said this, he addressed himself to the Germans, amiably recommending to them the benefits of a Republic; 'You got rid of my Emperor, I shall come to get rid of yours!' However, the Assembly ratified the Peace Treaty by 546 votes to 107, with 23 abstentions. Paris fumed in impotent rage and disgust; Gambetta and the deputies from Alsace-Lorraine resigned in a body, as did six of the extreme Left from Paris—including Rochefort and Pyat. They were followed on March 8th by Victor Hugo, after a debate in which he had vigorously opposed a motion to pronounce Garibaldi's election null and void. A rural *vicomte* had shouted at him, 'The Assembly refuses to listen to M. Victor Hugo, on the ground that he does not speak French.' No doubt the Assembly regarded the departure of the old demagogue with some relief, but his resignation came as yet another outrage to raw Parisian feelings.

The new Assembly could not, would not, comprehend the state of mind of the city which had for so long dictated to the provinces. 'We provincials were unable to come to an understanding with the Parisians', admitted the Vicomte de Meaux, a newly elected deputy and the son-in-law of the Catholic leader, Montalembert; 'It seemed as if we did not even speak the same language, and that they were prey to a kind of sickness.' What the nature of this 'sickness' was, most of the deputies did not inquire too deeply; preferring to accept, simply, Viollet-le-Duc's view that 'Paris is a monstrous agglomeration that must be liquidated for the peace of France and of all Europe. . . .' When the Parisian Deputies arrived at Bordeaux, 'still vibrating with patriotism, their eyes hollow but glowing with Republican faith',

s

wrote a left-wing chronicler savagely, 'they found themselves confronted by forty years of greedy hatreds, provincial notables, obtuse *châtelains*, grainless musketeers, clerical dandies ... a completely unsuspected world of towns ranged in battle against Paris;the atheistic, the revolutionary city which had created three Republics and shattered so many idols'.

There seemed to be no end to the extent to which the Assembly could rub salt into the wounds of Paris. Next, it was announced that General d'Aurelle de Paladines was to succeed Clément Thomas as commander of the Paris National Guard. It was not a happy choice. D'Aurelle was by repute a reactionary, a former Bonapartist and violently anti-Parisian; and moreover he was regarded now, not as the victor of Coulmiers, but as the man who had *failed* to come to the aid of Paris. It was also clear that by his appointment Thiers intended to curb the power of the National Guard.

Now, as the Assembly's session at Bordeaux neared its end, it hastened through a veritable flurry of legislation unpalatable to a wide variety of factions in the capital. In a deplorable *ex post facto* ruling, Blanqui, Flourens, and two other agitators were sentenced to death, *par contumace*, for their parts in the October 31st uprising; and six left-wing journals, including Pyat's *Le Vengeur* and the scurrilous but popular *Père Duchesne*, were suspended. But no act of the new Assembly caused more justifiable, and widespread, resentment than the Law of Maturities. This ordained that all debts, on which a moratorium had been declared during the war, were to be paid within forty-eight hours; while a similar law decreed that landlords could now also demand payment of all accumulated rents. The two bills were as cruel as they were stupid, and they dealt a staggering blow to hundreds of thousands of Parisians. With industry and commerce at a standstill for four months, and still virtually paralysed, only the wealthy minority had the funds with which to pay. At the same time, as yet another measure designed to diminish the National Guard's potential, the Assembly voted to end the pay of 1·50 francs a day, which for so many had provided a form of dole during the Siege. Thus with these three unenlightened strokes a vast cross-section of Parisian society— the *petite bourgeoisie* of clerks and shopkeepers, artisans and minor officials, few of whom owned their own dwellings—now found themselves thrust into the same camp as the under privileged proletariat, whom they had hitherto despised and distrusted. Their mood was rebellious, typified by Louis Péguret when he wrote to his sister: 'the landlords have no reclaim against those whose only fortune is in their daily work. ... We shall pay when we can, and there will be many who will never pay.'

The last act at Bordeaux of this 'Assembly of country bumpkins', as Gaston Crémieux described it, was to adjourn itself on March 10th and decide (by 427 votes to 154) to reconvene in Versailles on the 20th. Mindful of the humiliation Trochu and Favre had been subjected to on October 31st, and of the shootings of January 22nd, the Assembly certainly had reason to consider that somewhere outside of inflamed, disordered, atheistic Red Paris would be more conducive to good government. Reporting to Lord Granville, the Foreign Secretary, at the beginning of March, the British Ambassador, Lord Lyons, used some ominous words: 'The majority of the Assembly, which is decidedly anti-Republican, hardly expects to establish a Government to its taste, without some actual fighting with the Reds in Paris and other large towns. It therefore does not at all like the idea of moving the Assembly to Paris. . . . I cannot help thinking that the sooner the Government settles in the Capital, and has its fight (if fight there really must be) with the Mob over, the better.' The possible motives behind this latest slight were also apparent to the Parisians, but the choice of Versailles was taken as a sign not only of distrust, but—more dangerously—of weakness.

*   *   *

At the same time as the Assembly, in its heavy-handed insensitivity, was heaping injury upon injury from Bordeaux on to wounded Paris, the city itself had been subjected to the worst humiliation that any proud capital can know. France's part of the bargain by which Thiers had saved Belfort was to allow the Germans to make a triumphal march through Paris and occupy the city for two days. Unfeelingly Labouchere wrote, 'I am fully convinced that this vain, silly population would rather that King William should double the indemnity which he demands from France than march with his troops down the Rue de Rivoli', and indeed few Parisians felt that the fate of this distant provincial town merited submitting Paris—after all she had suffered—to such depths of shame. Indignation was universal and violent; and with it went an additional sense of betrayal, in that the Government had proclaimed on February 4th: 'The enemy shall not enter into Paris'. It recalled all too painfully Trochu's promise 'The Governor of Paris will not capitulate'—or Favre's 'not an inch of our territory, nor a stone of our fortresses'. Louis Péguret wrote to his sister, Octavie: 'What shame, what dishonour, these Royalists have brought upon their country! . . . The whole population has rage in its heart, and if the Prussians should give the least suspicion of mockery it would not be at all surprising if some patriot, for whom the shame was too much, fired a random shot.' The veteran Socialist, Louis Blanc, told Juliette Lambert that what was being said in the Clubs 'terrified' him, and that he 'feared some folly' if the Prussians should march through Paris. The Lyon brothers, who had just entered Paris, found that when the news became known, 'angry crowds of armed men were going about vowing vengeance on the Prussians', and added ominously that 'The National Guards had taken forcible possession of their arms and ammunition and were very excited'.

There were those in the German camp too, including the Prussian Crown Prince, who had their doubts about the wisdom of the triumphal entry, but on the appointed day the sheer splendour of the occasion swept all misgivings aside. At 8 a.m. on March 1st, a young lieutenant and six troopers of the 14th Prussian Hussars rode up to the Étoile, jumped their horses over the chains and other obstructions Parisians had placed around the Arc de Triomphe, and continued insouciantly through the sacred edifice. Edward Blount, who was watching, was 'astonished by the Prussians' bravery', and the populace too seems to have been taken by surprise. The march had begun.

Out at Longchamp, where less than four years ago another march past had been held in honour of the King of Prussia, but under rather different circumstances, the 30,000 troops picked for the triumphal entry were passing in review before him: 30,000 of the troops who had elevated him from a king to an emperor in those four years. Standing in the fallen Louis-Napoleon's pavilion, the Crown Prince noted that 'all the woodwork is burnt, and only the iron framework holds the walls precariously together. Obscene insults in word and picture scrawled on the bare walls revile the banished ruler'. As the men who had fought at Wœrth and Gravelotte, Orléans, and Dijon, and from Sedan to Paris, goose-stepped past, a sense of history overwhelmed Archibald Forbes who was attempting to record the event for the *Daily News*: 'Out rings the clarion of the trumpets, clash goes the silver music of the kettledrums, tempered by the sweet notes of the ophicleide. The horses, ever lovers of sweet sounds, arch their necks, champ the bits, and toss flecks of foam on the polished leathers of the riders. They are as proud as if they realised the meaning and the glory of the day.' As the procession formed up to move off, Forbes noted a touching encounter that seemed to epitomize the strength and solidarity of this new nation; 'The Kaiser turned his horse and met his son face to face. Hand went out to hand, and the grip was given of love and mutual appreciation.' Behind followed what looked to Forbes like 'half the Almanack de Gotha'.

On the way to Paris, there was an unplanned touch of the absurd when some of the Uhlans lost their way in the Bois de Boulogne and had to be redirected by French bystanders. But as the columns debouched into the Champs-Élysées, even Parisians—never able to resist a parade, nor stifle their curiosity—could hardly withhold grudging envy of the conquerors. 'A company of Uhlans, with their spears stuck in their saddles, and ornamented by the little flags of blue and white, headed the advancing column', Washburne reported to his Secretary of State; 'They were followed by the Saxons, with their light blue coats, who were succeeded by the Bavarian riflemen, with their heavy uniform and martial tread. Afterward followed more of the Uhlans, and occasionally a squad of the Bismarck cuirassiers, with their white jackets, square hats and waving plumes, recalling to mind, perhaps, among the more intelligent French observers, the celebrated cuirassiers of Nansouty and Latour-Maubourg in the wars of the First Napoleon. Now come the artillery, with its pieces of six, which must have extorted the admiration of all military men by its splendid appearance and wonderful precision of movement. . . .' 'What a solid and stately array', gasped O'Shea, homeward bound for England; 'The spectacle was one of the most thrilling I had ever witnessed.'

When the German troops were dismissed, they crowned themselves with laurels in the Tuileries, and strode proudly about the city in small groups. Some were followed by groups of urchins, hooting and whistling, while other elements booed from a safe distance. But, despite all the omens, no attacks were made on the Germans; in fact one of the British correspondents claimed 'there was a gala look about the place, which was revolting under the circumstances', and another noted how Parisian women 'openly expressed their admiration of the fine manly proportions, the martial look and gallant bearing, of the invaders'. There was an ugly moment when Bismarck found himself surrounded by a glaring crowd on the Place de la Concorde, but with superb aplomb he took out a cigar and asked the most hostile-looking spectator for a light. Writing from what they called 'Passy-Prusse' during those 'two sad days', the Rafinesque family reported that Belleville had 'barricaded itself, armed with cannons and machine-guns and swore that the Germans would never put a foot on its territory'. Fortunately, however, the Prussians were prudent enough not to enter this hornets' nest. Most of the shops in Prussian-occupied Paris remained firmly closed, their windows draped with black, and bistro-owners accused of having served the enemy had their windows smashed and premises sacked. Savage retribution was also meted out to civilians appearing to be too friendly to the conqueror, and a number of women had their clothes torn off them on the slimmest of pretexts. Forbes himself, observed doffing his hat to the Crown Prince of Saxony, was seized after the troops had passed by, beaten up, and narrowly escaped being thrown in the Seine.

Otherwise the Prussian occupation came to an end unchecked. On the morning of March 3rd, Goncourt was awoken 'by music, *their* music. A magnificent morning, with that fine sunshine indifferent to human catastrophes, whether they be called the Victory of Austerlitz, or the Capture of Paris. Marvellous weather, but with a sky filled with the cawing of crows, which one never hears here at this time of year, and which they bear in their train like black outriders of their armies. They are going! They are leaving us at last!' A *Times* correspondent who watched the departing German officers call for a cheer as they rode out through the Arc de Triomphe admitted: 'No matter, at that moment, upon which side one's sympathies might be, it was impossible not to catch the infection of the enthusiasm, not to feel one's heart beating and one's cheek flushing in harmony with the palpitating mass of men which went roaring and rolling past like some mighty torrent. . . .' On March 6th Bismarck and his entourage left for the Fatherland; it was, so the faithful Busch terminated his account, 'a beautifully fine morning. Thrushes and finches warble the signal for our departure'.

As soon as the last German had withdrawn from the city, Parisians set to scrubbing the streets the enemy feet had trodden with Condy's Fluid, and 'purifying' the tainted *pavé* by the fire of many bonfires. But an atrocious stain had been left behind which nothing would quite erase. To any Latin race, there are some insults that can only be wiped clean with blood. It would be another half century before France was strong enough to exact vengeance upon the Germans; in the meantime, the blood that was to flow would belong to her own people.

Seizure of the National Guard Guns

17. The Guns of Montmartre

'WHEN you know Paris', wrote Trochu's one-time aide, Captain d'Hérisson, about the city under siege, 'she is not a town, she is an animated being, a natural person, who has her moments of fury, madness, stupidity, enthusiasm.' That she was on the verge of or embarking upon one of her 'moments of fury' was sensed by some outside the city walls, including Lord Lyons, and on March 4th the Prussian Crown Prince entered in his diary: 'We must be prepared to see a fight in Paris between the Moderates and the Reds. . . . How sad is the fate of this unhappy people.'

But within Paris herself the city's true mood tended to be obscured by the thoroughly deceptive appearance she was beginning to give, superficially, of back-to-normal calm. After the harsh winter, spring now seemed to be just around the corner, and health was returning rapidly. By the week ending March 11th, the death rate had dropped by over a third compared with the first week of February. Business was reviving, and both traffic and gas lighting were seen once more on the streets. The Rev. W. Gibson, an English Methodist clergyman who had spent ten years before the war trying to 'convert' the Parisians, noted on first returning after the Siege how once-hefty coalmen shrank from carrying loads up to third and fourth storeys—but by March 9th it was the city 'assuming its former brilliant appearance at night' that occupied his attention.

To the casual spectator, keeping to the relit boulevards, people seemed more cheerful. Threads of life, broken by the Siege, were being picked up again. For Goncourt, February 24th was a red-letter day, for it was then he discovered his taste for literature had returned. Yet three days later he was brooding over some indefinable malaise: 'something sombre and unquiet... upon the physiognomy of Paris...'; and again the following day: 'impossible to describe the ambient sadness which surrounds you; Paris is under the most terrible of apprehensions, apprehension of the unknown.' If the perceptive Goncourt could not exactly diagnose what lay beneath the surface, it equally eluded even a shrewd, experienced observer like Washburne. William Brown, about to leave Paris for good, wrote lyrically to his wife: 'it is all over now I feel sure, thank God, and what with the prospect of peace and business, the abundance of every kind of food, the beautiful Spring weather, and last but not least the prospect of soon, I hope, seeing all your dear faces, I feel supremely happy.' Meanwhile, on March 5th, Jules Ferry was confidently telegraphing from Paris to his colleague, Jules Simon, in Bordeaux: 'The city is entirely calm. The danger has passed....'

The true mood of Paris should have been revealed by a savagely nasty incident that took place on the Place de la Bastille on February 26th. Already, two days previously, units of the National Guard had begun demonstrating there against suspected Government intents to disembody and disarm them, coupled with protests against the German triumphal entry (it also happened to be the anniversary of the creation of the Second Republic in 1848). On the 25th, the demonstration had turned into a veritable left-wing pilgrimage, and by evening the plinth of the July Column was heaped high with wreaths and oriflammes; and on the 26th (the day Thiers signed the Peace Treaty) it became a mass march past of the National Guard, lasting from 10 a.m. in the morning until 6 p.m. at night. Though none bore arms, each battalion marched with its own band and its colours draped in black. Some 300,000 Parisians took part, and many—like Louis Péguret—found it a particularly exalting, and even 'majestic', occasion. From the monument, leaders of the National Guard wearing red sashes across their chests made inflammatory speeches to any who could hear them. One regular Army officer heard a representative of the 238th Battalion of the National Guard declare—amid menacing references to 1793, 1830, and 1848—that 'the exploiters of monopoly seem to believe that the people are always in tutelage. They seem to forget that they sometimes wake up suddenly. . . .'

The temper of the crowd was ugly; it needed little to create an incident. Abruptly the speeches were interrupted by shouts of 'A spy! A spy! Arrest him!', and a man was dragged forth, beaten and kicked. His name appears to have been Vincenzoni, but just what his offence was remains vague; the Lyon brothers who witnessed the episode recounted that he had merely been recognized as a former Imperial police official, but left-wing sympathizers claimed that he was a Government spy noting down the numbers of units taking part in the demonstration. Whatever the truth, the mob was lusting for blood and the wretched man was dragged to the bank of the Seine, accompanied by yells of 'Beat him! Knock him on the head! Drown him!' According to the subsequent inquiry, he begged to be allowed to shoot himself, but the mob refused him this clemency, howling: 'Into the Seine with him, into the Seine!' He was then bound hand and foot and carried, 'like a parcel', across a line of moored barges, and thrown well out into the Seine. But the current kept bringing the unfortunate man back into shore, where 'some wretches, pushing ferocity to its ultimate limits, stoned him . . . .' These horrible scenes lasted not less than two hours, until the victim was finally drowned— under the eyes of several thousand unprotesting Parisian men and women.

That same day, insurgents forced their way into the Ste.-Pélagie prison to release, among others, a prisoner detained for his part in the January disturbances: one Lieutenant Paul-Antoine Brunel, who was to play a key role in subsequent events. Brunel, a determined disciple of *résistance à outrance* during the Siege, had been arrested by Vinoy shortly before the capitulation, on charges of having ordered his men of the 107th Battalion of the National Guard to seize the magazines and telegraphs, and to forestall any attempt of the Government of National Defence to leave Paris by balloon. At the same time as Brunel was released, other National Guards boldly descended on artillery parks in various parts of the city which the Germans were to occupy and removed some two hundred cannon. Most of these bore National Guard numbers, and had been 'bought' by public subscription during the Siege. In all honesty, the Guard felt that these guns were 'their' property, and its motives seem to have been activated purely out of determination to prevent them shamefully falling into German hands. Exasperated by defeat and all the further humiliation that they felt the new Assembly had piled upon it, the die-hard 'popular' elements of the National Guard now took it upon themselves to salvage what little remained of Parisian pride; and much of the rest of Paris was with them. Chanting the Marseillaise, with prodigious physical efforts they hauled the two hundred cannon up to Montmartre. Still only partially built up, with but one access road to it, Montmartre lay in 'friendly' territory and provided a redoubt difficult to approach. The removal of the guns was to have immense consequences, but—although the agitations of February 26th spread fairly widely across the city—as there had been no actual clash between the National Guard and the regular Army, the event passed by relatively unmarked.

At the end of January, after the shooting incident of the 22nd and the capitulation, the left-wing battalions of the National Guard with 'common interests' had gradually become grouped together under an executive organ calling itself the *Comité Central de la Garde Nationale*. By the beginning of March, after additional units, disaffected by the Assembly's unpopular measures, had drifted into its orbit, and after many 'bourgeois' battalions had been disbanded owing to the mass exodus from Paris of their members, the Comité Central wielded huge potential powers. It, and not d'Aurelle, the newly appointed chief, commanded the National Guard. Moreover, because of Favre's disastrous compromise at Versailles whereby (despite Bismarck's warning) the regular Army had been reduced to only one division while the National Guard retained its arms, the latter was now by far the most powerful armed force in France; and, as of February 26th, it had two hundred cannon at its disposal. On March 3rd, General d'Aurelle de Paladines arrived in Paris. He hardly enhanced his popularity by promptly proclaiming his 'firm intention to repress with energy all that could impair tranquillity'. When he summoned a meeting of battalion commanders of the National Guard, only some thirty out of two hundred and sixty turned up. The Government now suddenly became aware of the strength of the 'dissident' National Guard (who had given themselves the title of '*Fédérés*'), this Frankenstein it had created during the Siege. On March 5th, Blumenthal noted down in his journal doubts as to whether Vinoy, commander of the Paris garrison, would be master of the situation 'even with 40,000 men'.

Thus suddenly, literally overnight, had the balance of power in Paris—and, indeed, France herself—changed. To Thiers, the potential threat appeared too grave to leave unchallenged. On March 8th the regular Army was ordered to recover the purloined guns. Vinoy himself, as well as most of his officers, was burning with anger at the long chain of insults the 'rabble in arms' had offered his forces; ill-feeling between the regulars and the National Guard was at its peak, the provincial *Mobiles* in particular still recalling with contempt the performance of the latter during the Siege. But on the day Vinoy's men put up only the feeblest of performances. A new toughness seemed to have entered into the National Guard, and, confronted with a resolute refusal to hand over the cannon, the regulars backed away. Later that day, Duval, one of the members of the Comité Central, followed up this display of weakness by burning down an Army barracks on the Rue de Grenelle. Vinoy spluttered with impotent rage. Thiers, reaching Paris on the 17th,[1] realized that a full-scale military demonstration would have to be made to cow the National Guard into handing over the guns. A force of some 3,000 gendarmes and police, plus the 12,000 to 15,000 regulars at Vinoy's disposal, he reckoned, would be sufficient to impress a militia which Trochu had hesitated to send into action. The guns would be removed from Montmartre the next morning. 'Evilly-disposed men, under the pretext of resisting the Prussians, have taken control of a part of the city', Thiers proclaimed to the Parisians; 'You will approve our recourse to force, for it is necessary, at all cost . . . that order, the very basis of your well-being, should be reborn.' But he had misjudged the temper of both Paris and the National Guard as badly as he had gauged the morale of the defeated French regulars.

On the morning of the 18th, Minister Washburne set off to spend the day with some American friends, Mr. and Mrs. Moulton, at Petit-Val, some twelve miles from Paris. Before starting he called in at the Foreign Office, where he had detected some unspecified agitation; otherwise 'there was no excitement in the streets, and there appeared to be nothing unusual going on. . . .' Mr. Moulton mentioned hearing rumours of a collision at Montmartre, and that two generals had been killed, but after four months of siege Washburne no longer paid much attention to Parisian *canards*. When he returned that night he was to find the Thiers Government had fled Paris and the Commune had begun.

Vinoy's operation to disarm the National Guard comprised four separate movements; one body of troops was sent under General Faron to occupy the hotbeds of Belleville and the Buttes-Chaumont, where some of the cannon had also been dragged; General Wolff with a second column moved on the Bastille area; while a third under General Hanrion covered the Hôtel de Ville. The main effort of recovering the Montmartre guns fell to General Susbielle's division, consisting of two brigades commanded by Generals Paturel and Lecomte. It was, in fact, a far less impressive force than it sounded; Lecomte's brigade, for instance, to which the principal burden was

[1] Although the Assembly was to move to Versailles, most of the Government Ministries were still in Paris, which they had never left.

allotted, consisted largely of green and inexperienced young troops of the 88th Regiment. There was little enthusiasm as the regulars reached their objectives under a glacial rain, before dawn that Saturday morning; a Captain Patry, sent with his regiment to the Bastille, recalled being disgusted equally at the thought of anyone plunging the ruined country into a civil war, and himself being called out 'to bring back the House of Orléans to the Tuileries'. Yet, like so many of the disastrous battles during the Siege, the operation began auspiciously enough. Although today's Montmartre would not yet have gone to bed, by being in position at 3 a.m. Susbielle's division had caught the village fast asleep. Those sentries of the National Guard who were awake, standing watch over the sacred cannon, fled in terror; one alone, Guardsman Turpin, who was whiling away the time by greasing his bayonet, was wounded with a *chassepot* bullet. The guard-post in the Rue des Rosiers was captured and locked up in the cellars of the Tour Solférino restaurant, close to where Gambetta had climbed aboard his balloon. By 4 a.m. it was all over at Montmartre; the regulars had recaptured the guns.

By a piece of almost unbelievable incompetence, typical of that professional ineptitude which had lost France the war, Susbielle's division now discovered that it had come without the teams of horses needed to tow the guns away. It was Champigny, Le Bourget, and Buzenval all over again. (Said Thiers of the operation, in a superlative piece of understatement, 'It lacked the ardent vigilance which makes affairs of war succeed'.) There the regulars sat, with the guns they had recaptured, unable to move. In the meantime, Louise Michel— the Red Virgin—who had been assisting a National Guard *cantinière* to staunch Turpin's wounds at No. 6 Rue des Rosiers, somehow managed to escape. Down the hill she ran, with a rifle on her shoulder, crying 'Treason!' Quickly the Montmartre 'Vigilance Committee' mustered its supporters. As the sun came up and the horses had still not arrived, the denizens of Montmartre, realizing the stalemate, recovered their nerve. All over Paris the sinister tocsin was heard, alerting the National Guard. Everywhere immense, hostile crowds composed of National Guardsmen and the inevitable admixture of Parisian *canaille* sprang up around the regulars. Their aspect reminded one correspondent of *The Times* of pictures of Girondist revolutionaries, and he was terrified 'to see arms in the hands of such men'. Closer and closer they surged up to the regulars, whose officers were either too inexperienced or too dispirited to keep the mob at a distance. Down at the Bastille, Captain Patry claimed, 'I had never been more embarrassed in my life. My orders were to disperse any assemblages, and the streets were nothing but one vast assemblage in which my company was positively drowned. I myself had the greatest difficulty in moving.' Under such conditions it was impossible for the regulars to retain any initiative.

Up at Montmartre things became even worse. By 7.45 a.m., Lecomte's troops were virtually submerged by the mob, who fraternized with them, pouring every kind of seditious argument into their young ears. Suddenly, some of the 88th Regiment of the Line were seen to reverse their rifles, raising the butts in the air, accompanied by cries of 'Long live the Line! Down with Vinoy! Down with Thiers!' At approximately this moment, the twenty-nine-year-old Mayor of Montmartre, Dr. Georges Clemenceau, appeared on the scene requesting to remove Turpin to hospital. Clemenceau also warned Lecomte to get the guns away quickly, otherwise there would be serious trouble. Lecomte refused to allow Turpin to be moved; a decision which roused the mob—goaded on by the tempestuous Louise—to a new fury. Lecomte rashly gave the order to fire on the mob, but realizing he would no longer be obeyed, countermanded it and instead ordered his men to defend themselves with their bayonets. One order was as unrealistic as the other, and Lecomte, isolated by the defection of the troops of the 88th, was dragged from his horse.

What follows now bears the confusion of such events, depending as it did largely on the testimony of witnesses who were subsequently sentenced to death or to imprisonment for their participation. Beaten and insulted, General Lecomte—whom at one point the mob appears to have mistaken for Vinoy himself—was conducted to a National Guard post established in the 'Château-Rouge', a dance-hall similar to the famous 'Moulin de la Galette'. The post was commanded by Captain Simon Mayer, who promptly went to Clemenceau to report that he held Lecomte prisoner. Clemenceau instructed Mayer to be responsible for the general's safety, but on his return Mayer received a fresh set of orders from the 'Vigilance Committee of the 18th Arrondissement', composed of left-wing extremists such as Clemenceau's Deputy Mayor, a bearded Red fanatic called Théophile Ferré. Fearing that Clemenceau's intentions were to have Lecomte released, the 'Vigilance Committee' ordered that he should be transferred to another National Guard post in the Rue des Rosiers. Mayer obeyed.

On the way the procession, already composed of National Guards and some of Lecomte's own soldiers of the 88th, but chiefly of hangers-on, collected some of the worst riff-raff of the Montmartre slums. They included prostitutes and an appalling group of harpies who had been engaged in stripping an Army horse killed in the early scuffles—figures horribly reminiscent of the *tricoteuses* of the Terror. They howled for the blood of the captive, and it was with some difficulty that Mayer and his men kept him from their clutches. Progress as a result was slow, and it was not until 2.30 p.m. that the party reached the pleasantly named street which, 'with its pebbled road, its gardens, its low houses', made Alphonse Daudet, visiting the scene a few days later, think of 'one of those peaceful suburbs where the town straggles out and becomes diminished, eventually to die at the edge of the fields'. By this time Vinoy had called off the operation, leaving Lecomte to his fate.

At No. 6, Rue des Rosiers, to the accompaniment of an ever-increasing barrage of bloodthirsty imprecations, Lecomte's captors attempted to interrogate him. But at 4 p.m. a new escort of National Guards arrived, bringing with them a second captive, a tall white-bearded old man wearing a frock-coat and silk hat. It was General Clément Thomas, the recently retired ex-Commander of the National Guard. They had seized Thomas on the Place Pigalle whither, it appears, he had foolishly been drawn by curiosity. Long hated for his part in crushing the 1848 Revolution, Thomas was now regarded by those into whose hands he had fallen as chiefly responsible for the massacre of the National Guard at Buzenval. His presence was in effect a sentence of death for both generals. Beyond all control, the mob burst into the house, demanding their immediate extinction. Captain Mayer now rushed back to the Mairie to warn Clemenceau of the imminent danger confronting the two generals. According to a witness, one of the Guard officers yielded to the mob, calling for a show of hands. 'Everybody raised his hand', and General Thomas was dragged out into the little garden—'a real suburban garden in which every tenant has his corner for gooseberries and clematis, separated by green trellises with banging doors' (Daudet). No proper execution-squad was formed, and after a first ragged volley of shots the old general still stood there. One of the participants later told Rochefort in prison that Thomas had been superbly brave, crying out: 'Kill me! You won't prevent me from calling you cowards and assassins.' Shot after shot was fired until he finally fell, with a bullet through the eye, insulting his executioners to the last breath. Lecomte was then dispatched with one shot in the back. When a post-mortem was carried out, it was discovered that several of the generals' wounds had been caused by *chassepot* bullets, with which the National Guard was not equipped, and therefore presumably fired by Lecomte's own troops.

Some hideous scenes now ensued. The men continued to discharge their rifles into the dead and mutilated bodies, while mænads from the mob squatted and urinated upon them. Small urchins fought one another for a view of the corpses from the garden wall. At this point,

Clemenceau arrived, shouting distractedly, '*Pas de sang, mes amis, pas de sang !*', to be told 'It's too late'. In Clemenceau's own words:

... The mob which filled the courtyard burst into the street in the grip of some kind of frenzy. Amongst them were chasseurs, soldiers of the line, National Guards, women and children. All were shrieking like wild beasts without realizing what they were doing. I observed then that pathological phenomenon which might be called blood lust. A breath of madness seemed to have passed over this mob: ... men were dancing about and jostling each other in a kind of savage fury. It was one of those extraordinary nervous outbursts, so frequent in the Middle Ages, which still occur amongst masses of human beings under the stress of some primaeval emotion.

All that day Clemenceau seems to have been labouring under false optimism; first assuming that the guns would be delivered without incident, and secondly, that Lecomte would come to no harm. When he saw what had happened, he burst into tears; the last time, it was said, the tough doctor-politician was seen to weep in public until the victory of 1918. He too had grossly miscalculated the temper of the mob, and momentarily his own life seemed in jeopardy. Elsewhere in Paris, Chanzy emerging from the Gare d'Orléans in a general's full dress had been mistaken by another mob for d'Aurelle, and nearly shared the fate of Thomas and Lecomte; Vinoy too had a narrow escape, though for a time his death was widely rumoured; and Trochu held that he himself was saved only by a timely warning.

Amid these scenes of commotion and ferocity there passed incongruously, another manifestation of death. An old man, bare-headed and clad in deepest mourning, was marching at the head of a long, motley funeral procession, composed of men of letters, staggering drunks, and armed National Guards gathered up at random on the way to the Père-Lachaise cemetery. It was Victor Hugo, following the coffin of his son Charles, dead suddenly of apoplexy. '*Coup sur coup, deuil sur deuil, Ah ! L'épreuve redouble.*'[1] The words applied to France as well. Goncourt found himself shocked by the levity with which the fellow mourners around him joked about Thiers and 'the terrible revolution building up about us. I am very sad and full of the most painful presentiments.'

That same day, in marked contrast, Berlin in the most festive of moods was celebrating the triumphal return of her conquering monarch. From the statue of Frederick the Great floated a banner on which was inscribed a long poem, beginning 'Hail, Kaiser Wilhelm! Hail to thee and to the brave German host thou leadest back from

[1] 'Blow upon blow, loss upon loss, Ah! The ordeal is redoubled.'

victory, ghost-like from afar. . . . Old Fritz looks down with proud glance upon his descendants, approving greatly their valour.' For several days the festivities continued, during which the giant French cannon from Mont-Valérien was dragged triumphantly through the streets; but what seemed to please the jubilant Berliners most was the appearance on the royal balcony of their future ruler, thirteen-year-old Prince Wilhelm, dressed in the full regalia of an Uhlan. In the midst of all this, a shabby former Emperor of the French was released from his incarceration at Wilhelmshöhe and allowed to move without ceremony to his permanent place of exile in Britain.

By the time Generals Thomas and Lecomte were being done to death, Vinoy had withdrawn his troops from the trouble-centres of Paris, and concentrated them around the Invalides. Captain Patry had arrived there from the Bastille and was learning of the appalling news when he saw a carriage pass by, drawn by one horse, and containing a gentleman in a grey overcoat. 'It was the Minister of War effecting his retreat in good order to Versailles.' The Captain was astonished.

Since 5 a.m. that morning the leading members of Thiers's Government had been waiting anxiously at the Quai d'Orsay as bad news succeeded bad. After all the tribulations most of them had undergone since the previous September, nerves were not good. Towards the end of the morning, General Le Flô, the Minister of War—who had just escaped being mobbed at the Place de la Bastille—reckoned that no more than 6,000 out of 400,000 National Guards could now be counted on as loyal to the Government. The situation seemed desperate; it was no longer merely a question of retaking the Montmartre guns, but of maintaining ascendancy in Paris itself. Thiers's sense of history now dictated a fateful decision; the Government would withdraw from Paris to Versailles, 'completely and immediately'. During the Revolution of 1848 it was what he had told Louis-Philippe to do—'then return with Marshal Bugeaud and 50,000 men'—and he considered that, if his advice had been taken, the July Monarchy would still have been at the Tuileries; in that same revolutionary year, he recalled, Windischgrätz had done just this in Vienna, *reculer pour mieux sauter*, and returned to reconquer the insurrectionary city a few weeks later. With some reason, Thiers argued that if the Government remained in Paris, 'the moral contagion of the insurrection would spread to the regular Army, which would lose no time in abandoning us'. Simon, Favre, and Picard protested; it was unthinkable to abandon Paris. Why not instead create a centre of resistance around the Hôtel de Ville, so strongly fortified since last October 31st? But Thiers was adamant; besides, Ferry, as Prefect, had already reported from the Hôtel de Ville one attempt by followers of Blanqui to seize it.

The argument was settled by the appearance, at about 3 p.m., of several battalions of hostile National Guards on the Quai below the Foreign Office. 'We're done for!' cried Le Flô. By a concealed staircase Thiers escaped into the Rue de l'Université, and guarded by an escort hastily provided by Vinoy, he decamped to Versailles. The other Ministers followed shortly afterwards, and beind them marched the whole of Vinoy's regulars, jeered at by an amazed Paris.

All the events of March 18th had taken the various Red principals. as well as the Comité Central, thoroughly by surprise. None had anticipated the surprise Government move on Montmartre of that morning, nor the hideous retaliation it had engendered; but least of all had they foreseen that the Government, thwarted, would pull out. For such a contingency nothing like a plan had been prepared, and— like everything else that had happened that day—the reaction to the Government's withdrawal was completely spontaneous and uncoordinated. While the Comité Central staggered, Paul-Antoine Brunel, who had been liberated from Ste.-Pélagie prison during the demonstrations of February 26th, acted. A resourceful and effective leader, as soon as he realized that the Government forces were abandoning control, Brunel seized the initiative himself. At the head of a group of National Guards, he surrounded the Prince-Eugène Barracks which was tenanted by the 120th Regiment, locked up its officers, and disarmed the men, many of whom seemed disposed to take sides with the rebels. From there, joined by other National Guard units, Brunel marched on the Hôtel de Ville. At the Napoléon Barracks, linked to the Hôtel de Ville by its secret tunnel through which loyal troops had come to wave the Government on October 31st, there was a brief exchange of fire in which three people were hit. Then members of the line regiment inside came out shouting 'Vive la République!', and handed over their weapons.

By 7.30 that evening the Hôtel de Ville was completely surrounded. Fortified as it had been by the Trochu Government, it still represented a powerful stronghold, but gradually the troops and gendarmes manning it faded away, seeking refuge down the subterranean passage. Before much more than another hour had passed, Ferry found himself virtually deserted and out of touch with his Government. While Brunel and the hostile crowd still held off before the formidable building, Ferry escaped by ladder out of a back window. Hiding that night with a friend, he too departed for Versailles the next morning. Close on his heels, Brunel now entered the Hôtel de Ville, and amidst tumultuous applause unfurled a red flag from the belfry of the building.

T

Lest the Government should mount a surprise counter-attack, he quickly ordered that barricades be erected in the Rue de Rivoli and dispatched detachments to occupy the other Government buildings.

That night as Elihu Washburne returned from his day in the country with the Moultons, he was astonished to discover 'the movement of carriages interdicted on the principal streets, and I was obliged to turn into the by-streets. I soon found my way impeded by the barricades which had been improvised by the insurrectionary National Guard. After showing my card to the various commanders, I was enabled to go through the obstructed quarters. While I saw so many evidences of great public commotion, I had no adequate conception of how serious matters were until the next morning. . . .' For the first time since '93, revolutionaries were undisputed masters of Paris. With the superior force now at their disposal, would they go on to seize control of all France?

'Massacre' in the Place Vendôme

18. The Commune Takes Over

On the morning of Sunday, March 19th, Paris awoke to a day of brilliant spring sunshine; though still cold, it was sufficiently full of sparkling promise to gladden men's hearts after the passage of so harsh a winter. As people began to move about the streets, a festive atmosphere developed—at any rate in the proletarian districts—that was strongly reminiscent of the September 4th 'revolution' by which Louis-Napoleon had been overthrown. It contrasted curiously with the grim events at Montmartre the previous day. 'Paris could hardly be said to be "agitated"', noted the Rev. Gibson; 'the people promenading as usual on Sunday, and the National Guards marching along the middle of the streets. Indeed, all had a complete holiday air. Preceding most of the battalions of the National Guards were young women (one to each battalion) dressed in *képi* and Bloomer costume with a small cask suspended by a strap flung over the shoulders'. The only visible intrusion upon normal life was that 'the omnibus traffic was suspended'. Outside the Hôtel de Ville were an estimated 20,000 National Guards, peacefully encamped, with loaves of bread impaled upon the points of their bayonets. Edwin Child, now returned from England, strolled 'round the Louvre, meeting many battalions of National Guards promenading some for and some against the events of yesterday'. Goncourt was also out, his bourgeois aversions immediately . aroused by the ubiquity of the dissident National Guard: 'One was overcome with disgust at the sight of their stupid, abject faces, in which triumph and intoxication created a sort of dissolute radiance. . . . On the way home, I read on people's faces dazed indifference, sometimes melancholy irony, most often sheer consternation, with old gentlemen raising their hands in despair and whispering among themselves after looking cautiously all around.' Russell of *The Times*, who, going against the current, had just arrived from Versailles, observed Government employees at the Louvre packing up: 'There was a crowd of twenty men around the door of the *caserne*, watching with angry interest the men of the Garde de Paris and Gendarmerie, who were hastily removing and piling in a few carts at hand their military chests. . . .' In his opinion 'the surrender of the suffering capital of Western Europe to the foes who were more to be feared than "Goth or Vandal, or destroying Hun" ', was 'all but incredible'. He hastened to impart the news to Lord Lyons. The Ambassador viewed the departure of Thiers with considerable gloom, not untinged with personal feelings, in that he had only re-established himself in the Paris Embassy four days previously and, being of a distinctly sedentary disposition, did not relish the prospect of yet another move, to Versailles.

If there was relative calm on the streets of Paris, it was by no means reflected inside the captured Hôtel de Ville, where a widely diverse collection of 'revolutionaries' and dissidents of all hues was debating the circumstances that had been thrust upon them. All were astonished by it, some were appalled, most were overawed. Although later it became widely believed that March 18th had all been a carefully prepared plot engineered by that sinister and shadowy group, the International, no one was more surprised than its leaders, including Karl Marx. Everything that had happened that day bore the keynote of spontaneity, and—as has already been seen—it was only on the initiative of junior commanders like Brunel that the abandoned Government offices had been occupied at all. The Comité Central of the National Guard had organized nothing, planned nothing; with the result that it was now caught critically off balance. What course of action should be adopted? Who or what should fill the vacuum created by the departure of the Government?

Vigorously, and often chaotically, the argument raged. Brunel wanted to march on Versailles at once and arrest the Government, while Louise Michel was heard fiercely urging those who would listen to expedite the assassination of Thiers. One member of the Comité

Central declared: 'As for France, we do not presume to dictate laws to her—we have suffered too much under hers—but we do not wish any longer to submit to rural plebiscites.' This outraged the veteran Socialist, Louis Blanc, who in his later years had become imbued with a sense of the sanctity of the State; he protested, 'You are insurgents against an Assembly most freely elected!'[1] About all that emerged from the meetings was the ascendancy of the Comité Central as the only body capable of governing Paris. Under the chairmanship of an ineffective member of the International called Adolphe-Alphonse Assi, who had a passion for delicate embroidery and had helped mount the big Le Creusot strikes early in 1870, the Comité Central now took over the reins.

No single issue was debated more heatedly in those first sessions at the Hôtel de Ville than the killing of the two generals. Neither the Comité Central nor any individual Red leader bore responsibility for this spontaneous act of mob frenzy. Yet could they repudiate it? *Le Rappel* expressed its profound grief, while pointing out that National Guards on the spot did attempt to hold back the mob, and even some of the most extreme left-wingers were deeply shocked. André Gill the cartoonist gloomily predicted '*La Commune est foutue!*' and Babick, a Polish revolutionary on the Comité Central, protested against the killings and urged that the Comité should dissociate itself. But he was shouted down by another who cried, 'Beware of disavowing the people, lest in their turn they disavow you!' By and large, the feeling was—recalling '93—that such regrettable occurrences were unavoidable in revolutions. Great indignation, however, was provoked by the reading out of an editorial in the *Journal Officiel* of that morning; 'That frightful crime', it said, 'accomplished under the eyes of the Comité Central, gave the measure of the horrors with which Paris would be menaced if the savage agitators, who troubled the city and dishonoured France, should triumph.' It was decided that 'these calumnies' would have to be stopped at source, so that one of the first actions of the new regime was to dispatch emissaries to take over the publication. Reappearing under its new management the following day, the *Journal Officiel* promptly absolved the Comité of any responsibility for what it described as the 'executions' of 'two men who had made themselves unpopular by acts that as from today we rate iniquitous'. In its second issue, the *Journal* went further and spoke of the two generals as having been executed 'according to the laws of war'.

Beyond the ranks of the revolutionaries, the news of the lynching of the two old generals had widely disgusted Frenchmen; Goncourt

[1] Blanc was to play no part in the Commune.

said he experienced 'a sensation of weariness at being French'. Disastrously, the Comité Central through its utterances in the *Journal Officiel* now became identified with the outrage. At Versailles, anger surged through the officer's messes of the regular Army, and with it went a grim determination to avenge Lecomte and Thomas. What little prospect there now existed of conciliation between the Government and the insurgents was made clear by Jules Favre when he declared, in tougher language than he had ever been known to use about the Prussians during the Siege: 'one does not negotiate with assassins'. Yet at this juncture it was difficult to see, if negotiation were excluded, just how Thiers was going to implement his intentions of emulating Windischgrätz's reconquest of Vienna, and of taming Paris once and for all. He had already twice gravely under-estimated the situation. In the first place, although Marxists later claimed he had deliberately provoked a revolution, it is in fact quite clear that he had never anticipated that Vinoy's operation on March 18th would lead to open insurrection. Like most of the new Assembly, he had minimized the determination of the Parisian left wing. And now he had dangerously under-estimated the potential military power of the hostile National Guard, relative to his own. On the march out to Versailles during the evening of the 18th, the regulars had revealed the shakiness of their morale by insulting the loyal police and gendarmes who marched at their side. Once at Versailles, they went about refusing to salute their officers and openly declaring that they would not fight against their brethren in Paris. Lord Lyons reckoned that probably the only troops on whom Thiers could depend were the Papal Zouaves, and this view was supported by Captain Patry who, after spending three days 'reconnoitring' in Paris in civilian clothes, departed for Versailles to discover that all that remained of his company was one sergeant and three officers. All the rest had melted away. Moreover, owing to the exodus of the bourgeois during the armistice, the 'reliable' units of the National Guard in Paris, which under the Siege had once numbered between fifty and sixty battalions, could now be reckoned at little more than twenty; compared with some three hundred dissident battalions, now liberally equipped with cannon. It was with the greatest difficulty that Vinoy had established posts between Versailles and Paris, and the dawning of each day brought renewed and genuine fears of a descent by the insurgents in overwhelming force, before ever Thiers had a chance to build up his counter-offensive.

This was what Brunel and others had urged upon the Comité Central from the start, and Thiers was in fact saved only by the paralysis that confusion bred in the Hôtel de Ville, which ultimately would. cause the ruin of all Red dreams. Just as, in the state of euphoria which existed outside on the streets, there was no hint that a bloody civil war might be about to break out at any moment, so in the dazed revolutionary councils was there no sense of urgency, no suggestion that a rebellion had been launched that any legitimate Government would be bound eventually to suppress with force. Most of the discussions turned on the essentially parochial political issue of Parisian autonomy, on the election of a municipal council— the famous 'Commune'—and on the social issue of repealing the inequitable laws on debts and rents. Militarily, the first action of the Comité had been to place an unknown figure called Lullier in command of the National Guard, instead of the more obvious choice of Brunel. Lullier was an ex-naval officer discharged for bad conduct, and later described by a fellow Communard as 'an alcoholic fool without morals or talent', who on one occasion had had to be guarded by his colleagues to prevent him throwing himself out of the window. He seems to have been obsessed by fears of a surprise Government attack reoccupying the Hôtel de Ville by means of the subterranean passages which had already played so significant a role on recent occasions. Three were located and sealed off, but others believed to exist could not be traced. Thus a vast force was kept at the ready in the immediate area, and inside the building *mitrailleuses* appeared at the windows, mounted on tables and desks, and the windows themselves were stuffed with sandbags and feather beds. But apart from taking these quite unnecessary defensive precautions, Lullier did nothing. Worst of all, he made no effort to occupy Mont-Valérien, which had so effectively dominated the city's western approaches throughout the Siege. On the evening of the 18th, Thiers had ordered its garrison to withdraw and for nearly three days the huge fortress, key to both Paris and Versailles, remained untenanted. Then, reluctantly and under pressure from General Vinoy, Thiers sent some of his few regulars to resume occupation. The insurgents had lost the initiative and Versailles began to regain its badly shaken confidence.

For the rest, in those first days the Comité Central carried out none of the actions normally associated with revolutionary rule. Lord Lyons was agreeably surprised. To the Foreign Secretary he wrote on March 21st that its various proclamations in the *Journal Officiel* 'seem to me to be in form much more calm, dignified and sensible than the proclamations of the Government of National Defence used to be. In substance they are not specimens of political knowledge and wisdom. It is to be hoped that the Assembly will not make matters worse by violent and ill-considered resolutions.' He closed on a note of personal pessimism: 'Anyway, I should not be at all surprised if the Assembly transferred itself to some dismal French provincial town.' The next day, just as Dr. Alan Herbert returned, Lord Lyons received orders once more to leave Paris with his staff, and betake himself to Versailles. Once again, the British residents found themselves without an Ambassador. But, for the time being, there seemed little to worry about. On the 21st, the Rev. Gibson was writing: 'Paris is much quieter today . . . and the omnibuses are for the most part running as usual. Still there are groups of people talking most earnestly at the corners of the streets, and there is much excitement and but little business.' The next day he visited the scene where it had all begun, Montmartre, but there too 'all was quiet'. For several days Edwin Child had also been making the same observation, and took the opportunity to get out of hock forty watch-chains his employer had pawned during the Siege; but he thought there was something 'ominous' about the unusual 'silence and quietness' on the boulevards. The calm, however, led all talk around to the possibility of conciliation and, according to rumours which reached the Rev. Gibson, 'the Assembly at Versailles will not deal with the insurrection with a high hand, but will come to terms with the leaders of the National Guard'.

With the withdrawal of the Government, the last vestiges of legal authority left in Paris were embodied in the Mayors of the twenty *arrondissements*. As early as the 19th, Thiers had instructed them to mediate with the insurgents; although his motives were rather to stall for time, which he so badly needed, than to attempt any genuine conciliation. The Mayors themselves were as mixed, politically, as the various districts they represented. They ranged from Tirard, the conservative Mayor of the 2nd, the *arrondissement* of the banks and businesses, who was essentially Thiers's man, to Mottu of the 9th and Ranvier of the 20th, who were supporters of Delescluze. Most, however, were left of centre; while even the right-wingers resented the Assembly's 'decapitalization' of Paris, and wanted to restore her ascendancy by gaining some degree of municipal autonomy. All were anxious to avert any possibility of the situation heading towards civil war. The most important of them was the radical Mayor of Montmartre, Clemenceau, who was also a Deputy and who had attempted as early as March 8th to mediate between the Government and the National Guard over the disputed cannon. Under his lead, a series of meetings between the Mayors and members of the Comité Central had begun on the 19th, opening at 2 p.m. in the Bonvalet Restaurant. To the insurgents, Clemenceau pointed out the illegality of their position; 'Paris has no right to revolt against France and must recognize absolutely the authority of the Assembly. The Comité has only one means of getting out of this impasse: give way to the Deputies and Mayors who are resolved to obtain from the Assembly the concessions demanded by Paris.' Varlin responded by giving a surprisingly moderate list of demands: 'We want not merely an elected Municipal Council, but genuine municipal liberties, the suppression of the Prefecture of Police, the right of the National Guard to appoint its leaders and to reorganize itself; the proclamation of the Republic as the legitimate Government, the postponement, pure and simple, of payment of rent arrears, a fair law on maturities. . . .' The demands were by no means unreasonable.

Until 4 a.m. on the 20th the talks dragged on. When the appellation 'rebels' fell from Mayor Tirard's lips, tempers rose. Jourde, a fiery Auvergnat, was roused to mention the deadly words 'civil war', and went on to prophesy 'it will be ignited not only in Paris, but throughout France, and it will be bloody, I warn you . . . if we are conquered we shall burn Paris, and we shall turn France into a second Poland'. But to the voices of conciliation was added the influential one of old Louis Blanc, just returned from his long exile in England. At last, an agreement was reached whereby the Mayors would strive to get the terms of the Comité accepted by the Assembly; the Comité would postpone the municipal elections it was planning to hold on the 22nd until the Assembly should vote a municipal law for Paris; and it would hand the Hôtel de Ville over to the Mayors. But the next day the Comité Central came under heavy fire from the Vigilance Committees of the Twenty *Arrondissements*,[1] comprised of the more ardent revolutionaries, for having been too weak and compliant in their dealings with the Mayors. They had heard the fiercely uncompromising speeches being made at Versailles by Favre and others, and there was nothing to assure them that in fact the Assembly would yield to the Mayor's intercession. They could not rid their minds of instinctive distrust of the bourgeois 'Establishment', recalling how in every previous revolution it had somehow contrived to swindle the proletariat out of its presumptive birthright. Now, for the first time since the Great Revolution, the revolutionaries possessed temporary superiority in arms—a situation they had awaited throughout the century. But time was clearly not on their side—so could they afford to waste it on protracted negotiations?

On the 21st, the Comité informed Clemenceau that it was repudiating the agreement, as far as handing over the Hôtel de Ville was

[1] The Comité Central of the National Guard, formed only after the siege, should not be confused with the Comité Central of the Twenty *Arrondissements*, the essentially political grouping of the extreme Left formed the previous September.

concerned. But it would still adhere to the postponement of the elections. This in itself was no small victory for Thiers, though not for the cause of peace. Clemenceau was both annoyed and disappointed; from now on the Mayors were largely discredited by both parties, suspected by Versailles as being too extremist, and by the insurgents as being too moderate. Their suspicions of Thiers's motives were enhanced by a Government proclamation that day forbidding any civil or military functionary to have relations with the Comité. The next day, the 22nd, another Thiers proclamation declared in uncompromising language: 'The greatest crime with a free people, a revolt against national sovereignty, adds fresh disasters to the troubles of the country. Senseless criminals, on the morrow following a great misfortune, when the foreigner had scarcely evacuated our ravaged fields, have not blushed to carry disorder, ruin, and dishonour into Paris, which they pretended to honour and defend. They have stained the city with blood, which raises the public against them. . . .' Hardly the language of conciliation, but there was worse to come that day.

While with his left hand Thiers appeared to be offering conciliation, with his right he was testing the potential strength of his support within Paris. On the 19th he had appointed yet another officer to command the National Guard, in succession to the unpopular d'Aurelle. This was sixty-year-old Admiral Saisset, who had emerged with rare distinction from the Siege, in which he had also lost his son. He was promptly dispatched to Paris by Thiers, with the risky task of rallying round himself the 'loyal' units of the National Guard. How impossibly weak his position was, and what little likelihood there was of his mission succeeding, soon became apparent to him. As a factor to be reckoned with, the bourgeois National Guard had virtually disintegrated and no longer responded to any centripetal force its leaders could exert. Yet after the first paralysing shock had passed, a mild reaction had begun to build up in Paris. A motley of anti-revolutionary and 'moderate' elements, retired colonels, respectable shopkeepers, elderly gentlemen, and *petits crevés*, as well as the remnants of the bourgeois National Guard, gravitated around the Opéra and the Bourse, and especially Tirard's Mairie in the focal 2nd *Arrondissement*. Another rallying-point appears to have been the premises of a tailor in the Boulevard des Capucines, a M. Bonne, formerly a captain in the National Guard. In his window, Bonne displayed the following poster: 'Time presses for the formation of a dyke against the Revolution. Let all good citizens come to lend me their support.' It was signed 'Reunion of the Friends of Order', and the name stuck.

On the 21st, the 'Friends of Order' demonstrated, peacefully enough, outside the National Guard headquarters in the Place Vendôme. They were dispersed by the local commander, Bergeret, with the aid of two companies; but he, fearful lest the 'Friends' might be contemplating a serious coup to seize the H.Q., and would return in greater strength, called for reinforcements to seal off the Place. Sure enough, his fears seemed to be justified when a far larger force of the 'Friends' appeared the next morning. Now led by the intrepid old Admiral himself, they had assembled in the Place de l'Opéra with the aim of marching into the Rue de Rivoli, and thence to demonstrate in front of the Hôtel de Ville, collecting supporters as they went along. They deliberately came unarmed—with the exception of a few sword-sticks and pistols secreted about the persons of some of the more nervous. They bore banners inscribed '*Pour la Paix*', and proclaimed in alternate breaths as they marched, '*Vive l'Assemblée !*' and '*Vive la République !*' As they turned into the short Rue de la Paix, they collided with Bergeret's National Guards, ready and somewhat trigger-happy, who were drawn up across the entrance to the Place Vendôme. Insults were exchanged and tempers rose; according to the Comité, Bergeret ten times read the *sommation* ordering the demonstrators to disperse. But his voice was drowned by the noise, and all the time pressure from the rear was thrusting the leading 'Friends of Order' closer and closer on to the line of the National Guards. Then it happened, and as so often under these circumstances, no one ever knew which side fired first.

Just before the arrival of the 'Friends', Washburne's friend, the young and beautiful Lillie Moulton, reached the Place Vendôme on her way to visit the salon of Worth the English couturier. Picking her way through the barricades, she had entered his premises on the Rue de la Paix unmolested, and then heard the noise of the approaching cavalcade. Absent during the Siege, it was the first time she had seen anything like this in Paris. She rushed to an upstairs window, and fixed her eye upon a 'handsome young fellow' in the crowd, whom she recognized: Henri de Pène, a director of *Paris-Journal*, who seemed to be one of the leaders of the demonstration.

De Pène, seeing people on Worth's balcony, beckoned to them to join him; Mr. Worth wisely withdrew inside and shaking his Anglo-Saxon head said 'Not I'. . . This mass of humanity walked down the Rue de la Paix, filling the whole breadth of it. One can't imagine the horror we felt when we heard the roar of a cannon,[1] and looking down saw the street filled with smoke, and frightened screams and terrified groans reached our ears. Someone dragged me inside the window, and

[1] She seems to have exaggerated the noise of rifle-fire.

shut it to drown the horrible noises outside. De Pène was the first who was killed. The street was filled with dead and wounded. Mr. Hottinguer (the banker) was shot in the arm. The living members of *Les Amis* scampered off as fast as their legs would carry them, while the wounded were left to the care of the shopkeepers, and dead were abandoned where they fell until further aid should come. It was all too horrible!

Worth smuggled Mrs. Moulton out of a back exit. She returned home safely, was given a sedative of camomile tea, and put to bed after her harrowing experience.

Among those who had marched with the 'Friends of Order' was Gaston Rafinesque, a young medical student and son of the Passy doctor. After the first volley, fired by the National Guard, he claimed, 'then the shooters started to march continuing to fire, which was why some of them were wounded by their comrades who were left behind. . . .' When the firing died down, Gaston and another medical student helped pick up the dead and wounded; the first corpse they collected was that of an elderly gentleman wearing the Legion d'Honneur. Later Gaston recalled 'the whole scene lit up by the brilliant hot sun, unfeeling as it has been since eternity at the spectacle of human misery . . . .' It so disgusted him that he felt urged at once to take arms against the rebels, and his father, Jules Rafinesque, wrote in a letter to his brother-in-law in London, Louis Hack; 'Sometimes I wonder if it would not be wise to go and practise medicine in Switzerland.' The 'Massacre in the Rue de la Paix', as it came to be known, resulted in a dozen dead among the 'Friends of Order' and many more wounded, while Bergeret's National Guards lost one killed and two or three wounded. Each side accused the other of having fired first, and the true blame has never been apportioned; though it seems as if it were most likely to rest with Bergeret's men. But at the time this hardly mattered. What did matter was that, for the first time since the shooting outside the Hôtel de Ville on January 22nd, blood had been spilt. As Daudet wrote, 'the farce was turning towards the tragic, and on the boulevard people no longer laughed'. The rift between Paris and Versailles had now gone beyond conciliation.

The Comité had meanwhile invested the military command of the National Guard, pending the arrival of Garibaldi, to whom they had offered it,[1] in Brunel, Eudes, and Duval—all now raised to the rank of 'general'—in place of the bibulous Lullier who had been arrested for incompetence. The new commanders at once set about winkling out Thiers's remaining footholds in Paris. Tirard's Mairie in the 2nd

[1] Garibaldi, having had enough of French internal wrangles, wisely declined the invitation.

Arrondissement was occupied, as was that of Clemenceau in Montmartre; Clemenceau himself was incarcerated briefly by his insubordinate deputy, Ferré. As mediators, the Mayors had reached the end of the line. At Versailles, the talk was now all of 'suppression'. On the 25th, Thiers instructed Tirard: 'Do not continue a useless resistance; I am in the process of reorganizing the army. I hope that before two to three weeks we shall have a force sufficient to liberate Paris.' But when Tirard had asked Thiers for two regiments of gendarmes, he had been told, 'I have not got four men and a child to give you'; while Admiral Saisset, quitting Paris on foot and in disguise to report back to Thiers on the failure of his mission, gloomily pronounced that it would require 300,000 men to crush the insurgents. Not one of the facts seemed to support Thiers's optimism. Certainly nothing Washburne found at Versailles (he had decided to move his official residence there on the 24th, through still keeping a foothold in Paris) impressed him. Chaos and disorganization reigned. In the overcrowded conditions, some sixty of the Deputies were sleeping in the Council Chamber, sometimes appearing in their night-shirts in the midst of a debate; it was, thought Washburne, 'worse than a Western steamboat in emigration times'. They booed the Paris Mayors for their attempts at conciliation, but when Washburne visited the Assembly he found 'that august body fiddling while Paris burned'. Sitting between Washburne and Wickham Hoffman in the gallery of the theatre where Marie-Antoinette had spent her last evening at Versailles, Lillie Moulton heard Thiers declaim in his squeaky voice (with thorough hypocrisy) against the use of force; Favre then orated about the glorious 'destiny of France', remarks which were received with tremendous applause and much waving of feminine handkerchiefs. But Hoffman on one side of her growled 'How typical!', and Washburne on the other, 'What rubbish!'

In a dispatch to Secretary of State Fish dated March 25th, Washburne reported '. . . the appearance of things today is more discouraging than ever. The insurrectionists in Paris are gaining power and strength every hour. . . .' It was true. Still the seductive spring weather continued, as did the 'terrible silence' in Paris which had so alarmed Edwin Child. Underneath it was an acute nervousness, betrayed by 'shopkeepers who were brave enough to keep open, guarding their shutters close at hand so as to be ready to close at an instant's notice'. Now, on top of the realization that it was master of all Paris, deceptively good tidings from the provinces fortified the resolve of the Comité Central. There had been sympathetic uprisings, and Communes declared, in important centres as far apart as St.-Étienne and Marseilles, Le Creusot, Lyons, and Toulouse. Throwing to the winds its earlier undertakings to the Mayors, and in total defiance of the Assembly, the Comité decided to hold forthwith the postponed municipal elections.

On March 26th Paris went to the polls. From a register of 485,569, 220,167 voted. Thiers proclaimed a victory based on the apparent number of abstentions; but the truth was, and he knew it, that a large proportion of these represented the bourgeoisie who had 'abdicated' by quitting Paris during the armistice, or after the first flare-up on March 18th. In fact, compared with those of the municipal elections held the previous November, the results did denote a considerable advance in support of the revolutionaries; it was proof of just how seriously Thiers and the new Assembly had alienated Paris.

Now the wild-eyed men who with Flourens had strode up and down the table a few inches from Trochu's nose on October 31st had gained, belatedly, what they had demanded that day. Paris's new municipal council was controlled by Reds in a proportion of four to one, and they promptly assumed the title of 'Commune de Paris', with all the awe-inspiring associations that conveyed.

On Tuesday, March 28th, amid immaculate spring sunshine, the Commune officially installed itself at the Hôtel de Ville. Superbly stage-managed by Brunel, for sheer spectacle it was a day of brilliance such as the city had not seen—paradoxically enough—since the braver days of the despised Louis-Napoleon. Some Parisians even found themselves thinking back to the magnificent parades of the Great Exhibition. All Paris seemed to be there, and cheering wildly. In front of the Hôtel de Ville had been erected a platform decked in scarlet cloth on which stood the members of the newly elected Commune, also wearing red scarves, taking the salute as the massed units of the National Guard marched past. Never had this semi-trained militia, which had given so poor an account of itself during the Siege, marched better. There seemed to be a new spring in its step, a new swagger in its salute. At 4 p.m. salvoes of cannon-fire pealed out from batteries mounted on the quay. Assi, who stood near a bust of the Republic that wore a beribboned Phrygian cap, attempted to make a speech, but his words were drowned out by repeated roars of '*Vive la Commune!*' Abandoning his text, he shouted at the top of his voice: 'In the name of the people, the Commune is proclaimed!', and the crowd went mad. Thousands of National Guards stationed in the Place raised their képis on the points of their bayonets, as the massed bands thundered out the Marseillaise. All through the afternoon and late into the evening, two hundred battalions of them marched past; the officers saluting the Phrygian-capped bust of the Republic with their sabres. The sinking sun glittered fierily on the

Communard Barricade before the Hôtel de Ville

19. The Red Spectre

'Now that our Commune is elected, we shall await with impatience the acts by which it will make itself known to us. May God wish that this energetic medium will prove beneficial, and will procure us genuinely honest and durable institutions. That's what everybody wishes and desires, for we have been dissatisfied for a long time. That's why, I believe, everybody accords it his good wishes.' Thus wrote Louis Péguret, formerly Corporal of the National Guard, who admitted himself strongly in sympathy with the Commune, in a letter to his sister dated March 28th.

Just what was the Commune going to do ? This was the question which now lay uppermost in the minds of all Parisians, bourgeois and proletarian alike. But first of all, what *was* the Commune ? What, precisely, did it stand for, this mystical word 'murmured under the Second Empire, shouted under the Government of National Defence' ? Even many of those who shouted loudest, who were later to die unhesitatingly beneath the red standards of the Commune, could hardly give a coherent definition; and—reaching back over the years—today one's fingers clutch awkwardly at vague slogans, at conflicting ideologies and nebulous abstractions. Those who, like Delescluze and

Varlin, might have enlightened historians, were to be killed on the barricades or by the firing squads at Sartory before they had a chance to write their memoirs or record their creeds. Pyramids of tracts and books have been written since upon the social and philosophical content of the Commune, but much is so flagrantly biased in one direction or the other as to be worse than unhelpful. In its contemporary setting, the Commune came at a time when memories still recalled apprehensively the revolutions that had broken out all over Europe, when bombs thrown at princes killed innocent bystanders, when industrial unrest was everywhere at hand and behind it apparently the sinister red hand of Marx's International; and the period following the Commune saw still more anarchist bombs and more unrest. To the denizens of the otherwise tranquil nineteenth century, any threat to the established order of things was instinctively regarded as a far more pernicious heresy than it would to our world, its sensibilities long dulled by custom. During its lifetime, the Commune had few friends beyond the ranks of its immediate supporters in Paris, and these were rendered fewer by the unchallenged falsifications later put out by the eventually triumphant forces of legality, which spotlighted the bloody deeds of the Commune, while passing over the fact that they themselves had wreaked infinitely greater bloodshed upon the Communard supporters. For these reasons, over a prolonged period few respectable bourgeois historians were able to view the Commune, except through the most violently red-tinted spectacles. On the other side, for their own dialectic purposes the Marxists have distorted the Commune to create a myth portraying something it never was.

This present book is not the place, nor has it the space, to do more than try to sketch a brief course between the opposing untruths. But one may start by defining what the Commune was *not*. Despite the similarity of the names, as of March 1871 it had nothing to do with Communism. As Engels himself later admitted, 'The International did not raise a finger to initiate the Commune'.

At this time Karl Marx, now a mature fifty-two, sat in London operating like a skilful puppet-master the strings of the various branches of the International across the world, and dispatching a copious correspondence in all directions. Of the French branch he had no high opinion, and in 1868 had complained to his friend, Kugelmann, that 'these ragamuffins are half or two-thirds of them bullies and similar rabble.' Its receipts for the previous year had totalled only £63, and during the last years of the Empire it had been further weakened by successive trials and incarceration of its leaders. After the downfall of the Empire, Marx had abruptly switched his sympathies from Prussia to France, and had written to Engels

U

criticizing the desire of the Paris Internationalists to 'perform stupidities in the name of the International. They wish to overthrow the Provisional Government, establish a Commune of Paris, and recognise Pyat as the French ambassador to England.' Although he strongly disapproved of the bourgeois moderates who had taken over from Louis-Napoleon, he wrote again in the Second Manifesto, dated September 9th, that 'any attempt to overthrow the Government in the present crisis, while the enemy is beating practically upon the doors of Paris, would be a desperate folly'.

From the lessons of 1848, Marx had appreciated the dangers of inadequately prepared revolutions that went off at half-cock, and he now considered that the first duty of a revolutionary leader was laboriously to educate the masses towards their eventual destiny. Right up to March 18th, Marx remained strongly opposed to any outbreak of revolt in Paris, and its success thoroughly took him by surprise. Although he never held many illusions about its long-term prospects, he now suddenly, intuitively saw a vast potential significance in the new Paris revolution and, with all the nimbleness of an incomparable opportunist, leaped aboard the bandwagon. In the long run, the Commune would exercise a far profounder influence upon Marx than vice versa.

On March 23rd, Marx issued directives to the International in French provincial cities, urging it to help create 'diversions' to relieve pressure upon Paris, and at the same time sent one of his trusties, Serrailler, to act as a liaison officer in Paris. But meanwhile the Internationalists there vacillated, bickering with the revolutionaries of the Comité Central, many of whom they regarded as—to use more modern parlance—'deviationists', and awaiting advice from the Master. It was not until the revolution was firmly established and the Comité entrenched at the Hôtel de Ville that they actually decided to join in. But the world was conditioned to spotting the 'Red Spectre' behind all that was happening in Paris. The Rev. Gibson declared on March 24th that 'most of the members of the Comité Central are members of the *International* Secret Society'; although in fact they were a small minority, and even later at the peak of their influence there were never more than a score of Internationalists on the ninety-strong council of the Commune. It was also an illusion (though perhaps a lesser one) to say, as did Goncourt; '. . . What is happening is nothing less than the conquest of France by the worker . . . the convulsive agents of dissolution and destruction.' Certainly, as compared with the Revolution of 1848 where most of the leaders had belonged to the bourgeoisie, the founders of the Commune imparted a more proletarian flavour. But even so, only twenty-one of its members could be rated genuine workers, while another thirty were journalists, writers, painters, and assorted intellectuals, and thirteen were clerks and small tradesmen of the *petite bourgeoisie*; moreover, not one of the demands put forward at its inception in any way smacked of Socialism, let alone of Marxism.

Even a study[1] produced a generation after the Commune (though still under the spell of the Red Spectre) calls it erroneously the 'Communistical Republic of Paris'. But in fact the word 'Commune' had its origin many centuries before the publication of Marx's *Manifesto*, in the Middle Ages, where it eventually came to be used of any self-governing town. Such 'Communes' of townsfolk were often established in quest of independence from a local feudal baron. In 1789 a *Commune de Paris* had been improvised simply to assume responsibility for the administration of Paris, following the fall of the Bastille. Gradually, as the Great Revolution progressed, the extremists displaced the moderates until, on August 10th, 1792, they dissolved the earlier body to form a Revolutionary Commune. As Carlyle remarked of it, 'there never was on earth a stranger Town-Council. Administration, not of a great City, but of a great Kingdom in a state of revolt and frenzy, this is the task that has fallen it.' It was the Revolutionary Commune that forced the Assembly to dethrone Louis XVI, and, by default became itself the real provisional Government of France until such time as the *Convention Nationale* was elected. Led by the violent Danton, on the one hand it firmly established the first French Republic, while on the other it successfully chased the foreign, Royalist invaders from French soil; it was the combination of these two magical deeds that specifically first induced the Reds[2] during the Siege of Paris to reach back in history for the all-powerful amulet, *la Commune*. Even after the election of the Convention in September 1792, the Commune continued to be the real power behind the scenes, forcing the Convention to consult it at every turn, while being largely responsible for the worst excesses of the Terror. Until the downfall of Robespierre, nearly two years later, the Revolutionary Commune so effectively controlled France that it was frequently known as the 'Parisian Dictatorship'. This in itself endeared its memory to those Parisian revolutionaries of 1870 to whom the ascendancy of Paris over France was still sacrosanct; just as the historian Thiers would forever be haunted by the precedent of the simple,

[1] *Cassell's History of the Franco-German War.*
[2] To avoid confusion, it should perhaps be recalled here that the term 'Red' was applied to left-wing revolutionaries long before Marxist 'Communism' made its first appearance.

unambitious, semi-legitimate Commune of 1789 which had turned into an omnipotent, insatiably devouring monster.

Thus, by definition, the Commune as it came to power in 1871 was little more than a slogan with no ideology, no programme, constantly glancing over its shoulder to 1793—despite Marx's admonition of the previous September to the French proletariat 'not to begin the past over again, but to build the future'. (Typical of this backward-looking posture was the arrest on the day the Commune was proclaimed of a seventy-eight-year-old man called Bignon; he was accused of having denounced in 1822—half a century earlier—four sergeants of La Rochelle, who were subsequently executed for conspiracy.) In the words of one of the French historians of the Commune,[1] 'The title was too imprecise to proclaim a programme, but, waving in the wind like a flag, it united the traditionalist souvenirs of some with the dreams of others and thus rallied French revolutionaries. . . .' In the name of the Commune, its supporters tended to see either their own personal Utopia, or a means of settling a grudge against, or dissatisfaction with, the established order.

Of grudges and dissatisfaction there were no shortage. Although it was the residuum of the Siege that, directly, had ignited the Commune revolt, much of the inflammable material had been piling up long before. There was the resentment, mentioned earlier, keenly felt by the revolutionaries that the working class had been successively swindled out of their birthright inherited from the Great Revolution, and there were still savagely bitter memories of the brutality with which subsequent uprisings had been repressed; Manet for one, though no Communard, would never forget being taken as an art student to file past five or six hundred bodies, laid out 'under a layer of straw', of those massacred during the 1851 *coup d'état*. There was also the sense of disillusion, coupled to mistrust, that—as Louis Péguret complained—'since the 4th of September not a single Republican institution has been created' (although it was perhaps a little unrealistic to assume the Provisional Government could have spared time to create 'Republican institutions' while fighting the war).

But by far the biggest backlog of discontent stemmed from the poor social conditions existing under the Second Empire, from the reforms that Louis-Napoleon had not been allowed to complete. There were the appalling slums into which the workers were now concentrated despite (and partly because of) the works of Haussmann; the vastly inflated cost of living which had far outpaced wages; the

[1] Georges Laronze, *Histoire de la Commune de 1871 d'après des documents et des souvenirs inédits.*

long hours of work under disgraceful circumstances; child labour still involving several thousands of eight-year-olds in Paris alone; no security of employment, no sickness benefits, no pensions; restrictions on the right to affiliate, on freedom of the Press, and upon any means by which the workers might have achieved less intolerable conditions. Rossel, a regular soldier of middle-class extraction who later threw in his lot with the Commune, was moved by what he saw among the Parisians under his command to exclaim: 'These people have good reason for fighting; they fight that their children may be less puny, less scrofulous, and less full of failings than themselves.' The workers' attitude to all the glories left by the Second Empire was summed up simply by one who declared in Goncourt's hearing: 'What is it to me that there should be monuments, operas, café-concerts, where I have never set foot because I had no money ?' As the Communards would ultimately prove, there were those who would rather all these glories of civilization were expunged by fire than that the Parisian workers should continue to forfeit their claims to a better life.

Finally there were also those who were simply attracted to the Commune by its face value; by its demands of municipal independence for Paris. Ever since the removal of the Revolutionary Commune that had terrified France, executive power over the city had been placed in the hands of the Prefect of the Department of the Seine, so that in effect any small rural community possessed more real autonomy than this great, industrialized capital. Their claims for a municipal budget and local taxation, for control over local education and the police, and for the right of the city to choose its own magistrates, gained the Communards the sympathy of many outsiders; an aristocratic lieutenant-colonel on leave of absence from the Grenadier Guards, then working with the American Red Cross in Paris, the Hon. John C. Stanley, admitted: 'I have got into a strong unreasonable sort of sympathy with the best of the Reds. They are fighting for municipal liberties—what all our towns have always enjoyed.'

Nothing revealed the confusing multiplicity of ideas and aims more than the various components creating the Commune. The two biggest factions which dominated it from beginning to end were the Jacobins, headed by Delescluze, and the Blanquists. The Blanquists were Socialists of the old school—except in the eyes of Karl Marx, who considered them entitled to the name 'only by revolutionary and proletarian instinct'. They based their creed upon Proudhonist theories of a decentralized society comprised of small propertyowners; strongly individualistic with anarchist undertones, the Blanquists' ideals ran directly counter to the 'new' teaching of Marxism, dependent as it was upon the organization of the masses.

Innocent of any precise economic platform, the Blanquists were violently hostile to the Church and to the regular Army; the one they wished to disestablish, the other to hamstring by abolishing conscription. They were for the most part dedicated revolutionaries, and even Marx had grudgingly acknowledged the leader from whom they took their name to be the greatest revolutionary of the century. Sometimes called 'the Old One', or less affectionately the 'Spider of Revolution', or sometimes '*l'Enfermé*', on account of the twenty-eight years he had spent incarcerated in Mont-St.-Michel and various other French prisons, Auguste Blanqui was by far the most popular, and almost a legendary, figure among the Red leaders. Now sixty-six, his drawn, elongated features, white-cropped hair and thin beard gave him the look of a Greco apostle. The arch-priest of *résistance à outrance*, during the Siege it was Blanqui whose influence had lain behind most of the uprisings and demonstrations against the Provisional Government, although the long years of imprisonment had taught him to eschew the limelight. Nevertheless, for all his evasive cunning, the sudden sentence imposed upon him by the Assembly, *ex post facto*, for his part in the events of October 31st, caught him off balance and on March 17th he had been picked up by Thiers's police. Once again *l'Enfermé* languished in gaol, and his faction in Paris was left leaderless.

Still more lacking in any coherent programme was the large body of revolutionaries loosely classified as Jacobins. They were wedded to abstract ideas of political liberty, and were thoroughly conservative in the sense that they constantly looked to their namesakes of '93 for guidance; 'Their memory is always with me', admitted one of them. They mistrusted Marx's new fangled philosophy, and many Jacobins would have nothing to do with the Internationalists on the Commune. Their leader was Delescluze, the man around whom the mob had rallied on October 31st; his deeply eroded, tragic face still commanded support as well as sympathy, but he was old and ill. At sixty-two he was prematurely worn out, his physique ruined by long bouts of deportation to Devil's Island. Because of the state of his health, he had played no conspicuous part in the Commune's seizure of power, and he no longer felt capable of playing a leading role in its councils. Next to Delescluze, the best-known Jacobin in France was Rochefort, who had been returned as a Deputy for Paris in the February elections. But Rochefort, his aristocratic sensibilities possibly recoiling from the spectacle of the 'great unwashed' in command at the Hôtel de Ville—a situation which he, as the century's most outstanding polemicist, had done so much to assist—had not stood for election to the Commune. Instead he sat in his newspaper office, firing broadsides at Versailles, and occasionally the Commune too.

(The other great rhetorician whose rhodomontades had helped inflame Parisians to a revolutionary pitch, Victor Hugo, had absolved himself of all responsibility, withdrawing once again to Brussels, whence he cried a pox on both houses. As a reason for leaving Paris, he explained—with some truth—that his presence could 'only exacerbate the situation'.) Also at heart a Jacobin was Félix Pyat, Delescluze's pet aversion, whose paper *Le Combat* appeared revivified as *Le Vengeur*, as scurrilous as ever and destined to become the principal organ of the Commune; Pyat was both the most ineffectual and irresponsible of the leading Communards, as well as being among the noisiest.

The role of the Internationalist faction has already been discussed; but it too—unlike its descendants, the modern Communist Party— was far from being a monolithic structure. One of its leading lights, for instance, Benoît Malon, shocked Laura Marx by admitting he had never heard of *Das Kapital* and knew of her father only as 'a German professor'. That the bickering Paris International had thrown its weight behind the Commune was to a large extent due to Varlin, who had urged it to act 'as members of the Comité Central, rather than of the International'. Eugéne Varlin was a remarkably handsome thirty-one-year-old bookbinder, who under the Second Empire had taken refuge in Belgium. Returning after September 4th, he had recruited and commanded the 193rd Battalion of the National Guard, until it was dissolved following the October 31st uprising. He was to reveal himself one of the most sympathetic among the Communard leaders, and perhaps their most competent administrator. To his co-Internationalists, Theisz and the Hungarian Leo Frankel, the Commune later owed most of the social legislation that it was able to achieve during its short and disturbed life. Another interesting supporter of the International was a twenty-year-old Russian, Elizabeth Dimitrieff, an elusive figure somewhat reminiscent of one of Dostoevsky's self-willed heroines, who by her beauty and plurality of lovers injected a certain glamour into the Commune. The illegitimate daughter of a Tsarist ex-cavalry officer, she had been well educated in St. Petersburg, during which time she became an impassioned adherent to 'progressive' circles there. Contracting a *marriage de convenance* with an elderly, consumptive colonel, she then took off to Switzerland where she made contact with the International. In 1870 she moved to London, became a close friend of Karl Marx and his daughters, and at his impulsion went to Paris in March 1871; nominally to organize an Internationalist *'Union des Femmes'* to aid the Commune, but also to act as private rapporteuse to Marx.

Around the three main blocks comprising the Commune there hovered a nebula of assorted individuals: anarchists, intellectuals,

Bohemians, Gambettists, disgruntled petit bourgeois, general laya-
bouts, *déclassés*, and unclassifiables. Prominent among the anarchists
was the redoubtable Louise Michel. Like Elizabeth Dimitrieff, Louise
was a bastard, the daughter of a French *châtelain* and his chambermaid. Now forty, before the age of twenty she had fallen under the
spell of Hugo, with whom she had begun a long correspondence, and
to whom she dedicated a number of indifferent poems. As a school-
teacher, by 1853 she had already established a reputation of being an
anti-Bonapartist 'Red'. During the Siege, she had become a familiar,
somewhat masculine, figure, stalking into churches to demand money
for the installation of National Guard ambulances, wearing a wide red
belt and seldom without a rifle (with bayonet fixed) slung from her
shoulder. One of the principal mob-rousers during the shooting outside the Hôtel de Ville on January 22nd, it was Louise who wanted to
go to Versailles to assassinate Thiers after March 18th (subsequently
she even made the return trip in disguise, just to prove that it could
be done). In the months to follow, Louise would be found everywhere;
a member of both the male and female Vigilant Committees of
Montmartre, organizing the women with Elizabeth Dimitrieff, helping with the Commune ambulances, firing a rifle on the barricades,
and orating.

In marked contrast to the fiery Louise, among the intellectuals was
to be found Paschal Grousset, a twenty-six-year-old journalist later
appointed as the Commune's Delegate for External Affairs. Grousset
was a fiery, dapper little Corsican, so carefully groomed that Rochefort nicknamed him the 'ladies' hairdresser'; in January 1870 he had
challenged Prince Pierre Bonaparte to a duel, but in a fit of rage the
Prince had shot down Victor Noir, Grousset's second issuing the
challenge, thereby provoking one of the biggest anti-Bonapartist
demonstrations in the last days of the Empire. Upon the thoroughly
anti-Red Washburne, who was to see more of him than did any other
foreign diplomat, Grousset made a good impression. Washburne
may have been perhaps slightly prejudiced by his first interview, when
'unlike my previous visits to the Minister of Foreign Affairs, I did
not have to await my turn, for no representative of any foreign power
had ever called. . . .'; nevertheless, three weeks later Washburne was
still able to describe Grousset to Fish as a man of 'intelligence, education, and genteel personal appearance'. Two other distinguished
intellectuals were the Reclus brothers; Élisée, the famous geographer,
whose career with the Commune was cut short by his falling into the
hands of the Versailles forces, and Élie, who was nominated as
Director of the Bibliothèque Nationale. The writers included Jules
Vallès, permanently embittered by experiences of miserable poverty

THE RED SPECTRE 299

in his youth, and Verlaine—already partly estranged from his young wife and corrupted by drinking habits acquired during the Siege—who took over a humble post as chief of the Commune Press Office. The art world was represented principally by Gustave Courbet, gross and heavily bearded, and also sodden with drink which made him seem far older than his fifty-two years. Courbet, who became elected to the Commune at its subsidiary elections in mid-April, seems to have been motivated largely by the dismal treatment which l'art nouveau and the Impressionists had been accorded by the Establishment under the Empire. Pissarro also supported the Commune, while Renoir was sympathetic towards it because of Courbet's association with it.

There were a number of almost totally apolitical soldiers of fortune who had thrown in their lot with the Commune. Among them might be included the gasconading Flourens, the mob's leader during the demonstration of October 31st, who since his imprisonment, liberation, and subsequent sentence to death in absentia, had lain rather low in Paris, but was now elected to represent the turbulent Belleville. There were also a number of Polish exiles, among whom Dombrowksi and Wroblewski were to prove two of the Commune's ablest military commanders, drawn by the desperate belief that a blow for liberty anywhere represented a blow for oppressed and divided Poland. Motivated by less elevated ideals were pure terrorists like Montmartre's Théophile Ferré and the Bohemian layabout, Raoul Rigault, an Eichmann or a Beria born before his time; two sombre figures that come into their own in the final stages of the Commune. Finally, there were the representatives of the Red Clubs, still as full of wild and perfervid ideas as ever. They were typified by the lunatic Jules Allix who, thwarted in his ambition to mobilize Parisian women and equip them with his deadly doigt prussique during the Siege, now appointed himself Secrétaire d'Initiative of the 'Union of Women'; but such organization of the Communard women as existed was achieved principally by Louise Michel and Elizabeth Dimitrieff.

Thus, from the day it assumed office, the danger was apparent that the Commune might be overloaded, indeed overwhelmed, by the sheer diversity of desires as represented by so polygenous a multitude of personalities, ideologies, and interests. And there was no obvious leader to guide the multitude. Had Blanqui been there, it might have been quite a different story. But Blanqui was securely in the hands of Thiers, while Delescluze, the only other possible leader, was so ailing that. he would have preferred nothing better than to have retired from the scene altogether. Thiers, it now seemed, had at least made two excellent initial calculations; one was the seizure of Blanqui, and his other had been to force the Communards to commit themselves before either their plans or their policy had time to crystallize. His 'great hope', so Lord Lyons reported to London on March 30th, 'appears to be that the members of the Commune will quarrel among themselves. . . .' He had not long to wait.

On the night of the proclamation of the Commune, March 28th, its newly elected members met for the first time inside the Hôtel de Ville. At once there was an atmosphere of the fetid confusion prevailing in the Red Clubs. Nobody had been delegated from the Comité Central to hand over to the new body, whose representatives could not even find a room to convene in until a locksmith was sent to pick the locks of the Council Chamber. National Guards lolled, drunk or asleep, in corridors thick with tobacco smoke. In the fatigue generated by the stirring events of the day, personal squabbles erupted. There was immediate disagreement as to who should take the chair. Delescluze opposed a motion that his absent rival, Blanqui, be made '*Président d'Honneur*', and eventually the choice fell, by way of compromise, upon seventy-five-year-old Charles Beslay, as the oldest present. Between interjections proposing such irrelevant luxuries as abolition of capital punishment, there was much theoretical discussion concerning the legality of the Commune's position. (Indeed, in a country that over the past half-century had had four different forms of regime —Bourbons, Orleanists, Republicans, and Bonapartists—none of them elected, but each recognized abroad as the *legal* Government of France, it was an argument that could be continued indefinitely; the Commune certainly never resolved it.)

As it became clear that the majority present wished the Commune at once to arrogate to itself more than purely municipal functions, Tirard, the right-wing Mayor elected by the 2nd *Arrondissement*, seized the excuse to resign, followed by several others.[1] On the much more immediate issue as to whether or not the Commune should now march against Versailles, there were also lengthy debates; but these too were permeated with abstract considerations. Had the Commune been elected as a revolutionary body? Even some of those who were certain that it had been, and was, harboured hesitations. What would the Germans do if the Commune took the offensive against Versailles? Although, under the armistice, they had evacuated Versailles (on March 12th) and a large area to the south and south-west of Paris, they still occupied their old siege positions on the eastern half of the city's perimeter. Would the Germans now stand by and watch as the

---

[1] At the same time Clemenceau, who had not been elected to the Commune, resigned from the Assembly at Versailles in protest against the pusillanimity of its conciliation attempts.

protagonists of *résistance à outrance* crushed the Government with whom they had just concluded so favourable a peace treaty, or would Bismarck not intervene to crush the Commune instead? It seemed a real danger. On the other hand, there were those Communards who argued that the Germans had had a bellyful of war, that many of their best troops had already gone home, and that they were far from anxious to get further involved in French internal affairs. Nothing was decided, and the first session of the Commune broke up in discord and dissatisfaction after midnight.

The following day the Commune met again. This time it managed to agree to the formation of ten Commissions to carry out its various affairs. At the top of the list was the Executive Commission, consisting of Eudes, Tridon, Vaillant, Lefrançais, Pyat, Duval, and Bergeret. But despite its name, and although it was supposed to implement the decrees passed by the other Commissions, in effect it had no executive powers, as every measure had to be referred back to the Commune Council itself. Where the actual power of the Commune resided was by no means clear; and meanwhile, much as the original Commune of '93 had harassed the Convention, so the Comité Central continued to exist and to interfere with the working of the Commune's Executive Commission. Next in immediate importance came the Military Commission, whose best-known members were Eudes, Bergeret, Duval, and Flourens. (The more impressive Brunel appears to have been dropped for having shown too conciliatory an attitude towards the Mayors and their peace initiatives.) To the key posts in the *Sûreté Générale* went the sinister pair, Ferré and Raoul Rigault. Perhaps the Commission to achieve most under the Commune was that of Labour, Industry, and Exchange, operated by a heavy majority of Internationalists, including Malon, Frankel, Theisz, and Avrial. Another of great significance was the Finance Commission, comprising Clément, Varlin, Jourde, Beslay, and Régère.

For the most part, the delegates of the various Commissions assumed their functions with positively unrevolutionary diffidence. Theisz, appointed Postmaster-General, presented himself at the Post Office and 'invited' Rampont, the inaugurator of the balloon services during the Siege, to hand over his duties. Rampont replied that he would not, that he would only acquiesce to violence; in which case he and all the Post Office employees would decamp to Versailles. Theisz retired for further instructions. There was an even more comic situation when old Beslay—himself a failed banker—nervously arrived to 'take over' the Bank of France. Rouland, the Governor, had already fled to Versailles, leaving this mighty institution in the hands of the Marquis de Plœuc, who confronted poor Beslay with his four hundred employees drawn up outside, armed with sticks. There was a conversation, during which de Plœuc appealed to Beslay's patriotism, reminding him that 'the fortune of France' was in his hands. Obviously overawed, Beslay reported back to the Hôtel de Ville that if the Commune laid hands on the Bank there would be 'no more industry, no more commerce; if you violate it all promissory notes will become worthless'. In the meantime, Varlin and Jourde had assured the finances of the Commune temporarily by borrowing 500,000 francs from Rothschilds, and securing an advance of another million from the Bank. The National Guard could be paid, and immediate commitments met; thus removing any temptation to seize the Bank. This oversight was rated by both Marx and later Lenin as comprising one of the two cardinal errors committed by the Commune; for in the Bank's vaults lay over two milliards-worth of assets which could have provided the Commune with its most powerful weapon and hostage. Had it laid its hands on these assets, said Marx, 'the whole of the French bourgeoisie would have brought pressure to bear on the Versailles Government in favour of peace with the Commune'. Instead, Beslay amiably allowed himself to be installed in a small office next to de Plœuc's, completely under the latter's wing, while the astute Marquis doled out the advance to the Commune as slowly as possible, all the time smuggling out to Versailles the plates for printing banknotes and what money he could.

From March 29th onwards a flood of decrees began to pour out from the Commune, representing in their miscellany the extraordinary confusion over priorities that prevailed in the Hôtel de Ville. Great satisfaction greeted the repeal of the detested rent act, thereby exempting tenants from payment of rent for the previous nine months, as well as a decree suspending the sale of objects pawned at the notorious '*Monts-de-piété*'.[1] Gambling was banned; and on April 2nd the Church was disestablished. The Commune somehow found time to issue an *ordonnance* concerning the Ham Market, one of whose eighteen articles specified that Parisians should not relieve themselves 'elsewhere than in the public urinals'. There were edicts forbidding the public display of any announcements from Versailles, and threatening looters with the death penalty. Conscription to the regular Army was declared abolished; on the other hand all able-bodied citizens were to enroll for service with the National Guard.

---

[1] Under the Empire and its high cost of living, the pawnshops—the *monts-de-piété*—had become an inherent factor in the lives of the Paris poor; many of whom were regularly obliged to pawn their mattresses to provide food. During the Siege, the poor had fallen more and more into the pawnbrokers' clutches, pledging most of their few precious belongings at interest rates of 9½ per cent.

About the only other military measure taken at this time was the reoccupation of the southern forts which the regulars had abandoned; while it was sought to forestall any Versailles attack on the city by the following order sent to the officer guarding the western sector of the *Ceinture* railway; 'Place an energetic man at this post night and day. This man should mount guard equipped with a sleeper. On the arrival of each train, he must derail the train if it does not stop.'

Thus, as March drew to a close, the revolutionary masters of Paris had lost by their indecision thirteen priceless days since Thiers abandoned the city to them; days which Thiers himself had not wasted. By not taking advantage of their initial superiority to launch an offensive against Versailles, here, in the eyes of Lenin, lay the second of the Commune's fatal errors. As Marx had written about the Revolution of 1848, 'the defensive is the death of every armed rising; it is lost before it measures itself with its enemies'. The Commune was about to suffer the consequences of its error, one which Marx's pupil, Lenin—about to celebrate his first birthday far away at Simbirsk on the Volga—would not repeat when his turn came.

The Commune marches on Versailles, April 3rd, 1871

20. Monsieur Thiers Declares War

It astonished Dr. Powell, an English physician recently arrived in Paris, to learn that—except for the English Ambulance run by Dr. Cormack—all the others in operation during the Siege had closed down. Explained Dr. Powell; 'Strange to say, it was not imagined then that any more fighting would take place.' Once the excitements, alarms, and revolutionary zeal of the first days had calmed down, the bourgeois and uncommitted elements were agreeably surprised at how normal life in Paris still seemed to be. Although some of the extreme-Left Press, such as the reincarnated *Père Duchesne*, ranted and threatened as alarmingly as had any during the Siege, there were still few actual incursions into civic liberties. As yet there had been no expropriation of private property; two right-wing and extremely hostile newspapers, *Le Figaro* and *Le Gaulois*, had been seized, otherwise the rest continued unmolested. In the first flush, the revolutionaries —urged on by the new Police Chief, Raoul Rigault—had arrested over four hundred people between March 18th and 28th, but most of these (like Clemenceau) had been released again. Questing after a 'strayed' American subject, Washburne's private secretary, McKean, obtained a glimpse of a court martial which struck him as a chilling echo of 1793, and in his dispatch to Secretary of State Fish of March 25th, Washburne himself had singled out a curious report filed by the 'general' commanding Montmartre, Garnier, a former dealer in cooking utensils:

He says in the first place, that there is 'nothing new; night calm and and without incident'. He then goes on to say that at five minutes after ten o'clock two *sergeants de ville* were brought in by the franc-tireurs and immediately shot. He continues, 'At twenty minutes after midnight, a guardian of the peace, accused of having fired a revolver, is shot'. He closes his report of that calm night 'without incident' by saying that a gendarme, brought in by the guards of the twenty-eighth battalion, at seven o'clock, is shot.

But, despite these early excesses, there was no suggestion so far that a new Terror had been imposed upon Paris; anti-Communards did not yet go to sleep in constant fear of the knock on the door in the early morning.

Indeed, although the dispensation of law had all but come to a standstill with the 'disappearance' of most of the Parisian judges as well as the police (who were hardly encouraged to venture out on patrol by the kind of treatment recorded above), order was astonishingly well maintained. 'Robberies, assaults, and other crimes became', as Dr. Powell claimed with corroboration from many others, 'a very rare occurrence as far as I can remember.' The streets seemed unusually empty, and people went about calling each other '*citoyen*'; Rampont of the Post Office having carried out his threat and decamped with all his officials, both mails and telegraph services were temporarily halted (something which had never happened throughout the Siege); and Washburne noted occasionally meeting wedding parties on their way to the Mairie, the 'distracted' groom wondering whether he would find there a mayor who could marry him, or whether it had been turned into a Communard 'guard-house' instead. But people still got married, and everyday existence went on much as before. In fact, the Rev. Gibson reckoned that he had 'never seen the streets so well swept since the Siege'. Eight theatres were reopened on the Commune's orders, and, as the sunny spring weather settled in, so too did the euphoria of the simple supporters of the Commune. To the underprivileged, the oppressed, the frustrated of Paris, these last few days must have possessed an unimaginable magic, must have been golden with promise. There is something about these days that reminds one a little of the tragic optimism of the Hungarian freedom fighters during the brief period of revolutionary liberty in 1956, while Khrushchev was marshalling his tank divisions in the east; or of the heady euphoria of Polish 'solidarity' in 1980.

By the first days of April, Thiers, having scraped the bottom of the barrel, having brought in *Mobiles* from all over the provinces and mobilized the gendarmes and 'Friends of Order' National Guards escaped from Paris, had managed to muster over 60,000 troops at Versailles. This already exceeded by some 50 per cent the total permitted by the Peace Treaty with the Germans, and they were a mixed lot. No plan to reconquer Paris had yet been formulated, but in anticipation of this, on March 30th, two squadrons of cavalry carried out a reconnaissance in the Courbevoie area, just across the Seine from the suburb of Neuilly. It was apparently conducted on the sole initiative of the Marquis de Gallifet, the dashing general who had led the desperately heroic last cavalry charge at Sedan, now returned from a German prisoner-of-war camp. Later a close friend of the future Edward VII, Gallifet, the elegant, witty, and savagely sarcastic courtier, whose wife had been one of the Empire's most famous beauties, renowned for the extravagance of her costumes at Louis-Napoleon's masked balls, was to fill a prominent and dread role in the final chapter of the Commune. Though he seemed the very essence of the *panache-et-gloire* generals of the Second Empire, Gallifet had had experience which was perhaps peculiarly appropriate to the kind of warfare now facing the French regular Army. The influential Marquise had obtained him a command in Louis-Napoleon's Mexican campaign (no doubt to give herself greater freedom of action in Paris); a war against the irregulars of Juarez in which the French troops became accustomed to taking few prisoners. Gallifet had acquired there a reputation for being both fearless and ferocious, as contemptuous of his own suffering as he was of that of others. At a dinner party he had shocked young Mrs. Moulton with details of his Mexican experiences: 'He had been shot in the intestines and left for dead on the field of battle. He managed by creeping and crawling, "*toujours tenant mes entrailles dans mon képi*", to reach a peasant's house, where the good people took care of him. . . .' Now, so the impressionable lady was assured, he wore a silver plate with his name engraved on it 'to keep the above mentioned *entrailles* in their proper place.'

Light as it was, Gallifet's reconnaissance of March 30th succeeded in dislodging a small outpost held by the Commune National Guard; thus the report reaching Thiers cannot have given any impressive account of the state of the Paris defences. Two days later, an encouraged Thiers held a council, the proceedings of which were kept strictly secret, but to the Assembly he announced that same day:

The organization of one of the finest armies possessed by France has been completed at Versailles; good citizens can thus reassure themselves and hope for the end of a struggle which will have been painful, but short.

This was nothing less than a declaration of war; painful the struggle would certainly be, but not short.

In Paris, Thiers's announcement finally confronted Commune leaders, then involved in arguments over the disestablishment of the Church, with reality. Amid much disagreement and confusion, it was agreed that the Paris forces should march upon Versailles in five days' time; meanwhile, Bergeret would carry out a strong reconnaissance towards Courbevoie. But Thiers acted first. It was April 2nd, Palm Sunday. Goncourt, one of the 'good citizens' addressed by Thiers, began his diary for that day: 'A cannonade at about ten, o'clock, in the direction of Courbevoie. Thank God! Civil war has begun.' As the day went on, Goncourt noted that 'the cannonade died away. 'Is Versailles beaten ? Alas, if Versailles suffers the least reverse, Versailles is lost!' There were indeed ugly rumours as the ever-inquisitive Goncourt hastened into the centre of Paris. But there, as usual studying 'people's faces, which are like barometers of events during revolutions, I discerned a concealed satisfaction, a sly joy. At last a paper told me that the Bellevillites had been beaten! . . .'

Goncourt's entry was a fair summary of the day's skirmishing. Thiers had backed up Gallifet's reconnaissance with a strong attack on Courbevoie where the Communards, reinforced after the alert of the 30th, were entrenched at the Rond Point. The action was clearly visible from Paris. Washburne, disappointed at having seen none of the fighting during the Siege, found it 'a singular sight to my family on that Sunday morning to watch from the upper windows of my residence the progress of a regular battle under the walls of Paris, and to hear the roar of artillery, the rattling of musketry and the peculiar sound of the mitrailleuses'. But it was difficult to tell for some time who was winning. Indeed, at Courbevoie itself there was doubt to begin with. The Versailles regulars were repulsed, and one battalion of the line broke with ominous cries of '*Vive la Commune !*' On the other hand, the Zouaves were said to have attacked vigorously, shouting, '*Vive le Roi !*' Suddenly, it was the story of Buzenval all over again. Under pressure, the rebel National Guard, still no better trained or disciplined than in January, some drunk and all doped with over-confidence, panicked and abandoned their positions. Across

x

the bridge and up the Avenue de Neuilly they fled, offering to all
who would listen the excuses heard so often during the Siege; above
all, the dismal plaint, 'Nous sommes trahis!' Ex-Guardsman Child,
on his way home from Palm Sunday service, met some of them and
remarked acidly 'suppose they wanted what was most needful,
"pluck".' It was, he added, a 'dull day. Quite suitable to the événements.'

Almost without opposition Gallifet's men seized the vital bridge at
Neuilly. The success, small though it was, gave a boost of tremendous
importance to the shaky morale of Thiers's forces. Casualties had
been low on both sides, but among the victims had been the unfortunate inmates of a girls' school in Neuilly, hit by Government shells
as they were departing on a Palm Sunday outing. It was a prelude
to what lay ahead for the civil population of this part of Paris, but
there was also that day a casualty which was to set off an even more
tragic chain-reaction. With the Versailles troops had been Surgeon-
Major Pasquier of the Gendarmerie, the principal doctor attached to
Vinoy and apparently a much-beloved figure. According to the Government version, Pasquier had volunteered to go towards the Pont de
Neuilly, under a flag of truce, to negotiate with the insurgents;
according to the Communards, they simply saw a figure whose
sleeves were covered in gold stripes, assumed he was a general, and
shot him down. Wherever the truth lay, the killing caused great
indignation among the Versailles troops, and Thiers—condemning
it as an atrocity on a par with the murder of Thomas and Lecomte—
made maximum capital out of it.

Thoroughly shaken out of its tranquil euphoria by the news of the
Versailles attack, all Paris was trembling; some of it with rage. Larded
with references to 'Chouans, Vendéens, and Bretons of Trochu'
which betrayed the historical fixations of its Jacobin members, the
Commune emitted a hysterial proclamation, announcing:

> The royalist conspirators have ATTACKED.
> Despite the moderation of our attitude, they have ATTACKED. . . .

Those who still regarded the Commune as nothing more than a
legally elected municipal council were profoundly and genuinely
shocked. The boulevards 'were terribly agitated', reported Edwin
Child, 'at every turning almost were to be met battalions marching,
their drums and clarions creating a most awful discord. On arriving
Rue Royale, met them all united together and marching, so they
said, straight to Versailles, but doubt if they will ever get there.' At
the Hôtel de Ville there was the usual disunity. The 'generals' of the

Commune, Eudes, Duval, and Bergeret, demanded an immediate counter-attack; Pyat, who for the past three days had been clamouring for action in *Le Vengeur* in much the same tone as he had employed against Trochu during the Siege, now backed down, to the fury of Duval. Finally a plan was arrived at, under which massed units of the National Guard would march upon Versailles the following day, April 3rd, in three columns. On the right, Bergeret, and Flourens, heading on either side of Mont-Valérien towards the village of Rueil; in the centre, Eudes, advancing via Meudon and Chaville; with Duval securing the left flank by an attack on the same Châtillon heights that had so embarrassed Ducrot during the Siege. The plan itself was unexceptionable; but it relied too much on the striking-power of the National Guard, and ignored the fact that—through the disgraced Lullier's oversight—Mont-Valérien was now held by enemy gunners.

The force which set out from Paris early on the morning of the 3rd was more of a mob than an army; it proximated closely to the *sortie torrentielle* for which its leaders had pleaded throughout the first Siege. But in the haste and the disorganization the National Guard omitted to take along its most powerful military card—the two hundred cannon, the original *casus belli*, which still remained in the artillery park at Montmartre. What it lacked in equipment and train-ing, though, was more than compensated for by the National Guard's confidence in itself, despite the reverse of the previous day. All felt that one 'whiff of grapeshot' would suffice to disperse the demoralized 'royalists'. No one was more confident than the commanders. Bergeret, a former bookseller's clerk, who arrived at dawn at the assembly area in a phaeton, caparisoned in sashes and great knee-boots that re-minded one somehow of a Dumas musketeer, declared in a first dispatch: 'Bergeret *himself* is at Neuilly. Soldiers of the Line are all arriving and declaring that, except for the senior officers, no one wants to fight.' Flourens, too, was there, magnificent as ever in his Cretan uniform—blue pantaloons, immense scimitar, and Turkish belt crammed with pistols. In his turn, he telegraphed back to the Hôtel de Ville: 'We shall be the victors ... there cannot ever be a doubt of that.' Still the festive mood of those halcyon March days pre-vailed, and one Communard chronicler, Edmond Lepelletier, was reminded of 'a horde of turbulent picnickers, setting out gaily and uncertainly for the country, rather than an attacking column directing itself towards a formidable position'. In ragged but dense ranks, with-out any scouts, the Bergeret-Flourens column sauntered across the Seine, keeping to the centre of the road. Up on to the Bergères plateau they strolled, close to the scene of Trochu's final disaster.

Then one of the powerful guns spoke from the fortress of Mont-Valérien, towering above the expedition. The aim was not particular distinguished, but one shell fell amid the packed masses of Bergeret's column, followed by another. An officer was cut in two. It was enough. No one—least of all Bergeret—seems to have expected this, and like the detonation that ignites a powder magazine, panic flashed back along the whole straggling column. It split in two, the rear fragment scattering at top speed back across the Seine. On the far side of the river a *Times* correspondent came across 'two officers hiding in a house, and the men were begging the villagers to lend them clothes in order that they might not be caught in uniform by the troops'. Demoralization could hardly have been more complete. But, isolated at the head of the column, the ever-audacious Flourens and a now rather less confident Bergeret still decided to press on towards Versailles with the remnants of the vanguard, some 3,000 men, that still remained to them.

The Communards had fallen into a trap. As soon as Bergeret's troops deployed on to the plain, the Versailles cavalry swept down on them. He too fell back across the Seine. Flourens was now left alone with a handful of his faithful *Chasseurs* and Cipriani, his comrade from Cretan days. Displaying an almost suicidal courage, and ignoring Cipriani's exhortations to beat a retreat back to Paris, he continued sadly on to Rueil. At an inn in the village, he took off his famous belt, scimitar, and pistols, and flopped down, exhausted. During the night Rueil was surrounded by troops commanded by one Colonel Boulanger, who had fought with conspicuous gallantry at Ducrot's Great Sortie and would, at the end of the next decade, give his name to a bizarre episode in French politics, the Boulangist movement. According to one account, Cipriani and Flourens were denounced by the villagers; Cipriani was struck down at once, and Flourens led out unarmed. A mounted gendarmerie captain, apparently recognizing him, cleft his head in two with one savage sabre blow.

The body of the flamboyant adventurer was then thrown upon a dung-cart, and wheeled in triumph to Versailles (where, it was reported, elegant ladies prodded the corpse's shattered cranium with the ferrules of their umbrellas). The first of the Commune's leaders had been eliminated. Elsewhere other summary punishments were being exacted; at least five captured insurgents were put to death on Gallifet's orders, on the grounds that they were deserters from the regular Army, but it was fairly clear that these were regarded as reprisals for the shooting-down of Surgeon-Major Pasquier the previous day. Indeed, Gallifet issued a proclamation that same day, declaring that his soldiers had been 'assassinated', and that 'I proclaim war without truce or mercy upon these assassins. This morning I had to make an example; let it be salutary.' One woman at Cour-bevoie told a *Times* correspondent that many prisoners had been 'first treated with the grossest cruelty by the Gendarmes', and then shot. The same correspondent quoted rumours to the effect that General Vinoy himself had ordered the shooting out of hand of all surrendered National Guards, and the fate of Duval, the leader of the Communard left flank, suggests there may have been truth in these rumours. By the night of the 3rd, Duval had successfully installed himself, with some 1,500 men, on the Châtillon plateau. But the *Versaillais* counter-attacked the following morning, and Duval and his men were forced to surrender—apparently on promise of their lives. All who still wore any vestige of regular Army uniform were shot on the spot, while the remainder, including Duval, was marched off to Versailles. On the way they were intercepted by Vinoy. The general inquired if there was a leader among the Communards, and Duval stepped forward. Two others came to his side; Vinoy addressed them as 'hideous scum', turned to his staff and ordered the three prisoners shot.[1] The order was duly executed, and a captain dragged off the dead Communard 'general''s boots as a trophy. It was an episode that was to mark the beginning of the terrible tragedy of the Commune 'hostages'.

Everywhere the Commune drive on Versailles had collapsed in ruins. All that had been achieved was the recapture of the Pont de Neuilly. Paris was in a turmoil. In the afternoon Washburne en-countered a body of several hundred exhilarated women formed up in the Place de la Concorde, ready to march upon Versailles

in poor imitation of those who marched upon the same place in the time of Louis the Sixteenth. They paraded up the Champs Elysées and through the Avenue Montaigne. . . . Many of them wore the *'bonnet rouge'*, and all were singing the Marseillaise. Whenever they met an omnibus they stopped it, caused the passengers to get out, and took possession them-selves. One old woman, sixty years of age, mounted on the top of an omnibus, displayed the red flag, and gave the word of command. How far they went and what became of them I do not know.

Elsewhere the Rev. Gibson found National Guardsmen wandering about in twos and threes, looking extremely dejected; 'fatigued and worn, covered with dust; so changed in their appearance from what they were when they marched out on Sunday evening'. On the 6th,

---

[1] According to another (Versailles) account, Vinoy asked Duval: 'If I were your prisoner, what would you do to me?' 'I would have you shot.' 'Good. You have just passed your own sentence.'

there was a magnificent state funeral for the 'heroes' who had died in the two days of action. Three large hearses, containing the dead,[1] covered in black with red flags at each corner, were drawn solemnly through Paris. Delescluze and five Communard leaders, heads bare and wearing red scarves, led the procession. Behind came several battalions of National Guards; the men, thought Gibson, 'looking thoughtful and sad', though Edwin Child—less charitably—considered that 'a few hundredweights of soap would have done them good'. In the background muffled drums beat, and women sobbed as the corpses were lowered reverently into a communal grave at the Père-Lachaise cemetery.

It hardly needed the sombre procession, so reminiscent of those of a few months earlier, to make Parisians grimly aware that they were now under siege for a second time. The gates were shut and the trains ceased running. Hearing of this, the Rev. Gibson echoed the feelings of most Parisians when he exclaimed: 'So we are shut up as in a cage!'; his concierge admitted, 'I never felt afraid during the Siege, but now I shiver'. Despite the closing-down of communications, people contrived to leave Paris by the thousand; Gibson heard it said that they were leaving at a rate of 50,000 a day. Many men, fearful of being conscripted into the National Guard, took to their heels or went into hiding. As the Commune authorities required that a *laissez-passer* be obtained by anyone leaving Paris, Washburne (in his capacity as *chargé d'affaires* acting for the Germans) was besieged with Alsatians wanting a passport and claiming to have become German citizens. For the fourteenth time since the previous August, Edwin Child was instructed to pack up his shop's stock of watches and chains for the nervous M. Louppe to take them with him out of Paris. On Easter Sunday, he was surprised to notice how empty the church seemed; the boulevards had become more and more deserted; the principal shops shut because their owners had departed. Wandering into Voisin's on the Saturday, Goncourt asked for the *plat du jour*, to be told, 'There isn't any; there's no one left in Paris'. He spotted only one old lady whom he had seen there throughout the Siege. Outside, the emptiness gave him the impression 'of a city where there's a plague'.

At the Hôtel de Ville, the Commune rulers had reacted to the first military reverses in the true revolutionary spirit of '92. Assi and Lullier, suspected of treachery in their negligence at not occupying Mont-Valérien, were promptly flung into prison and the overconfident Bergeret followed them shortly afterwards. A brief announcement disclosed that a 'Citizen Cluseret is delegated to the Ministry

---

[1] The bodies of Duval and Flourens had not been recovered.

of War'. But shock at the dismal failure of the Commune's counter-attack was quite overshadowed by indignation and fury at the killing in cold blood of Duval and the other captured National Guardsmen. There was much talk about exacting 'an eye for an eye, a tooth for a tooth', and it was not long before an obscure Communard called Urbain proposed a measure that was to gain everlasting notoriety as the 'Law of Hostages'. Passed against some opposition on April 5th, the law opened with the preamble, 'Seeing that the Government of Versailles openly treads under foot the laws of humanity and those of war, and that it has been guilty of horrors such as even the invaders of French soil have not dishonoured themselves by . . .', it decreed as follows: every person accused of complicity with Versailles shall be imprisoned; juries to be instituted to try these parties within forty-eight hours; those convicted to be held as 'hostages of the people of Paris'; and the execution of any Commune prisoner of war to be followed immediately by the execution of three hostages, 'drawn by lot'. The ineluctable way that civil war has of escalating from atrocity to atrocity, horror to horror, was now clearly signposted in France. Who would be the hostages? A new chill of uneasiness settled over the anti-Communard elements of Paris; Goncourt predicted gloomily, 'If Versailles does not hurry up, we shall see the rage of defeat turn itself into massacres, shootings and other niceties by these tender friends of humanity. . . .'

But Thiers was in no hurry. It was not his plan. Like Napoleon III, he wanted to 'ne rien brusquer'. Despite the boost to morale provided by the hopeless performance of the Commune forces, he felt he could not yet rely too much upon his regulars.[1] There were still disquieting défaillances, soldiers going over to the Commune. If Moltke had hesitated to rush Paris, was not Thiers well advised to pause too? Until he possessed crushing superiority in numbers, he would take no risks of in-fighting inside the city, where revolution-aries entrenched behind their traditional barricades could slaughter

---

[1] In his excellent book, *The War against Paris 1871* (London 1981), Robert Tombs (who seemed to regard Thiers' success as a much finer run thing than historians had previously thought) describes well the delicate state of health of the Versailles Army, quoting a *chasseur* as having declared at the end of March: 'If they make me march against the Parisians, I shall march . . . but in no case will I fire on them, and every other member of the army must do the same.' On the other hand, if the Communards attacked, many soldiers were reported as having said 'they would defend themselves . . . but they would not march on Paris' [Tombs, pp. 69–70, 144]. But the Fédéré attack of 3rd April had changed all that. However, as Tombs goes on to point out, 'Even in the middle of the fighting, the generals could never be sure of the reactions of their men.' There was always the fear that they might be won over by the Communards, even after the main assault on Paris had begun in May.

his troops. Besides, he was determined that repression of the uprising must be thorough and lasting. Contrary to the pessimism of
Lord Lyons, Washburne, and others, Thiers was now convinced
that time was on his side. Abroad, apart from the lone voice of Karl
Marx and his Internationalists, the Commune had gained little or no
support;[1] even professional revolutionaries like Garibaldi and
Mazzini had turned their backs on it. So had Victor Hugo. In the
French provinces the sympathetic revolts there had all been
suppressed or were fizzling out, though Bakunin continued to cause
spasmodic trouble at Lyons. At Marseilles, where Gaston Crémieux
had proclaimed a Commune, the end came on April 8th after Government troops shelled the seized Prefecture at point-blank range,
killing over 150 rebels and arresting another 500. It looked as though
an investment of Paris could be maintained once again, so there would
be little danger of fresh revolt radiating outwards from it; and this
time there would be no Gambetta at large in the provinces to harry
the investing forces.

So, instead of attempting to follow up his successes of Holy Week,
Thiers settled down to 'regroup' his forces. On April 6th the elderly
and unpopular Vinoy was adorned with a Légion d'Honneur and
replaced as Thiers's commander by MacMahon, who, after seven
months of internment beyond the Rhine, was urging for an opportunity to requite the humiliations of Sedan. Meanwhile Favre, the
negotiator, had been sent to Prussian Headquarters to atone for his
grave miscalculations of January by obtaining permission to increase
the French regular Army beyond the limits prescribed in the Peace
Treaty. Bismarck, who had at first taken a cynically detached attitude
towards the humorous spectacle of Frenchmen killing Frenchmen,
was now beginning to fear the impact the Commune might have
upon his arch-enemies at home, the German Socialists, and he readily
acquiesced to the Army being inflated first to 80,000, then to 110,000,
and ultimately to 170,000 men. The return of the 400,000 French
prisoners of war was speeded up; back to France they poured, into
special camps organized by General Ducrot among others, to be
rehabilitated and prepared for their new role—the second Siege of
Paris.

[1] In England Frederic Harrison, the Positivist, was among the few non-
Marxists to sympathize with the Commune, and even the International leaders
were badly divided.

Elihu Wasburne

Adolphe Thiers

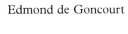

Edmond de Goncourt

Raoul Rigault

Charles Delescluze

Louis Rossel

Théophile Ferré

Louise Michel

N° 7. — Mardi 23 Mai 1871.　　　CINQ CENTIMES.　　　4 Prairial an 79. — N° 7.

LE SALUT PUBLIC

Rédaction, 11, rue du Fbg-Montmartre.　|　Directeur politique : GUSTAVE MAROTEAU　|　Bureau de vente, 8, rue de Crussol.

CITOYENS,

La trahison a ouvert les portes à l'ennemi; il est dans Paris; il nous bombarde; il tue nos femmes et nos enfants.

Citoyens, l'heure suprême de la grande lutte a sonné. Demain, ce soir, le prolétariat sera retombé sous le joug ou affranchi pour l'éternité. Si Thiers est vainqueur, si l'Assemblée triomphe, vous savez la vie qui vous attend : le travail sans résultat, la misère sans trêve. Plus d'avenir! plus d'espoir! Vos enfants, que vous aviez rêvés libres, resteront esclaves; les prêtres vont reprendre leur jeunesse; vos filles, que vous aviez vues belles et chastes, vont rouler flétries dans les bras de ces bandits.

AUX ARMES! AUX ARMES!

Pas de pitié. — Fusillez ceux qui pourraient leur tendre la main ! Si vous étiez défaits, ils ne vous épargneraient point. Malheur à ceux qu'on dénoncera comme les soldats du droit; malheur à ceux qui auront de la poudre aux doigts ou de la fumée sur le visage.

Feu! Feu!

Pressez-vous autour du drapeau rouge sur les barricades, autour du Comité de Salut public. — Il ne vous abandonnera pas.

Nous ne vous abandonnerons pas non plus. Nous nous battrons avec vous jusqu'à la dernière cartouche, derrière le dernier pavé.

Vive la République! Vive la Commune! Vive le Comité de Salut public!

LE SALUT PUBLIC.

Communard proclamation announcing the Versaillais entry into Paris

Place Blanche defended by the Communard Women's Battalion

May 23rd.—The capture of Montmartre

The Follies of the Commune by Cham

'Aren't they stupid! They hate us provincials, yet it's their city they burn!'

'Watch me, you poor amateur!'

'Execution of a trumpeter, during the Commune' —from a painting by Alfred Roll, 1871

'In all his glory', the Marquis of Gallife—from a drawing by Steinlen

The Tuileries Palace,
before the war

The Tuileries Palace,
June 1871

The Hôtel de Ville,
June 1871

'Appalled by her legacy.'—From a drawing by Daumier

The Second Siege of Paris: Inside the Porte Maillot

21. Besieged Again

WITH the death of Duval and Flourens, and the fall from grace in various degrees of Brunel, Lullier, Eudes, and Bergeret, a vacuum had been created in the military command of the Commune. A new figure was now drawn into it; Gustave-Paul Cluseret. Then aged forty-seven, Cluseret was a true soldier of fortune like Flourens. Although, as a character, he was altogether less colourful and less appealing, as well as deficient in the romantic idealism of Flourens, he could look back on an even more extraordinary career as an adventurer, and his military background was considerably wider. Commissioned at St.-Cyr, he had taken part in the suppression of the 1848 uprisings, but he then became involved with the Clubs and as a result was placed on the reserve. He was recalled during the Crimean War, where he was wounded, promoted captain, and awarded the Légion d'Honneur. From the Crimea he was sent to Algeria, to be cashiered in 1858 for complicity in the theft of stores, and from there he travelled to seek his fortunes in the United States. In the Civil War he re-emerged as a volunteer on the side of the North, attaining the rank of brigadier-general after a brief spell as A.D.C. to McClellan. Washburne recalled having been in conversation with President Lincoln at the Capitol when Cluseret was introduced by a Senator as a "gallant Frenchman" with the highest references, come over to offer his services to the Union. The Senator urged that Cluseret be appointed brigadier-general; Lincoln, according to Washburne, was not much taken by him and seemed disinclined to give him a commission at all, but eventually yielded to pressure. But soon after his appointment, the Union High Command apparently found him too incompetent for any operational duties and relegated him to an insignificant post in Baltimore. Cluseret, Washburne added acidly, 'remained in the army long enough to get his naturalization papers, which seemed to be his principal object'. After the Civil War, he hitched his waggon for a brief spell to the star of a kindred spirit, John C. Frémont, the 'Pathfinder', and then became involved with the Fenians, conspiring to raid Canada in the name of Irish freedom. Nominated their 'General-in-Chief', Cluseret followed the Fenian cause to England, where he took part in the 1867 attack on Chester Gaol. With England grown too hot, he returned to France and within a year had been sentenced to prison for seditious activities; but, on pleading his American citizenship, was deported instead. Having formed a tenuous link with the International, he was back in France after the overthrow of the Empire as an emissary of the anarchist, Bakunin, embarrassing Gambetta by proclaiming (on October 31st) a Commune at Marseilles and nominating himself 'Commander of the Armies of the South'.

According to his associate, Rossel, Cluseret was tall, 'with a white skin, black hair and beard, and a coarsely handsome face. He must have been rather a favourite with women. He had the fluency of a journalist, and knew how to introduce misplaced declarations of principle.' Seldom seen without a cheroot in the corner of his mouth —a habit picked up during the Civil War—Cluseret was a character whose shadiness gave rise to a variety of versions about his past career; one claimed that he had actually fought on the Confederate side during the Civil War; another that he had been condemned to death, *in absentia*, by the South, as well as by a British court for his complicity with the Fenians. Thus whatever he did, his motives tended to be open to mistrust. He was both cynical and lazy. When he took up his appointment at the beginning of April, he reckoned the prospects of Paris no greater than had Trochu during the first Siege; and, as an erstwhile regular, he shared Trochu's contempt for the National Guard. This opinion was something he was quite incapable of keeping to himself—with unfortunate results. Nevertheless, he possessed more practical experience than any other Communard on how an army should be run, and it was for this reason that he had been pushed forward by the Comité Central of the National Guard, chafing as it was at the display of military ineptitude the Commune leaders had shown to date. Although Cluseret had been appointed to be military commander of the Commune on April 2nd and strongly disapproved of the riposte projected for the following day, he had done nothing to stop it, beyond arresting Bergeret for 'insubordination' on his return. Now, after the calamitous failure of the April 3rd expedition (he said it reminded him of Bull Run), Cluseret ordered the Commune forces to take up a strictly defensive posture behind the forts and ramparts of Paris which had kept the Prussians at bay for so many months. In the breathing-space granted by Thiers's period of consolidation, he settled down leisurely to reforming the National Guard.

The hour was late, very late, and the task Augean. The bad habits acquired during the first Siege had become deeply rooted. At least two of the battalions deployed at Courbevoie on April 1st had been 'completely drunk'. With officers of the National Guard still elected (often on any basis but that of military efficiency) discipline was non-existent at any level; the moment an officer gave an unpopular order, a fresh election could be called to depose him. As one Communard admitted to Colonel Stanley: 'We are all ambitious, we all want to be commanders'.

With little exaggeration, Cluseret remarked of his take-over: 'never have I seen anything comparable to the anarchy of the National Guard in 1871. It was perfect of its kind. . . .' The whole force was impregnated with the thoroughly unmilitary, old-fashioned Jacobin beliefs (as it had been during the first Siege) that all that was needed for military victory was the surging, irresistible *levée en masse*; ignoring that the science of war had advanced somewhat since the eighteenth century. Anything that required staff-work was deficient; the commissariat, communications, and ambulance service were in a hopeless state of muddle; there were no cavalry and practically no engineers. It was hardly surprising that on April 3rd many of the National Guard had gone into battle unfed and short of cartridges, nor that the artillery was left behind. Despite the imposing number of battalions participating in Brunel's march past of March 28th, many of them had no commanders. At the top of the scale, 'generals' like twenty-eight-year-old Eudes had never even seen action in command of a battalion, and they were constantly drawn hither and thither by conflicting orders issued from their own headquarters in the Place Vendôme, from the Comité Central, from the Commune, as well as the local commissions in each *arrondissement*, none of which seemed to have any ascendancy over the others. 'The greater part of my time', declared Louis Rossel, a former lieutenant-colonel of the regular Army whom Cluseret designated as his Chief of Staff, 'was taken up by importunate and useless individuals; delegates of every origin, inquirers after information, inventors, and, above all, officers and guards, who left their posts to come and complain of their chiefs or of their weapons, or of the want of provisions and ammunition. There were also almost everywhere independent chiefs, who did not accept or did not carry out orders. . . .'

Following upon the example of the *Tirailleurs de Flourens* (who had now rechristened themselves the *Vengeurs de Flourens*), a proliferation of 'private armies' had sprung up. There were the *Lascars*, the *Enfants Perdus*, the *Éclaireurs de Bergeret*, the *Volontaires de Montrouge* and the *Turcos de la Commune*. Each was costumed according to its own whim, and the taste for bizarre and extravagant uniform had also infected many senior officers, who bedizened themselves superbly—on credit—at eminent army tailors. Some of their wives did not lag far behind; a frequently-seen, dashing figure at National Headquarters was Mme Eudes, who demanded to be known as '*la générale Eudes*', dressed either as a pistol-packing Amazone or (according to Alphonse Daudet) 'like the Empress, in *gants à huit boutons*'. Cluseret, perhaps mindful from his American Civil War memories of how slovenly had been the dress of that military giant, Ulysses Grant, was determined to begin by purging this unproletarian magnificence. On April 7th he announced the suppression of the rank of general, accompanying this with the qualification that, in future, there were to be 'no lanyards, no more glitter, no more gold braid rings . . . '. The order did not endear Cluseret to many Parisians, with their thoroughly Latin passion for 'glitter', and ultimately the Commune would have its generals back again.[1]

Cluseret's next reform made him even more unpopular. This was to split the National Guard (as Trochu had once attempted during the Siege) into 'active' and 'sedentary' battalions, by hiving off in the latter all the men of over forty. The Guardsmen grumbled that this measure 'broke up the bonds of solidarity and fraternity formed during the Siege', but it made sense if any of the National Guard battalions were to be made battle-worthy. Cluseret's greatest contribution undoubtedly lay in his choice of subordinates; Rossel as his Chief of Staff, and the thirty-five-year-old Pole, Jaroslaw

[1] The whole question of badges of rank raises some interesting comparisons with the Russian Revolution of October 1917, where epaulets were at first banned as a hangover from Tsarist days, and then reintroduced.

Dombrowski, as Commandant of Paris in succession to Bergeret. These were to prove the Commune's two ablest leaders, and it was greatly owing to Dombrowski's talents as a commander and to Rossel's energy in carrying through Cluseret's reforms that the fighting capacity of the Commune forces showed a striking improvement after their dismal performance on April 3rd.

Dombrowski belonged to the impoverished Polish nobility, had been commissioned into the Russian Army but condemned to fifteen years deportation to Siberia for taking part in the Polish insurrection of 1863. On his way through Moscow he escaped and made his way to Paris. During the Siege he had offered his services to Trochu, which were declined—no doubt out of mistrust, in so far as many of the troops fighting under Moltke were also of Polish origin. Now Dombrowski, entrusted with active command over the Commune's fighting troops, took up position at the threatened sector of Neuilly, with his brother Ladislas holding part of the line to the right. The appearance in the advance posts of Jaroslaw's slight figure and wispy moustache seems to have given new heart to the National Guards. (About Rossel, the chief-of-staff, more will be said in a later chapter.) On April 9th a surprise night attack by two Montmartre battalions inflicted a sharp reverse on the Versailles forces at Asnières, across the Seine to the north-east of Courbevois, capturing several guns. The rise in fighting spirit was noticeable even to Goncourt, no friend of the Communards: 'Why this stubborn resistance which the Prussians did not encounter?' he asked for a second time on April 12th concluding—with some accuracy—that it was 'Because in this war the common people are waging their own war and are not under the Army's orders'. In these days, he complained elsewhere, 'one cannot curse sufficiently that inept Government of National Defence for not having turned this valiance to its own advantage'.

Although no serious attempt to re-enter Paris was contemplated until the regrouping of the *Versaillais* could be complete, Thiers kept up the pressure on the suburb of Neuilly. The bridge was recaptured, but throughout most of the rest of April fighting surged back and forth from street to street, with Dombrowski's men defending from behind barricades built from ripped-up *pavé*, against an attack whose principal component was devastating and persistent artillery fire that echoed across Paris. Under it the Communards, now standing on the defensive, with their backs to their homes, instead of deployed on any ambitious offensive tactics, stood remarkably steady. Each day resistance increased with familiarity. During a lull in the fighting the ubiquitous Louise Michel was even to be found playing the organ in a deserted church. Casualties were not light. Colonel John Stanley of

the Grenadiers, sent to Neuilly with a British ambulance, found
nonchalant Communard doctors 'in stained aprons over their uniforms . . . smoking and stirring their coffee with the instruments with
which they had extracted the bullets'. A few days later, 'I saw one
man that was hit by a bit of a shell run for half a minute as though
nothing had happened, and then he fell. We picked him up; his leg
was cut off. . . .' Stanley was moved to pity[1] at the wretched condition of the wounded he tended, still suffering from the after-effects
of the Siege superimposed upon years of deprivation; 'what pains me
most is not the wounds but to see their poor shrivelled legs, really
not larger than a strong man's thumb'. Losses among the wounded
were discouragingly high: 'I am sorry to say that it is the old story,
out of 40 cases operated on hardly one recovers. Drink, drink, drink;
there is always the smell of drink, when they lie panting on the
wooden trestles, where they are put when their wounds are examined.
When they require all the calm and vitality they have to resist the
shock, they offer nothing but a feverish exhausted state of blood.'

At the overtaxed, makeshift hospitals that received the Communard
wounded in the centre of Paris there were spectacles no less distressing. Goncourt, visiting one where 'the picturesque of war was blended
with the disorder of a student's room', was shocked by the callous
gaiety with which the internees spoke of the appalling mutilations
they witnessed. One man, they told him, had had his jaw shot away;
'a real antique mask . . . and—imagine—the orderly persisted in
asking his name!' They pointed out to him a busy man in a black
skull-cap whose job was to undress the dead, at forty *sous* a time:
'It's his real passion . . . you should see with what an amorous eye
he looks around, spying out those who are going to kick the bucket. . . .'
Working at the Beaujon Hospital, Dr. Powell noted the critical shortage of trained nurses, many of whom had left Paris. Hygienic conditions were appalling: 'out of fifteen patients who had the leg
amputated all died of pyæmia or gangrene. . . . There was no
proper supervision and visitors came and went as they liked, also no
priests permitted to visit the wounded or the dying.' The hospital
became forced to add carbolic acid to bottles of alcohol, because it
'disappeared at one time so rapidly' down the throats of the attendants.

It was not only the combatants who suffered. The prosperous
village of Neuilly, largely spared during the Prussian bombardment, was being progressively destroyed and many of its inhabitants had been trapped in the ruins. Colonel Stanley wrote in the
last week of April:

[1] According to his descendant, Miss Nancy Mitford, he also reckoned 'that
no doubt the fellows . . . were glad to be attended to by a gentleman!'

every single tree is cut in pieces, and the ground is covered with grape, canister, shot and broken shells and flattened bullets. I entered what had been beautiful houses, with floors wobbling and held up only by a side, utterly wrecked, billiard tables, looking-glasses, sofas, and costly furniture all smashed to pieces, guns placed in lovely gardens, the walls broken through to enable them to pass from one garden to another. Bedding and furniture all piled up into barricades. . . . In many houses we found the dead laid out, where they had been placed some days ago . . . and the people had lived as they could in the cellars all this long time on bread and nothing else. . . .

What life under these circumstances was like for the inhabitants is revealed in an account written to his mother on April 20th by Charles Skelly, a type-compositor working on a Parisian English-language periodical. Skelly lived in the Avenue de Roule at Neuilly; he had two young children and his wife was imminently expecting a third. From his back window he had watched the shells from Mont-Valérien plunge down upon the advancing Communards, and the resultant débâcle. Three days later, on April 5th, Theresa Skelly gave birth, and the following morning (Thursday) her husband set forth as usual to his work in Paris:

. . . but in the evening when wanting to return I found that the insurgents had placed their guns in position on the ramparts at the Ternes and were sweeping our avenue; I slept in Paris that night. Next morning (Good Friday), at an early hour, I was fortunately permitted to pass through, after a close inspection of my passport. I sought my home with a heavy heart but, thank God, I found my wife and children safe. Theresa was too ill to be removed, but a neighbour dressed the children, and I succeeded by keeping close in by the side of the wall in bringing them safely into Paris, the shells bursting above and around us on our perilous way. Since that morning I have never been home, the gates have been closed, and it has been an eternal rain of shot and shell. Night and morning I visited the Ternes, from where I could see indistinctly our house enveloped in smoke . . . powerless to save them. . . .

On the morning of April 11th, Skelly managed to enter Neuilly, under fire from both sides, and reached

. . . within some yards of the house. I had but to bound across the Avenue du Roule and I could enter my home; but no that was impossible; it would have been certain death to expose myself to view within that deadly avenue; I should have passed under the very mouths of their guns. I saw the guards at the end of the Rue Victor Noir firing upon the soldiers of the *rond-point* of the Avenue Inkermann opposite our door. . . .

Having got so close, Skelly was forced reluctantly to return once more to Paris, 'amidst the awful howl and crash of shells as they travelled from the battery at Courbevoie to the Porte de Ternes and being answered from the ramparts'. After another week of misery in Paris, he applied to the British Embassy for assistance, but they were unhelpful. Then, like so many needy Britons during the Siege, he directed his footsteps towards Richard Wallace, who unhesitatingly gave him a letter to the American Ambulance, asking them to evacuate Theresa and child, at Wallace's own expense. But Skelly found the American Ambulance 'closed', and as a last report appealed to the chief of one of the French ambulances, who agreed to intervene:

... what was my joy when the next morning at five o'clock she entered my room in company with a National Guard. . . . As it was almost certain death to be exposed in the streets, they passed through holes previously cut in the walls, through gardens, and through houses, until they arrived at the end of Sallonville. . . . Our poor dear baby was quite black with dirt on the face. . . . I cannot tell you of all the horrors she has seen and heard of. A poor man who had bought them some sugar was retracing his steps, when he was shot dead in front of our house: two guards attempted to pick him up and one of them fell dead also. . . .

Gradually, as the guns and ammunition became available to the Versailles forces, the bombardment experienced by Neuilly spread to other suburbs on the western approaches to Paris. On the morning of Saturday, April 15th, Goncourt was working in the garden of his house at Auteuil, near the Bois de Boulogne, when there was a 'whistling of several shells'. Several burst very close and there were shouts of 'Everybody down in the cellars'. For nearly two hours the bombardment continued; there was one 'terrible explosion' so powerful that it shook the whole house above and knocked over his faithful housekeeper, Pélagie. Goncourt began to suffer from 'a sense of cowardice such as I never felt during the time of the Prussians. Physically one has reached bottom. I chose to have a mattress placed on the ground and, lying on it, I remained in a state of sleepy torpor, only vaguely perceiving the cannonade and death. . . .' Towards 3 p.m. the bombardment lifted and began to fall ahead on the ramparts where the Communards had installed some guns. When Goncourt emerged from his cellar, he found that three houses immediately behind his had been hit.

One of the ironies of the civil war was that, as the bombardment spread, it was the most staunchly anti-Communard parts of Paris that bore the brunt of Government gunfire. In an endeavour to strike back at Mont-Valérien, Cluseret had sited a battery of his biggest naval guns at the Trocadéro, and this in turn drew fire down on the smart residential area of Passy. Writing to his brother-in-law in London, Dr. Jules Rafinesque compared their situation there to travellers seized by bandits: 'When the gendarmes arrive the wretched travellers are exposed to blows from two sides. Siege by the Prussians was nothing by comparison . . . .' He described the 'bandits' occupying Passy as 'a veritable army of unpaid mercenaries, a dirty, lewd, sordid, vicious, indisciplined rabble, but well-armed and well able to resist behind walls and in the streets . . . .' To reach the few of his patients that still remained in Passy, the doctor frequently had to run a gauntlet of shellfire; he claimed the Communards had boasted of having positioned their guns at the Trocadéro (which evidently proved incapable of covering the 6,000 yards to Mont-Valérien) solely 'to draw cannon-balls down' on this detested bourgeois quarter.

Soon the shells from Mont-Valérien were reaching out still further into the centre of the city, as haphazardly and ruthlessly as at any time during the Prussian bombardment. On April 12th, Washburne recorded shell splinters striking the U.S. Legation near the Étoile 'within twenty feet of where I was writing'. Two days later he counted twenty-seven separate hits on the Arc de Triomphe itself, and Colonel Stanley passing by picked up an elbow that had been knocked off one of its bas-reliefs. Occasionally the shelling in the area grew so intense that no one was allowed farther up the Champs-Élysées than the Rond-Point. The great avenue was almost deserted. Anxious Americans living in the neighbourhood thronged the U.S. Legation morning and night applying for passports or 'protection papers', while at the British Embassy a Second Secretary thoughtfully repeated a notice Lord Lyons had issued before decamping the previous September, warning that 'British subjects who continue to remain in Paris now do so at their own risk and peril. . . .' By April 25th, Washburne decided it would be prudent to evacuate his family to the country, and the Rev. Gibson did the same. Militarily as ineffective as the Prussian endeavours of January, Thiers's promiscuous bombardment served chiefly to exasperate and depress his natural allies in Paris. Writing to his father on April 11th, Edwin Child, who had just witnessed a shell carry off both legs of a seventy-year-old lady outside his church, declared that 'at one time I was almost French in sentiment, but I now scorn them almost as much as I do the Germans'. On the 27th, noting the usual 'wastage of munitions', he wished 'the whole affair was finished one way or other. It is becoming absolutely sickening, during the siege at least people knew why they were suffering and for what end, but now it would be difficult to say which is the most preferable, the Commune or the Government. Both give such proofs of their incapacity.' A few days later Child remarked that the indiscriminate bombardment was 'deciding many hitherto neutral to join "the insurgents" although not in any way sympathising with the Commune'. An experienced soldier like Colonel Stanley was as contemptuous as ex-Guardsman Child about the procrastination of 'that too stupid little Thiers', while Goncourt, thoroughly unnerved and despondent, complained that 'at the end of all this terrible noise, nothing happens and one goes away saying to oneself: 'never mind, it will happen tomorrow!' And that tomorrow never comes. . . .'

Although the repeated rumours that the Government forces were about to force a re-entry into Paris continued to end in disappointment for the beleaguered bourgeoisie, as April moved to its close Thiers and MacMahon had in fact decided upon a formula under which to deploy the full weight of the troops they had been husbanding. Possibly better than any soldier, Thiers knew the strength—and weaknesses—of the Paris defences; it was he who had been the Minister responsible for their construction during the reign of Louis-Philippe. He had long been aware that the potential Achilles' heel of the system lay at the Point-du-Jour, the extreme south-western pinnacle of the city, close to where the Seine flows out towards Sèvres. It was here that his army would try to break in. But first they would have to capture Fort Issy, the imposing fortress controlling the approaches just across the river.

On April 25th, Thiers acceded to the Commune request for an armistice at Neuilly, in order to allow the evacuation of the wretched, half-starved inhabitants. There was by now hardly a house standing in the village, and many of its residents almost lacked the strength to leave their cellars. Under cover of the twelve-hour truce, Thiers now disengaged the weight of his artillery from the Neuilly sector and transferred it to that facing Issy-les-Moulineaux. No less than 53 batteries of guns, supported by powerful infantry contingents, were mustered there under the command of General Cissey. The next day Thiers announced the opening of 'active operations', and after a particularly intense bombardment captured the village of Les Moulineaux that evening. On the 27th, Cissey's troops succeeded in pushing a parallel to within 300 yards of Fort Issy, which was all the time being deluged with heavy fire. According to Lissagaray, the Commune chronicler, Issy—already badly battered by Moltke's artillery in January—was soon 'no longer a fort, hardly even a fortified position; a litter of shell-lashed earth and rubble. Through the smashed-in casements the countryside could be seen, and the powder magazines were exposed; half of Bastion No. 3 lay in the moat; one could have driven a carriage through the breach. . . .' The fort's commandant, a workman called Mégy who had killed a policeman come to arrest him the previous year, sent pleas to Cluseret for heavy reinforcements, but none came. By the 30th Cissey's men had sapped forward to the very foot of the fort glacis, and Mégy could no longer restrain the panic that had broken out among the garrison. Ordering the guns to be spiked, he now evacuated the fort.

It was the worst military blow yet to befall the Commune. At the Ministry of War, Cluseret at once realized the significance of the evacuation of Fort Issy, both to the defence of Paris, and to himself. Although there had been no major shocks since April 4th and his reforms had begun to return some dividend, his star had been steadily waning. Anger at the drowning of a large number of National Guardsmen when a bridge of boats had broken—apparently by mismanagement—on April 17th, had been directed against Cluseret, and his undisguised contempt for the National Guards' military attributes had caused growing resentment in Commune circles. Tact was not his strongest point, and the Executive Commission found itself constantly having to water down some of his more searing pronouncements; there was, for instance, one in which he had condemned the profligate expenditure of ammunition as a 'stupid and entirely Monarchist practice'. These were words that cut to the quick, and Cluseret came under constant fire at the Hôtel de Ville. In a heated session on April 20th, Vermorel had declared that 'for the past month we have been sleeping, we have had no organization', to which Delescluze responded with the lukewarm defence, 'We took Cluseret because we could find no other soldier'. Bitter rivalry had sprung up between the Comité Central and the Commune for control over the National Guard; the former was disinclined to subordinate its earlier powers. Thus every effort for reform made by Cluseret, never the most energetic of men, had been attacked by one side or the other, and much of his time had been wasted in playing one off against the other. A leader worth his salt would have seen the necessity to limit strictly the Comité's powers of interference in the conduct of war; but Cluseret, the eternal conspirator, could not help but exacerbate divisions between the two rival bodies.

By April 30th, after only four weeks of office, Cluseret was exhausted—worn out by the intrigues and the wrangling. Yet on hearing Mégy's report he summoned up a rare burst of energy, and marched out himself at the head of less than two hundred men, in pouring rain, to see what could be retrieved from the situation at Issy. Arriving at the fort, he found to his considerable surprise that it was still as Mégy had left it, unoccupied[1]—with the exception of 'an urchin of

---

[1] The Versailles Commander, Colonel Leperche, had apparently called on Issy to surrender; but, on receiving no reply from the empty fort, took this for a refusal, and therefore failed to take advantage of the garrison's withdrawal.

Nuns interrogated by Communards

22. The Return of the Jacobins

THE news of Cluseret's arrest was revealed in a public announcement the following day, Monday, May 1st. It provoked—according to Washburne—a great deal of excitement. The official reason was 'incapacity', but rumours swiftly buzzed through Paris that Cluseret had been apprehended plotting to overthrow the Commune; that he had sold himself to Versailles; or that, more specifically, he was an Orleanist agent. It was a measure of the new nervousness within the city.

To replace Cluseret, his former Chief of Staff, Louis Rossel, was designated 'provisional' Delegate of War. Completely apolitical, Rossel was one of the more unusual adherents to the Commune, and his attachment testified to how the bitterness felt by so many loyal Frenchmen at the shameful capitulation of the Government of National Defence had led up to the March insurrection and gained it such powerful initial support. At this distance in time, he, Varlin, and Delescluze strike one as being—in their different ways—the Commune's three most appealing figures; but Rossel was also by far its most efficient soldier. Had he been in charge in March, subsequent history might well have been different; had he survived, it seems almost certain that he would have left a mark of genius somewhere. Rossel was born in Brittany of a French father with military and Huguenot antecedents, and a Scottish mother. He had made a career as an engineer in the regular Army, graduating second in his class at the Polytechnique. At the beginning of the Franco-Prussian war Rossel held the rank of captain in Bazaine's Army, and from the first was disgusted at the ineptitude of the French High Command. Walled up in Metz, he seems early on in the siege to have toyed with the idea of 'deposing' Bazaine. He tried once to escape from the city, but was caught and led back by Prussian sentries; just as the capitulation was being arranged, he did succeed in getting away, disguised as a peasant, which would almost certainly have resulted in his being shot by the Prussians had he been discovered. He eventually reached Gambetta's forces, whose slovenliness shocked him, and when asked by Freycinet what job he wanted replied unhesitatingly: 'if all the places were to be distributed, I should choose the sole direction of operations'. Gambetta, at once recognizing genius in this strange, fierce young man with a straggly black moustache and penetrating eyes, promoted him colonel and sent him off to be Chief Engineer at Nevers. Rossel was then just twenty-six.

When news of the armistice reached him in Nevers, Rossel was appalled. In his *Posthumous Papers* he wrote: 'We are wanting in patience; we conclude peace as rashly as we went to war', adding with biting irony: 'as a general rule, a defence until death can never do harm to a people'. On March 19th, the day after the insurrection in Paris, he wrote to General Le Flô, the Minister of War:

Mon Général,

I have the honour to inform you that I am about to proceed to Paris, to place myself at the disposal of the Government forces which are being organized there. Having learnt by a Versailles despatch, published this day, that two parties are struggling for mastery in the country, *I do not hesitate to join the side which has not concluded peace, and which does not include in its ranks generals guilty of capitulation.* . . .

The letter must have been a delight to its recipient. Rossel now set forth for Paris, in the apparently genuine belief that—with the guns available in Paris and a revolutionary and fighting party in power— it would be possible somehow 'to snatch back victory' from the Prussians. Socialism, Proudhon, Blanqui, and Marx meant nothing to him; 'I did not know who the insurgents were, but I knew against whom they were rebelling and that was sufficient.' During a kind of ideological selection board to which he was submitted on taking up his new post, he admitted: 'I shall not tell you that I have profoundly studied social reforms, but I have a horror of this society which has just sold France with such cowardice. . . .' What he saw of the Commune soon shocked him even more than had Gambetta's levies, and he was about to quit Paris when Cluseret begged him, on April 3rd, to become his Chief of Staff; although, to the end, he maintained that 'the Parisian revolutionary party was, in my eyes, the lesser evil'.

Rossel had a self-confident manner, a deliberate and thoughtful way of speaking that reminded a *Daily News* interviewer more of an American or an Englishman, and—like Cluseret—he would have wished to introduce some Yankee efficiency into the National Guard. With an energy Cluseret never revealed, Rossel—well aware that time was now hopelessly against him—set to work to reorganize the Paris defences. On the very day of his appointment in succession to Cluseret he ordered the immediate construction of a ring of barricades behind the ramparts, as a second line of defence in the event of MacMahon breaking through the perimeter. There was much his engineering expertise could achieve here; on April 27th, Colonel Stanley noted critically, 'The embrasure in the barricade at the end of the Rue de Rivoli is so stupidly made, that it does not command half the Place de la Concorde'. Further within the city, three last-ditch 'citadels' were to be erected at the Trocadéro, Montmartre, and the Panthéon on the Left Bank. The whole of this southern side of Paris Rossel entrusted to another courageous and competent Pole, thirty-four-year-old Walery Wroblewski, while Dombrowksi was placed in direct control of the Right Bank. Eudes was sent, reluctantly, to Fort Issy, from which hot-spot he spent most of his time finding a pretext to return. For the first time, Rossel attempted to concentrate and centralize the Commune's powerful artillery; there were some 1,100 pieces which had hitherto been scattered uselessly about, many rusting in the compounds, their breech-blocks stored elsewhere, while the beleaguered gunners on the ramparts had for the most part only light 7- and 12-pounders with which to reply to Versailles's heavy naval guns.

Strategically, Rossel also appreciated that a purely passive defence would be powerless to prevent the eventual fall of the fortifications' and with this in mind he drew up a plan to create 'combat groups', each of five battalions, commanded by a colonel and supported by 40 guns, with the aim of seizing the initiative wherever possible before Paris. But his scheme was confronted with a serious, and growing, shortage of numbers; the 200 battalions parading in such triumph on March 28th had soon melted.[1] Levied on a parochial

---

[1] The *Journal Officiel* revealed that, out of a total National Guard strength of 190,425 on May 3rd, there were no less than 27,774 absentees, of whom 14,335 were absent without permission.

basis, the National Guardsmen showed a curious reluctance to serve in quarters other than where their own homes lay, as well as being fundamentally part-time militiamen; so that by the time of his take-over, Rossel could probably count on little more than 30,000 regularly available fighting troops, as against the 130,000 that Thiers and MacMahon had now mustered.

This was by no means Rossel's only headache. To raise the effectiveness of what troops he did have, he, like Cluseret, wanted to apply the disciplinary measures of a regular army. He wanted to bring those who had defaulted in the face of the enemy before a court martial, but the Executive Commission complained of his excessive severity: while Karl Marx's future son-in-law, Charles Longuet, accused Rossel of not showing the right 'political spirit'. When the sentence of death on one battalion commander found guilty of refusing to march on the enemy was commuted to imprisonment for the duration of the war, Rossel was driven to despair and fury. Just like Cluseret he too discovered his hands bound by the rival Communard bodies; Maxime Vuillaume, one of the Commune chroniclers, recalls a visit to the Ministry of War, when Rossel 'went to the window, pointed to a group of the Comité's officers gesticulating and arguing loudly below, and, turning to us, cold-eyed, muttered between his teeth: "If I were to have them shot, now, down there in the yard . . . ."' With the departure of Cluseret, the Comité Central had redoubled its efforts to gain control over military operations. Friction with the Commune Executive Commission grew worse, and when Rossel pleaded against any such transfer of responsibility, the Blanquists spread suspicion that he was scheming to set himself up as a military dictator. And, one day after his appointment, yet another new headache arrived in the form of the creation of a Committee of Public Safety; which, despite its dread connotations of absolutism, in fact—initially—only meant still further dissipations of the Commune's executive power, and graver rifts within it.

Throughout April and on into May, while on the one hand fighting for survival, the Commune had persisted in its zealous aims of reforming the world. From the Hôtel de Ville there poured out a mass of legislation—a mixture of incredibly irrelevant trivia and genuine attempts to right social injustices. On April 2nd a decree was passed limiting the salaries of all Government officials to 6,000 francs a year, roughly equivalent to a workman's wages; a step later praised by Lenin as making 'the break from a bourgeois democracy to a proletarian democracy'. On the 16th an edict ordained the 'nationalization' of all workshops abandoned by their bourgeois owners (but it was never carried out). On the 27th, the Commune abolished the system of fines imposed upon workers. On the 28th, it decreed an end to nightbaking, which had long been a grievance among the bakery workers (Frankel, who was responsible for it, considered the law the Commune's one big achievement, while many like Madame Rafinesque of Passy grumbled that it only meant 'all Paris is reduced to stale bread'). A serious effort was made to combat prostitution, but there were certain self-cancelling local discrepancies; as Colonel Stanley noted, 'It is very funny that the 1st Arrondissement forbid women in the houses and the second Arrondissement in the streets.... So I suppose the women will sleep in one quarter, and perambulate in the other.' The Commune proclaimed that it would 'adopt' all the wives and children of men who died 'in defending the rights of Paris'; the wives—'married or not', the Rev. Gibson was shocked to discover—were to receive pensions of 600 francs a year.

Nor was the Commune backward in cultural affairs; legislation was busily being prepared to laicize schools ('What', snorted one Communard, Gaston da Costa, 'should one think of this pedagogic Commission occupying itself at such a moment with educational reform.... This grandeur, this tranquillity, this blindness in an assembly of men already menaced by 100,000 *chassepots*, is one of the most stupefying facts ever given to a historian to record'), while on April 12th Courbet had been charged with the task of reopening the museums of Paris 'with the least possible delay', and of re-establishing the annual Salon.

On April 19th the Commune issued what was probably its most imposing and important politico-social proclamation, which was to become, in essence, its testament; at any rate its closest approach to formulating any coherent programme. In immense placards posted throughout Paris it declared the aims for which it was fighting:

... the recognition and consolidation of the Republic ... the absolute autonomy of the Commune extended to all the localities of France....

The inherent rights of each Commune are:

The control of the Communal budget, receipts and expenditures; the fixing and re-division of taxes; the direction of local services; the organization of the magistrature, of the police and of education....

The absolute guarantee of individual liberty, of the freedom of conscience and the freedom of labour....

Paris herself reserved the rights to make

administrative and economic reforms demanded by her population ... to universalize power and property according to the necessities of the moment, the wish of those interested, and the rules furnished by experience....

Rising to a powerful, grandiloquent climax, the proclamation continued:

The Communal Revolution, begun by the popular initiative of March 18th, inaugurates a new political era, experimental, positive, scientific.

It is the end of the old governmental and clerical world, of militarism, of monopolism, of privileges to which the proletariat owes its servitude, the Nation its miseries and disasters.

But nothing the Commune said or did faced up to the issue over which so many patriotic Parisians had originally sided with it—the humiliation at Prussian hands and the crushing peace terms. Nor, patently, had it ever had the military potential for any such action. With the Prussians ringed around the eastern perimeter of Paris, the Commune lived in constant fear that they might intervene to help Versailles crush the insurrection, and therefore went out of its way to avoid any incident that might upset the former enemy. And, if it lost adherents through its display of impotence towards the Prussians, as well as its military ineptitude in the fighting with Versailles, the Commune also lost many of its moderates when, in both word and deed, it revealed ambitions far beyond the scope of a mere municipal council.

By early April, through the resignation of such moderates, deaths, and other forms of erosion, the Commune Assembly found it had thirty-one vacancies, and on the 16th—with the fighting at Neuilly at its peak—chose to hold by-elections. Among the newcomers elected was the noisy and drunken old Courbet; Marx's future son-in-law, Longuet, the editor of the *Journal Officiel*, and his liaison officer, Serrailler; Johannard, a handsome heart-breaker and largely re-nowned for being the Commune's top billiards-player; and a con-tumacious hunchback called Vésinier. Its new blood did little to improve matters within the Commune. As the pressure from Versailles mounted, so the arguments and rifts grew; with each act of legislation the Commune threatened to divide into its various heterogeneous components.[1] Usually Félix Pyat, as ever the irresponsible polemicist, was to be found somewhere near the eye of the storm. Attacked by Vermorel for inconsistency between what he said at the Hôtel de Ville and what he printed in his paper, Pyat would retire to *Le Vengeur* to retaliate with a savage leader accusing Vermorel of

[1] Karl Marx, still minutely studying every move from London, wrote a warning letter in May to the two Internationalist leaders, Varlin and Frankel in which he remarked: 'The Commune seems to lose too much time in trifling affairs and personal quarrels. . . . None of this would matter, if you had the time to recover the time already lost. . . .'

being a police spy. There were few who were not at some time the target for Pyat's poisoned spleen, including Rossel, who he knew despised him.

In an attempt to bring some kind of order to the Commune's affairs, Delescluze proposed that the semi-impotent Executive Commission be replaced by a kind of War Cabinet formed from the Delegates of the other nine Commissions, and on April 21st this reorganization had been effected. But in practice it made little difference. Day after day the bickering continued. 'What gnawed the heart of the Commune', declared Rochefort with reason, 'was distrust. The Hôtel de Ville distrusted the Ministry of War, the Ministry of War distrusted the Ministry of the Marine, Vanves Fort distrusted Montrouge, which distrusted Issy. Raoul Rigault distrusted Colonel Rossel, and Félix Pyat distrusted me.' Delescluze was disgusted by it all, and in a fiery speech magnificent for one so sick and worn out he thundered to the Commune assembly:

> You complain that our decrees are not carried out. Well, citizens, are you not yourselves somewhat accessory to this fault? ... When a decree appears in the *Journal Officiel* with 13 negative votes and only 18 in the affirmative, and does not meet with the respect that this assembly deserves, can you be astonished? ...

'You should have replaced us sooner', he went on. But until then

> ... there are members who have remained at their posts, and will remain until the end despite the insults with which we are covered, and, if we do not triumph, we will not be the last to die, whether on the ramparts or elsewhere.

These were eloquently prophetic words.

On April 28th, an old Jacobin of the 1848 Revolution with a massive white beard, Jules Miot, proposed the creation of a Committee of Public Safety to take over the Commune's executive functions. For three stormy days the discussions continued over this proposal, so redolent with associations of Robespierre and the Terror. The Socialists, and above all the members of the International, were strongly opposed; Longuet scornfully described it as a talisman, while another with a long memory cried out; 'Under the Empire we stood for liberty, and in power we shall not abjure it.' Finally the Commune Assembly voted, 45 to 23, in favour of Miot's proposal. Next it went on to vote for five men to form the all-powerful Committee of Public Safety; with the exception of the inevitable Pyat, all unknown ciphers—although Washburne somewhat exaggeratedly described them as 'the most desperate and dangerous men in the Commune'. This time the Minority of 23 (including Beslay, Courbet,

Longuet, Malon, Serrailler, and Varlin) abstained from voting. The most fundamental split in the Commune so far had taken place, and henceforth its Assembly would consist of a Majority and Minority faction; the one, controlled by the Jacobins, wanting to exercise dictatorship and terror—the methods of '93—and blaming the failures of the Commune upon the sentimentality of the Socialists; the other desiring to govern by reasonably democratic methods, to observe moderation in order to leave, as Rochefort put it, 'the door at least half open to conciliation'. In the light of twentieth-century history, it seems perhaps ironical that the exponents of democracy and moderation should have been chiefly the Internationalists, the fore-fathers of Lenin's Bolsheviks.

Although at first the Committee of Public Safety proved as inef-fectual as anything that it was designed to replace, it was a milestone in the Commune's passage towards grimmer territory. For in the background personalities and trends had already emerged that would in the end for ever stigmatize the name 'Commune' in re-spectable eyes. Of all the leaders of the Commune, none was more responsible for shaping its final image than Raoul Rigault, its Police Chief, and later *Procureur* of the Revolutionary Tribunal introduced by the Committee of Public Safety. In at least one facet of his character Rigault typified the professional Bohemian and perpetual student still to be found today lurking purposelessly around the cheaper estaminets of St.-Germain-des-Prés—atheistic, amoral, left-wing, anti-Establishment, and lightly washed. A friend of Verlaine's, among others, Rigault before the war frequented the Café Madrid or any of the Left Bank haunts patronized by Rochefort, Pyat, and other vociferous enemies of the Second Empire. Though of steady middle-class origins, Rigault supported Blanqui as passionately as he hated the Church. But by instinct he was more of a Jacobin than a Socialist, spending most of his leisure time plunged into books about the Great Revolution, and especially the Terror. Not yet twenty-five at the outbreak of the war, he had already shown promise as a true disciple of *l'Enfermé* by receiving three separate sentences of imprison-ment for political agitation, during one of which he attempted to stir up a prison revolt with blood-curdling shouts of '*Vive la Guillotine!*'

'I want sexual promiscuity. Concubinage is a social dogma,' Rigault once declared, and, in and out of sordid Montparnasse garrets, he assiduously practised what he preached in the spare moments re-maining from his other commitments. His leer terrified poor Lillie Moulton when she had to apply to him for a passport to leave Paris. By then debauchery, probably more than the cares of office, had evidently aged him, for he 'appeared to me a man about thirty-five or forty years old, short, thick-set, with a full round face, a bushy black beard, a sensuous mouth, and a cynical smile. He wore tortoiseshell eyeglasses; but these could not hide the wicked expression of his cunning eyes.' In a voice loaded with insinuation, he voiced his regrets that she was leaving the city, because 'I should think Paris would be a very attractive place for a pretty woman like yourself.' Turning to the courteous Paschal Grousset (whose presence she felt probably saved her from something worse than just the refusal of a passport, and who later apologized to her for his colleague's behaviour), Rigault concluded, 'We don't often have such luck, do we Grousset?' Mrs. Moulton was afraid she might be about to faint.

One of the historians of the Second Empire, de la Gorce, claimed that one did not know whether 'to rank him among the dangerous lunatics or among the corrupt'. Rigault was much more than a mere Left Bank layabout. To this aspect he added an infinitely more menacing face. About him and his faithful lieutenant, Ferré, there was a touch of cold, twentieth-century professionalism notably lacking in the rest of the Communards. More than any other, Rigault had studied his part in advance. 'Nothing but a guttersnipe, but a policeman of genius', was old Blanqi's verdict on him. From his researches into the Revolution, while Marat deeply impressed him, Rigault reached the conclusion that Saint-Just was merely a feeble amateur in the art of terror. With this background knowledge, Rigault set himself to studying modern police techniques. Under constant observation himself by the Imperial police, young Rigault had turned the tables by spying on them. It was said he spent long hours with a spyglass propped up on a Seine bookseller's stall, peering into the Prefecture of Police across the water, and that he had a team of 'agents' posted outside to keep track of the coming and going of informers and plain-clothes men. Rochefort tells how Rigault plotted the undoing of a particularly harsh and licentious judge, Delesvaux, who delighted in sentencing revolutionaries. Rigault set an *agente provocatrice* to pick up the judge in a café; then, once the bait had been taken, Rigault arraigned the judge with seducing his sister, and—with the aid of three toughs—broke his nose and blacked both his eyes.

On the overthrow of Louis-Napoleon, Rigault had promptly offered his services to the Prefecture 'to dig out secret agents of the Bona-partist police, arrest them and prosecute them. . . .' Edmond Adam, then Prefect of Police, vaguely recalled noticing Rigault as a 'simple employee' busily searching for dossiers; until, on the night of October 31st, this same simple employee had presented himself at the head of three hundred National Guards as Adam's newly appointed successor. When the *putsch* failed, Rigault was sacked; but not, apparently, before he had been able to make off with a quantity of the secret files.

On March 20th, Rigault received the post coveted since the previous October, and with some zeal began arresting 'enemies of the Republic', many of whose names he had uncovered in the course of his counter-espionage against the police. Rigault and his work were at once a source of contention within the Commune; Jacobins like the embittered Vésinier claimed there 'never was a man who possessed a finer sense of justice', while Rossel accused him of having 'led the scandalous existence of a spendthrift rake, surrounded by useless persons, and giving up the greater part of his time to debauchery.'[1] As the pressure from Versailles mounted, and with it all the familiar manifestations of siege nerves, such as spy-mania, so Rigault stepped up the rate of his arrests until by May 23rd they totalled over 3,000. Many were clapped into gaol for long periods without any kind of hearing. The Communards themselves began to share the terror that Rigault and his 'twenty-year-old scoundrels', as Cluseret called them, exercised over the Parisian bourgeois, and on April 24th protests against the arbitrary arrests reached such a peak that both Rigault and his lieutenant, Ferré, were forced to resign. But Rigault's successor as Prefect of Police, Cournet, was in fact an ally of his; and three days later Rigault reappeared vested in the immensely greater authority of *Procureur*, State Prosecutor of the newly created Revolutionary Tribunal. It was yet another title with unpleasant connotations from '93, and under it Rigault emerged possessing more real power than any other member of the Commune.

If there was one issue over which the Communards instinctively and almost unanimously sympathized with Rigault, this was his violent anticlericalism. Left wing Paris had a long tradition of hating and distrusting the Church. At the door of the priesthood it laid the blame for much of the city's miseries, suspecting it of all manner of medieval malpractices.[2] When the Commune later entered various convents by force, incredible tales were circulated—and eagerly believed—to the

---

[1] One outside observer, Washburne—his feelings undoubtedly exacerbated by the proximity of events—observed no diplomatic moderation when describing Rigault; he was '. . . one of the most hideous figures in all history . . . consumed by the most deadly hatred of society and the most intense thirst for blood. All his associate assassins bowed before his despotic will. . . .'

[2] There were also certain specific economic grievances against the Church; for instance, more than half of the women working in industry in Paris were employed as seamstresses of one kind or another, while the convents also turned out exquisite work which could often undercut that produced by 'lay' workers by as much as 25 per cent.

effect that orthopædic irons found there were in reality instruments of torture; that bones found in the nuns' burial-vaults were the remains of victims done to death; that mad women had been confined in little boxes. On the bookstalls obscenely irreligious literature, bearing titles such as 'Confessions of a Breton Seminarist' or 'The Revelations of an Ex-Curé', began to replace scurrility at the expense of the former Empress. One of the Commune's very first acts had been to decree the disestablishment of the Church, together with the confiscation of its property, and subsequently a number of well-known churches were taken over, to be 'converted' into Red Clubs. St.-Nicolas-des-Champs—in which a red sash now adorned the crucifix—became the 'Club Montparnasse'; while at St.-Eustache Washburne listened to a *tricoteuse* ranting from the pulpit, in favour of the abolition of marriage. Then, on April 4th, Rigault had initiated the deed by which his name will be longest remembered. He arrested the Archbishop of Paris, Mgr. Darboy.

With the Archbishop were also arrested his Vicar-General, Abbé Lagarde, and the Empress Eugénie's confessor, the seventy-five-year-old Abbé Deguerry of the Madeleine, who was apparently seized in the act of trying to escape over his garden wall. The arrests were later followed by the wholesale round-up of priests.[1] Between a Jesuit and the atheistic Rigault, acting as interrogator, a famous interview took place:

Rigault. What is your profession?
Priest. Servant of God.
Rigault. Where does your master live?
Priest. Everywhere.
Rigault (to a clerk). Take this down: *X*, describing himself servant of one called God, a vagrant.

An English schoolmaster, Benjamin Wilson, was outraged at witnessing the arrest of one of the unfortunate priests, who, 'surrounded by half a dozen armed men and followed by a mob of hooting boys, was being taken to Mazas.[2] He was tall and distinguished-looking with an intellectual cast of countenance and he evidently felt the humiliation of his position keenly. His face gave signs of suppressed emotion and was as pale as a sheet of paper. To see one presumably a gentleman and a Christian in the hands of the vilest mob in Europe was enough to set one's blood boiling. Alighting from the omnibus I inquired of the bystanders what he had done. It was they said "*Une arrestation*

---

[1] Marx commented cynically: 'The priests were sent back to the recess of private life, there to feed upon the alms of the faithful in imitation of their predecessors, the Apostles.'
[2] The Mazas prison.

de prêtre—voilà tout" '. As the priest was about to disappear through
the forbidding gates of the Mazas Prison, Wilson 'pressed through the
crowd and shook him by the hand'; within a matter of minutes he too
found himself in custody in the Mazas.

Excuses of varying transparency were given for the arrests. It was
said (with complete truth) that the Archbishop was 'hostile' to the
Commune. It was also claimed that the priests, acting on the Archbishop's instructions, had offended the Disestablishment Decree of
April 2nd by smuggling out to Versailles church valuables which
were now the property of the state. Closer to the truth, however,
was the intent revealed in one Commune journal: 'This is a simple
security measure taken by the Commune to avert such tragedies as
that of which General Duval was the victim.' The arrests coincided
closely with the passage of the 'Hostages Bill', which had received
strong support from Rigault against the judgement of Delescluze and
other Commune principals, and although it was denied that the
Archbishop and his brethren had been seized as hostages, the link
was unmistakeable. The choice of the 'hostages' was emphatically
Rigault's, and while a few Communards bleated feebly at the facility
with which Rigault had been permitted to effect the arrests, the great
majority in their rabid anticlericalism did not oppose them. But in
his choice Rigault had a motive deeper even than mere hatred of the
clergy. From the beginning of the insurrection he had believed that,
in order to survive, the Commune must, above all else, get hold of
Blanqui to lead them. 'Blanqui', said da Costa, Rigault's twenty-one-
year-old 'secretary', 'was his constant obsession. Without Blanqui,
nothing could be done. With him, everything.' Blanqui alone could
resolve the Commune's squabbles. And Blanqui languished in one
of Thiers's gaols.

Reckoning upon the impact that news of the Archbishop's arrest
would have on the predominantly Catholic Assembly at Versailles,
Rigault dispatched da Costa on April 6th to obtain from the Archbishop and the Abbé Deguerry letters protesting at the summary
executions carried out by Vinoy and Gallifet. Ready by the 9th, these
were then entrusted to one of the other hostages, Abbé Bertaux, who
was given a safe conduct to Versailles, where—having delivered the
letters to Thiers in person—he was to offer to trade the Archbishop
for Blanqui. It was a ruthless but daring gamble. Thiers, however,
would have none of it. The tough old politician later claimed that he
had been 'profoundly moved, and shaken' by the Archbishop's letter.
But to hand Blanqui over to the Commune was, he calculated, 'to
send it a force equal to an Army Corps'. The deal could not be
contemplated.

As the war raged with ever-increasing fury around Paris, accusations of atrocities committed by the Versailles troops provoked repeated demands for the immediate execution, or even handing over to the mob, of the hostages. On April 25th, a Versailles cavalry officer shot down three surrendered National Guardsmen, of whom one survived to tell the tale. The next day there were loud calls for reprisals in the Hôtel de Ville, but moderation triumphed after one member insisted 'the Commune must live by its acts'. For the time being, the Archbishop seemed safe; and Rigault for one would not allow him to come to harm so long as there seemed the slenderest chance of freeing Blanqui.

*   *   *

For all the energy and sense Rossel had attempted to inject into the military conduct of the war, things did not go much better under him than they had under Cluseret. On May 4th there was another heated session of the Commune in which personalities and the usual irrelevancies had whittled away the time needed for serious discussion. Once again Pyat had taken the centre of the stage, complaining pathetically that the enemies he had made as a journalist were now sabotaging his work on the Committee of Public Safety. One of the latest of these enemies, the insulted Vermorel, intervened to ask whether Pyat had the right to characterize him a 'spy', and so it went on until suddenly the debate was broken up by an emissary of Rossel who burst in to announce the fall of the redoubt of Moulin-Saquet. Lying due south between Villejuif and the Communard-held fort of Bicêtre, the disquieting thing about Moulin-Saquet was more the manner of its taking than its strategic significance. Some 800 National Guards had been caught in their sleep by a surprise attack; 50 were slaughtered on the spot and a further 200 captured, at a cost of 36 casualties to the Versailles forces. There were ugly rumours (never substantiated) that the commander of the 55th Battalion of the National Guard had 'sold' the password.

But it was around the crucial position of Fort Issy that the most important fighting continued. In response to Colonel Leperche's call to the fort to surrender, Rossel, on taking over from Cluseret, had sent back the following message:

My dear Comrade,
The next time you send a summons so insolent as that contained in your yesterday's letter I shall have the man who brings it shot, according to the usages of war.

Your devoted comrade,
Rossel.

More than any other factor, Rossel's riposte was destined to bring
him before the firing-squad when Versailles had its day of reckoning;
but, for the present, there was no doubt that this display of spirit,
coupled with his reforms, was bearing fruit. At Issy, the National
Guards were fighting better than they ever had. There were bitter
odds against them. On the night of May 1st, Government Marines and
Chasseurs had seized Clamart railway station—little more than 300
yards distant on the fort's left flank. The Communards, rallied and
driven on by Louise Michel, recaptured it, then lost it again. All the
time Fort Issy was subjected to a bombardment resembling something out of 1916; it was, claimed survivors, far more intense than
any artillery fire brought to bear upon the Prussians during the
Siege. One by one the fort's guns were knocked out by the Versailles
fire; its prison was said to be packed with more than three hundred
corpses, piled six feet high; there were no doctors and provisions
were running out. In Paris, Goncourt watched troops relieved from
Issy re-enter the city, 'preceded by cheerful bands and a show of
gaiety which formed a contrast with the pitiful appearance of the men,
and the exhaustion with which they marched. . . . Behind follow two
vehicles full of rifles. It was said in the crowd that these are the
weapons of the dead and the wounded. . . .'

In his diary, one of the fort's officers wrote:

May 5th. The enemy's fire does not cease for a minute; our embrasures
no longer exist. . . . Rossel has been. He studied for a long time the
Versailles siegeworks. The *Enfants Perdus* serving the guns at Bastion 5
have lost a lot of people; they remain solidly at their posts. . . . All our
trenches, smashed in by the artillery, have been evacuated. The Versailles parallel is within 60 metres of the counter-escarpment. They are
advancing closer and closer.

May 6th. The battery at Fleury is sending us regularly six shots every
five minutes. They have just brought into the first-aid post a *cantinière*
who has been hit by a bullet in the left side of the groin. For four days
there are three women who go under the most severe fire to succour the
wounded. Now this one is dying and begs us to look after her two small
children. There is no more food. We are eating nothing but horse. This
evening, the rampart became untenable. . . .

May 7th. We are now receiving up to ten shells a minute. The ramparts
are completely uncovered. . . . With the exception of one or two, all the
guns have been knocked out. The Versailles earthworks are now almost
touching us. . . . We are on the point of being surrounded.

Disgracefully, Eudes, the nominal commander at Issy, had found an
excuse to pull out, leaving his deputies to bear the brunt. On one visit
to the fort Rossel was astonished to run into Dombrowski, his Right

Bank commander. Unbeknown to Rossel, Dombrowski 'had just received from the Committee of Public Safety an order investing him with the command of all the active forces, but leaving me the Ministry of War'. Rossel was exasperated by this further display of order and counter-order on the part of the Commune, but he and Dombrowksi —who were on the best of terms—concluded their own private arrangement, regardless of Pyat and his colleagues. On May 7th the battle had reached a point where, declared Rossel, 'there was only one chance left of improving the position of military affairs, which was becoming very threatening, and that was suddenly to take the offensive, with the troops just as they were, to interrupt the progress of the attack by inspiring the enemy with serious anxiety'. But when that night Rossel arrived at the front to supervise the offensive, the troops were not assembled; whilst one battalion was arriving, another disappeared .

In a fury, Rossel personally punished a number of National Guards who had deserted their posts, by cutting off their right sleeves,'commencing with the officers. They were all sobbing, and the guard which surrounded them was, perhaps, more affected than it would have been for a capital execution.' His action was bitterly resented, and may well have played some part in the reneguing, the next day, of a number of battalion commanders who had promised to furnish troops for Rossel's offensive (they included the unfortunate Bergeret, now returned to duty after a spell in the cells). This was the last straw for Rossel. After writing out a final fiery order to the effect that 'deserters and those hanging back at the rear will be sabred by the cavalry; if numerous, they will be cannonaded', on May 8th he dictated his resignation as Minister of War:

Citizen members of the Commune, I feel myself incapable of continuing to bear the responsibility of a command which everyone discusses and no one obeys. . . . The Commune discusses, and has resolved nothing. . . . The Comité Central discusses and has not yet been able to act. During this delay the enemy was surrounding Fort Issy by adventurous and imprudent attacks for which I should punish him had I the least military force at my disposal. . . . The nullity of the Artillery Committee prevented the organization of the artillery; the hesitations of the Central Committee hinder the administration; the petty preoccupations of the Battalion Commanders paralyse the mobilization of troops. My predecessor made the mistake of striving against this absurd situation. . . . I am withdrawing, and I have the honour to request from you a cell in the Mazas.

That same day, from Versailles, Thiers issued a proclamation to the Parisians warning them of the opening of the general attack on

the city: 'The moment has now come when, to shorten your sufferings, [the Versailles Army] must attack the fortifications themselves. It will not', he added in an aside hardly designed to impress
the residents of the Passy or Étoile districts, 'bombard Paris'. Commenting on the proclamation, Colonel Stanley wrote, 'I am sick of the
useless slaughter, poor misguided wretches, and by tonight's paper,
Versailles seems to be really in earnest. . . .' That this was so was at
once proved by a vast intensification of shellfire all the way from
Meudon to Issy, put up by over eighty heavy guns.

For Fort Issy, which had by now suffered somewhere over 500 dead
and wounded, this was the death-knell. Thiers had at last achieved
something which Moltke had failed to do—the capture of one of the
great Paris fortresses. At the Hôtel de Ville, Rigault was being subjected to cross-fire about police excesses when Delescluze interrupted
with the gravest news the Commune had yet received. 'You argue', he
cried, 'while it has just been announced that the *tricolore* now floats
over Fort Issy! Treachery threatens us at every hand. . . . Today the
National Guard no longer wants to fight, and you discuss matters of
procedure. We shall still save the country, though possibly now only
behind barricades;' but, he begged, 'put away your mutual hatreds'.
Deeply moved, the Commune applauded loud and long Delescluze's
impassioned speech; it was, said Lissagaray, the chronicler, 'sub-
jugated by this severe man, who was duty personified'. It was also
shaken by Rossel's bitter letter of resignation, and the session which
continued late into the evening degenerated once more into wrangling
and recrimination. Pyat attacked Rossel in his absence, declaring, 'I
warned you, citizens, that he was a traitor but you would not believe
me. You are young, unlike our Masters of the Convention you were
incapable of being wary of military authority.' The more extreme
members of the Jacobin 'Majority' clamoured for the arrest of Rossel
and the entire 'Minority' faction, while Malon of the International
counter-attacked Pyat with the apt accusation, 'You are the evil genius
of the Revolution! Shut up! Cease spreading your venomous suspicions and stirring up discord. It is your influence that is destroying
the Commune!'

At the Ministry of War Rossel had been receiving various deputa-
tions throughout the day. In the evening, just as he was about to
leave to dine with Dombrowski, five delegates from the Comité
Central which had come so severely under Rossel's flail arrived to tell
him of their Comité's decision to appoint him a military dictator,
which it considered was the last chance of saving Paris and the
revolution. But better than anyone else Rossel knew that the fall of
Fort Issy was the beginning of the end, that it was only a matter of

time now before MacMahon broke into the city itself; and Rossel had had enough of Pyat and the Commune's hopeless wrangling, the counter-orders and the impotence of his own position. He refused the Comité's proposition, pointing out that he had already sent in his resignation, which was irrevocable. On returning from dinner, Rossel found Delescluze and Avrial awaiting him with a warrant for his arrest—on the grounds of having posted up the news of the fall of Issy before consulting the Commune. After some discussion, Delescluze declared that he could not arrest Rossel without his first being heard before a plenary session of the Commune. An appointment was fixed for the next day, the 10th, but when the matter was brought up before the Commune Pyat and his allies refused to countenance a confrontation with so impressive a figure as Rossel, and demanded that instead he be tried by court martial, presided over by an officer named Collet. One of Rossel's friends slipped out to warn him what was afoot. 'I could not bear', Rossel wrote later, 'the idea of appearing as an accused before that Collet, whom I had seen cowering before the shells at Issy, and it was then that I determined to evade the justice of the Commune.' The insurgents' brightest, and last, military star now leaped into a carriage and disappeared, not to be seen again during the life of the Commune.

The Destruction of the Vendôme Column

23. 'Floreal 79'

THE Commune Assembly was listening half-heartedly to the ravings of Jules Allix, arrested for committing some bizarre outrage in his district, when a highly excited Avrial—who had been detailed to 'guard' Rossel—interrupted to tell of his flight. Rossel's fall struck the rest of Paris like a thunderclap; 'He was regarded by all', wrote the Rev. Gibson, 'as a man of talent and capacity, and his retirement is a great loss to the Commune ... the Commune is said to be dead, but it dies hard.'

Doomed though it might be, the Commune was far from dead, and it now handed authority to the one man who could inspire it in its last agonies; the one man who could rise above the Pyats and their petty factionalism. Delescluze! The sixty-one-year-old Jacobin who had led the attempted insurrection against Trochu on October 31st was himself slowly dying of consumption contracted through long years on Devil's Island; yet from the embers there still flickered a fire emitted by no other Communard. 'He no longer spoke, he hardly breathed; he was an ambulating corpse', said Rossel. But when he did speak, even Pyat listened. The son of a '92 revolutionary, by the time he was an adolescent Delescluze had already done his apprenticeship at the barricades, and the sum of his years in prison was exceeded only by Blanqui's record. To Washburne's secretary, McKean, who went to see him in May, he represented 'a most perfect type of the Jacobin and revolutionist of 1793. He affected to dress *à la mode Marat*, and had a coarse scarf about his neck; his hands were dirty and there was a large amount of "free soil" under his nails. He was an old man, with long hair, unclean, unshaven, and dressed in a shabby coat.' To another contemporary, Philibert Andebrand, Delescluze was 'small in stature, rather badly put together, and had none of the characteristics that Sallust exacted of those desiring to lead the multitude. The forehead had nothing noble about it; the eye observed fixedly, but without having the power to fascinate ... his face was eroded into deep wrinkles and strange zigzags denoting what Balzac described as the defeats of private life. A mouth devoid of nobility or smiles was concealed by a beard once upon a time red, but now more white than grey. From it came a tremulous voice, always tempestuous, and which occasionally brought to mind the grating of a prison gate. He had the yellow complexion of a Brutus. . . .'

Neither description was particularly flattering; yet in some of his portraits there is a touch of Lincoln in the ravaged face. There was something strangely noble about the dying Delescluze. He was as incorruptible as Robespierre—when Cluseret reported that Versailles had offered him one million francs to betray the Commune, Delescluze commented coldly, 'So much the worse for you, Monsieur Thiers would never make a similar proposition to Citizen Delescluze' —and every Communard knew that he would go on to the bitter end. Because of his age and the state of his health, Delescluze had not wanted to take any office under the Commune, but now, with the disappearance of Rossel, he could not escape taking over as Civil Delegate to the Ministry of War. At the same time he was appointed to a reconstituted Committee of Public Safety, from which Pyat had at last been purged. On the eve of disaster, the Commune now had something approaching control vested in one pair of hands; those of its most outstanding personality. It was the last chance of reuniting the Communards, but at the same time the coming to power of Delescluze completely changed its character. For Delescluze was the king Jacobin, and to the now ascendant Jacobins ideology and social reform were of secondary importance to living—and dying—in the heroic tradition of '93. The Jacobins were, in their own way, quite as conservative and reactionary as any restored Bourbon. To proclaim the spirit that moved them, the Committee of Public Safety began to date its proclamations with the Convention's old revolutionary calendar, starting on the '15th Floreal, year 79'. On May 15th the Committee of Public Safety announced that the Commune had abdicated all power in its favour. Thus of its two opposing conceptions, the Dictatorial Commune had triumphed over the Democratic Commune. Delescluze was its most powerful man; but close behind him, in the shadows, was Rigault, the exponent of that inseparable concomitant of Jacobinism—Terror.

The rift within the Commune did not heal automatically with the advent of Delescluze. On the contrary; on May 15th the Minority, composed largely of the Internationalists, openly issued a manifesto (which twenty-two of its members signed) declaring its opposition to the dictatorship the Committee of Public Safety had just established. The manifesto revealed to the public for the first time the existence of this fundamental split within the Commune. Nor was Delescluze to be granted any respite in his capacity as Minister of War. After the fall of Issy, morale had again slumped rapidly in the National Guard, with absenteeism and open desertion rising inversely. On his appointment, Delescluze issued a rousing Order of the Day to the National Guard:

> You know that the situation is grave.... To your ranks, therefore, Citizens, and stand firm before the enemy! Our walls are as stout as your arms, and as your hearts. Do not forget, too, that you are fighting for your freedom and for social equality, this promise which has so long escaped you; if your breasts are exposed to the shot and shells of Versailles, the prize assured you is the liberation of France, the security of your homes, the lives of your women and children....

But although Delescluze could, where professional soldiers like Rossel and Cluseret had failed, inspire by appealing to the revolutionary, civilian instincts of the National Guard, he was hopelessly at sea on military technicalities. He had brought to his post, as Lissagaray put it, 'nothing but his devotion'. His own paper, *La Justice*, might comment acidly that 'The Commune had revived and aggravated all the faults committed during the Prussian siege by the Government of the 4th of September', and speak of 'Trochu's plan without Trochu', but it was now far too late to set these faults right—even if Delescluze had been one of history's great captains.

On May 13th Fort Vanves fell to MacMahon's troops. Visiting it the previous day, Colonel Stanley described a scene of chaos: '... The confusion was awful. National Guards struggling to get into Paris, officers carrying despatches *violently arrested*, and accused of being cowards, scores of women trying to find their husbands ... the *rappel*

was beaten under our horses' noses, which made them unmanageable.'
On the 15th, the village of Issy, where for five days Brunel had been
conducting one of the Commune's most stubborn defensive actions,
surrendered while Brunel was absent at a council of war. A big
breach had been made in the outer defences covering the Achilles'
heel of Paris. The city itself was now directly menaced. At the same
time, just north of the Point-du-Jour salient on which Thiers had his
eye fixed, General Clinchant had crossed the Seine to establish himself at Longchamp and was now digging parallels across the Bois de
Boulogne almost up to the Porte de la Muette. Further to the north,
Ladmirault was still bogged down amid the ruins of Neuilly, held by
a hard-pressed Dombrowski. According to Lissagaray, at Dombrowski's headquarters in the Château de la Muette 'shells have opened to
the skies every room. . . . It has been worked out that his *aides de
camp* lived on an average eight days. . . . He received no reinforcements, despite his dispatches to the Ministry of War . . .' He had
apparently resigned himself to Slav fatalism, knowing the war to
be lost.

For the civilians in the threatened district within the walls, life
was becoming still more intolerable. 'I am writing to you above the
shells which are whistling over our heads', said Jules Rafinesque in a
letter from Passy, dated May 15th:

One fell five minutes ago in a garden next to ours, but it did not
explode—which undoubtedly saved Guli and Blanche, who were working
among the osiers, from being hit by splinters. . . . For the moment I
watch the number of the sick diminish without regrets; for the streets of
Passy are not safe, and I am the only doctor left.

Continuing the letter the following day, he noted that his family was
now forced by the bombardment to seek refuge elsewhere during the
day, returning to their home only at night:

The situation is extremely serious, although at this moment I can hear
Blanche playing the piano. Really I marvel at the courage of her and her
mother. . . . This morning the guns established at the Trocadéro,
endeavouring to hit the Bois de Boulogne, succeeded in landing their
projectiles on the houses at the corner of Rue de la Pompe and La
Tour.[1] . . . Bravo, bravo, they drink well, the Communard gunners, but
aim badly!

During these days, Edwin Child had also 'strolled' to the Trocadéro
to observe the cannonade, where he remarked that 'reply on the part
of the "Nationals" was almost out of the question, most of their
pieces being dismounted, and they altogether are becoming fast

[1] Roughly midway.

demoralised so that an end appears not far distant. . . .' From
Bordeaux Lillie Moulton received a laconic warning sent by her
friend, Prince Metternich, the Austrian Ambassador: 'Advise you to
go. Thiers is coming.' 'The Versailles troops are getting nearer and
nearer', wrote the Rev. Gibson on the 17th, 'and the general impression is that they will soon be within the ramparts.' It was an impression shared by many Parisians, but still the cautious Thiers—pushing
his saps across the Bois de Boulogne according to 'orthodox and
classical siege methods'—delayed the final assault.

Washburne, who up to the replacement of Rossel had tended to
over-estimate the military strength of the Commune, now also
recognized that 'the crisis seems to be really approaching'. At the
same time, as he observed to Secretary of State Fish, 'the worse
things grow, the more desperate the Commune becomes'. Threats to
confiscate private property were heard with increasing regularity,
while cases of pillaging (which Rigault's police seemed either powerless or unwilling to halt) grew more common. Colonel Stanley
reported that the Grand Hôtel, where Labouchere had luxuriated
during the Siege, had been methodically sacked; the looters 'took
all the silver for which the hotel is famous, women's boots, linen,
everything; they took 30 francs out of the pocket of a waistcoat of a
waiter, which was hanging up in his bedroom, they ate everything,
and drank themselves drunk, 200 bottles of wine'. On May 5th, the
Commune suppressed seven hostile newspapers, six more on May
11th, followed by another ten on the 18th. Fear and hatred mounted
hand in hand, inflamed by each successive charge of atrocities at the
front. There were accusations on both sides; Government troops
claimed to have found at Fort Vanves one of their men 'nailed to a
stake'; Communard leaders taken in the fighting for Clamart had been
shot on the spot, as Duval had been, and British correspondents in
Versailles heard regular units openly raising a cry of 'No quarter!'
A weighty portion of the Communards' wrath continued to be directed
towards the person of Thiers. 'Venomous toad' and 'serpent in
glasses', 'evil bandit' and 'old criminal', and 'the country's grave-
digger' were among the labels regularly attached to his name by the
Red Press; and they were not terms of endearment. One cartoon
portrayed him having obscenely unnatural relations with Bismarck;
while with his declaration of all-out war on May 8th and the stepped-
up bombardment that followed it, feelings against Thiers reached
new heights.

Henri de Rochefort, who, although he had declined to commit
himself to the Commune, was still capable of inspiring the Paris
mob to madness, now wrote in his paper:

M. Thiers possesses a wonderful mansion in the Place St.-Georges, full of works of art of all descriptions ... what would these property-owning statesmen say if the people of Paris replied to their ravages by using the pickaxe, and, if for every house at Courbevoie touched by the shells, a piece of the wall were knocked out of the palace in the Place St.-Georges? ... I am convinced that on the first news that even the door-knockers had been damaged, M. Thiers would order a cease-fire. ...

The article was to earn Rochefort a sentence of transportation for life to the South Pacific; for his suggestion was taken up with greater enthusiasm than he could possibly have foreseen. On May 11th the newly reconstituted Committee of Public Safety decreed that Thiers's house should be 'razed to the ground' and his belongings confiscated. Without delay twenty carts began clearing the house, distributing its various treasures among the city's libraries and museums, and the linen to the hospitals. On the 15th, Rigault's twenty-one-year-old aide, Gaston da Costa, 'gave an example' by climbing on to the roof and ripping off the first tiles; the next day Thiers wrote bitterly to a friend: 'My house is demolished. I have neither hearth nor home, and this dwelling where I received and entertained you all over the past forty years has been destroyed down to the foundations.' To Edwin Child, who watched the work of demolition, it was 'as striking an instance of futile spite, as perhaps any revolution can or has to furnish'.

Next, the backward-looking Jacobins—knowing they were about to perish and determined not to go without leaving their mark on Paris—embarked on one of the Commune's most memorable, as well as pointless, acts. The Vendôme Column had been erected by Napoleon I on the site where, in 1792, the mob had destroyed an equestrian statue of Louis XIV. In close emulation of Trajan's prototype in Rome, bronze bas-reliefs (cast from melted-down enemy cannon) celebrated Napoleon's campaign of 1805, winding for 840 feet round the column from the pedestal to the lantern. At the top had originally stood a massive effigy of the Emperor, clad in a toga. With the fall of the First Empire this had been removed, and an unsuccessful attempt made to demolish the huge shaft. Under Louis-Philippe the Column was crowned with a statue of Napoleon in the uniform he had worn at Austerlitz, but on the advent of Louis-Napoleon it too was changed, once again for his uncle, this time wearing his imperial robes. This restoration did much to revive old hatreds of the monument, which, in the eyes of even the moderate left wing of the Second Empire, had long represented all it most detested about militarism and imperialism. As early as September

1870 Courbet (who claimed an additional motive in so far as the Column offended his aesthetic senses)[1] had been urging Trochu to have the Column demolished, and finally the Commune had acceded to his pressure by passing the necessary decree on April 12th. But, apart from the erection of a scaffolding around its base, nothing much had happened. There were, if nothing else, considerable technical difficulties involving in bringing down this massive shaft, 155 feet high and immensely thick.

With the Jacobins in control, the Commune began to press for more active endeavours, threatening the contractors who had applied for the job with a 500-franc fine for every day's delay. According to a story later uncovered by Goncourt, an engineer who possessed a demanding mistress, and had been racking his brain for ways of making money, came up with the idea of applying a bevel-cut at the base of the column, to fell it like some gigantic tree. He was paid 6,000 francs for his brainwave (which he promptly passed on to his *amourette*), and workmen began laboriously to hew their way through bronze and stone. After more postponements the demolition was fixed for May 16th, the 26th Floreal. It was to be the biggest festivity since the proclamation of the Commune on March 28th, and no doubt there were hopes that the spectacle would distract minds from the grim realities drawing ever closer outside the city gates. Special 'invitation' cards stamped with a Phrygian cap were issued to permit entry into the Place Vendôme (now renamed Place Internationale). Three bands and several battalions of the National Guard were packed into the Place, transformed into a dense mass of red scarves and gold braid, with Félix Pyat swaggering about somewhere in the centre, enveloped in his conspiratorial black cloak with twin pistols at his belt. Paper strips had been stuck to the windows as a protection against shock, while, for fear that the falling column might penetrate straight through the *pavé* into the sewer, tons of manure, straw, and bracken had been spread to reduce the impact.

Engineers had installed capstans with ropes running from them to the top of the column, so that, as it had already been partially cut through, all that now remained was to winch the capstans and pull it over. Shortly after 3 p.m., the bands struck up the Marseillaise. On his own balcony in the Place, Colonel Stanley of the Grenadiers and two compatriots had a grandstand view of the proceedings:

The streets are densely crowded, about 10,000 people. The National Guards have driven back the mob halfway down the Rue de la Paix, it is

[1] As far as artistic taste was concerned, the values of the Proudhonist Courbet were simple; he once declared: 'I have no master; my master is myself. There is not, and never has been, any painter other than myself.'

a wonderful sight to see the buzzing mob, we are all expectation . . . the single officer watering the streets is a sight worth seeing alone. . . . It is a blackguard Vandalism but as it was to fall I would not have missed it for a great deal. . . . The first attempt commenced at 3.15. The rope, a double piece attached to a windlass anchored in the ground, began to be tightened at that moment. At 3.36 the snatch-block gave way and some two or three men were wounded, not anything very serious. . . .

There were cries of 'Treason', followed by a long pause during which the bands diverted the impatient crowd with patriotic airs. Meanwhile, at the base of the Column

workmen drove in extra wedges on the Rue St. Honoré side where it had been sawn. The other side had been largely cut out, wedge-like with picks, and extra rope was put round the top of the Column, and manned by 50 men on either side standing in the Rue de la Paix, and they, and not the windlass, caused it to lean over at 6.

Part of the great crowd in the Place began to stampede in terror, and then the Column

fell over on the heap of sand faggots prepared for it, with a mighty crash. There was no concussion on the ground, the Column broke up almost before it reached its bed, and lay on the ground, a huge mass of ruin. An immense dust and smoke from the stones and crumpled clay rose up and an instant after a crowd of men, National Guards, Commune, and sight-seeing English flew upon it, and commenced to get bits of it as remembrance, but the excitement was so intense that people moved about as in a dream.

A tremendous clamour broke out. Amid roars of '*Vive la Commune!*' Communard leaders attempted to make the customary speeches which nobody could hear from the stump of the column. National Guardsmen busied themselves in breaking up the bronze fragments with the butt ends of their muskets; one old lady purchased a piece of '*La Gloire*' for 500 francs from a sailor who afterwards denounced her to the Commune for another 500 francs. Other members of the crowd rushed up to spit on the remains of the great Emperor, which broken and fallen in the dust reminded the Rev. Gibson of when he had once stood 'in the midst of the shapeless ruins of Memphis, besides the one great prostrate statue, probably that of the great Rameses'. To the amorous engineer, as an additional reward, was given the little statue of Liberty on a globe held in Napoleon's hand. The echoes of the fall of the Column were heard afar; its disappearance was even apparent from Mont-Valérien; while in Brussels, Victor Hugo rebuked the Commune for its vandalism.

Moderate Parisians now began to dread increasingly where the Commune's next excesses would lead. The guillotine had been publicly burned at the foot of Voltaire's statue; the demolition of the Chapelle Expiatoire, erected in atonement for the execution of Louis XVI, had already been decreed and was to be saved only at the eleventh hour by the collapse of the Commune itself. The two arms of the cross surmounting the Panthéon had been cut off, replaced by a red flag, and the church—as in 1793—dedicated once again 'aux grands hommes'. On May 4th Goncourt had been horrified by Verlaine's revelation 'that he had had to combat a proposition calling for the destruction of Notre-Dame'; and he was extremely relieved to hear that the Venus de Milo had been hidden from Courbet's possible attention under a pile of dossiers at the Préfecture de Police.

Shortly before 6 p.m. on the day after the fiesta in the Place Vendôme, Edwin Child, chatting to a friend, was suddenly shaken by 'a terrific shock that made the house tremble, which we thought to be a terrible broadside from Montmarte'. In Passy, Dr. Rafinesque, who was almost knocked over by the force of the explosion, saw a huge column of smoke rising just across the Seine, and rushed home to discover the chandelier on the floor and his wife and daughter taking cover. An hour and a half later his son Gaston returned clutching a handful of blackened bullets; all that remained of an immense arsenal on the Avenue Rapp, a brief distance from the site of the Great Exhibition on the Champ-de-Mars. Visiting the scene of the explosion, Child 'could hardly believe my ears and eyes. Roofs torn off, not a window to be seen, sunblinds hanging by a broken hinge, fronts of shops smashed in and 4 houses of 5 stories thrown to the ground. The cafés even had the glasses and decanters splintered to pieces by the shock, and many serious accidents occurred to the wounded in the military hospital of the Gros Caillou.' Colonel Stanley's friend Lewis Wingfield, assistant surgeon to the American Ambulance during the first Siege, reported:'the number of human bodies is about 200, and he saw half a man thrown down from the roof of a neighbouring house, where it had been blown. . . . Poor women were crying and searching for the remains of their daughters.'

The catastrophe seems almost certainly to have been caused by the kind of carelessness so common during the Siege, but the Commune immediately cried treachery and arrested four unfortunate bystanders. In their hyper-nervous state, there were many Communards who automatically assumed that this was indeed the work of Thiers's agents; no doubt in retaliation for the shattering of the Vendôme Column. News of the explosion reached the Hôtel de Ville in the midst of fresh wrangling between the Minority and the Jacobin Majority, and it immediately provoked the latter to clamour for a stepping-up of the Terror. Urbain, a greasy, unattractive personality, rose to press for the application forthwith of the 'Hostages Law', which he had proposed on April 5th and on which so far no further action had been taken. Citing the recent killing of a woman ambulance attendant near Fort Vanves, he demanded that ten hostages be executed forthwith, five of them within sight of the Versailles forward posts. Urbain was promptly supported by Rigault, who jumped up with a decree already drafted to provide for the summary trial of prisoners, declaring that only those proven guilty, rather than hostages selected at random, should be executed; but he went on to qualify that, in his eyes, sympathy with Versailles or earlier complicity with the regime under the Second Empire was sufficient to constitute guilt. Protot, the Minister of Justice, contested the legality of Rigault's interpretation of guilt, and Urbain's savage proposal was rejected. But eventually a decree was passed constituting a 'Jury of Accusation' which was to render summary judgement upon anyone accused of 'complicity' with Versailles, and its sentences were to be carried out within twenty-four hours. Those found guilty would be retained as 'hostages' from whose number would be selected victims for reprisal executions under the original 'Hostages Act'.

The life of the Archbishop of Paris and his fellow prisoners was now clearly in the gravest jeopardy. So far the Commune had only executed three men (all for various military offences) and, despite the occasional demands of the mob to submit the hostages to lynch-law, the Archbishop seemed safe—protected as long as he remained a valuable pawn to trade with Blanqui. On April 18th, the Papal Nuncio, Mgr. Chigi, had written to Washburne to ask him—as the only senior diplomat still (partially) resident in Paris—to intercede on the Archbishop's behalf. Accordingly, Washburne sought an interview with Cluseret who, though receiving him affably enough, expressed his impotence and took him round to see Rigault. Although it was 11 a.m., Rigault was still in bed and Washburne noted an elegant breakfast for some thirty people being laid. Cluseret, however, entered Rigault's bedroom and came back with a permit for Washburne to visit the Archbishop at the Mazas Prison. Thoughtfully taking him 'a bottle of old Madeira and some newspapers', Washburne found him in 'a gloomy and naked little cell', about six feet by ten, such as housed common felons:

I was deeply touched at the appearance of this venerable man . . . his slender person, his form somewhat bent, his long beard, for he has not been shaved apparently since his confinement, his face haggard with ill-health. . . . I was charmed by his cheerful spirit and his interesting conversation. He seemed to appreciate his critical situation, and to be prepared for the worst. He had no word of bitterness or reproach for his persecutors, but on the other hand remarked that the world judged them to be worse than they really were. He was patiently awaiting the logic of events.

On returning from the prison, Washburne strongly urged Thiers to accept Rigault's offer to exchange the Archbishop for Blanqui, on the grounds that 'the French Government could lose nothing in placing Blanqui at liberty, and by doing so they would probably save the life of the Archbishop. I also stated that I considered him in the most imminent danger....' His intervention gained only Thiers's disfavour. 'They are very angry here with Mr. Washburne', Lord Lyons (who had also approached Thiers, perhaps rather less forcefully) wrote to Granville on April 28th, 'for interfering about the Archbishop, and they are still more displeased with him for being so much in Paris. In fact, although he has a room here he is much more in Paris than at Versailles.[1] Thiers observed to me last night that my American colleague had a *conduite très singulière*. They would not stand this in a European representative', his Lordship added in a condescending tone, 'but they allow a great latitude to the American, partly because he and his Government have nothing to say to European politics, and partly because they cannot well help it.' Washburne, like Lyons, found Thiers still adamant. The Communards were rebels, could expect none of the privileges of real warfare, and he could not possibly have dealings with them. Besides, if he agreed to trading Blanqui for the Archbishop, would the desperate rebels not seize additional hostages as a means of extracting new concessions from the lawful Government? So Thiers argued. There were, however, many anti-Communards who were to feel subsequently that Thiers could have made greater efforts to save the Archbishop. Washburne's assistant, Wickham Hoffman, thought he perceived wheels within wheels; 'The French authorities certainly were lukewarm in the matter. The Archbishop was a Gallican, a liberal Catholic, notably so. Had he been an Ultramontane, I think that the extreme Right of the Assembly—the Legitimists—would have so exerted themselves that his life would have been saved.'

The Archbishop's prospects were not improved by the behaviour of his fellow hostage, Abbé Lagarde, the Vicar-General. The Abbé had been released by the Communards in order to carry further negotiatory correspondence to Thiers, on condition that, his mission completed, he would then return. But, once reaching the sanctuary

[1] His diplomatic status enabling him to pass through the lines with little hindrance.

of Versailles, he found one pretext or another for not delivering himself up again into Rigault's clutches. According to Hoffman, the Archbishop referred to this desertion in a 'sad and resigned, but not bitter tone'. On Friday, May 19th, Washburne visited the Archbishop again; this time to bring him the bad news that it had, after all, proved impossible to effect his exchange for Blanqui. 'I am sorry to say', Washburne reported to Fish, 'I found him very feeble. He has been confined to his pallet for the last week with a kind of pleurisy; is without appetite, and very much reduced in strength. He is yet cheerful, and apparently resigned for any fate that may await him.' Washburne shook hands with him and 'bade him what proved to be a final adieu'.

That same day Rigault began the work of the summary Juries of Accusation. He had divided the hostages into two categories; first, the major figures who included the Archbishop and the other priests, Chaudey, Jules Ferry's deputy accused of being responsible for the 'massacre' outside the Hôtel de Ville on January 22nd, and a Second Empire banker called Jecker; and second the small fry, mostly police agents and gendarmes. The second category were tried first. The hearing of the fourteen before Rigault himself (who asked them such superbly pertinent questions as 'What would you have done in December 1851 ?) lasted little more than three hours, and twelve of them were sentenced to return to prison to await their fate as hostages. A hearing for the Archbishop and the first category was to be fixed for the following week; but events overtook it. Rigault's trials had cost the Commune the support of one of its powerful, albeit unpredictable, allies. Rochefort (earlier he had tried to obtain the release of one of the arrested priests) attacked in his *Mot d'Ordre* the principle of executing hostages, and the following morning, while still abed, he was visited by a young man from the Prefecture, come to warn him that he would probably be arrested that day. Like Rossel, he decided it was time to go. Accompanied by his secretary, with his beard shaven and his give-away bushy hair cut, Rochefort got out of Paris without much difficulty. Heading eastwards, he reached Meaux Station before being recognized and arrested by a Government agent. The prisoners were then escorted to Versailles, where it seemed as if the whole town had turned out to witness the arrival of the fettered rabble-rouser. Women crowded round, shaking their fists and screaming 'Kill them! Kill them! Kill them on the spot!' Instead of being taken at once to the cells, Rochefort claimed that they were driven through the town 'for more than an hour to feast the eyes of the population', and it seems he was lucky to escape lynching. Indicative of the prevailing mood at Versailles, the treatment of Rochefort was mild compared with what other prisoners of the lawful régime would shortly experience.

As tension increased in Paris, manifestations of phenomena familiar during the first Siege also recurred. The passion for crazy inventions was one. A Dr. Parisel, head of the 'Scientific Delegation', bombarded the Commune with ideas of 'armoured sharp-shooters', of explosive-carrying balloons that would wipe out not only Versailles and the Prussians, but for good measure the wicked English as well—because they were 'coveting Suez'. There was talk about mining the sewers of Paris, and more about that perennial fancy, Greek fire. Zealously abetted by Rigault, spy-mania had once more become a norm of life. The Rev. Gibson witnessed six people seized in the Avenue d'Eylau 'because they were looking towards Mont-Valérien, and their gestures made some National Guards believe they were making signals to the Fort!' Arrested by a drunk National Guard, Colonel Stanley was escorted to prison and flung into a hole 'two paces long and one broad . . . thickly coated with slippery filth'. There he was later joined by a drunk who promptly relieved himself; 'I gave him a small tap on the head . . . and I warned what would happen if he touched an Englishman, not a cowardly Frenchman as he fancied he had to do with.' Stanley was eventually released, through the intervention of the British Embassy, but while in prison he also met 'two poor *sergents de ville*, they both had families and expected to be shot', and 'two more supposed spies'.

Probably few had a luckier escape than Auguste Renoir. Oblivious of the world around, he was painting a sketch of the Seine which attracted the attention of some National Guards. They became convinced that he was a spy sketching plans of the river defences for Versailles. Renoir was arrested; a crowd gathered, and an amiable old lady proposed that the 'spy' should immediately be thrown into the river. 'You drown kittens', she said, 'and they don't do nearly as much harm.' Eventually, however, Renoir was dragged to the nearest *Mairie*, where (according to his son and biographer, Jean Renoir) 'there was a firing-squad on permanent duty'. Fortunately for Renoir, and posterity, Rigault also happened to be there and he now rendered his one great contribution to civilization by recognizing Renoir as the artist who had given him sanctuary at Fontainebleau some years previously, when he had been on the run from Louis-Napoleon's police. Rigault embraced the 'spy' touchingly, and promptly had him turned loose.

But in his zeal it was apparent that Rigault had been arresting the wrong spies and hostages. As Lissagaray observed, by far the best hostage held by the Commune was the Bank of France; 'Through it

they held the genital organs of Versailles; they could laugh at its professional experience, at its guns. Without expending a man, the
Commune had only to say to it: "Come to terms or die" '. Meanwhile,
under the myopic eyes of complaisant old Beslay, the Marquis de
Plœuc had continued to pass out of the back door of the Bank vast
funds that materially helped Thiers finance the expansion of his
forces. But apart from the issue of the Bank, there was also no doubt
that Paris was riddled with real spies who slipped through Rigault's
net. Numerous attempts were made by Thiers to 'buy' leading
Communards, and several of the conspiracies and rifts within the
Commune seem to have been caused by the work of his *agents
provocateurs*. Dombrowski (like Cluseret before him) was approached
by an agent with an offer of a million francs if he would 'open' one
of the gates under his command. Dombrowski promptly informed
the Commune. A short time later a 'peasant' forced his way into
Dombrowki's H.Q., purporting to bring news from the front, then
produced a dagger from underneath his smock, but was bayonetted
first by Dombrowski's bodyguard. At least such endeavours succeeded
in so far as they increased the nervous tension, suspicion, and mistrust
within the Commune, and by May 14th the Commune had decided
to issue identity cards.

In his fifth-column work Thiers was immeasurably aided by the
fact that, compared with the first Siege, Paris was only partially
invested. Over half the perimeter was still occupied by the Prussians,
supposedly neutral but in fact, for reasons of self-interest, increasingly
well-disposed towards Versailles. Thus, despite the battle raging in
the west and south-west, it was not all that difficult to leave or enter
Paris via St.-Denis or some other Prussian-held centre. As has already
been seen, Washburne travelled regularly between Paris and Versailles,
Louise Michel had entered Versailles in disguise and returned safely,
and in the latter part of April Edwin Child decided to make the
trip, purely for diversion. At first he thought of taking with him a
lady friend, Mlle Lassalle, but wisely changed his mind. He took a bus
to the Jardin des Plantes, walked from there to the Porte d'Italie and
thence to Sceaux on the road to Orléans, 'where I met the first post
of the Versailles troops, showed my passport, and got as far as Plessis
where I had to traverse a camp of soliders to arrive at the *Quartier-
Général* to obtain a *laissez-passer* to Versailles, here I was detained
upwards of three hours for what reason except being a stranger I
cannot say'. Having walked about sixteen miles and been arrested
five times, he reached Versailles at 9 p.m. and 'after about 3 hours
search all over the town found a bed, without a room, that is to say
in the room was 4 bedsteads, one occupied by a woman, but I was too

tired to search further'. The following day he returned by a long circuit around the north of Paris.

There were more people who wanted to get out and stay out. On April 21st, Goncourt expostulated in his *Journal* that he had heard the Commune was about to pass a decree under which 'every man, married or unmarried, between the ages of 19 and 55 will be conscripted and condemned to march against the *Versaillais*. Here I am, threatened by this law! Here I am, obliged within a matter of days to hide myself as at the time of the Terror!' When the Conscription Law was passed, and the Commune showed it meant business by actually entering houses to impress into the National Guard, according to Washburne, 'all who cannot prove that they are foreigners', thousands more Parisians went into hiding or took to flight. Every kind of ingenuity was practised; Dr. Powell smuggled two friends out on his English passport and a third 'escaped like Falstaff in a basket of dirty linen'; Alphonse Daudet described watching a *petit crevé* viscount depart disguised as a waggon-driver, piloting a team of horses through Vincennes. Fleeing himself from impressment, Daudet recalled with some contempt the fellow escaper who, having passed through the Commune posts in utter silence, 'became progressively more insolent, provocative, a real terror to the Communards the farther he got from the fortifications; he had threatened to put the lot of them to the bayonet'. After his narrow escape, Renoir too used his influence with Rigault to obtain a safe conduct to Louveciennes; Zola got out on a Prussian passport; while twelve-year-old Seurat fled with his parents to Fontainebleau. Several hundred thousand more Parisians had left since the Commune began,[1] and by mid-May Paris had begun to look like a city of the dead. Gulielma Rafinesque noted 'all the shops shut or half shut—a very few weary looking people shabbily dressed. . . .' What shops remained open had no customers, and even the Hôtel Meurice had closed down. In London, Karl Marx rubbed his hands: 'Wonderful, indeed, was the change the Commune had wrought in Paris! No longer any trace of the meretricious Paris of the Second Empire. No longer was Paris the rendezvous of British landlords, Irish absentees, American ex-slaveholders and shoddy men, Russian ex-serfowners, and Wallachian boyards.'

In at least one fundamental respect, the mass departures from Paris were a blessing in disguise for the Commune. As early as mid-April, the Rev. Gibson wrote in his diary:

Although the city is not really invested, the question of supplies is beginning to be a serious one. Country people don't care to bring their

[1] Wickham Hoffman estimated that 300,000 left during the first month alone.

provisions into a city bristling with cannon and abounding in barricades. Naturally prudent, they prefer to sell their provisions to the Prussians. . . . Hence the price of provisions is rising rapidly. Veal, which sold at 1·40 frs., now sells at 2 frs. the pound. . . . Our butcher said that in a week's time there would be no more beef to be had.

By the end of the month, Thiers had organized an effective blockade of food entering Paris, with the Prussians consenting to co-operate on their side of the city. Once again Edwin Child began laying in an emergency hoard of biscuits and concentrated milk; Colonel Stanley wrote an un-Guardsmanlike admission to his mother, 'I chiefly quarrel at having been asked to pay 75 centimes for washing an unstarched silk shirt. I revenge myself by wearing them three days.' Rising prices and food shortages reawakened grim memories of the first Siege, persuading further thousands to make their way out of Paris; but this in turn helped postpone a serious food crisis, so that as May entered its fateful third week Paris was experiencing nothing like the privations of the previous winter.

There were a variety of lesser ways in which, as the second Siege approached its climax, life in Paris continued to surprise the British and Americans still living there by its normality. The experiences of the first Siege, especially perhaps the Prussian bombardment, had conditioned many a Parisian to an unnatural phlegmatism out of which neither the Versailles bombardment nor the neo-Jacobin Terror of the Commune could really stir them. Returning to Paris from Versailles during the first battles of April 3rd, Benjamin Wilson had been astonished to see 'labourers peacefully at work on plots of ground white with blossoms, as if ignorant of all that was going on around them'. Nothing during the first Siege had managed to distract the Seine fishermen from their sport, and even when the shelling of Neuilly was at its peak they were still to be seen standing quiet and motionless, rods held in unshaking hands, as the cannon-balls whistled and rattled overhead. Towards the middle of April, the Rev. Gibson found delight in the spectacle, just outside the Madeleine, of 'A man in the middle of the broad asphalted pavement, with a crowd around him, performing feats with heavy weights, lifting them and throwing them over his head; a sight such as you might see on the green of a provincial village on a fête day.' More than a month later, he was commenting how Paris 'has never appeared to be cleaner and healthier than now'; there was a great improvement in the habitually 'sour smell' of Paris, which he attributed (rather than to any acts of the Commune) to the mass departure of its citizenry!

And beneath all the apprehension, the suffering, and the uncertainty, there still bubbled that irrepressible Parisian gaiety. Already by early April the Commune had reopened eight theatres, and the Rev. Gibson could not help exclaiming at the news 'that the museums are shortly to be opened to the public, and the usual annual exhibition of modern paintings is to be held!' On May 6th, as Fort Issy was tottering, the Commune threw open the Tuileries Palace for the first of a series of concerts to collect funds for the wounded. A great crowd of curious Parisians surged through the palace, pausing to goggle with particular fascination at the ex-Emperor's sumptuous private bath-room. Into the stately *Salle des Maréchaux*, where the belles of the Second Empire had once waltzed and where the fourteen life-sized portraits of the first Bonaparte's marshals were now discreetly covered over, they crammed to hear Mlle Agar recite the inevitable *Châtiments* of Hugo and to roar applause at Mme Bordas as she sang the current hit, which ended:

> *C'est la canaille,*
> *Eh ! bien, j'en suis !*[1]

The members of this essentially proletarian audience, for whose delectation tables groaning with brioches and beer had been laid out in the former banqueting hall, were 'not very orderly in their be-haviour', the *Illustrated London News* complained; while Colonel Stanley sniffed fastidiously that 'the stink became so bad I could not stay it out'. But for the organizers the distraction was a huge success, and it was repeated on the 14th and the 18th.

With the Tuilerie concerts, an extraordinary kind of exaltation, almost of valedictory gaiety, seemed to seize the supporters of the Commune as the final catastrophe became more obviously im-minent. Once again the boulevards filled; this time with strangers from the darker parts of Paris. It almost seemed as if they had come out to enjoy for the last time the opulence and grandeur of those foreign parts of the city which they loved with such possessive, destructive pride. Spring was at its splendid peak, and on the Concorde Communards replaced the withered laurels garlanding the statue of Strasbourg with offerings of flowers. To many it seemed as if there had never been quite so many flowers as that spring. 'In the young verdure and the bloom of vernal shrubs', Goncourt lyrically ob-served some National Guards 'lying alongside their arms which glistened in the sunshine, with a blonde *cantinière* pouring out a drink for a soldier with her Parisian grace.' But he could not avert his eyes from the unpleasant reminders of war inseparably mingled with this idyllic scene; 'a corpse being hoisted on to a cart, of which a man

---

[1] 'They're the rabble,
Ah well! I'm one of them!'

holds in his two hands the brain ready to escape from its open skull'. On Sunday, May 14th, Goncourt's raptures were less marred; 'All that still remains of the Paris population is at the bottom of the Champs-Élysées, under the first trees, where the gaily clamorous laughter of children seated in front of the Punch and Judy shows occasionally rises above the voice of the distant cannonade.' That same day Dr. Powell observed that the

Parisians were out in their Sunday best, usually morning attire, watching with interest the erection of formidable earth works at the top of the Rue de Rivoli and Rue Royale, the guns of which were to sweep the Place de la Concorde on the entry of the troops; the fountains were playing as usual, the water hoses being plied, whilst at the barricades a roaring trade was being driven in *sirop de vanille*, in the horrid periodical *Le Père Duchesne*, and in coarse illustrated skits on Napoleon, Eugénie, Thiers . . . and away towards the ramparts again might be seen a kite high in the air. . . .

The next Sunday evening, May 21st, the Commune threw its most ambitious entertainment yet in the form of a vast open-air concert in the Tuileries Gardens, at which fifteen hundred musicians took part. 'Mozart, Meyerbeer', claimed Lissagaray, 'and the great classics chased out the musical obscenities of the Empire'. Again it was a huge success. At the end, amidst heavy applause, a Communard staff officer mounted the conductor's stand with a brief announcement: 'Citizens, Monsieur Thiers promised to enter Paris yesterday. Monsieur Thiers did not enter; he will not enter. Therefore I invite you here next Sunday, here at this same place. . . .'

But at that identical moment the troops of Monsieur Thiers were beginning to pour into the city.

Versailles Troops Enter Paris

24. 'La Semaine Sanglante'—I

Up to the very last minute, Clemenceau, his fellow Mayors, the Deputies of Paris (jointly united as the 'League of Republican Union for the Rights of Paris'), and various other bodies had still been seeking anxiously to achieve a negotiated compromise between Paris and Versailles, before the disastrous final confrontation took place. At the end of April the Freemasons of Paris had massed together, and, in top hats, bearing their Masonic orders and banners, bravely mounted the ramparts to demand a parley with the *Versaillais*. A deputation had been received, but to them—as to all others—Thiers replied with his unwavering formula: 'Do you come in the name of the Commune? If so, I shall not listen to you; I do not recognize belligerents. . . . I have no conditions to accept, nor commitments to offer. The supremacy of the law will be re-established absolutely. . . . Paris will be submitted to the authority of the State just like any hamlet of a hundred inhabitants.' He did not intend, and never had intended, that there should be any compromise with the rebellious city. Now that he had the power he proposed to crush the Commune mercilessly. But when, following the fall of Fort Issy, he

362

began what he described as the 'orthodox and classic methods of siege', sapping his way forward across the Bois de Boulogne, his slow and methodical preparations received a nasty holt. Bismarck, growing as impatient as he had with Moltke during the first Siege, threatened Thiers that if he did not hurry up, the Prussian Army would itself enter Paris.

This would have been a political disaster of the first magnitude, and, as Thiers admitted, 'it was why we had now also thought of purchasing the entry of one of the gates to Paris'. Several attempts to open a way into the city by 'Fifth Column' work had failed, but one plan proposed by 'a very brave man who entered and left Paris every day' seemed to promise success. On the night of May 13th no less than 80,000 men stood by, concealed in the Bois de Boulogne, waiting for this modern Ulysses to lead them through the city gates. Thiers himself was there. But by 4 a.m. nothing had happened and the Army withdrew, disappointed. From now on Thiers spent every day at the front, full of Micawberish hopes. Still there was no sign of a breach in the walls, or the opening of a gate, so resignedly Thiers convened a Council of War at Mont-Valérien on Sunday, May 21st, to fix a date for the postponed general assault on the walls of Paris. He had reached the entrance to the fortress, when an excited staff officer galloped up to inform him that General Douay could not now attend the conference as he was occupied in entering Paris. Thiers hastened inside, where he found Marshal MacMahon studying the movements of Douay's troops through a spyglass. At first it looked as if they had been repelled, then—after about a quarter of an hour—Thiers saw 'two long black serpents, winding through folds in the ground, head towards the Point-du-Jour Gate, by which they entered'.

It had happened as follows. At Montretout, one of the objectives of Trochu's final sortie in January, the *Versaillais* had established what Wickham Hoffman (with memories of fighting at the Siege of Vicksburg under Ulysses Grant) described as 'probably the most powerful battery ever erected in the world'. This may have been a slight exaggeration; nevertheless, for several days it had pounded the Point-du-Jour area to such an extent that the ramparts had been partly demolished and the defenders had withdrawn some distance from the devastated area. On Sunday, May 21st, a civil engineer named Ducatel, an overseer in the Department of Roads and Bridges who felt no love for the Commune, happened to stroll near the battlements on his afternoon walk. He was astonished to perceive that near the Point-du-Jour there was not a defender in sight. After a brief reconnaissance, he discovered that no one was holding the gate there. (Why MacMahon's troops had not become aware of this, Colonel Hoffman claimed, could 'only be accounted for by the general inefficiency into which the French Army had fallen'.) Ducatel now mounted the ramparts, waving a white flag. A Versailles major came forward; Ducatel told his story; this was verified; and Douay's troops began to pour into Paris through the undefended gate. After all that had passed since the previous September, it was—as Hoffman remarked—'rather an anti-climax'.

Thiers now returned to Versailles to dine 'with my family and a few friends who shared my joy'.

At the Hôtel de Ville, the Commune had been busy formulating its last legislation. Apart from an order sending some staff officers, who had been caught philandering with *cocottes*, to the front with picks and shovels (the girls to a sandbag factory), in the four previous days there had been a Decree of Legitimacy, a new decision on the Secularization of Education, and a Decree on the theatres. Now the Assembly was in the midst of trying Cluseret for dereliction of duty. Suddenly, at about 7 o'clock that Sunday evening, Billioray, one of the members of the Committee of Public Safety, burst in shouting. 'Stop! Stop!', he cried, 'I have a communication of the utmost importance, for which I demand a secret session.' The doors were closed and Billioray read out a dispatch from Dombrowski reporting the Versailles entry. There was, according to Lissagaray, 'a stupefied silence', then uproar. Rigault, supported by Ferré, his successor as police chief, recommended that the Commune forces should blow up the Seine bridges and withdraw into the old Cité area for a last-ditch defence, burning all behind them. He also proposed that the hostages should be brought along too, 'and they will perish there with us'. Cluseret was released, and an hour later the Commune adjourned; the last time that it would ever hold a plenary session at the Hôtel de Ville.

Delescluze at the Ministry of War heard the news grimly, but with calm, and ordered Assi, the incompetent first Chairman of the Commune, off on reconnaissance of the threatened area. The haggard old Jacobin then dictated a street-by-street defence of the city, placing Brunel, who—once again in disfavour—had only been released from a spell in prison the previous night, in command of the key position around the Place de la Concorde. He completed his night's work with the issue of a rousing proclamation to the Citizens of Paris:

Enough of militarism! No more General Staffs with badges of rank and gold braid at every seam! Make way for the people, for the fighters with bare arms! The hour of revolutionary warfare has struck!

It was a call to the barricades, and the old appeal for the spontaneous, unorganized, torrential *levée en masse* heard so often from Delescluze and the Reds during the first Siege. But although for some days past 1,500 women had been set to work sewing sandbag sacks in the disused National Assembly building, at 8 centimes a sack, none of the second line of barricades recommended by Rossel had yet been completed. And now there would be no coherent plan of defence either. The barricades as prescribed by Delescluze were tactically more suited for guarding districts than for any integrated defence of the whole city. Rossel with his engineer's eye understood precisely the military significance of the obliquely intersecting streets of Haussmann's Paris, but his frequent warnings of how easy Haussmann had made it for regular troops to 'turn' a barricade went unheeded by the Jacobins with their memories of '48. At 5 a.m., leaving all his papers undestroyed, Delescluze abandoned his office for the barricades.

Outside the turbulent chambers of the Commune, Paris had spent the rest of that sparkling May Sunday in joyous oblivion. The city, thought the Rev. Gibson, 'seemed to be *en fête*. There have never been such crowds all around the Place de la Concorde except on some extraordinary occasion, such as the fete of the 15th of August under Imperialist rule, and everybody appeared to be in holiday dress.' In his diary, Edwin Child entered this account of his day:

> Up at 8. Church at 11. At 1 o'clock met Madame Clerc (rendezvous) at the Madeleine, breakfasted *au* Café du Helder ... afterwards strolled to Champs Elysées. There rested best part of afternoon. About 5 p.m. saw her home (Avenue Friedland), walked to my room, had tea, and then took bus to Johnson's, where I passed the evening. Lovely day.

As darkness fell, life continued. At the Gymnase there was a gala première of *Les Femmes Terribles* and the theatres had never been fuller. Pompeii on the night before its extinction can hardly have been gayer. At his 'usual place of observation', Goncourt, who had evacuated his house in the hazardous neighbourhood of Auteuil to lodge temporarily in the centre of Paris, saw a man arrested for shouting that the *Versaillais* had entered.

> I wandered around for a long time in search of information. . . . Nothing, nothing at all. . . . Another rumour. Finally I returned home. I went to bed in despair. I could not sleep. Through my hermetically closed curtains I seemed to be able to hear a confused murmur in the distance. In a street some way off there was the usual noise of one company relieving another, as happened every night. I told myself I had been imagining things and went back to bed . . . but this time there was no

mistaking the sound of drum and bugle! I rushed back to the window.
The call to arms was sounding all over Paris, and soon, drowning the
noise of the drums and the bugles and the shouting and the cries of
'To Arms!' came the great, tragic, booming notes of the tocsin being rung
in all the churches—a sinister sound which filled me with joy and sounded
the death-knell of the odious tyranny oppressing Paris.

It was not till the next morning that most Parisians learned of the
Versailles entry. Edwin Child recorded:

Was startled about ½ past 8 by Barbe knocking and calling out that
the troops had taken the town by assault. Immediately dressed, locked
all up and with him and Balfield proceeded by the Rue Lafayette, they
intending to try and leave Paris, but I made for Johnson's, leaving them
at the Faubourg St. Denis; crossed the Boulevard Strasbourg by Rue
St. Martin and Temple arriving safely R. de Braque, but not without
having assisted several times making barricades, that is to say, carrying
my 'pavé' to each, took my quarters up here, Johnson being very kind,
Madame also making me welcome. . . .

Paul Verlaine, who had been employing his literary talents in the
Commune Press Office and had spent the previous day at a Club
meeting in the Church of St.-Denis-du-St.-Sacrément, was awakened
by the voice of his wife dreaming aloud that the *Versaillais* had
entered Paris. A few moments later her pretty maid came in to tell
her that what she had dreamed was no fantasy. Mme Verlaine at
once packed to take refuge with her parents, leaving her husband
contemplating means of seducing the maid.

The Versailles entry at Auteuil had caught Dombrowski's forces
completely by surprise. There had been a desperate but brief defence
on the line of the *Ceinture* railway; then panic. A major come from
the lost ramparts assured Dombrowski that he had beaten his fleeing
troops 'with the flat of his sword till his arm ached; but he could not
stay the panic. Without losing his head, Dombrowski dispatched an
urgent request to Delescluze for reinforcements. But MacMahon's
troops, advancing through the friendly territory of Passy, had already
made remarkably rapid initial progress. At about 11 o'clock on Sunday
night, Assi reached the Trocadéro on his reconnaissance mission, but
turning into the darkened Rue Beethoven his horse slipped in a large
pool of blood and refused to budge. Along the walls Assi noticed what
appeared to be the figures of sleeping National Guards. Suddenly out
of the shadows regular troops rushed at Assi and seized him; the first
of the Commune leaders to be taken. Themselves fearing a trap (it
was rumoured that the Communards had mined and were intending

to blow up the whole area), the Versailles forces, with their habitual caution, paused before taking the dominating heights of the Trocadéro. But by 3 a.m. it was theirs, and through five gaping breaches in the walls between the Porte de Passy and the Porte St.-Cloud Mac-Mahon had already poured 70,000 troops; some 1,500 National Guards had surrendered. While in the centre Douay and Vinoy headed straight for the Étoile, on the right a column under General Cissey passed through Auteuil to infiltrate across the Pont de Grenelle, thereby opening up the Left Bank approaches too. Working left-wards along the inside of the walls, Clinchant and Ladmirault moved to take from the rear the Communard positions at Neuilly, then wheeled right to advance on the great fortress of Montmartre. By dawn the whole of Auteuil and Passy in the 16th *Arrondissement* had been 'liberated', as well as most of the 15th on the other side of the Seine. For residents like the Rafinesque family, almost overcome with joy and gratitude towards the Versailles Army, the ordeal of the past weeks appeared to be over; it seemed almost an augury that from an egg laid by one of the Rafinesques's pet birds a live chick should be hatched just as the fighting passed beyond Passy.

With the morning of Monday, May 22nd, a frenzy of desperate energy seized the Commune. Barricades that should have been constructed weeks earlier were being rushed up everywhere, and passing citizens—like Edwin Child—forced at bayonet point to assist by each contributing his *pavé*, prized out of the road. Dr. Powell, trying in vain to reach his place of work, the Beaujon Hospital some 500 yards down the Avenue Friedland from the Étoile, was several times deflected from his goal to build barricades, which he described as follows:

> If possible two or three trolleys, cabs or carts would form the foundation; all the apertures being filled with sand, the cubic paving stones from the road, sandbags, bricks or anything else . . . in such wide streets as the Rue Royale, the barricade was made by engineers, and were small fortresses with place for cannon, and very strong.

A vast new barricade, several metres high, was thrown up across the Rue de Rivoli, just in front of the Hôtel de Ville. Colonel Stanley awoke from a night out at the theatre to discover, from his hotel in the Rue de la Paix, that a barricade 'of water carts is across the Boulevard by the New Opéra, at the end of this street'. A quarter of a mile closer to the advancing *Versaillais*, Dr. Alan Herbert was disturbed to see, on looking out of his window just behind the Madeleine, 'several National Guards and dirty-looking fellows taking counsel together whether they should raise a barricade opposite my windows;

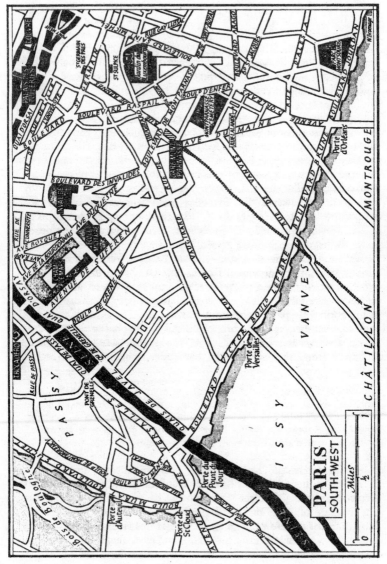

Map 2. Paris: south-west

and they were actually beginning it'. He was consoled, however, by the recollection that when he had been visited a few months previously by the up-and-coming young M.P. for Chelsea, Sir Charles Dilke, who already possessed a shrewd eye for a tactical situation, Dilke had suggested that the proper place for any effective barricade covering the Place de la Madeleine would be three doors further down. Sure enough, a senior officer (whom Herbert took to be Dombrowski himself) arrived and promptly ordered the barricade to be shifted to the point Dilke had indicated!

Herbert, like many another sensible Parisian, stayed quietly at home to await developments. Safely ensconced with his friends the Johnsons in the as yet unthreatened eastern part of Paris, Child did the same; 'Playing cards best part of day. We could hear the cannon now and then, but altogether it seemed quiet enough.' To many of the 'neutral' British and Americans, immured in their dwellings as the fighting of the next few days flowed and ebbed around them, was to be granted a view—terrifying in its proximity and historically all but unique—of warfare in a great western city; and warfare of a particularly atrocious kind. Of the French eyewitnesses, there were vast numbers like Louis Péguret who had ardently backed the Commune in the earliest days, but who also now unostentatiously went to ground, to avoid building barricades and to escape impressment by the Commune in its hour of need. Thus did its marginal supporters fade away when the crunch came.

Goncourt, however, his curiosity as ever gaining the upper hand, 'could not stay indoors today, I simply had to see and know.' Near the Madeleine he had found excited groups 'already plucking up the courage to boo the mounted orderlies'. Near the Opéra he saw 'a National Guard being carried along with his thigh broken. In the square, in a few scattered groups, they were saying that the Versailles troops had reached the Palais de l'Industrie. The National Guards, coming back in small bands, and looking tired and shamefaced, were obviously demoralized and discouraged.' Goncourt next went to call on Burty, the art critic, who lived just behind the Bibliothèque Nationale in the 2nd *Arrondissement*. There Goncourt found himself a prisoner in his apartment 'for I do not know how long. It was not safe to go out. . . .' As the hours passed by, 'Burty started copying out extracts of the *Correspondence found at the Tuileries*, while I buried myself in his *Delacroix* to the sound of exploding shells coming gradually nearer.' Curiosity had also induced Benjamin Wilson—'awakened strange to say by an unaccustomed still wave in the neighbourhood'—to poke his head outside, where he promptly met two National Guards, 'looking gloomy and crestfallen. In reply to my query whether there was anything new: "*Mon Dieu, Monsieur*", one of them said, "the tricolor is waving from the Arc de Triomphe, and we are completely betrayed as ever we were." A feeling of pity for those whose cause was lost and whose lives were possibly not worth a day's purchase prevented me from showing any satisfaction, though my heart was leaping for joy at the news'.

It was indeed true that Douay's men had occupied the Étoile; even though the Arc de Triomphe, heavily sandbagged, with a field-piece hoisted on to its top and provisions for a fortnight, had been converted into a minor fortress. Before the morning was over the Versailles troops could sweep all the way down the once-more deserted Champs-Élysées with their cannon. So far they had encountered practically no opposition. Their confidence was high; perhaps too high. Marching along the Quai they now headed towards the silent Place de la Concorde which, little more than twelve hours earlier, had been pullulating with gay, festive crowds. But all of a sudden concentrated volleys of fire flashed out from the terrace of the Tuileries Gardens. Struck at point-blank range and thoroughly caught off balance, the leading *Versaillais* suffered heavy losses; the survivors fled back as far as the Palais de l'Industrie. The advance had received its first check, administered by the tough and competent Brunel, and for the rest of the day Douay's force consolidated around the Étoile. The American Legation, now in Government-held territory, found itself once again under shellfire; this time from Commune guns positioned in Montmatre. The Minister (of whom Wickham Hoffman had once remarked, 'If we heard of any part of Paris where shells were likely to burst and bullets to whistle, Washburne was sure to have important business in that direction') was of course there. That afternoon he imperturbably mounted a horse to ride out to examine the state of his Residence near the Porte Dauphine. 'Besides the breaking of considerable glass, there was no material damage', Washburne reported with relief, and the house had not been looted. Along the line of the ramparts he saw many corpses in National Guard uniform, while all the time fresh regulars were pouring in from Versailles; 'It is estimated that from eighty to one hundred thousand troops of the line will be in the city before tomorrow morning. In all our part of the city they have been received with unbounded joy by the few people remaining.'

Later that same day Washburne rode over to see Marshal Mac-Mahon, who had now already established himself in Passy, 'to advise him of what I knew in relation to Archbishop Darboy, and to express the hope that the government troops might yet be enabled to save him. The interview was anything but reassuring to me, and I left the headquarters of the Marshal feeling that the fate of the Archbishop was sealed.'

Despite the check in the centre, MacMahon's turning movements on either flank were thrusting ahead with considerable speed. On the Left Bank, Langourian captured the École Militaire, including over a hundred Communard cannon parked uselessly outside. To his right, Cissey swept forward up Paris's longest street, the Rue de Vaugirard, to reach Montparnasse Station. There were only a score of National Guards defending this important position, but they fought hard until their ammunition ran out and then retreated up the Rue de Rennes, towards St.-Germain, where they took up position behind a hastily erected barricade. Their withdrawal was covered by a courageous Communard, who kept up a calm and steady fire into the station from a one-man stronghold inside a newspaper kiosk. At the other end of MacMahon's front, Ladmirault's and Clinchant's advance on Montmartre had been greatly facilitated by two characteristic Communard blunders. To the great discouragement of their fighters all over the city, up till 9 o'clock that morning the massed guns up in the principal Commune fortress of Montmartre had not yet fired a single shot against the Government troops. La Cécilia, sent by Delescluze to investigate, discovered the famous guns whose seizure in March had sparked off the whole civil war in a calamitous condition: 'Eighty-five cannon, a score of *mitrailleuses*, lay there, dirty and scattered about. Nobody, during these past eight weeks, had thought of getting them into action. There was plenty of 7-pounder ammunition, but no breech-blocks. At the Moulin de la Galette, three 24-pounders were the only ones equipped with gun-carriages; but there were no parapets, no side-armour, no platforms.' When the first shots were at last fired, 'the recoil buried the gun trails, and it took a lot of time to dig them out'.

Thus unopposed, Ladmirault moved right up to the Batignolles area at the foot of Montmartre, while to his right Clinchant was aided by the second Communard blunder. The Parc Monceau was captured when National Guards directed a murderous fire into the rear of their own front-line defenders, mistaking them for *Versaillais*. In the panic that ensued, Clinchant captured the park and began to sweep eastwards up the Boulevards Malesherbes and Haussmann, as well as the Faubourg St.-Honoré. The forces of law and order were now well into Paris. Before midday, the Beaujon Hospital, which Dr. Powell had tried in vain to reach earlier that morning, was in their hands. After being stopped several times to help build barricades, Powell had reach the Rue St.-Honoré, in the vicinity of the Place Vendôme, and—finding no more barricades ahead of him—still hoped

to be able to attain his destination. 'But I had not got far before several
bullets whizzed past my head . . . fighting was going on at the great
barricade across the Rue Royale and near the Church of the Madeleine
which was sadly damaged.' Unable to progress any further, Powell
stopped to give assistance at a temporary ambulance set up in the
Rue Royale. There he found all the painful confusion of civilians
caught up in the midst of war; 'Many ladies and children had also
come into the house for protection, and were all mixed up with the
wounded, and were much alarmed as it was then known that parts
of Paris were on fire. . . . There was little food or anything in the
house for the wounded and others, and no one dared to leave the
house, as the shutters (outside) were closed and often struck by
spent bullets . . . I felt my last hours were near. . . .'

The Rev. Gibson had left Paris to join his wife and family at
Chantilly, but M. Chastel, the librarian at his Methodist Chapel in
the Rue Roquépine (close to the Place St.-Augustin and the Boulevard
Malesherbes), had remained to find himself in the centre of the
fighting. In a detailed letter to Gibson, he wrote:

Since eight o'clock this morning there has been a fusillade in our
street. . . . This morning we were surrounded by National Guards, and
we heard the fusillade in the direction of the Faubourg St.-Honoré and
the Champs-Élysées. After a while the fight was close to Saint-Augustin,
in the Boulevard Malesherbes, and at last the soldiers reached our street.
We could not even put our nose through the window without the risk of
being struck by a ball. The soldiers are installed in the house next to
our chapel, and are firing in the direction of the Rue Neuve des Mathurins
(in a line with our Rue Roquépine on the other side of the Boulevard
Malesherbes). They are at the doorway and at the windows of each
storey. You can imagine the noise and confusion we hear outside. About
nine o'clock we had worship in our room; all in the house were present,
and we prayed earnestly to God to aid us. . . . I heard a poor wounded
man uttering a cry, I peeped out from under our window shutters. We
saw him carried off. Shortly afterwards a soldier was killed on the spot
close to our library. . . .

Later that afternoon, a *Versaillais* sapper entered the Roquépine
Chapel to inform M. Chastel that 'they have surrounded Paris, and
they are about to deliver us from the Commune. After having drunk
a glass of wine, he took his post at our chapel door and began
firing. . . .'

The fighting soon reached Alan Herbert's house, about a quarter
of a mile further to the east. At one moment the Communards
erecting the barricade outside had threatened to search all the houses
for able-bodied men to fight, but 'events were too rapid to allow them

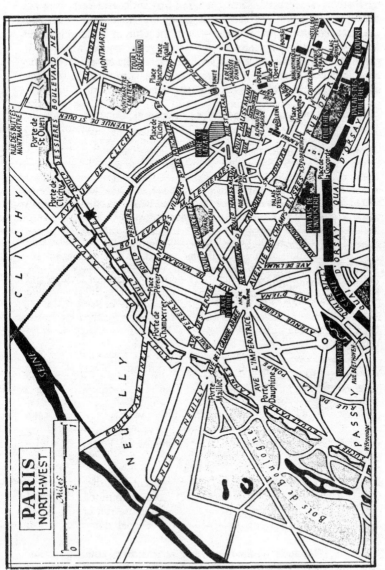

Map 3. Paris: north-west

to do so'. Dr. Herbert had then offered his services—which were not accepted—to a first-aid station set up in the Place de la Madeleine market; the proximity of which 'was very useful, as I was able to get some food sent to me through a window in my house, which looks upon it'. Two of the National Guards stationed outside declared to Herbert 'their intention of running away, taking off their regimentals and hiding themselves'. Then, at about 10 a.m.,

the firing became very bad, and cannon were brought up to be planted on the boulevards. . . . No one dared to stir out, and the sentries knew nothing. Towards the afternoon the fighting in the streets assumed another character. The troops had succeeded in taking posession of a house at the end of my street, Rue Chauveau Lagarde, and made their way from house to house by holes in the walls, till they arrived at the end of the street, and then they fired down on the barricade. The insurgents answered their fire from the Place de la Madeleine, but could not enter into the street.

Alan Herbert now found himself in an exceptional, but uncomfortable, position, as witness of the struggle that ensued. As the regulars worked their way through the houses on his side of the street, the only point whence the Communards could fire back at them under cover was from the opposite corner of the street, immediately facing Herbert's door. For the rest of the day Herbert watched, fascination and anxiety vying with each other:

The first who fired was a grey-headed, grey-bearded old man, who was the most bloodthirsty old fellow I ever saw. He hounded the others on, and had hot discussions, even with his own officers, so great was his determination to kill everyone he could see at the window, whether a soldier or not—so at least I interpreted through the bars of my prison. There were in all about twenty or thirty firing, and it was a horrible sight. They quarrelled as to who should have the most shots, whose turn it was to shoot, and from time to time one heard such expressions as these: 'Oh, that caught him!' It was just like boys rabbit-shooting. I do not believe, however, they *killed* many, but it would not have been possible to pass into the street, so hot was the firing. I was expecting every moment that one party or the other would endeavour to take possession of my house, but it was too much exposed to the firing. This fighting continued until night; no gas was lighted, and it was a very dark night, so we had a short respite.

At the Hôtel de Ville, something of the heat, confusion, and excitement of the March days had been recaptured. The Comité Central of the National Guard, the Artillery Committee, and all the various military services had concentrated there and were busy issuing contradictory orders. Noisy, anxious suppliants besieged the Committee of Public Safety and the War Commission, while the Comité Central inveighed in every direction against the incompetence of different members of the Commune. Early that morning some twenty Communards gathered around the venerable figure of Félix Pyat, whose *Le Vengeur* had just emitted stirring cries of '*Aux armes !*' It was very much Pyat's moment. 'Well my friends,' he intoned in an heroically avuncular manner, 'our last hour has come.' It distressed him to see the 'fair heads' of so many young men around him; but 'for me, what does it matter! My hair is white, my career is finished. What more glorious end could I hope for than to die on the barricades!' To prove to posterity, that he Félix Pyat, had done his duty he now called for a roll-call of all those present. Then, in his familiar fashion, he disappeared. His white hair was not seen on any barricade—in fact, not seen again at all until Pyat turned up safely in exile in London; far from his career being 'finished', he survived to be amnestied and elected Senator of France sixteen years later.

In the midst of all this commotion, a delegation arrived from the Liberal-Democratic Congress in Lyons, which had come—via Versailles—with last-minute offers of mediation. They were hardly received with warmth. It was too late. Elsewhere in the Hôtel de Ville, Raoul Rigault was busy executing two orders of the Committee of Public Safety. One detailed him to implement the Decree on Hostages finally approved five days earlier; the second, dated '*4 Prairial*, An 79', called for the immediate transfer of the Archbishop and the other leading hostages from the Mazas Prison to the condemned cells at La Roquette. The actual transportation of the hostages he passed on to his deputy, da Costa, who requisitioned two goods carts—like the tumbrils of another age—for the operation.

As far as military instructions for the hard-pressed National Guards went, little of sense was being transmitted from the Hôtel de Ville. The Commune had anticipated that, when the Versailles attack began, it would be a frontal assault; not, as it developed, a series of turning movements which took elaborately prepared defensive positions and impromptu barricades alike from a flank, or from the rear, with depressing ease. There was a certain irony in the fact that the groundwork of Louis-Napoleon and his Prefect, Haussmann, was contributing as much to the reconquest of Paris as the planning of his old adversary, Adolphe Thiers. A co-ordinated, mobile defence would have been the only means of coping with these turning tactics. But the Commune no longer had a Rossel, nor even a Cluseret to dispose its forces; and in any case the National Guard was already showing an in-built, parochial reluctance to fight elsewhere than in defence of its own district. So, just as the old Jacobins had fought until they were rounded up or slaughtered in 1848, Paris would be defended piecemeal and *ad lib.*, as it were—from barricade to barricade.

To those of its combatants with any military background, the total lack of direction from the Hôtel de Ville made the hopelessness of the situation abundantly plain. At about 10 o'clock on that night of May 22nd, some agitated National Guards brought Dombrowski into the Hôtel de Ville. Without a command since that morning, he had been seized while attempting—so it was claimed—to escape through the Prussian lines at St.-Ouen. Brought before the Committee of Public Safety, Dombrowksi vigorously denied that he had contemplated treason. The Committee 'appeased him affectionately'; Dombrowski shook hands all round in an unmistakeable gesture of farewell, and strode off grimly towards the fighting. 'There were', wrote Lissagaray, 'nights that were more clamorous, more streaked with lightning, more imposing, when the conflagration and the cannonade enveloped all Paris; but none penetrated more lugubriously into the soul.'

Yet despite the inertia and disarray of the Commune, already by the afternoon of the first day the main impetus of the Versailles attack had begun to slow down. In the Rue de la Paix, only a few hundred yards from where the front line was surging about Alan Herbert's house, all Colonel Stanley had to report by lunchtime was that his friend, Austin, had been 'slightly hit by a bullet, standing near the Louvre. A bit of shell killed a man this morning early on the Place Vendôme, and another bit fell in the yard of this hotel'. At 3 p.m. he added:

The line have got possession of the St. Lazare station, but they don't seem to advance very fast. I heard a citizen remonstrate with a National Guard for uselessly breaking windows. A brute ordered me to help to work on the barricade. I told him to go to the devil and insisted on passing with my friend. . . . Two bodies of National Guards have passed round the corner and down to the Place Vendôme, poor devils, singing '*Mourir pour la Patrie*'. A perfect silence has happened since. I suppose the Line are entrenching themselves half across Paris. It is a funny state of things. Guns and musketry are beginning again. I was ordered off from my balcony just now. I keep a jealous eye on the bronze on the Place Vendôme,ⁱ and shall take a bit as soon as the bother is over.'

At 10 p.m. that evening, he noted:

The National Guards are more cocky than ever. I suppose it is the wine they have had. [They] will insist on firing from the houses, which

The remnants of the friezes on the fallen column.

will entail retaliation. I have got a huge Union Jack hanging out of my balcony. Guns and musketry going on still, horses neighing and great talking; decidedly they mean to fight more.

Stanley was not far wrong in his assessments. About the only advance that afternoon had been to capture the grounds of the British Embassy on the Rue St.-Honoré. And everywherĕ there were signs of resistance stiffening. In their scattered little packets, the Communards were beginning to fight as never before—the fight of despair. General Clinchant had anticipated that three days would suffice to occupy the whole of Paris, once the entry had been effected, but his calculations were upset by the degree of caution thrust upon the 'liberating' troops. Their leaders were concerned about rumours of whole streets being mined and booby-trapped; apprehensive (unnecessarily) as to the weight of artillery the enemy could bring to bear, by employing the cannon captured on March 18th; and mindful from their experiences of 1848 of what a toll could be exacted by desperate men fighting from behind barricades in the areas of Paris less friendly to the Government than Passy and the Étoile. They were still dubious, too, of just how much could be expected of the mixture of green young troops and defeated ex-prisoners of war under their command. Above all, Thiers remained determined that the work of repression should be carried out without haste, systematically and thoroughly. Announcing to a jubilant Versailles Assembly that evening that 'the cause of justice, order, humanity, civilization has triumphed. . . . The generals who conducted the entry into Paris are great men of war . . . ', Thiers added ominously, 'Expiation will be complete. It will take place in the name of the law, by the law and within the law.'

In the final judgement of Paris that lay immediately ahead, it might be possible to perceive 'order'; but remarkably little of justice, humanity, or civilization.

The Hôtel de Ville on Fire

25. 'La Semaine Sanglante'—II

THE dawn of Tuesday, the 23rd, broke on yet another ravishing May day. As the front had been stabilized the previous evening, it lay roughly along a north–south axis, running from the Gare des Batignolles in the north, through the Gare St.-Lazare, the British Embassy, the Palais de l'Industrie, across the Seine to the Chamber of Deputies, and up the Boulevard des Invalides to the Gare Montparnasse. Behind it, on the one side, the western third of Paris lay solidly in Government hands, behind it on the other, no less than five hundred barricades had been started in the respite provided by MacMahon's slowing-down. But even before daybreak, his forces were on the move again. A short while later, Goncourt, still an involuntary 'prisoner' at his friend Burty's house, climbed up to the belvedere to look out upon an 'immense battle illuminated by the bright sunshine'. It was, he thought, 'at Montmartre that the main weight of the action seemed to be concentrated'.

At about 3 o'clock that morning, Ladmirault had opened another long flanking operation, moving along the inside of the city ramparts to take from the rear all the gates as far as the Porte de St.-Ouen.

Reaching the Porte de Clignancourt at the northernmost point of Paris, he wheeled right to face Montmartre from the north-east. At the same time, Clinchant moved frontally on Montmartre by smashing through the barricades at the Batignolles. Soon his troops had reached the Place Clichy, while Ladmirault's right wing occupied the Montmartre cemetery; thus confronting the Commune's most imposing fortress with an assault on three sides. As the Government troops moved beyond the Batignolles, a personal tragedy was recorded that was perhaps typical of what was being suffered wherever civilians found themselves caught between two fires. Just off the Boulevard Péreire lived a couple, M. and Mme Paris, who—according to their colleague, the Rev. Gibson—had been noted for their work of evangelization among the rag-pickers in this part of Paris. Throughout Monday fighting had raged about their house, dead and wounded had fallen all around them, and it was with immense relief that Mme Paris awoke the following morning to see the barricades outside abandoned. 'In her joy of seeing the fighting finished in our quarter', recorded the husband, 'she woke me up to come and watch the arrival of the soldiers who were taking possession of the station [Batignolles]. Everybody was at their window.... Unfortunately my brother-in-law, goaded by a fatal curiosity approached from the left side and lifted a corner of the curtain; at the same instant there was a rifle shot and hit in the lower stomach he fell backwards into the room.' Passing through his body, the same bullet then went on to kill Mme Paris too, who happened to enter the room at that moment carrying a cup of chocolate.

Benoît Malon, having conducted a vigorous rearguard action in the Batignolles, now found himself all but encircled in the Mairie of the 17th. Slipping through the *Versaillais* cordon, he managed to fall back on Montmartre, where he was greeted by a dismal spectacle of discouragement, half-completed barricades and unserviceable guns. Many of the defenders had faded away during the night, leaving only a hundred or so to man the defences on the northern slopes upon which Ladmirault was advancing with more than a division. About the only Communard detachment which showed spirit was a squad of twenty-five women from the Women's Battalion, headed by the redoubtable Louise Michel. Back along the Boulevard de Clichy they fought from barricade to barricade; past the Place Blanche, past the site of some of the more sordid night-haunts of modern Paris, back to the Place Pigalle, where most of them were forced to surrender. By this time only about fifteen of the women were left, including Louise Michel and Elizabeth Dimitrieff. Louise had orders to blow up, if necessary, the Butte-Montmartre. But it was too late. Near the Boulevard Barbés she met Dombrowski, falling back from Clignancourt, at about 2 o'clock that afternoon. 'We are lost!' he told her, and a few seconds later he fell mortally wounded in the Rue Myrha. As the Polish exile's body was carried back to the Hôtel de Ville, men at the barricades presented arms with un-Communard precision.

Up in Burty's belvedere with Goncourt, 'someone thought they perceived, through opera glasses, the *tricolore* flag floating over Montmartre. At that moment we were chased down from our glass observatory by the whistling of bullets.' The observation was accurate. By 1 p.m. Clinchant's *Chasseurs* hoisted the flag at the Tour Solférino, where the insurrection had first broken out on March 18th, recapturing more than a hundred of the original cannon. Now, at Montmartre, the repression of the Commune assumed for the first time a grimmer quality. 'I gave strictest orders', claimed Thiers *ex post facto* in his *Notes et Souvenirs*, 'that the rage of the soldiers was to be contained. . . .' But this was not how the Versailles Army interpreted his proclamation of the previous evening, calling for 'complete expiation'. In terms of bloodshed, the 'expiation' imposed upon the Commune was to eclipse by far either the 'Terror' of the first French Revolution, or even the St. Petersburg revolution of 1917. Immediately on the capture of Montmartre, some 49 Communards (including, Lissagaray claimed, three women and four children) were collected at hazard and marched to No. 6 Rue des Rosiers, the scene of the killing of Generals Lecomte and Thomas. There they were made to kneel down in front of the same wall and were shot without any semblance of a trial.

At the other extremity of their front, the Communards—under Varlin, Wroblewski, and Lisbonne—were now offering much tougher resistance. Varlin, firmly turning a blind eye to the conflicting orders that emanated from the Hôtel de Ville, had organized the nearest thing to a co-ordinated defence in his section on the Left Bank. At the Croix Rouge intersection between the Boulevards Raspail and St. Germain, he had set up a stronghold containing reserves which could be switched between the strongly manned barricades across the Rue de l'Université near the river, or at the Rue Vavin in Montparnasse. For the next two days there was bitter fighting, with heavy damage to property in this quarter, resulting in little progress by the Government troops.

As the day went on, it was the critical centre of the line that saw the severest fighting. Sweeping downhill from Montmartre and Pigalle, Clinchant's corps rolled up the Commune's flank towards the Opéra as it went. On his right Douay was reinforcing his efforts of the previous day in the direction of the Madeleine, as well as keeping up the heaviest frontal pressure on Brunel's position in the Place de la Concorde. Early that morning the tide of battle had finally surged past the Methodist Chapel in the Rue Roquépine; 'Midnight . . . We hear the bombs passing over the building. We *feel* the uncertainty of life, and that our existence hangs on a thread which may be broken at any moment', recorded M. Chastel, adding later:

God has kept us safely through the night . . . one bullet has just struck my window, pierced the glass, broken off a piece of stone in its course, and has fallen at the foot of my bureau . . . happily I was not there. At five o'clock the soldiers have driven away the insurgents from the barricade, and we could put our noses outside. I saw several soldiers lying dead, and others wounded. . . . At six o'clock the soldiers evacuated our street, and advanced towards the Madeleine.

With the Versailles forces pressing towards it on two sides, the Communard position at the Madeleine became a key bulwark to the Rue Royale and Brunel's stronghold. 'The sentries watched all night just opposite my house', said Alan Herbert,

and at early dawn the firing recommenced on both sides, and lasted all the morning, but less violent than the day before. Nothing whatever was known of passing events; we only knew just what we saw through the bars of my window. The monotony and the suspense was very great, and we felt that the barricades ought to be taken, as the force defending them was evidently small. I began to think that the capture of these barricades would be much like the rest of the war, and last ten times longer than anyone anticipated.

Towards evening, however, the firing became harder and harder, and after an hour and a half watching we saw the insurgents retreat from the different barricades and cross the Place. The troops then came in. A few scenes of horrid massacre and bloodshed, and then the streets were occupied by the regular troops. . . . I fear there is a very revengeful disposition amongst the regular troops, which is much to be regretted. . . .

While Douay's troops were closing in on the Madeleine, Dr. Powell, still working at his temporary first-aid post nearby on the Rue St.-Honoré, was sought out by some 'high officers of the Commune' who said they wanted to use his ambulance as a 'point of retreat' when the Madeleine barricades fell. He remonstrated with them, pointing out that they would all be put to death for violating the Geneva Conventions. 'The answer given to me was "well citizen, in that case we shall all go to hell together. . . ."' The Communard officers were evidently persuaded, however. Suddenly the cannonade ceased, and Powell peered out of the window to see men in red trousers taking position at the captured barricades. Some of the women with him 'fainted with joy'. Emerging into the open, he noticed all the columns of the Madeleine had been chipped and splintered, 'the figures in the Tympanum being sadly mutilated and railings twisted about and the street lamps also, into fantastic figures'.

Moving up the Boulevard Haussmann to join hands with Clinchant's right wheel, Douay also captured a barricade opposite the famous Printemps stores and with a few rounds of cannon dislodged the National Guards from the Trinité. Haussmann's still unfinished Opéra was soon hemmed in on three sides. Marine sharp-shooters mounted themselves in the top storey of the surrounding buildings, and directed a deadly fire down on to the Communards exposed behind their barricades; but here they fought back with desperate courage. At 6 p.m., after both sides had suffered substantial losses, the Opéra was carried; and a soldier climbed up on to the statue of Apollo at its entrance and ripped down the red flag. One of the *Daily News* correspondents was there to witness the event, and about the same time he watched another regular, 'a little grig of a fellow', run to take up position behind a tree, whence he began firing down the Boulevard Haussmann:

> He fired with an air; he loaded with an air; he fired again with a flourish, and was greeted with cheering and clapping of hands. Then he beckoned dramatically for he meditated firing up the Rue Lafayette, but changed his mind, and blazed away again up Haussmann. Then he turned and waved on his fellows as if he were on the boards of a theatre, the Federal bullets cutting the bark and leaves all around him.

A few seconds later the British journalist saw the 'little grig struck down with a bullet through his head'.

Clinchant's flanking right wheel was soon traversing the recently renamed Rue du 4 Septembre. The sound of the approaching rifle-fire brought hopes of early redemption to both Goncourt, still incarcerated with Burty behind the Bibliothèque Nationale, and an anxious Marquis de Plœuc in the Bank of France. Around Goncourt the signs of retreat began to multiply. First horse-drawn ambulances came past; then a bus filled with National Guards, followed by staff officers arriving at the gallop to warn the Communards stationed near Burty's house not to let themselves be cut off. Next came the artillery, followed by the stretcher-bearers. Some men began half-heartedly to start a barricade outside, but gave it up and sloped away. Shortly before 6 p.m., a mass of retreating National Guards came into sight, bearing with them 'a dead man with his head covered in blood, whom four men were carrying by his arms and legs like a bundle of dirty washing, taking him from door to door—none of which opened'. Soon *Versaillais* bullets were flying around Burty's house. Goncourt's curiosity was still unquenchable and, down on his knees in the dining-room, he peeped out through a corner of the curtain:

On the other side of the boulevard there was a man stretched out on the ground of whom I could see only the soles of his boots and a bit of gold braid. There were two men standing by the corpse, a National Guard and a lieutenant. The bullets were making the leaves rain down on them from a little tree spreading its branches over their heads. A dramatic detail I was about to forget; behind them, in front of the closed doors of a closed *porte-cochère*, a woman was lying flat on the ground, holding a peaked cap in one hand.

The National Guardsman, talking at the top of his voice, with violent and base gestures indicated to his fellows that he wanted to remove the corpse. Bullets continued to bring the leaves raining down on the two men. Then, the National Guardsman, whose face I could perceive was red with rage, flung his rifle on to his shoulder, butt upwards, and stepped out into the fusillade, an insult on his lips. Suddenly I saw him halt, put his hand to his forehead, lean for a second with his hand and his head against a small tree, then turn about and fall on his back, spreadeagled.

The lieutenant had remained motionless beside the first corpse, as tranquil as a man meditating in a garden. A bullet that had knocked down a small branch on to him, which he brushed away with a flick, did not draw him out of his immobility. For an instant, he contemplated his killed comrade. Then, without any hurry, he threw off his sword behind him, as if with scornful deliberation, bent down and tried to lift the dead man. The body was large and heavy, and, like any inert object, evaded his efforts and rolled about in his arms from left to right. At last he raised it; and clutching it across his chest, he was carrying it away when a bullet, smashing his thigh, made the dead and the living spin in a hideous pirouette, collapsing one upon the other. I think it is given to few people to to be witnesses of such a heroic and such a simple contempt of death. They told me that evening that the woman lying on the ground was the wife of one of the three men.

For all his loathing of the Communards, Goncourt could not withhold admiration for the courage and comradeship—senseless, perhaps—demonstrated in this small incident, nor could he stifle his compassion for the suffering of their wounded. As the *Versaillais* approached, 'I retained in my ear for a long time the rending cries of a wounded soldier[1] who had dragged himself to our door and whom the concierge, through a cowardly fear of compromising herself, refused to let in.' By nightfall the street was in the hands of the Versailles troops. 'We took the risk of looking at them from our balcony, when a bullet struck just above our heads. It was that imbecile of a lodger who had decided to light up a pipe at his window.'

---

[1] Possibly the lieutenant referred to above?

Even British correspondents accompanying the Versailles troops were struck by the joy with which this part of Paris greeted its 'liberators'. People sang and danced in the exhilaration of the moment. Bottles of wine and money were pressed upon the soldiers; women embraced them. Yet still Douay's forces could not frontally break Brunel's resistance in the Concorde and the Rue Royale; and, well after the capture of the Opéra and after Clinchant had swung round across the Rue du 4 Septembre, Colonel Stanley continued to find himself isolated in a pocket of Communard resistance in the Place Vendôme, the former H.Q. of the National Guard. At 3 p.m. he had jotted down for his mother's eyes:

It is a glorious day, but I am feeling low. We are surrounded. The Versailles people have not advanced as much as I expected, but they are gaining ground; after all there is a good deal of ground to get over. We have a battery of guns of the Reds at the end of Rue de la Paix, in the Boulevard 300 yards from the hotel which makes the windows rattle. The musketry has been very continuous and very heavy. Many of the National Guards are slipping away . . . I fear no letters will get out today.

(5 p.m.) For the last three quarters of an hour there has been an awful fire. The Reds have run past the Rue de la Paix in quantities with the greatest trouble . . . . It is a very grand sight, but the firing is of course a most pitiful one and also the cowardice of the people. We shall soon have the *red legs* in the streets, and they I shall not dare to bully as I do the Reds.

(5.30 p.m.) The barricade at the end of the street, which twenty minutes ago had been vacated by the Reds, has been taken by the Line and they have occupied a house and are firing down the street, making a most fearful noise. They are returning the fire near the Vendôme. . . .

Beyond the Place Vendôme, Stanley spotted National Guards 'flying across the Rue de Rivoli and St. Honoré, and their grand battery in Rue Castiglione is taken in reverse and is of course useless and empty'. Then, at 8 p.m., the Colonel recorded:

After forty minutes firing the Reds left the Place Vendôme. A quarter of an hour afterwards six men came back and have been firing ever since. The noise on both sides is awful, for those six men (it sounds like a joke), with their *tabatière* rifles, made as much noise as if they fired 6 pounders. I only observed two men wounded. It is getting dark . . . and the aim of course gets worse. . . .

An hour later the *Versaillais*, 'sick of the nonsense', brought up some guns, and fired five rapid rounds into the gathering dusk. The effect, continued Stanley, was wonderful, instant silence. The poor street is awfully cut up, glass and lamps have fallen all along; . . . I have chased away the maid who, like a little fool, would look out.

By 10 p.m. Stanley could hear people beginning to move about down in the street; 'Poor Street of Peace. I imagine it is in an awful state'. An hour later he made his last entry for the 23rd:

Well, this eventful day is closing quietly. The spent balls whistle through the still air, and can be heard at a great distance. . . . I have been looking at my English flag which sticks out of my window. It has several bullet holes in it.

Away in the distance he saw the red glow of a great fire, which he thought might possibly be the Tuileries Palace burning.

* * *

All through that day Brunel and his men had continued to hold out with the utmost tenacity at the barricades in the Rue Royale and the Place de la Concorde, and at the immensely strong one at the bottom of the Rue St.-Florentin which guarded the Rue de Rivoli, the street pointing so straight at the Hôtel de Ville and the very heart of the Commune. Douay had brought no less than sixty guns to bear on Brunel's position, against a meagre twelve. Their concentrated fire reduced the barricades to a shambles, killing scores of the defenders, whose flank all the time was becoming increasingly threatened by the turning movements from the direction of the Opéra. After the vital bulwark in the Place de la Madeleine fell, a new menace—that which had dispersed the Communards outside the Opéra—threatened them; deadly rifle-fire from sharp-shooters ensconced in the tops of the high buildings along the Rue Royale, which plunged down upon the defenders exposed behind their barricades. But Brunel was a soldier ruthless and resourceful enough to meet this kind of threat. Already during the first Siege he had acquired the nickname 'Brunel the Burner' on destroying a house that obstructed his field of fire, and now he swiftly ordered the firing of any houses capable of jeopardizing his defence. With alarming speed the flames spread up the famous street, consuming expensive *bijouteries* and elegant cafés alike.

The burning of Paris had begun; it was to become as integral a part of the legend of the Commune as the rats and balloons of the first Siege. For Brunel, however, the conflagration could only postpone the inevitable. His men (as Colonel Stanley spotted from his hotel) began to take flight in small packets down the Rue de Rivoli, and on the fall of the Place Vendôme his position became hopeless. An American friend of Wickham Hoffman, with an apartment overlooking the Concorde, witnessed what must have been the last minutes of 'the Burner's' stand there. At the great, sixteen-foot-high St.-Florentin barricade, in a scene that might have been painted by Delacroix, he saw

a young and apparently good-looking woman spring upon the barricade, a red flag in her hand, and wave it defiantly at the troops. She was instantly shot dead. . . .

When the barricade, stretching across what is now one of the busiest thoroughfares in Paris, was finally carried, Hoffman's friend watched while 'an old woman was led out to be shot. She was placed with her back to the wall of the Tuileries Gardens, and, as the firing party levelled their pieces, she put her fingers to her nose and worked them after the manner of the defiant in all ages. . . .' Some forty or fifty dead Communards were collected at the barricade, and thrown into the deep ditch from which the materials for its construction had been excavated. Quicklime was added and the ditch filled in, so that Douay's troops could without delay push their guns forward over it.

Up the vital Rue de Rivoli Brunel and his survivors now fell back towards the Hôtel de Ville in desperate haste. As they passed the Rue Castiglione they were caught in enfilading fire by regulars advancing from the Place Vendôme, who nearly succeeded in cutting off their line of retreat. Brunel escaped, although he and his men were silhouetted by an immense fire that had burst out behind them, the fire that Colonel Stanley had noted. Jules Bergeret, the Commune's earliest military commander, now released from prison and to some extent rehabilitated, had carried out a desperate action, actuated, apparently, more by vengeful motives than by tactical necessity; an action that might easily have led to perhaps the greatest tragedy of the whole civil war—the burning-down of the Louvre. Inside the *Salle des Maréchaux* of the Tuileries Palace, where only so recently the last of the famous concerts had taken place, Bergeret had piled barrel after barrel of gunpowder. The resplendent hangings in the great halls that had witnessed so many of the triumphs of the Second Empire in its hours of pride he smeared indiscriminately with tar and petroleum, and then withdrew. Shortly after 10 p.m. flames burst out all along the length of the palace. With a tremendous roar the central dome housing the *Salle des Maréchaux* disappeared. While Douay's men looked on impotently, fascination mingled with horror at this display of pyrotechnics dwarfing anything mounted by the former Emperor to divert his royal guests at the Great Exhibition, Bergeret scribbled a brief note to the Committee of Public Safety:

'The last relics of Royalty have just vanished.'

Even if this had so far eluded its grasp, the Commune was now certainly beginning to leave a permanent mark on the face of France. But at the Hôtel de Ville late on Tuesday night the signs of imminent defeat were multiplying. How remote seemed that halcyon day when the Commune had been proclaimed outside this same Hôtel de Ville; when it had seemed to so many of the oppressed and dissatisfied of Paris that Utopia was at last within their grasp! Could that day of splendour and sublime confidence really have been a bare two months ago? Now the flames rising high above the Tuileries cast a diabolic glow on the Hôtel de Ville's medieval façade, at the same time as it imparted an unnatural colour to the frightened faces of National Guards scurrying in and out of the building. The sounds of musketry were coming appreciably closer. Inside, the corridors were cluttered with wounded, groaning for water; the walls flecked with their blood. In men's eyes a real fear was betrayed, something beyond the transient panics of the past. The realization that, despite the slowing-down in the rate of the *Versaillais* advance, the 23rd had been—militarily—*the* decisive day was not restricted to the leaders of the Commune. That night most who visited the Hôtel de Ville became aware of being faced with a choice of death or flight. Some, like the vanished Pyat, had already chosen. So had Dombrowski, now lying in state in a blue satin bed in the Hôtel de Ville. Even in the Commune's last hours the irrelevant, as always, was to be found jostling the immediate; alongside Dombrowski a National Guard was occupied sketching the dead general's features.

Outside Delescluze's temporary office, a vigilant guard kept at bay the hordes of would-be suppliants. Within, a curiously unusual calm and quietness prevailed. According to Lissagaray's description, 'Delescluze is signing orders, pale, mute like a spectre. The agonies of the past days have drained what remained of his life. His voice is nothing but a croak. His gaze and his heart alone still live.' Again according to the usually reliable Lissagaray, at about 3 o'clock that same night a staff officer presented himself to the Committee of Public Safety, having come post-haste from Notre-Dame Cathedral. There, he reported, he had found a detachment of National Guards busily engaged in buidling up a large 'brasier' out of chairs and pews; but, the staff officer warned, there were some eight hundred Communard sick and wounded in the adjacent Hôtel Dieu hospital, to which the

flames would almost certainly spread if the cathedral were incendiarized. The Committee hastily dispatched him with orders for
Notre-Dame to be evacuated and left strictly alone. By so slender a
margin was one of the world's most famous monuments preserved.

But there was no one to check Raoul Rigault, then about to commit
an atrocity he had long been planning. Without any authority and
without consulting his colleagues, Rigault arrived at the Ste.-Pélagie
Prison claiming to have orders for the immediate execution of
Gustave Chaudey, one of the hostages who, as Jules Ferry's deputy,
had ordered the *Mobiles* to fire on the mob demonstrating outside
the Hôtel de Ville on January 22nd. Rigault informed Chaudey, 'You
killed my friend Sapia; you have five minutes to live.' Chaudey
pointed out that he had been merely carrying out his duty; that, in
the absence of any authenticated orders, Rigault would be responsible
for murder and not an execution. Rigault brushed all this aside and,
to a final objurgation by Chaudey that he had a wife and child, he
replied icily: 'The Commune will take better care of them than you.'
A reluctant firing-squad was hastily formed, of which Rigault personally took charge, but on its first volley only succeeded in wounding
Chaudey in one arm. Displaying admirable courage, Chaudey stood
there waving the other arm and crying '*Vive la République!*' until
prison warders finished off the job with their revolvers.

Not satisfied with his night's work, Rigault now ordered out three
of the lesser category of hostages, ordinary gendarmes seized on
March 18th. His firing-squad, quite unnerved by the execution of
Chaudey, demanded some kind of formal authorization. Compliantly,
Rigault dictated a farcical indictment in mock legal terms covering all
four men; 'Whereas', it read, 'the *Versaillais* are firing at us from the
windows, and whereas it is time to put an end to these events; in
consequence thereof they have been executed in the court of this
building.' A hideous ritual then ensued. Only one of the gendarmes
was killed outright by the half-hearted firing-squad; another tried
to escape, hiding like some hunted rodent in the shadows of the
courtyard until dragged out and shot. The episode shocked even
Rigault's aide and admirer, da Costa, who considered the killing of
Chaudey both the 'most fatally vengeful as well as the most justifiable'.

On May 24th, an Englishwoman living out at St.-Germain-en-
Laye noted in her journal that it was Queen Victoria's fifty-second
birthday. She added, 'God save the Queen, and long may she reign
over us. Paris is *burning*.' This last fact, so succinctly stated, was the
one which above all others stuck in people's memories for that day.
Edwin Child, still in Communard territory in the Marais district
where he continued to while away the time playing cards with his

friend Johnson, at first thought the news that the Tuileries were burning 'incredible'. But on the 24th 'it seemed literally as if the whole town was on fire and as if all the powers of hell were let loose upon the town'. From a distance the spectacle was almost more terrifying. The Rev. Gibson had returned from Chantilly as far as St.-Denis, to ascertain whether it was yet safe to re-enter the city, and from this vantage-point he saw 'a sight such as we shall never forget. Fires have been seen in various parts of the city throughout the whole day; but in the evening, towards nine o'clock, the heavens in the direction of the ill-fated city were completely lighted up.' Into his mind immediately came the passage in the Book of Revelations recounting the fall of Babylon:

Alas, alas that great city, that was clothed in fine linen, and purple, and scarlet, and decked with gold, and precious stones, and pearls!

For in one hour so great riches is come to nought. And every ship-master, and all the company in ships, and sailors, and as many as trade by sea, stood afar off.

And cried when they saw the smoke of her burning, saying, 'What city is like unto this great city!'

Biblical parallels also captured Dr. Powell's imagination, though he was reminded more of the destruction of Sodom and Gomorrah. Goncourt, who had returned to Auteuil to find his house still standing with only a hole in the roof and a shell-hole in the garden, could see behind him 'a cloud of smoke over Paris like that which crowns a gasworks. And all around us fall from the skies, like black rain, little fragments of burnt paper; the records and the accounts of France.' It reminded him of the ashes which had buried Pompeii, and that night the image recurred when he described the fire over Paris as resembling 'those Neapolitan *gouaches* of an eruption of Vesuvius done on black paper'. In a different vein, another Frenchman recalled dining at the chic Pavillon Henri VI on the Terrasse de St.-Germain, and his party pointing with detached cynicism at the various buildings that appeared to be alight. When someone declared that the Louvre was among those burning, 'a large lady exclaimed—"let's hope he doesn't mean the department store!"'

The list of buildings already incendiarized by the night of the 24th was appallingly impressive; it included the Tuileries, a large part of the Palais-Royal, the Palais de Justice, the Prefecture of Police, the Cour des Comptes, the Légion d'Honneur, and the Conseil d'État. Whole sections of streets like the Rue de Lille and much of the Rue de Rivoli were on fire, or already gutted. The Ministry of Finance housed in one wing of the Louvre was ablaze, having either caught fire from the Tuileries or been deliberately ignited. It was from here that the burnt fragments of bureaucracy descended on Goncourt; outside it one Parisian encountered a frantic civil servant dragging out vast leather boxes who requested him to keep an eye on them as they were 'the taxation files' (to his annoyance the following month he received a tax claim!). Already, early that morning, the Commune added to the flames one of the finest and most historic buildings of all Paris—the Hôtel de Ville itself. At 8 a.m. some fifteen members had met there to discuss its immediate evacuation, and only Delescluze and one other had protested. In its despair a scorched-earth policy had now become the retreating Communard's automatic response, and by 11 a.m. the Hôtel de Ville was a sea of flames.

It was perfect weather for arson. For the past month there had been an almost unbroken drought; the day of the 24th was one of mid-summer heat, and just to make matters worse the next day a wind approaching hurricane force had got up. With heartbreaking speed the fires jumped from one block to another, often before Thiers's forces could occupy the incendiarized area and put in hand fire-fighting measures. When they did, the equipment available would prove pathetically inadequate, 'Fancy putting out a house of 7 storeys', Edwin Child wrote his father, 'with pails of water.' Just as in the past days the Communards had impressed passers-by to help build barri-cades, so the Government troops called on all at hand to join in the work of saving Paris. Making his way from the Rue de la Paix to the British Embassy on May 24th, Colonel Stanley was 'requisitioned' three times by *pompiers*. From London, Mr. Gladstone inquired via Lord Lyons whether he could in due course send over some British firemen to help, and out in Chantilly the Rev. Gibson read notices pleading for young men of '*bonne volonté*' to come to Paris to man the fire-engines.

There is little doubt that many buildings would not have been burnt down but for the dry weather, others were probably set on fire fortuitously by *Versaillais* shells, whereas, among the acts of pure vengefulness carried out by the Commune, some—such as Brunel's initial operations on the Rue Royale—could possibly be excused on tactical grounds.[1] Yet now new rumours of mass terror began to spread among the Government troops and the anti-Communard

[1] Karl Marx, pleading justification on behalf of the Commune in *The Civil War in France*, pointed to the British burning of Washington during the War of 1812; 'To be burned down has always been the inevitable fate of buildings in the front of battle of all the regular armies of the world . . . . The Commune used fire strictly as a means of defence.'

inhabitants of Paris alike, rumours that agents of the desperate Commune were planning deliberately to raze the whole of Paris. The rumours fell on fertile ground, for Parisians could remember vividly all the wild talk about Greek fire emanating from the Red Clubs as far back as the first Siege, and more recently there had been constant threats by various Communards to mine the sewers of Paris. On May 19th, Washburne had reported to Fish the *canard* he had picked up to the effect that 'the Committee of Public Safety is decided to blow up Paris and bury everyone under its ruins rather than capitulate'. and, indeed, only two days previously there had appeared in the *Journal Officiel* a sinister decree ordering all owners of petroleum products to register them with the Hôtel de Ville. Word went around the Army that instructions for the burning of Paris had emanated from that twilight body in London, the *International*, while as early as the day after the fire Colonel Stanley heard it being said: 'The foreigners generally are accused of firing the Tuileries, as the vanity of the French will not accept of its being possibly the act of a Frenchman.' Edward Noble, an English silk-merchant who had spent most of the days of fighting in his bedroom, crouched behind an upturned bedstead, claimed to have been given 'a small bit of the electric wire which was laid with the intention of blowing up the whole of the Faubourg St. Germain'.[1] After the Civil War had ended, quantities of 'instructions' marked either *'Bon pour Brûler'* or *'Maisons à incendier'*, and franked with a Commune stamp, came to light; but these appear to have been forgeries designed to blacken still further the Commune's name.

No legend was more widely believed than that of the *pétroleuses*; fearful mænads from some infernal region who crept about the city, sometimes accompanied by their offspring, flinging fire-balls or bottles of petroleum into basement windows belonging to the bourgeoisie. On the 25th, Stanley recorded:

Last night three women were caught throwing small fire balls down the openings of the cellars in the street. There was no doubt of it of course. Already smoke was coming from some of them. They were driven into a corner and shot then and there through the head.

The previous day a woman was reported to have been arrested on the Rue du Bac with several bottles of petroleum slung round her from a belt fastened under her dress. M. Chastel of the Roquépine Methodist Chapel agreed that 'It is specially the women who are setting fire to

[1] This fragment of electric cable was in fact sent to the author for inspection by Mrs. W. M. Denham, into whose possession it had passed via Noble's daughter, together with his notebooks.

the houses. Many have been taken in the act and shot at once.' A 'Special Correspondent' of the *Daily News* described at great length the *pétroleuses* and their three different techniques. 'The part which the women play in this business is remarkable. It was no idle boast of M. Allix when he proposed to create a legion of Amazons of the Seine ready to fight.' Waxing to his theme, the journalist declared that in the Madeleine quarter these harpies enticed soldiers of the Line to drink with them, and then, 'it is said, poisoned their cups'. (*The Times*, though sceptical of the *pétroleuses* legend, repeated an almost equally improbable story; that unknown saboteurs working the fire-engines pumped petrol on to the flames instead of water.) Even the normally disbelieving and un-bloodthirsty Edwin Child wrote to his father that 'the women behaved like tigresses, throwing petroleum everywhere'; he added that 40 soldiers had been poisoned by them, commenting that 'shooting is far too good for these devils'.

What started the *pétroleuses* legend remains a mystery. Most of the wretched women seized were shot out of hand, and no acceptable evidence was ever subsequently produced before a court. Probably there was some basis of truth; in the feverish state of mind that prevailed in blazing Paris, one genuine case of women incendiaries caught *in flagrante delicto* (such as that cited by Stanley) might easily have sufficed to give birth to the whole legend. Certainly there was no shred of truth in one belief current among the Versailles Army; that the Communards had 'brigaded' together no less than 8,000 *pétroleuses* for their fell mission. To begin with, this degree of organization had always proved beyond them. Such eminently sensible witnesses as Washburne, Wickham Hoffman, and Dr. Alan Herbert remained sceptical. To Hoffman, petroleum was 'the madness of the hour';

Every woman carrying a bottle was suspected of being a *pétroleuse*. . . . I do not believe in the petroleum story, and I do not think that one-third of the population believed in it. Yet such was the power of suspicion in those days, and such the distrust of one's neighbour, that every staid and sober housekeeper bricked up his cellar windows, and for weeks in the beautiful summer weather not an open window was to be seen on the lower stories. . . .

But the burning of Paris had begun to drive the loyalist troops to a new excess of rage against the insurgents; a rage that swept away the restraints of reason and justice. In a dispatch to Secretary Fish of May 24th, Washburne reported how one of his assistants had 'counted this afternoon, on the avenue d'Antin, the dead bodies of eight children, the eldest not more than fourteen years of age, who had been seized while distributing their incendiary boxes, and shot

on the spot'. The summary executions multiplied. How many innocent old women thus met their deaths while returning empty milk
bottles to the *laitière* will never be known. To Fish, Washburne co-
tinued: 'The state of feeling now existing in Paris is fearful beyond
description.'

On both sides passions were rising to a dangerous pitch, and on the
night of the 24th they culminated in the most heinous and senseless
crime committed by the Communards; the murder of the Archbishop
of Paris. As noted previously, on May 22nd Gaston da Costa, Rigault's
twenty-one-year-old Deputy *Procureur*, had been entrusted with the
transfer of Archbishop Darboy and fifty other hostages from the
Mazas Prison to the more secure La Roquette. Some of the poor
bewildered priests evidently rejoiced, thinking they were about to be
set free. As the hostages crossed the Faubourg St.-Antoine in the
sordid Bastille area, a mob had crowded round the wagons shouting
'*À mort! À mort!* Hand them over! Let them be shot here and now!'
Da Costa recalled that, 'as always, it was the women who were the
most bloodthirsty'. However, guarded by a detachment of fifty men,
he succeeded in shepherding his charges safely inside the La Roquette
Prison. By the 24th this particularly tough and insalubrious area was
occupied by its own native 66th Battalion of the National Guard.
The previous day the 66th had fought a desperate action behind a
fragile barricade near the Opéra; several of its men had been captured and shot on the spot. Tempers were high and the battalion was
out for blood. Now, on the morning of the 24th, the battalion *cantinière*—a virago known as 'the woman Lachaise'—denounced a
Captain de Beaufort as having been responsible for the massacre.
She had, she claimed, overheard him declare his intention of 'purging' the battalion; and this was the result. De Beaufort, an elegant
young man of about thirty, was a renegade count whose motives for
throwing in his lot with the Commune remains obscure; he was a
natural target for the rampant suspicions of the hour. The Count
was arrested and taken to Battalion Headquarters, outside which
'the woman Lachaise' mustered a coterie of fellow *tricoteuses*, howling
for de Beaufort's head, and threatening to lynch the officers holding
him if their demands were not satisfied. In much the same way as the
National Guards had acceded to mob pressure for the killing of the
two generals on March 18th, de Beaufort was taken out and shot in
the street.

All the time the threat of the advancing Versaillais was increasing,
and with it came ever-fresh reports of more summary executions.
The 66th Battalion and its tigerish, goading female adherents had the
taste of blood in their mouths. 'Exasperation was reaching its peak',

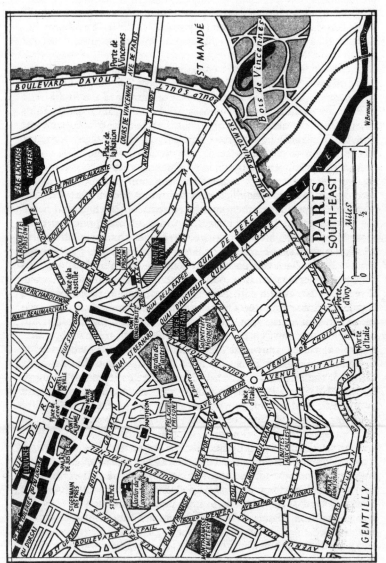

MAP 4. Paris: south-east

explained da Costa. 'This first killing accomplished, the survivors of the 66th Battalion did not judge themselves sufficiently revenged. They knew that prisoners "of note" had been transferred to La Roquette. . . .' As the day went on and the grim wounded men staggered back from the ever-approaching front, emotions mounted. The defence of the area now centred around the shop in which was located the H.Q. of the 66th Battalion. Here Théophile Ferré had arrived to co-ordinate operations. As Clemenceau's deputy on March 18th, the extremist Ferré had done much to undermine the Mayor of Montmartre's authority at the time of the shooting of Lecomte and Thomas. Since May 14th he had been Rigault's successor as Prefect of Police, for which post—as the purest kind of terrorist—he was admirably fitted. About twenty-five, he had a shock of black hair and heavy whiskers that surrounded a bird-of-prey face of extraordinary pallor and unmitigated melancholy. On his great hooked nose sat thick glasses through which peered black eyes full of all the myopic mildness of a Himmler. In relation to his upper body, his legs were almost deformedly short; he walked on tiptoe with a nervous tic of the shoulder. He envied Rigault his powers of attraction for women, while his own physical deficiencies—coupled to a youth of grinding misery as an impoverished clerk—filled him with misanthropy. In his capacity for taking ruthless, decisive action he and Rigault were as rare as each other in the Commune; McKean of the American Legation claimed that he 'never had seen a man who could dispose of matters so quickly and so readily'. An opportunity to display his talents to the full was now granted him.

As evening drew on, members of the 66th Battalion began to press Ferré for the execution of the hostages. Although the 'trial' at which Rigault and his supporters intended to designate the priests officially as 'hostages' had never taken place, Rigault's henchman Ferré needed little persuasion. He dispatched two officers, Fortin and Genton, with a terse note to the Governor of La Roquette ordering the execution of six unspecified hostages. On the way they were intercepted by 'the woman Lachaise' in tears of remorse over the morning's killing, and vainly imploring the officers not to pursue their mission. At the prison Fortin and Genton handed the order to the Governor, François, and then there ensued a discussion as to which of the prisoners should be selected. Fortin, it appears, insisted that the Archbishop head the list, but François, fearful of accepting the responsibility, declined to hand him over without specific authorization from Ferré. Fortin then returned to Ferré, who, declaring casually, 'All right, if they want the Archbishop they shall have him', took back the original order and wrote across it in large letters 'and particularly

The Last Barricade

26. 'Let us kill no more'

FROM the execution of the Archbishop, one important figure had been conspicuously absent—Raoul Rigault. That day, exchanging his civil garb as Public Prosecutor for the uniform of a National Guard major, he had gone off to help direct the fighting in his old hunting-grounds of the Latin Quarter. In the afternoon of the 24th, Cissey's corps had broken through and it looked as if the whole Panthéon district on the Left Bank would shortly fall. At about 3 p.m. Rigault withdrew to seek refuge in a hotel on the Rue Gay-Lussac where he kept lodgings, which he shared with an actress, under an assumed name. It was not long before the street was reached by Versailles troops, and they appear to have been informed that a National Guard major had been seen slipping into the hotel. Rigault's landlord was dragged out and threatened with instant death. On the entreaties of the hotelier's wife, Rigault intervened to save him, revealing his own identity. He was seized, so it was said, shouting '*Vive la Commune!*'; a regular sergeant then shot him several times through the head. For two days the *Procureur*'s body lay in the gutter, partly stripped by women of the

district, kicked and spat upon by passers-by, until one of his mistresses came to throw a coat over it.

For the best part of two terrible days Varlin and Lisbonne had put
up a spirited defence based on Montparnasse's Rue Vavin, against
enormous odds. By midday on the 24th, it was clear they could hold
out no longer. They now fell back, blowing up behind them the
huge powder magazine at the Luxembourg Gardens. The *Versaillais*
followed closely on their tracks, shooting batches of surrendered
Communards as they went. At Varlin's rear there were just three
barricades protecting the strategic Panthéon heights, and no longer
any organized reserves. By evening Cissey's troops had captured the
Panthéon and cleared most of the Boulevard St.-Michel. Varlin
escaped, still fighting. On the Left Bank the struggle had all but come
to an end. The sole exception was out on the extreme left flank where
Wroblewski, though isolated from the rest of the Commune forces,
was still keeping up a tough and professional defence from a stronghold atop the hill of the Butte-aux-Cailles, near the Porte d'Italie.
He was supported by fire from the forts of Ivry and Bicêtre which—
in disobedience of orders from Delescluze—he had stubbornly
refused to evacuate.

During the 24th, MacMahon's forces on the Right Bank had
captured the Gare du Nord, the Porte St.-Denis, the Conservatoire,
the Bank, and the Bourse. At the Bank they were greeted with more
than enthusiasm by the Marquis de Plœuc and his four hundred
employees, who during the last hours had been holding the buildings
more or less in a state of siege. Rescue had not come a minute too
early, for there had been serious talk of removing the Deputy
Governor to add to the hostages held at La Roquette. The building
itself was undamaged, as was the nearby Bibliothèque Nationale,
which the retreating Communards had fortunately not had time to
burn. In the markets of Les Halles, a bitter fight had gone on around
the Church of St.-Eustache, converted into a Red Club, which the
Communards had fortified with cannon and *mitrailleuses*. The way
was now open to the Hôtel de Ville, the red-hot ruins of which were
occupied at 9 p.m. that night. Delescluze, the remnants of the Committee of Public Safety, and the Comité Central all converged on the
Mairie of the 11th *Arrondissement*, half-way up the Boulevard
Voltaire, which became the temporary seat of the Commune. There
Delescluze addressed the survivors, in a voice little stronger than a
whisper: 'I propose that the members of the Commune, wearing
their sashes, should parade all the battalions that can be mustered, on
the Boulevard Voltaire. We can then lead them to the points that
have to be reconquered.'

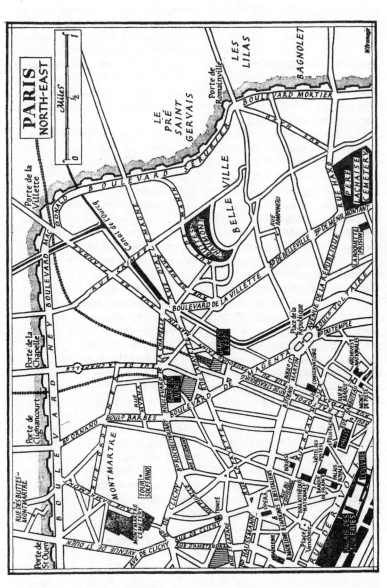

MAP 5.   Paris: north-east

Only the eastern part of Paris still remained in the hands of the Commune; but it would henceforth be fighting on home ground, surrounded by a sympathetic population. Elsewhere, in the parts of Paris already captured by the Government troops, Colonel Stanley was astounded to note the first little signs of life returning to normal; outside his hotel in the Rue de la Paix an 'active Frenchwoman had swept the pavement and door clear of rubbish'. That same day he was taken to see Pyat's house, where he found only the sabre and greatcoat of the vanished leader.

On Thursday the 25th, the fourth day of operations in Paris, MacMahon's plans were for Cissey to attack the Butte-aux-Cailles; Vinoy the Bastille; Clinchant and Douay the Château d'Eau area near the Gare de l'Est.[1] With the 101st Battalion, which had proved itself probably the Commune's most impressive fighting unit, Wroblewski was still holding the Butte-aux-Cailles, despite fresh orders from Delescluze to fall back on the 11th *Arrondissement*. One by one the supporting forts had fallen or been abandoned, the survivors of their garrisons trickling back to join Wroblewski on his hilltop. From dawn Cissey began hammering away at the narrow perimeter with a powerful concentration of fifty cannon. All morning the bombardment continued. Still Wroblewski held out; there was something about his stand that evokes the suicidal courage of the Warsaw uprising of 1944. Realizing by mid-afternoon that the enemy pincers were about to close behind him, he decided to carry out a fighting withdrawal through the Left Bank and across the river. As the remnants of the 101st pulled out, another tragic and senseless crime took place, for which it seems Wroblewski could probably not be held directly responsible. At Battalion H.Q. were held a score of Dominican monks, arrested by Rigault during his round-up of the priests. An officer now came to tell them that they were free to go, but as the bemused monks walked out of the building, they were shot down, one after the other, by some National Guardsmen, enraged at the summary execution of their comrades who had surrendered.

Miraculously Wroblewski reached the Pont d'Austerlitz, nearly a mile and a half away, and crossed into safe territory. With the handful of survivors that remained to him, he reported to Delescluze at the Mairie of the 11th. Delescluze offered him the over-all command of what remained of the Commune forces. 'Have you got several thousand resolute men?' inquired Wroblewski. Delescluze, having that morning inspected the troops in hand, replied 'at most several hundred'. Wroblewski decided he could not accept the responsibility of command in these conditions, and demanded to be allowed to

[1] The Place du Château d'Eau is now the Place de la République.

fight on as 'a simple soldier'. Picking up a rifle he disappeared towards the barricades.

One by one the leaders of the Commune were falling. From the barricades defending the Bastille, a wounded Frankel came back supported by Elizabeth Dimitrieff, herself wounded. Lisbonne fell with a bad wound, later resulting in an amputation. 'Burner' Brunel, who had continued to fight tenaciously ever since his stand at the Concorde and was now covering the Château d'Eau district at the head of a 'Youth Battalion', was crippled by a bullet through the thigh. Loyally his young boys bore him off to a place of safety at the rear. All that day Delescluze, looking more than ever like a man under imminent sentence of death, had hurried from barricade to barricade, supervising, encouraging, exhorting. But with the overwhelming pressure that the vastly superior Versailles forces were now bringing to bear he knew that it was only a question of time before any pretence of a co-ordinated defence came to an end, and the Communards were split up into isolated packets. He sat down to write a last letter to his sister;

Ma bonne soeur,

I do not wish, and am unable, to act as the victim and the toy of a victorious reaction. Forgive me for departing before you, you who have sacrificed your life for me. But I no longer feel I possess the courage to submit to another defeat, after so many others. I embrace you a thousand times with all my love. Your memory will be the last that will visit my thoughts before going to rest. . . . Adieu, adieu. . . .

Shortly before 7 p.m. that evening, Lissagaray saw Delescluze—dressed as always like an 1848 revolutionary in a top hat, lovingly polished boots, black trousers, and frock coat, a red sash around his waist, and leaning heavily on a cane—move off towards the Château d'Eau with some fifty men. Just before reaching the barricade across the Boulevard Voltaire, Delescluze met Pyat's old enemy, Vermorel, who had been mortally wounded. After gripping his hand and saying a few words of farewell, Delescluze walked on alone to the already abandoned barricade, some fifty yards further on. Before the eyes of Lissagaray and the detachment he had brought with him Delescluze slowly, painfully clambered up on top of the barricade. He stood there for a moment, silhouetted in the sinking sun; then pitched forward on his face. Four men rushed to pick him up; three of them were shot down too. In the moment of defeat, the old Jacobin had achieved a certain nobility denied to either Louis-Napoleon at Sedan, or Ducrot at the Great Sortie.

The Commune was now leaderless. Under cover of night it abandoned most of the Bastille area and the present Place de la République (then Château d'Eau), retreating back into the womb from which it had sprung—the narrow streets and squalid slums of Belleville. Behind it the Seine still gleamed red with the reflection of burning Paris. After nearly four days of card-playing incarceration with his friends, the Johnsons, Edwin Child had at last been liberated in the Rue Rambuteau. Throughout the previous day they had heard a 'terrible din that never ceased for an instant, not knowing at what moment our own time might arrive'. His grammar deserting him in the heat of the moment, he recorded that on the night preceding the 25th he

did not dare slept upstairs, bombs having fallen upon nearly every house in the *voisinage*. Fortunately part of the *maison* was occupied by a dealer in skins who kindly offered us *asile* (10 women 5 men). Slept upon bearskins almost as well as in my bed, much to the astonishment of the others who could not close their eyes for the sinister whistling of the bombs. Lovely day.

On being liberated the following afternoon, Child's first thought was to discover whether his shop and his lodging, were still safe:

... but had not gone far before I was stopped to work at the pumps, and what a sight met my eyes; destruction everywhere. From the Châtelet to Hôtel de Ville, all was destroyed, not a room left; worked about half an hour, then proceeded on my way. Saw three waggons of dead Communists [*sic*] taken out of *one* yard. ...

Reaching the Rue Scribe, he found the jeweller's shop undamaged. His own rooms appeared to be safe too, although he could not actually enter them as the adjoining houses were still blazing.

At the other end of Paris, after three days of painful waiting, M. Paris had managed to find a carpenter to make coffins for his dead wife and brother-in-law. No hearse was available, but on the 25th a funeral cart had arrived at the door. It already contained three corpses and was due to pick up another three in the same street. As the cemetery was outside the walls and the Versailles authorities were now strictly forbidding any Parisians to leave the city until the work of repression was completed, M. Paris was not allowed to accompany the forlorn little cortège. Situations like this were happening all over Paris as the Commune staggered to its end. At his rooms near the Château d'Eau, Paul Verlaine, the Commune Press chief, who had spent the past few days of battle ignobly toying with the seduction of

Mme Verlaine's maid, was suddenly confronted by Edmond Lepel-letier and another Communard, 'black with dust and powder, who had escaped from a barricade quite close by and were asking me for asylum':

> Naturally, I let them in and began the cremation of trouser belts and the destruction, also by fire, of képis. The metal buttons we threw down the lavatory, and took other precautions against a probable search. There was no longer any question of arms and ammunition; they had discarded those in the street.

The three men then settled down to a hearty meal, and all joined in teasing the pretty maid. That night they heard the approaching sound of MacMahon's *mitrailleuses*, and from the window they watched the deployment of a battalion of the *Vengeurs de Flourens*; 'youths of fifteen or sixteen, clad as light infantrymen of the Imperial Guard, with black-and-green trousers like Zouaves, and a broad white sash; they swaggered, they swaggered too much, but they were killed to the last man, next day, at the barricade of the Pont d'Austerlitz. . . .' At 4 a.m. the next morning, the doorbell rang and Verlaine found his mother, who had spent the whole night traversing Paris from the Batignolles. 'A short time ago, right nearby in the Rue de Poissy, she had witnessed a massacre of "insurgents", man, women and children.'

Friday, May 26th, was a day of savage killings on both sides. It was the day the struggle for Paris changed from a full-scale battle to a mopping-up operation, and it was also the day the rains came. 'Pouring wet day', Edwin Child noted in his meticulous fashion. Seldom can Parisians have greeted rain with quite such rapture. Swiftly it halted the spread of fires which the exhausted Versailles fire-fighters were beginning to get under control. The blaze in the Ministry of Finance was extinguished, and by a very narrow margin indeed the Louvre Museum had been saved. The world sighed with relief. But the rain could not quench the rage and hatred which had built up over the past five days in the hearts of the conquering army, many of them provincials with an instinctive loathing for the Parisian. The Versailles communiqué of the 25th had repeated the grim warning that 'justice will soon receive satisfaction'. Already the commanders in Paris had shown little heed for the various instructions of Thiers and MacMahon—that repression should abide strictly by the law—and Washburne was shocked by one officer he met who claimed to have orders 'to shoot every man taken in arms against the Government'. According to Wickham Hoffman, 'any lieutenant ordered prisoners to be shot as the fancy took him, and no questions were asked'. It was decreed that all windows must be kept closed, the shutters open, and the inhabitants of any house offending these regulations were liable to summary treatment for harbouring snipers. A friend of Wickham Hoffman 'saw a house in the Boulevard Malesherbes visited by a squad of soldiers. They asked the concierge if there were any Communists concealed there. She answered that there was none. They searched the house, and found one. They took him out and shot him, and then shot her.' Little time was wasted in weighing evidence; as Benjamin Wilson, who watched small squads of *Versaillais* search houses for hiding insurgents, noted, 'they were not at all particular as to whom they took, for, as several of them remarked to me, the '*triage*' or sifting could be done at Versailles'.

But a large proportion of the captured Communards were never to reach Versailles, and for a great many others the process of '*triage*' was carried out arbitrarily on the spot. From Montmartre, one of the Rev. Gibson's local preachers reported how he had 'just witnessed the execution of 25 women who were found pouring boiling water upon the heads of the soldiers'. On the morning of the 26th, a left-wing Deputy called Jean-Baptiste Millière was dragged in front of some officers in Cissey's corps who were breakfasting near the Panthéon. Millière was one of the Paris Deputies who had voted in the Assembly against both the peace treaty and the law of Maturities. He had been involved in the October 31st uprising, but had never participated in the Commune and had in fact been one of Clemenceau's associates in his various attempts at conciliation. Cissey's provost, a Major Garcin, declared however that he had read articles written by Millière, and they 'revolted' him; which was enough. Millière was marched off to the Panthéon, forced to kneel down on its steps ('to demand pardon of society for the evil he had done', Garcin explained later), and shot. Nearby, at St.-Sulpice, Dr. Faneau, a twenty-seven-year-old non-Communard, was in charge of a clearing-station full of National Guard wounded. Interrogated by Versailles troops, he explained that he 'only had casualties, whom I have had for a long time'. According to the (somewhat unconvincing) Versailles account, the regulars were then fired at by one of the wounded; they retaliated by killing Dr. Faneau, as well as a number of his casualties. The dispatching of Communard wounded was also corroborated elsewhere by Dr. Powell who noted with distress that, of the few casualties he had managed to save under the appalling conditions at the Beaujon Hospital, 'most of them were shot' when the Government troops arrived.

As more and more thousands of Communard prisoners, or suspects, fell into Versailles hands, the long dejected columns marching westwards through Paris, guarded by General Gallifet's cavalry, became a saddeningly common sight. Walking in Passy on the 26th, Goncourt encountered one batch of 'four hundred and seven, including sixty-six women':

The men had been split up into lines of seven or eight and tied to each other with string that cut into their wrists. They were just as they had been captured, most of them without hats or caps, and with their hair plastered down on their foreheads and faces by the fine rain that had been falling ever since this morning. There were men of the people there who had made themselves head coverings out of blue check handkerchiefs. Others, drenched to the skin by the rain, were carrying a hunk of bread. They came from every class of society; hard-faced workmen, bourgeois in socialist hats, National Guards who had not had time to change out of their uniforms. . . .

There was the same variety among the women. There were women wearing kerchiefs next to women in silk gowns. I noticed housewives, working girls, and prostitutes, one of whom was wearing the uniform of a National Guard. And in the midst of them all there stood out the bestial head of a creature whose face was half-covered with an enormous bruise. Not one of these women showed the apathetic resignation of the men. . . .

Goncourt was moved to pity, and admiration, by one of the women,

. . . who was singularly beautiful, with the implacable beauty of a young Fate. She was a girl with dark, curly hair, steely eyes, and cheekbones red with dried tears. She stood frozen as it were in a defiant posture, hurling insults at officers and men from a throat and lips so contracted by anger that they were unable to form sounds or words. . . . 'She's just like the girl who stabbed Barbier!' a young officer said to one of his friends.

Some of the women tried to protect their heads from the beating rain with their skirts. As the column prepared to move off, a colonel took up a position on its flank and shouted in a high voice with a brutality that Goncourt felt was affected to create terror:

'For any man who lets go of his neighbour's arm, it's death!' And that terrible *'it's death'* recurs four or five times in his brief speech; during which one heard the sharp sound of the escorts loading their rifles.

To Dr. Powell, the sight of the first convoy of about a thousand prisoners setting off on foot for Versailles was something 'I can never forget'. It extended:

from the Place de la Concorde to the Round Point of the Champs Élysées, nearly a quarter of a mile, rather more, and consisted of old men, women, girls and boys . . . some nearly in rags, and all being urged on by squadrons of cavalry—how they ever got to Versailles is a mystery, some must have

died on the way, or fainted and there were no ambulance carts following . . . near the Tour St.-Jacques I saw a procession coming along of
soldiers escorting two young men, who were being hissed by the crowd,
and suddenly the soldiers knocked them down with the butt-end of their
rifles and dispatched them by letting off a pistol placed in their ears.

As the prisoners passed through the anti-Communard parts of Paris,
it was often all the guards could do to prevent them from being torn
to pieces by enraged crowds. The British and the Americans in Paris
were particularly outraged by what they saw. 'The cowardly way the
Paris mob hoot after prisoners', thought Colonel Stanley, 'is simply
disgusting, but one must bear in mind that their houses are half burnt
down.' What impressed itself most strongly upon him was the
brutality of the women; more than once he tried to restrain them in
their savagery, and there were many others in Paris during that week
who came to agree with Voltaire's famous aphorism that the Parisienne
was composed of 'half tiger and half monkey'. One future Ambassador
of France never forgot the state of the wretched prisoners as they left
Paris; 'some of them bleeding, their ears torn off, their faces and
necks gashed as though by the claws of wild animals'.

The main burden of escorting the Communard prisoners to
Versailles fell to the cavalry commanded by General the Marquis de
Gallifet. The hero of Sedan, the sparkling gallant of Second Empire
days who had so shocked Lillie Moulton with the details of his
wounds, the man who had studied how to treat 'irregulars' under
Bazaine in Mexico, now established for himself a reputation for
ferocity that Paris would never forget. Out at the Porte de la Muette,
on the edge of the Bois de Boulogne, he set up his headquarters
whence he operated a private 'sifting' process of his own. 'I am
Gallifet', he told prisoners as they arrived; 'You people of Montmartre may think me cruel, but I am even crueller than you can
imagine.' A *Daily News* contributor who watched the General at work
confirmed that he was not making an idle boast. Walking slowly
along the halted ranks, and eyeing the prisoners 'as if at an inspection', Gallifet 'stopped here and there, tapping a man on the shoulder,
or beckoning him out of the rear ranks. In most cases, without further
parley, the individual thus selected was marched out into the centre
of the road, where a small supplementary column was thus soon
formed. The selected evidently knew too well that their last hour was
come, and it was fearfully interesting to see their different de-
meanours. . . .' One wretched woman picked out by Gallifet 'threw
herself on her knees, and with outstretched arms implored mercy,
and protested her innocence in passionate terms'. Gallifet's impassive
response was to gain enduring fame; 'Madame, I have frequented

every theatre in Paris; your acting will have no effect on me.' The basis of Gallifet's selection was apparently simplicity itself; men with grey hair were ordered to step forward, on the assumption that they must also have fought at the barricades of '48; those with watches were picked out as probable 'officials' of the Commune; while the balance was made up of unfortunates suffering from outstanding ugliness or coarseness of feature. Needless to say, any Communard found to have been a former member of the regular Army was automatically shot.

Just how many hundreds of Communards were thus 'purified' in the Bois de Boulogne by General Gallifet, on their way to Versailles, will never precisely be known. Of those who avoided the general's attention, still many of the weaker ones—as Dr. Powell had predicted —never reached Versailles. Stragglers received little mercy. In a column of prisoners at Montmartre, Benjamin Wilson noticed one woman, who 'unable or unwilling to advance any further sat down by the road side on which she was at once shot by one of the escort and her body placed within a *porte-cochère* next door to a music seller's'. He added, 'I have since heard that she was an Englishwoman.' There could hardly have been a more atrocious act than the one witnessed by Alphonse Daudet on the Avenue de Clichy:

A large man, a true southerner, sweating, panting, had difficulty in keeping up. Two cavalrymen came up, attached tethers to each of his arms, around his body, and galloped. The man tries to run, but falls; he is dragged, a mass of bleeding flesh that emits a croaking sound; murmurs of pity from the crowd: 'shoot him, and have done!' One of the troopers halts his horse, comes up and fires his carbine into the moaning and kicking parcel of meat. He is not dead . . . the other trooper jumps from his horse, fires again. This time, that's it. . . .

Stanley, in front of whom the cavalry had repeatedly struck at stragglers, 'and not with the flat of their sabres either', was appalled when his friend Wingfield told him of an old couple he had spotted among the prisoners, unable to walk very well:

The woman was a cripple. She said 'Shoot me; I cannot walk any further.' The husband stood by her. They were shot down after thirty shots of revolvers. I am glad I did not see it; I think I should have been ill. They are a cowardly race, these French. . . .

Stanley had just about had enough. He was disgusted by all he had seen and experienced in *la ville lumière*; in his own frank admission, 'frightened at noting that my nerves are giving way'. On the afternoon of the 26th, he packed up and departed for England. In one of his last letters home, he wrote: 'Five thousand people have been shot (after being made prisoners) today. They are digging deep trenches. . . .' but as a final note of hope he added, 'I really think a re-action has set in'. He was wrong. The killing still had a long way to go.

*   *   *

During the 26th, the Prussians had obligingly moved up 10,000 troops behind the Communards' rear, to seal off their line of escape eastwards; also neutralizing their last remaining fortress at Vincennes. But, despite the hoplessness of the Commune's predicament, that day MacMahon in fact made less territorial progress than on any other. By the evening he held the Commune in a semicircle, stretching from the Ourcq Canal in the working-class district of La Villette in the north, down along the Boulevard Voltaire, to the Porte de Vincennes at the eastern extremity of Paris. Within this semicircle, the only *arrondissement* still wholly in Commune hands was the 20th, embracing Belleville and Ménilmontant. Here the Communards were truly at home. As at Warsaw and Leningrad in the Second World War, a whole population was now fighting. Every man, woman, child in the district was ready to serve and die on the barricades. The honeycomb of dingy narrow streets and tortuous alleyways, untouched by the reforming hand of Haussmann, made it ideal terrain for a last-ditch stand. Barricades here were not so easy to turn as they had been on the *grands boulevards*. Also, on the prominent features of the Buttes-Chaumont and the famous Père-Lachaise cemetery there was artillery, which, though greatly inferior to MacMahon's, still possessed a strong nuisance value. But, above all, the defenders—knowing that they could now expect no quarter—were fighting with all the despair of trapped animals. At Belleville, an English medical student observed in admiration the performance of a woman's battalion (probably Louise Michel's); 'they fought like devils, far better than the men; and I had the pain of seeing fifty-two shot down, even when they had been surrounded by the troops, and disarmed. I saw about sixty men shot at the same time.' He overheard one woman, taken alive and accused of having killed two of the attackers, tell her interrogators that she had two sons killed at Neuilly, two at Issy, and that her husband had died at the barricade she had been defending. She too was put to death forthwith.

Despair, coupled with the Communards' fury at fresh reports of atrocities being committed by the Government forces, had placed the lives of the hostages still remaining inside Commune prisons in the gravest jeopardy. That morning a posse of five National Guards had forced their way into La Roquette and at pistol-point ordered Governor François to hand over Jecker, the Swiss banker whose financial manipulations were reputed to have been among the causes of Louis-Napoleon's disastrous Mexican adventure. Jecker was led into an alleyway off Père-Lachaise, called Rue de Chine; there he was shot and left in a ditch, a note with his name scribbled on it pinned to his hat. It so happened that Émile Gois, president of one of Rigault's 'courts', and now presumably the next in succession to the dead *Procureur*, was lunching nearby and was drawn to the scene of the execution by the shots. Gois was piqued to learn that 'justice' should have been carried out behind his back, and determined not to be outdone. Commandeering from Eudes a squad of his *Enfants Perdus*, Gois now marched to La Roquette himself and ordered a thoroughly frightened François to hand over fifty hostages. These included thirty-six gendarmes, most of whom had been under arrest since March 18th, ten priests, and four assorted civilians—loosely described as Imperial 'police spies'. Accompanied by a mob as vicious and blood-lusting as any that was rending the columns of captured Communards, the hostages were taken to the Mairie of the 20th *Arrondissement*. Here Ranvier, the Mayor of Belleville, had set up what passed for the Commune's last headquarters following the death of Delescluze. Varlin pleaded forcefully against resorting to any desperate measures, while Ranvier feebly washed his hands of the whole business. In any case, the surviving remnants of the Commune legislature no longer exercised much power over its last fanatical adherents. The final, and greatest, killing carried out under the reign of the Commune, as at the beginning when the two generals were lynched and at every other crime since, did not recive the official stamp of the Commune as a body.

Gois and his fifty hostages marched on, still trailed by their terrible escort of drunk and jeering rabble, clamouring for immediate carnage. At the top of a long hill approached by what is now the Avenue Gambetta, they stopped in the Rue Haxo. Here they were so close to the city walls that they could hear snatches of waltz music being played on German accordions, a few hundred yards away beyond the wall. Again Varlin attempted to intercede on behalf of the hostages, and but for his popularity might well have shared their fate, such was the mood of the mob. In a small courtyard the massacre took place, hideous in its disorganized butchery. There was no co-ordinated execution-squad. Anyone who had a weapon appears to have fired it into the huddled group of priests and gendarmes. Several of Eudes's *Enfants Perdus* were themselves wounded in the haphazard volleys, and when the killing was done fifty-one corpses—not fifty—were picked up. 'Definitely one too many', Gois was said to have re-marked mildly. The supernumerary victim was probably a National

Guardsman who came too close; as it was, one body was later dis-covered to have been hit by sixty-nine bullets in the fury of the moment, another to have received some seventy bayonet thrusts.

Saturday the 27th opened on another gloomy day of torrential rain. At La Roquette Prison it matched the misery and terror that now existed in the hearts of the remaining hostages. Since Gois had marched off fifty of their fellows the previous day, the survivors had few illusions about the fate in store for them. It seemed but a matter of time; and yet, how tantalizingly close sounded the guns of Mac-Mahon's troops! The arrival of the dreaded Ferré on the morning of the 27th increased the hostages' sense of despair. According to one of them, the Abbé Lamazou, Ferré 'rushed and sprang about like a panther afraid of losing its prey', with a revolver in one hand and a rifle slung from his shoulder. But events at the front seem to have distracted him from his quarry, and for the rest of the morning the hostages were left alone. At 3 p.m. in the afternoon, the Abbé Lamazou heard the bolts of his cell drawn back. He thought that his hour had come. In fact, by what seemed almost a miracle, freedom, not death, was in attendance outside. One of the warders, a man named Pinet, had received orders to let the prisoners out in twos for immediate execution. The killings of the recent days, however, had sickened him; he had had enough. He now hurriedly released all the hostages—some ten priests, forty gendarmes, and about eighty cap-tured regulars—and urged them to barricade themselves within the prison. After the mental agonies to which they had been subjected, many of the hostages distrusted Pinet, reckoning that this was some kind of insidious trap. Eventually they were persuaded by him, and frantically began creating barricades out of the iron bedsteads and ripped-up floor-boards.

Later in the afternoon an execution-squad of National Guardsmen arrived. Unable to force an entry, they tried to smoke out the prisoners with burning mattresses. But the hostages fought back with a despair only equalled by the Communards dying on the last barricades outside. A few priests lost their heads and tried to run for it; they were instantly shot down. Meanwhile, the Communards' own position was becoming desperate. Ranvier had issued what was to be the Commune's last proclamation, its 395th: 'Citizens of the XXth *Arrondissement*, if we yield you know what fate is in store for us! To arms! Vigilance, especially at night! I ask you to carry out orders loyally. . . . Forward! Long live the Republic!' At 11 that morning a small group of all that remained of Commune leadership collected in the Mairie of the 20th. Jules Allix, more lunatic than ever, arrived beaming with pleasure at a plan he had evolved to launch a counter-attack into the central districts of Paris, now emptied of Versailles troops, and thus take the enemy from the rear. The vapidity of the discussion made it seem just like old times at the Hôtel de Ville, until Ranvier appeared. With a brusque command of 'Go and fight instead of arguing!', he dispatched all available hands to the Buttes-Chaumont. It was, noted Lissagaray, 'the last encounter of these perpetual deliberators'. The Commune's strongest remaining position at the Buttes-Chaumont was being threatened by MacMahon's final turning manœuvre. Ladmirault had swung down from the north, through the blazing docks and the cattle-market of La Villette, with the aim of driving a wedge between the bastion defences on the city ramparts and the rear of the Buttes-Chaumont. After some progress his advance was checked by desperate resistance. On Ladmirault's right, Clinchant now attacked the formidable Buttes frontally. Through most of the afternoon his men pressed up the steep slopes at bayonet point, suffering heavy losses; the Communards held out until their ammunition was gone, until 10 p.m. that night.

In the centre, where Vinoy had attacked after a massive dawn bombardment, the Communards were less successful. By 4 a.m. the regulars had reached the Père-Lachaise cemetery, the second of the Commune's remaining strongholds. Possessing what is still one of the finest views in all Paris, the vast cemetery dominated all to the west of it; the whole smouldering city seemed to lie at its feet. It was defended by two batteries of guns and some two hundred National Guards. But they were an indisciplined assemblage, and in their habitual carelessness had omitted to poke loopholes or firing-parapets through the thick and high external walls. Vinoy's men had little difficulty in infiltrating round these walls, thus encircling and isolating the cemetery. At 6 a.m. his guns smashed in the main gate from point-blank range, and the infantry surged forward. Their ammunition nearly exhausted, the Commune artillery could not prevent them carrying the barricades that protected the entrance. Amid the massive family vaults of the bourgeoisie and the less imposing tombs of France's famous poets, painters, and musicians a terrible carnage now ensued. Bullets splintered the sanctified white marble, ricocheting off it; blood sullied the pretentious gravestones. From an emplacement just in front of the monument that had been recently erected in memory of Louis-Napoleon's illegitimate half-brother, the Duc de Morny, cannon fired one of the last rounds to leave a Communard gun-barrel. As the merciless hand-to-hand combat drew to its close in this macabre battlefield, the last of the Père Lachaise-defenders was winkled out near Balzac's tomb.

The Mairie of the 20th had become a refuge for untended wounded, hysterical women, and whimpering, terrified children; but even before Père-Lachaise was completely cleared the Versailles troops were pushing on to capture it—the Commune's terminal headquarters. At La Roquette that evening the hostages were still holding out, surrounded by a howling mob. Part of their improvised barricades had been set on fire, and it looked as if the end had come when some National Guards wheeled up two cannon and a mortar. Before they could begin to bombard the prison, however, word came that the enemy had made a breakthrough and were advancing rapidly on La Roquette. The National Guards scattered in panic, but still relief did not come. After the shooting-down of the escapees earlier in the day, no one yet dared emerge from the prison. The hostages spent a night of hideous anxiety, waiting and praying, uncertain as to whether morning would bring rescue—or only a return of the maddened Communard mob. But the life of the Commune was beginning to flicker out. When the 27th came to its close, the Communards had been pressed into a tight quadrilateral, between Père-Lachaise and the Buttes-Chaumont, and astride the boundary of the 19th and 20th *Arrondissements*. Morale was cracking. Despite the draconian treatment they knew they could expect, thousands were laying down their arms. Of the leaders, only Ferré, Varlin, Ranvier, Jourde, and Trinquet were left; they, and a few dispersed handfuls of other loyal followers, fought on.

At Champrosay some fifteen miles outside Paris, Alphonse Daudet who had escaped there on the 25th (to find still written in large Gothic letters above the door '5th Company Boehm, *Feldwebel* and three men') could hear plainly the sounds of the Commune's death agony. Whenever the wind blew from Paris it brought with it 'that rumbling of cannon and *mitrailleuses* . . . shaking the horizon, pitilessly ripping up the rosy mists of morning, upsetting with its storms the beautiful, clear nights of May, those nights of nightingales and crickets'. On the evening of the 27th, the noise had seemed particularly 'desperate', like 'a great ship in distress, furiously firing off its maroons'. The simile reminded him of the wreck of a ship filled with Italian mimes, which he had once seen from Bastia some ten years earlier. He could not help comparing the last moments of the Commune to the drowning of those wretched clowns and harlequins off the rocks of Corsica;

> I felt that the Commune, about to go down, was firing its last distress rockets. At every minute I could see the wreck heave up, the breach in it grow bigger, and then inside I could see the men of the Hôtel de Ville clinging to their stage, and continuing to decree and decree amid all the din of the wind and the tempest. Then one final surge of the sea and the

great ship sank, engulfing its red banners, its golden sashes; its Delegates dressed in judges' robes and generals' uniforms; its gaitered and be-plumed battalions of Amazones; its circus soldiers rigged up in Spanish képis and Garibaldian caps; its Polish lancers and fantastic Turcos, furiously drunk, singing and whirling about. . . .

The next morning, May 28th, Thiers's army moved in for the kill. It was Whit Sunday. For a whole week the Commune had fought back against enormous odds, but now it was the end. As the sun came up, the besieged hostages in La Roquette were horrified to see fighting recommence outside, but at 5.30 a.m. Government Marines took possession of the building. Even then some of the priests, half-crazed with the mental anguish of the past weeks, refused to believe that the Marines were not Communards in disguise, and could hardly be persuaded to leave the prison. By 10 a.m. the last survivors of the Commune, led by Varlin, were hemmed into a tiny square fragment of Paris. As the morning ended, there was only one barricade left in Belleville's Rue Ramponneau. Here, for a quarter of an hour, a solitary unknown defender was seen to hold off the attackers with a cool and deadly aim. Having fired what appeared to be his last cartridge, he walked calmly away and disappeared. Some 2,000 Communards surrendered in the Rue Haxo alone, and the leaders still surviving tried to make their escape as best they could. Varlin, who had fought to the very last moment, got as far as the Rue Lafayette when he was recognized by a *Versaillais* officer. His hands were bound behind his back and he was marched up to Montmartre, beaten with rifle butts all along the way, and half-lynched by jeering crowds of Parisians. By the time he reached the sinister Rue des Rosiers, which had become a regular 'expiation' centre, his face was a pulp and one eye was dangling out of its socket. No longer able to stand, he was carried out into the garden, to be shot seated in a chair. When the collapse came Louise Michel sought refuge with a friend, then went in search of her mother. Learning that she had been seized by the *Versaillais* as a pawn for Louise herself, and that her life was in imminent danger, Louise gave herself up. She was marched out to Versailles to await trial.

That afternoon Edwin Child read a proclamation by Marshal MacMahon, addressed to the 'Inhabitants of Paris':

The Army of France has come to save you. Paris is delivered.[1] At four o'clock our soldiers captured the last position occupied by the insurgents. Today the struggle is ended; order, work, and security will be reborn.

[1] Beyond the city walls, at Vincennes, a Communard detachment did in fact hold out inside the fortress until Monday (May 29th). On its surrender nine out of its twenty-four officers were promptly shot, on what is one of France's best-known execution-grounds, close to the spot where the Duc d'Enghien was executed in 1804, and Mata Hari in 1917.

The whole operation, including the preliminaries from April 3rd onwards, had cost the Government forces 83 officers and 790 men killed. In the fighting of 'Bloody Week' alone the Communards had lost somewhere over 3,000 in dead and wounded. But it was only a beginning. At Père-Lachaise cemetery Vinoy's troops had found the unburied corpse of the murdered Archbishop. That Whitsun morning they marched 147 of the captured Communards out to the cemetery, lined them up against a wall in its eastern corner, and mowed them down.

When the last of the Communards had surrendered, the 'expiation' promised by Thiers began in earnest. The insurgents were given forty-eight hours in which to surrender all weapons; for Parisians found with any in their possession after that, justice was summary. Society clamoured for merciless measures. Wrote *Le Figaro*, 'Never has such an opportunity presented itself for curing Paris of the moral gangrene that has been consuming it for the past twenty years. The Parisians must submit to the laws of war, however terrible they may be. Today, clemency equals lunacy. . . .' Little exhortation was needed. Dr. Jules Rafinesque wrote to his brother-in-law, Louis Hack, in England that—in the emotional atmosphere prevailing at the end of May—not 'a single young girl has been upset by the sight of people shot up against a wall, summarily and justly. Everyone had wanted to kill a scoundrel, and for the time being the statue of Pity has her face covered with a very thick veil.' The mood was catching; even a young Englishman, Edward Noble, who had spent most of the past week under his bed, commented on hearing that five hundred prisoners had been shot down by *mitrailleuses*: 'That is the only way to deal with these wretches.' There was a positive orgy of denunciations, more than 350,000 of which were received by the authorities within the first fortnight of June. As was to happen again after the liberation of France in 1944, many denunciations proved to have a lamentable element of personal revenge. The shibboleths applied to suspects as the Commune collapsed were crudely simple; a discoloration of the right shoulder that might have been caused by a rifle butt, or the wearing of a pair of Army boots—these were enough. But the favourite one, the hand test, was simplicity itself. Anyone with blackened hands was assumed either to have been involved in incendiary operations, or to have been firing a *tabatière* rifle which had a habit of leaving tell-tale powder stains. One well-known French writer told the author how his grandmother, longing with all the instincts of a houseproud Frenchwoman to get her home in the Rue St.-Honoré cleaned up after the long months of neglect, employed a chimney-sweep even before the fighting at the far end of Paris had actually ended. As the soot-stained sweep left, before her horrified eyes he was seized by the Versailles troops, hands examined, put up against a wall close to where the elegant shop of Hermès now stands, and shot. It was a memory that haunted her throughout her life.

How many innocents like the wretched sweep perished during the first hysterical days of repression can only be guessed at from the numbers of Communard 'leaders' falsely reported to have met their end. A man denounced by a crowd as Billioray promptly had his brains blown out by a Versailles patrol, and was even sketched in death by a passing artist; the real Billioray was arrested a short time later, and the victim turned out to be an unfortunate hosier called Constant. At one time or other Cluseret, Vallès, Ferré, Longuet, Gambon, Lefrançais, Ulysse Parent, and Courbet were all said by *Le Figaro* to have been executed; in fact none of them had been. The death of Jules Vallès (who had already escaped across the frontier) was reported no less than three times, and one British correspondent claimed to have seen both Vallès and Longuet shot, having been seized at a barricade. Karl Marx heard one or two versions of how 'Burner' Brunel also had been shot, with his mistress, in the Place Vendôme; but Brunel too was well on his way to the enjoyment of a ripe old age in England.

The savage, incidental killings continued for some days still in the streets of Paris; one of the Rev. Gibson's preachers was horrified to see some wretch 'coolly pricked to death by a soldier, and then lifted up on the point of the bayonet for the inspection of the lookers-on. No sympathy was evinced for the poor old man, and two ladies (?) suggested that the soldier should "chop the rat's head off!" ' But it was behind the austere walls of the prisons and temporary detention-centres that the real work of repression was carried out. For the mass shootings, cemeteries like Montparnasse, parks normally frequented by Parisians on their Sunday-afternoon walks like the Parc Monceau and the beautiful Jardin du Luxembourg, and Army barracks like the Casernes Lobau near the Hôtel de Ville, and even the railway stations, were employed. As Goncourt was walking past the Lobau on the 28th, a squad of twenty-six prisoners was marched in through the gates which slammed heavily behind them. Goncourt claimed to have no idea what was about to happen, until he heard a 'bourgeois', who had been phlegmatically counting the prisoners, remark to his neighbour:

'It won't be long, you'll soon hear the first rattle.'
'What rattle ?'
'Well, they're going to shoot them!'
Almost at that same moment there was an explosion, like a violent noise enclosed within those gates and walls, a fusillade, with something

of the mechnical regularity of a *mitrailleuse*. There was a first, a second, a third, a fourth, a fifth murderous *rrarra*—then a long interval—and yet a sixth, and finally two rattles coming closely upon each other. . . .

A few minutes later, the gates were opened

and while two closed waggons entered the courtyard, there slipped out a priest whom one could see for a long time, moving along the outside of the barrack wall, with his thin back, umbrella, and legs unused to walking.

Maxime Vuillaume, himself a captured Communard, provides a terrible, unforgettable picture of prisoners 'queuing-up' to be shot in sixes in the Luxembourg. All over Paris the shots echoed out incessantly for several days more; La Roquette, with such grim memories for the hostages of the Commune, some 1,900 prisoners are said to have been shot in two days, and at the Mazas Prison another 400.[1]

The blood shed during these ferocious days of repression somehow even found its way into the Seine; wrote *La Petite Presse* (one of the papers suppressed by the Commune), 'yesterday one could see on the Seine a long streak of blood following the current passing under the second arch on the side of the Tuileries. . . .' All night the waggons clattered through the streets, occupied in the gruesome task of disposing of the corpses. At the forts outside Paris and up at the Buttes-Chaumont huge funeral pyres were built, polluting the air for days on end with the hideous smell of burning flesh. Many of the executed men were hastily buried beneath levelled barricades, and the Rev. Gibson was not the only person to be shocked on returning to Paris by the knowledge 'that there are dead men underneath the newly-laid road. . . .' So hasty was the liquidation and disposal of the captives that terrible stories (apparently not without foundation) went the rounds of men buried while still alive; of arms appearing out of shallow-dug graves in the Square de la Tour-St.-Jacques.

For those lucky enough actually to reach Versailles, the terror was by no means over. In their thousands the Communards were crammed into 'reception centres' prepared in the stables and the Orangerie at Versailles, and in the nearby military camp of Satory. They were kept short of water, food—and medical attention. A number died of suffocation in the hopelessly crowded atmosphere. Here too the shootings went on. Camp Satory, where Communard women and children slept in the open on ground that had become a clay quagmire, became a favourite outing for the ladies of Versailles, come to gaze

---

[1] By comparison, the total executions carried out under the Commune numbered under 500.

at the strange wild beasts held within. Not until the next century would Europe see human beings confined in such squalor; or their sufferings viewed with so little humanity. Only as the threat of widespread disease manifested itself were the inmates gradually combed out and dispersed among various fortresses and hulks throughout France, still to await their trial.

There seemed to be no end to the horror. Abroad it had already aroused bitter comment. There were meetings of protest in London, addressed by John Stuart Mill; and Thiers was not being entirely truthful when he claimed that the British Press 'declared that greater humanity had never been displayed towards greater criminals'. Exclaimed *The Times* on 29 May: 'The laws of war! They are mild and Christian compared with the inhuman laws of revenge under which the Versailles troops have been shooting, bayonetting, ripping up prisoners, women, and children during the last six days. So far as we can recollect there has been nothing like it in history . . .' and two days later:

The French are filling up the darkest page in the book of their own or the world's history. The charge of ruthless cruelty is no longer limited to one party or to one class of persons. The Versailles troops seem inclined to outdo the Communists [*sic*] in their sheer lavishness of human blood . . . They should remember that the blood shed by the Versailles troops cannot be laid at the door of their neighbours; for the Marquis de Gallifet and the other officers who have commanded in Paris are surely French . . .

Finally, on 1 June

Human nature shrinks in horror from the deeds that have been done in Paris. The crimes of the Insurgents have surpassed the most gloomy forebodings of what would be accomplished under the Red Flag. The burning of Paris was diabolical; the shooting of the hostages 'a deed without a name.' But it seems as if we were destined to forget the work of these maddened savages in the spectacle of the vengeance wreaked upon them. The wholesale executions inflicted by the Versailles soldiery, the triumph, the glee, the ribaldry of the 'Party of Order', sicken the soul.

Even France herself was beginning to sicken of the slaughter. There were many who shared Alphonse Daudet's misgiving that the 'Marats' of Versailles were proving themselves still more terrible than those of the Commune. On June 2nd the *Paris-Journal* implored:

Let us kill no more, even murderers and incendiaries! Let us kill no more!

* * *

The work was nearly completed. Estimates on the numbers of Parisians killed in the process of 'expiation' during and after 'Bloody

Week' vary between the grotesquely wild extremes of 6,500 and 40,000. A platform figure is however provided by the French Government's own subsequent revelation that the Municipality of Paris alone paid for the burial or disposal of 17,000 corpses. Reliable French historians today seem more or less agreed on a figure of between 20,000 and 25,000.[1] Whichever set of statistics is accepted, the total is still staggering. No single battle of the Franco-Prussian war cost so many French lives. The blood shed in those relatively few days far exceeded the number of heads that had rolled during the whole Reign of Terror, spread out as it was over more than a year of time, of the Great Revolution.[2] Not even Lenin's October Revolution of 1917 in St. Petersburg (excluding the Civil War which later spread across Russia) would cause quite so many deaths. Yet, what is most difficult for the imagination to grasp is that this dark holocaust took place not in some remote African territory, or by the whim of some long-dead Oriental despot, but amid a recent age perhaps rather more enlightened than our own; and in a city which, only so short a time previously, had regarded itself as *the* Citadel of Civilization. Recalling the extreme reluctance in March of Thiers' army to march on Paris at all, the *semaine sanglante* provided a terrible example of how swiftly a civil, urban conflict can become degraded into such unbridled ferocity.[3]

---

[1] Over 40,000 Communards still remained to be tried, though of these only 23 more would actually be executed.

[2] Just over 2,500, executed by the Paris Revolutionary Tribunal.

[3] In *The War against Paris*, [pp. 107–11, 187] Robert Tombs offers three useful explanations for this savage metamorphosis: first of all the Army saw itself as representing order against the mounting anarchy of the Commune. Predominantly bourgeois, the officers of 1871 feared and hated the Communards' seizure or destruction of private property, culminating in the wilful conflagration of large parts of Paris during the *semaine sanglante*. Secondly, it represented the nation against faction. Thirdly, it held itself to be the champion of liberty against tyranny.

Paris in Ruins: Avenue de la Grande Armée

27. Aftermath

On June 29th, 1871, 120,000 troops of MacMahon's victorious army marched past in review at Longchamp racetrack. It was only a few months since those same fields had echoed to the sounds of Germanic 'Hurrahs' as Kaiser Wilhelm I inspected his armies before they set forth on the triumphal entry into Paris. In the minds of those present on that magnificent June day, the occasion evoked all that had been sweetest and most bitter in the four years that had passed since that other great June review when Louis-Napoleon entertained his guests to the Great Exhibition; but at the same time it seemed to set a seal on events. At 1.30 p.m. Thiers arrived to take up his position in the stand where the ex-Emperor had once stood with the Tsar and the King of Prussia at his side, hastily redecorated to cover the scars left by the first Siege. There was none of the wild cheering that had marked each of the two earlier occasions. As General Gallifet galloped past at the head of his cavalry, foreigners present sensed a particularly uneasy silence. The glitter of the uniforms of 1867 was absent, too. As Thiers explained, the men were 'still not fitted out in new equipment, but in the veritable panoply of war; possessed of a confident air,

419

and proud of having forced the walls of Paris which had halted the Prussians . . .'. At the head of a division marched Ducatel, the civil engineer who had opened the gate at the Point-du-Jour to Mac-Mahon's troops, also honoured with a decoration. After galloping past on a coal-black Arab charger, MacMahon joined Thiers in the presidential box. Silently the two men wept on each other's shoulders. To the few Prussian officers of the army of occupation observing the parade, there was about it a soberly impressive quality which caused them tingles of indefinable apprehension for the future.[1] Thiers described the occasion as according 'the joy of a happy convalescence upon a day of wonderful weather'.

Convalescence! This was indeed the keynote of Thiers's review. France is an astonishingly resilient patient, and now—shamefully defeated, riven by civil war, bankrupted by the German reparation demands and the costs of repairing Paris—she was to amaze the world and alarm her enemies by the speed of her recovery.

The defeat of the Commune meant the loss, once and for all, of Paris's special claim to independence; but it was still the recovery of Paris which set the pace for the convalescence of the country at large. At the end of May, the city presented a terrible sight. In the Place de la Concorde, the Tritons in the fountains were twisted into fantastic shapes; the candelabras torn and bent; the statue of Lille decapitated. Théophile Gautier, returning to a city whose silence oppressed him, was particularly appalled by the Rue de Lille, on the Left Bank, where his colleague Mérimée had once lived; 'it seemed to be deserted throughout its length, like a street of Pompeii'. Of Mérimée's old house, nothing remained but the walls; his famous library was in ashes. 'A silence of death reigned over these ruins; in the necropolises of Thebes or in the shafts of the Pyramids it was no more profound. No clatter of vehicles, no shouts of children, not even the song of a bird ... an incurable sadness invaded our souls. . . .' But at the Hôtel de Ville, Gautier found a certain Gothick romanticism and beauty about the ruins. The immense heat had imparted to the stone and the metal the most exotic colours; 'All pink and ash-green and the colour of white-hot steel, or turned to shining agate where the stone-work has been burnt by paraffin, it looks like the ruin of an Italian palace . . .', sighed Goncourt. Penetrating to conquered Belleville, he was confronted by 'Empty streets. People drinking in cabarets, mute in a sinister fashion. The appearance of a quarter conquered,

---

[1] In Berlin, just two weeks earlier, a triumphal march had been held at the Brandenburger Tor, when the old Emperor had received the keys of the city from a deputation of white-clad virgins—remarking to his young grandson, the future Wilhelm II, 'This is a day you will never forget.'

but not subjected. . . .' Also touring the ruins, Edwin Child went to see the murdered Archbishop lying in state. As an additional reminder of the horrors only so recently past, other Britons noticed Parisians for a long time walking in the road rather than on the pavements—to avoid any suspicion that they might be *pétroleuses* intent on popping their incendiary packets through basement windows.

Yet more of the city had survived than people thought. The Louvre and its treasures had been saved; but only just. Gautier recalled the irrepressible excitement when the Venus de Milo was brought forth from her hiding-place in the incendiarized *Préfecture de Police*, where by a miracle a burst water-pipe had apparently preserved her. As she was removed from her 'coffin', 'everybody leaned forward avidly to contemplate her. She still smiled, lying there so softly . . . this vague and tender smile, her lips slightly apart as if all the better to breathe in life. . . .' It seemed like a symbol of the return of life to Paris herself. June brought with it many pleasant surprises for private individuals; people, like Louis Péguret's neighbours, reported to have been killed at the barricades or in the repression turned out to be still alive; all the Rafinesques' valuables and Jules's medical notes, which they had evacuated to safe keeping in the Rue de Lille and which they heard had all gone up in flames, also turned out to have been unharmed.

While the last fighting raged overhead, Georges Rouault the painter had been born in a cellar. It seems, now, symbolic of the regeneration of the city. Now life was returning to normal at a remarkable pace. Already by June 2nd, Washburne noted 'a marvellous change . . . the smouldering fires have been extinguished and the tottering walls pulled down'. Worth, the couturier, bought up part of the wreckage of the Tuileries to make sham ruins in his garden, and the work of rebuilding Paris was already beginning. Writing to his father on June 12th, Edwin Child remarked 'in about 6 months and we shall wonder where all the fires took place', and then went on to express annoyance at not receiving a rise of pay in his job. On the 15th, he recorded in his diary 'opened *magasin* for the first time since the siege, but did not see many clients . . . hot sultry day.' For this young Englishman the extraordinary events of the past year, to which he had been so close a witness, were at an end.

It was not long before even the famous façade of Paris was back in place, too. Omnibuses and *fiacres* were plying the streets again, *bateaux-mouches* bustling up and down the Seine. As early as the beginning of June, the enterprising Thomas Cook was sending special excursions to visit the 'ruins' of Paris, and soon a horde of English tourists began to descend; looking for, and finding, the immortal diversions that Paris has to offer. *Polichinelle* was back on the boulevards, and the Rev. Gibson noted in a slightly aggrieved tone that this modern Babylon did not in any way seem 'saddened by the disasters' that had befallen it. For some time the sale of petroleum and all inflammable products was banned, and cafés were required to close by 11 p.m., but on June 3rd the theatres reopened. Although only the previous day Goncourt had complained how dowdy and provincial the Parisians—now flooding back from the country—looked, on June 6th he remarked upon the 'reappearance of the crowds on the Boulevard des Italiens, even on the thoroughfare, deserted only a few days ago. This evening, for the first time, one begins to have difficulty in pushing a way between the lounging men and the women prostituting themselves.' Paris was recuperating fast.

In July 1873, the National Assembly voted the erection of an immense basilica—'in witness of repentance and as a symbol of hope' —to be called the Sacré-Cœur, and to be at Montmartre on the spot where the Commune had broken out in March 1871.[1] But, before the foundation of this great epitaph to the Commune could be laid, there still remained a residue to be disposed of. Justice had to be apportioned among the more than 40,000 prisoners held in Government hands. Twenty-six courts martial were instituted, and the work continued until 1875. The first trial, held in the riding-school close to the Palace of Versailles, began in August. Before it appeared fifteen former members of the Commune and two of the Comité Central. Of them Théophile Ferré and Lullier were condemned to death. Despite the intervention by Victor Hugo, Ferré was executed, but Lullier was subsequently reprieved. Urbain, the author of the 'Hostages' Decree' was sentenced to hard labour for life; Assi, Billioray, Paschal Grousset, and four others, transportation to a fortified place. Jourde, the last Minister of Finance, who had behaved so scrupulously in office that his wife continued to the end as a laundress, and who had made a point of formally handing over to the authorities 9,770 francs of Government moneys that he was carrying on him when arrested, was sentenced to simple transportation.[2] Courbet received a sentence of six months imprisonment, and (if ever there was a case of the punishment fitting the crime) was ordered to pay up 250,000 francs towards the reconstruction of the Vendôme Column. Rather than find this astronomic sum of money, he fled to Switzerland where he spent the remainder of his days.

---

[1] It was not in fact completed until 1919.
[2] Old Beslay, whose compliance with the Marquis de Ploeuc had saved the Bank of France from depredation by the Commune, was never brought to trial, but was quietly led across into Switzerland by a grateful Government.

Many of the trials were held *in absentia*, since quite a remarkable number of the leading Communards had somehow made their getaway abroad. Altogether twenty-three death sentences were carried out; seventy-two death sentences were commuted, including that passed on young Gaston de Costa who was made to wait seven months in the condemned cells before reprieve; 251 were sentenced to forced labour for life; 1,160 to transportation to a fortified place; 3,417 to simple transportation (principally to New Caledonia in the South Pacific, where Berezowski, the young Pole who had shot at the Tsar in 1867, was already doing time), while there were another five thousand lesser sentences passed.

Rochefort, too—the darling of the mob who had eventually taken flight from the Commune—was condemned to lifelong transportation to New Caledonia. In vain he had appealed for assistance to his former chief, Trochu; in whose Government he had served during the first Siege. Among the women, Louise Michel (not brought into court until December 1871), wearing a black veil in mourning for the recently executed Ferré, impressed the court with her defiant spirit, totally devoid of any sense of self-preservation; yes, she had helped in the burning of Paris, because 'I wanted to oppose the Versailles invaders with a barrier of flames'; she wanted to die with her friends, and if you let me live, she cried, 'I shall never cease to cry vengeance'. Her sentence was transportation to a penal colony in Nouméa. But no trial aroused quite so much emotion as that of Rossel, captured on emerging from the hiding-place where he had sought to escape trial by the Commune. Many a patriotic Frenchman identified himself with the brave but misguided Rossel, and at his first trial even the prosecutor was observed to have tears in his eyes as he demanded the death sentence. A campaign was started on Rossel's behalf; the death sentence was annulled and a new trial ordered. But it was Rossel's background as a senior officer in the regular Army, as well as the brash threat he had issued to the would-be captor of Fort Issy, that were his undoing. On October 7th he was tried anew, and in a note scribbled to Rochefort, lodged in an adjacent cell, he wrote: 'MY DEAR NEIGHBOUR, It is death again. I'm beginning to get used to it.' This time there was no reprieve. On November 28th, courageous to the end, Rossel—accompanied by the ice-cold terrorist, Ferré—was led out on to the wind-driven plain of Satory, tied to a post, and shot. The next February saw the execution of three men accused of complicity in the murder of Generals Lecomte and Thomas; in March, one man for the killing of Chaudey. In April, Genton was executed for his part in the shooting of the Archbishop; he was followed that July by Francois, the Governor of La Roquette; and in September by young Lolive and two others involved in the death of the Archbishop (Lolive had already been previously sentenced for lesser offences, but was later overheard blurting out that he had been one of the Archbishop's firing-squad). It was not until June 1874 that the last official executioners did their work; this time shooting a soldier accused of participation in the drowning of Vincenzoni in February 1871.

After spending a long, grim winter in the hulks, over 20,000 of the Communard prisoners were finally acquitted in 1872. But with the killings of the previous year, the banishments and the voluntary exiles of those lucky enough to escape, the face of Paris remained changed in one curious way for some years; half the house-painters, half the plumbers, the tile-layers, shoemakers, and zinc-workers had disappeared. At Belleville there were streets which seemed to be tenanted solely by old women. For some time Parisian industry was hamstrung. There was bitter irony in the fact that, for all the Commune's endeavours of social reform, it was as much its defeat which, by creating such a rarity value among the artisan class, enabled them to obtain better terms of employment.

Following trial, the Communards sentenced to transportation were herded into cattle-trucks for journeys to Cherbourg or Brest often lasting forty-eight hours. Aboard the penal ships, conditions seem to have belonged to the age of Botany Bay. Sometimes prisoners were not allowed on deck for three months on end. Many died of scurvy or heat exhaustion on their way to the South Pacific. Even in their eventual place of exile, life was harsh. Several of the Communards tried to escape, and were drowned or eaten by sharks. Finally Rochefort (who had already tried unsuccessfully to escape from La Rochelle Prison), Jourde, and Paschal Grousset, after a remarkable saga of adventure, managed to escape penniless to Australia. They cabled to Edmond Adam, Trochu's one-time police chief, for funds, and after he and Gambetta organized a popular subscription the fugitives were helped back to Europe, where Rochefort's account of the miseries of transportation moved Frenchmen to plead for an amnesty for the Communards. But it was not until 1880 when, introduced by Gambetta, an amnesty bill was finally adopted.

A quite astonishing number of the leading Communards had nevertheless escaped the trials, the death sentences, and the transportations. Bergeret, condemned to death *in absentia*, fled to Jersey and thence to the United States, where he died in 1905. Cluseret, who was about to be tried by the Commune on the eve of the *Versaillais* entry, took no part in the fighting of 'Bloody Week' but devoted his energies to finding a means of escape. Having been hidden by a priest for several weeks, he left France in clerical disguise and claimed (as an American citizen) protection from the American Minister in Belgium. When this was turned down, he wandered in exile through Switzerland, Turkey, Britain, and the U.S.A.; returning to France after the amnesty to be elected as a (Socialist) Deputy. The beautiful Elizabeth Dimitrieff, wounded in the last days of the Commune, took refuge in Switzerland, then returned to Russia and married an exile to Siberia, where she died. Paul Verlaine (who was not arrested) took increasingly to drink, fell under the spell of Rimbaud in October 1871, and was left by his wife.

Many of the Communards sought exile in London, where they lived in close contact with each other. Longuet and Lafargue each married one of Karl Marx's daughters. Pyat remained there, fulminating, until the amnesty when he returned to France and eventually became a Senator; in 1888 the British Ambassador described seeing him in the Chamber of Deputies 'with a flowing white beard, the image of all that is venerable'. Mounting the tribune he addressed the Chamber as '*Citoyens*', and 'delivered with great seriousness and vehemence a speech which was greeted with convulsions of laughters'. Wroblewski, also condemned to death *in absentia*, managed to get to London on a false passport provided by a fellow Pole; when the amnesty came he too returned to France, to live quietly near Nice. After serving her time on Nouméa, Louise Michel was repatriated to France—a violent anarchist—in 1880. She appeared in court three times more to receive terms of imprisonment for her revolutionary activities, and eventually sought refuge in London where she made a strong impression on a young art student with anarchist leanings, called Augustus John, who recalled how 'a little old lady in black, pointed a denunciatory claw at a Society of mammon worshippers....' She died in 1905, exultant at the news of revolution in Russia. Of all the ex-Communards who migrated to England, probably none had a more surprising career than Brunel, the Burner. Though badly wounded, he slipped through the Versailles net (escaping a death sentence) and four years later found employment on the staff of the Royal Naval College, Dartmouth. There he remained until he died in 1904; the very pillar of respectability, known as 'Mons Brunel' to the cadets whom he taught French—one of whom appears to have been the future King George V.

Another exile in Britain of rather a different kind was the ex-Emperor, Louis-Napoleon, who—on being liberated from Germany —spent the last two unhappy, painful years of his life at Chislehurst, Kent. His Empress, Eugénie, was to survive him by many years, until 1920; long after the last hope of the dynasty, the young Prince Impérial, had perished by a Zulu assegai in South Africa. Louis-

Napoleon's marshal at Sedan, and later the conqueror of Paris, MacMahon succeeded Monsieur Thiers as President of the Third Republic. Ducrot soldiered on, but in 1878 was dismissed from command for expressing 'anti-Republican' views and died four years later. Trochu, having refused both a marshal's baton offered by Thiers as well as the Légion d'Honneur for his services during the first Siege, disappeared—as he had always promised—into total obscurity, to write two verbose volumes of memoirs. In contrast, Victor Hugo managed to remain in the limelight during his declining years; having made Brussels too hot with his noisy intercessions on behalf of the exiled Communards, he retired to Vianden in Luxembourg with a new, eighteen-year-old mistress, Marie Mercier, who is said to have inspired his great work on the Commune, L'Année Térrible. Léon Gambetta continued to be the scourge of the right wing, as well as the voice of true Republicanism, in French politics until a bullet fired by a jealous woman put an end to a brilliant but mercurial temperament on New Year's Eve, 1882. Soon after his return to France, the stormy Rochefort had to flee once again, following the Boulangist attempt to establish a military dictatorship. Back in France at the end of the century, he was to be found telling Queen Victoria, after the Franco-British dispute over Fashoda, not to make her annual visit to Nice, and he lived almost to the eve of the Great War. Goncourt went on writing his *Journal* until twelve days before he died (in 1896), publishing it in instalments—to the dismay of his contemporaries, friends and foes alike. The dreaded Marquis de Gallifet became Minister of War in the regime under which the Dreyfus case exploded.

Of the Britons and Americans who had lived in Paris during L'Année Terrible, Richard Wallace—given a baronetcy for his services in the Siege—was as disillusioned by Thiers's new administration as he had been disgusted by the Commune, and began preparations for moving his incomparable collection of paintings to London; an immeasurable benefit for Britain. On leaving Paris he gave another million francs for the relief of the poor and for the erection of drinking fountains—which still bear his name. In 1890 he died, crippled with rheumatism. Dr. Alan Herbert continued to live in Paris, and was buried in the Clichy Cemetery in 1907; but his pet hen, Una, who survived the first Siege, travelled to England, where she lived to a venerated old age at Thornbury Castle. Edwin Child married four years after the Commune, returned to London to manage a watch shop in London, and eventually came to Stockport in Lancashire as representative of an Amiens hat firm, owned by his friend Johnson with whom he had spent *la semaine sanglante* in refuge. He died, aged eighty-five, the year Hitler came to power. Elihu Washburne remained another six years as American Minister in Paris. Labouchere, the 'Besieged Resident', returned—as noted earlier—to British politics. It was observed by his friends that the Siege had markedly aged him, giving him a somewhat more reverend appearance; and perhaps as a result of what he had seen in Paris, he retained a loathing for jingoism all his life. Like his fellow correspondent, Tommy Bowles also entered politics. Thirty years later, as a veteran Member of Parliament, he cosseted and prompted a nervous young M.P., who had also once been a war correspondent, about to make his maiden speech in the Commons; his name was Winston Churchill.

Once Paris had recovered, France herself was not far behind. After sketching dead Communards at the barricades, Manet was back at Boulogne painting *La Partie de Croquet*. Renoir and Degas came back to find studios in Paris; Monet and Pissarro returned from refuge in London. Suddenly, as if in reaction against the grim drabness and the horrors of the Siege and the Commune, the Impressionists burst forth into a new, passionate, glorious blaze of colour, redolent with the love of simple, ordinary existence. France had come back to life again. Her industry blossomed forth in a new renaissance; this time based on firmer foundations than those that had existed under the Second Empire. To the astonishment of the world, the first demi-milliard of the five milliard francs in reparations that France was to pay Germany were handed over just one month after the collapse of the Commune. The rest followed with a rapidity no European banker would have predicted; by September 1873 the crushing bill had been paid off, and the last German soldier removed from French soil. In 1872 the French Assembly passed the first of the laws designed to restore the efficiency of her humiliated Army; and with it went a new spirit. Already by June 15th, 1871, the Rev. Gibson was writing with gloomy foresight:

> I regret to find that the determination to seek to take their revenge sooner or later on Prussia is again manifesting itself among the Parisians. . . . Alas for France, and alas for the hope of the peace of Europe! . . . Germany, when within the next few years she again encounters France in arms, will find her a very different foe from the France of 1870; and who knows but that before the end of this century there may be a similar triumph in Paris to that which is now being celebrated in Berlin? I vainly hoped that France would feel herself fairly beaten and be willing to accept her inferior position. . . .

Throughout the next forty-three years Frenchmen would ponder in silence Edgar Quinet's remark at the time of the debate on Bismarck's peace terms:

FF

The cession of Alsace-Lorraine, it is war to perpetuity under the mask of peace!
For a nation like France could not possibly accept an 'inferior position' in Europe; nor, in the long run, would it prove acceptable to Europe.

*   *   *

Together and separately, each in its different way, the Siege and the Commune had left the structure of the old world fundamentally altered. Nothing would ever be quite the same. The Franco-Prussian War, of which the Siege of Paris was both its central and climactic feature, upset the whole balance of power as it had existed in Europe since the downfall of the first Napoleon. Englishmen, basking in the late noon sunlight of Victorian splendour and introvertively pre-occupied with liberal experiments, and Americans, still recovering from their own Civil War and about to plunge into the era of Big Business, little reckoned that one day they would both be called in—twice—to redress the balance which Louis-Napoleon and Bismarck had upturned. Because of the chronic and endemic weakness of post-1871 France in relation to her former enemy, the new resurgent Germany was bound sooner or later to be enticed on to further ideas of grandeur; which would ineluctably bring her into conflict with the world's greatest remaining force, British sea-power. On the other hand, France clearly would never herself have the capacity to restore the balance until the powerful industrial areas of Alsace and Lorraine were once more back in her hands; and she could never regain them without calling upon the help of others.

Materially, France herself would recover from the after-effects of war and civil war with astonishing speed. Even the amputation of Alsace–Lorraine might not prove mortal; perhaps, who could tell, there might even come a day when the lost territories would be restored by negotiation ? But far more serious for so proud a nation were the unseen wounds; the shame, the outrageous reversal of fortune, the slur on her virility. The deep insult of the German Emperor being crowned in the palace dedicated 'à toutes les gloires de la France' while Paris was in her death throes was something no people could forget. Soon a new generation would grow up in France; a generation to whom defeat would be unthinkable, and who in the unspeakable mire of Verdun would turn Gambetta's slogan 'résistance à outrance' into a terrible reality. With uncanny accuracy, the Illustrated London News had predicted in December 1870, '. . . it may be that young officers who are now watching the strife will come to the front and renew the race of Marshals'. There was Ferdinand

Foch who would always remember as a teenager the spectacle of Louis-Napoleon dragging himself sick and defeated through Metz; Pétain, then a schoolboy, already dedicating himself to a military career; and Joffre, an apprentice gunner on the fortifications of Paris . . . all would be brought up with but one idea; to expunge the shame, to repurchase the lost glory—whatever the cost. 'Everything was rotten in France.' Thiers had told officers during the war, 'only the army remained clean and honourable' [quoted Horne, *The French Army and Politics*, op cit, p. 14]. Hence what better starting point for a spiritual spring-cleaning than the army? Hand in hand with a wave of piety in the nation, a new mood of dedication ran through the whole army; there followed far-reaching reforms, a new code of discipline—modelled on German success—and new plans to meet the menace of a fresh war against those triumphant Germans. Foch, Pétain and Joffre, they would be old men before the shame was purged, inside that same Hall of Mirrors where the German nobility had huzzahed their Emperor; and the price paid, not just for France but for the whole world, would have been well-nigh unbearable.

The echoes set up by the Commune were of a different kind, and, in terms of historical significance, they have resounded more powerfully even than the long-range effects of the first Siege and of France's defeat at Prussian hands. The social achievements of the Commune during its two brief, turbulent months of existence were minimal; one of its leading reformers, Frankel, rated the ending of night-work in the Paris bakeries as the Commune's single most important contribution. Yet for all the ephemeral, and so often foolish, content of its acts, the image of the Commune would linger long, and potently.

There was one person above all others who was determined that the image of the Commune should not fade. When it first broke out, Karl Marx had had misgivings—in that, as a revolution, it was unlikely to succeed—and these were misgivings to which he returned later in life. But he had swiftly perceived that the real importance of the Commune lay elsewhere; as early as April 17th, when Thiers had just begun to hammer on the doors of Paris, he prophesied to his friend Kugelmann:

The struggle of the working class against the capitalist class and its state has entered upon a new phase with the struggle in Paris. Whatever the immediate results may be, a new point of departure of world-historic importance has been gained.

Out of the fabric of the Commune Marx was to weave social and revolutionary myths of immense portent. Within a matter of days, he had written *The Civil War in France*. Next to the *Communist*

Manifesto, it was probably the most powerful tract Marx ever wrote, as well as being a remarkable *tour de force* of up-to-the-minute journalism. From his listening-post on Haverstock Hill, he got most of the events of the Commune right—plus the reasons for its failure —then distorted the facts for his dialectic purposes. 'After Whit Sunday, 1871', concluded Marx,

... there can be neither peace nor truce possible between the working men of France and the appropriators of their produce ... the battle must break out again and again in ever-growing dimensions. .... And the French working class is only the advance guard of the modern proletariat.

'Working-men's Paris, with its Commune', he predicted, 'will be for ever celebrated as the glorious harbinger of a new society. Its martyrs are enshrined in the great heart of the working class.'

The Civil War in France attracted immediate attention. 'It is making the devil of a noise', Marx wrote to Kugelmann on June 18th, 'and I have the honour to be the best calumniated man in London. That really does one good after a tedious twenty years' idyll in my den.' Marx's whole-hearted support for the Commune split the *International* movement down the centre. On one side the split led indirectly to the birth of the moderate British Labour Party and the German Social Democrats; on the other, to Lenin's extremist Bolshevik party. Overnight Marx ceased to be a still somewhat obscure German-Jewish professor, and achieved universal notoriety as the 'Red Terrorist Doctor'. But he had succeeded in creating a heroic, Socialist legend. He was right about the Commune's 'martyrs'. Still to this day, the *Mur des Fédérés* where the 147 Communard survivors were shot down at Père-Lachaise is a Mecca for mass left-wing pilgrimages every May 28th. Despite the rift caused in the *International* by Marx's pamphlet, the numbers of its branches began to multiply, its strength to grow.

In France, although the defeat of the Commune meant the death also of the 'sacred cause', the independence of Paris, the struggle had achieved one result; there would now be no question of France taking the risk of replacing the Republic by any kind of monarchist restoration. With some justification, the surviving Communards could claim to have 'saved' the Republic. With equal justification, Thiers could say that he had saved France from anarchy. He also claimed, 'we have got rid of Socialism'. He was, of course, totally wrong: history was to prove that the death of the Commune, with all the mythology it left behind, fanned by Marx, was far more important than its life. A deep trench had been dug between the French bourgeoisie and the masses, between the professional army and the Left, so much more profound than that left by the conflict of 1848, and which would stretch on into the far distance, suddenly yawning open to bedevil France at various critical moments in the years ahead.[1] Although the process of social reform and of emancipating the workers was seriously slowed down over the next twenty years (certainly in comparison to developments in Britain and Germany), in fact the crushing of the Commune only postponed the 'arrival' of Socialism in France. When it did arrive, it was to assume a more virulent form than in perhaps any other Western country. For 'Bloody Week' and its martyrs whose memory Marx would not permit to fade injected into French politics rifts not yet bridged today, accompanied by bitterness never paralleled in Britain or the U.S.A. As Colonel Stanley remarked on his last day in Paris, May 25th, 1871: 'What provokes me is that there seems no middle opinion ever expressed.' Nearly a hundred years later, it is still hard to find a 'middle opinion' about the Commune in France. From the 'secession' of the proletariat after May 1871 stemmed the receptiveness, later, of many a French Socialist to conversion to Marxist Communism. From the bitter hostilities engendered in 1871 was to spring the *Front Populaire*, the Socialist–Communist alliance of the 1930's, which so devitalized France; leaving her once again an easy prey to a new German menace—this time in 1940.

But it was through the medium of Vladimir Ilyich Ulyanov, one year old at the time of the Commune and later known as Lenin, that the Commune and Marx's interpretation of it was to have the most cosmic effect. All through his life Lenin studied the Commune; worshipped its heroism, analysed its successes, criticized its faults, and compared its failures with the failure of the abortive Russian revolution of 1905. In his mind, two mistakes committed by the Commune stood out above all others; as he declared in an often quoted article written on the anniversary of March 18th, in 1908:

---

[1] One immediate legacy of the nightmare of the Franco-Prussian War and the Commune was to persuade France's political leaders that henceforth the Army would have to be treated with the utmost tender loving care. 'The army had been brought into politics by civil war,' Dr. Tombs writes of its aftermath [Tombs, op cit, p. 200]:

> The extreme Right saw it as a bulwark of society . . . but even with MacMahon as President, the army made no move to stem the tide of Left-wing advance, however much its officers would have liked to try. The lesson of March 18th seems to have been learnt: that the cohesion of the army itself was put at risk by involvement in internal disputes . . . The army had won a military victory in 1871, but had been forced to realise the limits of military victory.

This was to apply for many years to come.

The proletariat stopped half-way; instead of proceeding with the 'expropriation of the expropriators', it was carried away by dreams of establishing supreme justice in the country . . . institutions such as the Bank were not seized. . . . The second error was the unnecessary magnanimity of the proletariat; instead of annihilating its enemies, it endeavoured to exercise moral influence on them; it did not attach the right value to the importance of purely military activity in civil war, and instead of crowning its victory in Paris by a determined advance on Versailles, it hesitated and gave time to the Versailles government to gather its dark forces. . . .

When the moment came for the revolution for which his whole life had been a preparation, Lenin would not repeat the Commune's 'half-measures' and 'unnecessary magnanimity'. There could be no question of accepting, as the Commune had demonstrated, 'the available ready machinery of the State', and adapting it; everything had to be smashed and re-created in a new, proletarian image. To Lenin and his followers, the supreme lesson of the Commune was that the only way to succeed was by total ruthlessness.

On the outbreak of the First World War, Lenin declared (on November 1st, 1914), 'The transformation of the present imperialist war into a civil war is the only effective slogan of the proletariat, indicated by the experience of the Paris Commune. . . .' This was his objective throughout the war. When on the eve of success he was forced to flee briefly to Finland, Marx's *The Civil War in France* was one of the two books he took with him on his final exile. When he returned, it was to impose Communism upon Russia by means of a revolution that never would have succeeded had it not been for the 'dummy run' attempted by Delescluze and his martyrs; and to impose it by resorting to ruthlessness with a flavour that also had its origins in those savage days. Lenin appears to have been constantly obsessed with fears that the October Revolution would go the way of the Commune; each day that it outlived the Commune, he is said to have counted 'Commune plus one'. To ensure that the revolution would not be frittered away by the paralysing squabbles such as had arisen within so feebly democratic a body as the Commune, Lenin split with his more moderate allies, the Mensheviks; then proceeded remorselessly to crush the left-wing Constituent Assembly, until the extreme Bolshevik dictatorship was complete. 'The Commune was lost,' explained Lenin, 'because it compromised and reconciled.' His Red Army commissar, Trotsky, criticized the Commune for not meeting the 'white terror of the bourgeoisie with the red terror of the proletariat', and when civil war broke out in Russia neither Trotsky nor Lenin was backward in the dispensation of terror. How much

of the ferocious brutality with which the Russian Reds fought for
survival was attributable to the ever-present memory of May 1871,
may be judged by the comment in retrospect of an old Bolshevik:

> In those grave moments we said; 'Look, workers, at the example of the
> Paris Communards and know that if we are defeated, our bourgeoisie
> will treat us a hundred times worse.' The example of the Paris Commune
> inspired us and we were victorious.

When Lenin died, his body was appropriately shrouded in a Communard flag, and his mantle passed to Stalin. Stalin once described
the Commune as 'an incomplete and fragile dictatorship', a charge
which he made sure would never be levelled against his tenancy of the
Kremlin. If the course run by the Commune could perhaps be held
responsible for contributing to the oppressively monolithic character
assumed by the Bolshevist regime in Russia, well might one also
speculate as to how much Stalin, when deciding on the wholesale
liquidation of those Communists whose views in any way diverged from
his own, had at the back of his mind the lessons of the destructive
discord created by Pyat and the wranglers at the Hôtel de Ville.

In perhaps the most eloquent epitaph on the Communards ever
uttered by a non-Marxist, Auguste Renoir (who so narrowly escaped
with his life in those days) said of them:

> They were madmen; but they had in them that little flame which
> never dies.

The memory of Louis-Napoleon's glittering masked balls at the
vanished Tuileries has been swallowed up by the mists of the past;
little enough is still recalled about Trochu's spiritless defence of
Paris; and in France even the humiliation at Bismarck's hands is
largely forgotten. But the 'little flame' of the Communards continues
to be kept alight. The link between the brave balloonists of Paris and
the spacemen of ninety-five years later may seem a tenuous one. But
the course of history often flows down strange and unexpected
channels. In 1964, when the first three-man team of Soviet cosmonauts went up in the *Voskhod*, they took with them into space three
sacred relics; a picture of Marx, a picture of Lenin—and a ribbon off
a Communard flag.

Bibliography

Adam, Mme Edmond (pseudonym 'Juliette Lambert'), *Le Siège de Paris. Journal d'une Parisienne*. Paris, 1873.

Allem, Maurice, *La Vie Quotidienne sous le Second Empire*. Paris, 1948.

The Amberley Papers, The Letters and Diaries of Lord and Lady Amberley. Edited by Bertrand and Patricia Russell. London, 1937.

Audebrand, Philibert, *Histoire Intime de la Révolution du 18 Mars*. Paris, 1871.

Baldick, R., *Pages from the Goncourt Journal*. London, 1962.

Bankwitz, Philip C. F., *Maxime Weygand and Civil-Military Relations in Modern France*. Cambridge, Mass., 1967.

Bellanger, Claude; Godechot, Jacques; Guiral, Pierre and Terrou, Fernand (eds.), *Histoire général de la presse Française*. 3 vols. Paris, 1971.

Bennett, Enoch Arnold, *The Old Wives' Tale*. London, 1908.

Berlin, Isaiah, *Karl Marx*. London, 1939.

Blount, Sir Edward, *Memoirs of Sir Edward Blount, 1815–1902*. Edited by S. J. Reid. London, 1902.

Blume, Carl Wilhelm von, *Die Beschiessung von Paris, 1870–71*. Berlin, 1899.

—— *Campaign 1870–1: The Operations of the German Armies in France. From Sedan to the End of the War*. Translated by E. M. Jones. London, 1872.

Blumenthal, Leonard von. *Journals of Field Marshal Count von Blumenthal for 1866 and 1870–71*. Translated by A. D. Gillespie-Addison. Edited by Constantine von Blumenthal. London, 1903.

Bourgin, Georges, *Les Premières Journées de la Commune*. Paris, 1928.

—— *La Guerre de 1870–71 et la Commune*. Paris, 1939.

—— *Histoire de la Commune*. Paris, 1907.

Bowles, Thomson Gibson, *The Defence of Paris*. London, 1871.

Brecht, B., *Die Tage der Commune*. East Berlin, 1957.

Brogan, D. W., *The Development of Modern France, 1870–1939*. London, 1940.

Bruhat, Dautry, and Tersen. *La Commune de 1871*. Prague, 1960.

Brunel, Georges, *Les Ballons au Siège de Paris, 1870–71*. Paris, 1933.

Brunet-Moret, Jean, *Le Général Trochu, 1815–1896*. Paris, 1955.

Brunon, General, B. C., *Siège de Paris, Journal du Fort de Vanves*. Paris, 1887.

Burnand, Robert, *La Vie Quotidienne en France de 1870 à 1900*. Paris, 1947.

Bury, J. P. T., *Gambetta and the National Defence. A Republican Dictatorship in France*. London, 1936.

—— *Gambetta and the Making of the Third Republic*. London, 1973.

Busch, Moritz, *Bismarck in the Franco–German War*. Translated. London, 1879.
—— *Our Chancellor. Sketches for a Historical Picture*. Translated by W. Beatty-Kingston. London, 1884.
Carr, E. H., *Karl Marx: Study in Fanaticism*. London, 1934.
Cassell's History of the War between France and Germany, 1870–71. London, 1894.
Castelot, Henri, *Paris: Turbulent City 1783–1871*. Translated by D. Folliot. London, 1963.
Chastenet, Jacques, *L'Enfance de la Troisième. 1870–1879*. Paris, 1952.
Chevalet, Émile, *Mon Journal pendant le Siège et la Commune. Par un Bourgeois de Paris*. Paris, 1871.
Chevalier, Louis, *Classes laborieuses, Classes dangereuses*. Paris, 1978.
Clarétie, Jules, *Paris Assiégé. Tableaux et Souvenirs*. Paris, 1871.
Clark, T. J., *Image of the People; Gustave Courbet and the 1848 Revolution*. London, 1973.
Cluseret, G.-P., *Mémoires du Général Cluseret*. Paris, 1888.
Cobb, Richard, *Tour de France*. 1976.
Costa, Gaston da, *La Commune Vécue*. Paris, 1903–5.
Craig, Gordon A., *The Politics of the Prussian Army, 1640–1945*. 1968.
Cresson, E., *Cent Jours de Siège à la Préfecture de Police*. Paris, 1901.
Dabit, Eugène, *Faubourgs de Paris*. Paris, 1935.
Daily News, War Correspondence of the Daily News, 1870–71. London, 1871.
Dansette, Adrien, *Origines de la Commune de 1871*. Paris, 1894.
Daudet, Alphonse, *Souvenirs d'un Homme de Lettres*. Paris, 1888.
—— *Notes sur la Vie*. Paris, 1899.
Dayot, Armand, *L'Invasion, le Siège, la Commune. D'après des Peintures, Gravures, &c*. Paris (no date).
Du Camp, Maxime, *Souvenirs d'un Demi-Siècle*. Paris, 1949.
Ducrot, A. A., *La Défense de Paris (1870–1871)*. Paris, 1875–8.
Duveau, Georges, *Le Siège de Paris, Septembre 1870–Janvier 1871*. Paris, 1939.
—— *Le Vie Ouvrière en France sous le Second Empire*. Paris, 1946.
Edwards, H. Sutherland, *The Germans in France*. London, 1874.
Edwards, Stewart, *The Paris Commune*. London, 1971.
Elton, Lord, *The Revolutionary Idea in France, 1789–1871*. London, 1923.
'Englishwoman' (Emma Georgina Elizabeth Ward), *Outside Paris during the Two Sieges*. London, 1871.
Evans, Thomas W., *History of the American Ambulance Establishment in Paris during the Siege of 1870–1871*. London, 1873.
—— *Memoirs: Recollections of the Second French Empire*. Edited by E. A. Crane. London, 1905.
Falk, Bernard, *Old Q.'s Daughter. History of a Strange Family*. London, 1937.
Favre, Jules, *Le Gouvernement de la Défense Nationale*. Paris, 1872.

Flaubert, Gustave, *Letters*. Edited by Richard Rumbold. London, 1950.
—— *The Selected Letters of Gustave Flaubert*. Translated and edited by Francis Steegmuller, London, 1954.
Fleischmann, H., *Les Secrets du Second Empire: Napoleon III et les Femmes*. Paris, 1913.
Fleury, Comte Maurice, and Sonolet, Louis, *La Société du Second Empire. 1867-70*. Paris (no date).
Flourens, Gustave, *Paris Livré*. Paris, 1871.
Fonvielle, Wilfrid de, *Le Siège de Paris vu à Vol d'Oiseau*. Paris, 1895.
Forbes, Archibald, *My Experiences of the War between France and Germany*. London, 1871.
François, L., *Les Correspondences par Ballon Monté du Siège de Paris*. Amiens, 1925.
Franklyn, Henry Bowles, *The Great Battles of 1870 and Blockade of Metz*. London, 1887.
Frederick III, *The War Diary of the Emperor Frederick III, 1870-1871*. London, 1927.
French, Army: État-Major, Section Historique. *La Guerre de 1870-71. L'Investissement de Paris*. Publié par la Revue d'Histoire rédigée à la Section historique de l'État-Major de l'Armée. Paris, 1901-13.
Gaillard, Jeanne, *Commune de Province, Commune de Paris, 1870-1871*. Paris, 1971.
Galliffet, General Gaston de, 'Mes souvenirs', *Journal des Debats*, 19, 22, and 25 July 1902.
Gautereau, A., *Les Défenseurs du Fort d'Issy et le Bombardement de Paris. 1870-71*. Paris, 1901.
Gautier, Théophile, *Tableaux du Siège. Paris 1870-1871*. Paris, 1886.
German Army; *Sammlung der Offiziellen Kriegsdepeschen von 1870-1*. Leipzig, 1896.
—— *The Franco-German War, 1870-1871*. Translated by Capt. F. C. H. Clarke. London, 1854-84.
—— Heft 4. *Die Tätigkeit der Belagerungs-Artillerie vor Paris im Kriege 1870-71*. Berlin, 1884.
Gibson, Rev. W., *Paris during the Commune*. London, 1895.
Goncourt, Edmond and Jules de, *Journal. 1851-95*. Paris, 1887-96.
Gorce, Pierre de la, *Histoire du Second Empire*, Paris, 1896.
Goure, Léon, *The Siege of Leningrad*. Stanford (U.S.A.), 1962.
Grouard, A., *Le Blocus de Paris et la Première Armée de la Loire*. Paris, 1889-94.
Guedalla, Philip, *The Second Empire*. London, 1922.
Guérard, Albert Léon, *Napoleon III*. Cambridge (U.S.A.), 1943.
Guillemin, Henri, *L'Héroïque Défense de Paris*. Paris, 1959.
—— *Cette Curieuse Guerre de Soixante-Dix*. Paris, 1956.
d'Hérisson, Comte Maurice, *Journal of a Staff Officer during the Siege of Paris*. Translation. London, 1885.
Hernu, Charles, *Citoyen-Soldat*. Flammarion, Collection 'Le Poing Rose', Paris, 1977.

d'Heylli, G. (pseudonym for A. E. Poinsot), *Journal du Siège de Paris*. Paris, 1871–4.

Hoffman, Wickham, *Camp, Court and Siege*. New York, 1877.

Hooper, George, *The Campaign of Sedan. The Downfall of the Second Empire, August–September 1870*. London, 1887.

Horne, Alistair, *The French Army and Politics, 1870–1970*. London, 1984.

Howard, Michael, *The Franco-Prussian War*. London, 1961.

Hurst, Michael (ed.), *Key Treaties for the Great Powers 1814–1914*. 2 vols, 1972.

Jackson, Hampden, *Clemenceau and the Third Republic*. London, 1946.

Jellinek, Frank, *The Paris Commune of 1871*. London, 1937.

Jollivet, Gaston, *Le Siège de Paris et la Commune*. Paris, 1928.

Kranzberg, Melvin, *The Siege of Paris, 1870–71. A Political and Social History*. Ithaca, N.Y., 1950.

Kunz, Hermann, *Die Kämpfe der Preussischen Garde um Le Bourget während der Belagerung von Paris*. Berlin, 1891.

Labouchere, Henry, *Diary of the Besieged Resident in Paris*. London, 1871.

Lamazou, Abbé, *The Place Vendôme and la Roquette. The First and Last Acts of the Commune*. Translated by C. F. Audley. London, 1872.

Lanoux, Armand, *Une Histoire de la Commune de Paris*. 3 vols. Paris, 1971.

Laronze, Georges, *Histoire de la Commune de 1871 d'après des documents et des Souvenirs inedits*. Paris, 1928.

Lefèvre, Henri, *La Proclamation de la Commune*. Paris, 1965.

Lenin, V. I., *The State and Revolution*. London, 1919.

Lindencrone, L. de Hegermann, *In the Courts of Memory*. New York, 1912.

Lissagaray, P.-O., *Histoire de la Commune de 1871*. Brussels, 1876.

Loliée, Frédéric, *Les Femmes du Second Empire: La Fête Impériale*. Paris, 1907.

Lowndes, Mrs. Belloc, *'I, too, have lived in Arcadia'. A Record of Love and Childhood*. London, 1941.

Maillard, Fermin, *Les Publications de la Rue pendant le Siège et la Commune*. Paris, 1874.

Mallet, François, *Les Aéronautes, les Colombophiles du Siège de Paris*. Paris, 1909.

Marichy, Jean-Pierre, *Le Système Militaire Français*, Toulouse, 1977.

Marx, Karl, *The Civil War in France*. Introduction by F. Engels. Translated E. B. Bax. London, 1937.

—— *Letters to Doctor Kugelmann. 1862–74*. London, 1934.

Mason, E. S., *The Paris Commune*. London, 1930.

Maurois, André, *Histoire de la France*. Paris, 1947.

—— *Olympio. Ou la vie de Victor Hugo*. Paris, 1954.

Mérimée, Prosper, *Lettres à Panizzi. 1850–1870*. Paris, 1881.

Michel, Louise, *Mémoires*. Paris, 1886.

Michell, E. B., *Siege Life in Paris by One of the Besieged*. London, 1870.

Molinari, Gustave de, *Les Clubs Rouges pendant le Siège de Paris*. Paris, 1871.

Moltke, Helmuth von, *The Franco–German War of 1870–71*. New York, 1892.

Moser, Françoise, *Une Héroine—Louise Michel*. Paris, 1947.

Müller, Hermann von, *The Bombardment of Paris*. Translated. London, 1905.

—— *Die Tätigkeit der Deutschen Festungsartillerie bei den Belagerungen, Beschiessungen und Einschliessungen im deutsch-franzsiöschen Kriege 1870–71*. Berlin, 1899–1904.

Nass, Dr. Lucien, *le Siège de Paris et la Commune. Essais de Pathologie Historique*. Paris, 1914.

Newton, Lord, *Lord Lyons. A Record of British Diplomacy*. London, 1913.

O'Shea, John Augustus. *An Iron-Bound City*. London, 1886.

'Oxford Graduate', *Inside Paris during the Seige*. London, 1871.

Parris, John, *The Lion of Caprera*. London, 1962.

Patry, Léonce, *Le Guerre telle qu'elle est (1870–71); Metz—Armée du Nord—Commune*. Paris, 1907.

Paz, Maurice, 'Le Mythe de la Commune, relations avec les Prussians', *Est et Ouest*, no. 479 (Feb. 1971), 20–4; and no. 485 (March 1972), 22–4.

—— 'Le Mythe de la Commune, les deux reproches majeurs', *Est et Ouest*, no. 482 (Feb. 1972), 23–28.

Peat, Anthony B. North, *Gossip from Paris during the Second Empire. Correspondence (1864–1869)*. Selected and arranged by A. R. Waller. London, 1903.

Perruchot, Henri, *Manet*. London, 1962.

Peyrefitte, Alain, *The Trouble with France*. New York, 1981.

Pinkney, David H., *Napoleon III and the Rebuilding of Paris*. 1972.

Plamenatz, John, *The Revolutionary Movement in France, 1815–71*. London, 1952.

Powell, O. C., *Reminiscences of La Commune and the Second Siege of Paris. March to May 1871*. Privately printed, 1914.

Pratt, S. C., *Saarbruck to Paris 1870*. London, 1904.

Prévost-Paradol, Lucien Anatole, *La France Nouvelle*. Paris, 1868.

Ralston, David B., *The Army of the Republic: the Place of the Military in the Political Evolution of France, 1871–1914*. London, 1967.

Reitlinger, Frédéric, *A Diplomat's Memoir of 1870*. London, 1915.

Remy, Tristan, *La Commune à Montmartre, 23 mai 1871*. 1970.

Rihs, C., *La Commune de Paris, sa Structure et ses Doctrines*. Geneva, 1955.

Roberts, J. M., 'The Myth of the Commune'. Article from *History Today*. London, May, 1957.

—— 'The Paris Commune from the Right', *English Historical Review*, supplement 6. 1973.

Robinson, G. T., *The Fall of Metz*. London, 1871.

Rochefort, Henri, *Les Aventures de ma Vie*. Paris, 1896.

Rossel, Louis, Posthumous Papers. Translated. London, 1872.

Rougerie, Jacques, *Paris Libre 1871*. 1967.

Russell, William Howard, *My Diary during the Last Great War*. London, 1874.

Ryan, Charles E., *With an Ambulance during the French–German War*. London, 1896.

Saint-Edmé, Ernest, *La Science pendant le Siège de Paris*. Paris, 1871.

Sarcey, Francisque, *Le Siège de Paris*. Paris, 1871.

Sheppard, Nathan, *Shut up in Paris*. London, 1871.

Sheridan, Philip Henry, *Personal Memoirs of Philip Henry Sheridan*. London, 1888.

Smith, Charles Harvard Gibbs, *Ballooning*. London, 1948

Thiers, L. Adolphe, *Notes et Souvenirs (1870–1873)*. Paris, 1904.

Thomas, Édith, *Les Pétroleuses*. Paris, 1963.

—— *Rossel, 1844–1871*. Paris, 1967.

—— *Louise Michel*. Canada, 1982.

Thompson, J. M., *Louis Napoleon and the Second Empire*. London, 1954.

Tissandier, Gaston, *En Ballon! pendant le Siège de Paris. Souvenirs d'un Aéronaute, etc*. Paris, 1871.

Tombs, Robert, and Bury J. P. T., *Thiers*. London, 1986.

Tombs, Robert, *The War Against Paris, 1871*. Cambridge, 1981.

Trailles, Paul et Henri de, *Les Femmes de France pendant la Guerre et les Deux Sièges*. Paris, 1872.

Trochu, Louis Jules, *Pour la Vérité & Pour la Justice*. Paris, 1873.

—— *L'Armée Française en 1867*. Paris, 1867.

—— *Œuvres Posthumes*. Tours, 1896.

Verdy du Vernois, Julius von, *Im Grossen Hauptquartier. (With the Royal Headquarters in 1870–1.)* London, 1897.

Verlaine, Paul, *Confessions*. Paris, 1899.

Vésinier, Pierre, *The History of the Commune of Paris*. Translated J. V. Weber. London, 1872.

Victoria, Queen, *Leaves from a Journal*. London, 1961.

Vinoy, Joseph, *Campagne de 1870–1871. Siège de Paris*. Paris, 1872.

Viollet-le-Duc, Eugéne Emmanuel, *Mémoire sur la Défense de Paris 1870–1*. Paris, 1871.

Vizetelly, Henry, *Paris in Peril*. London, 1882.

Vuillaume, Maxime, *Mes Cahiers Rouges*. Paris, 1914.

Washburne, Elihu Benjamin, *Recollections of a Minister to France. 1869–1877*. London, 1877.

—— *The Correspondence of E. B. Washburne*. Washington, 1878.

Weber, Eugene, *Peasants into Frenchmen, the Modernization of Rural France 1870–1914*. London, 1977.

Whitehurst, F. M., *My Private Diary during the Siege of Paris*. London, 1875.

Williams, Roger L., *Gaslight and Shadow: the World of Napoleon III, 1851–70*. New York, 1957.

Zeldin, Theodore, *The Political System of Napoleon III*. London, 1958.

—— *France 1848–1945*. 2 vols. Oxford, 1973–7.

Zola, Émile, *La Débâcle*. Paris, 1892.

Reference Notes

The foregoing bibliography contains the principal published works used either to a greater or lesser extent by the author, but is far from complete. Books on the Commune alone would fill a small library. In addition, and (for reasons of space) not included in the bibliography, a mass of contemporary periodicals, Government reports, *affiches*, and various other documents were consulted; most of which can be found in the Bibliothèque Nationale in Paris. But, as mentioned in the Preface, one of the richest sources of material for this book (at least in the author's opinion) proved to be the unpublished letters, journals, and diaries chiefly provided by the descendants of Britons and Americans in Paris during 1870–1.

Certain sources—both published and unpublished, such as the writings of Washburne, of Goncourt, and of Edwin Child—have been used in almost every chapter. When quoting the Goncourt *Journal*, I have principally relied upon my own translation of the complete works; but I have also made use of the translated abridgement, *Pages from the Goncourt Journal*, by Robert Baldick—to whom I am greatly indebted. As a source, Goncourt was occasionally carried away by his own feelings, sometimes he exaggerates and sometimes bias distorts his vision; but when it comes to supplying the mood of the moment he is in a class by himself. Of the other principal eyewitnesses, I hope my evaluation of their various worths should be clear from the text itself.

For the actual military details of the first Siege as well as the war outside Paris, in addition to the sources specifically listed below and the official archives, I have probably leaned most heavily on Michael Howard, *The Franco-Prussian War*; a book which as an objective study in military history towers above any other recent book on any campaign. As a more contemporary history, I have also drawn extensively on *Cassell's History of the War between France and Germany* (published in 1894,) which covers both the war and the Commune. Provided its biases are taken into account (notably its anti-Communard line), it is a fund of much rich material gleaned from most of the sources available at the time.

For a more sympathetic general treatment of the Commune, Bourgin's large illustrated work, *La Guerre de 1870–71 et la Commune* is valuable. A still more partisan recent work, published in Prague under Communist auspices, is Bruhat, Dautry, and Tersen's *La Commune de 1871*, which is particularly notable for its bibliography and dossiers of the leading Communards contained as appendices, For a reasonably dispassionate account of the political-social content of the Commune, a recent (Swiss) work by C. Rihs is also especially to be recommended.

Over the twenty-five years since this book was first written, a number of new works have appeared, a number of which have been included in the bibliography above. Specifically on the Commune, Robert Tombs' *The War against Paris, 1871* is to be recommended among works written in English; on the more general background, Eugene Weber, *Peasants into Frenchmen, The Modernization of Rural France 1870–1914* and Theodore Zeldin's monumental two-volume study, *France 1848–1945*.

The following notes list the principal source material utilized specifically in each chapter. Works to be found in the bibliography bear the author's name only; where there is more than one by the same author, the appropriate number is given; where a work is not listed in the bibliography the title is given in full. With comments made by the various eyewitnesses, the source is generally self-evident; when this is not so, special mention has been made in the following notes but has otherwise been omitted. References below neither to be found in the bibliography nor entered in full relate to unpublished material, acknowledged in the Preface.

PART ONE

Chapter 1

Description of the Great Exhibition and its accompanying ceremonies is drawn from numerous sources, but principally: de la Gorce, von Klass (*Die Drei Ringe*), Guedalla, Allem, Fleury and Sonolet, Perruchot, Goncourt, Gautier, Child diaries, Guérard, Mérimée, Peat, Hoffman, *Illustrated London News*.

Chapter 2

Second Empire morals: de la Gorce, Allem, Fleury, Peat, Burnand, Loliée, Fleischmann, Guedalla, Thompson. Social and political conditions under the Second Empire: Guedalla, Duveau (2), de la Gorce, Burnand, Plamenatz, Allem, Goncourt, Elton, Guérard Maurois (1), Brogan, Chastenet, Newton.

Chapter 3

Causes and outbreak of Franco-Prussian War: de la Gorce, *Illustrated London News*, Howard, Newton, Brogan. State of the opposing Armies: Howard, Hooper, Pratt, Edwards, de la Gorce, Brogan, Guedalla (*The Two Marshals*), Fuller (*Decisive Battles of the Western World*, vol. iii). Opening phases of the war: Zola, de la Gorce, Hooper, Fuller, Cassell, *The Times*, *Illustrated London News*, Sheridan, Mérimée, Forbes. Appointment of Trochu: Trochu (2) and (3), Brunet-Moret. Revolution of September 4th: Duveau (1) de la Gorce, Kranzberg, Washburne (1), Rochefort, Trochu (3), Chastenet, Hoffman, Sheppard, d'Hérisson.

Chapter 4

Paris prepares for the Siege: Ducrot, Trochu (3), Duveau (1), Viollet-le-Duc, Brogan, Kranzberg, Cassell. Comparisons to Siege of Leningrad, here and elsewhere: Goure. Spy-mania: Péguret, Goncourt, Clarétie, Bowles, Washburne (1), O'Shea. Character of Trochu: Duveau (1), Brunet-Moret, d'Hérisson, Washburne (1), Hoffman, Trochu (1), (2) and (3), Rochefort.

Chapter 5

Prussian approach march: Forbes, Sheridan, *Daily News*, Müller (1), Busch (1), Blume (1), Russell, Frederick III. Battle of Châtillon: Ducrot, Trochu (3), Duveau (1), d'Hérisson, Grouard, O'Shea. Favre–Bismarck negotiations: Newton, Howard, Chastenet, Cassell, Busch (1), Frederick III. Gambetta flies to Tours: Bury, Brogan, Flaubert (1) and (2), Fonvielle, Grouard, Tissandier, Washburne (1), Trochu (3).

Chapter 6

Lack of news and rumours: Labouchere, Blount, Bowles, Goncourt, Whitehurst, Kranzberg. Introduction to 'Reds': Duveau (1), Jellinek, da Costa, Mason, Guillemin (2), Flourens, Chevalet, Bowles. The National Guard: Child diaries, Péguret, Duveau (1), Kranzberg, Nass, Labouchere, Flourens, Bowles.

Chapter 7

First Battle of Le Bourget: Adam, Washburne, Ducrot, Trochu (3), O'Shea, Labouchere, Forbes, Kunz, Grouard. Surrender of Metz: *Daily News*, Robinson, Cassell, Rochefort. Uprising of October 31st: Bowles, O'Shea, Labouchere, Ducrot, Trochu (3), Whitehurst, Adam, 'Oxford Graduate', Washburne (1), Flourens, Duveau (1), d'Hérisson, Michell, Rochefort, Mason, Lissagaray, Sheppard, Clarétie, Goncourt, Hoffman, Mason.

Chapter 8
The Balloons of Paris: Smith, Tissandier, François, Gautier, Saint-Edmé, Fonvielle, Mallet, Brunel, Nass, Reitlinger, Robinson. Inventors and inventions: Saint-Edmé, Kranzberg, Nass, Labouchere. Bowles, Sheppard, Maillard, Cassell, Ducrot, O'Shea, *Mid-week Pictorial*.

Chapter 9
'*Le Plan*': Trochu (3), Ducrot, Grouard, Duveau (1), Brogan, Brunet-Moret. Gambetta's campaign on the Loire: Bury, Grouard, Howard. Imperfections of French security: Goncourt, Frederick III, Forbes, Blumenthal, Blume (1). Flight of the *Ville d'Orléans*: Brunel, Mallet, François, Tissandier, Cassell.

Chapter 10
Mood in Paris before the Great Sortie: Whitehurst, O'Shea, Child letters, Washburne (1), Goncourt, Adam. The Great Sortie: Bowles, Labouchere, Adam, Clarétie, O'Shea, Goncourt, Grouard, Ducrot, Trochu (3), Forbes, Busch (1), Duveau (1), d'Hérisson, Cassell, Whitehurst, Blumenthal, Frederick III, Blume (1), Russell, Chevalet.

Chapter 11
British relations with the combatants: Collins and Abramsky (*Karl Marx and the British Labour Movement*), Roy Jenkins (*Sir Charles Dilke*), Fonvielle, Newton, Amberley, Harbord, Reitlinger, *Illustrated London News*, Kranzberg, Labouchere, Forbes, Frederick III, Pierce, Spears, Brown. The British and American communities in Paris: Falk, Washburne (1), Sheppard, Hoffman, Brown, Michell, Blount, Herbert, Burnley, Bowles, Thom, Whitehurst, Labouchere, O'Shea. Hospitals and 'ambulances': Adam, Sheppard, Evans (1), Gautier, Goncourt, Whitehurst, Bowles, Trailles, Labouchere, Ducrot, Ryan, Kranzberg, Hoffman, Sarcey, Forbes, Russell, O'Shea.

Chapter 12
Food supplies (sources used on this section are almost too numerous to list more than a few of the principal ones—the well-known correspondents whose names appear in the text are also omitted): 'Oxford Graduate', Maurois (2), Spears, Gautier, Nass, Washburne,

Hoffman, Verlaine, Adam, Saint-Edmé, Sheppard, Herbert letters, Pierce, Duveau (1), Howard, Michell, Kranzberg, *Illustrated London News*, Vizetelly, Lowndes, Burnand, Péguret, Carter, Sarcey, Blount, Brown, Jollivet, Child diaries and letters, *Daily News*, Goure. Morale in December: Labouchere, Duveau (1), Goncourt, Michell, d'Hérisson, d'Heylli, Spears, Bowles, Goncourt. The second Le Bourget: Ducrot, Trochu (3), Adam, Busch (1), Kunz, Blumenthal, Forbes O'Shea, *Daily News*, Duveau (1).

Chapter 13
The Prussian camp: Russell, Forbes, Viollet-le-Duc, Blumenthal, Busch (1) and (2), Carter, Frederick III, Ryan. Discussion on the bombardment of Paris: Blume (1), Müller (1) and (2), Forbes, Frederick III, Busch (1), Russell, Blumenthal, Howard. The war in the provinces: Brogan, Bury, *Daily News*, Howard, Cassell, Parris, Sheridan, Hoffman.

Chapter 14
The shelling of Avron: Viollet-le-Duc, Forbes, Labouchere, Müller (1), Frederick III, Blumenthal. Shelling of the southern forts; Gautereau, Brunon, Viollet-le-Duc, Moltke. Bombardment of Paris; Moltke, O'Shea, Bowles, 'Oxford Graduate', *Daily News*, Cassell, Lowndes, Whitehurst, Blount, Washburne (1), Goncourt, Kranzberg, Trochu (3), Müller (2), Forbes, Frederick III, Russell. Shortage of fuel in Paris: 'Oxford Graduate', O'Shea, Hoffman Adam, Goncourt, Kranzberg, Sheppard. Government of National Defence plans last sortie: Trochu (3), Brunet-Moret, Ducrot, Duveau (1).

Chapter 15
State of the National Guard: Child diaries, O'Shea, Labouchere, 'Oxford Graduate'. The Buzenval sortie: Goncourt, Ducrot, Adam, Bowles, Blumenthal, Frederick III, Trochu (3), Busch (1), Russell, Herbert, d'Hérisson. The replacement of Trochu: d'Hérisson, Blount, Labouchere, Maurois (2), Washburne, Hoffman. The shootings of January 22nd: Ducrot, Labouchere, O'Shea, Kranzberg, Duveau (1), Washburne (1) and (2), Clarétie, Moser, Mason. Favre's negotiations with Bismarck for an armistice: Howard, d'Hérisson, Frederick III, Duveau (1), Busch (1), Newton, Chastenet, Child diaries and letters, Gautereau. The end of the war in the provinces: Chastenet, Bury, Brunel, Rochefort, Brogan.

PART TWO

Chapter 16
The revictualling of Paris: Child letters, Hoffman, Blount, Cassell, *Daily News*, Forbes, Sheppard, Lyon, Nass, Brown, Herbert. 'Obsidional fever': Nass, Saint-Edmé, Dansette, Duveau (1), Adam, Labouchere, Kranzberg. The exodus from Paris: Mason, *Daily News*, Plamenatz, Daudet (1), Chevalet, Perruchot. Elections and the new Government: Chastenet, Bourgin (1), *Daily News*, Cassell, Brogan, Bowles, Elton, Jellinek, Bourgin (2), Dansette, Mason. Thiers's first legislation: Chastenet, Cassell, Maurois (1) and (2) Péguret, Plamenatz, Bourgin (2), da Costa, Brogan, Dansette, Washburne (2). The German triumphal march: Lyon, Nass, Labouchere, Adam, Washburne, Frederick III, Blount, Blumenthal, Forbes, du Camp.

Chapter 17
Deceptive return to normal of Paris: d'Hérisson, Gibson, Goncourt, Dansette, Brown. The lynching of Vincenzoni: Bourgin (2), Lyon, Jellinek, Lissagaray. Seizure of the National Guard cannon: Bourgin (2), Péguret, Lissagaray, Rihs, Mason, Hoffman, Cassell, Patry, Jellinek, Gibson, da Costa, Washburne (1), Thiers. Killing of Lecomte and Thomas: Chastenet, Bourgin (2), da Costa, Brogan, Jackson, Daudet (1), Rochefort, Thomas, Jellinek, Bourgin (1), Trochu (3), Maurois (2), Bruhat. The retreat of the Thiers Government to Versailles: Patry, Bourgin (1) and (2), Mason, Lissagaray, da Costa, Washburne (1) and (2).

Chapter 18
First discussions of the insurgents: da Costa, Russell, Newton, Lissagaray, Brogan, Bourgin (2), Moser, Michel, Chastenet, Plamenatz, *Journal Officiel*, Dansette, Mason, Gibson. Mediation of the Mayors: Jellinek, Plamenatz, Chastenet, Bourgin (1) and (2), Lissagaray, da Costa. Massacre in the Place Vendôme: Washburne (2), Jellinek, da Costa, Lindencrone, Gibson, Spears. The situation at Versailles: Hoffman, Washburne (1) and (2), Lindencrone, Thiers. Installation of the Commune. Bourgin (2), Gibson, Castelot, Jellinek, Mason.

Chapter 19
Definition of the Commune and Marx's relationship with it: Rihs, Chastenet, Mason, Bourgin (2), Berlin, Jellinek, Brogan, Elton,

Carlyle (*The French Revolution*), Aulard (*The French Revolution*), Laronze. Political and social background to the Commune: Brogan, Jellinek, Rihs, Chastenet, Bruhat, Rossel, Bourgin (1), Elton, da Costa, Marx (1), Berlin, Mason, Plamenatz. Factions within the Commune: da Costa, Marx (1), Berlin, Michel, Thomas, Mason, Elton, Plamenatz, Maurois (2), Rihs, Bruhat, Duveau (1), Jellinek, Verlaine, Bourgin (2). First acts of the Commune: Rihs, Jellinek, Lissagaray, Mason, Gibson, Washburne (1), Castelot, da Costa, *Journal Officiel*.

Chapter 20

Life in Paris during first days of the Commune: Powell, Washburne (1), Cassell, Gibson, Bourgin (2). Thiers attacks: Bourgin (2), Bruhat, da Costa, Cassell, Gibson, Jellinek, Brogan, Child diaries, Mason, Lissagaray, Rochefort, Cole, Thiers. Reaction in Paris: Washburne (1) and (2), Child diaries and letters, Gibson, Strang, *Journal Officiel*, Bourgin (2). Thier's plan: Bourgin (2), Cassell, Newton, Thiers, Tombs.

Chapter 21

Notes on Cluseret: Mason, Jellinek, Bruhat, Washburne (1), Rossel, Cluseret. Cluseret's reform attempts: Lissagaray, Rossel, Bourgin (2), da Costa, Cluseret, Mason. The fighting at Neuilly: Cassell, Young, Powell, Moser, Stanley. Thiers's bombardment of Paris: Goncourt, Child diaries, Strang, Spears, Washburne (1), Gibson. Evacuation and recovery of Fort Issy: Jellinek, Lissagaray, Bruhat, Cluseret.

Chapter 22

Notes on Rossel: Washburne (1) and (2), Bourgin (2), da Costa, Rossel, Cassell, Vuillaume, Mason. The Commune's political decrees: Elton, Lenin, Bruhat, Mason, Stanley, Bourgin (2), Gibson, Rihs. Creation of the Committee of Public Safety: Gibson, Mason, Rochefort, Lissagaray. Notes on Rigault: Mason, da Costa, Jellinek, Washburne (1), Duveau (1), Lindencrone, de la Gorce, Renoir, Adam. Arrest of the hostages: Washburne (1), Mason, Lissagaray, Cassell, Nass, Bourgin (2), da Costa, Cole, Maillard, Thiers. The final struggle for Fort Issy: Michel, Lissagaray, Jellinek, Rossel, da Costa.

Chapter 23

Notes on Delescluze and his coming to power: Audebrand, Lissagaray, Rossel, Rihs, *Journal Officiel*, Bourgin (2). Destruction of

Thiers's house: Washburne (2), Bourgin (2), Rochefort, da Costa. Felling of the Vendôme Column: Gibson, Cassell, Jellinek, Goncourt, Powell, Hoffman, Washburne (1), Stanley, Rihs. Explosion of Rapp arsenal: Child diaries, Spears, Stanley, Gibson. Negotiations over Archbishop: *Journal Officiel*, Washburne (1) and (2), Hoffman, Newton, Jellinek. Spies 'and spy-mania: Lissagaray, Bourgin (2). New exodus from Paris: Powell, Daudet (1), Child diaries and letters, Hoffman, Gibson, Spears, Goncourt, Daudet (2), Washburne (2). Parisian gaiety on eve of Versailles entry: Gibson, Goncourt, Castelot, Bourgin (2), Lissagaray, Thomas.

Chapter 24
Last attempts at mediation and the Versailles entry into Paris: Thiers, Jackson, Bourgin (2), Hoffman, Chastenet, Bruhat. Eyewitness accounts (such as those of Herbert, Stanley, and Child) of *La Semaine Sanglante*, both here and in succeeding chapters, are generally named and therefore source self-evident. Otherwise general sources used: Lissagaray, da Costa, Bruhat, Bourgin (2), *Journal Officiel*, Jellinek, Brogan, Cassell, Thiers, Goncourt, Cole, Chastenet, Moser, Michel, Thomas, Washburne (1) and (2), Jollivet.

Chapter 25
The burning of Paris and the *Pétroleuses*: Goncourt, Child letters, Stanley, Nass, Thomas, Jellinek, Marx (1), Cassell, Hoffman, Washburne (2), Michel. Death of the Archbishop: da Costa, Bourgin (2), Washburne (1) and (2), Brogan, Lissagaray, Cassell.

Chapter 26
Versailles atrocities: Chastenet, Verlaine, Bourgin (2), Jellinek, Lissagaray, Bruhat, Mason, Gibson, Hoffman, Denham, Cole, da Costa, Cassell, Nass, Powell, Goncourt, Stanley, Castelot, Daudet (2), Moser. Death of Delescluze: chiefly Lissagaray. The shootings of the remaining Communard hostages: Bruhat, Lissagary, Cassell, da Costa, Mason. The siege of La Roquette Prison: Cassell, Lamazou, Washburne (1), Bruhat, Lissagaray, Jellinek. Daudet's passage on the end of the Commune comes from Daudet (1); the story of the execution of the sweep was told the author by M. Cécil Saint-Laurent. Other notes on 'expiation' following the end of the Commune: Mason, Bruhat, Péguret, *The Times*, Gibson, Cassell, Goncourt, Bourgin (2), Brogan, Elton, Gautier, Maurois (2), Thiers, Daudet (2), Chastenet, Castelot, Vuillaume, Tombs.

Chapter 27

The review of June 29th: chiefly Thiers. Ruins and recovery of Paris: Child diaries, Buss, Goncourt, Gautier, Gibson, Spears, Péguret, Castelot. Trials and sentences of Communards: Rossel, Rochefort, Buss, Lissagaray, Jellinek, da Costa, Bruhat, Thiers, Bourgin (2). Much of the details of the subsequent life of the Communard surviviors comes from Bruhat; Augustus John's description of Louise Michel in old age is from *Chiaroscuro*; for confirmation of 'Burner Brunel's' more peaceful employment in England, I am indebted to the Royal Naval College, Dartmouth; the notes on Rochefort's later career were partly furnished by Frank Harris, in *My Life and Loves*. The notes on Richard Wallace come partly from Falk and the Wallace Collection; on Edwin Child, from Miss E. Child; on Labouchere from Hesketh Pearson's *Labby*; on Tommy Bowles, from Winston Churchill's *My Early Life.* Notes on the Marxist-Leninist interpretation of the Commune: Marx (1) and (2), Berlin, Bruhat, Lenin, Rihs, Mason. Auguste Renoir's quote, 'little flame which never dies', is drawn from Jean Renoir.

Index

458 INDEX

Conference, 47, 49; predicts Siege of Paris, 48; as Governor of Paris, 49–50; accepts post of President, 56; notifies Palikao of Republic, 57; doubts about National Guard, 62, 92; works on Paris defences, 63, 69–70, 72, 83; physical appearance, 70; character, 71; pessimism of, 71–72; 80; and battle of Châtillon, 77, 80; on Gambetta's balloon flight, 84; love of bombast, 89; opposition to, 90–91, 97, 99–100; reaction to Le Bourget attack, 104–6; and surrender of Metz, 107; during 'Black Monday' uprising, 107 ff.; and *le plan Trochu*, 136 ff.; changes Basse-Seine plan, 142; failure of efforts to contact Gambetta, 144–6; reluctant to let foreigners leave, 170; second sortie and, 190–2; resignation of, demanded, 193; opportunities missed by, 200; protests against bombardment, 214; prays for a miracle, 222; determines on 'supreme effort', 224; disbands battalions of National Guard, 229; plan for final break-out attempt, 231; receives last salute, 233; relieved of military command, 234–6; withdraws into oblivion, 253, 426; escapes from death, 273; refuses help to Rochefort, 423; little now recalled of, 433

Troplong, 33
Turpin, guardsman, 270

Urbain, 353, 422

Vaillant, Marshal, 68, 301
Vallès, Jules, 119, 289, 298, 415
Van der Goltz, 33
Vanves, Fort, 202–3, 212, 346–8, 353
Varlin, Eugène, 100, 283, 291, 297, 302, 327, 380, 398, 409, 412–13
Vengeur, Le, 260, 297, 309, 332, 375
Verlaine, Paul, 59–60, 95, 179, 299, 334, 366, 402, 425
Vermorel, 119, 332, 339, 401
Versailles, as Prussian headquarters, 196 ff., 211, 217–18, 258; as French Government headquarters, 269 n., 278 ff., 306 ff.; travel between Paris and, 357–8

Vésinier, 332
Victoria, Queen, 3, 20, 24, 36, 67, 79, 82, 162, 165, 289, 426,
Villejuif, 80
Villiers plateau, 151, 153, 155–7
Vincenzoni, 267, 424
Vinoy, General, 61, 152, 156, 231, 235–8, 267–9, 273–5, 281, 311, 367, 400, 411
Viollet-le-Duc, Colonel, 63, 195, 259
Vivandières, 149
Vizetelly, Henry, 157
Vuillaume, Maxime, 330, 416

Walewski, 33
Wallace, Richard, 167–70, 249, 253, 256 n., 322, 426
Washburne, E. B., xi, 66, 68, 71, 73, 81, 84, 87, 90, 102, 113, 211, 215, 217, 219, 221, 223, 236, 238, 251, 253, 263, 265, 269, 276, 287, 298, 305, 316, 323, 327, 333, 336 n., 345, 348, 353–5, 357–8, 370, 391–3, 403, 421, 427
Werder, General von, 207, 243
Whitehurst, Felix, 108, 158, 166, 173, 193, 215, 220
Wilhelm, King of Prussia, 8, 11, 37, 75, 81–82, 197, 199, 202, 211, 262, 419; proclaims himself Kaiser of Germans, 218
Wilhelm, Prince (Wilhelm II), 240, 274, 420 n.
Wilson, Benjamin, 337–8, 359, 369, 404, 407
Wimpffen, General de, 51–52, 81
Wingfield, Lewis, 352, 407
Wissembourg, 43
Wodehouse, Secretary, 168, 170
Wœrth, 44
Wolff, General, 269
World War I, comparisons with, x, 49, 75–76, 104, 137, 153, 185, 191–2, 206
World War II, comparisons with, x, 49, 51, 79, 106, 201, 206, 214–15, 408. *See also* Leningrad, Siege of
Worth, balloonist, 130
Wroblewski, Walery, 299, 329, 380, 400, 425

Zola, Émile, 43, 49, 358
Zouaves, 38, 52, 77–78, 80, 153, 231, 280, 307